Y0-BRV-204

THE PRESS AND SOCIETY

A Book of Readings

Edited by

GEORGE L. BIRD, Ph.D.

Chairman, Graduate Division, School of Journalism
Syracuse University

and

FREDERIC E. MERWIN, Ph.D.

Director, School of Journalism
Rutgers University, the State University of New Jersey

NEW YORK
PRENTICE-HALL, INC.

PRENTICE-HALL JOURNALISM SERIES
KENNETH E. OLSON, EDITOR

First printing ....April 1951
Second printing ......March 1952
Third printing ....April 1955

PREFACE

In preparing the revised edition of this book, the editors have found that the period of World War II produced relatively little research devoted to the press. Since that period excellent studies have been published with increasing frequency, however, and upon these latter years the editors have drawn heavily.

The primary purpose of the editors has been to preserve the historical depth of the book, so that young students may learn what critics of the press formerly held to be true. These students may decide from their own experience and from the writings of present-day critics whether the old opinions are still tenable. A few statements about the press have become landmarks of scholarly reference. These have been retained. Citations that relied heavily upon statistics of the day have been replaced in order to give a truer postwar picture.

Comparison of this edition with the earlier one will show that the editors have made an effort to broaden the book's scope. This was done in order that many of the issues discussed might be placed before the student not only in terms of the newspaper but of other mass media as well. Wherever possible, the chapter introductions were employed to point up comparative aspects of the communications picture.

A careful effort has been made to present the pros and cons of controversial issues, such as the mooted influence of advertisers and the effect of concentration of ownership upon editorial independence. It seems clear in most aspects of press criticism that little of an entirely new character has been added in recent years. What was said ten or twenty or even thirty years ago is still being said. But criticisms today are more precise and often better documented. Also, new evidence has been produced which indicates that some of the dreaded weaknesses of the press are not weaknesses at all but a source of strength, e.g., the increased financial stature. Various new instruments for study of the press are in process of being developed and sharpened. Representative findings from these have been included.

The editors believe that the recent studies of the press, herein cited, show an increasing strength of the press as well as increased freedom. They believe that many changes apparent in the press since 1941 have been for the best. Some unexpected weaknesses, however, have been revealed when public trust in press accuracy has been compared with public trust in radio accuracy. The attitudes of younger age groups are of particular interest to students and publishers.

This volume attempts to show how and why the press influences the public and how and why the public reacts to the press. To show how influence operates it has been necessary to begin with definitions of public opinion, since it is always public opinion that the press seeks to change, one way or another, directly or indirectly. In addition, since public opinion so often reacts to the manipulations of the propagandist, and since the press is a standard vehicle for the dissemination of propaganda, selections on the meaning of propaganda follow the definitions of public opinion. Finally, without freedom of utterance the press would not be free to exercise choice in the matter it presents to its readers. A discussion of freedom of the press, therefore, was deemed a third necessary element. The reader should be alert to the fact that these three chapters merely furnish a basic introduction to the rest of the book.

Part Two is a compilation of material on various internal factors in press influence. How news takes shape, how the press views major contemporary problems, its conception of its function, and the meaning of its physical appearance—all these are treated. A completely satisfactory division of topics was difficult; the editors have from time to time combined some chapters and subdivided others. Ever present was the knowledge that space limitations required the complete exclusion of certain interesting aspects. In the main, topics were selected to meet the needs of students and teachers of journalism, the working press, and those in other fields who are interested in problems of communications.

The concluding section, which deals with outside influence in press practices, comes to grips with the major forces—organized and unorganized—that are conceded to have powerful roles in the course of contemporary journalism. The impact of an industrial civilization, the activities of interest groups, the ever-increasing role of the radio, and the recent rise of employee groups in editorial and business departments receive attention. A determined effort has been made to present fair and significant views in each chapter.

Those desiring to delve more deeply into the topics may do so through the selected bibliographies appended to each chapter. The chapter introductions, written by the editors, are designed to serve as keys to the doors that lead to discussion. The review questions and suggested assignments may help all who find occasion to use the book.

Thanks are due to many individuals and organizations for their help in making possible publication of the two editions of this work. The editors feel a particular debt of gratitude to the copyright owners of the original works from which the various selections were taken. Book and magazine publishers and individual authors have proved both accommodating and gracious when approached with a request for permission to reprint. We would like to thank especially on this score Dr. Raymond B. Nixon, editor of the *Journalism Quarterly,* Dr. Thorstein Sellin, editor of the *Annals of the American Academy of Political and Social Science,* Mr. Louis M. Lyons, curator of the Nieman Foundation at Harvard, and Dr. Wilbur Schramm, director of the Institute for Communications Research at the University of Illinois. Full credit has been accorded all copyright owners in the footnotes accompanying the citations.

Much helpful advice and criticism from various individuals spurred the editors to their task. When the first edition was prepared especially valuable suggestions were received from Dean Kenneth E. Olson of the Northwestern School of Journalism, Dr. Ralph D. Casey of the Minnesota School of Journalism, Dean M. Lyle Spencer of the Syracuse School of Journalism, and Dr. W. Brooke Graves, head of Temple University's Department of Political Science. Many leaders in the field of journalism offered constructive criticism for the guidance of the editors in the preparation of the new edition. The editors appreciate in particular the help received once more from Dean Olson and from Dr. Henry Ladd Smith of the Wisconsin School of Journalism. The many students who have used the book as a text proved a continuing source for sound suggestions.

The great amount of detail involved in compiling a book of readings requires the assistance of many hands. The editors owe a perpetual debt of gratitude to Jeanne Bird, Jacqueline S. Merwin, Evelyn Outcalt, Evelyn Smith, and Gladys E. Frisch for the help they gave in typing the selections, checking original sources, locating evasive items, and handling correspondence.

While many individuals have read and criticized all or parts of the manuscript, the editors must assume full responsibility for any errors, particularly of omission, that might appear in a work of this type.

George L. Bird
Frederic E. Merwin

CONTENTS

PART ONE

PUBLIC OPINION, PROPAGANDA, AND PRESS FREEDOM

PAGE

PART TWO

THE PRESS AT WORK IN SOCIETY

PART ONE

PUBLIC OPINION, PROPAGANDA, AND PRESS FREEDOM

1. CONCEPTS OF PUBLIC OPINION

INTRODUCTION

THE NEWSPAPER, the radio, and other mass media of communication play upon public opinion by disseminating to wide audiences many different types of news, opinion, comment, and entertainment. An obvious and significant connection exists between the content of the media and public attitudes, standards, morals, and tastes. This relationship always has been of fundamental importance in the development of American democracy. It has become a matter of critical significance in the uncertainties and perplexities of the postwar years. The fate not only of the nation but of the entire world hinges to a major extent on what flows through the arteries of communication to the publics.

Until comparatively recent times, much of the interest shown by scholars in public opinion centered on efforts to arrive at a satisfactory definition of the meaning of the term. Bauer, Bryce, Lowell, Lippmann, and many others offered still famous concepts of the nature of public opinion. In most cases, these concepts represented theorizing on the nature of the public and publics in a democracy. Observations on the meaning of *opinion* in early discussions of the term are couched in much more scientific terms.

All the efforts to achieve a definition of public opinion that would satisfy the many different groups interested in the term ran into many difficulties. A common fault still marks attempts at definition: the tendency on the part of students in different disciplines to apply the meaning of the term to their own special interests.

In the nineteenth century, James Bryce asked: "How is the drift of Public Opinion to be ascertained? That is the problem which most occupies and perplexes politicians."

In recent years, scholarly interest in the nature of public opinion has evidenced a widespread acceptance of the challenge thrown down by Bryce. Today there is increasing use of certain tables of figures that reveal percentages of "Yes," "No," and "I don't know." On the basis of these figures, the investigator is able to postulate the opinions a selected public holds on an issue stated in the form of a question. Dr. George Gallup of the American Institute of Public Opinion was one of the earliest users of this method of actually trying to count the pulse of the public.

There is equal and corollary interest in content analysis studies, in which Dr. Harold D. Lasswell has played a leading role. The studies involve an examination, usually during a specified period, of words used by the media in connection with a given issue, such as a labor strike. The words are classified under such headings as "favorable," "unfavorable," "neutral," and the like.

Dr. Hadley Cantril of Princeton has been a leader in the application of sampling methods in charting trends of opinion. These methods involve a repetition of the same question on comparable cross sections of the population with the idea of showing by means of a chart what Bryce probably had in mind when he referred to the drift of opinion.

The application of scientific methods in studies of public opinion undoubtedly posits serious questions for the owners and managers of the mass media. They are the ones who hold the responsibility for content. And they can hardly help but respond to findings that indicate that the opinions of their publics seem to be moving in one direction or another.

The change in the economic structure of the mass media in the twentieth century greatly complicates the situation. As Dr. Paul F. Lazarsfeld, director of the Bureau of Applied Social Research at Columbia University, has pointed out, the old arrangement whereby the media represented the citizens in their relations with the government, no longer exists. Now we have a triangle, with the citizens in one corner, the media in the second, and the government in the third.

STATIC AND DYNAMIC PUBLIC OPINION

—From Wilhelm Bauer, "Public Opinion," *The Encyclopedia of the Social Sciences.* By permission of The Macmillan Company, publishers, 1934, Vol. 12, pp. 669–670. The author was on the staff of the University of Vienna when he wrote this article.

ALTHOUGH the term *public opinion* was a coinage of the late eighteenth century, a number of approximate equivalents may be traced to much earlier periods. The Greek concepts *ossa, pheme,* or *nomos* were familiar in Athens and were even accorded on occasion a niche in the Hellenic pantheon; the Romans spoke of *fama, fama popularis, rumores,* and, in the closing days of the empire, of *vox populi.* The mediaeval *consensus,* modeled on the Stoic *sensus communis,* was repeatedly cited by jurists of both papal and imperial camps as synonymous with the prevailing body of traditional opinion. At the beginning of the modern period Machiavelli called attention to the force of *publica voce, e fama,* and Shakespeare's Henry IV in apostrophizing "opinion that did help me to the crown" anticipated the phraseology if not the temper of the eighteenth-century revolutionists. The civil struggles of seventeenth-century England represent the first step in clarifying the nature and function of public opinion. William Temple in his "Essay Upon the Original and Nature of Government" (written 1672) traces the source of political authority to the prevailing "opinion" as to the wisdom, goodness, and valor inhering in the ruler, while Locke in his "Essay Concerning Human Understanding" (1690) first sought to supply a juristic and ethical orientation for the phenomenon of public opinion. . . . From England the concept spread during the eighteenth century to France. Montesquieu's *esprit général* and Rousseau's *volonté générale,* the prototypes of the *Volksgeist* of the German romantic schools, may be considered rough approximations of public opinion. On the eve of the revolution the term *opinion publique* began to gain currency, particularly in Necker's circle, whence it gradually found its way not only throughout France but into the most treasured rhetoric of virtually all western nations.

Repeated usage, during the century and a half of democratic consolidation, has robbed the term of much of its initial incisiveness. Invoked with little discrimination by the astute politician and by the special pleader in all lines of public and semi-public enterprise, it has lost not a little of its original richness of overtone. Suspected by the systematic historian, who seeks a less exploited substitute in such partial equivalents as "popular sovereignty," "conventions," "mores," "climate of opinion," *idées directrices, Zeitgeist,* it has been taken over as a rule by the journalist and social psychologist and in the process frequently stripped of many of its historical associations.

In the absence of a carefully defined set of connotations a great deal may pass as public opinion which in reality is merely the publicly expressed opinion of an individual or small group that happens to possess the knack of making itself heard. In an attempt to reach a working definition a distinction should therefore be drawn first of all between public opinion proper and opinion which is voiced in public. The latter, essentially personal in character, strives to impose itself on the collective mind of the community, just as poems of a folk character, although the work of an individual poet, are able under certain circumstances to develop into genuine folk *Lieder*. Public opinion, on the other hand, is a deeply pervasive organic force intimately bound up with the ideological and emotional interplay of the social groupings in which since earliest times gregarious individuals have come together; it articulates and formulates not only the deliberate judgments of the rational elements within the collectivity but the evanescent common will, which somehow integrates and momentarily crystallizes the sporadic sentiments and loyalties of the masses of the population.

Analysis of the particular forces and processes which are instrumental in shaping homogeneous group attitudes and pressures calls for emphasis upon such broader social factors as the general level of civilization and the cultural media of expression prevailing at a given period; the racial and national characteristics of the group; the framework of political, legal, and economic institutions within which the process operates; and the particular set of objectives toward which it may be directed. There are two main types of public opinion, the static and the dynamic. The static, which need not imply rigidity, manifests itself in the form of traditional customs, mores, and usages and bears the same relation to the dynamic as costume does to fashion or customary law to parliamentary enactments. The preponderance of the one or the other of these types is determined by the larger social and economic relationships prevailing at a particular period. The static form is found as a rule in most agrarian and barter economies, such as prevailed in mediaeval Greece, Rome, Japan, and western Europe. This essentially irrational complex of opinion coincides closely with the relatively unchanging preconceptions and sympathies of the masses of people. It was a collective consciousness of this type, an irrational consensus of opinion, that the traditionalists and mediaevalists of the romantic period sought to reinvoke in their formula of *Volksseele* and *Volksgeist*. Dynamic public opinion, on the other hand, being predominantly rational in character, is built upon the cultivated arts of persuasion and systematic publicity and draws upon definite historical events or contemporary happenings as the material for its propaganda and agitation.

THE VIEW, OR SET OF VIEWS, OF THE MAJORITY

—From James Bryce, *Modern Democracies*. By permission of The Macmillan Company, publishers, 1921, Vol. I, pp. 153–156. Mr. Bryce achieved fame as a student of government.

WHAT is public opinion? The term is commonly used to denote the aggregate of the views men hold regarding matters that affect or interest the community. Thus understood, it is a congeries of all sorts of discrepant notions, beliefs, fancies, prejudices, aspirations. It is confused, incoherent, amorphous, varying from day to day and week to week. But in the midst of this diversity and confusion every question as it rises into importance is subjected to a process of consolidation and clarification until there emerge and take definite shape certain views, or sets of interconnected views, each held and advocated in common by bodies of citizens. It is to the power exerted by any such view, or set of views, when held by an apparent majority of citizens, that we refer when we talk of Public Opinion as approving or disapproving a certain doctrine or proposal, and thereby becoming a guiding or ruling power. Or we may think of the opinion of a whole nation as made up of different currents of sentiment, each embodying or supporting a view of a doctrine or a practical proposal. Some currents develop more strength than others, because they have behind them larger numbers or more intensity of conviction; and when one is evidently the strongest, it begins to be called Public Opinion *par excellence,* being taken to embody the views supposed to be held by the bulk of the people. Difficult as it often is to determine the relative strength of the different streams of opinion—one cannot measure their strength as electric power is measured by volts—every one admits that when one stream is distinctly stronger than any other, i.e., when it would evidently prevail if the people were called upon to vote, it ought to be obeyed. Till there is voting, its power, being open to doubt, has no legal claim to obedience. But impalpable though it may be, no sensible man disputes that power, and such governing authorities as ministries and legislatures are obliged to take account of it and shape their course accordingly. In this sense, therefore, the people are always ruling, because their will is recognized as supreme whenever it is known, and though it is formally and legally expressed only by the process of counting votes, it is frequently known for practical purposes without that process. . . .

How is the drift of Public Opinion to be ascertained? That is the problem which most occupies and perplexes politicians. They usually go for light to the press, but the press, though an indispensable, is not a safe guide, since the circulation of a journal does not necessarily measure the prevalence of the views it advocates. Newspaper accounts given of what men are thinking may be colored and misleading, for every organ tends to exaggerate the support its views command. Neither are public meetings a sure index, for in populous centers almost any energetic group can fill a large hall with its adherents. Stray elections arising from the death or retirement of a legislator or (in the states of the North American union) of an elected official, are much relied on, yet the result is often due rather to local circumstances than to a general movement of political feeling. There is, moreover, such a thing as an artificially created and fictitious opinion. The art of propaganda has been much studied in our time, and has attained a development which enables its practitioners by skilfully and sedulously supplying false or one-sided statements of fact to beguile and mislead those who have not the means or the time to ascertain the facts for themselves. Against all these sources of error the observer must be on his guard.

PUBLIC OPINION MUST BE REALLY PUBLIC

—A. Lawrence Lowell, *Public Opinion and Popular Government,* Longmans, Green, 1921, pp. 4–7, 9, 11, 12–14. Mr. Lowell, president of Harvard University from 1909 to 1933, wrote extensively on government.

Each of the two words that make up the expression "public opinion" is significant, and each of them may be examined by itself. To fulfil the requirement an opinion must be public, and it must be really an opinion. Let us begin with the first of these qualities.

If two highwaymen meet a belated traveller on a dark road and propose to relieve him of his watch and wallet, it would clearly be an abuse of terms to say that in the assemblage on that lonely spot there was a public opinion in favor of a redistribution of property.

Nor would it make any difference, for this purpose, whether there were two highwaymen and one traveller, or one robber and two victims. The absurdity in such a case of speaking about the duty of the minority to submit to the verdict of public opinion is self-evident; and it is not due to the fact that the three men on the road form part of a larger community, or that they are subject to the jurisdiction of a common government. . . . In short the three men in each of the cases supposed do not form a community that is capable of a public opinion on the question involved. May this not be equally true under an organized government, among people that are for certain purposes a community?

To take an illustration nearer home. At the time of the Reconstruction that followed the American Civil War the question whether public opinion in a southern state was, or was not, in favor of extending the suffrage to the Negroes could not in any true sense be said to depend on which of the two races had a slight numerical majority. One opinion may have been public or general in regard to the whites, the other public or general in regard to the Negroes, but neither opinion was public or general in regard to the whole population. Examples of this kind could be multiplied indefinitely. They can be found in Ireland, in Austria-Hungary, in Turkey, in India, in any country where the cleavage of race, religion, or politics is sharp enough to cut the community into fragments too far apart for an accord on fundamental matters. . . .

In all these instances an opinion cannot be public or general with respect to both elements in the state. For that purpose they are as distinct as if they belonged to different commonwealths. You may count heads, you may break heads, you may impose uniformity by force; but on the matters at stake the two elements do not form a community capable of an opinion that is in any rational sense public or general. . . . If we are to employ the term in a sense that is significant for government, that imports any obligation moral or political on the part of the minority, surely enough has been said to show that the opinion of a mere majority does not by itself always suffice. Something more is clearly needed.

But if the opinion of a majority does not of itself constitute a public opinion, it is equally certain that unanimity is not required. To confine the term to cases where there is no dissent would deprive it of all value and would be equivalent to saying that it rarely, if ever, exists. Moreover, unanimous opinion is of no importance for our purpose, because it is perfectly sure to be effective in any form of government, however despotic, and it is, therefore, of no particular interest in the study of democracy. . . .

A body of men are politically capable of a public opinion only so far as they are agreed upon the ends and aims of government and upon the principles by which those ends shall be attained. They must be united, also, about the means whereby the action of the government is to be determined, in a conviction, for example, that the views of a majority—or it may be some other portion of their numbers—ought to prevail; and a political community as a whole is capable of public opinion only when this is true of the great bulk of the citizens. Such an assumption was implied, though usually not expressed, in all theories of Social Compact; and, indeed, it is involved in all theories that base rightful government upon the consent of the governed, for the consent required is not a universal approval by all the people of every measure enacted, but a consensus in regard to the legitimate character of the ruling authority and its right to decide the questions that arise. . . .

Leaving out of account those doctrines whereby political authority is traced to a direct supernatural origin, government among men is commonly based in theory either on consent or force, and in fact each of these factors plays a larger or smaller part in every civilized country. So far as the preponderating opinion is one which the minority does not share, but which it feels ought, as the opinion of the majority, to be carried out, the government is conducted by a true public opinion or consent. So far as the preponderating opinion is one the execution of which the minority would resist by force if it could do so successfully, the government is based on force. . . .

One more remark must be made before quitting the subject of the relation of public opinion to the opinion of the majority. The late Gabriel Tarde, with his habitual keen insight, insisted on the importance of the intensity of belief as a factor in the spread of opinions. There is a common impression that public opinion depends upon and is measured by the mere number of persons to be found on each side of a question; but this is far from accurate. If 49 per cent of a community feel very strongly on one side, and 51 per cent are lukewarmly on the other, the former opinion has the greater public force behind it and is certain to prevail ultimately if it does not at once. The ideas of people who possess the greatest knowledge of a subject are also of more weight than those of an equal number of ignorant persons.... One man who holds his belief tenaciously counts for as much as several men who hold theirs weakly, because he is more aggressive, and thereby compels and overawes others into apparent agreement with him, or at least into silence and inaction. This is, perhaps, especially true of moral questions. It is not improbable that a large part of the accepted moral code is maintained by the earnestness of a minority, while more than half of the community is indifferent or unconvinced. In short, public opinion is not strictly the opinion of the numerical majority, and no form of its expression measures the mere majority, for individual views are always to some extent weighed as well as counted. Without attempting to consider how the weight attaching to intensity and intelligence can be accurately gauged, it is enough for our purpose to point out that when we speak of the opinion of the majority we mean, not the numerical, but the effective majority.

PUBLIC OPINION A MANIFESTATION OF THE SOCIAL MIND

—Clyde L. King, in the introduction to *Readings in Public Opinion,* edited by W. Brooke Graves, Appleton-Century, 1928, pp xxiii-xxviii. The late Professor King taught political science at the University of Pennsylvania.

PUBLIC OPINION is but one of the many manifestations of the social mind—one of the many ways by which individuals think, will, and feel together. To public opinion has been so often ascribed the fatuities and fickleness of certain of these manifestations that it is advisable to define public opinion and distinguish it from other kinds of public action with which it has been thus associated.

Public opinion is the social judgment reached upon a question of general or civic import after conscious, rational public discussion....

Public opinion is not the offspring solely of impulse; it is not merely a "re-action" along the grooves of habit or custom. It implies conscious departure from custom and tradition. The people are conscious of the question at issue and are aware that a decision is being reached upon it. Public opinion readapts old principles to new conditions, creates new social norms, sets up new group standards, develops new rules of action for a new social situation. Public opinion is born out of and contains the customs, traditions, and norms of a people and yet it is the chief instrument for affecting changes in them.

The group faces a crisis. There is an awareness of the needs and wants of others that makes possible team play. Leaders arise to state the issue, propose solutions, and endeavor to get their solutions adopted. Then follows rational discussion in which experiences are declared and in which each man begins to know or at least gets interested in learning what his fellows think and know about the subject. Expectation of a change for the better is aroused; evil consequences are depicted. Discrimination is used, discussion takes place in the street, in the office, in the club room; some one or all of the agencies of public opinion brings facts, sentiments, prejudices, hopes, fears, dogmas, experiences, principles, prophecies, traditions to bear in order to change or to conform men's minds. The conflict of interests becomes clear. Individuals "take sides" and a judgment is finally reached. This judgment may be the same or it may be different from what any leader wanted it to be; it is a social judgment, the highest creation of the social mind, the product of both the conservative and progressive forces of the day. By the sanity and wisdom of these judgments, groups survive or perish; nations progress or decay.

Public opinion is thus very far from mob action with which it has been so frequently associated. Mob action is a violent reaction along pre-established prejudices or social standards; public opinion is a rational judgment reached after discussion—rational in the pragmatic sense that it seems right to the majority. The decision of the mob is reached amidst the excitement of the multitudes; in the process by which public opinion is formed the individual is not under morbid pressure from an excited crowd. In public opinion there is consciousness of *what* is being done; in mob action there is only consciousness that *something* is being done. . . .

The processes by which public opinion is reached are also quite in contrast to the psychology of the crowd. The crowd is activated by a simple emotion; in public opinion the emotions are as diverse as group interests. In the crowd, individuality is suppressed; in public opinion each individual takes a part—some more, some less. Crowds think in images and are subject to hallucinations. In public opinion most people are thinking in terms of their economic and social interests and are guided by open discussion. Government officials can never long remain indifferent to the demands of an aroused, sustained public opinion.

Public opinion is likewise to be distinguished from public indignation. The public is indignant when its anger is aroused by that which is unjust, ungrateful, or base; when its anger is mingled with contempt or abhorrence. . . . There is much government through indignation when public officials have been negligent or indifferent to public needs and demands. Indignation is reaction; public opinion is a product.

Public opinion is also to be distinguished from public sentiment. Public sentiment is the feeling of admiration or abhorrence, respect or derision by which the public expresses its approval or disapproval of acts that conform to or are at variance with its habitual attitudes. Public sentiment is the way people feel together; public opinion is the result of their thinking together. . . .

Nor is public opinion to be confused with popular impressions. . . . Popular impression is the unthinking reaction of men. It is the natural thought or wish which an occurrence evokes; it is the result of suggestion. It does not contain the element of conflict that characterizes public opinion nor does it have in it adjusting power. In its popular impressions the public unwittingly approves what is "in vogue" just as it approves the day's fashions. One who does not conform is dowdy, and while not discredited is not warmly accepted. Popular impression is that unanimity of interest, feeling, or opinion among a group of communicating individuals resulting wholly from suggestion and imitation. . . .

There may be also a preponderant opinion on a subject that is in no sense a public opinion. A preponderant opinion is simply the conclusion of a preponderant number of people in a group, a conclusion reached without discussion, without any new readjustment of values. Thus the preponderant opinion in Philadelphia on co-education is not what it is in Chicago or St. Louis. The opinion that prevails as to the moral effects of religious revivals is different in some rustic center from what it is in New York City. . . . a preponderant opinion is a hereditary attitude. There is all the difference between a preponderant opinion and a public opinion that there is between a habit and a judgment. . . .

The almost entire unanimity in the attitude of individuals in a community toward a given question may be characterized as a general opinion. In this general opinion nearly every one shares in part, though to be sure there may be an infinite number of interpretations of this general opinion such as those held by the farmers, the labor unions, the clergymen, the church goers, the club men, the rich, and the poor. A general opinion is wanting in the element of recent discussion and criticism. In general opinion, as in public opinion, there is a like-mindedness among individuals. But in general opinion this like-mindedness is the result not so much of current discussions as of the amalgamation of past discussions with customs and tradition; it is not the creative force that public opinion is. . . .

There is a difference also between a public judgment and the social judgment called public opinion. A public judgment is the public's choice of alternative measures; its approval or disapproval of an act as good or bad, noble or ignoble. It is not the mature, aroused, social judgment that public opinion is. The number of subjects upon which a public opinion may be forming in any group at any time must necessarily be few in number, limited by the amount of time left from private business for public affairs. Public judgments are more easily made and the number of subjects upon which it can be pronounced is legion. Public judgment, however, is supportive only, not creative.

THE PICTURES INSIDE OUR HEADS

—From Walter Lippmann, *Public Opinion*. By permission of The Macmillan Company, publishers, 1922, pp. 29, 81, 87–90, 124–125. Mr. Lippmann, well known as a journalist, is the author of numerous books and articles dealing with public affairs.

THE WORLD that we have to deal with politically is out of reach, out of sight, out of mind. It has to be explored, reported, and imagined. Man is no Aristotelian god contemplating all existence at one glance. He is the creature of an evolution who can just manage his survival, and snatch what on the scale of time are but a few moments of insight and happiness. Yet this same creature has invented ways of seeing what no naked eye could see, of hearing what no ear could hear, of weighing immense masses and infinitesimal ones, of counting and separating more items than he can individually remember. He is learning to see with his mind vast portions of the world that he could never see, touch, smell, hear, or remember. Gradually he makes for himself a trustworthy picture inside his head of the world beyond his reach.

Those features of the world outside which have to do with the behavior of other human beings, in so far as that behavior crosses ours, is dependent upon us, or is interesting to us, we roughly call public affairs. The pictures inside the heads of these human beings, the pictures of themselves, of others, of their needs, purposes, and relationships, are their public opinions. Those pictures which are acted upon by groups of people, or by individuals acting in the name of groups, are Public Opinion with capital letters. . . .

For the most part we do not first see, and then define; we define first and then see. In the great blooming, buzzing confusion of the outer world we pick out what our culture has already defined for us, and we tend to perceive that which we have picked out in the form stereotyped for us by our culture. . . .

There is, of course, some connection between the scene outside and the mind through which we watch it, just as there are some long-haired men and short-haired women in radical gatherings. But to the hurried observer a slight connection is enough. If there are two bobbed heads and four beards in the audience, it will be a bobbed and bearded audience to the reporter who knows beforehand that such gatherings are composed of people with these tastes in the management of their hair. . . .

There is economy in this. For the attempt to see all things freshly and in detail, rather than as types and generalities, is exhausting, and among busy affairs practically out of the question. . . .

The subtlest and most pervasive of all influences are those which create and maintain the repertory of stereotypes. We are told about the world before we see it. We imagine most things before we experience them. And these preconceptions, unless education has made us acutely aware, govern deeply the whole process of perception. They mark out certain objects as familiar or strange, emphasizing the difference, so that the slightly familiar is seen as very familiar, and the somewhat strange as sharply alien. They are aroused by small signs which may vary from a true index to a vague analogy. Aroused, they flood fresh vision with older images, and project into the world what has been resurrected in memory. Were there no practical uniformities in the environment, there would be no economy and only error in the human habit of accepting foresight for sight. But there are uniformities sufficiently accurate, and the need of economizing attention is so inevitable, that the abandonment of all stereotypes for a wholly innocent approach to experience would impoverish human life. . . .

That is the one reason why it is so dangerous to generalize about human nature. A loving father can be a sour boss, an earnest municipal reformer, and a rapacious jingo abroad. His family life, his business career, his politics, and his foreign policy rest on totally different versions of what others are like and how he should act. These versions differ by codes in the same person, the codes differ somewhat among persons in the same social set, differ widely as between social sets, and between two nations, or two colors, may differ to the point where there is no common assumption whatever. That is why people professing the same stock of religious beliefs can go to war. The element of their belief which determines conduct is that view of the facts which they assume.

That is where codes enter so subtly and so pervasively into the making of public opinion. The orthodox theory holds that a public opinion constitutes a moral judgment on a group of facts. The theory that I am suggesting is that, in the present state of education, a public opinion is primarily a moralized and codified version of the facts. I am arguing that the pattern of stereotypes at the center of our codes largely determines what group of facts we shall see, and in what light we shall see them.

THE IMPORTANCE OF ATTITUDES

—Leonard W. Doob, *Public Opinion and Propaganda,* Henry Holt, 1948, pp. 35–37. The author is a professor of social psychology at Yale University.

ALTHOUGH most writers who use the term public opinion seldom indicate its referent and thus contribute to general confusion, it is possible to come up with numerous definitions by conducting a diligent search through various intellectual sources. Definitions begin with the simple word "people" and end with the semi-mystical idea of "a more or less rational collective judgment formed by the action and reaction of many individuals." No one can quarrel with a definition which is precise unless the question of its accepted usage is raised. "Public opinion," however, is such an ambiguous term that usage is no guide to clarity. Here is a definition that seeks to be precise and at least not sensationally different from the way in which the term is frequently employed: *public opinion refers to people's attitudes on an issue when they are members of the same social group.*

The key psychological word in this definition is that of "attitude." Before such a concept can carry the burden of the definition, it is necessary to recall from the previous chapter the characterization of an attitude as the socially significant, internal response that people habitually make to stimuli. Presumed, therefore, is a series of experiences which have produced within people more or less similar responses; various gradients of generalization and discrimination along which the evoking stimuli are arranged; and some connection with overt behavior. In this sense it might appear as though public opinion exists whenever people have attitudes. Most Americans, for example, drink coffee for breakfast and therefore may be presumed to have a favorable attitude toward this beverage; but should one say that American public opinion favors coffee?

According to common usage, it is fairly certain that this attitude would not be included in the category of public opinion. "American public opinion favors coffee"—no, it does not sound right. The definition of public opinion here proposed, moreover, also rules out the use of the expression to apply to coffee-drinking, *unless* an issue is at stake. An issue involves a controversy or conflict among people and therefore results in the interruption of a habit with consequent non-reduction of drives. If the price of coffee suddenly rises so high that it is beyond the budget of the average American family, then the attitude can no longer find its normal outlet in drinking the beverage but affects other behavior. There are public demonstrations or there is petty grousing against the government, coffee merchants, or the capitalist system. At this point public opinion regarding coffee arises.

In addition, the people who have attitudes more or less in common regarding an issue must be members of a social group before there is public opinion. Each group has a distinctive organization that regulates the behavior of its members. A crowd's organization is very simple; participants have face-to-face contact with one another and their behavior results from their pre-existing knowledge, attitudes, and drives as well as from mutual stimulation. Photographers scattered throughout the country belong to a social group, although they may not be members of a formal association: they are conscious of one another to a certain degree and they obviously share an interest in pictures. Citizens of a country also are members of a social group, the nation, while simultaneously they belong to local groups as well as those also scattered throughout the land.

The social structure of a group, as Warner and Lunt (*Yankee City Series:* Vol. II, *The Status System of a Modern Community,* 1942) have vividly demonstrated in the American society, assigns to each individual a status which in turn determines a large part but not all of his social behavior. The group, moreover, places at the disposal of its members certain media of communication through which public opinion can be expressed. These media can be quite diverse. Orally they range from the informal conversation of friends to the speaker whose voice is transmitted by a national hookup at one of the favorable evening hours. Visually they vary from a private letter received from a relative to a syndicated column reaching the more or less literate at their breakfast tables each day. They include the poorly focused snapshot in the family album as well as the most extravagant effusion from Hollywood.

PUBLIC OPINION INFLUENCES THE MEDIA

—Bernard Berelson, "Communications and Public Opinion," in *Communications in Modern Society,* Wilbur Schramm (editor), University of Illinois Press, 1948, pp. 169–171. Dr. Berelson is dean of the Graduate Library School of the University of Chicago.

. . . It is clear that one factor, among others, that conditions what the media of communications say on social and political issues is the desire or expectation of the readers-listeners-seers to be told certain things and not others. The reporter or commentator or editor or producer may know or may think he knows "what his public wants" on a given issue, and to the extent that such knowledge affects what he communicates, to that extent public opinion becomes a determinant of communications. This aspect of the relationship between communication and public opinion is not always admitted, or even recognized, because of the immorality of suggesting that anything but "truth" or "justice" contributes to the character of communication content. However, everyone knows that communication channels of various kinds tell people what they want to hear. In such cases, public opinion sets limits upon the nature of what is typically communicated.

This determination (or really, partial determination, since this is of course not the only factor responsible for communication content any more than communication content is the only factor responsible for public opinion) can operate in two ways, once the communication channel (newspaper, magazine, political writer, radio commentator, and so forth) has attracted to itself a distinguishable audience. The two ways are themselves interrelated and can coexist. First, it can operate through conscious and deliberate and calculated manipulation of the content in order to coincide with the dominant audience opinion. Sometimes this operates by rule of thumb, as when someone on the production line in the communication process decides that "our public won't take this, or won't like it." Sometimes it operates through elaborate machinery organized precisely for the purpose, as when thousands of research dollars and hours are spent in finding out what kinds of people the audience is composed of and what kinds of opinions they hold on controversial issues. Whether the decision to conform to audience predispositions is taken on the front line or in the front office is for the moment immaterial; so is the question of why it happens, e.g., the desire or need for constant and large audiences for economic reasons. The important point is that overt consideration of audience opinion does (help to) shape the social and political content of the mass media. Everyone recalls the story of the foreign correspondent who cabled a thoroughgoing analysis of a relatively obscure Hungarian crisis to the home office only to be told: "We do not think it advisable to print it because it does not reflect Midwestern opinion on this point."[1]

The other method by which public opinion can affect communications is implicit, through the sincere and more or less nonconscious correspondence of ideology between producers and consumers. The two groups often see the world through the same colored glasses. The correspondence is achieved through a two-way process: the audience selects the communications which it finds most congenial and the producers select people with "the right viewpoint" to prepare communications for other people with "the right viewpoint." Although this latter process also occurs through deliberate decision, it also happens through the most laudable and honest motives that people of the same general persuasion as their audience are found in influential positions in particular communication agencies. This is all the more true in specialized enterprises like trade papers or magazines like *Fortune* or *The Nation*. In such cases, producers react to new issues and events like the modal members of their audience; and their communications fit audience predispositions, not through a process of tailoring, but through correspondence in outlook. "The daily re-

[1] Leo Rosten, *The Washington Correspondents,* Harcourt, Brace, 1937, p. 231.

election of the editor" serves to make the editor quite sensitive to the wishes of the electors. Here again the economic necessity to hold an audience and the political desire to do so are relevant factors, as well as the "correctness" of outlook. The point is that the nature of one's audience places certain limits upon what one can say to it—and still have an audience. The need of the audience is not only to be informed but also to be satisfied, and the latter is sometimes evaluated more highly than the former.

It is important to take account of this direction in the flow of influence between communication and public opinion in order to appreciate the reciprocal nature of that influence, i.e., to recognize that it is not all a one-way process. It is also important to note that the total effect of this reciprocal process is probably to stabilize and "conservatize" opinion since ideologies are constantly in process of reinforcement thereby. The over-all picture, then, is that of like begetting like begetting like.

THE ROLE OF THE PUBLIC OPINION POLL

—George Gallup, *A Guide to Public Opinion Polls* (2nd Edition), Princeton University Press, 1948. Dr. Gallup, director of the American Institute of Public Opinion, is widely known for the Gallup Poll.

(EDITORS' NOTE: *There is no more intriguing concept of public opinion than the one which is based on the theory that public opinion can be scientifically tested when issues arise. Dr. George Gallup, who sums up the contributions made by polling, has been one of the leading exponents of the theory ever since 1935, the year in which he undertook periodic surveys of public opinion on important issues. Dr. Gallup wrote the following justifications of polling just a few months before he and his fellow pollsters found themselves under terrific pressure because of their failure to forecast correctly the election of President Truman in November, 1948. The subsequent widespread criticism was summed up to some extent in Lindsay Rogers' book* The Pollsters.)

PUBLIC OPINION polls have been thoroughly tested in times of both peace and war. Virtually every important issue since 1935 which has come before the country has been covered in periodic surveys. The value of polls to democracy is written into the record of this era.

The reliability of methods now employed to gauge public opinion has been demonstrated time and again, not only in the United States but in a dozen different nations. Polls have met successfully the test which any scientific method must meet. They have proved equally reliable when applied in completely different circumstances and by different organizations.

Students of government have noted many contributions to our democratic process made by polls. . . . Suffice it here to review the ten which seem most important.

1. Public opinion polls have provided political leaders with a more accurate gauge of public opinion than they had prior to 1935.

No responsible person in the field of public opinion research would assert that polling methods are perfect. On the other hand, no one who has studied all the methods of gauging public opinion would maintain that other methods are superior to polling methods. Certainly the indices which were relied upon most in the past—letters, newspaper editorials, self-appointed experts, and the like—have been found to be highly inaccurate as guides to public opinion.

2. Public opinions polls have speeded up the processes of democracy by providing not only accurate, but swift, reports of public opinion.

Modern poll procedures make it possible to conduct a nationwide referendum or plebiscite in a matter of hours, and to report results that would differ by only a few percentage points from the results which would be obtained if the entire voting population of a nation went to the polls. In fact in many situations—particularly those in which a substantial portion of the population fails to take the trouble to vote—the poll results might be even more accurate as a measure of public sentiment than the official returns.

3. Public opinion polls have shown that the common people do make good decisions.

The arguments which have continued from the early days of the country regarding the political wisdom of the common people can now be settled on the basis of a mountain of factual data. The views of the people have been recorded on hundreds of issues, and enough time has elapsed to judge the soundness of majority opinion on scores of these problems.

The people have displayed such good sense, and have made such a good record, that the faith of many persons in the basic premises of democracy has been rekindled. There is little disposition today to refer to the people in slighting terms, as was the case after the first World War, when it was common to think of the people as comprising a "boobocracy."

4. Public opinion polls have helped to focus attention on major issues of the day.

They have provided what Walter Lippmann, in his book *Public Opinion,* asserted was greatly needed by this democracy—a machinery for scoring. By injecting the element of controversy, by showing the division of opinion, in fact by helping to simplify major issues by expressing them in language understandable to the great mass of people, polls have helped to increase public interest in many national issues.

5. Public opinion polls have uncovered many "areas of ignorance."

In performing this service they have brought out certain fundamental weaknesses of our educational system and have pointed to the shortcomings of the whole process of keeping the public well-informed on vital issues of the day.

6. Public opinion polls have helped administrators of government departments make wiser decisions.

The problem of dealing intelligently with the public is one that confronts not only the heads of many government departments, but state and local officials everywhere. Government is learning what business learned years ago—that any program designed to influence the public must be based upon accurate knowledge of public attitudes. Millions of dollars can be wasted by following wrong hunches about the public's information and thinking on important policies.

7. Public opinion polls have made it more difficult for political bosses to pick presidential candidates "in smoke-filled rooms."

The "open" primary was originally intended to give voters a chance to help guide the parties in choosing presidential nominees and candidates for other political office. It was designed to strip political machines of their power to select candidates without respect to the wishes of the people.

Polls can perform this service which the open primary was intended to provide. They can report the popularity of various candidates with the voters. And in doing so they can make it that much more difficult for professional politicians to hand-pick candidates.

8. Public opinion polls have shown that the people are not moti-

vated, in their voting, solely by the factor of self-interest, as many politicians have presumed.

Time after time, poll results reveal the fairness of the people in spreading the tax load to all segments of the population, their resentment at "log rolling" methods, and their concern about the national good, as contrasted with the selfish interests of their own community or state. Too often, officeholders assume that the only road to popularity and to re-election is to grab as much political booty as possible for their own electorate—a fact disproved by poll results.

9. Public opinion polls constitute almost the only present check on the growing power of pressure groups.

Many students of government have been concerned with the great influence exerted upon legislation by lobbyists for the various pressure groups in the country. By exploding the claims of these lobbyists to represent the "unanimous" or "overwhelming" sentiment of the pressure group which employs them, public opinion polls have revealed their real status.

Poll results show that pressure-group spokesmen often represent only a minority of those within their own groups, and prove baseless their threats of political reprisal if legislators do not bow to their wishes.

10. Public opinion polls help define the "mandate" of the people in national elections.

Inevitably many wrong conclusions are drawn from the attempt to read the will of the people on national issues, by examining election returns on individuals. Some of the greatest mistakes of the last thirty years have come about by trying to decide what the public really thought on issues, when it cast its vote for candidates.

Not until elections are changed to permit the public to vote on all the issues which come up in a campaign will it be possible to draw accurate conclusions about the opinion of the majority on specific problems. Meanwhile public opinion polls can perform this service. At the same time that the views of voters are obtained on candidates, the views of these same voters can be recorded on issues. In this way, election results can be interpreted much more accurately than in the past.

REVIEW QUESTIONS AND ASSIGNMENTS

1. How would you outline an "ideal relationship" between the press and public opinion?

2. What differences in influencing the formation of opinion can you cite among the mass media of communication?

3. Do you feel that reader-interest surveys are providing a better picture of the relationship between the newspaper and public opinion?

4. Why has newspaper opinion seemed so far removed from public opinion in many recent presidential elections?

5. Do you feel that, if all the mass media were controlled by the government, we could expect an improved state of public opinion?

6. What reasons can you give, based on your own responses, to support the idea that public opinion, when faced with a controversial question, tends to fatigue rather quickly?

7. How would you define: (*a*) a public, and (*b*) an opinion?

8. What are some of the factors that hinder the formation of a healthy climate of opinion?

9. How much influence do you feel is exerted by external forces on the expression of opinions in the newspaper and other mass media?

10. Viscount Bryce says politicians often go to the press for light when seeking the drift of public opinion, and adds this warning: "But the press, though an indispensable, is not a safe guide, since the circulation of a journal does not necessarily measure the prevalence of the views it advocates." Discuss.

11. Discuss Walter Lippmann's statement that there is economy in man's reliance on stereotypes.

12. Do you feel that the newspaper in your home community is a true mirror of the community's publics and their opinions?

13. What weaknesses do you see in public opinion polling as it has developed to date?

14. Write a brief summary of your concept of public opinion in a democracy.

ADDITIONAL REFERENCES

Albig, William, *Public Opinion,* McGraw-Hill, 1939.

Allport, Gordon, and Leo Postman, *The Psychology of Rumor,* Henry Holt, 1947.

Angell, Norman, *From Chaos to Control,* Century, 1933.

Bailey, Thomas A., *The Man in the Street,* Macmillan, 1948.

Beard, Charles A., *The Discussion of Human Affairs,* Macmillan, 1936.

Berelson, Bernard, "The Effects of Print Upon Public Opinion," in *Print, Radio, and Film in a Democracy,* Douglas Waples (editor), University of Chicago Press, 1942, pp. 41–65.

Bernays, E. L., *Crystallizing Public Opinion,* Liveright, 1923.

Blankenship, Albert B., *Consumer and Opinion Research,* Harper & Brothers, 1943.

Bruner, Jerome S., *Mandate From the People,* Duell, Sloan and Pearce, 1944.

Cantril, Hadley, *Gauging Public Opinion,* Princeton University Press, 1944.

———, *The Psychology of Social Movements,* John Wiley, 1941.

Carroll, Wallace, *Persuade or Perish,* Houghton Mifflin, 1948.

Childs, Harwood L., *A Reference Guide to the Study of Public Opinion,* Princeton University Press, 1934.

———, *An Introduction to Public Opinion,* John Wiley, 1941.

Commager, Henry Steele, *The American Mind,* Yale University Press, 1950.

Cottrell, Leonard, and Sylvia Eberhart, *American Opinion on World Affairs,* Princeton University Press, 1948.

Dewey, John, *The Public and Its Problems,* Henry Holt, 1927.

Eldridge, Seba, *Public Intelligence,* University of Kansas Press, 1935.

Ernst, Morris L., and David Loth, *The People Know Best,* Public Affairs Press, Washington, 1948.

Flint, L. N., *The Conscience of the Newspaper,* Appleton-Century, 1925.

Freeman, Ellis, *Conquering the Man in the Street,* Vanguard Press, 1940.

Friedrich, Carl J., *New Belief in Common Man,* Little, Brown, 1942.

Gallup, George H., *Public Opinion in a Democracy,* Princeton University Press, 1939.

———, and Saul Forbes Rae, *The Pulse of Democracy,* Simon & Schuster, 1940.

Graves, W. Brooke (editor), *Readings in Public Opinion,* Appleton-Century, 1928.

Hull, Clark L., *Principles of Behavior,* Appleton- Century, 1943.

Irion, Frederick C., *Public Opinion and Propaganda,* Thomas Y. Crowell, 1950.

Kardiner, Abram, *The Psychological Frontiers of Society,* Columbia University Press, 1945.

King, Clyde L., *Public Opinion as Viewed by Eminent Political Theorists,* University of Pennsylvania Lectures, Vol. 3, 1916, pp. 417–453.

Koop, Theodore, *Weapon of Silence,* University of Chicago Press, 1946.

Lazarsfeld, Paul, Bernard Berelson, and Hazell Gaudet, *The People's Choice: How the Voter Makes Up His Mind in a Presidential Campaign,* Duell, Sloan and Pearce, 1944.

Lerner, Max, *Ideas Are Weapons,* Viking Press, 1943.

Lippmann, Walter, *The Phantom Public,* Harcourt, Brace, 1920.

Lydgate, William A., *What America Thinks,* Thomas Y. Crowell, 1944.

McCallum, Ronald B., *Public Opinion and the Last Peace,* Oxford University Press, 1944.

MacDougall, Curtis D., *Hoaxes,* Macmillan, 1940.

McDougall, William, *The Group Mind,* G. P. Putnam's Sons, 1920.

Markel, Lester, *Public Opinion and Foreign Policy,* Harper & Brothers, 1949.

Meier, Norman C., and Harwold W. Saunders (editors), *The Polls and Public Opinion,* Henry Holt, 1949.

Merton, Robert K., *Mass Persuasion: The Social Psychology of a War Bond Drive,* Harper & Brothers, 1946.

Murphy, Gardner, *Public Opinion and the Individual,* Harper & Brothers, 1938.

Myrdal, Gunnar, *An American Dilemma,* Harper & Brothers, 1944.

Nevins, Allan, *American Press Opinion, Washington to Coolidge,* D. C. Heath, 1928.

Odegard, Peter H., *The American Public Mind,* Columbia University Press, 1930.

Parten, Mildred B., *Surveys, Polls and Samples,* Harper & Brothers, 1950.

Rice, Stuart A., *Quantitative Methods in Politics,* Alfred A. Knopf, 1928.

Robinson, Claude E., *Straw Votes,* Columbia University Press, 1932.

Rogers, Lindsay, *The Pollsters,* Alfred A. Knopf, 1949.

Schramm, Wilbur (editor), *Mass Communications,* University of Illinois Press, 1949.

Smith, Bruce, Harold D. Lasswell, and Ralph D. Casey, *Propaganda, Communications and Public Opinion,* Princeton University Press, revised 1947.

Smith, Charles W., *Public Opinion in a Democracy,* Prentice-Hall, 1939.

Thorndike, Edward L., *Human Nature and the Social Order,* Macmillan, 1940.

Thurstone, L. L., and E. J. Chave, *The Measurement of Attitude,* University of Chicago Press, 1929.

Wallas, Graham, *Human Nature in Politics,* Alfred A. Knopf, 1921.

Waples, Douglas (editor), *Print, Radio, and Film in a Democracy,* University of Chicago Press, 1942.

Weyl, Walter E., *The New Democracy,* Macmillan, 1916.

Wright, Quincy, *Public Opinion and World Politics,* University of Chicago Press, 1933.

Young, Kimball, *Source Book for Social Psychology,* F. S. Crofts, 1927, pp. 722–723.

2. THE ROLE OF PROPAGANDA

INTRODUCTION

Propaganda is the technique frequently employed by those in a position to influence the formation of opinion through reliance on the mass media of communication. The dissemination of propaganda undoubtedly exerts great influence on why people think and act the way they do. The true proportions of propaganda, therefore, must be understood by anyone who deals with the place of media in contemporary society.

Propaganda is employed by governments, institutions, groups, and individuals for many different purposes and reasons. Its use normally represents a systematic effort to obtain the consent of those at whom it is directed with respect to some goal.

Propaganda thrives on controversy. When conflict arises (and armed warfare represents the extreme example), the employment of propaganda techniques becomes evident at once. When we consider the hundreds of different groups in society with as many different programs, certain of which are controversial, a continuous use of propaganda is seen to be inevitable.

In its original meaning, propaganda was confined to the efforts of the Roman Catholic Church to propagate the faith in the Middle Ages. It was adopted later by temporal forces in the great upheaval that accompanied the rise of the modern national state. The word was not a part of the vocabulary of the average man until a group of scholars began to investigate the use of propaganda in World War I. Largely as a result of this research and subsequent investigation of the employment of propaganda in times of peace, the word became common, with many connotations.

Studies of the use of propaganda in World War I showed that atrocity stories had been widely disseminated as a means of influencing the attitudes of both allied and neutral nations. Many of these stories were later proved to have been falsehoods, and many scholars felt that atrocity symbols had been deliberately employed to achieve hoodwinking on a world scale. The result was that as propaganda became widely known it was regarded by many as promotional activity with menacing and evil attributes.

This reaction led to insistence on the part of certain students of propaganda that a distinction be made between "bad" and "good" promotion, according to source, procedure, and objective. Propaganda designed to enrich some corporation or advance the program of an interested group or to propagate a silly idea is labeled "bad," and doubly so if the source is concealed. If, however, the source is known and accepted, if the procedure is understood, and if the objective squares with public welfare, then the persuasive effort is called "good." The trouble at this point, of course, arises from the difficulty in achieving a precise determination of the true value or meaning of a given program. And the effect of the propaganda, in the final analysis, is what counts.

Despite discussion of the true nature of propaganda, no one questions its value in time of war. During World War II, Mr. Elmer Davis, the director of the Office of War Information, developed a domestic and overseas propaganda program based on what he called a policy of truth. Mr. Davis felt the greater the truth in persuasive operations, the greater the effect. The military operations during the war involved extensive use of psychological warfare. This warfare met with considerable success, despite the inability of President Roosevelt to make policy determination and propaganda operations coincide.

During the summer and fall of 1950 when American and other United Nations troops were forced to fight the aggression of North Korean Communists, the U. S. State Department's "Voice of America" vigorously continued the propaganda policy laid down by Mr. Davis. Daily broadcasts were directed at the peoples of Asia and Soviet-dominated areas in Europe in an effort to give them the truth about the postwar East-West crisis.

The representations involved in the dissemination of propaganda may take spoken, written, pictorial, or musical form. The media available to the propagandist are those that permit these representations or symbols to pass from source to object. The greater the audience of the media, the greater the area of operations of the manipulators. The newspaper, the radio, motion pictures, speeches, pamphlets and the drama are universally used channels.

Various devices may be employed in the utilization of the communications channels. The now defunct Institute for Propaganda Analysis drew up a list of seven devices shortly before the outbreak of World War II. Selection of the proper device depends on the circumstances facing the propagandist. It may be forceful or subtle, expensive or cheap, clever or vicious. Its success will be determined in pragmatic fashion by the amount of consent it wins.

There are a number of principles of propaganda that meet with wide acceptance:

1. Propaganda is an inevitable part of the communications system, both in war and in peace.
2. Propaganda probably is a necessity in populous countries.
3. Propaganda will succeed only if a responsive audience exists. That is to say, propaganda is always based on non-coercive appeals.
4. Propaganda can be controlled only through the exercise of intelligent responsibility by the owners and managers of the mass media.

THE AGE OF PROPAGANDA

—Eduard C. Lindeman and Clyde R. Miller, Introduction to *War Propaganda and the United States* by Harold Lavine and James Wechsler, Yale University Press, 1940. The authors were, respectively, president and executive secretary of the Institute for Propaganda Analysis.

WE LIVE in a propaganda age. Public opinion no longer is formulated by the slow processes of what Professor John Dewey calls shared experience. In our time public opinion is primarily a response to propaganda stimuli.

Whether or not the above statements are regarded as true depends upon one's definition of propaganda. If, for example, one condemns all propaganda as being vicious, then the above statements cannot possibly be true. On the other hand, if one assumes that propaganda is a method utilized for influencing the conduct of others on behalf of predetermined ends, it appears that every articulate person with a purpose is a propagandist. From this viewpoint it would hence be more fair to state that ours is an age of competing propagandas. The task of the thoughtful citizen, who still believes that it is his responsibility to formulate the principal ends of life, then becomes that of distinguishing and choosing between rival propagandas. And the task of the propaganda analyst is to assist the citizen in this performance. Propaganda is a method, a device for conditioning behavior. It represents nothing new in human affairs, except a refinement of techniques and the appropriation of new instruments for exerting the stimuli. Propaganda has no doubt always existed and will continue to exist so long as human beings contrive to formulate new goals and purposes.

The individual who wishes to acquaint himself with the character of contemporary propagandas begins, therefore, not with moral discriminations but rather with technical analysis. If there is a right and a wrong in propaganda, it is to be found in the relation between means and ends, methods and purposes, and not in propaganda itself. At any rate, in a relatively free society it is to be assumed that each individual or each group which has a purpose also has the right to propagate that purpose, that is, to win converts. As individuals, for example, we believe in education: we are propagandists in behalf of reasonableness. We strive, therefore, to win converts to our purpose, especially do we labor with those who believe in force because from our viewpoint they are in error. We do not assume, in any case at the outset, that those who believe in force rather than education are inferior to us either intellectually or morally. We are in competition with them in the attempt to influence public opinion. The citizen's responsibility is to choose between us, and it is at this point that propaganda analysis enters the equation. His task, the citizen's, is to examine our methods in order to discover (a) what devices we utilize in our attempts to condition his thought and behavior, (b) whether our methods are consonant with our goals, (c) whether our ostensible ends are the real ends we seek, and (d) the extent to which our methods lead to over-simplification, confusion, or falsification. . . .

Although we have attempted to provide a point of view regarding propaganda in a relatively free society, we are obliged to admit that there are in our time societies which are not free. In these societies there are no competing propagandas. This freedom has already been lost, and, alas, lost partly through propaganda. When a society reaches this stage, that is, when all ends are predetermined by dictators, the process of propaganda becomes something quite different from our descriptions. How is it possible to distinguish truth from falsehood when no one possesses the right to question the dictator's pronouncements? Our basic assumption is that this stage need not be reached so long as various propagandas may compete.

TYPES OF PROPAGANDA

—Leonard W. Doob, *Public Opinion and Propaganda,* Henry Holt, 1948, pp. 250–253.

A CLASSIFICATION of phenomena into types is usually a makeshift arrangement that is evolved for some practical reason. Women may be called vaguely or precisely "tall" or "short" in order to indicate which size coat they should buy or which size man they should love or marry. When a particular woman is so classified, obviously only her height is being considered and not the thousand-and-one other characteristics she possesses.

Innumerable schemes are available which can serve as the basis for classifying propaganda campaigns. All of them are arbitrary and hence the selection of one rather than another is a function of which aspect of propaganda, then, may refer to the motive of the propagandist; the methods he employs; the recognition or non-recognition of his objectives by the propagandees; or the consequences of his propaganda.

A classification of the basis of the propagandist's motives has already been suggested: propaganda may be intentional or unintentional. This distinction refers only to the propagandist's awareness of what he is doing: is he deliberately or unwittingly attempting to influence other people? It does not take into account all the other ways in which propaganda may be characterized, nor should it be required to.

It is difficult to classify propaganda on the basis of methods because those methods are so diverse. A dichotomy may be derived from a moral judgment and then propaganda may be called "honest" or "dishonest." Or propaganda may be labelled with reference to a particular method: there is "repetitious" and "non-repetitious" propaganda. Propaganda may also be characterized in terms of the media of communication employed: "newspaper," "radio," "motion-picture," "magazine," "leaflet," and "rumor" propaganda are the principal categories. Each of these schemes has its merits and each, consequently, should be employed as the occasion demands.

An extremely useful criterion for classifying propaganda is to refer to propagandees' recognition or non-recognition of the propagandist's objectives. Every normal adult in American society, for example, knows that the goal of an advertisement is to increase sales: the presence of the propaganda is thus appreciated and variously evaluated. The praise lavished upon the product by a housewife may be considered quite disinterested and objective, as indeed it is if she is merely an unintentional propagandist. Conceivably, however, she may be an intentional propagandist who is simply not revealing her interested motive to the propagandee: she or her husband may own stock in the company manufacturing the product or she may be paid to recommend the product as part of the company's promotion campaign. Regardless of her conscious intention, she is affecting the person with whom she is talking, and that person is not aware of the fact that he is being propagandized. Propaganda, consequently, may be *revealed, concealed,* or concealed at first and then revealed (*delayed revealed*).

Propaganda is revealed when the propagandees are aware of the fact that propaganda is affecting them. Voters during a campaign never or seldom forget that the candidates' immediate objective is to be elected. Concealed propaganda, in contrast, affects people even though they do not know that someone else—intentionally or unintentionally—is seeking to control their reactions. Fifth columnists pose as sincere patriots and try to prevent people from learning that they are being paid and directed by some outside power.

The division between revealed and concealed propaganda cannot be clearcut for two reasons. In the first place, the nature of the propaganda may be concealed at first but then later—because the propagandist makes the decision or is forced to make it or because the propagandees secure additional insight—it is revealed. The shrewd street-corner speaker does not reveal his purpose until he has attracted a crowd and aroused their interest; then he names his party or nostrum. Then, secondly, propagandees differ in their reactions to the propaganda which is affecting them: some may and others may not know what is happening to them. The same item on a radio newscast, for example, is revealed propaganda for the few who appreciate its origin and social implications, but it is concealed propaganda for the greater number who consider it an objective, important presentation of the "facts." Since minute analyses of propagandees are usually impossible and since, consequently, their own appraisal of the propagandist's objective cannot be obtained, any classification of propaganda into one of the three types must always be somewhat arbitrary. Sometimes a sample of the propagandees can be interviewed or otherwise observed, but the representativeness of the sample may remain open to question. More frequently it is possible to make reasonably probable inferences about the propagandees' reactions from the stimuli which constitute the propaganda. No investigation is required to decide that a political speech is a form of revealed propaganda for American adults, but one is necessary to determine whether members of a radio audience are able to recognize that a "news" item about a candidate has been smuggled into the press association's file.

Propaganda may also be classified in terms of its objectives. It may be called "good" or "bad" on the basis of some social, philosophical, or simply prejudiced criteria. The most obvious and distinguishing characteristic to single out is the field of human activity which the propaganda is attempting to affect. Common sense suggests types such as commercial propaganda, political propaganda, war propaganda, anti-semitic propaganda, communist propaganda, etc.

Sometimes it is useful to refer to the effort of one individual to influence others as *counter-propaganda.* This term emphasizes the negative objective of weakening customary responses which people make or of preventing responses desired by an opponent from occurring or being reinforced. In a sense, however, all propaganda involves some counter-propaganda, inasmuch as the drive strength of pre-existing competing responses must be weakened before learning can occur. The manufacturer may have a monopoly and therefore he is not forced to carry on counter-propaganda against a competitor, but he nevertheless is competing with other interests possessed by the propagandees. The term "counter-propaganda," therefore, has little psychological significance and should be employed only when it is necessary to indicate that a propagandist is seeking, intentionally or unintentionally, to counteract a competing propaganda which has been previously, is concurrently, or may eventually begin operating.

TRUTH IN WAR PROPAGANDA

—Elmer Davis, "The Government's News Service: Shall It Be Continued?" *Journalism Quarterly,* Vol. 23, June 1946, pp. 151–152. Mr. Davis, well known as a radio news commentator, was director of the Office of War Information during World War II.

... WHAT is propaganda? The late A. E. Housman once said that he could not define poetry any more than a terrier could define a rat, but that the terrier knew a rat when he saw one. That is about the way I feel about propaganda; so long as the material you send out is true, whether it is propaganda or information depends on the intention, and still more on the effect, rather than on the actual content of the material. We have recently had an instance. The blue book issued by our State Department on the pro-Nazi activities of the Argentine government was news; it was factual information. But, if the Argentine voters accepted it as true, and if they were permitted to express their feelings in the election, it would probably influence their votes. Was the State Department radio guilty of propaganda, then, in sending a report of the contents of this American official document to Argentina? If so, the AP and UP were equally guilty of propaganda, for they sent long news stories about it, too.

All those agencies, governmental and private, were reporting news; but it was news which would have a propagandistic effect. The truth is that a fact—an incontrovertible, undisputed fact—is often the most powerful propaganda. In the old war, the war of 1914, the most effective anti-German propaganda was nothing that was said by Northcliffe or Creel or any other allied propagandist; it was the German invasion of Belgium, violating a neutrality which Germany had guaranteed by treaty—an act which shocked the far more civilized world of 1914 as perhaps nothing could shock us now. The biggest anti-German propaganda in this war was Hitler's record—his broken promises, the bestiality of his rule. And the most powerful anti-Russian propaganda this winter was Mr. Vishinsky's behavior at the recent London conference; factually and objectively reported, it had a powerful propaganda effect, just as the most powerful anti-American propaganda, at present, is the knowledge, in the rest of the world, that we are letting our army and navy go to pieces, so that whatever the policies of the United States, we lack, at the moment, the force to back them up.

The definition of propaganda is not so simple. Certainly false information may be propaganda, but propaganda, as I have suggested, is not always or even often false. Falsehood is too easy to detect; and when it is exposed, your propaganda backfires. During the war the Office of War Information did make propaganda against our enemies —both to their home publics, to the inhabitants of occupied countries, and where necessary to neutral countries; but we stuck to the truth. Luckily the truth was on our side. We could stick to the truth and tell an effective story; but we told the truth to advance the interest of the United States at war, and we told it to the enemy, to occupied countries, and on occasion to neutrals, with such selection and emphasis as best to advance that interest. That was propaganda and I am not ashamed of it.

At the same time, addressing allied countries, and generally in addressing the neutrals, we provided as best we could a straight information program about American policy and American life—not glossing over the bad news such as strikes and race riots, but endeavoring to present a complete and rounded picture in which bad and good would be seen in proper perspective. That is the kind of program that the State Department proposes to conduct.

There are, of course, certain obvious types of propaganda, not for one's own country but against the government of a foreign country—what is known as the war of nerves, such as the Germans conducted against the Czechs in the summer of 1938, against the Poles in the summer of 1939, and against other nations later as their policy required. It might be noted that words are usually only one weapon in the war of nerves; propaganda is apt to be accompanied by certain governmental acts, diplomatic or economic measures. It is a milder form of political pressure than shooting war; but like shooting war, it is a carrying out of the political policy of one government against another—and like shooting war, the question whether it is justifiable or not depends on the soundness of the policy, and on the question whether the aims of that policy could not be attained by milder methods.

THREE DEFINITIONS OF PROPAGANDA

(Editors' Note: *There are many different definitions of propaganda. One authority speaks of "pre-determined private ends"; another refers to "veiled promotion"; in World War II it was called "psychological warfare." The variations result from the different outlooks and purposes of those who deal with the term. The effect of the propaganda, of course, is of much greater importance than a precise, all-encompassing definition. The following brief definitions of propaganda represent the thoughts of men from different fields of life.*)

The Manipulation of Representations

—From Harold D. Lasswell, "Propaganda," *The Encyclopedia of the Social Sciences*. By permission of The Macmillan Company, publishers, 1934, Vol. 12, pp. 521–522. Dr. Lasswell, professor of law at Yale University, is a leading authority on content analysis.

Propaganda in the broadest sense is the technique of influencing human action by the manipulation of representations. These representations may take spoken, written, pictorial, or musical form. The expected disproportion between the specific consequence and the general reaction which is behind some political assassination justifies the category "propaganda of the deed." Many official acts of legislation and administration derive their significance from the general as distinguished from the circumscribed results anticipated; these are the propaganda aspects of public policy. Both advertising and publicity fall within the field of propaganda. . . .

It is true that techniques have value implications, even though values do not necessarily depend upon technique. Nevertheless, the processes by which such techniques as those of spelling, letter forming, piano playing, lathe handling, and dialectic are transmitted may be called education; while those by which value dispositions (hatred or respect toward a person, group, or policy) are organized may be called propaganda. The inculcation of traditional value attitudes is generally called education, while the term *propaganda* is reserved for the spreading of the subversive, debatable, or merely novel attitudes. If deliberation implies the consideration of a problem without predisposition to promote any particular situation, propaganda is concerned with eliciting such predispositions.

The Altering of Man's Pictures

—From Walter Lippmann, *Public Opinion.* By permission of The Macmillan Company, publishers, 1922, pp. 26, 248–249.

BUT what is propaganda, if not the effort to alter the picture to which men respond, to substitute one social pattern for another? . . .

That the manufacture of consent is capable of great refinements no one, I think, denies. The process by which public opinions arise is certainly no less intricate than it has appeared in these pages, and the opportunities for manipulation open to anyone who understands the process are plain enough.

The creation of consent is not a new art. It is a very old one which was supposed to have died out with the appearance of democracy. But it has not died out. It has, in fact, improved enormously in technique because it is now based on analysis rather than on rule of thumb. And so, as a result of psychological research, coupled with the modern means of communication, the practice of democracy has turned a corner. A revolution is taking place, infinitely more significant than any shifting of economic power.

Within the life of the generation now in control of affairs, persuasion has become a self-conscious art and a regular organ of popular government. None of us begins to understand the consequences, but it is no daring prophecy to say that the knowledge of how to create consent will alter every political calculation and modify every political premise. Under the impact of propaganda, not necessarily in the sinister meaning of the word alone, the old constants of our thinking have become variables. It is no longer possible, for example, to believe in the original dogma of democracy; that the knowledge needed for the management of human affairs comes up spontaneously from the human heart.

The Effort To Propagate Ideas

—Ivy L. Lee, ***Publicity,*** Industries Publishing Company, 1925, pp. 21–22. Mr. Lee is remembered as a pioneer in the development of the theory and practice of public relations.

The effort to state an absolute fact is simply an attempt to achieve what is humanly impossible; all I can do is to give you my interpretation of the facts.

If my interpretation of the facts appeals to you tonight as correct and sincere; if my interpretation seems to embody accurate observation and sound processes of reasoning, and I speak to you again tomorrow, you are going to pay considerable attention to me, you are going to believe in me to a considerable extent. And then if you find the next day it is the same way, and again the next day, and the next, you are going to believe in me more and more. But if after thinking it over tomorrow, you find my interpretation of the facts tonight does not ring true, that it is contradicted by other facts you have ascertained, then when you come to hear me speak tomorrow night, you will discount a good deal of what I say because you will have found that what I said tonight did not stand the test.

That is the whole process with reference to propaganda. It is a bad word; I wish I had some subsitute for it, but after all it means the effort to propagate ideas, and I do not know any real derivative to substitute for the word; all that can be involved in propaganda is a demand, which the public is entitled to make, that when it is given information upon which it is expected to form conclusions, it shall know who is doing the telling, who is responsible for the information.

The essential evil of propaganda is failure to disclose the source of information, and arises when the person who utters it is not willing to stand sponsor for it.

THE COMMON DEVICES OF PROPAGANDA

—Institute for Propaganda Analysis, "How To Detect Propaganda," *Propaganda Analysis*, Vol. I, November 1937, pp. 1–4.

. . . We can more easily recognize propaganda when we see it if we are familiar with the seven common propaganda devices. These are:

1. The Name Calling Device.
2. The Glittering Generalities Device.
3. The Transfer Device.
4. The Testimonial Device.
5. The Plain Folks Device.
6. The Card Stacking Device.
7. The Band Wagon Device.

Why are we fooled by these devices? Because they appeal to our emotions rather than to our reason. They make us believe and do something we would not believe or do if we thought about it calmly, dispassionately. . . .

Name Calling

"Name Calling" is a device to make us form a judgment without examining the evidence on which it should be based. Here the propagandist appeals to our hate and fear. He does this by giving "bad names" to those individuals, groups, nations, races, policies, practices, beliefs, and ideals which he would have us condemn and reject. . . . Today's bad names include: Fascist, demagogue, dictator, Red, financial oligarchy, Communist, muck-raker, alien, outside agitator, economic royalist, Utopian, rabble-rouser, trouble-maker, Tory, Constitution wrecker.

"Al" Smith called Roosevelt a Communist by implication when he said in his Liberty League speech, "There can be only one capital, Washington or Moscow." When "Al" Smith was running for the presidency many called him a tool of the Pope, saying in effect, "We must choose between Washington and Rome." That implied that Mr. Smith, if elected President, would take his orders from the Pope. Recently, Mr. Justice Hugo Black has been associated with a bad name, Ku Klux Klan. In these cases some propagandists have tried to make us form judgments without examining essential evidence and implications. . . .

Use of "bad names" without presentation of their essential meaning, without all their pertinent implications, comprises perhaps the most common of all propaganda devices. Those who want to *maintain* the *status quo* apply bad names to those who would change it. . . . Those who want to *change* the *status quo* apply bad names to those who would maintain it. . . . .

Glittering Generalities

"Glittering Generalities" is a device by which the propagandist identifies his program with virtue by the use of "virtue words." Here he appeals to our emotions of love, generosity, and brotherhood. He uses words like *truth, freedom, honor, liberty, social justice, public service, the right to work, loyalty, progress, democracy, the American way, Constitution defender.* These words suggest shining ideals. All persons of good will believe in these ideals. Hence the propagandist, by identifying his individual group, nation, race, policy, practice, or belief with such ideals, seeks to win us to his cause. As Name Calling is a device to make us form a judgment to *reject and condemn,* without examining the evidence, Glittering Generalities is a device to make us *accept and approve,* without examining the evidence. . . .

Transfer

"Transfer" is a device by which the propagandist carries over the authority, sanction, and prestige of something we respect and revere to something he would have us accept. For example, most of us respect and revere our church and our nation. If the propagandist succeeds in getting church or nation to approve a campaign in behalf of some program, he thereby transfers its authority, sanction, and prestige to that program. Thus we may accept something which otherwise we might reject.

In the Transfer device symbols are constantly used. The cross represents the Christian church. The flag represents the nation. Cartoons like Uncle Sam represent a consensus of public opinion. Those symbols stir emotions. At their very sight, with the speed of light, is aroused the whole complex of feelings we have with respect to church or nation. . . .

Testimonial

The "Testimonial" is a device to make us accept anything from a patent medicine or a cigarette to a program of national policy. In this device the propagandist makes use of testimonials. "When I feel tired, I smoke a Camel and get the grandest 'lift'." . . . This device works in reverse also; counter-testimonials may be employed. Seldom are these used against commercial products like patent medicines and cigarettes, but they are constantly employed in social, economic, and political issues. "We believe that the John Lewis plan of labor organization is bad; C.I.O. should not be supported."

Plain Folks

"Plain Folks" is a device used by politicians, labor leaders, businessmen, and even by ministers and educators to win our confidence by appearing to be people like ourselves—"just plain folks among the neighbors." In election years especially do candidates show their devotion to little children and the common, homey things of life. . . . They would win our votes by showing that they're just as common as the rest of us—"just plain folks"—and, therefore, wise and good. Businessmen often are "plain folks" with the factory hands. Even distillers use the device. "It's our family's whiskey, neighbor; and neighbor, it's your price."

Card Stacking

"Card Stacking" is a device in which the propagandist employs all the arts of deception to win our support for himself, his group, nation, race, policy, practice, belief, or ideal. He stacks the cards against the truth. He uses underemphasis and overemphasis to dodge issues and evade facts. He resorts to lies, censorship, and distortion. He omits facts. He offers false testimony. He creates a smoke-screen of clamor by raising a new issue when he wants an embarrassing matter forgotten. He draws a red herring across the trail to confuse and divert those in quest of facts he does not want revealed. He makes the unreal appear real and the real appear unreal. He lets half-truth masquerade as truth. By the Card Stacking device, a mediocre candidate, through the "build-up," is made to appear an intellectual titan; an ordinary prize fighter a probable world champion; a worthless patent medicine a beneficent cure. By means of this device propagandists would convince us that a ruthless war of aggression is a crusade for righteousness. . . .

The Band Wagon

The "Band Wagon" is a device to make us follow the crowd, to accept the propagandist's program en masse. Here his theme is: "Everybody's doing it." His techniques range from those of medicine show to dramatic spectacle. He hires a hall, fills a great stadium, marches a million men in parade. He employs symbols, colors, music, movement, all the dramatic arts. He appeals to the desire, common to most of us, to "follow the crowd." Because he wants us to "follow the crowd" in masses, he directs his appeal to groups held together by common ties of nationality, religion, race, environment, sex, vocation. . . . All the artifices of flattery are used to harness the fears and hatreds, prejudices and biases, convictions and ideals common to the group; thus emotion is made to push and pull the group on to the Band Wagon. In newspaper articles and in the spoken word this device is also found. "Don't throw your vote away. Vote for our candidate. He's sure to win." Nearly every candidate wins in every election—before the votes are in. . . .

Keeping in mind the seven common propaganda devices, turn to today's newspapers and almost immediately you can spot examples of them all. At election time or during any campaign, Plain Folks and Band Wagon are common. Card Stacking is hardest to detect because it is adroitly executed or because we lack the information necessary to nail the lie. A little practice with the daily newspapers in detecting these propaganda devices soon enables us to detect them elsewhere—in radio, news-reel, books, magazines, and in expressions of labor unions, business groups, churches, schools, political parties.

REVIEW QUESTIONS AND ASSIGNMENTS

1. What is your definition of propaganda?

2. How would you distinguish between news and propaganda?

3. What steps would you take as a newspaper editor to combat what has been called "the menace of propaganda"?

4. What kind of a propaganda policy do you think the United Nations should adopt?

5. Would you favor the passage of a Federal law that would require all media to identify clearly the source of all disseminated information and opinion?

6. Discuss the statement of Elmer Davis that truthful propaganda is the most effective type of all.

7. Do you think the Federal Government would be justified in establishing a "Voice of America" program on a domestic basis?

8. Can you cite any essential differences between the propaganda output of the United States Department of Agriculture and the National Association of Manufacturers?

9. Study the reports of the Institute for Propaganda Analysis and write an evaluation.

10. Can you devise a yardstick that might be employed in attempting to measure the effect of a selected propaganda campaign?

11. Study your home-town paper for examples of the seven propaganda devices listed by the Institute for Propaganda Analysis.

12. Discuss the claim that propaganda disseminated by radio is more effective than printed propaganda.

13. Study the methods being employed at present by leaders in the field of media analysis and write an evaluation.

14. Discuss the relationship between public opinion polling and the activities of the propagandist.

ADDITIONAL REFERENCES

Bailey, Thomas S., *The Man in the Street*, Macmillan, 1948, pp. 291–303.

Bartlett, F. C., *Political Propaganda*, Macmillan, 1940.

Biddle, William W., *Propaganda and Education*, Columbia University Press, 1932.

Bornstein, Joseph, *Action Against the Enemy's Mind*, Bobbs-Merrill, 1944.

Bryson, Lyman (editor), *The Communication of Ideas*, Harper & Brothers, 1948.

Cantril, Hadley, *The Psychology of Social Movements*, John Wiley, 1941.

Carroll, Wallace, *Persuade or Perish*, Houghton Mifflin, 1948.

Casey, Ralph D., "Propaganda and Public Opinion," in *War in the Twentieth Century*, Willard Waller (editor), Dryden Press, 1940, pp. 429–477.

———, "The Press, Propaganda, and Pressure Groups," *The Annals of the American Academy of Political and Social Science*, Vol. 219, January 1942, pp. 66–75.

Chase, Stuart, *Democracy Under Pressure*, Twentieth Century Fund, 1945.

Childs, Harwood L., *Propaganda and Dictatorship*, Princeton University Press, 1936.

———, and J. N. Whitton, *Propaganda by Short Wave*, Princeton University Press, 1942.

Clarke, Edwin L., *The Art of Straight Thinking,* Appleton-Century, 1929.

Creel, George, *How We Advertised America,* Harper & Brothers, 1920.

Davidson, Philip, *Propaganda and the American Revolution,* University of North Carolina Press, 1941.

Doob, Leonard W., *Propaganda, Its Psychology and Technique,* Henry Holt, 1935.

Eastman, Max, *Artists in Uniform,* Alfred A. Knopf, 1934.

Ellis, E. (editor), "Education Against Propaganda," *Seventh Yearbook of the National Council for Social Studies,* 1934.

Evans, Bruce, *The Natural History of Nonsense,* Alfred A. Knopf, 1946.

Farago, Ladislas, *German Psychological Warfare,* G. P. Putnam's Sons, 1942.

Godfrey, J. L., "Propaganda and Public Opinion," in *American Society and the Changing World,* 2nd edition, by C. H. Pegg and others, F. S. Crofts, 1947.

Gordon, Matthew, *News Is a Weapon,* Alfred A. Knopf, 1942.

Graves, W. Brooke (editor), *Readings in Public Opinion,* Appleton-Century, 1928.

Gruening, Ernest H., *The Public Pays,* Vanguard Press, 1931.

Harper, Manly H., *Social Beliefs and Attitudes of American Educators,* Columbia University Press, 1927.

Hovland, C. I., *et al., Experiments in Mass Communication,* Vol. III of *Studies in Social Psychology in World War II,* Princeton University Press, 1949.

Hummel, William, and Keith Huntress, *The Analysis of Propaganda,* William Sloan Associates, 1949.

Huxley, Aldous, "Notes on Propaganda," *Harper's Magazine,* Vol. 174, December 1936, pp. 36–39.

Irion, Frederick C., *Public Opinion and Propaganda,* Thomas Y. Crowell, 1950.

Irwin, Will, *Propaganda and the News,* McGraw-Hill, 1936.

Jacobson, David J., *The Affairs of Dame Rumor,* Rinehart, 1948.

Kris, Ernst and Nathan Leites, "Trends in 20th Century Propaganda," in *Psychoanalysis and the Social Sciences,* International University Press, 1947.

Lasswell, Harold D., *Propaganda Technique in the World War,* Alfred A. Knopf, 1927.

Lee, Alfred M., and Elizabeth B. Lee (editors), *The Fine Art of Propaganda,* Harcourt, Brace, 1937.

Linebarger, Paul M., *Psychological Warfare,* Infantry Journal Press, 1948.

Lochner, Louis P. (editor), *The Goebbels Diaries 1942–1943,* Doubleday, 1948.

Lumley, Frederick E., *The Propaganda Menace*, Appleton-Century, 1933.

Margolin, Leo J., *Paper Bullets*, Froben, 1946.

Miller, Clyde R., *The Process of Persuasion*, Crown Publishers, 1946.

Millis, Walter, *Road to War*, Houghton Mifflin, 1935.

Mock, James R., and Cedric Larson, *Words That Won the War*, Princeton University Press, 1939.

Munson, Gorham B., *Twelve Decisive Battles of the Mind*, Greystone Press, 1942.

Overstreet, H. A., *The Mature Mind*, W. W. Norton, 1949.

Parsons, Talcott, "Propaganda and Social Control," *Psychiatry*, Vol. 5, November 1942, pp. 551–572.

Peterson, H. C., *Propaganda for War*, University of Oklahoma Press, 1939.

Raup, Robert B., *Education and Organized Interests in America*, G. P. Putnam's Sons, 1936.

Read, J. N., *Atrocity Propaganda, 1914–19*, Yale University Press, 1941.

Sington, Derrick and A. Weidenfeld, *The Goebbels Experiment*, Yale University Press, 1941.

Smith, Bruce, Harold D. Lasswell, and Ralph D. Casey, *Propaganda, Communication and Public Opinion*, Princeton University Press, 1947.

Taylor, Edmund, *Strategy of Terror*, Houghton Mifflin, 1940.

Thomas, Ivor, *Warfare by Words*, Penguin Books, 1942.

Waples, Douglas, Bernard Berelson, and Franklyn R. Bradshaw, *What Reading Does to People*, University of Chicago Press, 1940.

Warburg, James P., *Unwritten Treaty*, Harcourt, Brace, 1946.

3. FREEDOM OF PRESS IN THE UNITED STATES

INTRODUCTION

THE MOST controversial phase of journalism is the question of its right to print the news and to criticize individuals in public life. Never, since the establishment of the first newspaper, has there been a period when this right was not disputed and when its exercise was not in jeopardy. Probably that state of affairs will exist as long as there is even the semblance of a free press; nevertheless in America the press has never been so free of legal and legislative restraints as it is today. In spite of attempts to gag the press and in spite of adverse court decisions, the trend has been toward greater security for the press in is right to print the facts and to voice its opinion in all fields.

In this chapter, the editors attempt to set forth the principles upon which a free press rests. To this end excerpts from the now famous Hutchins report, *A Free and Responsible Press*, are included. This statement is among the best ever made on the subject, and it appears certain to become a lighthouse for journalistic guidance for some years to come. Because of its importance to the free press in America, the eloquent plea of Andrew Hamilton, the Philadelphia lawyer, in the trial of John Peter Zenger in 1735, is quoted at length. It is commonly held to be the most brilliant and important defense ever presented for press freedom. From a later period come the statements of Alexander Hamilton to show that not all the founding fathers of the American Constitution believed in constitutional guarantees of freedom of the press.

The remarks of Salmon throw emphasis upon five of the great crises in the fight to establish and maintain the freedom of the press. Although other crises have since occurred, this citation throws them into excellent historical perspective. From the late William Allen White, vigorous journalistic voice, comes a presentation of one of the sources of danger to press freedom. One of the most thoughtful and far-seeing suggestions to the press comes from Herbert Brucker in his

Freedom of Information. The student would do well to read all of this work.

In its conclusions, the Hutchins Commission on Freedom of the Press offered 13 recommendations to clarify the general status of press freedom in America. These suggestions, without their accompanying explanation, are presented by way of summarizing this chapter.

A FREE PRESS AND A FREE SOCIETY

—The Commission on Freedom of the Press, Robert M. Hutchins, chairman, *A Free and Responsible Press,* University of Chicago Press, 1947, pp. 6–11. This is the joint effort of the entire committee of 13 members.

FREEDOM of the press is essential to political liberty. Where men cannot freely convey their thoughts to one another, no freedom is secure. Where freedom of expression exists, the beginnings of a free society and a means for every extension of liberty are already present. Free expression is therefore unique among liberties: it promotes and protects all the rest. It is appropriate that freedom of speech and freedom of the press are contained in the first of those constitutional enactments which are the American Bill of Rights.

Civilized society is a working system of ideas. It lives and changes by the consumption of ideas. Therefore it must make sure that as many as possible of the ideas which its members have are available for its examination. It must guarantee freedom of expression, to the end that all adventitious hindrances to the flow of ideas shall be removed. Moreover, a significant innovation in the realm of ideas is likely to arouse resistance. Valuable ideas may be put forth first in forms that are crude, indefensible, or even dangerous. They need the chance to develop through free criticism as well as the chance to survive on the basis of their ultimate worth. Hence the man who publishes ideas requires special protection.

The reason for the hostility which the critic or innovator may expect is not merely that it is easier and more natural to suppress or discourage him than to meet his arguments. Irrational elements are always present in the critic, the innovator, and their audience. The utterance of critical or new ideas is seldom an appeal to pure reason, devoid of emotion, and the response is not necessarily a debate; it is always a function of the intelligence, the prejudice, the emotional biases of the audience. Freedom of the press to appeal to reason may always be construed as freedom of the press to appeal to public passion and ignorance, vulgarity and cynicism. As freedom of the press is always in danger, so is it always dangerous. The freedom of the press illustrates the commonplace that if we are to live progressively we must live dangerously.

Across the path of the flow of ideas lie the existing centers of social power. The primary protector of freedom of expression against their obstructive influence is government. Government acts by maintaining order and by exercising on behalf of free speech and a free press the elementary sanctions against the expressions of private interest or resentment: sabotage, blackmail, and corruption.

But any power capable of protecting freedom is also capable of endangering it. Every modern government, liberal or otherwise, has a specific position in the field of ideas; its stability is vulnerable to critics in proportion to their ability and persuasiveness. A government resting on popular suffrage is no exception to this rule. It also may be tempted—just because public opinion is a factor in official livelihood—to manage the ideas and images entering public debate.

If the freedom of the press is to achieve reality, government must set limits on its capacity to interfere with, regulate, or suppress the voices of the press or to manipulate the data on which public judgment is formed.

Government must set these limits on itself, not merely because freedom of expression is a reflection of important interests of the community, but also because it is a moral right. It is a moral right because it has an aspect of duty about it.

It is true that the motives for expression are not all dutiful. They are and should be as multiform as human emotion itself, grave and gay, casual and purposeful, artful and idle. But there is a vein of expression which has the added impulsion of duty, and that is the expression of thought. If a man is burdened with an idea, he not only desires to express it; he ought to express it. He owes it to his conscience and the common good. The indispensable function of expressing ideas is one of obligation—to the community and also to something beyond the community—let us say to truth. It is the duty of the scientist to his result and of Socrates to his oracle; it is the duty of every man to his own belief. Because of this duty to what is beyond the state, freedom of speech and freedom of the press are moral rights which the state must not infringe.

The moral right of free expression achieves a legal status because the conscience of the citizen is the source of the continued vitality of the state. Wholly apart from the traditional ground for a free press—that it promotes the "victory of truth over falsehood" in the public arena—we see that public discussion is a necessary condition of a free society and that freedom of expression is a necessary condition of adequate public discussion. Public discussion elicits mental power and breadth; it is essential to the building of a mentally robust public; and, without something of the kind, a self-governing society could not operate. The original source of supply for this process is the duty of the individual thinker to his thought; here is the primary ground of his right.

This does not mean that every citizen has a moral or legal right to own a press or be an editor or have access, as of right, to the audience of any given medium of communication. But it does belong to the intention of the freedom of the press that an idea shall have its chance even if it is not shared by those who own or manage the press. The press is not free if those who operate it behave as though their position conferred on them the privilege of being deaf to ideas which the processes of free speech have brought to public attention.

But the moral right of free public expression is not unconditional. Since the claim of the right is based on the duty of a man to the common good and to his thought, the ground of the claim disappears when this duty is ignored or rejected. In the absence of accepted moral duties there are no moral rights. Hence, when the man who claims the moral right of free expression is a liar, a prostitute whose political judgments can be bought, a dishonest inflamer of hatred and suspicion, his claim is unwarranted and groundless. From the moral point of view, at least, freedom of expression does not include the right to lie as a deliberate instrument of policy.

The right of free public expression does include the right to be in error. Liberty is experimental. Debate itself could not exist unless wrong opinions could be rightfully offered by those who suppose them to be right. But the assumption that the man in error is actually trying for truth is of the essence of his claim for freedom. What the moral right does not cover is the right to be deliberately or irresponsibly in error.

But a moral right can be forfeited and a legal right retained. Legal protection cannot vary with the fluctuations of inner moral direction in individual wills; it does not cease whenever a person has abandoned the moral ground of his right. It is not even desirable that the whole area of the responsible use of freedom should be made legally compulsory, even if it were possible; for in that case free self-control, a necessary ingredient of any free state, would be superseded by mechanism.

Many a lying, venal, and scoundrelly public expression must continue to find shelter under a "freedom of the press" built for widely different purposes, for to impair the legal right even when the moral right is gone may easily be a cure worse than the disease. Each definition of an abuse invites abuse of the definition. If the courts had to determine the inner corruptions of personal intention, honest and necessary criticisms would proceed under an added peril.

Though the presumption is against resort to legal action to curb abuses of the press, there are limits to legal toleration. The already recognized areas of legal correction of misused liberty of expression—libel, misbranding, obscenity, incitement to riot, sedition, in case of clear and present danger—have a common principle; namely, that an utterance or publication invades in a serious, overt, and demonstrable manner personal rights or vital social interests. As new categories of abuse come within this definition, the extension of legal sanctions is justified. The burden of proof will rest on those who would extend these categories, but the presumption is not intended to render society supine before possible new developments of misuse of the immense powers of the contemporary press.

THE KEYSTONE OF PRESS FREEDOM IN AMERICA

—Livingston Rutherford, *John Peter Zenger, His Trial, His Press,* Dodd, Mead & Company, Inc., 1904, pp. 218–221, 223–224, 226–227, 229–240. Andrew Hamilton was among Philadelphia's most noted Colonial lawyers.

MR. HAMILTON. Sure, Mr. Attorney, you won't make any Applications; all Men agree that we are governed by the best of Kings, and I cannot see the Meaning of Mr. Attorney's Caution; my well known Principles, and the Sense I have of the Blessings we enjoy under His present Majesty, makes it impossible for me to err, and I hope, even to be suspected, in that Point of Duty to my King. May it please Your Honour, I was saying, that notwithstanding all the Duty and reverence claimed by Mr. Attorney to Men in Authority, they are not exempt from observing the Rules of common Justice, either in their private or publick Capacities; the Laws of our Mother Country know no Exemption. It is true, Men in Power are harder to be come at for wrongs they do, either to a private Person, or the publick; especially a Governour in the Plantations, where they insist upon Exemption from Answering Complaints of any kind in their own Government. We are indeed told, and it is true they are obliged to answer a Suit in the King's Courts at *Westminster,* for a Wrong done to any Person here: But do we not know how impracticable this is to most Men among us, to leave their families (who depend upon their Labour and Care for their Livelihood) and carry Evidences to Britain, and at a great, nay, a far greater Expence than almost any of us are able to bear, only to prosecute a Governour for an Injury done here. But when the Oppression is general there is no Remedy even that Way, no, our Constitution has (blessed be God) given Us an opportunity, if not to have such Wrongs redressed, yet by our Prudence and Resolution we may in a great measure prevent the committing of such Wrongs, by making a Governour sensible that it is his interest to be just to those under his Care; for such is the Sense that Men in General (I mean Freemen) have of common Justice, that when they come to know, that a chief Magistrate abuses the Power with which he is trusted, for the good of the People, and is attempting to turn that very Power against the Innocent, whether of high or low degree, I say, Mankind in general seldom fail to interpose, and as far as they can prevent the Destruction of their fellow Subjects. And has it not often been seen (I hope it will always be seen) that when the Representatives of a free People are by just Representations or Remonstrances, made sensible of the sufferings of their Fellow-Subjects, by the Abuse of Power in the Hands of a Governour, they have declared (and loudly too) that they were not obliged by any Law to support a Governour who goes about to destroy a Province or Colony, or their Privileges, which by His Majesty he was appointed, and by the Law he is bound to protect and encourage. But I pray it may be considered, of what Use is this mighty Privilege, if every Man that suffers must be silent? And if a Man must be taken up as a Libeller, for telling his sufferings to his Neighbour? I know it may be answered, *Have you not a Legislature? Have you not a House of Representatives to whom you may complain?* And to this I answer, we have. But what then? Is an Assembly to be troubled with every Injury done by a Governour? Or are they to hear of nothing but what those in the Administration will please to tell them? Or what Sort of a Tryal must a Man have? And how is he to be remedied; especially if the Case were, as I have known it to happen in *America* in my Time; That a Governour who has Places (I will not [say] Pensions, for I believe they seldom give that to another which they can take to themselves) to bestow, and can or will keep the same Assembly (after he had modeled them so as to get a Majority of the House in his Interest) for near *twice Seven Years* together? I pray, what Redress is to be expected for an honest Man, who makes his Complaint against a Governour, to an Assembly who may properly enough be said, to be made by the same Governour against whom the Complaint is made? The Thing answers itself. No, it is natural, it is a Privilege, I will go farther, it is a Right which all Freemen claim, and are entitled to complain when they are hurt; they have a Right publickly to remonstrate the Abuses of Power, in the strongest Terms, to put their Neighbours upon their Guard, against the Craft or open Violence of Men in Authority, and to assert with Courage the Sense they have of the Blessings of Liberty, the Value they put upon it, and their Resolution at all Hazards to preserve it, as one of the greatest Blessings Heaven can bestow. And when a House of Assembly composed of honest Freemen sees the general Bent of the Peoples Inclinations, That is it which must and will (I'm sure it ought to) weigh with a Legislature, in Spite of all the Craft, Carressing and Cajoling, made use of by a Governour, to divert them from harkning to the Voice of their Country. As we all very well understand the true Reason, why Gentlemen take so much Pains and make such great Interest to be appointed Governours, so is the Design of their Appointment not less manifest. We know his Majesty's gracious Intentions to his Subjects; he desires no more than that his People in the Plantations should be kept up to their Duty and Allegiance to the Crown of *Great Britain,* that Peace may be preserved amongst them, and Justice impartially administered; that we may be governed so as to render us useful to our Mother Country, by encouraging us to make and raise such Commodities as may be useful to *Great Britain.* But will any one say, that all or any of these good Ends are to be effected, by a Governour's setting his People together by the Ears, and by the Assistance of one Part of the People to plague and plunder the other? The Commission which Governours bear, while they execute the Powers given them, according to the Intent of the Royal Grantor, expressed in their Commissions, requires and deserved very great Reverence and Submission; but when a Governour departs from the Duty enjoyned him by his Sovereign, and acts as if he was less accountable than the Royal Hand that gave him all that Power and Honour that he is possessed of; this sets People upon examining and enquiring into the Power, Authority and Duty of such a Magistrate, and to compare those with his Conduct, and just as far as they find he exceeds the Bounds of his Authority, or falls short in doing impartial Justice to the People under his Administration, so far they very often in return, come short in their Duty to such a Governour. For Power alone will not make a Man beloved, and I have heard it observed, That the Man who was neither good nor wise before his being made a Governour, never mended upon his Preferment, but has been generally observed to be worse: For Men who are not endued with Wisdom and Virtue, can only be kept in Bounds by the Law; and by how much the further they think themselves out of the Reach of the Law, by so much the more wicked and cruel Men are. I wish there were no instances of the Kind at this Day. . . . I beg Leave to insist, That the Right of complaining or remonstrating is natural; And the Restraint upon this natural Right is the Law only, and that those Restraints can only extend to what is *false;* For as it is Truth alone which can excuse or justify any Man from complaining of a bad Administration, I as frankly agree, that nothing ought to excuse a Man who raises a false Charge or Accusation, even against a private Person, and that no manner of Allowance ought to be made to him, who does so against a publick Magistrate. *Truth* ought to govern the whole Affair of Libels, and yet the Party accused runs risque enough even then; for if he fails in proving every Tittle of what he has wrote, and to the Satisfaction of the Court and Jury too, he may find to his Cost, that when the Prosecution is set on Foot by Men in Power, it seldom wants Friends to Favour it. And from thence (it is said) has arisen the great Diversity of Opinions among Judges, about what Words were or were not scandalous or libellous. I believe it will be granted, that there is not greater Uncertainty in any Part of the Law, than about Words of Scandal; it would be mispending of the Court's time to mention the Cases; they may be said to be numberless; and therefore the utmost Care ought to be taken in following Precedents; and the Times when the Judgments were given, which are quoted for Authorities in the Case of Libels, are much to be regarded.

I think it will be agreed, That ever since the Time of the Star Chamber, where the most arbitrary and destructive Judgments and Opinions were given, that ever an *Englishman* heard of, at least in his own country: I say, Prosecutions for Libels since the Time of that arbitrary Court, and until the glorious Revolution [the English Revolution of 1688], have generally been set on Foot at the Instance of the Crown or its Ministers; and it is no small Reproach to the Law, that these Prosecutions were too often and too much countenanced by the Judges, who held their Places at Pleasure (a disagreeable Tenure to any Officer, but a dangerous one in the Case of a Judge). To say more to this Point may not be proper. And yet I cannot think it unwarrantable, to shew the unhappy influence that a Sovereign has sometimes had, not only upon Judges, but even upon Parliaments themselves.

It has already been shewn, how the Judges differed in their Opinions about the Nature of a Libel, in the Case of the seven Bishops. There you see three Judges of one Opinion, that is, of a wrong Opinion, in the Judgment of the best Men in *England,* and one Judge of a right Opinion. How unhappy might it have been for all of us at this Day, if that Jury had understood the Words in that Information as the Court did? Or if they had left it to the Court, to judge whether the Petition of the Bishops was or was not a Libel? No they took upon them, to their immortal Honour! To determine both *Law* and *Fact,* and to understand the *Petition* of the Bishops *to be no Libel, that is, to contain no falshood nor Sedition,* and therefor found them *Not Guilty.* And remarkable is the Case of Sir *Samuel Barnardiston,* who was fined 10,000 *L.* for Writing a Letter, in which, it may be said, none saw any Scandal or Falshood but the Court and Jury; for that Judgment was afterwards looked upon as a cruel and destestable Judgment and therefor was reversed by Parliament. . . .

If then upon the whole there is so great an Uncertainty among Judges (learned and great Men) in Matters of this Kind; If Power has had so great an Influence on Judges; How cautious ought we to be in determining by their Judgments, especially in the Plantations, and in the Case of Libels? There is Heresy in Law, as well as in Religion, and both have changed very much; and we well know that it is not two Centuries ago that a Man would have been burnt as an Heretick, for owning such Opinions in Matters of Religion as are publickly wrote and printed at this Day. They were fallible Men, it seems, and we take the Liberty not only to differ from them in religious Opinions, but to condemn them and their Opinions too; and I must presume, that in taking these Freedoms in thinking and speaking about Matters of Faith or Religion, we are in the right: For tho' it is said there are very great Liberties of this Kind taken in *New-York*, yet I have heard of no Information preferred by Mr. Attorney for any Offences of this Sort. From which I think it is pretty clear, That in *New-York*, a Man may make very free with his God, but he must take special Care what he says of his Governour. It is agreed upon by all Men, that this is a Reign of Liberty; and while Men keep within the Bounds of Truth, I hope they may with Safety both speak and write their Sentiments of the Conduct of Men in Power I mean of that Part of their Conduct only, which affects the Liberty or Property of the People under their Administration; were this to be denied, then the next Step may make them Slaves: For what Notions can be entertained of Slavery, beyond that of suffering the greatest injuries and Oppressions, without the Liberty of complaining; or if they do, to be destroyed, Body and Estate, for so doing?

It is said and insisted on by Mr. Attorney, *That Government is a sacred Thing; That it is to be supported and reverenced; It is Government that protects our Persons and Estates; That prevents Treasons, Murders, Robberies, Riots, and all the Train of Evils that overturns Kingdoms and States, and ruins particular Persons; and if those in the Administration, especially the Supream Magistrate must have all their Conduct censured by Private Men, Government cannot subsist.* This is called *a Licentiousness not to be tollerated.* It is said, *That it brings the Rulers of the People into Contempt, and their Authority not to be regarded, and so in the End the Laws cannot be put in Execution.* These I say, and such as these, are the general Topicks insisted upon by Men in Power, and their Advocates. But I wish it might be considered at the same Time, How often it has happened, that the Abuse of Power has been the primary Cause of these Evils, and that it was the Injustice and Oppression of these great Men, which has commonly brought them into Contempt with the People. The Craft and Art of such Men is great, and who, that is the least acquainted with History of Law, can be ignorant of the specious Pretences, which have often been made use of by Men in Power, to introduce arbitrary Rule, and destroy the Liberties of a free People. . . .

These, I think, make out what I alledged, and are flagrant Instances of the Influence of Men in Power, even upon the Representatives of a whole Kingdom. From all which I hope it will be agreed, that it is a Duty which all good Men owe to their Country, to guard against the unhappy Influence of ill Men when intrusted with Power; and especially against their Creatures and Dependants, who, as they are generally more necessitious, are surely more covetous and cruel. But it is worthy of Observation, that tho' the Spirit of Liberty was born down and oppressed in *England* at that Time, yet it was no lost; for the Parliament laid hold of the first Opportunity to free the Subject from the many insufferable Oppressions and Outrages committed upon their Persons and Estates by Colour of these Acts, the last of which being deemed the most grievous, was repealed in the first Year of *Hen. 8th.* Tho' it is to be observed, that *Hen. 7th.* and his Creatures reap'd such great Advantages by the grievous Oppressions and Exactions, *grinding the Faces of the poor Subjects,* as my Lord *Coke* says, by Colour of this Statute by information only, that a Repeal of this Act could never be obtained during the Life of that Prince. The other Statute being the favourite Law for Supporting arbitrary Power, was continued much longer. The execution of it was by the great Men of the Realm; and how they executed it, the Sense of the Kingdom, expressed in the *17th of Charles 1st.* (by which the Court of Star-chamber, the soil where Informations grew rankest) will best declare. In that Statute *Magna Charta,* and the other Statutes made in the Time of *Edw. 3d.* which I think, are no less than five, are particularly enumerated as Acts, by which the Liberties and Privileges of the People of *England* were secured to them, against such oppressive Courts as the Star Chamber and others of like Jurisdiction. And the Reason assigned for their pulling down the Star Chamber, is *That the Proceedings, Censures, and Decrees of the Court of Star Chamber, even tho' the great Men of the Realm, nay and a Bishop too* (holy Man) *were Judges, had by Experience been found to be an intolerable Burthen to the Subject, and the Means to introduce an arbitrary Power and Government. And therefor* that Court was taken away, with all the other Courts in that Statute mentioned, having like Jurisdiction.

I don't mention this Statute, as if by the taking away the Court of Star Chamber, the Remedy for many of the abuses or Offences censured there, was likewise taken away; no, I only intend by it to shew, that the People of *England* saw clearly the Danger of trusting their Liberties and Properties to be tried, even by the greatest Men in the Kingdom, without the Judgment of a Jury of their Equals. They had felt the terrible effects of leaving it to the Judgment of these great Men to say what was *scandalous and seditious, false or ironical.* And if the Parliament of *England* thought this Power of judging was too great to be trusted with Men of the first Rank in the kingdom, without the Aid of a Jury, how sacred soever their Characters might be, and therefore restored to the People their original Right or tryal by Juries, I hope to be excused for insisting, that by the Judgment of a Parliament, from whence an Appeal lies, the Jury are the proper Judges, of what is *false* at least, if not, of what is *scandalous and seditious.* This is an Authority not to be denied, it is as plain as it is great, and to say, that this Act indeed did restore to the People Tryals by Juries, which was not the Practice of the Star Chamber, but that did not give the Jurors any new Authority, or any Right to try Matters of Law, I say this Objection will not avail; for I must insist, that where Matter of Law is complicated with Matter of Fact, the Jury have a Right to determine both. As for Instance; upon Indictment for Murder, the Jury may, and almost constantly do, take upon them to Judge whether the Evidence will amount to Murder or Manslaughter, and find accordingly; and I must say I cannot see, why in our Case the Jury have not at least as Good a Right to say, whether our News Papers are a Libel or no Libel as another Jury has to say, whether killing of a Man is Murder or Manslaughter. The Right of the Jury, to find such a Verdict as they in their Conscience do think is agreeable to their Evidence, is supported by the Authority of *Bushel's* Case in *Vaughan's Reports, pag.* 135 beyond any Doubt. For, in the Argument of that Case, the Chief Justice who delivered the Opinion of the Court, lays it down for Law, *That in all General Issues, tho' it is a Matter of Law, whether the Defendant is a Trespasser, a Disseizer, etc. in the particular Cases in Issue, yet the Jury find not (as in a special Verdict) the fact of every Case, leaving the Law to the Court; but find for the Plaintiff or Defendant upon the Issue to be tried, wherein they resolve both Law and Fact complicately.* It appears by the same Case, that tho' the discreet and lawful Assistance of the same Judge, by Way of Advice to the Jury, may be useful; yet that Advice or Direction ought always to be *upon Supposition, and not positive, and upon Coercion.* The Reason given in the same Book is *because the Judge (as Judge) cannot know what the Evidence is which the Jury have,* that is, *he can only know the Evi-*

dence given in Court: but the Evidence which the Jury have, may be of their own Knowledge, as they are returned of the Neighborhood. They may also know from their own Knowledge, that what is sworn in Court is not true; and they may know the Witnesses to be stigmatized, to which the Court may be strangers. But what is to my Purpose, is, that suppose the Court did really know all the Evidence which the Jury know, yet in that Case it is agreed, *That the Judge and Jury may differ in the Result of their Evidence as well as two Judges may,* which often happens. And in pag. 148. the Judge subjoins the Reason, why it is no Crime for a Jury to differ in Opinion from the Court, where he says, *That a man cannot see with another's Eye, nor hear by another's Ear; no more can a Man conclude or infer the Thing by anothers Understanding or Reasoning.* From all which (I insist) it is very plain, *That the Jury are by Law at Liberty (without any affront to the Judgment of the Court) to find both the Law and the Fact, in our Case,* as they did in the case I am speaking to, which I will beg Leave just to mention, and it was this. Mr. *Penn* and *Mead* being Quakers, and having met in a peaceable Manner, after being shut out of their Meeting House, preached in *Grace Church Street* in *London,* to the People of their own persuasion, and for this they were indicted; and it was said, *That they with other Persons, to the Number of* 300, *unlawfully and tumultuously assembled, to the Disturbance of the Peace etc.* To which they pleaded, *Not Guilty.* And the Petit Jury being sworn to try the issue between the King and the Prisoners, that is whether they were Guilty, according to the Form of the Indictment? Here there was no Dispute but they were assembled together, to the Number mentioned in the Indictment; But *Whether that Meeting together was riotously, tumultuously and to the Disturbance of the Peace?* was the question. And the Court told the Jury it was, and ordered the Jury to find it so; *For* (said the Court) *the Meeting was the Matter of Fact, and that is confessed, and we tell you it was unlawful, for it is against the Statute; and the Meeting being unlawful, it follows of course that it was tumultuous, and to the Disturbance of the Peace.* But the Jury did not think fit to take the Court's Word for it, for they could neither find *Riot, Tumult,* or any Thing tending to the Breach of the Peace committed at that Meeting; and they acquitted Mr. *Penn* and *Mead.* In doing of which they took upon them to judge both the *Law* and the *Fact,* at which the Court (being themselves true Courtiers) were so much offended, that they fined the Jury 40 Marks a piece, and committed them till paid. But *Mr. Bushel,* who valued the Right of a Juryman and the Liberty of his Country more than his own, refused to pay the Fine, and was resolved (tho' at great Expence and trouble too) to bring, and did bring, his *Habeas Corpus,* to be relieved from his Fine and Imprisonment, and he was released accordingly; and this being the Judgment in his Case, it is established for Law, *That the Judges, how great soever they be, have no Right to fine imprison or punish a Jury, for not finding a Verdict according to the Direction of the Court.* And this I hope is sufficient to prove, That Jurymen are to see with their own Eyes, to hear with their own Ears, and to make use of their own Consciences and Understandings, in judging of the Lives, Liberties or Estates of their fellow Subjects. And so I have done with this Point.

This is the second information for Libelling of a Governour, that I have known in *America.* And the first, tho' it may look like a Romance, yet as it is true, I will beg Leave to mention it. Governour *Nicholson,* who happened to be offended with one [of] his Clergy, met him one Day upon the Road and as was usual with him (under the Protection of his Commission) used the poor Parson with the worst of Language, threatened to cut off his Ears, slit his Nose, and at last to shoot him through the Head. The Parson being a reverend Man, continued all this Time uncovered in the Heat of the Sun, until he found an Opportunity to fly for it; and coming to a Neighbour's House felt himself very ill of a Feaver, and immediately writes for a Doctor; and that his Physician might the better judge of his Distemper, he acquainted him with the Usage he had received; concluding that the Governour was certainly mad, for that no Man in his Senses would have behaved in that Manner. The Doctor unhappily shews the Parsons letter; the Governour came to hear of it; and so an Information was preferred against the poor Man for saying *he believed the Governour was mad;* and it was laid in the Information to be *false, scandalous and wicked,* and *wrote with Intent to move Sedition among the People,* and bring His Excellency into *Contempt.* But by an order from the late Queen *Anne,* there was a Stop put to that Prosecution, with sundry others set on foot by the same Governour, against Gentlemen of the greatest Worth and Honour in that Government.

And may I not be allowed, after all this, to say, That by a little Countenance, almost any Thing which a Man writes, may with the

Help of that useful Term of Art, called an *Innuendo*, be construed to be a Libel, according to Mr. Attorney's Definition of it, *That whether the Words are spoke of a Person of a public Character, or of a private Man, whether dead or Living, good or bad, true or false* all make a Libel; for According to Mr. Attorney, *after a Man hears a Writing read, or reads and repeats it, or laughs at it, they are all punishable.* It is true, Mr. Attorney is so good as to allow, *after the Party knows it to be a Libel,* but he is not so kind as to take the Man's Word for it. . . .

Mr. Hamilton. If a Libel is understood in the large and unlimited Sense urged by Mr. Attorney, there is scarce a Writing I know that may not be called a Libel, or scarce any Person safe from being called to an Account as a Libeller; for Moses, meek as he was, libelled *Cain*; and who is it that has not libelled the Devil? For according to Mr. Attorney it is no Justification to say one has a bad Name. *Echard* has libelled our good King *William*: *Burnet* has libelled among many others King *Charles* and King *James;* and Rapin has libelled them all. How must a Man speak or write, or what must he hear, read or sing? Or when must he laugh, so as be secure from being taken up as a Libeller? I sincerely believe that were some Persons to go thro' the Streets of *New-York* now-a-days, and read a Part of the Bible, if it was not known to be such, Mr. Attorney, with the help of his *Innuendo's,* would easily turn it into a Libel. As for instance, *Is.* IX. 16. *The Leaders of the People cause them to err, and they that are led by them are destroyed.* But should Mr. Attorney go about to make this a Libel, he would read it thus; *The Leaders of the People* (*innuendo,* the Governour and Council of *New-York*) *cause them* (*innuendo,* the People of this Province) *to err, and they* (the People of this Province meaning) *that are led by them* (the Governour and Council meaning) *are destroyed* (*innuendo,* are deceived into the Loss of their Liberty) which is the worst Kind of Destruction. Or if some Persons should publickly repeat, in a Manner not pleasing to his Betters, the 10*th* and 11*th* Verses of the LVI. *Chap.* of the same Book, there Mr. Attorney would have a large Field to display his Skill, in the artful Application of his *Innuendo's.* The Words are, *His Watchmen are all blind, they are ignorant, etc. Yea, they are greedy dogs, that can never have enough.* But to make them a Libel, there is according to Mr. Attorney's doctrine, no more wanting but the Aid of his Skill, in the right adapting his *Innuendo's.* As for Instance; *His*

Watchmen (*innuendo*, the Governour's Council and Assembly) *are blind, they are ignorant* (*innuendo,* will not see the dangerous Designs of His Excellency). *Yea, they* (the Governour and Council meaning) are greedy Dogs, which can never have enough (*innuendo,* enough of Riches and Power). Such an Instance as this is seems only fit to be laugh'd at; but I may appeal to Mr. Attorney himself, whether these are not at least equally proper to be applied to His Excellency and His Ministers, as some of the Inferences and *Innuendo's* in his Information against my Client. Then if Mr. Attorney is at Liberty to come into Court, and file an Information in the King's Name, without leave, who is secure, whom he is pleased to prosecute as a Libeller? And as the Crown Law is contended for in bad Times, there is no Remedy for the greatest Oppression of this Sort, even tho' the Party prosecuted is acquitted with Honour. And give me Leave to say, as great Men as any in *Britain,* have boldly asserted, That the Mode of Prosecuting by Information (when a Grand Jury will not find *Billa vera*) is a national Grievance, and greatly inconsistent with that Freedom, which the Subjects of *England* enjoy in most other Cases. But if we are so unhappy as not to be able to ward off this Stroke of Power directly, yet let us take Care not to be cheated out of our Liberties, by Forms and Appearances; let us always be sure that the Charge in the Information *is made out clearly even beyond a Doubt; for the matters in the Information* may be called *Form* upon Tryal, yet they may be, and often have been found to be *Matters of Substance* upon giving Judgment.

Gentlemen; The Danger is great, in Proportion to the Mischief that may happen, through our too great Credulity. A proper Confidence in a Court, is commendable; but as the verdict (whatever it is) will be yours, you ought to refer no Part of your Duty to the Discretion of other Persons. If you should be of the Opinion, that there is no Falsehood in Mr. *Zenger's* Papers, you will, nay (pardon me for the Expression) you ought to say so; because you don't know whether others (I mean the Court) may be of that Opinion. It is your Right to do so, and there is much depending upon your Resolution, as well as upon your Integrity.

The loss of liberty to a generous Mind, is worse than Death; and yet we know there have been those in all Ages, who for the sake of Preferment, or some imaginary Honour, have freely lent a helping Hand, to oppress, nay to destroy their Country. This brings to my

Mind that saying of the immortal *Brutus,* when he look'd upon the Creatures of *Caesar,* who were very great Men, but by no means good Men. "*You* Romans *said* Brutus, *if yet* I *may call you so, consider what you are doing; remember that you are assisting Caesar to forge those very chains, which one day he will make your selves wear.*" This is what every Man (that values Freedom) ought to consider: He should act by Judgment and not by Affection or Self-Interest; for, where those prevail, No Ties of either Country or Kindred are regarded; as upon the other Hand, the Man, who loves his Country, prefers it's Liberty to all other Considerations, well knowing that without Liberty, Life is a Misery.

A famous Instance of this you will find in the History of another brave *Roman* of the same name, I mean *Lucius Junius Brutus,* whose story is well known and therefore I shall mention no more of it, than only to shew the Value he put upon the Freedom of his Country. After this great Man, with his Fellow Citizens whom he had engag'd in the Cause, had banish'd *Tarquin* the Proud, the last King of *Rome,* from a Throne which he ascended by inhuman murders and possess'd by the most dreadful Tyranny and Proscriptions, and had by this Means amass'd incredible Riches, even sufficient to bribe to his Interest, many of the young Nobility of *Rome,* to assist him in recovering the Crown; but the Plot being discovered, the principal Conspirators were apprehended, among whom were two of the sons of Junius Brutus. It was absolutely necessary that some should be made examples of, to deter others from attempting the restoring of *Tarquin* and destroying the Liberty of *Rome.* And to effect this it was, that *Lucius Junius Brutus,* one of the Consuls of *Rome,* in the Presence of the *Roman* People, sat Judge and condemned his own Sons, as Traitors to their Country: And to give the last Proof of his exalted Virtue, and his Love of Liberty: He with a Firmness of Mind (only becoming so great a Man), caus'd their Heads to be struck off in his own Presence; and when he observ'd that his rigid Virtue, occasion'd a sort of Horror among the People, it is observ'd he only said, "*My fellow-citizens, do not think that this Proceeds from any Want of natural Affection: No, the Death of the Sons of Brutus can affect Brutus only; but the Loss of Liberty will affect my Country.*" Thus highly was Liberty esteem'd in those Days that a Father could sacrifice his Sons to save his Country, But why do I go to Heathen *Rome,* to bring Instances of the Love of Liberty, the best Blood in Britain has been shed in the Cause of Liberty; and the Freedom we enjoy at this Day, may be said to be (in a great Measure) owing to the glorious Stand the famous *Hamden*, and other of our Countrymen, made against the arbitrary Demands, and illegal Impositions, of the Times in which they lived; who rather than give up the Rights of *Englishmen*, and submit to pay an illegal Tax, of no more, I think, than 3 shillings, resolv'd to undergo, and for their Liberty of their Country did undergo the greatest Extremities, in that arbitrary and terrible Court of Star Chamber, to whose arbitrary Proceedings (it being compos'd of the principal Men of the Realm, and calculated to support arbitrary Government), no Bounds or Limits could be set, nor could any other Hand remove the Evil but a Parliament.

Power may justly be compar'd to a great River, while kept within it's due Bounds, is both Beautiful and Useful; but when it overflows, it's Banks, it is then too impetuous to be stemm'd, it bears down all before it, and brings Destruction and Desolation wherever it comes. If then this is the Nature of Power, let us at least do our Duty, and like wise Men (who value Freedom) use our utmost Care to support Liberty, the only Bulwark against lawless Power, which in all Ages has sacrificed to it's wild Lust and boundless Ambition, the Blood of the best Men that ever liv'd.

I hope to be pardon'd Sir for my Zeal upon this Occasion; it is an old and wise Caution. *That when our Neighbours House is on Fire, we ought to take Care of our own.* For tho' Blessed be God, I live in a Government where Liberty is well understood, and freely enjoy'd: yet Experience has shewn us all (I'm sure it has to me) that a bad Precedent in one Government, is soon set up for an Authority in another; and therefore I cannot but think it mine, and every Honest Man's Duty, that (while we pay all due Obedience to Men in Authority) we ought at the same Time to be upon our Guard against Power, wherever we apprehend that it may affect ourselves or our Fellow-Subjects.

I am truly very unequal to such an undertaking on many Accounts. And you see I labour under the Weight of many Years, and am born down with great Infirmities of Body; yet Old and Weak as I am, I should think it my Duty if required, to go to the utmost Part of the Land, where my Service cou'd be of any Use in assisting to quench the Flame of Prosecutions upon Informations, set on Foot by the Government, to deprive a People of the Right of Remonstrating (and complaining too), of the arbitrary Attempts of Men in Power. Men who injure and oppress the People under their Administration provoke them to cry out and complain; and then make that very Complaint the Foundation for new Oppressions and Prosecutions. I wish I could say there were no Instances of this Kind. But to conclude; the Question before the Court and you Gentlemen of the Jury, is not of small nor private Concern, it is not the Cause of the poor Printer, nor of *New-York* alone, which you are now trying: No! It may in it's Consequence, affect every Freeman that lives under a British Government on the main of *America.* It is the best Cause. It is the Cause of Liberty; and I make no Doubt but your upright Conduct, this Day, will not only entitle you to the Love and Esteem of your Fellow-Citizens; but every Man who prefers Freedom to a Life of slavery will bless and honour You, as Men who have baffled the Attempt of Tyranny; and by an impartial and uncorrupt Verdict, have laid a Noble Foundation for securing to ourselves, our Posterity and our Neighbours, That, to which Nature and the Laws of our Country have given us a Right,—the Liberty—both of exposing and opposing arbitrary Power (in these Parts of the World, at least) by speaking and writing Truth.

OPPOSITION TO A CONSTITUTIONAL GUARANTEE

—Alexander Hamilton, *The Federalist,* No. LXXXIV. Mr. Hamilton, leading statesman of the Federalist Party in the period following the Revolution, was an advocate of a strong central government.

I GO further, and affirm that Bills of Rights, in the sense and to the extent in which they are contended for, are not only unnecessary in the proposed Constitution, but would even be dangerous. They would contain various exceptions to powers not granted; and, on this very account, would afford a colorable pretext to claim more than were granted. For why declare that things shall not be done, which there is no power to do? Why for instance, should it be said, that the liberty of the Press shall not be restrained, when no power is given by which restrictions may be imposed? I will not contend that such a provision would confer a regulating power; but it is evident that it would furnish, to men disposed to usurp, a plausible pretence for claiming that power. They might urge with a semblance of reason, that the Constitution ought not to be charged with the absurdity of providing against the abuse of an authority which was not given, and that the provision against restraining the liberty of the Press, afforded a clear implication that a power to prescribe proper regulations concerning it was intended to be vested in the National Government. This may serve as a specimen of the numerous handles, which would be given to the doctrine of constructive powers, by the indulgence of an injudicious zeal for bills of rights.

On the subject of the liberty of the Press, as much has been said, I cannot forbear adding a remark or two. In the first place, I observe that there is not a syllable concerning it in the Constitution of this State [New York]; in the next, I contend that whatever has been said about it in that of any other State, amounts to nothing. What signifies a declaration, that "the liberty of the Press shall be inviolably preserved"? What is the liberty of the Press? Who can give it any definition which would not leave the utmost latitude for evasion? I hold it to be impracticable; and from this I infer, that its security, whatever fine declarations may be inserted in any Constitution respecting it, must altogether depend on public opinion, and on the general spirit of the people and of the Government.[1] And here, after all, as intimated upon another occasion, must we seek for the only solid basis of all our rights. . . .

(EDITORS' NOTE: *The remainder of this selection is from Hamilton's address in 1804 to the court in defense of Harry Croswell, who had been indicted for libel of President Jefferson.*)

[1] To show that there is a power in the Constitution, by which the liberty of the Press may be affected, recourse has been had to the power of taxation. It is said, that duties may be laid upon publication so high as to amount to a prohibition. I know not by what logic it could be maintained, that the declarations in the State Constitutions, in favor of the freedom of the Press, would be a constitutional impediment to the imposition of duties upon publications by the State Legislatures. It cannot certainly be pretended, that any degree of duties, however low, would be an abridgement of the liberty of the Press. We know that newspapers are taxed in Great Britain, and yet it is notorious, that the Press nowhere enjoys greater liberty than in that country. And if duties of any kind may be laid without a violation of that liberty, it is evident that the extent must depend on Legislative discretion, regulated by public opinion; so that after all, general declarations respecting the liberty of the Press, will give it no greater security than it will have without them. The same invasions of it may be effected under the State Constitutions which contain those declarations, through the means of taxation, as under the proposed Constitution, which has nothing of the kind. It would be quite as significant to declare, that Government ought to be free, that taxes ought not to be excessive, etc., as that the liberty of the Press ought not to be restrained. [Footnote by Hamilton.]

The liberty of the Press consists, in my idea, in publishing the truth, from good motives and for justifiable ends, though it reflect on government, on magistrates, or individuals. If it be not allowed, it excludes the privilege of canvassing men, and our rulers. It is in vain to say, you may canvass measures. This is impossible without the right of looking to men. To say that measures can be discussed, and that there shall be no bearing on those who are the authors of those measures, cannot be done. The very end and reason of discussion would be destroyed. Of what consequence to show its object? Why is it to be thus demonstrated, if not to show, too, who is the author? It is essential to say, not only that the measure is bad and deleterious, but to hold up to the people who is the author, that, in this our free and elective government, he may be removed from the seat of power. If this be not to be done, then in vain will the voice of the people be raised against the inroads of tyranny. For, let a party but get into power, they may go on from step to step, and, in spite of canvassing their measures, fix themselves firmly in their seats, especially as they are never to be reproached for what they have done. This abstract mode, in practice can never be carried into effect. But, if under the qualifications I have mentioned, the power be allowed, the liberty, for which I contend, will operate as a salutary check. In speaking thus for the freedom of the Press, I do not say there ought to be an unbridled license; or that the characters of men who are good, will naturally tend eternally to support themselves. I do not stand here to say that no shackles are to be laid on this license.

I consider this spirit of abuse and calumny as the pest of society. I know the best of men are not exempt from the attacks of slander. Though it pleased God to bless us with the first of characters, and though it has pleased God to take him from us, and this band of calumniators, I say, that falsehood eternally repeated would have affected even his name. Drops of water, in long and continued succession, will wear out adamant. This, therefore, cannot be endured. It would be to put the best and the worst on the same level. . . .

Some observations have, however, been made in opposition to these principles. It is said, that as no man rises at once high into office, every opportunity of canvassing his qualities and qualifications is afforded, without recourse to the Press; that his first election ought to stamp the seal of merit on his name. This, however, is to forget how often the hypocrite goes from stage to stage of public fame, under false array, and how often, when men attain the last object of their wishes, they change from that which they seemed to be; that men, the most zealous reverers of the people's rights, have, when placed on the highest seat of power, become their most deadly oppressors. It becomes, therefore, necessary to observe the actual conduct of those who are thus raised up.

FIVE CRISES IN AMERICAN PRESS FREEDOM

—Lucy M. Salmon, *The Newspaper and Authority*, Oxford University Press, 1923, pp. 268–278, 280. Professor Salmon, long connected with the History Department of Vassar College, studied the press from the standpoint of the social historian.

THE ABSTRACT THEORY of the benefit of a free press has prevailed in America from the time of the difficulties with England and the establishment of the Constitution until the present time. It has often, however, been more honored in the breach than in the observance and its exact meaning has never at any time been more clearly defined than it is today. The varying degrees of freedom of the press have in America, as elsewhere, been confused with justifiable criticism, seditious libel, censorship, and regulation of the press; popular conceptions of it have been confused with judicial interpretations of it; judicial interpretations have been based on the English common law; but, says Chaffee, "the founders (of the Constitution) had seen seventy English prosecutions for libel since 1760, and fifty convictions under that common-law rule, which made conviction easy. That rule had been detested in this country ever since it was repudiated by jury and populace in the famous trial of Peter Zenger." And it must not be forgotten, he goes on to say, "that the controversy over liberty of the press was conflict between two views of government, that the law of sedition was a product of the view that the government was master, and that the American Revolution transformed into a working reality the second view that the government was servant, and therefore subjected to blame from its master, the people."[1]

During the period preceding the adoption of the Federal Constitution, it was inevitable that the theory of the sovereignty of the people should be adopted. The two theories had first crossed swords in the Zenger trial, where the Assembly of New York, representing

[1] Z. Chaffee, Jr., *Freedom of Speech*, pp. 22–24.

the people, and the governor of New York, representing the king, had ostensibly argued the question whether a person was at liberty to criticize authority adversely and whether such criticism, even though true in itself constituted libel. John Peter Zenger had criticised unfavorably a much-disliked governor of New York and was tried for libel in 1735. He was ably defended by Andrew Hamilton, a noted Philadelphia advocate of Scotch birth, and acquitted by the jury. The defense made was that the statements of *The Weekly Journal* were true and therefore not libellous. The Court held that the greater the truth the greater the libel, but it was unwilling to put to the test either the truth or the falseness of the criticisms made in *The Weekly Journal.* The acquittal of Zenger "first established in North America the principle that in prosecution for libel the jury were the judges of both the law and the facts."[2] Freedom of the press was secured and new courage to combat arbitrary power was infused into the Province of New York. While the main point at issue in the trial itself had been the question what constituted a libel, the point really gained was the assertion by implication of the right of the people to criticise the government. "The liberty of the press was secure from assault and the people became equipped with the most powerful weapon for successfully combating arbitrary power, the right of freely criticising the conduct of public men."[3]

The position taken by Jefferson in opposing the Alien and Sedition Acts of 1798 was but the natural outcome of his earlier utterance on the same general subject. He had written to James Currie, January 18, 1786, "Our liberty depends on the freedom of the press, and that cannot be limited without being lost."[4] A year later, writing to Edward Carrington from Paris on the general good sense of the public, he had said: "The people are the only censors of their governors; and even their errors will tend to keep these to the true principles of their institutions. To punish these errors too severely would be to suppress the only safeguard of the public liberty. The way to prevent these irregular interpositions of the people, is to give them full information of their affairs through the channel of the public papers, and to contrive that those papers should penetrate the whole mass of the people. The basis of our government being the opinion of the people,

[2] Rutherford, *John Peter Zenger,* p. 131.

[3] *Id.*

[4] T. Jefferson, *Writings,* Ford edition, IV, 132.

the very first object should be to keep that right; and were it left to me to decide whether we should have a government without newspapers, or newspapers without a government, I should not hesitate a moment to prefer the latter. But I should mean that every man should receive those papers, and be capable of reading them."[5] In the same spirit he later wrote to Charles Yancey, saying, "where the press is free, and every man able to read, all is safe."[6] To Washington he had written: "No government ought to be without censors; and where the press is free, no one ever will."[7] And towards the end of his life he wrote to Lafayette, indicating no change in spirit, "An hereditary chief, strictly limited, the right of war vested in the legislative body, a rigid economy of the public contributions, and absolute interdiction of all useless expenses, will go far towards keeping the government honest and unoppressive. But the only security of all, is in a free press. The force of public opinion cannot be resisted when permitted freely to be expressed. The agitations it produces must be submitted to. It keeps the waters pure."[8]

All of these attestations of a belief in the theory of a free press were not inconsistent with an entire disapproval of much printed in the press and place Jefferson in the same class with Voltaire in upholding the abstract right of freedom while disagreeing with its concrete expression. The corollary that followed was an opposition to prosecution of the press even where it was flagrantly in the wrong, though later, exasperated by the attacks of the Federalist press, he thought that "the press ought to be restored to its credibility if possible. The restraints provided by the laws of the state are sufficient if applied. And I have long thought," he continues, "that a few prosecutions of the most prominent offenders would have a wholesome effect in restoring the integrity of the presses. Not a general prosecution, for that would look like persecution: but a selected one."[9] Jefferson's opposition to the Sedition Law had thus been three fold—the Federal Government had exceeded its powers in passing it, the law in itself was objectionable; in the enforcement of the law its original purpose was merged into a persecution of the Republican press.

The most bitter of all these controversies over freedom of the press

[5] January 16, 1787, *Works*, Monticello edition, VI, 55–59.
[6] January 6, 1816, *Writings*, Ford edition, X, 4.
[7] September 9, 1792, *Works*, Monticello edition, VIII, 406.
[8] November 4, 1823, *ib.*, XV, 491.
[9] *Writings*, Ford edition, VIII, 218–219.

was that between the upholders and the opponents of slavery over the printing and the circulation of so-called incendiary literature. The weapons used by one side in the controversy were the destruction of printing-presses—four presses of E. P. Lovejoy were destroyed in succession; the type and other printing material of the Utica *Standard and Democrat,* the Abolition paper of the city, were thrown into the street; the breaking up of meetings in support of a free press; personal assaults; burning of property; suits for libel and rebukes by courts; attempted restriction through legislation; the inspection of mails and detention of papers; defamatory articles published in the press, and every other device that could be invented to suppress freedom of the press.

The effect of these efforts was only to add fuel to the flames. Attacks on the press in one community led to its reappearance in another; the suppression of a paper under one name led to its revival under another; attempts to suppress free speech in a community roused a courageous press to come to its support—during the anti-slavery agitation "when attempts were made to prevent the abolitionists from holding meetings in Nantucket, *The Islander* championed the cause of the lecturers and dealt vigorous blows against those who attempted to break up the meetings."[10] When Wendell Phillips had hurled defiance at a Boston mob with the words, "Howl on, I speak to thirty millions here," at least a part of the press realized that the real question at issue was less that of the abolition of slavery than that of free speech and a free press. A jury brought in a verdict for the leaders of the mob that killed Lovejoy, but it must be remembered that a jury had previously brought in a verdict in favor of his supporters. When the Rev. Edward Beecher, at a meeting in Alton, November 2, 1837, presented a series of resolutions in support of freeom of the press and demanding the protection of Lovejoy, the resolutions were referred to a committee and the meeting adjourned until the following day—when resolutions condemning Lovejoy's paper were adopted, but "the idea that the supporters of Mr. Lovejoy were not acting as abolitionists, but as friends of law and good order, and that a large portion of them were not abolitionists, and that they were not a party, but merely friends of their country and opponents of mob law, does not seem to have occurred to the committee at all."[11]

[10] H. B. Fuller, in R. A. Douglas-Lithgow, *Nantucket,* p. 333.
[11] E. Beecher, *Riots at Alton,* p. 83.

It had, however, occurred to many others, and the columns of *Niles' Register* all during these years indicate vigorous protest against all efforts on the part of the pro-slavery party to curb freedom of the press. Even the cautious New York *Herald* reminded the South that "When they . . . demand of the North to pass laws infringing the liberty of the press we must tell them frankly that they are running into a similar degree of fanaticism to that which they object to in the abolitionists." The Boston *Courier* expressed its opinion vigorously in rhyme and the concludng stanza of one selection ran:

> Rail on, then 'brethren of the south'—
> Ye shall not hear the truth the less—
> No seal is on the Yankee's mouth,
> No fetter on the Yankee's press!
> From our Green Mountains to the sea
> One voice shall thunder—WE ARE FREE![12]

And even Calhoun realized that the law proposed by President Jackson in his message of December 1835 would be unconstitutional and would moreover act as a two-edged sword since to give Congress the right to determine what papers were incendiary would in effect "clothe Congress with the power to abolish slavery,"[13] though his own bill that placed with postmasters the responsibility of deciding what was incendiary literature was undoubtedly equally unconstitutional.

The fourth great crisis in the history of freedom of the press in America came during the time of the Civil War when an attack on it was made in the effort to suppress sympathy with the South and to suppress criticism of the Federal Government, but these efforts received little support. Carl Schurz has described his first experience of being attacked and vilified by political opponents who raised the familiar cry that he was "in the pay" of those whose cause he was supporting. This called forth the question whether it would not be advisable to pass restrictive measures preventing the license of the press in attacking public men. But to this his emphatic answer was, "In spite of many provocations I have had to suffer, I have always been opposed to such a policy." He argues that while freedom of the press in the discussion of public characters is liable to gross abuse, restrictive legislation would be liable to far more dangerous abuse. "I

[12] *Niles' Register,* XLIX, 65.
[13] J. C. Calhoun. *Works,* V, 196–197.

do not know," he adds, "of a single instance of a public man in our political history being destroyed or seriously injured in his standing or influence by unjust attacks upon his character." Public men are often justly criticised and conscientious attacks would be discouraged were more restrictive laws in force. While it is often said that persons of fine sensibilities do not enter public life on account of the liberties the press would take with their names, such persons he compares with men who are willing to serve as soldiers only on condition that they are not compelled to march over muddy roads. But as roads are made better and therefore less muddy, so the remedy for these conditions lies in improving the press. "The American people," he concludes, "can not be too careful in guarding the freedom of speech and of the press against any curtailment as to the discussion of public affairs and the character and conduct of public men. In fact, if our newspaper press has become at all more licentious than in olden times, it is in the way of recklessly invading social privacy and of the publication of private scandals. The discussion of public matters and the treatment of men in office, especially in high office, has gradually become very much more discreet and lenient than it was in the early times of the Republic. Private scandal may perhaps be repressed by a strengthening of the libel laws. . . ."

During the Civil War, Lincoln was urged to suppress the Chicago *Times*, but he protested against such action and wrote his correspondent: "I fear you do not fully comprehend the danger of abridging the liberties of the people. A government had better go to the very extreme of toleration than to do aught that could be construed into an interference with or jeopardize in any degree the rights of the people."[14] He subsequently yielded, however, and General Burnside gave the order suspending it. But he still had misgivings and wrote to Stanton, June 4, 1863, "I have received additional despatches, which, with former ones, induce me to believe we should revoke or suspend the order suspending the Chicago *Times* and if you concur in the opinion, please have it done."[15] But the matter still would not down and he wrote to I. N. Arnold, May 25, 1864: "In regard to the order of General Burnside suspending the Chicago *Times*, now nearly a year ago, I can only say I was embarrassed with the question between what was due to the military service on the one

[14] *Suppression of the Chicago Times*. Pamphlet.
[15] *Works*, Nicolay and Hay, Tandy edition, VIII, 290.

hand, and the liberty of the press on the other, and I believe it was the despatch of Senator Trumbull and yourself, added to the proceedings of the meeting which it brought me, that turned the scale in favor of my revoking the order.

"I am far from certain to-day that the revocation was not right; and I am very sure that the small part you took in it is no just ground to disparage your judgment. . . ."[16]

But Secretary Welles had had no such misgivings and he wrote in his *Diary*, "The arrest of Vallandingham and the order to suppress the circulation of the Chicago *Times* in his military district issued by General Burnside have created much feeling. . . . These acts . . . are Burnside's, unprompted, I think, by any member of the administration. . . . The President—and I think every member of the Cabinet—regrets what has been done. . . ."[17]

At the opening of the war in August 1914, the American press, in common with the press of all neutral nations, came within the pale of neutrality prescribed by government. When America entered the war in April 1917, the American press was released from the obligation to be neutral, but it was tacitly expected to support the war to the utmost, and many held that it also incurred the obligation not to criticise the Federal Government; in common parlance, "the shoe was on the other foot." Whenever war on a large scale has been declared, the freedom of the press of all countries, both those at war and neutral nations, has thereby become seriously impaired. "When war is declared, the first casualties are free press and free speech."

But during the same period, the press of the nations actively engaged in war was never expected to be neutral, but on the contrary from the first day it was relied upon to support both war and the governments behind it. No change of policy amid stream is therefore found. But the American press during this period was much less free than was the English press. So displeasing had been the efforts made to prevent an alliance between America and the European Allies that scarcely an American periodical ventured to print anything that could be construed into an expression of sympathy or good will towards Germany or an individual German. The American press was as definitely suppressed on this one point by the public opinion of the day as if it had been controlled by definite restrictive legislation. In

16 *Works*, Tandy edition, X, 108.
17 Gideon Welles, *Diary*, June 3, 1863, I, 321.

England, with a much smaller percentage of German population, without a German-British press, and far less under the influence of German propaganda, the press at every point seemed more free than did the press of America. This is but one illustration of the limitations on the freedom of the press in a critical period due to semi-official action, vigorously supported by public opinion.

It is thus seen that in the history of freedom of the press in America five great crises have come that have threatened to stifle all free, spontaneous expression of opinion. In the Zenger trial, authority in the person of the state sought to suppress the criticism made of public officials, but the result of the trial was to secure to the people and to the press the right of such criticism. Through the alien and sedition laws, authority sought to prop up its own position, though in reality to suppress the press of the opposite political party, but its policy in the end resulted only in its own dethronement from political power. The effort to prevent the printing and circulation of incendiary literature grew out of a desire to avoid offending a wealthy and influential section of the country, but the effort only postponed the inevitable day of retribution. During the Civil War period, the effort on the part of the Federal Government to suppress sympathy with the South brought only criticism against itself and the policy was quickly repudiated by it. During the recent war, the effort to suppress the press charged with pro-German sympathy or with radical tendencies has met with a temporary partial success, but the end is not yet. In all of these five great crises, authority in the person of the government has held the whip hand, but wherever even partial success has been achieved, the victory has been a Pyrrhic one. Freedom of the press has from time to time suffered a temporary defeat, but by the path of an ever-ascending spiral, it has ultimately won the day. . . .

It seems impossible to avoid any other conclusion than that absolute freedom of the press is an ideal that does not exist outside of the imagination and that it never has, and never can be obtained. Preceded by censorship and by regulation, followed by government control and by press bureaus, publicity committees, and organized propaganda, freedom of the press seems reduced to a mere mathematical point. The conception of it has always been fluctuating, never stable. It has been limited in one country by government action, in another by vested wealth, in another by political parties; elsewhere it has been controlled by the church, in another country by the ascendant industry, in another by chauvinism, and everywhere by authority. Reasonable limitations are put on it by laws against libel and fraud—unreasonable limitations vary with every changing breeze. Freedom for the press is as unattainable as is freedom for the individual, and yet—we still believe, and rightly, that a country's freedom is measured by the freedom accorded its press.

PUBLISHERS MENACE THEIR OWN FREEDOM

—William Allen White, *Canons of Journalism* (IX), pamphlet reprinted from the Chicago *Times,* July 2, 1939, pp. 23–27. The late Mr. White achieved world fame as the editor of the Emporia (Kansas) *Gazette.*

The most serious danger that menaces the freedom of the American press is the obvious anxiety of rich publishers about the freedom of the press. They make so much noise about the threat to the freedom of the press that they have persuaded many people, particularly unthinking people, that the freedom of the press is merely a private snap for editors who wish to exploit the public by selling poisoned news. It is not a universal rule, but the rule is fairly workable that a newspaper which is eternally agonizing about the freedom of the press is a newspaper which is endangering the freedom of the press by abusing that freedom.

In the last 50 years the cost of printing machinery—by that I mean presses, linotypes, stereotypes, and photoengraving machinery—has risen so that a publisher has to be a capitalist with real standing at the town or city bank. For instance, the machinery to publish a paper in a village of 1,000 would cost, if bought new, $3,000 or $4,000. The machinery necessary to print a decent little daily newspaper in a town of 10,000 would cost from $25,000 to $40,000. The machinery to publish a daily newspaper in a town of 50,000 would cost nearly $100,000 and as towns grow into cities these figures advance until the publisher of a daily newspaper in a town of half a million needs an investment in machinery and working capital of two or three million dollars if he expects to compete with an established daily. So the publisher becomes a capitalist.

If he is a smart go-getting-up-and-coming publisher in a town of 100,000 to 1,000,000 people, the publisher associates on terms of equality with the bankers, the merchant princes, the manufacturers, and the investing brokers. His friends unconsciously color his opinion. If he lives with them on any kind of social terms in the City club or the Country club or the Yacht club or the Racquet club, he must more or less merge his views into the common views of the other capitalists. The publisher is not bought like a chattel. Indeed he often is able to buy those who are suspected of buying him. But he takes the color of his social environment.

He is pretty generally against organized labor. He is too often found opposing the government control of public utilities. He instinctively fears any regulation of the stock exchange. The right to strike seems to the rich publisher and his Chamber of Commerce friends to be sheer anarchy. It is inevitable that the managing editor and the editorial writers who want to hold their jobs take their professional views and get their professional slant from their boss, the man who signs the payroll check.

So it often happens, alas too often, that a newspaper publisher, reflecting this unconscious class arrogance of the consciously rich, thinks he is printing news when he is doctoring it innocently enough. He thinks he is purveying the truth when much that he offers seems poison to hundreds of thousands of his readers who don't move in his social and economic stratosphere. So when this rich publisher sees any kind of a threat to the freedom of the press and when he protests in big black type at what he sees or at what he thinks he sees in the menace to his freedom, the net of it is that thousands of his readers get a notion that the freedom of the press is merely a political gadget to allow rich publishers to make money by coloring the news against the poor folks! This is unfair to the rich publisher.

That it is unfair is not the worst of it. The worst of it is that, bad as he is, the crookedest, rich, property-minded publisher is vastly better than he would be if he was operating under a government controlled press. For on seven sides out of ten, the most prejudiced, unscrupulous publisher is fair and his columns in those areas are reasonably dependable.

In a government controlled press, nothing is fair, nothing is left to the routine professional judgment of the editor. A crooked, kept press, privately owned and operated, dominated by an arrogant, class-conscious individual or group of individuals, at its worst blinds only one eye of the public. But a government censored press blinds both eyes. And sometimes one objectionable newspaper in a community is mean only on one side and another mean newspaper is good on its rival's bad side. So by shopping around, the public gets the truth is a free press. . . .

But the sad thing is that the biased editor—whether he is a plutocrat or a proletarian—by his continual blatting about the freedom of the press deafens people to the truth that the freedom of the press is not primarily for the newspapers, that it is not primarily to give purse-proud publishers a chance to make money by lying to the poor. If the unthinking minorities grow into majorities who are persuaded by the property-minded editors or radicals clamoring for a free press that the free press is only a license for class-conscious lying on one side or the other, then these unthinking minorities may not protest when real freedom of the press is menaced.

So whenever I read a rabid editorial by a reactionary newspaper whooping it up for the freedom of the press I am scared stiff. For every boost that kind of a paper makes for freedom is a knock against it. That kind of press in czarist Russia, in prewar Germany and Italy of the Kingdom must have made the public sentiment that stood by and let the freedom of the press on continental Europe go to pot. A kept government press is a kept press whether it is kept by the dictatorship of the proletariat or by the dictatorship of the military plutocracy of Germany or by the dictatorship of state capitalism in Italy. A kept press is the first sign that human liberty is being crushed.

OBJECTIVITY AND PRESS FREEDOM

—Herbert Brucker, *Freedom of Information,* pp. 277–280. Copyright 1949 by Mr. Brucker. Used with the permission of The Macmillan Company. Mr. Brucker, former professor of journalism at Columbia, is editor of the Hartford (Connecticut) *Courant.*

FREEDOM of information requires nothing more drastic than encouraging the natural growth that has already given us the tradition of objective reporting. But extending that growth necessitates a sharp change of purpose and direction by the corporations that operate our newspapers, radio, moving pictures, and other means of mass communication; for more is involved here than continued progress toward objectivity in news reports to the point where they no longer display even occasional lapses from fairness; we shall not have freedom of information until we make a courageous leap into the future by broadening the tradition of objectivity to include not only news, but the interpretation of news.

Here is where the most significant and necessary change from present practice comes in. Editorials, columns, commentaries, features, cartoons, and special articles are by nature expressions of opinion; but to achieve freedom of information the orientation of that opinion must be more objective than it is today. Instead of arguing for a preconceived point of view, as now, they must be dedicated, in a spirit of scientific inquiry, to the search for truth.

At this point I can hear all Americans who are distressed at the preponderantly conservative animus of our information system groan as one man and say, "Good Lord, does this fellow expect us to trust those old buzzards who run the newspapers and radio to get religion of their own accord, and give us an honest slant on what is happening in their editorials, columns, and political tirades?" The only possible answer is, "Yes." I challenge anyone to find an approach more likely to carry us toward freedom of information than reliance on this indigenous American growth. Time passes. With it pass old men, and even young men whose ideas are old. We have come far in the past century. Is there any reason why the spiritual growth that has given us truth in the news should suddenly halt before it gives us objectivity in the evaluation of the news?

To begin with, we are not so badly off as our Cassandras would have us believe. When war came in 1939 President Roosevelt told us we were "the most enlightened and best informed people in all the world." We were. We still are. Despite the preponderantly conservative bias of our information media, no people, at any time in history, in any country, has had so complete, so accurate, and so fair a report on the world it lives in as the American people today. This is of enormous significance.

We still have a long way to go. But we shall have difficulty in going the rest of the way if we ignore the fact that we have already covered the greater part of the long, long road toward the ideal. Our system does function, and function far better than any other that has ever existed anywhere, despite what a Seldes or an Ickes, a Goebbels or a Molotov may say about it. No doubt you recall, for example, Henry Wallace's celebrated speech in 1942 to the effect that this is the century of the common man. At the time it was made, that speech was, to put it mildly, inadequately reported by the standard press. But

PM and others, making much of the incident, came out with the full text, and—well, you remember the speech still, don't you? At the time, this was cited as one more proof that a capitalist press suppresses truth. But if our press tried to suppress the Wallace speech it did not do a good job. It never does, under the American tradition. The fact is that in one way or another the American public finds out what is going on. If a too conservative press and radio ignore something that is noteworthy, it comes out anyway. Nothing is suppressed for long. Minorities, wise and foolish, public-spirited and selfish, do get their views into the open if only through minority publications. And if what they have to say is important enough, then all the resources of newspapers, radio, magazines, films, and books spread the word to the people.

The fact that our system works as well as it does ought to give us the courage to believe that it holds within itself the seeds of all we need for the future. What is conspicuously lacking is a conviction in most publishers and editors, network executives, and film producers that it is up to them to make a jump into the future like that made by the newspaper pioneers of the nineteenth century. Where is the publisher with the vision of the twenty-year-old Adolph Ochs who, when he took over the sickly Chattanooga *Times* in 1878, saw that success lay in abandoning the universally accepted habit of allegiance to a political party, political idea, religious sect, or industry? Ochs resolved instead to take the entire community for his constituency, and to publish the news as it happened for the benefit of *all* the members of that constituency. The result was that the Chattanooga *Times* and the New York *Times,* with which he subsequently repeated the formula, turned into gold mines. The publishers of today who have Ochs' vision and courage stand to win similar rewards. In fact, the newspapers that take the next and final step toward independent journalism will find themselves prospering far beyond their most fantastic dreams. There is, in other words, a commercial as well as a moral reason for a change. But if the managers of today's vastly complicated information system are to win a financial reward and a world-wide esteem like that won by Adolph Ochs, they must take a forward step as positive and as radical as the one he took. They must apply to editorial policy the same standard of service to the entire community that Ochs applied to the coverage of news. Only when an entire newspaper is put together with the thought of reflecting the desires and the needs of society as a whole will the newspaper owners and managers of the twentieth century achieve the moral greatness of their predecessors of the nineteenth.

To those publishers who insist that this is precisely what they do now it must be pointed out that, like them, the editors who dipped their news in partisan colors before publishing it also fancied they were serving their fellow men. Salvation lay through the particular political doctrine they preached. Why not, therefore, present the news only as colored by that doctrine? Once we achieved objective reporting, we could see how wrong they were. So it is now. The demands our times make on the men responsible for journalism are not easy. Our publishers and editors must give up, not only outwardly but in their hearts, all liaison with economic and political groups. They must sponsor no Committee for Constitutional Government, no partisan tax doctrine or labor policy, nor any cause at all other than independent journalism. They must not hanker after political office. They must not own a paper as an incident to owning or managing some other business. They must fight until there is not a paper left in the country with the hooks of a bank in its financial nerves. They must battle for independence until no paper or power company, no department store, no great copper or chemical industry is so much as suspected of participating in the ownership of any medium of public information.

It is difficult to see, in short, how we can realize freedom of information to the full until our publishers and editors are just that, and nothing more. Such professional independence is little enough. As we have noted long since, despite the convictions of our liberals it is not advertising or any other direct financial inducement that orients the press toward conservatism. Rather it is the fact that the men who make our newspapers live and breathe the same atmosphere as the men in the top posts elsewhere in the national economy. Therefore the severance of such economic ties with industry and finance as remain is only the beginning of independence. Our editors and publishers must also develop a healthy skepticism toward their own prejudices. They must scrupulously and suspiciously inspect the base of their own editorial policies. If they find themselves at the club, agreeing with the manufacturers and the corporation lawyers, the brokers and the real-estate men, as to the significance of the latest political speech or as to the rights in the newest labor dispute, it is a sign that they have wandered out of the Fourth Estate. Would the laboring men themselves agree in full with these better citizens at the club? Would the white-collar workers, the office girls, the housewives who do not live in the best residential districts? But why go on? All of us know already the difference between viewing the world from a particular point of view and viewing it with the objectivity of a Fourth Estate.

SUGGESTIONS FOR PRESS IMPROVEMENT

—From the Commission on Freedom of the Press, Robert M. Hutchins, chairman. *A Free and Responsible Press,* University of Chicago Press, 1947, extracted from pp. 79–100.

THE THIRTEEN recommendations made in this chapter reflect the conviction. . . . that there are no simple solutions of the problem of freeing the press from the influences which now prevent it from supplying the communication of news and ideas needed by the kind of society we have and the kind of society we desire.

. . .

1. We recommend that the constitutional guarantees of the freedom of the press be recognized as including the radio and motion pictures.

2. We recommend that government facilitate new ventures in the communications industry, that it foster the introduction of new techniques, that it maintain competition among large units through the antitrust laws, but that those laws be sparingly used to break up such units, and that, where concentration is necessary in communications, the government endeavor to see to it that the public gets the benefit of such concentration.

3. As an alternative to the present remedy for libel, we recommend legislation by which the injured party might obtain a retraction or a restatement of the facts by the offender or an opportunity to reply.

4. We recommend the repeal of legislation prohibiting expressions in favor of revolutionary changes in our institutions where there is no clear and present danger that violence will result from the expressions.

5. We recommend that the government, through the media of mass communication, inform the public of the facts with respect to its policies and of the purposes underlying those policies and that, to the extent that private agencies of mass communication are unable

or unwilling to supply such media to the government, the government itself may employ media of its own.

We also recommend that, where the private agencies of mass communication are unable or unwilling to supply information about this country to a particular foreign country or countries, the government employ mass communication media of its own to supplement this deficiency.

6. We recommend that the agencies of mass communication accept the responsibilities of common carriers of information and discussion.

7. We recommend that the agencies of mass communication assume the responsibility of financing new, experimental activities in their fields.

8. We recommend that the members of the press engage in vigorous mutual criticism.

9. We recommend that the press use every means that can be devised to increase the competence, independence, and effectiveness of its staff.

10. We recommend that the radio industry take control of its programs and that it treat advertising as it is treated by the best newspapers.

11. We recommend that nonprofit institutions help supply the variety, quantity, and quality of press service required by the American people.

12. We recommend the creation of academic-professional centers of advanced study, research, and publication in the field of communications. We recommend further that existing schools of journalism exploit the total resources of their universities to the end that their students may obtain the broadest and most liberal training.

13. We recommend the establishment of a new and independent agency to appraise and report annually upon the performance of the press.

REVIEW QUESTIONS AND ASSIGNMENTS

1. Why must freedom of press precede other freedoms?

2. Did rivalry among the Colonies increase or decrease the need for journals of opinion? Why?

3. Why might the American press at the end of the eighteenth century be said to exercise more freedom than at any other time before or since?

4. Name five of the great crises in the history of the fight for press freedom.

5. What were the two principles involved in the trial of Peter Zenger?

6. What principle did the trial of Zenger establish?

7. Give Jefferson's position with regard to freedom of the press.

8. What were Jefferson's reasons for opposing the Sedition Laws?

9. How did the fight over slavery make itself shown in the press?

10. What stand did Lincoln take during the Civil War with respect to the freedom of the press?

11. What restrictions were placed upon the American press at the outbreak of war in Europe in 1914? After April 1917? In September 1939? After December 1941?

12. Discuss the statement that freedom within any country is measured by the freedom accorded the press.

13. Set forth the main arguments used by Alexander Hamilton in opposing a constitutional guarantee of freedom of the press.

14. What was the contention of the court upon the defendant's right to prove the truth of the facts in the Zenger case?

15. The main issue in press freedom today is said to be economic independence. What does this mean?

16. What evidence have you seen of newspapers menacing their own freedom?

17. Discuss Brucker's ideas on objective reporting. To what extent is current reporting on an objective basis?

18. Discuss the 13 recommendations of the Hutchins report in the light of current practice. How feasible are these suggestions?

ADDITIONAL REFERENCES

Barth, Alan, "Freedom from Contempt," *Nieman Reports,* Vol. 3, April 1949, pp. 11–16.

Chafee, Zechariah, Jr., *Free Speech in the United States,* Harvard University Press, 1941.

———, *Government and Mass Communications,* University of Chicago Press, 1947, Vols. 1 and 2.

Dawson, S. A., *Freedom of the Press,* Columbia University Press, 1924, pp. 48–64.

Ernst, Morris L., *The First Freedom,* Macmillan, 1946, pp. 57–124.

Gerald, J. Edward, *The Press and the Constitution, 1931–1947,* University of Minnesota Press, 1948, pp. 1–19.

Gosnell, C. B., and R. B. Nixon, *Public Opinion and the Press,* Emory University Press, 1933.

Hanson, E., "Life, Liberty, and Property," *Vital Speeches Magazine,* Vol. 4, February 1, 1938, pp. 254–256.

Hocking, William Ernest, *Freedom of the Press,* University of Chicago Press, 1947.

Hughes, Charles E., *Proceedings U. S. Supreme Court,* Vol. 283, p. 697.

Hughes, Frank, *Prejudice and the Press,* Devin-Adair, 1950.

Ickes, H. L. (editor), *Freedom of the Press Today,* Vanguard Press, 1941.

Johnson, G. W., "Freedom of the Newspaper Press," bibliography, *The Annals of American Academy of Political and Social Science,* Vol. 200, November 1938, pp. 60–75.

Larson, Cedric, "OWI's Domestic News Bureau," *Journalism Quarterly,* Vol. 26, March 1949, pp. 3–14.

Lash, Robert, "A Real Threat to Freedom," *Nieman Reports,* Vol. 1, July 1947, p. 7.

Lee, Alfred M., *The Daily Newspaper in America,* Macmillan, 1937.

McCormick, Robert R., *The Freedom of the Press,* Appleton-Century, 1936.

Meiklejohn, Alexander, *Free Speech and Its Relation to Self-Government,* Harper & Brothers, 1948.

Milton, John, "Areopagitica: An Essay on the Liberty of the Press," cited in Frank L. Mott and Ralph D. Casey, *Interpretations of Journalism,* F. S. Crofts, 1937, pp. 3–15.

Price, B., "Freedom of Press, Radio and Screen," *The Annals of the American Academy of Political and Social Science,* Vol. 254, November 1947, p. 137.

Rowell, C. H., "Freedom of the Press," *The Annals of the American Academy of Political and Social Science,* Vol. 185, May 1936, pp. 182–189.

Rudd, M., "Democracy and the Press," *Scholastic,* Vol. 32, March 26, 1938, pp. 25s–28s.

Schramm, Wilbur (editor), *Communications in Modern Society,* University of Illinois Press, 1948, pp. 220–221.

——— (editor), *Mass Communications,* University of Illinois Press, 1949.

Seldes, George, *Freedom of the Press,* Bobbs-Merrill, 1935, pp. 296–309.

———, "Is a Free Press Possible?" *Scholastic,* Vol. 27, October 26, 1935, pp. 14–15.

Siebert, F. S., *Rights and Privileges of the Press,* Appleton-Century, 1934, Chapter I.

Steigleman, Walter A., *The Newspaperman and the Law,* William C. Brown, 1950.

Steinberg, Morton, "Only a Free Press Can Enable a Democracy To Function," *Journalism Quarterly,* Vol. 23, March 1946, pp. 11-19.

Swindler, William F., "The AP Trust Case in Historical Perspective," *Journalism Quarterly,* Vol. 23, March 1946, pp. 40–57.

Thayer, Frank, *Legal Control of the Press,* Foundation Press, 1950.

Whipple, Leon, *The Story of Civil Liberty in the United States,* Vanguard Press, 1927.

Yost, Casper S., *The Principles of Journalism,* Appleton-Century, 1924, pp. 115–122.

PART TWO

THE PRESS AT WORK IN SOCIETY

4. THE PRESS AN INSTITUTION OF SOCIETY

INTRODUCTION

THE MASS MEDIA of communication—newspapers, radio, news magazines, and the cinema—sharply influence the course and shape of events in society. Social, political, and economic developments, in turn, control to a large extent the day-to-day performance record of the media.

The influence exerted by the media, as we shall see in later chapters, is inevitably the outgrowth of a combination of internal factors: the private profit motive, attitudes of the publisher or owner, the news and entertainment evaluation pattern, relations with news sources, technological resources, and type of personnel employed. These factors are constantly making themselves felt in a determination of the character and quality of the content of the media.

We dare not underemphasize "the force of the impact of external forces" on the conduct of the media, despite the tendency of so many observers to look inside for the explanation whenever criticism of any one or all of the media makes itself felt. The desires, interests, and wishes of the mass audiences reached by the media, the power exerted by institutions and groups, the control enjoyed by those who stand at the sources of events, and sudden changes in the course of national and world affairs are among the many types of external influence constantly being felt by the owners and managers of the media.

Of all the mass media, the newspaper's institutional role probably is the most significant and, at the same time, controversial, because of the First Amendment to the Federal Constitution, which protects the newspaper from interference at the hands of the Congress. Magazines enjoy the same protection, but radio and the motion pictures do not. Newspaper publishers, working through groups like the American Newspaper Publishers Association, have been vociferous in claiming a privileged position in society despite the fact that their properties are private business enterprises which must be operated at a profit.

What emerges in the case of the newspaper and, to a large extent, the other mass media as well, is of a dual character: a commercial undertaking on the one hand and an institution with marked social attributes on the other. The existence of this dualism tends to keep the press constantly on the defensive. It must show that it can operate in conformance with the rules of a capitalist economy and still provide the public with the accurate, reliable, and unprejudiced information and comment it must have in order to deal intelligently with those issues that confront it. As the contributors to this chapter point out, the press cannot permit its devotion to property rights to obscure its role as a "common carrier of information."

What may be called routine news flows through the media to the public in an honest fashion. Stories about the weather, births and deaths, traffic accidents, fires, sports contests, meetings, and social gatherings reach the audience in a form both reliable and complete. Such happenings are easy for the communicators to record; they lack complexity and are non-controversial. When such accounts err, usually human carelessness or stupidity will be found to be the cause.

Suspicion and criticism of the way in which the media discharge their responsibility for disseminating a truthful flow of information do exist with respect to the treatment of events that arise from complex, controversial, and unscored developments. The charge that the press does not record news about government, foreign affairs, labor strikes, financial dealings, and crime waves in a completely unprejudiced and authoritative fashion is constantly heard. Similarly, the media often are accused of failing to provide the clarification and explanation so badly needed by the public if it is to have a true understanding of events.

The media do have imperfections; they do fall into error on occasion; they still haven't developed the specialists needed in the baffling task of recovering facts in a complex civilization.

However, it is easy to be unfairly critical of the performance record of the press. Uncovering the basic realities in a given situation and presenting them in an approximately truthful manner is not a simple task. The sources may refuse to co-operate; censorship may play a part; a portion of the record may feel the touch of the hand of the special pleader; lack of time may permit only a partial investigation. And in the case of many complex issues, the communicator knows in advance that reader interest will be trifling.

It is perfectly proper to expect the media to make an effort to provide the public with the information it must have. And, with few exceptions, the press does a remarkable job in meeting this responsibility. It is definitely unfair, however, to expect the press to solve in single-handed fashion all our communications problems for us.

THE PRIVILEGED POSITION OF THE PRESS

—Willard Grosvenor Bleyer, "Does Press Merit Privileged Place?" *Editor & Publisher*, Vol. 67, July 21, 1934, pp. 214–216. The late Professor Bleyer was for many years director of the School of Journalism at the University of Wisconsin.

LIKE OTHER forms of business and other social institutions, the American newspaper, during the last half century, has undergone a greater change than in all its previous history. As a privately owned business enterprise it has been swept along by the powerful economic currents that have transformed all business and industry. The monopolistic tendency evident everywhere in the business world has affected newspapers. The number of daily papers during the last decade has been steadily decreasing, until now many cities have but a single paper, while others have but two, one morning and one evening paper, both owned by the same company. Chains of newspapers have grown up along with chain grocery stores, chain drug stores, chain ready-made garment shops, and chain shoe stores.

As units of business and industry have become larger and larger, so newspapers have become bigger and bigger business enterprises. Large new buildings have been built to house them; improved machinery has been necessary to keep pace with the increasing size of the papers and their ever growing circulations; electricity has supplanted steam as the motive power; every new form of transportation and communication has been used to obtain more news and to distribute papers more widely. Illustrations are now transmitted by wire and wireless from one end of the country to the other, as well as from foreign countries. All these improvements have meant higher costs of production and the investment of more capital. These changes have also led to the supplanting of the great editorial leaders of the nineteenth century, men like Greeley, Raymond, Dana,

Bowles, the elder Bennett, Watterson, and Godkin, by the business-man type of newspaper publisher. . . .

The United States is the greatest newspaper-reading country in the world. Enough copies of daily papers are published to supply every family with one copy. Daily newspaper circulation is no longer confined to the city and its suburbs in which the paper is published. In typical agricultural states in the Middle West it has been found that from two-thirds to nine-tenths of the farm homes take a daily paper. Automobiles, good roads, motor trucks, and rural free delivery have extended widely both the circulation areas of the daily papers and the trading areas within which their local advertising is of value. Because of its low price and efficient methods of distribution, daily papers are now available to the great majority of the people in city and country.

But the newspaper is not fulfilling its mission if it is merely a profitable business enterprise, producing and selling cheaply a necessary commodity. Newspaper publishing is more than the mass production and mass distribution of a more or less standardized, low-price product designed for mass consumption, like bread, soap, shoes, ready-made garments, and automobiles. . . .

The newspaper, it is generally agreed, must perform a threefold function in the formation of public opinion: First, it must furnish the day's news in as complete and accurate a form as possible, because, as President Woodrow Wilson once said, the "food of opinion is the news of the day"; second, it must explain and interpret current news and current issues, in order to aid readers to form intelligent opinions; and third, it must guide public opinion, after presenting impartially both sides of every issue, by pointing out to readers what measures seem to promise the greater good for the greater number.

The answer to the question, "Does the Newspaper Merit Its Privileged Position?" depends upon the answer to the question, "Do the Newspapers as a Whole Perform Their Three-Fold Function in the Formation of Public Opinion?"

Because of the frequent criticisms of the press made both by leaders and by the rank and file of newspaper readers, as well as those recently expressed by organized newspapermen themselves, this question cannot be answered in a way that will satisfy all who are interested in newspapers.

Last year, when Dean Carl W. Ackerman of the Columbia School of Journalism interviewed a number of leaders in all walks of life, he found that they made a number of serious charges against American newspapers. Here are some of the faults that they pointed out:

First—That newspaper standards are determined by circulation; that the press gives the public what it wants, rather than what the public needs.

Second—That news values are often superficial and trivial.

Third—That most reporters are inaccurate when writing interviews.

Fourth—That newspapers are interested primarily in day-by-day news developments, and do not follow through to give readers continuous and complete accounts of what is happening.

Fifth—That the press utilizes its freedom as a license to exploit policies which make for circulation rather than for service.

Sixth—That news and photographs are sometimes deliberately falsified.

Seventh—That the press overemphasizes irrational statements made by public officials, particularly members of Congress.

Eighth—That in all civilized countries at present newspapers exist for the purpose of concealing the truth.

Ninth—That headlines frequently do not correctly reveal the facts and the tenor of the articles.

Tenth—That many men and women hesitate to express their real opinions about the press because of the uncharitable attitude of editors toward criticism and because of the fear of retaliation.

Eleventh—That the basic fault with the press is its ownership; that the press cannot be an impartial and true advocate of public service so long as its owners are engaged or involved in other businesses.

From a review of all these various criticisms of daily newspapers, it would seem that a number of them at least have fallen short of the high standards expected of them by prominent leaders, by many newspaper readers, by liberals and students of our social and economic problems, and even by working newspapermen themselves. Undoubtedly the volume of criticism has grown during the last year, because all business and industry, as well as our social and political institutions, have been subjected to closer scrutiny than ever before in an effort to find out wherein they have failed to render the fullest service. In such a re-examination, the newspaper's faults could not escape criticism. In a period like the present when we are more than usually critical of everything in American life we are prone to condemn all banks, all businesses and industries, all schools and colleges, all motion pictures, all newspapers. In thus failing to discriminate between the good and the bad, critics are manifestly unjust to those leaders and those institutions that have made honest efforts to maintain high standards. All these criticisms of the press do not apply equally to all newspapers. Undoubtedly critics of American journalism would be willing to admit that there are notable exceptions among newspapers to which most, if not all, of their strictures are inapplicable.

An analysis of these faults shows that the basic cause of them is to be found in the dual character of the newspaper; that is, it is both a private business enterprise operating under the prevailing conditions of our profit economy, and a quasi-public institution essential to the successful existence of our democratic society and government. On the one hand it must make every effort to attract as many readers and as much advertising as possible, and, in order to make a profit, must pay out for wages, salaries, and other costs of production no more than is absolutely necessary. On the other hand, it is supposed to render disinterested public service at an extremely low cost to the public. Every business operated for a profit finds it difficult to render disinterested service to the public; in fact, it is generally true that no business renders much more disinterested service than is consistent with operating on a profitable basis. Because the business of newspaper publishing has grown tremendously in the last half century, newspaper publishers, rather than newspaper editors, are the dominant element in American journalism today. As business men they are likely to take the point of view of other business men. Since the dominant motive in our profit economy is the making of money, there is always the danger that money making rather than disinterested service to the public may become the dominant factor in newspaper publishing.

Because of its dual character, the newspaper is unlike other social institutions, such as schools and colleges, libraries, and art galleries, which are either endowed or tax supported and are not dependent for their existence on the money they make; it differs also from the church, which is supported by voluntary contributions. In its dual character, the press resembles the theater.

THE NEWSPAPER AND RIGHTS OF PROPERTY

—William Allen White, "Annual Address by the President of the Society," *Problems of Journalism,* Proceedings of the 17th Annual Convention of the American Society of Newspaper Editors, 1939, pp. 15–20.

Any discussion of the American press as a public institution should begin with the modest hypothesis that the American press is honest according to its lights, which are clearer and more penetrating than the illumination of any other section of American public life. We invite comparison in our conduct and morals with the politicians who run our government, with the lawyers who interpret and give direction to our laws, with the doctors who heal our bodies, with the preachers who guide our spiritual life, with the teachers who channel our youth, with the business men who keep the wheels of economic progress moving, with industrial leaders on both sides of the bargain counter, and with the manipulators of the banking institutions that finance our commerce. Stand any one of these callings or orders beside the press, measure our leadership with theirs, their best against our best, their worst against our worst, and the common run of their ways and works with our daily outgivings, and no one would question that, measured by integrity and intelligence, American journalism is worthy to hold up its head in the presence of any other estate of our American life. Few editors are in jail or are on their way there. Few editors obviously and shamelessly defend malefactors of great wealth. The class consciousness of our profession does not seal our lips when one of our own calling makes a mistake. Our code does not require us to put the double hush on charges made against us either as individuals or against our calling. Yet when an offender from any other group of our professional friends, the lawyers, the doctors, the teachers, the preachers, the labor leaders, the great enterprisers, or the farmers in any community or in the nation at large is indicted either in the courts or at the bar of public opinion, the newspapers first of all carry the story of his misdeeds.

To no other agency of publicity, neither the radio nor the moving pictures, do the people turn in time of stress when the shadow of suspicion begins to weaken any man, any class, any party, any group of leaders. Indeed when the truth, the whole truth, and nothing but the truth will make the people free, they get the truth more quickly, more surely, more freely from the press than from any other agency. By the press, I don't mean every newspaper but I mean all newspapers. When one journal shields a public malefactor another turns its light upon him. Taken by and large on the whole the American newspapers are the most dependable source of public information. In this country American journalism, with all its faults, and they are many, is the only free, unfettered, unbossed, unlicensed vehicle through which one way or another finally and surely the truth comes to the American people. Before the Congress begins to inquire, the press has taught the people to suspect. Before the church has begun to denounce, the press has illuminated the evils that are banned. Before the teachers have become alarmed, the editors have given the teachers the facts which disturb them. Years before the organized lawyers begin to pass resolutions, the press has made the public sentiment that forces the lawyers into action.

Whom do the great crooks fear, the public enemies either from the underworld or from the plug-hat section of the upper world? Listen to them snarl at the press! Whom do crooked politicians on the right or ignorant amiable demagogues on the left denounce first of all? It's the press! If any group of bigots should attempt to undermine the liberties of the American people in the blind zeal of noble fanaticism, what institution would they seek to throttle and discredit? It would be the American press.

Yet we must not ignore the bald fact that in the last decade a considerable section of the American press, and in particular the American daily newspaper press, has been the object of bitter criticism in a wide section of American public opinion. In certain social areas a definite minority, sometimes perhaps a majority of our readers, distrust us, discredit us. It is wise and well to ask ourselves exactly what is wrong with our attitude that we should suffer these indignities from those who should be our friends. Wherein have we failed? In what section of our news gathering are we weak? Is it that we do not print the news of the churches and their differences, difficulties, or aims and aspirations? The answer is obviously no. In that area our enterprise is obviously satisfactory. Do we fail to give a fair picture of the condition of the organization of business called commerce? Are we remiss in quoting prices from hour to hour and day to day on any of the great stock exchanges where American business is reflected in its passing phases? There again our accusers must acquit us of dereliction. Do we cover up malfeasance or crime as it appears in the courts? The answer must be no. We may be justly accused of bad taste and in so far as bad taste is low morals we are perhaps reprehensible in our court reporting. But we do as editors state the truth as it is developed in the proceedings of the American courts. Anyone who has a dime to spend to buy two or three papers with two or three viewpoints may get the truth, the whole truth, and nothing but the truth out of any great trial or cause that is grinding through our courts. We might ask our accusers and critics if they are satisfied with the way we print the news of literature, science, invention, education, or the arts, and they would give us a clean bill.

But they would point the accusing finger at us if we should ask what about politics. "There," our disgruntled friends would say, "the American press is not dependable." We might well answer that so far as party politics is concerned we are vastly more reliable than the press was fifty years ago, when every newspaper was a party organ. We might call attention to the fact that the great American newspapers are independent of party control, that as editors commenting on the news or reporters gathering the news, we treat partisan Republican and Democratic leaders pretty much alike. We might answer that the American press gives every authentic political leader his full say inside of quotation marks with little bias, and on the first page if as a public figure he belongs there. Our enemies would say, "Yes, but that is not the point." If we ask, "Well, what is the point?" they would reply that the fundamental differences in American political beliefs today are not represented in the parties and that, while it is true in the campaign of 1936, for instance, we printed the speeches of Governor Landon and President Roosevelt in full and played them up with a first page lead, still the bias which spread the poison is not visible but in our inherent attitude, not toward parties, not even party leaders but toward controversies arising out of the changing status of property revealed in our politics. At the end of their indictment, our accusers might free us on every count. But our adversaries and the jury of public opinion might vote guilty on the count which charges us with a strong and poisonous bias in favor of the *status quo* as it affects the rights of property.

How are those rights of property threatened with change in the present state of our politics? Let us examine the portending change for a moment. For in that examination we may find what all the shooting is about, directed pretty generally from the left of center at our editorial heads. First of all we should remember that to the left of center a lively minority, indeed possibly a majority, of our fellow citizens, rightly or wrongly are deeply interested in seeing a change in American property rights. They are not for confiscation. They do not advocate a "divvy"—share and share alike—nothing of the sort. In social reform they believe in taxation as an instrument of social justice. In industry they would limit property right by establishing absolute collective bargaining. In financial reform this lively left center group would limit our present property rights by redefining commercial honesty.

Now property rights shift with the years. A generation ago, men who owned the railroads had a property right to issue passes on the railroads to whom they pleased. That property right gave the railroad owner great political power. The property right was taken away from them—screaming! Also the railroad owners crying socialism at the top of their lungs lost the property right to make rates on their own rails. Government had to be consulted. Sixty years ago a man who invested a dollar in an industrial concern asked no odds of government. He could do as he pleased with his industry, cut prices, destroy competition, take and give rebates, and run his own business in his own way. Government, amid cries of treason, stepped in and changed that property right with an Anti-Trust Law. Eighty years ago man had a property right in slaves. That right passed—in blood and rebellion. A hundred years ago a man could buy votes with his dollar and no one gainsaid him. That property right disappeared after a terrible turmoil. Thirty-five years ago under *caveat emptor* a man could sell any kind of food that he could fool the buyer into buying. That property right in the invested dollar also disappeared under the threat that anarchy was among us, with the passage of the Pure Food and Drug Act of June 1906. With the establishment of the Federal Trade Commission a quarter of a century ago, many property rights were curtailed; some of the property rights in swindling vanished. Year after year the laws of the land have been curbing the rights of property. We shall go on narrowing property rights under the democratic process as new inventions produce new moralities and require new checks to establish a fair balance in the relation between the dollar and the man.

At the moment, we are curtailing the property rights of the dollar invested in public utilities, of the dollar invested in the stock exchange, and we are making new limitations of the property rights of the man who hires labor. These three limitations of property rights which are no greater than a score of limitations that have been placed upon property in the memory of men now living make an acute situation. The country is divided—not into Democratic and Republican camps—nothing like that! The divisory line cuts Americans into two or three groups having definite opinions about how far the proposed limitations of the rights of property in these three areas, public utilities, the stock exchange, and labor relations shall be curtailed. Of course all sorts of caterwauling and name calling fill the air. That's nothing new. The extreme right group calls the extreme left group a bunch of socialists and communists. And the left group calls the right group a bunch of fascists. And the middle group, the third group, led by the Honorable Caspar Milquetoast and associates, the same being your Society's presidential orator and I suspect most of his fellow workers, are baffled and bewildered and only hope for the best.

But the newspapers of our country by reason of the large sums of money required to buy the tools of the trade in our business are unusually affected by a property interest. We feel, at least our publishers and owners often feel, of whom again your speaker is sometimes one, that if the rights of property are curtailed, the foundations of the Republic may be shaken. We forget that democracy has always triumphed, the flag keeps right on waving, and—thank all the gods at once—the smoke goes up the chimney just the same, even when property rights were curtailed by the eight-hour railroad law under Woodrow Wilson, even under the income tax and the parcel post in the days of William Howard Taft, even under the railroad legislation and the conservation laws of the first Roosevelt, and so even back to tariff reform in Grover Cleveland's day. And the same charges of socialism and anarchy were hurled at the reformers who advocated inheritance taxes, income taxes, the government control of trusts and railroad rates and food sales. These are the same rhetorical brickbats that are now being tossed back and forth by the reformers and the conservatives today. Then nothing happened. Now nothing will happen.

But we, we newspaper people, editors and owners, because of our large property investment, have taken the side of property unconsciously in many cases. That unconscious attitude toward the property which is the investment in our business is what makes us seem to be unfair to those who are seeking these new reforms in property rights. They will admit that we print official documents on both sides, speeches of both leaders, for instance. But because our editorials are in the main conservative, because we criticize the methods of those whom we call radical leaders, their followers are bitter. They do not realize that the right of criticism after the news is printed fairly is an inherent American right guaranteed by the Bill of Rights. Of course emotion has entered into the controversy on both sides. Our critics are sore and being sore are unfair. But what are we going to do about it?

There is our problem. We represent more than the press of any other nation in the world today, a comparatively large property investment in the tools of our trade. That property investment consciously or unconsciously gives us a bias in the narrow area where politics is now concerned with changing property rights. To recognize this situation frankly and treat it with kind, courageous candor is half the battle. If we know what is the matter with us we can prescribe for ourselves. That doesn't mean that we should retreat. That doesn't mean that we should change our opinions if they oppose the current shift in property rights. But it does mean that we cannot afford to call names. It does mean that we should recognize that when it is all over, even though property rights do shift, they will shift under the democratic process and in the shift the Republic will live and life will adjust itself through new conditions and liberty will survive. If our opponents emotionalize their logic, it will pay us to calm down. We can well afford to take it easy. We can well afford to continue to print both sides, to editorialize after the dictates of our own conscience. But we should also not emote too heavily. Nothing is gained by working up a temperature, by jiggling our hair shirts. We can say what we want more convincingly if we are kind than if we are all hot and bothered. . . . We can rage if we will against sin and the sales tax and political corruption and other devices of the devil. But for the prestige of our calling, for the good of the order, we can afford to be nobly logical for a time while these problems affecting property are grinding through the public mill.

THE MAIN FUNCTION OF THE PRESS

—James S. Pope, "On Understanding the Press," *Nieman Reports,* Vol. 2, April 1948, pp. 7–8. Mr. Pope is the managing editor of the Louisville (Kentucky) *Courier-Journal.*

NOW IT IS OBVIOUS that the main burden of [press] responsibility lies with owners and editors. As a group we have done too little to improve and modernize our product. We have adhered too closely to threadbare concepts of what news is and how it should be presented.

I am glad to report stirrings of conscience on many of these items. Experts on typography and readability have been employed by many editors who once thought they knew it all. The American Press Institute at Columbia University is shaking hundreds of editors and reporters out of such lethargy and smugness as they have let invade their work.

And in Detroit last October [1947], managing editors delivered eight reports which lashed out in friendly but unreserved fashion at the best news service in the world, the Associated Press. This has become a continuing study which will go on around the clock and calendar.

There is plenty more that we need to do, but we are never going to do all of it until the readers' responsibility to the press begins to be discharged. And they do have one—as students, as teachers, as readers, and just as Americans.

Particularly as Americans. It takes only a brief look at the true function of the press to make clear how broad is the responsibility involved, because the true function of a newspaper in a democracy is to make it sure that the democracy can work.

I do not see how that relationship can be challenged without ignoring history. The first guarantee of the Bill of Rights was freedom of the press, but the first concern of all those guarantees was the freedom of all of us. The Bill of Rights could not have had as an aim the accumulation of power by individual newspaper owners because it was dead against accumulations of power; and it could not have been concerned with the privilege of printing comic strips and crossword puzzles because these ornaments of the press had not appeared.

A group of Nieman Fellows has written a book called *Your Newspaper,* and in the introduction Louis M. Lyons, Curator of the Nieman Foundation, makes this point compactly. He says:

"There is only one function which justifies the exalted protection given the press in our Constitution: that is as a common carrier of information."

The conveying of this information is vital for a manifest reason: people who govern themselves have to know the score. Nevertheless, hundreds of newspapers habitually carry this information, this news so essential to the life of a democracy, in the most horribly butchered and distorted form, as something stuffed into the paper where a hole occurs, and the less holes the better. These papers feel many compulsions, but not the compulsion to give their readers a comprehensive and balanced picture of what goes on.

Some, especially where competition is keen, feel the human compulsion to promote street sales, though the Bill of Rights seemed indifferent to street sales. I know publishers, honorable men, who cast out of their shop patently dishonest advertising, yet their front pages are a mass of dishonest 8-column streamers nearly every day—frequently dishonest in words, usually dishonest in emphasis.

Some papers feel the compulsion to propagate their owner's social, political and economic ideas in their own columns, unaware that freedom should include freedom of news from color and distortion.

And most do surely feel the compulsion to make money. Too many of them use news merely to plug gaps in their advertising; it is rare that the news space on these papers is altered to fit the flow of copy after the dummies are laid out in the advertising department, unless some overwhelming event comes along. To be sure advertisements and financial stability are essential to any good newspaper that is to be its own master. Still, it is noteworthy that the Bill of Rights threw no safeguards around this. On the contrary its authors seemed to assume that no editor in a democracy would ever throw away significant news merely to get in another ad for a New Look.

Meditate on this problem from any and all aspects. I believe you will wind up agreeing with Louis Lyons. The main function of the press as an institution guaranteed certain constitutional rights, is to protect and strengthen the democracy which that Constitution was undertaking to assure.

WHAT THE PEOPLE EXPECT IN A NEWSPAPER

—Charles E. Swanson, "Midcity Daily: What the People Think a Newspaper Should Be," *Journalism Quarterly*, Vol. 26, June 1949, pp. 173–176. Professor Swanson is director of the Research Division of the University of Minnesota School of Journalism.

(EDITORS' NOTE: *The following data are based on questions asked of 373 adults in a mid-western community called Midcity. Professor Swanson was seeking to test two hypotheses: (1) Midcity had certain values as to what its daily newspaper should be, and (2) these values operated as one kind of control upon the news policies of the*

Daily *in the sense that the staff was inevitably responsive to reactions of readers.*)

In approaching the problem of what values Midcity had about its newspaper, one would expect these Midwesterners to have values about "freedom of speech and press," religion, and "individual rights." How much "freedom" would they allow "newspapers"? A question was designed to measure the agreement about this value. Its results follow:

Which of these things do you believe newspapers ought to do:
Print only ideas or opinions most people agree with? (4.02%).
Or print all ideas or opinions? (92.4%).
No opinion. (3.49%).

This printing of "all ideas or opinions" would appear to be a value, a moral requirement on "newspapers."

More detail on the outlines of this and related values was obtained by recording 1,826 comments on this and 11 related questions. The themes of these comments are grouped in the order of their frequencies in Table II.

Table II

MAJOR THEMES ABOUT WHAT THE NEWSPAPER SHOULD BE

(These themes were obtained by content analysis of 1,826 volunteered remarks made by 373 Midcity adults in replies to 12 questions on what the newspaper in Midcity should print.)

Theme	*Frequency*	*Proportion of 1,826 Comments (Percentages)*
1. "The newspaper should stand for what I think is the public interest."	505	27.7
2. "The newspaper should print enough news to keep me adequately informed."	400	21.9
3. "The newspaper should conform to my standards of decency and good taste."	278	15.2
4. "The newspaper should print what I think are both sides of an issue."	233	12.8
5. "The news should be what I consider true and accurate."	172	9.4
6. "I believe in freedom of the press and speech."	170	9.3
7. "The news should be condensed, easy to understand, and interesting to me, so I may read it in as little time as possible."	38	2.1
8. "The newspaper is justified in making a profit."	30	1.6
	1,826	100.0

One should note that each comment was made in response to a question which related to values. Therefore, it is not surprising that the themes about "public interest," "decency," printing "both sides of an issue," and "true and accurate news" account for 64.06 per cent of the 1,826 comments.

Even the news function, or the demand that the newspaper supply "adequate" information, is overshadowed by the value which requires the newspaper to act in what these people consider the "public interest."

The personal nature of these comments and these themes should be emphasized. These remarks nearly always included "I think" or "we think." Midcity expected the newspaper to conform within the limits of "what I think is right."

Midcity had favored the printing of "all news or opinions"—including items which might oppose the values or interests of groups in this U. S. native white, Protestant, midwestern culture. What would happen to this 92 per cent majority for "all ideas or opinions" when put to the test of questions which posed value-conflict situations?

The *Daily* was noted for its "crusades" and for its "plain speech" in its editorial columns. It was "against the New Deal," and it criticized books, movies, public officials, the President of the United States, labor unions, business, and other groups. Would Midcity allow its newspaper to "attack," to "criticize," or to print "objectionable" material on certain topics?[1]

Table III shows how Midcity retreated from applying the value to its newspaper that newspapers should be free to "print all ideas and opinions."

Did the *Daily's* columns show that the staff was aware of these values or these areas of conflict about what it should print? In the 20 months of this study, the newspaper—in greater or lesser degree—took these actions:

Criticized each day the movies shown locally and on Sundays criticized books.

Printed beer advertisements—but no liquor advertisements.

Criticized the mayor and other local officials.

Criticized the President of the United States and his policies.

[1] Characteristics of the Midcity sample showed U. S. native white 71.3 per cent, Protestant 75.6 per cent, and non-union 75.6 per cent.

TABLE III

MIDCITY OPINIONS ON WHAT THE *DAILY* SHOULD PRINT

Item	*Proportion of Sample (N = 373) (Figures in Percentage)* Yes	No	Don't Know
Question: Do you believe the *Daily* should be allowed to:			
Criticize a book or a movie?	82.3	12.6	5.1
Print beer advertisements?	76.7	20.9	2.4
Attack the mayor?	75.9	18.7	5.4
Attack the President?	64.8	31.4	3.8
Criticize the labor policy of an employer?	58.2	33.2	8.6
Attack labor unions here?	56.0	36.5	7.5
Print divorce hearings?	54.2	42.6	3.2
Print pictures of bodies of dead people?	53.3	42.4	4.3
Criticize gasoline quality?	50.7	40.5	8.8
Print painting of a nude?	35.9	61.2	2.9
Criticize your religion?	18.8	79.4	1.8

Criticized the labor polices of employers. (One wealthy Midcity citizen inquired privately whether "Communists had gotten into" the news staff.)

Criticized the local labor unions. (A front-page editorial made direct attack on one union policy.)

Printed divorce hearings—but not with "all the details." (When a Midcity couple's marital antics involved police and courts, a metropolitan newspaper gave a detailed report on its front page and its copies sold that day in Midcity. The *Daily* told the story in a third as much space on an inside page.)

Printed pictures of bodies—including one of two Midcity girls who had drowned and one of an injured auto racer, his eyes staring, his throat slit and bleeding. (He died a few minutes after the picture was taken.)

On the other hand, the *Daily* did not criticize the quality of a brand of gasoline—but it did report on page one the names and addresses of restaurants charged by state officials with violating health laws. Nor did it print artistic paintings of nudes or criticize religion directly. In general, the newspaper avoided open conflict with these moral requirements.

The range of difference of Midcity opinion on these items shows also how group and personal experiences were related to the values about the newspaper. A book or a movie is a shadow of experience compared with being a member of a church with one's family and friends, knowing the minister, going to Sunday School. A glance at Table III will show that the more closely these topics related to the interests, group or personal, of an individual, the less willing these Midwesterners were to support "the moral right of free public expression," or the printing of "all ideas or opinions."

THE QUESTION OF FAIRNESS IN MEDIA CONTENT

—Paul F. Lazarsfeld and Patricia L. Kendall, *Radio Listening in America,* Prentice-Hall, Inc., 1948, pp. 53–58. The authors are staff members of the Bureau of Applied Social Research, Columbia University.

(EDITORS' NOTE: *No more serious question faces the owners of newspapers and radio stations than that of fairness. The material that follows represents an analysis of questions asked on this subject in a nationwide survey conducted by the National Opinion Research Center at the University of Chicago. An earlier comparable survey by the Research Center was summarized in* The People Look at Radio *by Paul F. Lazarsfeld and Harry Field, University of North Carolina Press, 1946.*)

FOR Americans, "fairness" is a quality which invites high praise; "unfairness" in any activity, whether a sports contest, a political campaign, or a radio program, brings only strong censure.

Another facet of the public's over-all evaluation of radio is their appraisal of its fairness. Do they feel that radio stations present "both sides" of every issue, that they present all the facts of any situation? These are the requirements of fairness in the field of communications.

The question used to determine attitudes on this point, and the answers which it elicited in both surveys, are presented in Table 25.

TABLE 25

"I'd like to ask you how fair radio stations and newspapers generally are. For example, do you think radio stations are generally fair in giving both sides of public questions? How about newspapers in general?

	Per Cent Saying "Fair"	
	1945	1947
Radio stations	81%	79%
Newspapers	39	55

At both times of questioning, the great majority of listeners felt that radio stations were fair in their handling of controversial issues.

When one realizes how many listeners would disagree with the individual opinions of various commentators, this fact is impressive.

Table 25 should not be used for invidious comparisons of newspapers and radio. After all, newspapers are entitled, by tradition, to editorial opinion and they do not claim to present both sides of every argument. The present question just shows that, barring further evidence to the contrary, the American public feels that radio is usually fair in its treatment of controversial issues.

A second observation is that, although the judgment of radio's fairness remained virtually constant between our two surveys, newspapers made a large gain in this respect. Previously, only slightly more than one-third of the respondents considered newspapers fair; now, over one-half do. We may speculate for a moment as to the meaning of this change. It may be that the less favorable judgment in the earlier period is due, partially at least, to the fact that for many years before 1945 American newspapers had generally been hostile to the Roosevelt administration, whereas the public had favored it. This disagreement expressed itself in the feeling that newspapers were unfair; and it came to an end with Roosevelt's death in 1945. The more widespread feeling in 1947 that newspapers were fair is probably also a reflection of the more important role which newspapers achieved during the postwar era.

The great majority of listeners consider radio fair. Still there is a minority which is critical in this respect. In the light of previous findings it is no surprise to learn that these critics are more likely to appraise radio less favorably on other questions as well. The relationship between the different evaluation questions is, in fact, a marked one. And, just like the critics of other features of radio, the listeners who consider radio stations unfair are relatively more numerous in the better educated groups.

To some extent a feeling that radio stations are unfair is also associated with relative lack of interest in radio: Light listeners, on all educational levels, find radio more unfair than do heavy listeners. Strictly speaking, our data do not permit us to determine which of these two factors is the cause and which the effect. There can be little doubt from a psychological point of view, however. It is psychologically unrealistic to suppose that light listeners are such because they feel that radio is unfair: There are so many programs in which the question of fairness or unfairness is irrelevant that listeners who wanted to avoid programs they considered unfair could do so and still listen a great deal. It is more probable, therefore, that amount of listening is in some way a "cause" and judgment of fairness an "effect." Or, as seems most likely, the same lack of interest which brings about light listening may also lead to a negative attitude toward radio's fairness.

We might expect that members of the working class would find radio less fair than do professionals or business men. One does occasionally hear that labor unions have difficulties in buying air time, in getting their side of a dispute presented, and so on. Our data indicate, however, that the rank and file members of the working class do not share these critical attitudes to any degree: Even when education is taken into account there are no differences in judgments of radio's fairness either according to socio-economic status or according to occupation.

A new feature of the present survey was an attempt to determine who was blamed for the unfairness of either radio or the newspapers. Individuals who said they thought radio or newspapers unfair were asked the questions reported in Table 26.

TABLE 26

RESPONSIBILITY FOR UNFAIRNESS OF RADIO OR NEWSPAPERS

"Who do you think is chiefly responsible for radio's (the newspapers') unfairness —the radio station (newspaper) owners, the commentator or announcer (columnist or reporter) who gives the news, the advertisers who sponsor the news, or someone else?"

Radio			*Newspapers*
Advertisers	32%	7%	Advertisers
Station Owner	26	53	Newspaper owner
Commentator or announcer	18	16	Columnist or reporter
Someone else	12	13	Someone else
Don't know	12	11	Don't know
	100%	100%	
The 13% saying Radio is "Unfair"			The 37% saying Newspapers are "Unfair"

The first point to note is the similarity between radio and newspapers on the last three lines of this table. Newspaper columnists and reporters are blamed as frequently as radio commentators and announcers; the miscellaneous personnel collected under the heading "Someone else" share equal responsibility; and the "Don't know" answers are as frequent in the case of radio as they are in the case of newspapers.

It is only when advertisers and owners are considered that we find discrepancies between the two media. Our interviewees hold sponsors and station owners about equally responsible for radio's unfairness. They overwhelmingly blame newspaper owners and publishers for any unfairness which they detect in the press. Or, to put it another way, radio advertisers are blamed more than four times as frequently as newspaper advertisers; station owners are blamed only half as frequently as publishers.

It is interesting to see how certain technical differences between the two media are reflected in this result. In the first place, advertisers do not sponsor columns of news or comment in papers as they do on the radio; their connection with, and influence on, the editorial content of newspapers is perhaps not as apparent therefore. Secondly, we may speculate that newspapers seem to have a greater number of small and diversified advertisers than does radio. It is true, of course, that many commercial announcements are sponsored by local companies, and we have no evidence that listeners are not aware of this fact. But the most popular programs, the "big-name" programs, are often sponsored by large corporations. This may lead to the feeling that radio advertisers are more powerful and influential. Finally, it is easier not to see the advertisements in newspapers than it is not to hear them on the radio, and their number may therefore be underestimated. All of these factors, inherent in the current systems of operation, make the role of advertisers more noticeable in radio than in the newspapers. The result is that responsibility for unfairness is much more frequently placed at the feet of radio sponsors than is the case with newspaper advertisers.

On the other hand, radio stations are relatively de-personalized institutions, with their alphabetic call-letters, their combination into large networks, and what seems to be the almost intentional avoidance of publicity on the part of station owners. This is in marked contrast to the fame and public notice of such publishers as Hearst, McCormick, Gannett, Knight, and so on. It is quite likely that, if put to the test, more people could name the publishers of newspapers in their communities than could correctly identify the station owners. Furthermore, many newspaper owners are frank to admit that they publish their papers in order to express their opinions and foster the causes which have their support. For reasons such as these, the newspaper publisher is blamed more frequently than the station owner for the unfairness which listeners find in the two media.

THE CANONS OF JOURNALISM

—Adopted by the American Society of Newspaper Editors at its first annual meeting in 1923.

THE PRIMARY FUNCTION of newspapers is to communicate to the human race what its members do, feel, and think. Journalism, therefore, demands of its practitioners the widest range of intelligence, or knowledge, and of experience, as well as natural and trained powers of observation and reasoning. To its opportunities as a chronicle are indissolubly linked its obligations as teacher and interpreter.

To the end of finding some means of codifying sound practice and just aspirations of American journalism, these canons are set forth:

I

Responsibility.—The right of a newspaper to attract and hold readers is restricted by nothing but considerations of public welfare. The use a newspaper makes of the share of public attention it gains serves to determine its sense of responsibility, which it shares with every member of its staff. A journalist who uses his power for any selfish or otherwise unworthy purpose is faithless to a high trust.

II

Freedom of the Press.—Freedom of the press is to be guarded as a vital right of mankind. It is the unquestionable right to discuss whatever is not explicity forbidden by law, including the wisdom of any restrictive statute.

III

Independence.—Freedom from all obligations except that of fidelity to the public interest is vital.

1. Promotion of any private interest contrary to the general welfare, for whatever reason, is not compatible with honest journalism. So-called news communications from private sources should not be published without public notice of their source or else substantiation of their claims to value as news, both in form and substance.

2. Partisanship, in editorial comment which knowingly departs from the truth, does violence to the best spirit of American journal-

ism; in the news columns it is subversive of a fundamental principle of the profession.

IV

Sincerity, Truthfulness, Accuracy.—Good faith with the reader is the foundation of all journalism worthy of the name.

1. By every consideration of good faith a newspaper is constrained to be truthful. It is not to be excused for lack of thoroughness or accuracy within its control, or failure to obtain command of these essential qualities.

2. Headlines should be fully warranted by the contents of the article which they surmount.

V

Impartiality.—Sound practice makes clear distinction between news reports and expressions of opinion. News reports should be free from opinion or bias of any kind.

1. This rule does not apply to so-called special articles unmistakably devoted to advocacy or characterized by a signature authorizing the writer's own conclusions and interpretation.

VI

Fair Play.—A newspaper should not publish unofficial charges affecting reputation or moral character without opportunity given to the accused to be heard; right practice demands the giving of such opportunity in all cases of serious accusation outside judicial proceedings.

1. A newspaper should not invade private rights or feelings without sure warrant of public right as distinguished from public curiosity.

2. It is the privilege, as it is the duty, of a newspaper to make prompt and complete correction of its own serious mistakes of fact or opinion, whatever their origin.

VII

Decency.—A newspaper cannot escape conviction of insincerity if while professing high moral purpose it supplies incentives to base conduct, such as are to be found in details of crime and vice, publication of which is not demonstrably for the general good. Lacking authority to enforce its canons, the journalism here represented can but express the hope that deliberate pandering to vicious instincts will encounter effective public disapproval or yield to the influence of a preponderant professional condemnation.

REVIEW QUESTIONS AND ASSIGNMENTS

1. What reasons can you list to explain the persistent criticism of the content of the mass media?

2. Do you agree that a communications channel that is operated for the private profit of one individual or one group can still serve as a reliable purveyor of intelligence to society?

3. If you think that society should have better control over its institutions, including the press, then how would you reconcile your point of view with the tradition of press freedom in this country?

4. Would you favor the establishment by the media of self appraising "courts" which would rule on questions of irresponsibility?

5. How much of the responsibility for making the media perform in an enlightened fashion rests with the public?

6. Do you see any notable distinctions between the news-dissemination roles of the newspaper and radio?

7. Do you feel that the newspaper in your home town helps or hinders the processes of democracy in the community?

8. Do you feel that the same newspaper provides a fairly accurate mirror of the social climate of the community?

9. Why is it that among the media the newspaper is credited with enjoying the greatest intimacy with its public?

10. State in your own words what you consider to be the actual meaning of the term "the responsibility of the press."

11. Do you feel that the United Nations can deal effectively with the issue of responsibility in the dissemination of information?

12. How well do you think that the press conforms to the ideals set forth in the "Canons of Journalism"?

13. The managers of the media often claim that they are "the watchdogs of democratic government." Do you agree?

14. List those steps that the press might follow in improving the quality of the flow of news.

ADDITIONAL REFERENCES

Angell, Norman, *The Press and the Organization of Society,* Cambridge University Press, 1933.

Bent, Silas, *Ballyhoo: The Voice of the Press,* Liveright, 1927.

Bleyer, Willard G., *The History of American Journalism,* Houghton Mifflin, 1927, pp. 389–429.

——— (editor), *The Profession of Journalism,* Atlantic Monthly Press, 1918.

Brucker, Herbert, *Freedom of Information,* Macmillan, 1949.

———, *The Changing American Newspaper,* Columbia University Press, 1937.

Bryson, Lyman (editor), *The Communication of Ideas: A Series of Addresses,* Institute for Religious and Social Studies, New York, 1948.

Cantril, Hadley, and Gordon W. Allport, *The Psychology of Radio,* Harper & Brothers, 1935.

Casey, Ralph D., "Communications Channels," in *Propaganda, Communication, and Public Opinion,* Princeton University Press, 1946, pp. 4–30.

Chafee, Zechariah, Jr., *Government and Mass Communication,* University of Chicago Press, 1947.

Cummings, A. J., *The Press and a Changing Civilization,* John Lane, London, 1936.

Desmond, Robert W., *The Press and World Affairs,* Appleton-Century, 1937.

Flint, L. N., *The Conscience of the Newspaper,* Appleton-Century, 1925.

Gerald, J. Edward, *The Press and the Constitution, 1931–1947,* University of Minnesota Press, 1948.

Given, John, *Making a Newspaper,* Henry Holt, 1907.

Gramling, Oliver, *AP—The Story of News,* Farrar & Rinehart, 1940.

Herzberg, Joseph G. (editor), *Late City Edition,* Henry Holt, 1947.

Ickes, Harold L., *America's House of Lords,* Harcourt, Brace, 1939.

Jones, Robert W., *Journalism in the United States,* E. P. Dutton, 1947.

Keezer, Dexter M., "Press," in *Encyclopaedia of the Social Sciences,* Vol. 12, Macmillan, 1934, pp. 325–344.

Kingsbury, Susan M., and Hornell Hart, *Newspapers and the News,* G. P. Putnam's Sons, 1937.

Kobre, Sidney, *Backgrounding the News,* Twentieth Century Press, Baltimore, 1939.

Landry, Robert J., *This Fascinating Radio Business,* Bobbs-Merrill, 1946.

Lazarsfeld, Paul, F., and Frank N. Stanton (editors), *Communications Research, 1948–1949,* Harper & Brothers, 1949.

Lee, Alfred M., *The Daily Newspaper in America,* Macmillan, 1937.

Liebling, A. J., *The Wayward Pressman,* Doubleday, 1948.

Lundberg, Ferdinand, *America's 60 Families,* Vanguard Press, 1937.

MacNeil, Neil, *Without Fear or Favor,* Harcourt, Brace, 1940.

MacDougall, Curtis D., *Newsroom Problems and Policies,* Macmillan, 1941.

Mott, Frank L., *American Journalism,* Macmillan, 1950.

———, and Ralph D. Casey (editors), *Interpretations of Journalism,* F. S. Crofts, 1937.

Problems of Journalism, Proceedings of the American Society of Newspaper Editors, issued annually since 1923.

Rothenberg, Ignaz, *The Newspaper: A Study in the Workings of the Daily Press and Its Laws,* Staples Press, 1948.

Schramm, Wilbur (editor), *Communications in Modern Society,* University of Illinois Press, 1948.

——— (editor), *Mass Communications,* University of Illinois Press, 1949.

Seldes, George, *Freedom of the Press,* Bobbs-Merrill, 1935.

———, *Lords of the Press,* Julian Messner, 1938.

Sinclair, Upton, *The Brass Check,* Boni, 1936.

Svirsky, Leon (editor), *Your Newspaper: Blueprint for a Better Press,* Macmillan, 1947.

Tebbel, John, *An American Dynasty,* Doubleday, 1947.

Thorpe, Merle H., *The Coming Newspaper,* Henry Holt, 1915.

Villard, Oswald Garrison, *Some Newspapers and Newspapermen,* Alfred A. Knopf, 1923.

———, *The Disappearing Daily: Chapters in American Newspaper Evolution,* Alfred A. Knopf, 1944.

Walker, Stanley, *City Editor,* Frederick A. Stokes, 1934.

Waples, Douglas, "Communications," *American Journal of Sociology,* Vol. 47, May 1942, pp. 907–917.

Warner, W. Lloyd, *Democracy in Jonesville,* Harper & Brothers, 1949.

White, Llewellyn, *The American Radio,* University of Chicago Press, 1947.

Willey, Malcom M., and Stuart A. Rice, *Communication Agencies and Social Life,* McGraw-Hill, 1933.

5. WHAT THE PRESS PRINTS

INTRODUCTION

As early as the last decade of the nineteenth century, efforts were being made to measure the content of newspapers. Sometimes the purpose of these attempts was to determine the reading habits of newspaper subscribers, and at other times it was to measure the influence of the press. The measurement in both cases was an awkward and inaccurate means to the end in view. Numerous studies also were made during the second and third decades of the present century. A careful reading of the best of them shows a great variation in the measurements used, but to date no study has been completed that is not open to criticism for patent flaws of methodology.

The fourth and fifth decades brought forth studies that were far more scientific and scholarly. First-rate efforts were made to evaluate such aspects of the press as reader interest, readability of editorial matter, and bias in printed news. The readings that follow are cited because they are representative of recent research. Inasmuch as interest is upon the findings and not upon the methods used, readers who wish to study the latter are referred to the complete studies.

In the first reading, Mott states that the change in news emphasis in recent decades has been scant, though in the next item Garnett indicates that certain changes have occurred. The Lostutter quotation is based upon a readability study of a typical newspaper. It indicates relative ease of reading among certain types of news, and the influence of training upon the way reporters write. The Getzloe article gives a more pointed explanation of how difficult some news is to read.

That the newspapers neglect certain broad fields of interest is brought out by Vincent S. Jones, editorial director of the Gannett newspapers. In the Klapper-Glock citation, a point is made clear that should be more widely recognized—namely, that the newspapers often print different facts about the same people or set of circumstances. While that is to be expected in a free and competitive press, it is also desirable for all stories to be as objective as possible.

The data gleaned from the newpaper readership surveys conducted by the Advertising Research Foundation offer the external side of the content problem. They show what men and women like and do not like about the material offered by the press.

STABILITY OF CONTENT

—Frank Luther Mott, "Trends in Newspaper Content," *The Press in the Contemporary Scene, The Annals of the American Academy of Political and Social Science,* Vol. 219, January 1942, pp. 60–61. Mr. Mott, famed historian, has enjoyed a notable career in journalism education at Iowa and Missouri.

THE PUBLISHER is a merchant, and the editorial art is largely one of merchandising, as respects general newspaper content. In taking a position on a public issue, the editor and the publisher may be, to a certain extent and under certain conditions, individualists; but in providing the general menu spread in the 75 to 225 nonadvertising columns of a metropolitan daily, editors and publishers attempt to provide, as closely as possible, satisfaction for the desires and tastes of what they conceive to be their proper reader audience.

Occasional newspaper failures testify that mistakes are sometimes made in this catering business, but the upward curve of aggregate circulations is evidence of the skill of newspaper makers in answering faithfully to the wishes of readers. The old "able editor," himself a part of the social group for which he prepared his paper, and united to it by economic, political, and institutional backgrounds and training, believed that he knew through a sixth sense what his readers wanted; and since he himself felt the same desires and responded to the same symbols, this was often true enough. But in a more complicated society, modern techniques for the study of reader interest have afforded helpful guidance. Even editors who are somewhat contemptuous of such supposedly "theoretical" devices are affected by them through their imitation of the successes of those who are less cynical, for imitation of successful newspaper practices is the oldest and most consistent secondary cause of general newspaper trends.

The existence of wide divergencies in what has been called the socialization index[1] of a newspaper signifies only that reader audiences

[1] Susan M. Kingsbury, Hornell Hart, and associates, "Measuring the Ethics of American Newspapers," *Journalism Quarterly,* Vol. 10, June 1933, pp. 93–108.

are different. The New York *Times,* the New York *Mirror,* the Baltimore *Sun,* and the Boston *Post* are all edited alike for newspaper readers; but their audiences are found on different economic and intelligence levels. All of them are subject to the weekly referendum and recall offered when the delivery boy collects his money and his stops.

This intimacy with the popular audience which is the essence of journalism gives newspaper content high validity as an index of social desires and responses. What a nation of newspaper readers wants to read and what it finds pleasure in reading are shown pretty definitely in a sympathetic journalism.

But the student who begins to analyze and measure newspapers to discover trends in content—and thereby trends in popular tastes and desires—soon finds that his percentages change but little from year to year. Apparently there are two reasons for this comparatively static condition. In the first place, basic desires are essentially static; and in the second place, when circulation holds up, it seems like tempting fate to change the offering. But beyond these consideration, it is undeniable that newspapers in general are fairly conservative in policy. In studying the history of the evolution of any new technique—say the comic strip or the front page banner—one is impressed by the caution and slowness with which it was adopted. There are always experimenters, but the great bulk of newspapers are slow to change. The accompanying table indicates few striking changes.[2]

	1910		1920		1930		1940	
	Cols.	*Prop.*	*Cols.*	*Prop.*	*Cols.*	*Prop.*	*Cols.*	*Prop.*
Foreign News and Features	2.4	.031	6.2	.088	6.8	.048	14.0	.079
Washington News	4.7	.061	5.0	.071	5.7	.040	10.6	.060
Columns Dealing with Public Affairs			.4	.006	1.0	.007	2.5	.014
Original Editorials	3.0	.039	2.8	.040	3.0	.021	3.1	.018
Business, Financial, Marine, etc.	16.0	.211	11.4	.160	53.2	.375	56.6	.320

[2] The table is presented with the following warnings against improper reading. The categories are not mutually exclusive; pictures, for example, are included under both illustration and the category of the story illustrated. The averages represent measurements of ten prominent newspapers (excluding tabloids) in New York, Chicago, Philadelphia, Boston, and Baltimore for the first week of each year named. . . .

Average Number of Columns Given Certain Categories of Content in Each Issue in Ten Leading Metropolitan Newspapers at the Beginnings of Four Decade Years, with Proportions in Decimals on the Base of Total Nonadvertising Space

	1910		1920		1930		1940	
	Cols.	*Prop.*	*Cols.*	*Prop.*	*Cols.*	*Prop.*	*Cols.*	*Prop.*
Sports	7.1	.094	10.4	.146	18.2	.128	20.9	.118
Society	1.4	.019	1.8	.026	4.5	.032	6.4	.036
Women's Interests	1.1	.015	1.4	.020	2.3	.016	6.7	.038
Theatre, Movies, Books, Art, etc.	2.2	.029	2.2	.031	4.4	.033	7.4	.042
Radio Announcements and News					2.5	.018	2.5	.014
Comic Strips and Singles	.8	.010	2.0	.028	5.1	.036	10.8	.061
Illustration (excluding comics)	4.0	.054	4.0	.057	8.5	.060	19.8	.112

CHANGES IN CONTENT

—Burrett P. Garnett, "Changes in the Basic Newspaper Pattern," *The Press in the Contemporary Scene, The Annals of the American Academy of Political and Social Science,* Vol. 219, January 1942, pp. 54–55. Mr. Garnett is co-founder of *Editorial Research Reports.*

As EDITORS cultivated the dormant or changing interest of readers in various manifestations of American life, the contents and sometimes the physical form of the newspapers were altered.[1] Newspaper readers in the middle age groups will recall that in their lifetime the number of sports pages has increased and that much greater emphasis is given now than formerly to features for women. They will recall also that when the automobile was a new and exciting novelty, nearly all Sunday papers carried automobile pages or whole sections devoted to motor cars and motoring.[2] At one time there were radio pages and aviation columns. Currently, news of travel and resorts—particularly resorts in the Western Hemisphere—appear to be on the increase.[3]

These special pages are, in most cases, additional pages. Nearly every metropolitan paper contains more pages per edition than it did thirty years ago. The addition of pages has not greatly affected format, except that newspapers in large cities have two sections. In many cases the first page of the second section is made up as attractively as the Page 1 "show window." Sports stories and pictures; the stories and pictures of enticing resorts, steamships, and streamlined

[1] In the sense that a 6- or 12-page paper became a 24- or 36-page paper, for example.

[2] Such pages and editions are now confined principally to the period when new models are introduced to the public by manufacturers.

[3] Naturally, all of the special pages, with the exception of sports, are influenced to some extent by the business office. Pages addressed to prospective travelers attract advertisements of resort hotels and travel utilities.

trains; and the features on the women's page, are fitted into the chase much as pictures and stories of the new Buicks and Packards used to be on the automobile pages.

Through the use of matrix picture services, syndicated columns, and other materials, the smaller papers have tried to keep pace with the metropolitan press, but it has been a losing battle for many in the non-metropolitan field. They have changed less in appearance, perhaps, than the big city dailies, by reason of the fact that they have had less opportunity to attract advertising in large volume.

READABILITY OF NEWSPAPER CONTENT

—Melvin Lostutter, "Some Critical Factors of Newspaper Readability," *Journalism Quarterly*, Vol. 24, No. 4, December 1947, p. 308 and pp. 310–312. Mr. Lostutter is a member of the journalism faculty of Michigan State College.

In this investigation a former newspaperman took the newspaperman's approach to readability in an effort to determine the critical factors involved in applying objective measurement to the daily and weekly journal. Selected for study was the *State Journal,* published daily in Lansing, Mich., a city of approximately 80,000 population. For our purpose this paper with its circulation of 50,496[1] may be considered representative of papers of its own size and many much larger and much smaller, because it is big enough to have an editorial staff with some variety of background and specialization yet small enough to take the folksy attitude toward the news of the community that is characteristic of the non-metropolitan press of the United States. In addition, investigation disclosed that it was no more conscious of its readability than the average newspaper gives evidence of being.

One hundred fifty articles written by eighteen regular members of the staff were analyzed. Also ten published letters from readers, ten Associated Press stories, and ten staff-written articles from the Detroit *Free Press* were measured for comparison. . . .

Sampling the material in the *State Journal* indicated that the easiest reading in the paper was written by outsiders. The readers' letters averaged well under the staff-written material and the AP stories from the front page. The Detroit *Free Press* articles averaged lowest of the four categories studied. The *Free Press* was chosen for comparison because it is one of those newspapers with a well-administered readability program. . . .

[1] *Editor & Publisher 1947 International Year Book.*

The discovery that the *State Journal* amateurs were, on the whole, more "readable" than its professionals, raised some questions that this investigation did not answer. One is the relationship of education and experience to the writing of readable newspaper copy. Interviews and a study of individual scores failed to shed much light on this relationship.

For instance, the two staff members who had taken college journalism had relatively low scores but not as low as some working in the same departments who had not taken it. Another writer who took no college journalism but was reared in a newspaper family ranked about midway on the staff's readability scale.

Of the six with college training, three (in the society department) were among the easiest writers and another (on general assignments) was among the hardest.

The three with only grammar school preparation wrote neither the easiest nor the hardest copy. They were about midway. The rest, all high school graduates, ranked from second to eighteenth.

When analyzed on the basis of experience, the readability of the *Journal* staff fell into no clearer pattern. The writers with two years or less included high and low scores. So did those with more than ten years in the field. For example, A with the lowest score, and R with the next to highest, both have been with the paper for twenty years or more.

In short, little traceable relationship between readability and formal education, experience, and special interests was found. Those elements are so interwoven with such considerations as subject matter, departmental policy, and individual and traditional outlook that it did not seem possible to isolate the critical factors in a small sample.

When the material of this study was classified by types, measurement indicated that its readability was affected about as much by habitual or conventional approach to certain types as by the subject matter itself. However, here again there did not seem to be enough possibility of isolating those factors for the results to be too conclusive.

Ranking second and third for easy reading were sports and society. Both deal with rather obvious facts, but departmental policy unquestionably is a factor in their readability. The two men who write sports for the *Journal* tend to tell the story and let it go at that, while the three women who do society eschew much of the flowery and complicated treatment noted often in other newspapers.

Scores ran high for stories on local government, politics, business, a series on rent control, and reports on public addresses. Practically all such stories measured were of college reading level by Flesch's formula.

Perhaps the best evidence of the effect of subject matter was found in analysis of the "spot news" classification. Here material that was rather elemental was involved—deaths, fires, accidents, police news—and the way four general assignment reporters wrote it could be compared directly to the way they handled matter somewhat more subtle. In every case by the Flesch measurements and in half the cases by Lorge the scores for "spot news" were lower than the reporters' average for all types of stories.

Two classes of writing in which opinion was expressed freely were near the opposite extremes of the readability scale.

Six columnists, commenting on fields such as sports, music, aviation, society, and general news, were studied. In each case, by both formulae, the writer had a lower score for his column than for his writing as a whole.

On the other hand, the editorials, written by two men not otherwise represented by material in this investigation, had high scores—college graduate level. Here the influence was obviously not subject matter; the editorials, like the columns, covered a wide range of subjects. It seemed rather to be the writer's approach to the matter. Columns are traditionally free and easy, chatty, personal in their relationships between the writer and reader. The editorial, however, often follows a tradition of formality and profundity, and it is stretching it to consider the "editorial we" a "personal reference." Really profound writing is likely to go over the heads of readers with an eighth grade education, and specious profundity is almost sure to.

Evidence that editorials need not be hard reading is contained in the Getzloe report mentioned earlier.[2] It says: "After the foreign correspondents had brought in the news at a 14 level, the editorial writers shed their light on it at a 12 level. That was the average grade of editorials on foreign affairs appearing in 16 different newspapers between July 8 and July 18, 1946." The ratings ran from 8 for the New York *Daily News* and Philadelphia *Record* to 15 for the New York *Sun* and *Herald Tribune*. This is a rather clear case of the writer's approach rather than his subject matter governing his readability.

[2] Lester Getzloe, "The Ohio Newspaper," *Ohio State University Bulletin*, Vol. XXVIII, No. 2, November 1946.

Another thing disclosed was that the leads of the *Journal* stories raised the scores of the stories as a whole. Twenty-four articles were measured both with and without their leads, and in only one case did a story score lower by both formulae without its lead than with it. Four were higher by Flesch but lower by Lorge; four, vice versa; fifteen, lower by both.

SOME NEWS IS HARD TO READ

—Lester Getzloe, "Wide Variation in Washington News Coverage Shown by Readability Test," *The Ohio Newspaper*, Vol. 27, No. 1, October 1945, pp. 2–3. The author is a professor of journalism at the Ohio State University.

MORE THAN a thousand Washington stories, most of them dated between July 2 and 31, were tested for readability. *The average reader level of all these stories was 13. That is, although the average American adult has a little less than a ninth-grade education, his Washington news is coming to him on the reading level of a college freshman.*

The average level of the I. N. S. was 12, the United Press 12-plus, and the Associated Press 13-plus. This is just a little tougher reading than *Harper's Magazine* and about five grades tougher than the *Reader's Digest*. United Press Radio copy, processed from UP, graded 10.

The Akron *Beacon Journal* showed most readable among individual newspapers, grading 11, the same level as the Washington bureau of the Scripps-Howard Newspapers. The New York *Times*, as might be expected, writes at a college graduate level, averaging 17-plus. (Incidentally, ten editorials chosen at random from "Days of Decision," a collection of *Times* editorials, averaged 10.4.) More surprising, however, is the fact that the New York *Journal American* rated next to the *Times* in relative difficulty, averaging 15-plus.

The following table gives the reader level of Washington news from ten different sources:

	Average	*Mean*
United Press Radio	10	9
Scripps-Howard Washington Bureau	11	11
Akron *Beacon Journal* Washington Bureau	11	12
International News Service	12	11-plus
United Press	12-plus	12
Associated Press	13-plus	13-plus
Chicago *Sun* Washington Bureau	15	14-plus

Christian Science Monitor Bureau	15	15
New York *Journal American* Bureau	15-plus	16
New York *Times* Washington Bureau	17	16-plus
Average	13	

There are serious implications in these figures, and it would be best not to minimize them, but several observations may be made in explanation, perhaps in extenuation:

1. Much Washington news is inherently dull, inevitably high in abstractions, usually low in human interest. Considering its nature, the average reading level of 13 is not necessarily disturbing. Readable News Reports, the Gunning organization, recently found that all United Press news showed an average reading level of 11.7. The 12.4 average for its Washington news is not bad in comparison.

2. There is no way of removing the pressure and the need for speed which are responsible for much bad newspaper writing. The old excuse for prolixity might be paraphrased for the Washington correspondent, "Excuse these long words and long sentences. I didn't have time to write shorter ones." He normally doesn't have the chance for the rewriting which is responsible for the greater clarity of, say, the *Reader's Digest*, or even of *Time*.

3. Even if written in the language of the ninth grade, the real meaning of much Washington news would still escape many ninth-grade students.

4. Newspapers with special audiences, like the New York *Times* or the *Christian Science Monitor*, have less need to gear their readability level to the needs of an "average" reader.

These statements have validity. On the other side remains the contention of the circulation manager, "There's no use printing it if the people can't understand it."

WOMEN'S INTERESTS IN THE PRESS

—Vincent S. Jones, "Bold Experimentation Needed to Improve Newspaper Content," *Journalism Quarterly*, Vol. 25, No. 1, March 1948, pp. 20–21. Mr. Jones is editorial director of the Gannett newspapers.

MOST NEWSPAPERS are edited by men—for men. Yet women are the greatest readers of both news and advertising. Why they haven't deserted us years ago is a mystery.

Women's interests follow a narrow but very vital range. They are emotional, personal, practical, and, of course, unpredictable. Most of our efforts to take care of them are too crude to fool that sharp-eyed breed of born shoppers. Any readership study will show how wide is the gap between male and female readers on most items. It's a rare story or feature which pleases both in equal proportion.

At the Press Institute, the editor of *Good Housekeeping* magazine told about the continued dominance of fashions, the perennial search for youth, and the rise in what the trade calls "shelter books"—information about homes and interior decorating. He said that there never had been an unsuccessful cook book, and also told why: Most women don't give a hoot about cooking. But, since they are stuck with the job of feeding the world, they want to know how to do it.

He asked some pointed questions of newspaper editors. He wondered why we didn't hire competent people to shop the stores, to explore the interior decorating triumphs of local ladies, or to correlate cooking advice with the state of the local market. He said we could save him all kinds of trouble by answering simple questions.

Most newspapers regard their women's departments as appendages to appease the grocery advertisers and the stores. They pay little attention to them and get about what they deserve. Syndicate material is on the shoddy side. Why? Because we don't pay enough to get results. *Good Housekeeping* pays its departmental editors fat salaries. And they don't even have to be able to write their own names! A "production department" does that. The editors and consultants are merely required to know their own fields.

We have made some timid experiments in this line. The County Home Bureau is glad to provide a weekly market survey, plus advice on how to exploit the stuff that is in good supply. . . .

The other things are harder to do. Perhaps they're things which might be attempted on a cooperative basis. It won't be easy to find the right people, either, because the girls who go into journalism are looking for romance. Even the big schools say they can't find anybody who wants to get rich writing about cooking.

One immediate solution is for every boss editor to go over his whole paper and examine every piece of reading material to see whether there is a "women's angle" and whether it has been exploited to the hilt. If he has an array of hairy-chested, big-muscled characters on the comic page, he's in for trouble. A great majority of the comics fail to click with women. But the best of them all, "Blondie," is a hit with both sexes.

Frank Tripp once coined a happy and homely phrase to the effect that the Gannett Newspapers were "as local as the town pump." That's a pretty good slogan for any newspaper to adopt. Readers are quick to vote for the home town news, too, and it's the field which no competitor ever can take away from us if we cultivate it properly.

The same thing goes for local columns. They're more expensive than the fancy-name boys, but they earn their keep.

VARIATION IN NEWSPAPER REPORTING

—Joseph T. Klapper and Charles Y. Glock, "Trial by Newspaper," *Scientific American,* Vol. 180, No. 2, February 1949, pp. 18–21. The authors are research associates in the Bureau of Applied Social Research, Columbia University.

(EDITORS' NOTE: *On March 2, 1948, a subcommittee of the House Committee on Un-American Activities denounced Dr. Edward U. Condon, director of the National Bureau of Standards, in a statement dealing with atomic security. The drama that followed was extensively reported by the media. Treatment of the case by nine New York City dailies is discussed in the selection that follows.*)

THE GENERAL FINDING (in the "trial by newspaper" of Dr. Condon, of which an investigation was requested by *Scientific American* and six eminent scientists) is that in the New York press taken as a whole there was a preponderance of statements favorable to Dr. Condon. Of the 3,909 analyzed statements, 745 or 19 per cent were unsympathetic to Condon, and 971 or 25 per cent were sympathetic. These proportions, applying as they do to the total coverage by the entire New York press, are not particularly meaningful: few persons would consistently have read all nine papers and been exposed to this comprehensive coverage. More significant are the differences among the papers. The range of these differences is indicated in the percentages of pro-Condon and anti-Condon statements in the individual newspapers:

	Pro	*Con*
Times	65	35
Herald Tribune	64	36
Star	63	37
Post	57	43
World-Telegram	50	50

	Pro	Con
News	49	51
Mirror	47	53
Sun	43	57
Journal-American	18	82

(Because the *Journal-American* published relatively little on the Condon case, the findings for this paper may be less meaningful than for the others.)

Most of the pro-Condon statements were contributed by the first four papers—*Times, Tribune, Star* and *Post*—which accounted for nearly two thirds of the total New York coverage of the story in terms of number and statements. In the four papers taken as a group, statements sympathetic to Dr. Condon outnumbered unsympathetic ones in a ratio of 17 to 10. In the other five papers, which have a much larger total circulation than the first group, statements unsympathetic to Dr. Condon predominated in a ratio of 13 to 10 for the group as a whole.

Analysis of the two categories of statements on each side of the case—i.e., those relating directly to Dr. Condon and those relating to the Committee—revealed another interesting difference in the handling of the case by the two groups of papers. There were few statements in praise of the Committee's treatment of the case: of the total of the anti-Condon statements in all the papers fewer than one in 13 supported the Committee itself. When it came to the pro-Condon statements, however, there were contrasting results in the amount of criticism of the Committee in the two newspaper groups. In the *Times, Tribune, Star* and *Post,* more than one third of the statements on Dr. Condon's side consisted of criticisms of the Committee's procedure. In the other five papers, this proportion was nearer one fourth. In other words, the second group published a substantially smaller proportion of statements criticizing the Committee than did the first group.

The statements favorable and unfavorable to Dr. Condon taken together accounted for 44 per cent of the 3,909 on the case. Of the rest, a surprisingly large group—some 15 per cent of all statements—concerned the struggle between Republican Congressmen and the Administration over the release of the FBI letter. The remaining 41 per cent of the statements in the case were classified as descriptive background of a neutral character.

A further breakdown showing how the treatment of Dr. Condon

fluctuated during the progress of the case also yields significant information. In April, when the battle over the FBI letter reached its peak, the reflections of this event were markedly different in the two groups of newspapers. The *Times, Tribune, Star* and *Post* continued to give greater attention to the Condon case itself and to publish more pro-Condon than anti-Condon statements, although the ratio for the group fell to 12 to 10. In the other five papers, however, statements about the letter actually outnumbered statements about the Condon case proper, and the ratio of statements unsympathetic to Condon rose to 23 to 10. When the Atomic Energy Commission cleared him in July, the *Times, Tribune, Star* and *Post* presented a 14-to-10 ratio of statements favorable to him, but the other five papers, in spite of his clearance, remained on the other side of the fence; in that month, they printed an average of 11 anti-Condon statements for every 10 pro-Condon. Thereafter there was relatively little press activity on the Condon case, but in September, when the Un-American Activities Committee promised new "shocking revelations," the statements published in the group of five papers were 26 to 10 anti-Condon. In other words, two months after his AEC exoneration, the five papers were still presenting a predominantly unsympathetic picture.

These are simply objective data revealed by the analysis. Whether they show that the New York press was fair or unfair in its coverage of the case is a matter of interpretation which is beyond the scope of this analysis. The interpretation will depend on the standards applied by the observer. Some may consider that justice would have been served by a perfect balance of pro- and anti-Condon statements in a paper's reporting. On this point, however, the analysis developed certain other pertinent data.

The data had to do with the sources, character and repetition of statements on the case. Because this analysis dealt with statements concerning Dr. Condon himself, the findings from this point will include only statements directly pro- and anti-Condon: i.e., they exclude the statements for and against the Committee. Of the statements against Dr. Condon, 88 per cent were made by members of the Un-American Activities Committee directly or in excerpts that they quoted from the FBI letter. The accusations against Dr. Condon were virtually a monopoly product of the Committee, for some of the remaining 12 per cent of anti-Condon statements were made by Dr.

Condon himself or by his defenders in reviewing what the Committee had said about him.

On the other hand, the sources of the pro-Condon statements were legion. They included two departments of the executive branch of the government, the Commerce Department Loyalty Board, the Atomic Energy Commission, entire departments of leading universities, and dozens of scientists and scientific societies. Analysis of the weight given by the various papers to the source of these statements yielded significant differences. The *Times, Tribune, Star* and *Post* gave considerably more attention to the width of Dr. Condon's support than did the other papers; 21 per cent of their pro-Condon statements were attributed to scientists and scientific societies, while in the other five newspapers only 4 per cent of the statements favoring Condon came from these sources. Indeed, it appears that those five dailies all but ignored the multitude of meetings, letters and statements in defense of Condon by reputable scientists and institutions. As a result, 77 per cent of the case for Dr. Condon as presented to the readers of those papers came from Dr. Condon himself, from representatives of the Administration, or from unnamed sources.

A similar analysis was made of the bases of the anti-Condon and pro-Condon statements and the relative weight given to them. The case against Dr. Condon was made up almost entirely of three charges: 1) that he associated with suspected persons, 2) that he was lax in regard to U. S. security, 3) that he was unfit in some other unspecified way.

Of the statements making the first charge, 89 per cent identified Dr. Condon's associates only in vague terms or did not identify them at all. His associates were generally described as persons "alleged" or "known" to be espionage agents, or as Soviet or Soviet-satellite diplomats, or as persons suspected of being subversive, without any specification as to why they were under suspicion or any evidence that Condon knew that his associates were under this vague cloud. Only eight per cent of the statements regarding association actually named his associates, and in most of these cases the charges were equally vague. With regard to Dr. Condon's "laxity," nearly all of the statements were simply assertions, most of them being repetitions of the phrase "the weakest link"; there was little or no specific indication as to how he may actually have endangered national security. In the third category, the allegations were even more vague.

Indeed, whatever impression may have been produced on casual readers, the content analysis indicates that the case against Dr. Condon as presented in the newspapers may well have raised a question in careful readers' minds as to whether there was any case at all.

The case *for* Dr. Condon contains a substantial amount of specific material. About a quarter of the pro-Condon statements rest on the fact that he was cleared by official investigations. Other favorable statements are based on "two exhaustive FBI investigations" and several documents, still others on testimonials to Dr. Condon's loyalty and competence from a variety of sources. Yet in comparison with the case against Condon these facts were lightly treated by a majority of the New York papers, which throughout the case gave far heavier emphasis to the allegations by the Un-American Activities Committee than to the support of Dr. Condon from various sources.

A description of what the press said and what it omitted can give only a relatively superficial picture of its coverage. Equally important is the nature of the treatment, and the manner in which newspaper techniques affected the picture presented to the reader. These factors are difficult to analyze in any objective fashion, but the Bureau [Bureau of Applied Social Research, Columbia University] approached the problem from several new angles and obtained some fruitful results.

One approach was a test of the material by the criterion of the repetition of statements. In any continuing news story, it is to be expected that a newspaper will frequently find it necessary to review past events as background. In making the selection of what background information to print, the newspaper obviously exercises more selective judgment than it can with respect to the new material, for the background provides many more items from which to choose. If, for example, the Un-American Activities Committee announced that it intended to hold a hearing on the Condon case, the "news" was pretty well restricted to that fact, but in injecting background into the report, a paper could choose from among a number of statements, such as that Dr. Condon had been accused of associating with spies, that he had been cleared by the Loyalty Board, and so on. Thus it is of considerable interest to see what the papers chose to include as background in their reports as the news developed.

In the analysis of this phase of the newspapers' coverage, all statements printed within two days after an occurrence were classified as "new" and all others as "old." The general finding that resulted from this analysis was that in eight of the nine dailies the "old" or repeated statements built up the case against Dr. Condon more than the case for him. About 57 per cent of the case against him in the papers consisted of revivals of the original charges. On the other hand, criticism of the Un-American Activities Committee were seldom repeated; only 11 per cent of the statements in this category were revivals.

In every category of statements on the case except the one that covered criticisms of Condon, new statements outnumbered the old. The newspapers repeated general denunciations of him six times as often as they repeated general statements in his support. If they had published no "old" statements at all, the score for statements directly naming Condon would have been 416 pro to 301 anti, instead of 695 to 631 the other way.

There is no reason to believe that this result was deliberate. But the fact remains that the reporting techniques employed by the papers served to inflate the case against Condon far beyond its native size.

Another significant finding concerns the newspapers' handling of the Committee's promises of a hearing to Dr. Condon, and of the breach of that promise. All the papers reported the promises much more often than the breach. Here again, however, there were substantial differences between the two groups of papers. The *Times, Tribune, Star* and *Post* published 14 statements on the Committee's promises for every 10 statements on its failure to keep the promise. In the other five papers as a group the ratio was about eight to one.

Thus the content analysis produced these principal findings: the nine New York papers showed wide variations in their news treatment of the case, although all were reporting the same story. Some presented a picture predominantly favorable to Dr. Condon, some predominantly unfavorable. As reported in all the papers, the charges against Dr. Condon were vague. The width of the support of Dr. Condon received substantial attention in the *Times, Tribune, Star* and *Post,* but very little attention in the other five papers. The background material revived for use in the running news stories had the effect of building up the case against Dr. Condon but did not build up his defense to anywhere near the same degree. All the papers reported the Committee's promise to give Dr. Condon a hearing far more often than they reported its failure to do so.

Such are the objective findings. The writers have attempted to avoid judgments, or have labeled them clearly when they seemed unavoidable. How or why the press treatments here described took the form that they did, and whether the papers should be commended or condemned are questions to be considered by interested students of the press.

READING OF TYPES OF CONTENT

—Advertising Research Foundation, *100-Study Summary,* The Continuing Study of Newspaper Reading, 1946, pp. 10–11.

(EDITORS' NOTE: *The following data on the readership of different types of newspaper content are based on 100 separate studies of newspaper reading conducted by the Advertising Research Foundation in co-operation with the Bureau of Advertising of the American Newspaper Publishers Association.*)

HOW CONTEMPORARY EVENTS may influence reading habits is reflected in readership patterns established for newspapers studied during the prewar, wartime and postwar periods.

The first 47 studies, conducted from July, 1939, to December, 1941, comprise the so-called prewar group. Studies 48 through 90 report the examinations made during active American participation in World War II. They were made between January, 1942, and June, 1945. The postwar group includes Studies 91 through 100, those made from August, 1945, to May, 1946.

Two important factors should be borne in mind in connection with wartime and postwar studies. Because of newsprint rationing, space for advertising and editorial content was severely curtailed during the war. This situation carried well over into the postwar studies. Secondly, of the ten newspapers studied since V-J Day, only one—the Indianapolis *Star*—had a circulation over 100,000. The others in this group ranged from 15,000 to 78,000 circulation. Hence, the postwar tabulation is primarily a tabulation of smaller newspapers. This probably accounts for the decline in radio program readership and increase in society news readership noted in the last 10 studies—a tendency which has been noted in studies of smaller papers. (By City Size Groups.)

Outstanding in the postwar studies is the intensified interest in newspaper advertising, especially among men. This is reflected in medians compiled for readership of all advertising departments in the postwar group. In all such cases, the postwar medians for men exceed the corresponding prewar and wartime medians, as well as those for all 100 studies. The same holds true for women except for readership of national advertising.

That serious events may arouse more serious thinking is apparent in the greater readership of editorials by both men and women during the war. Although the postwar studies indicate a moderate falling off in such readership, the median readership of editorials for the 100 studies has been boosted above that recorded for the prewar studies —a result, of course, of the wartime influence.

During the war, men also paid more attention than before to items on editorial pages and to classified advertising. Their medians for all other editorial and advertising departments show a decline of one to 14 percentage points from prewar medians.

Women's readership of classified advertising also increased considerably during the war, and a slight increase may be noted in the attention they gave national advertising and editorial page items. But their wartime medians for all other editorial and advertising departments either remained unchanged or dropped one to 21 percentage points below prewar levels.

In the postwar studies, a dropping off of interest in editorials, editorial page items and radio programs is noted. But gains ranging from five to 18 percentage points over wartime levels are shown for male readership of all other editorial and advertising departments, with the exception of financial news and comics which remained constant.

While women's readership of financial news has held fast to its wartime level, there has been some decrease in their readership of national advertising. This is in contrast to male readership figures which show that the median for men in the postwar period is 23% higher than during wartime. For women, all other departmental reading medians show an increase of one to eight percentage points.

The sharpest postwar increases in readership percentages are recorded for department store advertising and society news or pictures. Men's readership of department store ads has increased 18 percentage points over the wartime figure, while women's has risen eight percentage points. Similarly, male readership of society news or pictures has advanced 12 percentage points over the wartime median, while that for women is up six percentage points. Women's median for amusement advertising also has risen six percentage points.

TABLE I

READING OF TYPES OF CONTENT

Prewar, Wartime and Postwar Medians

Men Percentage of Those Interviewed Who Read	*Studies 1–100* High	Low	Median	*Studies 1–47 Prewar* Median	*Studies 48–90 Wartime* Median	*Studies 91–100 Postwar* Median
Editorials	77%	17%	45%	41%	54%	47%
Editorial Page Items	96	50	85	83	87	83
Comics	96	53	80	84	77	77
Financial News	49	4	26	29	21	21
Radio Programs or News	76	5	40	42	41	28
Society News or Pictures	86	1	37	42	28	40
Sports News or Pictures	95	29	77	80	71	76
Advertising (Except Classified)	97	55	80	80	77	84
National Advertising	92	23	53	53	48	59
Local Advertising	94	48	73	74	67	77
Department Store Advertising	75	2	38	39	31	49
Classified Advertising	69	12	37	32	40	51
Amusement Advertising	66	15	43	44	42	47
Women						
Editorials	63%	9%	29%	25%	35%	32%
Editorial Page Items	96	43	80	80	81	75
Comics	94	50	78	82	73	77
Financial News	36	1	9	10	8	8
Radio Programs or News	83	9	51	53	49	38
Society News or Pictures	98	34	84	86	75	81
Sports News or Pictures	82	6	35	48	27	29
Advertising (Except Classified)	100	81	95	95	95	96
National Advertising	89	20	60	59	62	57
Local Advertising	99	75	94	94	93	94
Department Store Advertising	96	16	84	87	80	88
Classified Advertising	68	11	43	38	48	51
Amusement Advertising	78	19	60	59	59	65

REVIEW QUESTIONS AND ASSIGNMENTS

1. Why has suppression of news almost ceased to be a topic in discussions of the American press?

2. Does the newspaper assume more or less responsibility for its accounts than is demanded by law?

3. Discuss the facts revealed in Mott's table on the content of various newspapers. Does this show that he is correct in stating that the content of newspapers has changed but little?

4. What variations in newspaper content have you observed?

5. What justification is there for the fact that the "labor press" prints news almost exclusively for labor?

6. Discuss how readability affects the extent to which people at different educational levels tend to favor reading the various parts of the newspaper.

7. Should news space be apportioned according to public interest in the various news subjects?

8. Do you agree with Jones that women's interests have been neglected by the press? Why?

9. How can the fact be defended that two or more newspapers give widely different accounts of the same conditions and situations?

10. What are the cases for and against the press tendency toward increasing similarity?

11. Compare the handling of one or more outstanding news events in five or more newspapers. How do these accounts differ? Why?

12. What may the newspapers learn from such news magazines as *Time* and *Newsweek?*

13. Discuss the relative reliability of financial and political reporting.

14. To what extent does the public trust what it reads in the press?

15. Which would tend to be more accurate in local reporting, daily or weekly newspapers? Why?

16. How has careless reporting affected the willingness of competent men to serve in public office?

17. What changes in reporting and editing would you suggest to improve the newspapers?

ADDITIONAL REFERENCES

Allen, Frederick Lewis, "Newspapers and the Truth," *The Atlantic Monthly,* Vol. 129, January 1922, p. 44.

Bent, Silas, *The Nation,* Vol. 123, December 8, 1926, pp. 580–581. (Figures on Hall-Mills case.)

———, *The New Republic,* Vol. 53, January 25, 1928, pp. 274–275. (Figures on Snyder case and Hardy's death.)

Bird, Charles, "The Influence of the Press upon the Accuracy of Reports," *Journal of Abnormal and Social Psychology,* Vol. 22, 1927, pp. 123–129.

Brucker, Herbert, *The Changing American Newspaper,* Columbia University Press, 1937, pp. 2–4, 19–27.

Cole, Virginia Lee, "The Newspaper and Crime," *University of Missouri School of Journalism Bulletin,* Vol. 28, No. 4, January 21, 1927, pp. 42–44, 45.

Dickey, Carl, "The Truth About the Newspapers," *World's Work,* Vol. 49, December 1924, pp. 203–211.

Donovan, H. L., "Content of Ordinary Reading," *Elementary School Journal,* Vol. 25, January 1925, pp. 370–375.

Fenton, Frances, *The Influence of News Presentation upon the Growth of Crime and other Anti-Social Activities,* University of Chicago Press, 1911.

Flesch, Rudolf, *The Art of Plain Talk,* Harper & Brothers, 1946.

Garth, T. R., "A Statistical Study of the Contents of Newspapers," *School and Society,* Vol. 3, January 22, 1916, pp. 140–144.

Gerberich, J. R., and J. A. Thalheimer, "Reader Interest in Various Types of Newspaper Content," *Journal of Applied Psychology,* Vol. 20, August 1936, pp. 471–480.

Gilman, Mildred, "Truth Behind News," *American Mercury,* Vol. 29, June 1933, p. 139.

Goodman, Jack (editor), *While You Were Gone,* Simon & Schuster, 1946.

Graves, W. Brooke (editor), *Readings in Public Opinion,* Appleton-Century, 1928, pp. 306–311.

Greene, Ward (editor), *Star Reporters and 34 of Their Stories,* Random House, 1948.

Harris, Frank, *Presentation of Crime in Newspapers,* Sociological Press, 1932.

Irwin, Will, *Propaganda and the News,* McGraw-Hill, 1936, Chapter 5.

Kingsbury, S. M., and others, *Newspapers and the News,* G. P. Putnam's Sons, 1937, pp. 77–78, 88–90, 147–148.

Kobre, Sidney, *Backgrounding the News,* Twentieth Century Press, 1939.

Lahey, Thomas A., *The Morals of Newspaper Making,* Notre Dame University Press, 1924.

Lippmann, Walter, and Charles Merz, "A Test of the News," *The New Republic Supplement,* Vol. 23, August 4, 1920, pp. 41–42.

Mott, Frank L., "Trends in Presidential Campaigns," *Public Opinion Quarterly,* Vol. 8, Fall 1944.

Nafziger, Ralph O., and Marcus M. Wilkerson, *An Introduction to Journalism Research,* Louisiana State University Press, 1950.

Riis, R. W., "Are Newspapers Doing Their Duty?" *Independent,* Vol. 112, March 1, 1924, pp. 117–118.

Snyder, Louis L., and Richard B. Morris (editors), *A Treasury of Great Reporting,* Simon & Schuster, 1949.

Steinberg, Morton, "Only a Free Press Can Enable Democracy to Function," *Journalism Quarterly,* Vol. 23, March 1928, pp. 11–19.

Stewart, Kenneth, *News Is What We Make It,* Houghton Mifflin, 1943.

Storey, Moorfield, "The Daily Press," *The Atlantic Monthly,* Vol. 129, January 1922, pp. 41–44.

Villard, Oswald G., "Press Tendencies and Dangers," *The Atlantic Monthly,* Vol. 121, January 1918, pp. 62–66.

Willey, M. M., *The Country Newspaper,* University of North Carolina Press, 1926, pp. 65, 85, 101.

Wiseheart, M. K., *Public Opinion and the Steel Strike,* supplementary volume to Interchurch World Movement Report on the Steel Strike of 1919, Harcourt, Brace, 1921, pp. 87–162.

6. SELECTION AND SUPPRESSION OF NEWS

INTRODUCTION

THE INFLUENCE of the mass media on what the public thinks may be sharply affected by the withholding of information for one reason or another. This is particularly true with respect to the newspaper because of the relatively large amount of space it has available for many different pieces of news.

This situation prompts critics of the press to charge that the newspapers—through failure to print all the news (and particularly items of interest to the critics)—are often guilty of suppression. Yet one of the most significant aspects of criticism of the press is that critics have almost ceased to mention suppression as a major or minor vice of the newspaper. The topic has almost disappeared from recent literature on journalism. The once-feared influence of advertisers—to be discussed in the next chapter—is no longer what it perhaps once was. And so with many other restraining influences.

Few newspapermen take the trouble to deny that all the available news on a given publishing day sees print. The managing editor of the New York *Times* recently answered a critic of news selection to the effect that the *Times* receives some 450,000 words of news a day of which only slightly more than 200,000 words can be printed. Many smaller papers do not print all the news from their local fields because of financial inability to maintain a staff sufficiently large for complete coverage. Similarly, news may go unreported because of oversight or failure of the reporter to recognize its value. Some news, therefore, never reaches the newspaper office.

In all such cases, where the news later reaches public light—perhaps through another channel—the charge of "news suppression" usually is heard. In most instances the charge is unfounded. Careless or poor journalism may be involved, but not suppression in the sinister meaning of the word.

Suppression occurs when known facts that a newspaper could print are withheld from publication. Suppression is of several types, and it arises from various reasons. Much news, reaching both large and small newspapers, is not printed because of the practices of selection and rejection. But to give to all these processes the name of suppression is a manifest injustice to the press. News that reaches the hands of the editors may not be published for any of the following legitimate reasons: (1) It reaches the newspaper too late to be printed. (2) It was eliminated because there was no room for it or because more important items demanded the space. (3) The item was partly cut down because other news equally important also had to be represented in the same edition.

Most news stories that are wholly or partly thrown out are rejected for the foregoing reasons. Although it would be impossible to arrive at an estimate of the percentage of "suppressed" stories that were rejected for these reasons, every newspaperman knows that a hundred stories are cut or "killed" for every one actually suppressed because of a demand from an advertiser or other influential individual. Further, it is just as important to know how significant a suppressed story was as to know how many stories were suppressed.

Many newpapers have made it a policy to suppress stories that involve minors committing their first offense. The practice can be found in operation on metropolitan newspapers as well as on small-town papers. Editors who fear no type of pressure nevertheless may suppress such items so that a delinquent may have the opportunity to "go straight" without having a public criminal record to live down, and in so doing the editor believes he is contributing directly to public well-being.

Suppression because of duress and other forms of suppression that affect public welfare adversely are of quite another type than that referred to above, and it is this form that most critics of the press have in mind when they talk loosely of "suppression." Of this type was the failure of certain Chicago newspapers in 1933 and 1934 to warn visitors to the "Century of Progress" fair of the dangers of amoebic dysentery infection at certain hotels and restaurants near the fair grounds, although some of them knew long before the fair was over that scores of people had been infected.

During periods of national crisis, particularly wars, suppression takes the form of "voluntary censorship," a type of patriotic news control designed to safeguard not only national welfare but also the conduct of a determined policy. This procedure, if successful, either obviates or delays imposition of compulsory control by the government.

STANDARDS OF SELECTION

—James Russell Wiggins, "The News Is the First Concern of the Press," *Journalism Quarterly*, Vol. 23, March 1946, pp. 20–21. Mr. Wiggins was formerly editor of the St. Paul (Minnesota) *Pioneer Press* and *Dispatch*, and later was named managing editor of the Washington (D. C.) *Post.*

IT IS POSSIBLE to select and present news so as to shape customs, morals, conventions, and beliefs; but it is immoral for those who pretend to be engaged in mirroring human affairs to distort the news to such an end.

As long as the news function is fulfilled without conscious direction to such a purpose, the press is only a substitute for the natural environment of the tribal community; its unrelated and undirected mirrorings of human affairs only help make effective the natural motivations which otherwise would be missing. It is fitting, proper, and safe to entrust private individuals, neither elected nor appointed by public authority, with the task of telling what has happened. It would not be prudent to trust thousands of private persons, controlling the press through the happenstances of the private enterprise system, with the task of fabricating a predetermined picture of events calculated to give readers a motivation that would impel them toward someone's idea of how they should behave, in their own interest and in the interest of the state.

The purposeful presentation of the news, to achieve some given effect on customs and morals of society, is not the proper province of the news editor. The news is the "raw material of opinion" but it should not be manipulated with an eye to the finished product. Editors, exercising such power, could alter our customs, conventions, compulsions, and inhibitions and induce conformity to entirely different standards of behavior, remaking the rules by which we live. The diversity of ownership of the press under the private enterprise system is one protection against this.

All news should be "good" news to the editor. It is not his proper task to weigh the unpredictable consequences of the news and then pick and choose material for publication on the basis of his guess about what forces the news may set in motion.

News editors who mistakenly assume that it is their responsibility to decide what news is "good" for the public or "safe" for the readers expose themselves to many dangers. Not the least of these is the danger that their judgment, in an area where absolute values are so difficult to establish, will conveniently conform, by the sheerest coincidence, with the interest of their friends and their friends' friends.

The proper question the news editor should ask himself is: "Is it news?," not "Is it good news or is it bad news?" Who is going to decide what news is good for the public and what news is bad for them, and by what rules are the decisions to be made? The news of evil acts may furnish society precisely the urge it requires to correct a bad situation. The public profits by news of bad behavior (by revulsion) as well as from news of good behavior through imitation. The news that is good, bad, and indifferent must be held up to scrutiny so that newspaper readers are enabled to see life and see it whole—not just that part of it some editor thinks the public ought to see.

LIMITATIONS OF NEWSPAPER SPACE

—Casper S. Yost, *The Principles of Journalism,* Appleton-Century, 1924, pp. 30–31. Mr. Yost was editor of the St. Louis (Missouri) *Globe-Democrat* when he wrote this book.

THE PROBLEM always before the editor, and renewed afresh each day, is, What shall I print, and what reject? This involves much more than a judgment as to propriety or as to relative values of the various items presented on their merits. Each day he is obliged to consider limitations of space. He has so many columns available for news. The news that comes to him from his various reporting agencies usually far exceeds the space at his disposal. In consequence he is often obliged to reject much that he would print if room at his command would permit it. And this space is an unstable quantity. It varies from day to day, and not infrequently from hour to hour, as other requirements of publication alter in their needs. And the supply of news is as variable in its volume and importance. Today may be filled with news; tomorrow comparatively newsless. Today may furnish a great quantity of news, none of which is of much importance; tomorrow may bring a rush of big news commanding many columns for its presentation. Or, again, a relatively uneventful day may proceed to near its end when news of great importance suddenly demands large space for its telling, requiring the rejection of much that is in type or that has been printed perhaps in earlier editions. There is, therefore, a continuous process of selection and rejection, of adjustment and readjustment to events and to mechanical restrictions.

Moreover, the editor never has before him at one time all the news of the day from which to pick and choose in accordance with his deliberate estimate of relative values. It is coming to him in a flowing stream, and the necessities of time and the limitations of mechanical facilities compel the exercise of his judgment upon a moving current instead of upon a static mass. He cannot see the news of the day as a whole until the printed paper comes to his desk, and then it is too late to exercise his judgment from the viewpoint of the whole.

But notwithstanding these inescapable difficulties under which editorial judgment labors there is and must be discrimination in the selection of news, and it is largely upon the quality of that discrimination that journalism depends, both for its success and for its usefulness. Where that discrimination is wise and its standards high journalism attains its loftiest elevation and contributes most to public service. But in the exercise of it there are many things to be considered.

REJECTION AND SELECTION OF NEWS

—Casper S. Yost, *The Principles of Journalism*, Appleton-Century, 1924, pp. 42–44, 45–46, 53–55.

It has been shown that constant and varying limitations of available space compel a constant adjustment of news to meet the varying restrictions of room. Always there is more news than can be printed. Always there must be more or less rejection and condensation. The newspaper does not create events nor do events consider its convenience. It must take events as they come, whether in great volume or less, and adjust accounts of events to the capacity of publication. The item that is rejected today might have found a place yesterday. The item that fills a column today might have been entirely excluded, or greatly condensed, yesterday. Or an item accepted early in the day may be necessarily rejected before the paper goes to press.

Conditions under which discrimination is exercised are, therefore, different each day and change with the hours. But in reducing the volume of news to fit the capacity of publication, that which is of least importance or of least interest is first sacrificed, the effort being to crowd into the paper, not all of the news of the day, for that is rarely, if ever, possible, but the best of the news. In the exercise of this discrimination the editors in direct charge of the news must act upon their judgment of news values, and act instantly as a rule. When doubt arises there may be deliberation and conference, but in the daily publication there is little time or opportunity for this. In nearly all cases immediate decision is essential. In the continuous stream of news that flows through the hands of news editors items are accepted or rejected, given full space or condensed, upon their instantaneous estimate of relative importance or interest, always subject to sudden and unexpected demands for space for fresh and important news, requiring radical readjustment of all that has been done, and the elimination or reduction of much that has been previously accepted.

In all other productive enterprise the relation between demand and capacity is comparatively uniform, or is at least calculable for a short period of time. The editor is always confronted by unknown quantities. Each day he begins a new creation with no definite knowledge of the volume or the nature of the materials with which he must create. He has, to be sure, the expectation of certain routine sources of daily news, but he does not know what will develop from them nor what they will demand from him. No foreknowledge or prescience can enable him to see through the day, or even through the hour, to make definite calculations in advance. The news, most of it utterly unexpected, may come to him in a steady flow or it may fall upon him as an avalanche. He knows not, nor can he know, what the day may bring forth. All he can be sure is that he will have more news than he can print, and that he must be prepared for the worst. . . .

A veteran newspaperman once said that the judgment of "what not to print" was the supreme test of editorial ability. This may be an exaggeration, but at any rate the negative side of discrimination is as important as the positive. The limitations of space compel a continuous balancing of values for this reason alone, upon a basis of value that may vary with each day or each hour, according to the volume of the news. Often the weight of a hair influences decision for or against publication, but judgment upon each item must be rendered and rendered instantly. To "kill" an item that ought to be used is as bad judgment as to use an item that ought to be "killed." But all this refers to decision in response to the insistent demands of space.

Decisions upon the considerations of safety and considerations of propriety are no less essential and no less important. . . .

It is the business of the newspaper to print the news, as has been repeatedly said, yet "suppression of the news" is one of the most frequent complaints against journalism. It is, however, one of the least justified, if any sinister significance be given to the charge. All the problems of discrimination that have been under discussion involve rejection of news for many proper reasons. And the failure to print news for which there is no room, or which in the judgment of the editor ought not to be printed, whether because it is unimportant, unfit, or relatively uninteresting to his reader, is the only basis for most of the complaints that are made, usually by people who have been disappointed by the absence from the paper of items in which they were personally interested. It is the duty of the newspaper to print the news that is important; it is to its own interest to print the news that is attractive to the public, within the limits of propriety that have been mentioned. But what is important, either actually or relatively, and what is attractive, are questions that must be decided by the individual judgment of the editors of each newspaper, acting always of necessity under the pressure of time and space. There should, however, be no exterior or ulterior influence on that judgment. It should be founded solely upon the conception of news value in general, and, in particular, of its values for the section of the public which the newspaper serves. While a considerable proportion of news is of manifest importance to all newspapers alike, or to all alike in a country, region, or community, there is much news whose importance depends upon the nature and purposes of the publication and the character of its readers. That is to say, some news that is of value to one newspaper may be of no value, or relatively little value, to another. The editor must consider not only the comparative importance of news of general interest but the particular interests and tastes of his territory and constituency. Naturally, too, there are differences of judgment among editors, resulting from individual variations of temperament, association, and opinion, which cause one editor to reject an item which another would print, or to put in a few lines what another would present with prominence. These, however, are but the differences of personality that give variety to life, as they do to journalism, which is an epitome of life. But whatever these differences, the conscientious editor—most editors are conscientious and all should be—holds the publication of news that is of real importance to his readers to be a paramount duty.

VOLUNTARY NEWS SUPPRESSION IN WARTIME

—Byron Price, "The American Way," in *Journalism in Wartime,* Frank Luther Mott (editor), American Council on Public Affairs, 1943, pp. 29–33. Mr. Price was director of the Office of Censorship throughout World War II.

...ON DECEMBER 16, 1941, the President announced the appointment of a Director of Censorship, using these words:

"All Americans abhor censorship, just as they abhor war. But the experience of this and of all other nations has demonstrated that some degree of censorship is essential in war time, and we are at war.

"The important thing now is that such forms of censorship as are necessary shall be administered effectively and in harmony with the best interests of our free institutions."

As in 1917, various approaches to a voluntary system had been made in advance through isolated requests issued by various branches of the government. The first was a Navy request early in 1941 for secrecy regarding the repair of British warships in American shipyards. The Maritime Commission, the Weather Bureau, and various other agencies followed with requests of their own. Obviously the first thing for the new Office of Censorship to do was to tie these requests together, eliminate those which seemed unnecessary, and draft others so that the field would be covered comprehensively and in organized fashion.

Fortunately, the undertaking was launched without bitterness in any quarter. The declaration of the President for a voluntary system of censorship was hailed generally by the press, which came forward with a universal pledge of cooperation. There had been no prelude of controversy in Congress as in the case of the First World War. It is quite true that some disagreements had arisen within the Administration itself. The President had been urged strongly by some of his higher-ranking aides to ask Congress for a compulsory censorship statute. He had declined to do so. But all of this controversy, such as it was, had taken place within confidential official precincts, and no public incident developed. On the whole the venture of 1941 was launched on smooth waters.

The problem of codifying the government's requests was far from a simple one. Fevered day and night conferences among the government agencies and with representatives of the newspaper industry ensued. The United States government, already gigantic and complex almost beyond belief, was expanding its operations rapidly in the first desperate effort to grapple with a surprise attack. Even at the last moment, when we thought the provisions of the new Code had been pretty well settled, and we were about to make them public, we discovered that another government agency without any authority at all had prepared a complicated code of its own and was in the act of announcing it to the press of the country. It was more by luck than otherwise that we were able to learn of this prospective development and forestall it.

The President's statement of December 16, 1941, was the rock upon which we were attempting to build, and it has remained ever since the true foundation of all of our operations. In addition to declaring that censorship of the press should be voluntary, the words of the statement laid down three cardinal principles: that censorship was an instrument of war, that censorship must be so administered as to be effective, that this was to be an American censorship, in harmony "with the best interests of our free institutions."

As to the first of these considerations, there was little difficulty in theory but much complication in practice. Everyone recognized, as an abstract proposition, that requests to the press ought to be confined to matters related to the war and to national security. Nevertheless, when it came to concrete cases, there was no absence of attempts to smuggle into the Code certain things which might suit the convenience of the government but which dealt with peace-time statutes or with situations where the war effort, as such, was only remotely involved.

The invariable method of dealing with these situations was to inquire over and over just what issue of national security was involved. In other words, the Office of Censorship adopted at the very beginning the old legal stratagem of requiring the litigant to "show cause." Unless a definite consideration of national security could be shown, the request was omitted from the Code.

The second stipulation of the President was that censorship must be "administered effectively" even though there was no statute behind it. Obviously this meant that confidence in our operation had to be established, not only on the side of the press but on the side of the government itself. In other words, to be effective, the Code must be recognized by other government agencies, including the armed forces, as sufficient to cover the needs of security; and it must be recognized by the press as reasonable and workable.

We had always on the one hand the possibility that some powerful government department would lose faith in the virility of our program and would initiate a broad-gauge censorship crusade on its own account in a zealous effort to fill the gap. We had always on the other hand the possibility that some individual, newspaper or magazine, or group, would lose faith in our honest intentions and our reasonableness and would decline to have any part in the experiment.

This dilemma we sought to resolve, as best we could, by once more applying strictly the rule of national security. The Code is based throughout on a belief that no government agency has a right to be unreasonable in its requests and that the press will be willing always to accept and abide by any request which can be defended on the score of reasonableness. In such a manner only could effective censorship be established.

Finally, the President stipulated that we must remember we were dealing with free institutions. This meant that relations with the press must not be harsh or bureaucratic. It meant also that there was to be no infringement upon the guarantee in the First Amendment.

Much has been said about the seeming incongruity of the terms "censorship" and "free press" and there always is a certain bristling when any restraint whatever is put upon the operation of a printing press. The cry of government meddling and interference with free expression always is an especially handy tool for politicians when censorship in any guise enters the arena. But there is a reasonable basis for distinction here as there is everywhere else in law and practical government.

The rights conferred by the First Amendment are by no means absolute rights. No one would contend, for instance, that freedom of the press meant a freedom to commit libel or slander or to indulge in indecency of expression. When it is examined in all of its aspects, the Constitutional guarantee resolves itself into a guarantee of freedom to express opinion, to petition, to criticize, to protest. The language of the Amendment certainly cannot be reasonably stretched to include a guarantee of freedom to be criminally careless with information in war time, or to commit treason, which is expressly dealt with in another clause of the Constitution.

It is, therefore, the basic characteristic of the present Code and of all of our incidental relations with the domestic press that the Office of Censorship in no way and to no degree seeks to influence editorial opinion.

Such is the theory of our present censorship of the domestic press. Space does not permit a detailed discussion of actual experience, but it is appropriate to recognize, in conclusion, that no one can claim perfection either for what has been attempted or for what has been accomplished.

From an operational viewpoint, the weakness of voluntary censorship has lain not so much in the lack of legal penalties as in the vast expanse of the American publishing industry and the inevitable differences of interpretation which arise among editors widely separated and always under the pressure of approaching deadlines. This disadvantage would arise whether there were penalties or not. It is inescapable under any system which stops short of absolute government regimentation, with every line of type controlled exactly by one central authority.

Censorship, for example, issues its rule book—a set of requests written as plainly as a trained staff can write them after long consultation with the war agencies and the industry. Yet whatever the painstaking effort, no Code can be devised which covers every human possibility exactly. Hence the event is always happening which is either just outside the letter, but inside the purpose of the mind of the censor.

A painstaking editor will think this through, will see that a security issue may conceivably be involved despite the loophole left by the language of the Code, and will decide to give security the benefit of the doubt and put the story on the dead-hook. His neighbor, however, may be more literal-minded, less thoughtful, more influenced by lifelong habits of initiative formed in the hard school of journalistic competition.

Not only does such a situation present a pretty tangle for those who administer censorship, but it weakens by just so much the strategic position of that school of thought which clings to the voluntary theory. If dangerous information gets into print through such a succession of events, the doubters shake their heads, and there is an audible rustling of bills and resolutions which propose to deal with censorship on a statutory basis. The advocates of such measures do not split hairs. They are not inclined to be impressed with the virtues of a free press in time of war. They are not schooled to be concerned about the problems of the press or of the people, but only with the immediate physical problems of making war on the battlefield.

The desertions from the French warships in American harbors early in 1943, the Guadalcanal sit-down reports, and certain aspects of the Darlan episode in North Africa all fell within this foggy area of being partly but not too explicitly covered by the language of the Code. In each instance there was some trace of a security issue, yet no book of rules brief enough to be workable could ever cover these or similar situations, with finite thoroughness. Should some borderline case arise where innocently intended but thoughtless publication actually and visibly cost American lives, there might easily be a public opinion over night that voluntary censorship had failed.

This is the Field of Darkness. It is well that every devotee of a free press understand the danger. Yet we must not be dismayed by it, for, after all, these are simply the hazards which every free institution must face in time of world upheaval.

The important consideration is that we recognize the perils, but never lose our faith. With all their faults, free institutions still are best; and with all its weaknesses, voluntary censorship still is vastly to be desired above all other methods of dealing with a free press in war time.

NEWS DEFINITION CHANGES

—Eric W. Allen, "The Newspaper and Community Leadership," *The Press in the Contemporary Scene, The Annals of the American Academy of Political and Social Science*, Vol. 219, January 1942, pp. 26–27. Mr. Allen was dean of the School of Journalism, University of Oregon, when he wrote this article.

WHAT, THEN, besides his often potent editorial page, is left to the American editor who wants to use the power of the press to forward worthy causes and obstruct bad ones? The answer lies in the shifting character of "news." Not only does public interest focus on different things at different times, but there is a no man's land between news and not-news where there may or may not be a latent public interest which the newspaper itself, merely by publishing the facts in an interesting way, can fan into a lively flame. The editor who can discover and first exploit the largest number and the most judiciously selected of these previously unrecognized fields, is likely to have the newsiest paper. Here is where his many daily visitors may be a real help. Not all of their proposals are useless. Here and there is one which his professional instinct tells him has lively possibilities.

An editor obviously has a wide moral latitude. He may know or convincingly suspect that there is a strong latent interest in anti-Semitism, in ideological witch-hunts, in sexual aberrations, in religious controversies, in "ganging-up" on unpopular scapegoats, or in friction between economic classes, and may deliberately decide not to exploit it. Who shall say, in any given case, how close this comes to suppression of news? Is the *Christian Science Monitor* unethical in its attitude toward death and despair? Or are the other papers wrong in the way they handle catastrophes and disasters? On the other hand, the editor may decide that his community is ripe for a discussion of police reorganization, fundamental tax reform, civic beautification, or "progressive" education. He can, if he wishes, lend powerful help to movements, first by giving more reportorial space to the subject than any existing public curiosity calls for, then by reporting fully the controversy that arises (unless the proposition falls flat), and later by taking sides editorially, and perhaps, if the project looks hopeful, by plunging into an all-out "campaign" to bring about action.

Public attitudes (and professional opinion, too) concede wide latitude to the editor for partisanship, even eccentricity, on the editorial page, though it has lately become customary to give greater representation to opposing views in "columns," signed articles, letters from the public, and quoted material. This liberalization becomes ethically the more necessary as papers become fewer, and as an approach toward monopoly is made; as in everything else, progress is gradual. Feature, sports, dramatic, music, entertainment, home economics, and other cultural pages campaign mildly and continuously in a semi-editorial manner for what the editor (or his assistants) consider superior amenities and better practices, though they seldom affront any large body of public feeling. But on the news pages the larger and more intelligent demand is for objectivity, fairness, or even a close approach to neutrality between good and evil where the issue is controversial. An occasional "campaign," publicly acknowledged editorially, with reasons constantly stated, is regarded as a legitimate incursion of editorial motives into the news pages, provided there are not too many of them, and that there is an underlying truthfulness and fairness. One reason the editor must say "no" to most of his visitors is because he will lessen his influence if he champions at one time too many "social control" projects; his main business is news.

PROS AND CONS OF SUPPRESSION

—L. N. Flint, *The Conscience of the Newspaper,* Appleton-Century, 1925, pp. 71–73, 77–78, 98–100. Mr. Flint was head of the Department of Journalism, University of Kansas, when he wrote his study of press ethics.

THE PHRASE, suppression of the news, has an evil import to most minds, arising from the fact, no doubt, that the cases of suppression we hear most about are coupled with intimations of venality or graft on the part of the editor, or sinister influence by some powerful individual or group. Experience with the problem, however, or even study of it from the outside, soon reveals that it has its laudable aspects as well as its evil ones. A veteran in journalism, looking back over his career, may very possibly take as great satisfaction in the remembrance of acts of news suppression as in those of fearless news publication or any other of his achievements.

The public says little regarding the newspapers' practice as to suppression, except when some portion of it protests at failure to eliminate the indecent, or another portion complains at failure to print adequate reports of some special interest. The general feeling of the public seems to be that people with influence can keep things out of the paper and that unimportant people cannot. Not many people nowadays believe that newspapers accept money to keep things out. Some prominent people call newspapers ruthless and profess to hate them. Our purpose is to get a broad view of this most complex matter and to discover the general direction of correct procedure.

It would be impossible for anyone to say confidently how much newspaper material is being withheld from publication for some other reason than its inferiority of news value or lesser importance to the public. Only this can properly be called suppression.

One editor of a metropolitan daily ventures the opinion that, "suppression of news has come to be a topic of conversation largely because some people have disagreed with newspapers about the relative importance of news. A committee organizes a political party and then complains that the newspapers suppress the news about it. The trouble is that the doings of the committee interest so few people that the editors do not feel justified in giving much space to them."

Moreover, if one looks at the reading matter in almost any issue of any newspaper, with the question in mind as to how much of it would have been suppressed if everybody's selfish interest or personal preferences had been considered, he will find plenty of evidence that remarkable independence is maintained by the press. It is printing the news without much fear or favor. A view behind the scenes will, however, show that this is not the whole story. . . .

Among the reasons given for asking that news be withheld from publication are some of doubtful propriety or plausibility and some which may be accepted as convincing. Some of the more familiar and interesting reasons are:

That the withholding of an item about a misdemeanor would constitute a threat calculated to prevent further offenses by the same person.

That the publication of the item would hurt the business of the person concerned.

That the item of news would hurt the town.

That publication of the item would hurt the business of the editor.

That suppression of the item would be a favor to the editor's friends and in line with his social obligations.

That suppression of the truth about an incident would be proper because of the paper's previous acceptance of a formal statement, though untrue, as covering the case.

That the item refers to a first offense.

That the item relates to a juvenile offender.

That sympathy for parents justifies the suppression.

That suppression would promote peace in the community.

That suppression would avoid embarrassment of innocent persons.

That the paper is not sure of all the facts.

That the matter is a delicate one involving affairs of state or similar public matters.

That the item involves the reputation of a woman or a girl.

That the story looks like propaganda.

That the story was obtained in confidence.

That the story is morbid in tone and content.

That the item is to be regarded as free publicity.

Among the obvious reasons against suppression, the following are to be regarded seriously:

That the newspaper has an implied contract with the public to give complete information of the day's events.

That omission is one way of telling an untruth.

That the suppression gives rise to rumors while publication of the facts protects the public against anxieties growing out of baseless reports.

That the news can be published with substantial fairness to all concerned and with better results than to attempt to favor certain ones through suppression.

That by refusing to suppress news, a newspaper demonstrates its independence.

That the knowledge that publicity may be "a part of the penalty" will act as a wholesome deterrent from wrong doing.

The question naturally arises as to whether it is fair to the journalist to expect him to sacrifice his financial interest in order to conserve the public interest. Why should we say that it is the duty of the editor to make enemies, if necessary, in giving the public the news and in performing other kinds of community service? Why cannot the editor run his business as other men conduct theirs—in the manner that will insure him the greatest returns?

The answer is, of course, that the newspaper is not merely a business concern. In the very nature of things it cannot be a good newspaper if run on the controlling principle of business, that the good will of everybody is at the basis of success. No man should enter the field of journalism unless he is willing to take the losses that are sure to come from following the policy of representing the interests of the unorganized public against those of powerful individuals and groups. That is an essential part of the editor's career. It calls for courage; it appeals only to the man with a vigorous strain of altruism. That men of other ideals are financially successful in journalism and are not ashamed to maintain that their vocation is nothing more than a business means nothing except that in every business and profession are men who do not accept the best standards of that business or profession. They are the dead weight carried by their colleagues who are blessed with clearer vision.

Nor, after all, is so much more required of the journalist than of those in other professions. The doctor, in protecting the public by a strict adherence to quarantine laws, makes enemies who represent for him a financial loss; in fact, much of the modern physician's labor is towards lessening the need for physicians. The lawyer, in lending his strength to the protection of causes that are unpopular, though entitled to protection for their legal right, sometimes loses valuable good will. The minister whose preachings and whose activities are directed at concrete evils rather than at evil in general must pay the price. He should not have entered the ministry unless he could cheerfully accept the penalties. So with the editor. To make an enemy by refusing to suppress a piece of news to which the public is entitled should be to him merely a part of the day's work. Of course, this is easier said than done. It is easier in the city than in the small town. It may properly be avoided, so far as good nature and diplomacy and sympathy can avoid it; but there is a line of professional conduct on which courage stands firm.

Nothing would be more ridiculous than to attempt to reach a decision in a doubtful case by a mechanical method of weighing the arguments for and against suppression. Broadly speaking, every case is different and must be settled on its merits. But to do this wisely is to bring to bear a judicial mind on all the considerations. This process may well be illustrated graphically in a table presenting the reasons, properly weighed, for and against suppression. To be sure, there is no time in the editor's day to refer to such a table, even if he were academic enough to make one. Most decisions must be made on the instant. But the fact remains that the editor with the ability to look at all sides of a question without being paralyzed thereby into indecision is the one who will have the least occasion to regret "bad guesses."

REVIEW QUESTIONS AND ASSIGNMENTS

1. Discuss the theory that it is the newspaper's duty to refuse to print certain types of news.

2. Discuss the statement that the *Christian Science Monitor* is the nearest approach to an ideal newspaper in the United States.

3. Distinguish between selection, rejection, and suppression of the news. What are the common defenses offered for each type?

4. Discuss the possibilities of creating a more thoughtful press by diminishing the public demand for speed in news dissemination. Is this speed demanded by the public, or is it a product of newspaper competition? Is the same haste shown in cities in which there is but one newspaper?

5. Within your own experience, what cases of suppression have you known, and what was the reason for the suppression?

6. Is there any way of ameliorating those conditions that now force the editor to pick and choose from the stream of news as it enters his office in order to meet his deadlines?

7. Should the press present a cross section of all the news, or only that part of the news in which the reading public is interested?

8. To what extent should the interests, degree of education, and character of the readers influence the newspaper's choice of news?

9. Is the amount of the newspaper "copy" that is destroyed an accurate index to the amount of vital news that is suppressed?

10. To what degree do charges of suppression arise from groups or individuals attempting to influence the printing of certain news items?

11. Discuss the ethics of suppressing news of epidemics and financial conditions that might hurt the business of the town.

12. What are the arguments for and against the suppression of news items involving the reputation of juveniles and women?

13. Discuss the theory that omission of news is one way of telling an untruth.

14. Is it fair to the journalist to expect him to suppress news the publication of which would injure his own business?

15. What are the obligations to print the news that are assumed by any newspaper in operating under the constitutional guarantee of freedom of the press?

ADDITIONAL REFERENCES

Allen, Frederick Lewis, "Newspapers and the Truth," *The Atlantic Monthly,* Vol. 129, January 1922, pp. 44–54.

Angell, Norman, *Let the People Know,* Viking Press, 1942.

Anonymous, "Censorship," *Fortune,* Vol. 23, June 1941, pp. 88, 153–154, 158, 160.

———, "Creeping Censorship," *Editor and Publisher,* Vol. 82, January 1, 1949, p. 24.

———, "Freedom of Press Curbed During 1948, Survey Shows," *Editor & Publisher,* Vol. 81, December 25, 1948, p. 7.

Bailey, Thomas A., *The Man in the Street,* Macmillan, 1948, pp. 304–319.

Chafee, Zechariah Jr., *Free Speech in the United States,* Harvard University Press, 1942.

Cooper, Sanford Lee, "Censorship" in *Newsmen's Holiday, Nieman Essays,* First Series, Harvard University Press, 1942, pp. 112–126.

Crawford, Nelson A., *The Ethics of Journalism,* F. S. Crofts, 1924, pp. 103–105.

Gilman, Mildred, "Truth Behind the News," *American Mercury,* Vol. 29, June 1933, pp. 139–146.

Harrington, Harry F., "Can a Newspaper Tell the Truth?" *National Printer Journalist,* Vol. 40, January 1922, pp. 30–31.

Henning, A. F., *Ethics and Practices in Journalism,* Ray Long and Richard R. Smith, 1932, pp. 105–113.

Hocking, William Ernest, *Freedom of the Press,* University of Chicago Press, 1947, pp. 135–160.

Hughes, Helen MacGill, "The Social Interpretation of News," *The Annals of the American Academy of Political and Social Science,* Vol. 219, January 1942, pp. 11-17.

Koop, Theodore, *Weapon of Silence,* University of Chicago Press, 1946.

Lloyd, A. H., "Newspaper Conscience: A Study in Half-Truths," *American Journal of Sociology,* Vol. 27, September 1921, pp. 197–210.

MacDougall, Curtis D., *Newsroom Problems and Policies,* Macmillan, 1941, pp. 351–386.

Mayer, M. S., "Amoebic Dysentery in Chicago," *Forum,* Vol. 92, July 1934, pp. 3–9.

Older, Fremont, *My Own Story,* Macmillan, 1926.

Rogers, Charles E., "The Role of the Weekly Newspaper," *The Annals of the American Academy of Political and Social Science,* Vol. 219, January 1942, pp. 151–152.

Villard, Oswald G., *Some Newspapers and Newspapermen,* Alfred A. Knopf, 1923, pp. 119–120, 164–167.

Williams, J. C., A. Brown, "Forum: Is Censorship Justifiable in a Democracy?" *Forum,* Vol. 110, October 1948, pp. 228–234.

Wittenberg, Philip, *Dangerous Words,* Columbia University Press, 1947.

7. THE ROLE OF ADVERTISING

INTRODUCTION

DISCUSSION in print and in public forums of the role of advertising in the American economy has been gradually shifting from the sociological to the economic aspects. Today there is less fear of the influence of advertisers upon newspaper and magazine editors and the managers of radio stations than upon the economic system itself. Although critics have written much to the effect that the media have suppressed news at the request of advertisers, in recent years increasing inquiry has been directed at the cost and influence of advertising in the distributive processes. One extremely serious question concerns just how much of the expense of an expanding communications network advertising will be able to bear.

Advertising revenue always has been the major source of income for the press; circulation receipts occupy a secondary position. The income percentages achieved through these two sources were changed somewhat during World War II when most daily newspapers adopted a five-cent retail price with a consequent sharp increase in circulation revenue. The great amount of money made by the newspapers through sale of advertising space and the many problems connected with advertising messages have made advertising income a focal point for much criticism of the performance record of the press.

Radio and television, of course, rely on advertising income for almost all their income. The chunk taken out of the advertising dollar by the cost of expensive television shows has forced consideration of the possibility that advertisers may discover that there are limits on the amount of money they can spend on sales appeals. This, in turn, may bring serious readjustments in the whole advertising picture, with all the media affected in one way or another.

The economic arguments, pro and con, on newspaper advertising are set forth by Frey. These arguments cover the ground over which most controversy rages today. Borden, in the second selection, gives his opinion on the place of advertising in a capitalistic society. The growth of controls on advertising through the *Printers' Ink* model statute is covered in the selection from Lund.

One of the best summations on the contributions of advertising is made by Presbrey. This is an older opinion but one that has changed very little among most influential voices in advertising. A specific example of how advertising "influence" may react upon the advertiser is given in the quotation from Harry Lewis Bird. The criticism by Batten is the work of one who has spent a lifetime in producing advertising and, therefore, one who speaks with great insight.

ECONOMIC CONSIDERATIONS OF ADVERTISING

—Albert Wesley Frey, *Advertising*, Copyright 1947 by The Ronald Press Company, pp. 654–656. Mr. Frey is professor of marketing at Dartmouth College.

To APPRAISE advertising adequately from an economic viewpoint, one should have in mind the desirable objectives of our economic system. Although there may be some difference of opinion as to what those objectives should be, most persons would probably agree on the following:

(a) High productivity
(b) A low cost of obtaining this productivity
(c) An equitable distribution of the fruits of this productivity
(d) Production of wanted merchandise, that is, production based on the general interests of the community, with the most important wants filled first
(e) Use of resources with proper regard for the correct balance between present and future needs
(f) A correct balance between productive activity and leisure

In general we may say that in judging advertising and other business activities with the public welfare in mind we should give consideration to their effects on the standard of living of all the people and on the manner in which, and the efficiency with which, the country's resources are utilized.

The views of those persons who believe that advertising aids in the attainment of at least some of the foregoing objectives and does not interfere with the attainment of any of them, may be stated somewhat as follows:

1. Advertising increases the sales volume of a product, permitting large-scale manufacture and distribution. The result is reductions in cost which are passed on to consumers in the form of lower prices.

2. Advertising creates utility and thus leads to greater satisfaction on the part of the consumer-buyer.

3. Advertising stimulates production through making people work harder to obtain the merchandise and services advertised.

4. Advertising stimulates businessmen to attempt to reduce costs in order to make possible the selling appeal of lower prices.

5. Advertising leads to an increase in the range of merchandise available to consumers and to a continual improvement in its quality. As it encourages the introduction of new merchandise, it brings about new investment and increased employment.

Opponents of advertising claim that much of it tends to hinder the attainment of the desired objectives. They contend that if much advertising were eliminated, we would be better off. They argue that while productivity and the standard of living may be high in this country, they would be higher with less advertising. Specifically they state:

1. Advertising is an unnecessary cost of doing business and therefore raises prices unnecessarily. It encourages costly yet unimportant product differentiation.

2. Advertising is too often merely competitive, that is, it attempts to induce consumers to cease buying one brand and to start buying another which is identical in quality and price. The result is often a stalemate, with the sales of all competitors remaining relatively the same, and too frequently absolutely the same, as they were before advertising was undertaken. The resources tied up in this sort of endeavor could be put to better use.

3. Advertising gives some manufacturers a monopoly control which enables them to exert an undesirable influence on supply and prices. Often the monopoly is based not on a superior product but on a larger advertising appropriation. If "monopoly control" seems too strong a term, at least it can be said that advertising enables manufacturers to avoid price competition.

4. Advertising may enable a manufacturer to continue to compete on an equal footing with other manufacturers not because he is

equally efficient but because he has a larger advertising appropriation.

5. Advertising results in an inefficient use of our resources at any one time, and in an undesirable rate of use, considering the correct balance between the present and the future.

6. Advertising accentuates cyclical fluctuations in general business conditions.

7. Advertising goes beyond informing consumers as to how they may best fill their wants and actually creates the wants in many instances.[1]

From those two sets of arguments, we can conclude that the fundamental questions involved are:

1. Is advertising productive?
2. Does advertising increase the range of merchandise available to consumers and does it lead to improvements in merchandise?
3. What effect does advertising have on demand, costs, and prices?
4. Does advertising lead to concentration of supply and monopoly?
5. Is some advertising solely "competitive" and therefore wasteful?
6. Does advertising lead to improper use of our resources?
7. Is advertising uneconomic because it creates wants rather than merely catering to existing wants?

ADVERTISING IN A CAPITALISTIC ECONOMY

—Neil H. Borden, *The Economic Effects of Advertising*, Richard D. Irwin, Inc., 1944, pp. 880–882. Mr. Borden is professor of advertising in Harvard Graduate School of Business Administration.

In the end, what role of social significance does advertising play in our capitalistic economy? On the whole, does it add to consumer welfare? The discussion has shown that its use is accompanied by certain dangers, particularly those attending the tendency of businessmen to compete in advertising and thus to bring into prices a large amount of selling costs. On the other side of the ledger, what is advertising's offsetting contribution, if any?

[1] "And what comfort is to be derived from the thought that demand is the governor of production, when demand is the plaything of the arts of advertising hypnotism?" J. M. Clark, *Social Control of Business* (McGraw-Hill Book Company, 1939), p. 41.

Advertising's outstanding contribution to consumer welfare comes from its part in promoting a dynamic, expanding economy. Advertising's chief task from a social standpoint is that of encouraging the development of new products. It offers a means whereby the enterpriser may hope to build a profitable demand for his new and differentiated merchandise which will justify investment. From growing investment has come the increasing flow of income which has raised man's material welfare to a level unknown in previous centuries.

In a static economy there is little need of advertising. Only that minimum is necessary which will provide information regarding sources of merchandise required to facilitate exchange between buyers and sellers who are separated from each other. Clearly in a static economy it would be advisable to keep informational costs at a minimum, just as it would be wise to keep all costs at a minimum.

In a dynamic economy, however, advertising plays a different role. It is an integral part of a business system in which entrepreneurs are striving constantly to find new products and new product differentiations which consumers will want. Without opportunity to profit relatively quickly from the new products which they develop, entrepreneurs would not be inclined either to search for them or to risk investment in putting them on the market. Advertising and aggressive selling provide tools which give prospect of profitable demand.

The critic must realize that progress in product improvement comes slowly; merchandise does not come on the market in full perfection. The constant seeking for product improvements, with which advertising and aggressive selling are intimately related, has been essential to an ever-increasing variety of new merchandise.

For much of this new merchandise advertising and other forms of aggressive selling play the significant role of aiding the expansion of demand and the responsiveness of demand to price reductions upon which widespread enjoyment of the products among the populace depends. Widespread usage is made possible by low prices, which in turn require low costs. For many industries low costs of production depend upon large-scale operations which are not possible until there is a large volume of sales not only for the industries, but also for individual producers. Advertising may make increased sales possible not only through shifting demand schedules but also through increasing the elasticity of demand for products. Thereby it provides business concerns with the opportunity to increase dollar sales volume through price reductions and makes it worth their while to do so as production costs decrease. In past years in industry after industry the economies which have come from large-scale operations and technological development have been passed along in lower prices.

As an industry matures and new differentiations, upon which expansion rests, become less important, then it is particularly desirable that counterbalancing forces which tend to check and reduce competition in advertising, and which prevent innovators from profiting over long periods of time from their innovations, should have free opportunity to operate. Probably the most important of these counterbalancing forces is that provided in the competition of business firms which do not make substantial outlays in development work on which growth depends, either in product development or in promotion of new merchandise. The price competition of these concerns serves to hold down the costs of competition in advertising and other non-price forms. The price competition of such concerns is to be encouraged rather than discouraged by restrictive price legislation, such as has been embodied in recent years in price control acts of one type or another.

To the counterbalancing force of price competition may be added that of increased education of consumers permitting them to choose intelligently among the variety of goods offered them.

Since advertising has in large part been associated with the promotion of new and differentiated merchandise, a substantial part of advertising costs should be looked upon economically as growth costs. They are the costs incurred in raising the economy from one level to another. From the standpoint of social welfare these costs have been far more than offset by the rise in national income which they have made possible. Such costs should not be prevented or decried. In the future if man's material welfare is to be raised to higher levels in our free economy, the spark of enterprise must be kept glowing brightly; the chance to profit from the new should continue to exist. So long as individual enterprise flourishes and a dynamic economy continues, advertising and aggressive selling will play a significant social role.

LEGAL CONTROLS ON ADVERTISING

—John V. Lund, *Newspaper Advertising*, Prentice-Hall, Inc., 1947, pp. 429–431. Mr. Lund is a member of the journalism faculty, State University of Iowa.

The Federal government exerts certain controls over advertising through the Post Office Department, the Securities and Exchange

Commission, and the Federal Trade Commission. The basis of jurisdiction by the Federal government is in its controls over use of the mails and over activities of interstate commerce.

Through the Post Office Department the Federal government regulates advertising of lotteries, publication of obscene matter, publication of advertising supplements, and the marking of paid advertising which appears in the guise of reading matter. The Federal Trade Commission regulates certain fraudulent and misleading advertising practices which constitute unfair competition and enforces the Wheeler Lea Act regulating advertisements of food, drugs, devices, and cosmetics. The Securities and Exchange Commission regulates advertising practices in regard to securities.

Twenty-six states and the District of Columbia have enacted the model statute or satisfactory modifications of it, making false advertising a misdemeanor. These states are Alabama, Colorado, Idaho, Illinois, Indiana, Iowa, Kansas, Kentucky, Louisiana, Michigan, Minnesota, Missouri, Nebraska, Nevada, New Jersey, New York, North Dakota, Ohio, Oklahoma, Oregon, Rhode Island, Virginia, Washington, West Virginia, Wisconsin, and Wyoming. Five states have no general false advertising statute: Arkansas, Delaware, Georgia, Mississippi, and New Mexico. The remaining 17 states have less inclusive statutes covering false advertising.

The *Printers' Ink* model statute is as follows:

> Any person, firm, corporation or association who, with intent to sell or in any wise dispose of merchandise, securities, service, or anything offered by such person, firm, corporation or association, directly or indirectly, to the public for sale or distribution, or with intent to increase the consumption thereof, or to induce the public in any manner to enter into any obligation relating thereto, or to acquire title thereto, or an interest therein, makes, publishes, disseminates, circulates, or places before the public, or causes, directly or indirectly, to be made, published, disseminated, circulated, or placed before the public, in this state, in a newspaper, or other publication, or in the form of a book, notice, handbill, poster, bill, circular, pamphlet, or letter, or in any other way, an advertisement of any sort regarding merchandise, securities, service, or anything so offered to the public, which advertisement contains any assertion, representation, or statement of fact which is untrue, deceptive, or misleading, shall be guilty of misdemeanor.[1]

Many states have enacted laws governing the publication of politi-

[1] For a discussion of legal interpretation of the statute see *Legal Control of the Press*, by Frank Thayer, Foundation Press, Chicago, 1944.

cal advertising. In addition, some states have enacted laws governing the advertising of special groups such as dentists and optometrists. Fair Trade acts in some states regulate price advertising on merchandise for which a minimum resale price has been established by the manufacturer. Information on all such state laws should be available in the advertising department and may be obtained through the newspaper's attorney or through the state publishers' association.

ADVERTISING SPEAKS ON ITS OWN BEHALF

–Frank Presbrey, *The History and Development of Advertising*, Doubleday, Doran & Company, Inc., 1929, pp. 598–604, 608–611, 613–618. Mr. Presbrey was founder of *Public Opinion* and an advertising executive.

EXAMPLES of the profound effect of advertising results on economic development are numerous. In the automobile we have, besides the creation of a six-billion-dollar industry and what that means in employment, the effect of automobile production on the steel, glass, copper, lumber, railroad equipment, petroleum, and other industries, on railroad haulage of raw materials, and especially, the effect of motor transportation on suburban real estate development. To the large-scale advertising of automobiles which began in 1903 and made possible mass production, low price, and ownership of a score of millions of cars by the American public, is attributable, directly and indirectly, the major part of the increase from $55,000,000,000 to $336,000,000,000 in our national wealth in twenty-five years. Suburban and agricultural land values, greatly enhanced by the facility afforded by automobile communication, represent the largest item in the increased national wealth and in nearly all items the influence of the automobile may be found.

Advertising of fruits has added millions to the income of growers and more millions to land values. Breakfast-food advertising has had a like effect on land, besides creating factories. . . . In practically every industry the output has been increased by the force of advertising.

Advertising is, as President Coolidge said, "the most potent influence in adapting and changing the habits and modes of life, affecting what we eat, what we wear, and the work and play of the whole nation." It is the influence which causes John Smith to desire something John Doe makes and John Doe to desire something that Sam Jones makes and leads to each producing more in order to gratify his own desire for new comforts and pleasures, with the result of a higher standard of living all around. . . .

If all advertising were to be forbidden tomorrow American business would have the problem of keeping sales volume by other methods. The first thought probably would be to add traveling salesmen to perform the service which advertising now renders as an urge on the dealer to stock. There are 500,000 or more traveling salesmen in the United States. Merely doubling that force at $4,000 a year salary and expenses for each man would mean $2,000,000,000 in added cost of distribution. If house-to-house canvassers were to attempt to do what advertising now does in reaching the consumer and creating demand on the dealer, five billions of dollars—it is anybody's guess—might be spent without getting the results that are now obtained through advertising. Doors would be closed against a procession of bell ringers such as would be necessary. And if the whole job could be done with salesmen, the Fuller Brush Company, which sells through door-to-door salesmen exclusively, doubtless would not be spending $300,000 a year on advertising. Experience of department stores during periods when labor strikes have stopped publication of newspapers has demonstrated that their business cannot go on in present volume without advertising. . . .

If we estimate all retail turnover and various services at eighty billion dollars a year and charge to it a billion and a quarter for national and local publication, outdoor, radio broadcast, and display card advertising, we get 1½ per cent as the advertising cost. That includes not only advertising to the ultimate consumer but advertising by the raw material and machinery man to the manufacturer and by the manufacturer to the dealer. Advertising of cost-reducing materials and machinery to the manufacturer has had, and continues to have, a large influence in lowering the price of products to the ultimate consumer, and is a legitimate inclusion in the price of the final product.

Advertising of an article or group of articles which brings people to a store leads to the sale also of unadvertised articles in that store. Advertising the uses of a product sells the same article made by manufacturers other than the advertiser. Thus advertising has an influence in practically all sales. But if we assume that advertising sells only half the goods sold and charge all the cost to people who buy the goods specifically advertised, the advertising cost still represents only 3 per cent. If the estimated cost of direct mail is added the figure goes to 5.8 per cent.

. . . Advertising is a volume-producing, cost-reducing machine. Without it the consumer would be paying much more than is represented by 1½ per cent, 3 per cent, or even 5.8 per cent. Production of unadvertised goods would go down with the rest because education in the use of articles had ceased, and manufacturing and distribution costs would go up all around. Things would cost more and income would at the same time be reduced, for that part of the consumer's income which is due directly or indirectly, to sales and general prosperity made by advertising would be lost. This reduction of income, which undoubtedly would come to farmers, artisans, bookkeepers, stenographers, and all people alike, would represent a figure per capita considerably greater than the per-capita cost of advertising. . . .

There appears to be a growing realization among those who trace for the rest of us the factors which bring about profound changes that advertising is a civilizing influence comparable in its cultural effects to those of other great epoch-making developments in history. In the United States, advertising, by creating a demand for the products of labor, has been instrumental in obtaining a wide diffusion of the national wealth among the people. It has helped to bring about an all-around easing of toil and a consequent greater interest in the finer things of life. In England it has exerted its power and done big things in the face of economic and social conditions that present greater obstacles than advertising has found in the United States. Elsewhere in the world it will be acting in its full power when means are found for adaptation of methods to various social conditions and giving a start to the beneficent circle of which advertising is an indispensable part.

Some future "History of Civilization" perhaps will give advertising credit as the power that in the nineteenth century began to make a large part of the world so speedily a more comfortable sphere for the human family to be on. . . .

There is no refinement in modern American life which advertising has not helped to spread. If it did not first educate, advertising would not sell the article which the manufacturer is seeking to distribute. To the person unaccustomed to the toothbrush an announcement "Tooth Brushes for Sale" has no direct interest. But when the physical and social advantages of a clean mouth are portrayed in text and illustration he becomes converted to the idea. The clean mouth habit of Americans in every station of life has cost the nation much less to create through advertising than education of the same effectiveness would have cost by some other method.

In the spread of formal education itself advertising perhaps has made a hundred students where without it there would have been one. Advertising copy technique has been effective, not only in enrolling hundreds of thousands of persons each year in the correspondence schools but in creating a desire to go to some school and obtain the concrete advantages which the advertisements have pictured. Home study likewise undoubtedly has been stimulated throughout the population by the strong appeal which correspondence-course advertisements employ. Perhaps no advertising has been subjected to more fun-poking than that which uses scenes out of everyday business and social life and graphically portrays the triumphs of "the man who knows" or the humiliation of "the man who doesn't." We all enjoy the columnists' burlesques on the study-course advertisements, but when we return to the serious mood we wonder if that class of advertising is not one of our most widely effective impelling forces to mental improvement. The advertising of cultural courses shows as keen a knowledge of human nature as is found anywhere.

Since Barnum brought Jenny Lind to America and through his human interest stories of her piety and her charity aroused interest in her and gave the better kind of music its start here, advertising has been a chief factor in the spread of musical knowledge in the United States. If the commission that some day may set out to prove what advertising has done digs to the roots it doubtless will find that most of our American talent in music has developed from the purchase of a piano, a phonograph, or a radio receiving set, and that desire to possess the instrument was awakened by an advertisement which sold the idea of music first and the instrument next.

Whatever superficial opinion based on prejudice may be, a good picture is a good picture whether it appears in an advertisement or is viewed at an art gallery. The high grade of pictorial art which is an outstanding feature of modern advertising has made the physical form of advertising itself an influence for development of taste in art. The influence of advertising illustration on dress, manners, interior decoration, architecture, landscaping, and all that goes to make up the refinements of life is undoubted, and is deep-going.

Advertising probably is our greatest agency for spreading an understanding and love of beauty of all things. The advertising man who discovered that beauty is an added selling point for any article, often a point of more importance than other attributes, gets credit for the effort which the modern manufacturer makes to get beauty of line and color into his product, though the article be one primarily of utility. . . .

In the newspaper national advertisers have a medium whose local and regional influence often is so permeative that an idea appearing in it with some degree of regularity will be adopted by the whole community it serves, as in Chicago, where the *Tribune's* potency, which is equally great on the socially far-apart Lake Shore Drive and Back-of-the-Yards, and the districts in between, is a tribute to good management. Other examples of deep-going influence on large communities by advertising mediums are the Chicago *Daily News,* the Brooklyn *Eagle,* the Cleveland *Plain Dealer,* the Kansas City *Star,* the Philadelphia *Bulletin,* the San Francisco *Examiner* and the Los Angeles *Times.* . . .

Our twentieth-century diversity in diet among all the people owes its wide diffusion in a large measure to advertising. Salads and desserts and other dishes which formerly appeared on the tables of a limited part of the population have become common to practically the whole population. The makers of salad dressing have taught how to make salads, and have spread this beneficial eating habit to millions of homes in which bread, meat, and potatoes formerly constituted the unvarying diet. Advertising for the orange and pineapple growers has given every woman scores of ideas for new and intriguing desserts. Shredded Wheat advertising, besides spreading the beneficence of the whole wheat, has induced great numbers of people to eat various fruits by suggesting the delicious dishes to be obtained by combining them with Shredded Wheat. Scores of other manufacturers have contributed to give the housewife in her magazine or newspaper a cookbook which provides the most delectable dishes from all the world's famous cuisines. As a by-product the food manufacturers' advertising thus is helping to turn a proverbial nation of dyspeptics into a people of better eating habits.

Also good for the soul, directly and indirectly, are the vacuum cleaner, the kitchen cabinet, iceless refrigeration, and the many other labor-saving or convenience devices which advertising has brought into the homes of people of ordinary means. To many of their owners such physical comforts give, besides relief from toil, a pleasure which others get only from the possession of a fine painting or some other object of which appreciation is limited to a relatively small percentage. The extra leisure obtained from employment of time-saving devices in the home is reflected in a wider reading of books and periodical literature and in other cultivation of the mind and the social graces, thus promoting a higher grade of culture.

The eager interest displayed by the average housewife in the advertisement picture of a dining table set with silver and other appointments is an index to the influence this class of advertising has for the diffusion of home-refinement ideas. The neat appearance of the housewife who is pictured cooking the advertiser's food product or operating a vacuum cleaner undoubtedly has raised the standards of dress. Many a husband also owes the trim appearance of his wife at breakfast to the suggestive power of the good-looking woman who is pouring the coffee in the advertisement. Probably half the advertisements in the women's magazines contain definite household or dress ideas a woman can use, often without purchasing the advertiser's product.

The modern sanitary bathroom in the American workman's home is given prominence among the evidences of America's high standard of living. Those millions of porcelain tubs and the self-respect they engender in their possessor were put into homes of all classes as a result of advertising by a handful of manufacturers. On this one item alone advertising has earned place as a powerful instrument for raising the common level of refinement. . . .

Up to the date of this volume advertising has been employed mainly for commercial purposes. The social work it has been doing has been a part of the job of selling a product or service. World War I, however, demonstrated the power of advertising to rouse social thought and active cooperation by the individual in broad movements for the good of all. In this field probably lies a future development of magnitude which will give advertising full recognition as a great socializing as well as business force. The health advertising of the Metropolitan Life Insurance Company, which that company credits with a very definite reduction of mortality, and the recent publicity campaign of the American Society for the Control of Cancer, are examples of what might be done for the health of the nation. There are other big tasks of education. No newspaper or periodical can do such work in its news columns with the necessary persistence and maintain its popular circulation. Advertising, moreover, has forms and methods which obtain attention for a subject that in the news columns would be skipped as dull reading by the class of people it is most desired to reach.

Advertising, by reason of its technique, possesses peculiar power as an educative force. An extension of this power, into fields now scarcely dreamed of for it, is not improbable. Who knows what it may some day be doing? A sociologist whose plan for social betterment is contained in the two volumes of his dynamic sociology finds that fundamentally there is one thing the matter with the world—ignorance. If everybody had all the knowledge that exists and is available, and applied it, there would be very little unhappiness. His method for giving happiness to everyone is education of every human being in the sciences and all real knowledge. Then we should all *know* how to be happy.

DO ADVERTISERS "INFLUENCE" NEWSPAPERS?

—From *This Fascinating Advertising Business,* by Harry Lewis Bird. Copyright 1947, used by special permission of the publishers, The Bobbs-Merrill Company, Inc. Mr. Bird is a magazine and advertising executive.

THE RESPONSIBILITY for producing a newspaper that is an efficient advertising medium rests almost solely with the publisher and his editorial and circulation staff. Occasionally a campaign will be secure because of special favors granted to the advertiser, such as free publicity, but the great majority of newspapers maintain vigorous and even insolent independence of any effort to dictate their editorial policies.

A classic example of this occurred some years ago with the Chicago *Tribune.* Little Orphan Annie, a comic-strip heroine, was taking a cross-country bus trip. In several issues she encountered discomforts not at all flattering to motor-coach travel. The advertising manager of one of the bus companies, or perhaps one of the top executives, evidently took umbrage, and needled his advertising agency into writing a letter of protest. Unwisely the agency man mentioned that his concern advertised heavily in the *Tribune,* the innuendo being that if Annie didn't quit knocking bus travel, the ads might be placed elsewhere. The *Tribune* printed the letter in its "Voice of the People" department. On the same page appeared an editorial calling attention to the letter and announcing that the publisher had no intention of changing a single blurb in any comic strip to placate an advertiser. The *Tribune,* the editorial pointed out, was edited for its readers, and if they liked the paper it would automatically become a good advertising medium. So as far as Mr. Blank was concerned, concluded the diatribe, he could take his business elsewhere if he so chose. Meanwhile let him confine himself to handling the advertising for the PDQ Bus Company, and "we shall confine ourselves to editing the Chicago *Tribune.*"

Not all requests from advertisers are treated so cavalierly, however. Untoward incidents occurring in department stores—an elevator accident, the arrest of a shoplifter, a near-panic caused by a small blaze—are often reported as happening in "a downtown department store" without specific identification. The debut or wedding of the daughter of an important local merchant or banker may receive undue prominence. But as far as national advertisers are concerned they seldom get consideration in the news columns; when they do, it is because of some newsworthy happening or the ingenious creation of some synthetic publicity story that took the editor's fancy. And this can happen to a nonadvertiser. A case in point is that of Franklin Reynolds, the ball-point pen manufacturer, who bought an army plane and hired a veteran pilot to fly him around the world. Reynolds got a million dollars' worth of newspaper publicity on himself and his plane, the *Reynolds Rocket,* and promptly brought out a new pen named the Rocket to cash in. He advertised the pen extensively in newspapers, *after* the flight. Obviously his advertising had nothing to do with the columns of news items and photographs he obtained.

Are newspapers "friendly" to advertisers in their editorial policies and treatment of news? Only, in the writer's opinion, to the extent that they are advocates of the capitalistic system and its American manifestations: free enterprise, free speech, a minimum of government regulation, the right to make a profit. A majority of American newspapers opposed President Franklin D. Roosevelt, not at the dictates of their advertisers but because they felt that their own privileges and opportunities were in jeopardy. Most newspapers have taken a stand against unrestricted use of force and intimidation by labor unions for the same reason.

The "right to advertise" is a corollary of the right of free speech. So while newspapers reserve the right to censor advertising on the ground of fraudulent or misleading copy, few will reject an advertisement because it expresses views contrary to its own policies. During the agitation over the Taft-Hartley Labor Bill advertising by the unions appeared frequently in many papers. And often the same issues would carry editorials and columnists' dissertations voicing the opposite position.

THE AGENCY MAN CRITICIZES ADVERTISING

—H. A. Batten, "An Advertising Man Looks at Advertising," *The Atlantic Monthly,* Vol. 150, July 1932, pp. 53–56. Mr. Batten is president of N. W. Ayer & Son, Inc.

One of the most consistent charges leveled against the American commonwealth, both at home and abroad, concerns the blatancy, vulgarity, and charlatanism of our industrial life. We are accused, not without justice, of being a nation of materialists. We are represented as producing badly made goods; of distributing them by unfair trade methods; of selling them by means at once insincere and misleading and offensive to good taste. We are, in short, left with very little of that dignity or natural virtue which is commonly associated with the humanely civilized state.

This is a serious indictment, and one which is of particular interest to me because my profession is advertising, and advertising is, and always must be, the handmaiden of industry. Advertising is the channel through which much of this blatancy, this vulgarity and sharp practice, must necessarily be manifested. Any charge against our industrial system must, therefore, be considered and dealt with, at least in part, by the professional advertising man.

Just how much truth, then, is there in this indictment? I will say unhesitatingly that in my opinion there is a great deal of truth in it. So far as advertising goes, we are fallen upon evil days. Even a brief excursion through the average newspaper and magazine is, for the advertising man who respects his calling, a disheartening experience.

Here, for example, is an article recommended to the American public because it has found favor (almost certainly at a price) with a popular radio crooner. Here is an advertisement which is systematically creating and fostering the fear—in the great majority of cases absolutely unfounded—of unpleasant breath. Here, on the following pages, are its horrendous foster brood—awesome medical terms seized upon by purveyors of various remedies and antiseptics to inspire fear, and thereby to increase sales. In this newspaper one finds what purports to be a comic strip, but turns out to be an almost incredibly inane dialogue about a common home product. In that magazine one is regaled with a hysterical domestic drama of lost love resulting from failure to use a certain toilet accessory.

It would be possible to cite further instances, *ad nauseam* and *ad infinitum*; but everyone is familiar with this sort of thing. Such antics would be mildly amusing if they were not so tragically symptomatic. But to the responsible advertising man they are no joke. It means that the great power with which he is concerned—the power of the printed page—must slowly but surely become discredited.

Already there are indications that this is so.

One product, which for several years has featured the testimonials of moving-picture actresses and other professional endorsers, has been forced by public skepticism to state in the advertising itself that no money is being paid for these encomiums (leaving discreetly in the air the question of how much has been paid for them in the past).

An organization which investigates and returns confidential reports upon the value and utility of all kinds of products has gained thousands of members without a line of advertising or promotion—simply because a great many people are beginning to turn from advertising (even at a nominal cost to themselves) in order to supply themselves with some source of information which they can trust.

And finally we have the very significant phenomenon of a group of magazines which have recently sprung up, devoted entirely to the gentle art of burlesquing advertising—magazines which carry to their logical conclusion all its absurdities, exaggerations, and misrepresentations.

This is a situation which exists, and one which is poles apart from the true nature and purpose of advertising. Advertising is, or should be, nothing more than the dissemination of truth. Every product worthy of being advertised at all has certain qualities to recommend it to the public. It is the function of advertising to make these qualities known. That this should be done as interestingly and effectively as possible goes without saying. But it is not within the province of advertising to make for any product a single claim unfounded upon fact, or to exceed the bounds of candor or good taste in the statement of those facts which are at hand. . . .

Perhaps it will be enlightening if we traced in a characteristic industry the rise and spread of this process of contamination.

Let us take one of the more conservative manufacturers in the industry. He is not the largest manufacturer, but he has always done very well. One of his chief competitors, however, is doing better than very well. He is forging ahead. He is using advertising of a sensational and misleading nature. He is also using five times as much of it.

The advertising of this competitor is a mixture of paid testimonial, specious claims, and an occasional excursion into the realms of pseudo-science. It shouts, it shrieks, it blares from the pages of newspapers and certain magazines, and from every other bill-board. It sells the product.

Under the pressure of this competition our manufacturer grows restless. He does not believe he can afford to spend any more money on advertising, but he thinks that perhaps he can get more for what he is spending by changing the nature of his advertising. "Fight fire with fire," he says. He calls upon his advertising agent, therefore, to produce something "with more punch in it." He wants a new idea.

Now the advertising agent, no matter what his standards or ethics, has his choice of one of two courses. He can either produce an idea "with punch in it," or resign the account to somebody else who will.

First, of course, he tries to stay within the bounds of good taste and reason. If, however, his client is not satisfied with what he offers, he has the choice of surrender or the Pyrrhic victory of declaring his moral independence.

If he is big enough and strong enough, and feels that way about it, he will part company with the manufacturer and let somebody else take the business. If, on the other hand, he cannot afford to lose the account, he will swallow his scruples and try to give the customer what he wants.

We will assume that the agent needs the business very badly indeed. (In days like these, everybody needs the business very badly indeed.) He possesses his soul, therefore, in silence, and retires to formulate an idea of sufficient blatancy and idiocy to compete with its model. In a week he returns. He has it. With due solemnity he reveals it. It is Sex Appeal.

Thus within a short time we read in the newspapers that this manufacturer's product merits our patronage because, after using it, one may kiss without exhaling an offensive odor.

Now it is easy enough for the observer of this little moral tragedy to pass judgment upon the actions of both the manufacturer and his advertising agent; but before doing so it would be well if he were to ask himself the question, "What would I have done in their place?"

My own feeling is that there are few of us here on earth with enough moral courage to sacrifice our bread and butter during a period of financial depression for the sake of an abstract ideal. As a matter of fact, our unhappy advertising man is no whit different from the lawyer who knowingly defends a guilty client, the minister who preaches sermons made to order for his wealthy parishioners, the editor who sets forth the opinions of the newspaper publisher who hires him, or the stock-market operator who participates in bear raids.

I venture to say that there is no one of us who is not forced, at some point in his daily affairs, to make compromises with his conscience and his bow to Mammon. The instinct for self-preservation is still stronger than the passion for perfection. The spirit is willing, but the flesh is weak.

This, of course, is an explanation, not an excuse. I do not wish to appear as an apologist, but if possible as a constructive critic. Before prescribing a remedy, it is necessary to diagnose the disease.

I have suggested that the blame for this condition of affairs rests no more with the advertising agent than with the manufacturer. But there is a third party, a silent accessory after the fact. That party is the public. Such advertising as we see today in this country could not possibly be made to pay if the public did not respond to it by buying the goods it promotes. It is true that a great portion of the patronage thus obtained is drawn from population levels so low as to be unable to distinguish between truth and untruth, good taste and bad. Yet there remains a large body of informed citizens who can, if they will, do much to correct the evil.

I must explain, in passing, that when I say that advertising of this sort is being made to pay, I do not mean that it is profitable by reason of its nature. It must be remembered that most of these malodorous campaigns are supported by huge appropriations. They are in all but the most scrupulous newspapers and magazines. It is entirely possible, and even probable, that a similar expenditure upon better advertising would produce similar, or better, results. The fact remains, however, that such advertising is, as it stands, successful, and that it is a stench in the nostrils of the civilized world.

REVIEW QUESTIONS AND ASSIGNMENTS

1. What arguments can be offered in support of Presbrey's theory that advertising is responsible for the major part of the increase in national wealth in the last 25 years? Against it?

2. What can be said for the argument that advertising is "the most potent influence in adapting and changing the habits and modes of life"?

3. Discuss the statement that advertising is a civilizing influence.

4. What contributions has advertising made to formal and general education?

5. How has advertising changed the eating habits of the public?

6. What contributions did advertising make to the part America played in World War II?

7. What influence has advertising had on public health?

8. Consult a representative number of issues of the local papers, and present your findings on the quality of the advertising.

9. If advertising were done away with, what would become of those now dependent upon the trade for a livelihood?

10. What would be the effect of a discontinuance of all advertising upon distribution and production?

11. Would it be sufficient merely to announce in the news columns, or in the advertising columns, the fact that a new product or new process has been made ready for public use?

12. How long does it take for a socially useful invention to be generally adopted by those able to afford it? What role does advertising play therein?

13. How does advertising make its influence felt when bills to control advertising come before the Congress?

14. How does the advertising "red clause" affect newspaper policies?

15. Discuss the statement that the truth assures greater sales appeal for advertising.

16. Discuss the implications of the statement that the advertising writer knows little or nothing of the product of which he writes.

17. What concrete evidence can you offer from your own experience that advertisers have tried to control or have succeeded in controlling the policies of a newspaper?

18. Is the enormous advertising revenue a real menace to the freedom of the press?

ADDITIONAL REFERENCES

Borden, Neil H., *The Economic Effects of Advertising*, Richard D. Irwin, 1944.

Broun, H., "Shoot the Works," *The New Republic*, Vol. 93, December 22, 1937, p. 195.

Chase, Stuart, "Advertising, an Autopsy," *The Nation,* Vol. 138, May 16, 1934, pp. 567–568.

———, and F. J. Schlink, *Your Money's Worth,* Macmillan, 1927, pp. 2–3.

Cherington, Paul T., *The Consumer Looks at Advertising,* Harper & Brothers, 1928.

Coates, R., "Do You Offend?" *The New Republic,* Vol. 86, April 8, 1936, pp. 246–247.

Crawford, N. A., *The Ethics of Journalism,* Alfred A. Knopf, 1929, pp. 5–24.

Falk, A. T., *Advertising–The Accelerator of Civilization* (pamphlet), Advertising Federation of America, 1931.

Flint, L. N., *The Conscience of the Newspaper,* Appleton-Century, 1925, pp. 116–123, 244–250.

Frey, Albert Wesley, *Advertising,* Ronald Press, 1947, pp. 642–729.

Harding, T. S., "Truth in Advertising," *The Commonweal,* Vol. 22, June 21, 1935, pp. 206–208.

Hattwick, Melvin S., *How to Use Psychology for Better Advertising,* Prentice-Hall, 1950.

Hotchkiss, G. B., *An Outline of Advertising,* Macmillan, 1937, pp. 62–84.

Kenyon, B., "Housewife Looks at Advertising," *American Mercury,* Vol. 29, June 1933, pp. 181–189.

Lasker, A. D., "Freedom of Advertising and a Free Press," *Vital Speeches Magazine,* Vol. 1, October 8, 1934, pp. 27–32.

Liebling, A. J., *The Wayward Pressman,* Doubleday, 1947, pp. 155–166.

Lyon, Marguerite, *And So to Bedlam,* Bobbs-Merrill, 1943.

Phillips, Mary C., *Skin Deep,* Vanguard Press, 1934.

Rorty, James, *Our Master's Voice,* John Day, 1934, Chapters 22, 23.

Salmon, Lucy M., *The Newspaper and the Historian,* Oxford University Press, 1923, Chapter 13.

Thayer, Frank, *Legal Control of the Press,* Foundation Press, 1944, pp. 500–548.

Vaile, Ronald S., *Economics of Advertising,* Ronald Press, 1927.

Veblen, Thorstein, *Absentee Ownership and Business Enterprise in Recent Times,* Viking Press, 1923.

Wakeman, Frederic, *The Hucksters,* Rinehart, 1946.

Woody, A. T., "Dilemma of the Newspaper," *The Christian Century,* Vol. 51, June 13, 1934, pp. 797–798.

8. THE INFLUENCE OF PHYSICAL PRESENTATION

INTRODUCTION

THE PHYSICAL CHARACTERISTICS of the mass media constitute a most significant factor in the influence they exert on their audiences. They represent the "first-impression impact," which many readers, listeners, and viewers find more pervasive than the other forms of influence that lie behind physical appearance. There are obvious variations among the physical characteristics of the media. Some maintain that since a newspaper is a personal possession it enjoys an intimacy advantage not shared by either radio or television. The latter, however, possess striking qualities in such things as the tone of the voice of the person speaking and the musical background.

The physical appearance of the newspaper deserves painstaking and penetrating appraisal because it is the only mass medium that relies for its effect on the printed word and picture. What the newspaper says through its headlines, its philosophy of makeup, its style of printing, and its policy on pictures determines in large measure the amount and type of influence it wields. The effect, although possibly not so immediate as the radio often exerts, tends to produce a somewhat lasting impression on the public mind.

Contemporary physical characteristics of the newspaper grew out of a revolution in news presentation late in the nineteenth century. Joseph Pulitzer and William Randolph Hearst offered many innovations during their epic battle for New York City circulation. Improvements in printing and typographic equipment made possible the introduction of novel and even sensational ideas on news, opinion, and entertainment display. The Spanish-American War and World War I provided the dramatic news needed to encourage the experimentation. From this background sprang still-current patterns of headline forms and makeup styles, although ever since World War I the press has grown increasingly conservative in appearance.

America has been called "a nation of headline readers." That statement may be a dangerous generalization, but the newspaper headline is written with the idea that it, and perhaps it alone, will be read by everyone who sees the paper in which it appears. No other explanation suffices for the American practice of making the headline serve as a highly condensed summary of the story it covers. Consequently, what the headline says is of intrinsic importance. Coloration, bias, and distortion are possible, and, when they are employed, they give the headline a relationship to public intelligence more powerful in possible influence than anything else in the newspaper.

A similar situation is apparent in newspaper makeup. Newspapers arrange news in their pages according to values placed on available stories for one day or one edition. Value, in turn, is based on the editors' concept of reading habits. Certain stories, particularly "spot-news breaks" concerning disasters and accidents, receive high value, and it is proper that they do. However, the same high value is not necessarily placed on consequential, albeit nonsensational, political, social, and economic news. Such news often receives poor display as the result of either ignorance or misunderstanding. Likewise, a so-called "policy story" can be either featured or "played down" according to the views of the publisher and his assistants. The influence resulting from repeated major display of certain types of crime and "drama-of-life" stories is too obvious to be worth discussion.

The reader must remember that lay critics often overlook factors that control a paper's appearance. For example, an important story appearing on page one in an early edition may be forced far inside by a late-breaking yarn without proving that the editor is responding to some internal pressure. The change is purely mechanical: The newspaper page has only eight columns, each two inches wide and roughly 20 inches deep, and a great amount of selection and rejection is necessary from edition to edition. Likewise, undue emphasis on a trivial story may merely represent absence of other "street-sales news" rather than deliberate distortion.

The influence of the picture is vast. All studies of readership show that almost any kind of an illustration will attract a much greater percentage of both men and women than will a printed news story, column, or editorial. In the ten years that elapsed between the first and second editions of this book, pictorial journalism "came of age" in the sense that many of the ethical issues posed by early illustrations seemed to have disappeared. Photographers are increasingly conscious of the great influence wielded by their product.

The advent of television after the close of World War II gave radio an appearance element of new significance. While more directly comparable to the cinema than to the newspaper, television still may outstrip all the other media in the exertion of influence through physical characteristics.

THE HEADLINE IN THEORY AND PRACTICE

—Frederic E. Merwin, a summary written especially for this book.

THE HEADLINE that catches your eye in your favorite newspaper is distinctly a product of American ingenuity. There is nothing like it anywhere else in the world. Its form and style reflect the vigorous efforts of a host of editors to present news about the more exciting occurrences in the nation's history to their readers in a vivid, appealing, and, at times, shocking manner.

Early American newspapers presented the news under label headings in direct imitation of foreign contemporaries. Events from abroad were captioned "Foreign Intelligence," while news from Washington often appeared under "From the Capital." The label head, which merely segregates and classifies news, might still be popular had the course of the nation remained peaceful and had newspapers escaped the competitive duress of circulation wars. Its lack of effectiveness became apparent, however, when editors were forced to struggle with the problem of presenting news about bigger and bigger wars to a group of readers who had to be stimulated to buy one paper rather than another. War news was simply too momentous to "bury" under an inactive, dull label head, and a substitute form, which would carry the gist of the news to the reader as a come-on for the pennies in his pocket, was devised. The change came slowly—mild experiments in 1848, some use of the active voice in 1861, a virtual revolution in 1898, which was aided and abetted by the Pulitzer-Hearst circulation battle in New York City. The new theories were put to the acid test from 1914 to 1918, and they remain in vogue today despite the decline in newspaper competition and circulation struggles.

The function of the headline is to summarize in just a few words the most important elements of the story it covers. It conveys the highlights in short, easily understood, emphatic words. Strong verbs, colorful words, and the positive statement are characteristics. In effect, it is a miniature replica of the story and provides the reader with an opportunity not only to select at a glance what he cares to read but also to read the top of the news during the preceding 24 hours as he speeds for the 8:15 local.

Newspapermen justify the headline that tells the news by pointing out that it "sells" the contents of the paper to the prospective reader just as the department store show window lures the shopper inside. If it is properly written, it plays upon man's curiosity to a point where he will stop and then buy to get the complete account.

Just how valid this justification of the headline is at the present time is a moot question. Recent years have witnessed a strong trend toward home-delivered circulation, with a consequent decline in the importance of street sales in all but a few metropolitan centers. This change indicates that the long-felt necessity to catch the reader's eye with a graphic headline no longer has any basis in fact. Or, stated another way, a sensational headline is no longer a positive guarantee of street sales.

As long as newspapers continue to display the news under summary headings, the vastly important (and often slighted) relationship between the headline and public opinion will continue. An influence of extreme significance is at work here. The headline is more than an emphatic, dramatic version of a news event. It appears in large, bold type; it often extends over two or more columns; it is easy to read and understand; and it is always the first aspect of the story to be seen. All these characteristics make its impact upon the reader of obvious importance. No other part of the paper reaches its audience with such telling force. No other part of the paper is permitted to compete with it in influence.

Various problems exist with respect to the way in which the influence of the headline on the newspaper-reading public operates.

There is, for example, an ever-present tendency toward overemphasis growing out of the effort to achieve a smash effect in the wording in order to increase the appeal of the day's occurrences. Stories substantiated by nothing more than vague rumors are headed as positive happenings because headline writers like to avoid any word that might "weaken" the effect. Occasionally, coloration results when a story is developed in the head all out of proportion to its true significance.

The headline writer's choice of words is a second problem. He must pick and choose among several possibilities in casting the head in what he considers the most effective and emphatic form. The result may produce a certain vagueness, or a possible double meaning, or, worst of all, bias. The effect, thus, is to give the reader a first impression of the story which may be distorted in terms of the real significance of the event. Occasionally, the necessity of selection is relied upon to achieve deliberate misrepresentation if the story happens to involve an issue in which the paper possesses more than a casual interest. Whenever this occurs, the traditional objectivity of the news columns is dealt a blow.

Most headline styles require the utmost effort on the part of the copy reader in the direction of condensation. The combination of large type sizes in major heads and the narrow width of the newspaper columns produces the problem. In order to stay within specifications (make the head fit), the thought of the headline often appears somewhat out of line with the story. "Bus Crashes, 20 Aboard," conveys one meaning, while "Two Hurt When Bus Hits Culvert" conjures a different kind of picture.

Various authorities have long felt that a healthier relationship between the headline and public opinion would result if certain mechanical changes in headline forms were effected. Their theories have taken form in recent trends toward the so-called "flush-to-left" headline, in which the requirements for exact fitting within the column are eliminated, and the use of type families that assure more freedom from condensation of ideas.

Many other changes appear likely in view of the aforementioned decline in circulation competition. An editorial writer for *Editor & Publisher,* the leading newspaper trade weekly, neatly summed up a discussion of present headline practices aimed at selling papers by declaring, "We leave the thought with managing editors that maybe it's time to overhaul the whole philosophy of headlines in the light of modern communications, modern newspaper circulation practices, and the general information possessed by readers in 1940, as contrasted to that of 1898."

MAKEUP AND THE CHARACTER OF THE NEWSPAPER

—Albert A. Sutton, *Design and Makeup of the Newspaper,* Prentice-Hall, 1948, pp. 326, 331. The author is professor of journalism at the Medill School of Journalism, Northwestern University.

In recent years, more serious attention has been given to matters of typography and makeup than ever before. Much experimentation has been made in the direction of simpler and more attractive headlines and the building of newspapers that are more pleasing and more effective in the presentation of news and advertising. Many of the customs and traditions that shackled editors for so many years have been replaced by practices that permit far greater freedom and designs that are more pleasing and readable.

When a new reader picks up a newspaper for the first time and begins to turn through its pages, he immediately begins to gain certain impressions regarding it and regarding the persons responsible for its publication. And these first impressions often are lasting ones.

If the display is quiet and reserved, he classifies the paper as conservative; if the headlines shout their wares in types that are heavy in tone, he forms an entirely different opinion.

Carefully planned makeup, orderliness on editorial and other special pages, attractive advertising, and pleasing design all have a desirable effect. If pages are poorly printed, or if the body-type and headlines are hard to read, he draws conclusions that are not so favorable. Even the texture of the paper, which may stand up crisply, or fall limply in his hands, helps to shape this new reader's likes and dislikes. Another consideration that enters sharply into his reactions is the similarity of this newspaper to others with which he is familiar.

Alert makeup editors and others responsible for the design of a newspaper know these things. They also are aware that a sudden change from one style of makeup to another style strikingly different even though the new methods are based upon sound principles of design, might be resented seriously by readers who have been accustomed to practices followed for many years. Habits of long-standing are not easily broken.

Many readers of the Kansas City *Star,* famous for its quiet, conservative makeup and display, undoubtedly would raise their voices in protest if that paper should change overnight to the style of makeup followed by the Chicago *Herald-American* or the New York *Herald Tribune.* On the other hand, readers of these papers in Chicago and New York probably would find the design and makeup of the Kansas City *Star* stodgy and uninteresting. . . .

The front page of a newspaper frequently is referred to as the "show window." It is the one the reader sees first, and consequently the editor who disregards this fact would be forfeiting his best opportunity to build confidence and readership.

Here he has a chance to display the most important stories and pictures of the day and to set the stage for the rest of the paper typographically. The treatment used on the front page will have much to do with influencing a reader to turn to the inside, and careful attention should be given to building a design that is both pleasing and interesting.

The first requirement is that all elements going to make up the page should harmonize and be placed in proper relationship with one another, as well as with the news they accompany. Although headlines form the major part of the front-page design, several other significant elements also are included. The appropriateness of each of these elements should be determined, since their combinations into a unified pattern are what establishes a newspaper's character and personality.

HOW APPEARANCE MAY CONFUSE THE READER

—Herbert Brucker, *The Changing American Newspaper*, Columbia University Press, 1937, pp. 56–58.

LAY CRITICS of the press have long complained that they get a confused picture of the news from our newspapers, and if newspaper men can put themselves in the position of the conveniently objective man from Mars they may agree. For if one forgets for a moment the standards and traditions and habits of American newspaper make-up and news display, one discerns a surprising lack of orderliness in the way in which news is presented to the reader. Consider, for example, the man who became interested in a story about British affairs in his newspaper and who read on down to this last paragraph:

> The problem of getting a seat or standing room along the coronation route or a glimpse of the new king and queen at one of the great ceremonial occasions during the coming spring and summer is one of the main worries of the loyal British subjects.
>
> ---
>
> TOWN REQUIRES
> SNAKE OWNER
> TO POST BOND
>
> *By United Press*
>
> Gettysburg, Pa., Jan. 18.—The town council here acted on the petition of a number of housewives and passed an ordinance providing that any person desiring to harbor

> snakes, rodents, skunks, "or any dangerous and loathsome creatures," must take out a $5 license and post a $500 bond.

The jolt felt by this reader on bumping suddenly into snakes and skunks when his mind was attuned to the pageantry of George VI's coronation is experienced daily by American newspaper readers. The stories quoted here happened to appear in the South Bend *Tribune,* but so long as American newspapers retain their present methods of makeup and news display, the shift from King George to snakes in the space of a quarter of an inch, and countless similar mixtures of news, can be duplicated in almost any of them.

The American newspaper displays the news by putting over each item a headline which is a tabloid version of the story itself. But there its organization of the news on behalf of the reader all but ceases. The front page, to be sure, is a sort of headline for the whole paper, in the sense that it lifts out of the day's news the most important, interesting, or spectacular stories and presents them at once for the reader's inspection. This practice, however, may be as much of a hindrance as a help to the man who wants to get the essence of the day's news. Playing on page one all sorts of stories which have nothing in common except that they stand out above the rest of the day's supply means that there is grouped together a collection of wholly unrelated items.

The theory is, of course, that the news is clearly identified by its headlines and that by skimming them both on the front page and inside the reader can sample all the news there is. He does not have to wade through each story itself to find out whether he thinks it is worth reading or not. Millions of copies sold and read every day demonstrate the soundness of this theory. It is a question, however, whether the system of selecting, displaying, and organizing the news could not be carried farther. If all the news throughout the paper were grouped into departments containing stories dealing with the same general subject matter, the news could be seen in orderly perspective, and some at least of the confusion complained of would disappear.

It is true that on the inside pages of our papers there is a tendency to segregate some of the news into certain broad classifications. Sports, finance, and society, for example, are usually grouped together in one or more pages. Usually, too, some effort is made to bring together in one place the local news, the foreign news, and the national news. Nevertheless these classifications are by no means rigid, nor are they thoroughgoing. Something of the habits of page one with its mixture of the important and the sprightly, the sublime and the ridiculous, usually carries over to these loose groupings of the news within. There is nothing to keep the makeup man from sandwiching an extra local story into a convenient space in the sports form, or from putting into adjoining columns on the general news page items bearing as little relation to each other as "British Regency Bill Assailed in Commons" and "2 Women Killed on New Parkway."

In recent years editors have given signs of dissatisfaction with the results of this kind of thing, and by means of news indices, news digests, special-writer columns, and week-end reviews, they have sought to bring order out of the surrealist headline procession.

THE INFLUENCE OF THE TABLOID

—Taken from *Jazz Journalism, the Story of the Tabloid Newspapers,* by Simon M. Bessie, published and copyright by E. P. Dutton & Company, Inc., New York, 1938, pp. 229–235. Mr. Bessie, now an editor at Harper & Brothers, has been a staff writer and contributor to newspapers and magazines and has served on the staffs of *Market Research Monthly* and *Look Magazine.*

IN MODERN SOCIETY newspapers play a double role. As an active force, they exert influence upon the development of journalism and, to a certain extent, upon the habits of their readers. And, in a more passive sense, they act as mirrors of contemporary life reflecting the atmosphere of their time and place. The meaning of the tabloid is disclosed by the manner with which it has discharged this double function.

In 1927 *The New Republic* estimated the importance of the tabloid in these words:

> A quarter of a century ago, 90 per cent of the influence of Hearst on public manners and morals was exerted, not through the columns of his papers, but through those of his imitators whose sheets outnumber his own a hundred to one. In the same manner, we find today that even papers which seem safely beyond the reach of tabloid competition are alarmed by their mushroom growth and tend to imitate many of their most undesirable characteristics. It is not really true that there is a Gresham's Law of journalism by which the baser metal drives out the

true coinage, but since the publishers seem to believe that this is the case, we get, temporarily at least, the same gravely undesirable results.

Except for the familiar note of disapproval which marked most utterances on the subject, this was an accurate diagnosis. In 1919 publishers had been certain that the tabloid was a fleeting stunt. But as the picture papers spread across the country and acquired unprecedented followings, scorn gave way to doubt and soon the inevitable process of imitation had begun. By the middle twenties the journalistic procession had moved so far along the new path that Silas Bent could assert, "The daily eight-column newspaper, in very truth, is tarred with the stick of the tabloid; tarred with its pictures, its format, its headlines, its sensationalism, its rowdyism, its meddlesomeness."

Even the eminently respectable New York *Times* reflected the influence of the tabloid. During the twenty days of the Hall-Mills trial, the *Times* poured forth 528,000 words of information and comment upon the lurid case while the *Daily News* was able to produce only a paltry 223,000. For the first Tunney-Dempsey prize-fight in 1926, the *Times* used the same size front-page headline with which it had announced the Armistice.

When the *Times* of 1920 is compared with that of the present day, one gets a more complete picture of the change. The issue for March 1, 1920, did not contain a single picture, had less than one full page of sports news, and the entire feature content consisted of two inches on the theater by Alexander Woollcott, a half column of movie reviews, the "Topics of the Times," and a short poem. On an average day in 1938 the same paper had a picture on almost every news page, five full pages of sports, a full page of society news, and these features: columns on books, art, music, dance, sports, politics, theater news, movie gossip, reviews of plays and pictures, "Topics of the Times," and the perennial poem. In tabloid manner, the *Times* had adopted the practice of heading important news stories with a brief digest of the highlights (a "tabloid" of the story).

The tendencies manifested by the nation's most austere daily were echoed with greater emphasis by every newspaper in the country. Taking their cue from the tabloid, editors were learning that it is profitable to concentrate upon one story at a time, playing it up until the last drop of interest has been drained. For two weeks in February 1925, every front page in the land was devoted to the story of an obscure man who had been imprisoned by a landslide in a Kentucky cave which he had been exploring in an effort to find a lure for tourists. Floyd Collins became a national hero. A short while later, more than fifty men were killed in a North Carolina mine but the incident was hardly mentioned. The excitement over Collins had killed the drama of subterranean stories.

In their selection of stories, all newspapers came to adopt the values of the tabloid. Attention was concentrated upon sex, crime, sport, and sentiment. More than 12,000,000 words—enough to fill 400,000 pages of ordinary book size—were sent out by the wires from the scene of the Hall-Mills trial. During the Scopes "monkey" trial, in which evolution was declared contrary to Tennessee law, more than 2,000,000 words were dispatched by telegraph alone. Bobby Jones, Red Grange, Babe Ruth, Mary Pickford, Doug Fairbanks, Peaches Browning, and, above all, Charles Augustus Lindbergh, were the heroes of the day. Nor did this emphasis upon personalities and sensations die with the coming of the depression. Though in a less excited manner, today's front page is still devoted to the same interests.

Even greater than its effect upon the presentation of the news was the tabloid's influence upon other parts of the newspaper. Devotion to features became so intense that "the side-shows threatened to swallow the main tent." Like the modern drug store, the daily newspaper adopted so many supplementary items that the article upon which its name had been based became almost an incidental. In addition to material which can be classed as news or editorial interpretation, the typical American daily in 1938 contained the following miscellany: cartoons, recipes, style patterns, child advice, health comment, question and answer column, society column, beauty information, comics, romance assistance, contests, puzzles, games, radio comment, Hollywood gossip, Broadway items, book reviews, sports features, oddities, fiction, etiquette, and pictures. These were just the standard items; each paper had several additional specialties.

But the greatest influence of the tabloid was exerted in the field of photography. Before the war, pictures had been a sort of fillip used to spice an occasional story. Cameramen were regarded as just above the level of manual laborers, useful at times, but hardly essential. When the tabloid taught its readers to expect a picture with every story, the large papers were forced to imitate this popular practice.

They did not attempt to produce an illustration for each account. but the sports, entertainment, and society pages were always decorated with pictures, and the rotogravure section became a weekly feature of every newspaper in the country. When anything really important occurred—a big athletic event, a major political happening, a great tragedy, or a stirring crime—the big papers learned to carry as many, if not more, pictures than the tabloid.

The Louis-Braddock prize-fight elicited two full pages of pictures in the New York *World-Telegram.* During the fall of 1937, the Sunday rotogravure section of the *Times* contained more pictures of football than of any other single subject. When President Roosevelt was inaugurated, every paper in New York devoted several pages to pictures of the event. The recent explosion of the dirigible Hindenburg put a grim scene upon every front page in the country. And when Ronnie Gedeon, "the beautiful artist's model," was murdered on Easter morning in 1937, many of the large-size papers outdid the tabloids in exploiting her much-photographed body.

This was the pattern stamped upon the American daily newspaper during the post-war years—concentration upon one story, play-up of crime, sensation, and sport, increasing devotion to features, and greater use of pictures. The tabloid, of course, was not the only factor behind these changes. They were entirely harmonious with the course of American journalism since the Pulitzer-Hearst days. What happened after 1919 was merely a modernization and extension of the yellow technique. Furthermore, these changes were so consistent with the current of popular desires that they would probably have come in the course of time even without the tabloid stimulus. How well these changes were rooted in popular tastes is shown by a survey of "What the Readers Read in Newspapers" compiled by Dr. George Gallup and printed in 1938.

This study showed that men's attention is accorded in the following order: (1) one news story, (2) picture page, (3) comics, (4) editorial cartoon, (5) oddities cartoon, (6) leading sports story, (7) weather report, (8) radio program and so forth. Women show a similar preference for one news story, pictures, and comics, but, instead of sports, they turn next to style pictures. The best read parts of the newspaper are precisely those upon which increasing emphasis has been placed in recent years—a single news story, pictures, features and sports.

Since these were the dominant interests of the reading public, they would inevitably have expressed themselves by evoking changes in daily journalism similar to those noted above. But the tabloid was the active agent which dramatized popular desires and compelled publishers of large-sized newspapers to imitate its ways. Whether this influence was good or bad is a problem for psychiatrists and sociologists. One fact, however, is evident. Whatever its effects and whatever its moral worth, the attitude embodied in the tabloid was but a journalistic reflection of the currents which were sweeping through every phase of post-war American life.

THE NEWS PICTURE ATTAINS MATURITY

—Henry Ladd Smith, a summary written especially for this book. Mr. Smith is a professor of journalism at the University of Wisconsin.

Mr. Gladstone is said to have made the statement, all too readily accepted, that "the camera cannot lie." This, of course, was as false a statement as the prime minister ever made (if he *did* make it). Any movie actress who has ever had a news picture taken from the wrong angle can tell you that the camera is a downright liar.

Yet the public on the whole appears to believe that the camera shows us the world "as is." Actually, the camera shows us the world as it was for just a fraction of a second. In the hands of an able photo journalist the camera may indeed give us an incomparable report of the passing scene. Certainly the pictures of the *Noronic* disaster at Toronto in the fall of 1949 described the horror of that night far better than any number of words. But in the hands of the irresponsible photographer the camera is a dangerous implement, if for no other reason than because of the blind faith of the public in pictorial representation.

Because of this credence pictures have extremely high propaganda effect. The elaborate indictments of the Nazis and Fascists for their conquests of Poland and Ethiopia were made convincing to many doubters by the atrocity photographs that accompanied the texts. One picture of a screaming baby sitting in the rubble of Shanghai probably did more to arouse sympathy for the Chinese during the undeclared war with the Japanese than hundreds of thousands of words sent out by correspondents reporting the bombardment.

The news picture is the last stand of the scoop, and that fact also increases its value as a medium. One newspaper or wire service may be on top of a story a few minutes before a rival has the yarn, but the public may not be aware of that fact, if the next editions carry the news. But the photographer who "shot" the Tacoma bridge as it collapsed had a scoop that no rival could duplicate even a few seconds later.

Little wonder, then, that publishers set such store on picture coverage. Editors have known for generations that illustrations had a high reader interest count. Hearst depended heavily on pictures to build up circulation when he invaded New York. The largest newspaper in the United States based its success upon the news photo. In the 1930's, when depression made competition all the keener, publishers went all out for photo coverage. Fast new lenses, small cameras, better films and developers, and the synchronized electric flash gun made pictures all the more popular. That was the reason hard-pressed executives were willing to spend heavily for wire-transmitted photo services. The concensus appears to be that the investment was worth while. The *Continuing Study of Newspaper Reading* consistently reports the high reader interest in pictures. When *Life* and *Look* magazines were launched on the idea that picture popularity was based on more than mere novelty, the proponents of pictorial journalism believed they had been completely justified.

Like any new medium of expression, the news picture was badly abused. The early Corontos, the first penny papers, the new tabloids, and radio were all at one time or another severely criticised for the misuse to which they had been put. So it was with pictorial journalism. In the hands of Erick Salomon the "candid camera pictures," as a London paper called his product, were excellent examples of honest reporting by means of the new medium. Imitators abused this new art, until the candid camera shot was synonymous with bad taste, invasion of privacy, and outright libel. No picture page was complete without at least one shot of a famous athlete in an embarrassing pose; a statesman wolfing his lunch; or an actress photographed through the transom in a thrilling stage of undress.

The denouncement came when the Lindberghs fled to Europe after a too-enterprising news photographer took pictures of the youngest Lindbergh child sometime after the kidnapping and murder of the older son. The Lindberghs had been pestered before. Many a reporter had no patience with them because of the somewhat arrogant attitude of the Colonel toward the press. But when one of our foremost citizens rebelled against the gutter ethics of certain newspaper editors, the public was aroused. Cried A. F. Payne, speaking over New York's powerful radio station, WOR, ". . . I think we have about ten million too many laws right now, but why can't we have a law that it is a criminal offense to publish pictures of anyone without that person's consent?"

Typical of public reaction was an editorial in the New York *Times*, which said: ". . . I promise never again to buy or subscribe to any newspaper that attempts to discover or reveal Col. Lindbergh's place of refuge in England. . . . Who will join me in this pledge?"

A follow-up was the letter of Fred Ferguson, president of Newspaper Enterprise Association (a syndicate) to all clients saying that neither NEA nor its affiliate, Acme Newspictures, would issue any more pictures of the Lindbergh baby without the consent of the parents.

There were many more violations, needless to say, but either the new medium was adjusting itself, or the press was making a sincere effort to mend its ways in picture coverage, for the more nauseous aspects of news photography began to improve. On the whole, the press appeared to be learning how to use the news picture. It would be interesting to know how many editors who turned down the Nazi war criminal execution pictures would have used them in the early 1930's—despite the fact that, after the war, death pictures are no longer necessarily shocking. War pictures were generally good. Some, such as the raising of the flag on Iwo Jima, have become photographic classics. If there are criticisms today, they are likely to be more legal than ethical in nature. The status of the camera in the courts, for example, is still uncertain. But at least the threatened "holy war" against the ubiquitous cameraman has long since been forgotten. Yet, with the wave of yellow journalism that is almost certain to coincide with a release of public tension and a return to true peacetime living, the same problems can arise again.

REVIEW QUESTIONS AND ASSIGNMENTS

1. What are the major distinguishing characteristics of the physical form of the newspaper and radio?

2. Study television newscasts for one week and compare them with the presentation of news in the newspaper you read regularly.

3. "The prayer of the modern, longing to sway the hearts of a people, might well be: 'Let who will make their laws if I may write their headlines'." Discuss.

4. Observe the headlines in your local paper for a week and clip any that appear to reflect bias, coloration, or distortion.

5. The statement has been made that the chief influence wielded by the newspaper during election contests is through headline display rather than through editorial comment. Discuss.

6. What is the relationship between the technical problems of the headline and possible bias and coloration?

7. Do you agree that the press might well scrap its present headline system and re-adopt the "label head" of the Colonial press as a means of solving headline faults?

8. Outline in 2,500 words or less your interpretation of the ethics of the headline.

9. Compare the makeup of ten newspaper front pages for one day and discuss them as to (1) what each attempts to do with its front page display; (2) the degree of variation in news emphasis; (3) possible influence of each page on the minds of the readers.

10. What is your reaction to Herbert Brucker's thesis that current practice in newspaper makeup tends to give the reader a confused picture of the news?

11. Compare the news picture provided by the front page of an evening newspaper and an evening 15-minute news broadcast.

12. Clip ten newspaper pictures that you consider to be in bad taste and ten that appear to you worthy of publication. Defend your classifications.

13. If you were the managing editor of an evening paper with a large home circulation, what policy would you follow on the use of news pictures?

14. Write your own code of ethics for news photographers.

ADDITIONAL REFERENCES

Allen, John E., *Newspaper Designing,* Harper & Brothers, 1947.

———, *Newspaper Makeup,* Harper & Brothers, 1936.

———, *The Modern Newspaper,* Harper & Brothers, 1940.

Anderson, Milton, *The Modern Goliath,* David Press, 1935.

Bastian, George C., and Leland D. Case, *Editing the Day's News,* Macmillan (third edition), 1943.

Bent, Silas, *Ballyhoo: The Voice of the Press,* Liveright, 1927, pp. 21–45.

Brandenburg, George A., "Cartoons Revived Fifty Years Ago," *Editor & Publisher,* Vol. 67, July 21, 1934, p. 47.

Butterfield, Roger, *The American Past,* Simon & Schuster, 1947, pp. 291–312.

Crawford, N. A., *The Ethics of Journalism,* Alfred A. Knopf, 1924.

Doob, Leonard W., *Propaganda, Its Psychology and Technique,* Henry Holt, 1935, pp. 345–347.

English, Earl, "A Study of the Readability of Four Newspaper Headlines Types," *Journalism Quarterly,* Vol. 21, September 1944, pp. 217–229.

Garst, R. E., and T. M. Bernstein, *Headlines and Deadlines,* Columbia University Press, 1940.

Graves, W. Brooks (editor), *Readings in Public Opinion,* Appleton-Century, 1928.

Herzberg, Joseph G. (editor), *Late City Edition,* Henry Holt, 1947, pp. 175–187, 199–220.

Hogben, Lancelot, *From Cave Printing to Comic Strip,* Chanticleer Press, 1949.

Johnson, Isabel S., "Cartoons," *Public Opinion Quarterly,* Vol. 1, July 1937, pp. 21–44.

Luckiesh, Matthew, and Frank K. Moss, *Reading as a Visual Task,* Van Nostrand, 1942.

MacNeil, Neil, "The Presentation of News," in *The Newspaper: Its Making and Its Meaning,* by members of the staff of the New York *Times,* Charles Scribner's Sons, 1945.

Mahin, Helen O., *The Development and Significance of the Newspaper Headline,* George Wahr, 1924.

Merz, Charles, *The Great American Bandwagon,* John Day, 1928, pp. 215–229.

Mich, Daniel D., and Edwin Eberman, *The Technique of the Picture Story,* McGraw-Hill, 1945.

Neal, Robert M., *Editing the Small City Daily,* Prentice-Hall, 1939.

Nevins, Allan, and Frank Weitenkampf, *A Century of Political Cartoons,* Charles Scribner's Sons, 1944.

Olson, Kenneth E., *Typography and Mechanics of the Newspaper,* Appleton-Century, 1930.

Price, Jack, *News Pictures,* Round Table Press, 1937.

Price, Matlack, *Advertising and Editorial Layout,* Whittlesey House, 1949.

Robinson, Boardman, *Cartoons on the War,* E. P. Dutton, 1915.

Seldes, George, *Freedom of the Press,* Bobbs-Merrill, 1935, pp. 161–168.

Svirsky, Leon (editor), *Your Newspaper: Blueprint for a Better Press,* Macmillan, 1947, pp. 161–187.

Tinker, Miles A., and Donald G. Paterson, "Differences Among Newspaper Body Types in Readability," *Journalism Quarterly,* Vol. 20, June 1943, pp. 152–155.

Updike, Daniel B., *Printing Types: Their History, Forms, and Use,* Harvard University Press, 1927.

Vitray, Laura, *et al., Pictorial Journalism,* McGraw-Hill, 1939.

Waugh, Coulton, *The Comics,* Macmillan, 1947.

Wheeler, Kittredge, "Art of the Copy Reader," *American Mercury,* Vol. 26, July 1932, p. 352.

Winship, Elizabeth C., and Gordon W. Allport, "Do Rosy Headlines Sell Newspapers?" *Public Opinion Quarterly,* Vol. 7, 1943, pp. 205–210.

Yost, Casper S., *The Principles of Journalism,* Appleton-Century, 1924.

9. SYNDICATED CONTENT

INTRODUCTION

THE PRESS SYNDICATE, which has grown during the last century to be one of the chief sources of non-local news and feature material disseminated by the mass media, exerts a persistent and powerful influence on both the content of the press and the minds of the mass audiences.

Two major types of syndicated material are available to the media. The first consists of the news reports furnished on a 24-hour basis every day of the year by the great news-gathering associations—Associated Press, United Press, and International News Service. The second is composed of the varied offerings of the so-called feature syndicates, such as Newspaper Enterprise Association and King Features. Both sources make their offerings available to clients who pay a charge usually based on the size of audience reached.

The news-gathering associations constitute the source for the great bulk of international, national, and state news offered to the public by the newspaper as well as by the other mass media. They maintain large staffs of correspondents who "protect" them on all news developments except those deemed to be of purely local interest.

Most of the media distribute press association reports to their publics without essential change, except possibly condensation. This means that a news service account of a coal mine strike will be seen and heard by untold millions in precisely the form given it by the reporter and editors of the central agency. If the account is fair and accurate, no problem exists. But if it is prejudiced or omits essential elements, then it will reach the attention of the public in a garbled state, because no newspaper or radio station can afford to check back and make its own examination of such facts. This means, of course, that public opinion on all recorded events except those of purely local origin is shaped to some extent by news-gathering agencies.

After the close of the Civil War, the emergence of the modern newspaper, with an increased number of pages as a result of advertising and large Sunday editions, made it necessary for editors to rely increasingly on non-local sources for many different types of content, particularly those of a so-called entertainment nature. The feature syndicate proved to be both an efficient and an inexpensive source for most of the material deemed desirable in the new concept of what the press should offer the public. It offered a veritable flood of items—serial stories, comics, menus, advice columns, cartoons, feature stories dealing with news events, and pictures. Later, editorials and columns became common offerings. No matter what the press might seek in the way of a feature, it could be found in the offerings of some one of the syndicates. The syndicates grew in number, prospered, and expanded, and emerged in the twentieth century as one of the "big business" auxiliaries in the communications industry.

The syndicates are undoubtedly efficient. Publication of a column, such as the one written by Walter Lippmann, in a large number of daily and weekly newspapers across the country would be impossible without the use of the syndication system. Few dailies or weeklies, or radio stations, can afford to develop and maintain the staffs of specialists that would be required if they were to attempt to produce all their own news and features. And even if they could, what reporters and artists could duplicate the output of the highly paid stars employed by the major syndicates? Thus, no matter what faults may be ascribed to the syndicate, its economic advantage in the communications pattern makes it impossible for the media to disregard it without radical changes in content.

The dominant role played by the syndicates has produced, as the selections in this chapter illustrate, a hotly debated question concerning the impact of standardization in news and features on the public mind. The battle cry sounds when a gruesome incident is pictured in the adventures of Dick Tracy, when Little Orphan Annie expresses critical ideas about the government, when a press association story is found to be tendentious, when a medical adviser urges his readers to abstain from a certain type of food, or when a questionable news picture is taken. Many critics feel that many slogans that become widely accepted as a result of syndicate distribution produce a uniformity in mass opinion and ideas that increases the burden of those seeking to inform and enlighten. They argue, in effect, that syndicated content tends to partly nullify the true role of the media in a democracy.

THE SYNDICATE IN AMERICAN JOURNALISM

—Elmo Scott Watson, *A History of Newspaper Syndicates in the United States, 1865–1935,* Western Newspaper Union, 1936, pp. 78–85. The late Mr. Watson, authority on certain aspects of American history and well-known editor, taught journalism at Illinois, Northwestern and Denver.

THE NEWSPAPER has been an American institution for 230 years. The syndicate, as a distinct enterprise, has a history of only 70 years.

Approximately 5,000 newspapers were being published in the United States when the syndicate idea became a reality in 1865. Their combined circulation was nearly 17,000,000. Today, a total of 13,700 newspapers have an estimated circulation of almost 74,000,000.

In 1865 three small syndicates were in operation. They supplied only a limited amount of material, consisting mainly of news items, a story, and miscellaneous matter which was little more than "filler." Today 130-odd syndicates offer the publisher more than 1,600 separate features which cover a wide range of topics and appeal to every interest of the newspaper reading public.

During the first 150 years of American journalism both the numbers of newspapers and their circulation gained slowly. But during the last 70 years there was a rapid increase in both, and in that increase the use of syndicated material played an important role. It reduced the cost of producing a newspaper and that encouraged the founding of new publications. The information, but more particularly the entertainment, which syndicated features afforded newspaper readers was a factor in increasing circulation during the early history of the enterprise and it is an even more important factor today.

The first great increase in the number of newspapers came in the decade from 1870 to 1880. In those ten years 5,484 new papers were started, three times as many as in the previous decade. The increase was particularly noticeable in the South and in the West.

It was the era of Reconstruction in the South. Thither Northern "carpetbaggers" flocked to occupy public offices and to loot public treasuries. To sustain their corrupt administrations, it was necessary to establish a party press. So innumerable political organs sprang up over night and were heavily subsidized from public funds.

Then, too, some of the more intelligent Negroes, rejoicing in being freed men, expressed their consciousness of the altered status of their race by establishing newspapers to circulate among their people. The use of syndicated service in the form of readyprint was a convenient aid to issuing imposing-looking publications. Although such sheets could scarcely be dignified with the title of "newspaper," yet they did help swell the number of weeklies and were taken into account in the statistical data of the period.

The great increase in the number of newspapers in which syndicate service played a part, however, was in the West. The trans-Mississippi empire was rapidly opening up to settlement. "Boom towns," built along the route of proposed railroads, dotted the map. Local pride in these communities demanded that they have newspapers to cater to the optimistic belief of their citizens that their mushroom village would grow into a metropolis. So one of its first business establishments was invariably a newspaper office.

Sometimes this office was only a tent pitched along the main street which wandered crookedly through the collection of "soddies," log huts, or one-story frame "false-fronts." In this canvas shelter the adventuring editor, equipped with an old Army press or a "G. Wash." and the traditional "shirttailful of type," began operations as an exponent of frontier journalism. If the final railroad surveys revealed the fact that this future metropolis would not be on its route, "ye ed," like the other business men, loaded his equipment in a wagon and drove away to the new town-site along the railroad right-of-way.

To such pioneering and peripatetic journalism, the readyprint was an invaluable aid and it was a life-saver to more than one publisher, struggling under the handicaps of inadequate equipment and an uncertain future. If he had had to depend upon local news and advertisements to fill his paper, it would have been little more than a two-page handbill. But with two, four, six and eight-page readyprints available, he could get out a newspaper whose size suggested that it was published in a flourishing little city.

So the pioneer form of syndicate service helped to bring into existence hundreds of newspapers on the Western frontier, and the convenience and economy of the service encouraged the establishment of many new publications in the more settled parts of the East, South, and Middle West. In fact, the increasing number of weeklies during this period, made possible by syndicate service, resulted in an ominous prediction for the future of the country press by the editor of the Cleveland *Herald*. Declaring that rural journalism was deteriorating and laying the fault at the door of syndicate service the *Herald* said:

> The "patent insides" and "patent outsides" have damaged it seriously by coaxing into feeble life a host of little rivals published in the smaller towns. Formerly in counties like Lake, Geauga, Portage, Summit and Trumbull there were but two papers—one of each party and sometimes a minority party failed to sustain an organ. Now, the small cost of issuing a paper on a "patent inside" or "outside" has encouraged the starting of new sheets at almost every petty village. Of course, they divide the total business of the county and draw away a part of the support of the older and larger journals. . . .

Immediately the editor of a country weekly, the Ravenna (Ohio) *Republican Democrat,* took up the cause of his brethren and declared that the competition of the city newspapers was the real cause of any definite decline in the country press because the city papers, with their big weekly editions made up from type saved from their daily editions, gave more reading matter than the country papers could hope to do. He continued:

> The country weekly is irretrievably dwarfed. It has not the capital nor the power to cope with the strong financial newspaper printing combinations and corporations of the city. We have sometimes thought that but for the co-operative plan of publishing, the city weeklies would nearly, if not quite, root out the country weeklies—as it is, the latter have but comparatively a feeble, sickly existence and a hard struggle for life.

During the next few years the service was "improved as it might be" and the syndicates offered to the publisher, through an economical and convenient medium of supply, a variety and quality of material that he could not possibly have given his readers otherwise. The addition of the stereotype plate, while it did not help increase the number of newspapers so noticeably as had the readyprint, did extend the popularity of syndicated material and aided in its widespread use, especially in the East.

The decade from 1880 to 1890 was marked by the greatest increase in the number of newspapers American journalism has ever known. They multiplied at the rate of two new publications every day during those ten years. But more significant were the soaring circulation figures during this decade and the next. From 1880 to 1890 more than 37,000,000 Americans became newspaper subscribers, as compared to less than 11,000,000 during the previous decade, and from 1890 to 1900 another 37,000,000 were added.

The principal factors in these phenomenal gains, which was indicative of what was coming during the next half century, were a vastly increased and better educated population, improved transportation, speedier means of communication, lower postal rates, and cheaper paper. The rapidly rising tide of culture and a keener interest in public affairs, coupled with a greater prosperity and more leisure (now that the nation's pioneering was virtually ended), resulted in a never-ceasing demand on the newspapers for more and more reading matter to supplement the local and telegraphic news and editorials. The syndicate was the instrument by which they were able to meet this demand. By the turn of the century it had developed the four media of service through which it was able to supply the needs of every type of newspaper, from the smallest country weekly to the largest metropolitan daily.

During the three decades of the present century, each ten-year period has witnessed even more phenomenal gains in circulation. During that time the syndicates have enlarged the scope of their operations, added to the variety of their features, and adapted their service readily to changing public tastes. The part which they have played in the swift increase in the number of papers and in the phenomenal increase in newspaper circulation is impossible to state exactly. But the conclusion is inescapable that they must have had a tremendously important part in both. The fact that fully 90 per cent of all newspapers in the United States now use syndicate service in one form or another is the best evidence of the position the syndicates hold in American journalism today. Certainly, they, with the class-of reading material which they supply, have done more than any other element in journalism to make the modern American newspaper "the people's library."

Another effect of the syndicate on American journalism has been the so-called "standardization" of newspapers because their use of its material results in a certain similarity of appearance and content. With every force in American life during the last half century showing a trend away from the individual and toward the standardized, it is not so unusual that journalism should reflect this tendency in its own development.

But the syndicate has been only one of the agents of newspaper standardization. Press associations share with it the responsibility for duplication of reading matter in our daily and weekly journals. If a subscriber in Maine and another in Oregon see the same comic strip, the same health talk, and the same installment of a serial story, they also read the same cable dispatches about the war clouds hovering over Europe, the same story about the latest legislation passed by the Congress in Washington, and the same details of the kidnaping or murder mystery currently attracting nation-wide attention.

The widespread use of syndicated material has had both unfavorable and favorable effects upon American newspapers. In some cases it undoubtedly has weakened editorial initiative by encouraging the publisher to neglect adequate coverage of local news and local features. If the knowledge that he can fill up his columns with syndicated material and still issue a full-size newspaper leads him to do so, then syndicate service has been used as a harmful influence in diverting the newspaper from one of its important roles—that of being a faithful mirror of the community.

On the other hand, intelligent use of syndicate service—the blending of its material with that produced by the newspaper's staff—makes for the type of well-rounded journal of news, information, and entertainment which the modern American reader has come to believe his newspaper should be. The syndicate has enabled newspapers of every class to give their readers that "balanced ration" of mental food, and, through the cheap medium of the newspaper, has brought to the masses the stimulation of reading the words of outstanding leaders of thought in the world today. That fact, perhaps, has been the syndicate's greatest contribution to American journalism.

BUSINESS ASPECTS OF THE SYNDICATES

—Curtis D. MacDougall, "Newspaper Syndication and Its Social Significance," in *The Press in the Contemporary Scene, The Annals of the American Academy of Political and Social Science,* Vol. 219, January 1942, pp. 76–78. Professor MacDougall teaches journalism at Northwestern University.

. . . NEWSPAPER SYNDICATION is Big Business in the aggregate. Reliable figures do not exist, but best guesses range from $15,000,000 to $40,000,000 as the total value of gross sales obtained annually by approximately two hundred and fifty companies. This does not include the straight news services of press associations, such as Associated

Press, United Press, and International News Service, or news picture services such as Acme, Underwood & Underwood, and Pacific and Atlantic. Although these associations and services operate on the same principle of providing identical material to thousands of clients, the term "syndicate" is restricted to those agencies which specialize in other than "spot news" material.

Comic strips, for instance, are still the backbone of the syndicate business. The average daily newspaper uses ten or fifteen comic strips and has a choice of about three hundred on the market. It is all but impossible to find a strictly local comic strip. Many begin with individual newspapers, but as soon as they prove successful they are syndicated, and this is true of cartoons also; a strip not good enough to syndicate is rarely considered good enough for use by a single paper.

Health columns, gardening columns, advice to the lovelorn, fashion hints, food suggestions, Hollywood gossip, short stories, serialized novels, household hints, oddities, advice on child rearing, Washington and other political columns—everything, in fact, that a newspaper uses in addition to straight news—are obtained from syndicates, although there is more local talent engaged in producing features of the types indicated for individual newspapers than is true in the case of comic strips.

A few of the largest and best syndicates are still owned or controlled by newspapers, notably Chicago *Tribune* and New York *News* (jointly), Philadelphia *Public Ledger* (suspended 1942), Des Moines *Register* and *Tribune*, Chicago *Times*, and New York *Herald Tribune*; but generally, newspaper syndication today is an independent business. Most features, furthermore, are for sale individually, but some of the large companies—notably King's, Bell, Newspaper Enterprise Association, and United Features—offer, for a fixed weekly sum, budget or blanket services intended to supply all of a small newspaper's needs.

Despite the huge profits which enable syndicates to pay the "big names" among columnists and cartoonists salaries which run into five and six figures, it is decidedly a buyer's market. Theoretically, size of circulation and exclusive territorial rights are the determining factors; yet local situations differ so much that rate cards generally are meaningless. With so many first-class alternative features on the market, the metropolitan daily without competition in a trading area with a hundred-mile radius is a very different prospect than another daily, with comparable circulation, in a densely populated section of the country where there are a dozen other papers in a territory of similar size.

Furthermore, competing newspapers may have different demands for exclusive territory, ranging from an area smaller than a county to five states. Outside the metropolitan areas, the usual circulation area in which exclusive rights are granted is only fifty miles; but there are few cities under 100,000 population with more than one newspaper and the trend toward consolidation is reaching even larger metropolitan areas.

The net result of such factors is that a syndicate may receive $5.00 a week for a feature from one newspaper, $10 a week for exactly the same feature from another newspaper of comparable size, and $15 from a third. For an identical feature the range may be from $3.00 in a small city to $50 or more in a large city; and for a budget service, from $20 for small papers of about 5,000 circulation to $350 for large papers of 200,000 circulation. Syndicate managers deplore the present cutthroat competitive system, but the few feeble attempts to bring order out of chaos have been unsuccessful.

From the standpoint of the subscribing newspaper, the financial value of syndicate material is equally difficult to measure. A small weekly newspaper can obtain all the feature material it is able to use for $1.00 or $2.00 a week, and it is futile to estimate what it would cost a weekly newspaper to employ a staff able to produce copy of comparable quality. The difficulty of arriving at an estimate is equally true for metropolitan papers and for the small-city daily with a circulation of from 10,000 to 15,000. Small-city dailies can obtain a blanket service from a syndicate for about $35 a week. A newspaper-owned syndicate may pay its writers three times as much in the aggregate as the combined pay roll for a newspaper editorial staff with a much larger personnel.

STANDARDIZATION REPLACES INDIVIDUALISM

—Oswald Garrison Villard, "The Press Today," *The Nation,* Vol. 130, June 1930, pp. 646–647. The late Mr. Villard, a thoughtful critic of the press, was for many years editor of *The Nation,* liberal weekly.

TODAY when one travels through the country on a Sunday on a fast train and buys successively the Buffalo, Cleveland, Chicago, Indianapolis, Toledo, and St. Louis Sunday papers it is hardly possible to tell which city is represented in a given mass of printed pages without carefully scanning the page headings. One finds the same "comics," the same Sunday magazines, the same special "features" in almost all of them and, of course, in most of them precisely the same Associated Press news. I have looked through the Sunday editions of nine big Eastern and Midwestern papers and I found "Little Orphan Annie" in seven of them, and she doubtless graces hundreds of others. "The Gumps," I am sorry to say, are not so popular, as they appear only five times. I was shocked to find "Mutt and Jeff" in only three of them, and the "Katzenjammer Kids," once the leading American comic, in only two. A cursory examination of the Philadelphia *Inquirer,* for example, reveals twenty features that have appeared in eight other newspapers, and probably as many more have appeared in other Sunday issues not included in this study. The special services of the New York *Times, Herald Tribune, American,* and the other New York dailies are as widely syndicated as possible. The truth is that people in or out of journalism, facing the same problems, having great economic stakes in the existing order, are bound to react in the same way if they do not happen to be infected by the germ of liberalism or radicalism. The newspaper profession has turned out to be a business and as a result there was bound to be standardization of the mentality of owners and editors which had its effect upon the editorial and the news pages, too.

So we have a steady waning of the individualism of the daily, marked first by the disappearance of the great editor whose personality shone through its pages—men such as Watterson, Medill, the Bennetts, Godkin, Dana, Greeley, Raymond, Nelson—and then by the extinction of typographic originality. You could tell the *Tribune* of Horace Greeley, the Springfield *Republican* of the Bowleses, the old Boston *Post,* the *Evening Post* of Godkin, as far as you could see the format. They were distinctive institutions bearing the impress of owners and editors. Now they have nearly all yielded to the tremendous pressure every owner is under to increase circulation in order to get more advertising at higher rates, in order, in turn, to meet his steadily increasing costs. No wonder he turns to syndicates, to combinations, or to special services. What more natural, too, than to make up your pages just like one of the New York dailies with your editorial pages, "opposite-editorial" pages, society and sports pages in the same relative positions? The appearance of the tabloid is, of course, a variation from the old standardized type of daily, but it is significant that the tabloids themselves imitate one another with complete fidelity.

In the sports pages above all others the opportunity for standardization is of the best. But here we have the offset that there is a tremendous thirst for the views of the distinguished commentators on sports who are paid very large salaries and are bid for by the rival dailies because they carry with them, as they migrate from one daily to another, a following of "fans" whose numbers run into the thousands. Read the leading dailies in the East and see how much alike their financial pages are. As for the editorial pages, standardization is at work there with a vengeance. The same "columnist" and the same editorial cartoons may appear in a dozen or more dailies, and the same half-column of medical advice and the same personal gossip from Washington. I have personally received as many as sixty clippings of an editorial commenting upon some words of mine from as many small dailies all over the Union—all of which had received the editorial from the same source and doubtless accepted its facts and comment without subjecting them to any critical examination whatever. The Newspaper Enterprise Association, one of the leading syndicates of the country, sends out daily about five editorials. It is the belief of the managers that 80 to 90 per cent of the 800 to 900 newspapers they serve use one or more of these "canned" editorials a day.

As for the syndicates, they play an ever-increasing role. Thus the Newspaper Enterprise Association, which is a Scripps-Howard organization, spends $2,225,000 annually on its service. Of this, $500,000 goes for pictures only, to obtain which quickly no expense is spared. Thus, to rush to New York a few photographs of the stranded German airplane which was the first to cross the Atlantic from east to west it hired a special train as well as airplanes—the modern press photographer in his daring outranks the special correspondents of old. Sometimes it has spent $12,000 for a single picture; sometimes it hires a whole fleet of airplanes to distribute its photographs. This association offers three kinds of service—the difference being in the quantity of matter offered. It sells, besides editorial matter, foreign correspondence of the gossipy, "feature" variety, and letters from Washington, comics, radio, aviation, and other features.

On the other hand, the North American Newspaper Alliance is

most eager to let one know that its chief aim is to get away from standardization. It serves no chain of newspapers, only independent dailies, and but one in each city. It is not interested in factual, but in interpretative articles. Most of its clients belong to the Associated Press and, like that organization, the Alliance is cooperative and non-profit-making. It is especially strong in financial and business articles, is distinctly dignified, believes itself "conservatively liberal," and also supplies "women matter," news of Hollywood daily(!) and . . . gives plenty of attention to sports, but offers no comics.

There is, of course, another side to syndication which, in all fairness, must be set forth. Without the syndicate small town newspapers would be much duller and much less informed than they are. They could not print any news pictures; they could not broaden their pages; they could not have much—if any—news of New York, Washington, or other centers; their foreign features would probably almost disappear, except in so far as they were brought to them by the news associations. Some of the syndicated Washington and European correspondence is of genuine educational value.

MASS INTEREST IN SYNDICATED FEATURES

—Stephen J. Monchak, "Syndicate Features Appeal Equally to Men and Women," *Editor & Publisher*, Vol. 73, Section Two, September 21, 1940, p. 1. Mr. Monchak was a staff writer for *Editor & Publisher* when he wrote this article.

THE AMERICAN PEOPLE read their daily newspaper features in much the same manner whether they live in Maine or California. Both in metropolitan areas and in the smaller communities, they have the same entertainment interests in the daily press.

The common denominator among them, irrespective of the size of the city in which their papers are published, is their interest in syndicated comic strips, oddity and "gag" panels, and other syndicated features.

Approximately the same percentage of readers of syndicate features exists alike among both men and women in every city. The type of feature that appeals to one, however, does not appeal in the same degree to the other.

For example, women prefer human interest, children's doings, and heroines in a feature, while men lean heavily to adventure in such reading.

A minority of both likes puzzles and patterns.

Those are some findings culled from a study of the reports and a summary of the Continuing Study of Newspaper Reading, conducted by the Advertising Research Foundation of the Association of National Advertisers and the American Association of Advertising Agencies in co-operation with the Bureau of Advertising of the American Newspaper Publishers Association.

. . .

The writer's tabulation of the percentage readership of every comic strip in each of the 21 papers studied to date revealed there were exactly 200 strips carried in those papers. Some strips are duplicated many times. Of these 116 are classified as humor strips, the remaining 84 as adventure strips.

Further breakdown shows that men read more of the adventure type of strip than women, while women out-read slightly the men on humor strips. Men, these figures show, read more comics than women.

The approximate percentage figures in the two classifications follow:

Adventure strips: men, 62%; women, 52%.
Humor strips: men, 53%; women, 57%.

Oddity panels, the studies reveal, attract more men and women readers than any other syndicated feature. A summary of the first 15 papers studied, released recently, showed that 88% of the men read such panels, as did 80% of the women.

The appeal of such a feature, it may be assumed, is its combination of information and entertainment.

In comic strip readership, according to the summary, men registered 82%, while women totaled 76%.

Humor, or "gag," panels also score well in reader traffic stops, with 79% of the men and 84% of the women being attracted by them.

Syndicated features such as New York, Hollywood, political, and health columns are less widely read.

Among both men and women readers, local columns consistently outpull the big-name syndicated columnists, probably because of the advantage of local subjects treated entertainingly.

Of the syndicated columnists, however, results show that political writers fare better in the ratings, especially among men, but still bow in popularity to the local columnists in the papers studied.

Serial stories attract a small percentage of readers, although women give them more attention than men.

Crossword puzzles also attract few readers, averaging about the same among men and women, according to the summary.

. . .

Comic strips, the studies bring out, are better read if they are grouped together on a single page or on two pages facing each other than if they are spotted throughout the paper.

The strategy of spotting strips and panels in newspapers, of course, is obvious. It is a technique that magazine editors use to good advantage. By putting cartoons on back pages of their books, they have increased the reader traffic on those pages. In a newspaper, however, it seems to result differently.

The reason for that may be that one comic is more popular than another in a reader's eyes. A reader who would scan the ones he prefers on a page of strips might include some others in his reading but would not read a lone comic that does not appeal to him.

. . .

No matter where the oddity panel is spotted, it consistently gets the greatest reader traffic stops of the features on that page. For example, one such appeared on the editorial page of a Southern daily.

It was an average editorial page with letters to the editor, questions and answers, and short paragraphs. Yet, while men and women read everything that appeared on the page, readership of the oddity panel far out-distanced any other item on the page.

On the page opposite the editorial page of the same daily, two Washington columns, one written by a team, the other by a woman, attracted about half the readers who read the editorial page, the men favoring the team, while the women readers paid more attention to the woman writer.

It is interesting to note, however, that although the men outnumbered the women readers more than four to one in reading the team of writers, the women only outnumbered the men two to one in reading the woman columnist, bearing out again that the men readers are more politically minded than the ladies.

An oddity and a humor panel, both extremely popular with both types of readers, shared about equally in reader traffic stops among both men and women who went to the next page.

This daily's comic strip make-up put them on back pages of the paper. Three each were spotted on two facing pages among classified advertisements; and three more were placed on another classified page. All had bottom right hand position. Reader traffic stops for all the comics ranged from 60% to 80%.

On two pages of the three, advertisements utilizing comic strip technique were included. Their readership in comparison to the legitimate strips was poor, neither of them attracting more than a third of the readers, both men and women, who read the regular comics on the same page.

THE INFLUENCE OF THE SYNDICATED COMIC

—John K. Ryan, "Are the Comics Moral?" *Forum*, Vol. 95, May 1936, pp. 301–302, 304. The author, a noted educator, is professor of philosophy at the Catholic University of America, Washington, D. C.

(Editors' Note: *Ten years after Mr. Ryan wrote the following article, the* 100-Study Summary *of the Continuing Study of Newspaper Reading, published in 1946 by the Advertising Research Foundation, showed* Dick Tracy *at the top of the men's list of 15 best-read comics, with a median readership of 70 per cent. Among women readers,* Blondie, *a non-adventure humorous strip, stood first with a median score of 74.* Dick Tracy *ranked fourth. Very few adventure comics were listed among the first 15 favored by both men and women. It should be pointed out, however, that interviewers conducting the Research Foundation surveys question only men and women 18 years and older.*)

Sadism, cannibalism, bestiality. Crude eroticism. Torturing, killing, kidnaping. Monsters, madmen, creatures half-brute, half-human. Raw melodrama; tales of crimes and criminals; extravagant exploits in strange lands and on other planets; pirate stories; wild, hair-raising adventures of boy heroes and girl heroines; thrilling accounts in word and picture of jungle beasts and men; marvelous deeds of magic and pseudo science. Vulgarity, cheap humor and cheaper wit. Sentimental stories designed for the general level of a moronic mind. Ugliness of thought and expression. All these, day after day, week after week, have become the mental food of American children, young and old.

With such things are the comic strips that take up page upon page in the average American newspaper filled. Repeated and drilled into their readers countless times by vivid pictures and simple words, the crude, trivial, debased, and debasing features of the comic strips are more than a sign of the prevailing infantilism of the American mind. They are at once an effect and a powerful contributing cause of that infantilism. The number and character of the comic strips at the present time are a cultural phenomenon and psychological portent of the most serious kind.

The change that has come over the comic section in recent years is an episode in journalism that most Americans have watched with interest. Perhaps the interest has been in many cases unconscious, but it has been extremely real. The fact that the comic section has reached its present size and power is ample proof of the tremendous interest it holds for American readers of all ages and classes. The power of a popular strip over circulation is notorious. For a paper to lose its best strips means disaster, almost ruin. The Supreme Court itself had to decide which Washington paper was to have exclusive rights to the deeds of Andy Gump, Dick Tracy, and their friends. . . .

Is a continuous diet of lurid melodrama, told by pictures of brutal men doing brutal deeds, good for children or for adults who are mentally immature and emotionally unstable? There are comic strips that now provide such a diet, day after day, to avid thousands. *Secret Agent X-9, Red Barry, Dick Tracy, Dan Dunn, Radio Patrol, Inspector Wade*—this last written, seemingly, from the grave by Edgar Wallace—represent the detective-criminal strip so popular at present.

What they offer can be illustrated by one Sunday's installment of the adventures of Dick Tracy. Dick and his young assistant, Junior, are caught in a net lined with fishhooks. The repulsive hunchbacked villain who has caught them in this trap tells the detective and the boy that if they move they will be torn to shreds. A vicious dog is then brought on the scene, and the hunchback says that he is going to infect the dog with a serum that "produces instant rabies." Then the hunchback will release the dog and watch the fun. But the dog gets out of control, seizes the hunchback by the throat and kills him. In crude but vivid pictures the dog is shown tearing at the hunchback's throat while Junior and Tracy look on in horror.

It was for the right to publish such pictures that the Hearst papers fought a losing battle with the Washington *Post.* The momentous issue, who would purvey these scenes to the peoples of the District of Columbia, was finally decided by the Supreme Court of the United States.

Crimes, killings, torturings, not all so horrible or pictured as vividly as the death of Doc Hump, are essential ingredients in the criminal-detective strips. It is true that virtue is invariably triumphant, that the law is vindicated, that the police are the heroes and the criminals the villains. But the evil effects of prolonged and repeated brutalities are not wiped out by a final and rather hurried triumph of law and virtue. In fact, this triumph itself may take the form of more death and carnage, of more crude scenes. . . .

In such preposterous tales . . . the vicious elements are made more vivid by the pictures than would ever be possible by words alone. The repulsive brutes that figure in these pictures; their repellent activities; the horrible practices that are hinted at, described, or threatened; the emphasis upon madness, degeneracy, cruelty, and lust all unite to produce something that can for the most part bear only the word *obscene.* This ugly element cannot be justified as being realistic; it has no connection with life and reality. Its exhibitionism and cheap emphasis on sex are utterly without aesthetic defense. Its horror motifs and vulgar melodramatics are completely devoid of literary value. There is nothing substantial that can be urged in its favor.

These vicious features are found for the most part in the melodramatic strips such as those described. Most of the scores of comic features that are being published in American newspapers are in themselves harmless enough. Some of them consistently maintain a fairly high plane of genuine humor and human interest. In some, like *Moon Mullins,* there is a strain of what may be called a sort of wholesome and robust vulgarity. Others tell stories that are harmless enough and often develop characters and situations that justify their existence. But the multiplication of such features and their steady consumption by an immense public can hardly be considered encouraging. Not degraded or degrading in themselves, they are yet a sign and a cause of intellectual and cultural infantilism in America.

REVIEW QUESTIONS AND ASSIGNMENTS

1. How would you appraise the present position of the syndicate in American journalism? Do you regard it from a critical or a favorable point of view?

2. Select a major feature syndicate and classify all the offerings it markets. Write an analysis based on content.

3. Do you think that the extreme competition among the syndicates has produced unfortunate results for the press?

4. Compare the accounts of the three major news-gathering associations on a half-dozen different stories and point out similarities and differences.

5. Can you find any examples of stories that were built up by one of the syndicates?

6. Summarize your position with respect to the common charge that the syndicates have promoted a dangerously standardized press.

7. Study the comics in a selected newspaper for one month and then write an estimate of their possible influence on English usage, sense of humor, desire for excitement, and so forth.

8. Do you subscribe to the theory that the lurid melodrama in certain comic strips, as well as in radio and television shows, is a dangerous influence on the mind of the growing child?

9. If you were the managing editor of a newspaper in a city of 100,000 population, what policies would you follow with respect to the use of pictures?

10. Study the contents of ten weekly newspapers in your state and prepare a report on the amount of syndicated material used, the types that appear most popular, and the use of material not credited to regular commercial syndicates.

11. Would you be willing to have the government syndicate free features on the activities of the various administrative departments to the press?

12. If you were a media manager, what would your answer be to a demand from an outside group that a certain syndicated feature be banned?

13. How far do you think the press should try to go in having its feature content produced by local staff effort?

14. Would you favor a law requiring the media to indicate in clear fashion the source of all non-local content?

ADDITIONAL REFERENCES

Anderson, Carl T., *How To Draw Cartoons Successfully,* Greenberg, 1935.

Anonymous, "(AP)," *Fortune,* Vol. 15, February 1937, p. 89.

———, "The Funny Papers," *Fortune,* Vol. 7, April 1933, p. 92.

———, "The Newspapers as Childhood's Enemy," *Survey,* Vol. 27, February 24, 1912, p. 1794.

Benet, Stephen Vincent, "United Press," *Fortune,* Vol. 7, May 1933, p. 67.

Bent, Silas, *Ballyhoo: The Voice of the Press,* Liveright, 1927, pp. 245–268.

Bleyer, Willard G. (editor), *The Profession of Journalism,* Atlantic Monthly Press, 1918.

Bok, Edward W., *The Americanization of Edward Bok,* Charles Scribner's Sons, 1920.

Bowers, Claude G., *The Tragic Era,* Houghton Mifflin, 1929.

Briggs, Clare A., *How To Draw Cartoons,* Harper & Brothers, 1926.

Britt, George, *Forty Years—Forty Millions,* Farrar & Rinehart, 1935.

Cochran, N. D., *E. W. Scripps,* Harcourt, Brace, 1933.

Desmond, Robert, *The Press and World Affairs,* Appleton-Century, 1937.

Editor & Publisher, Annual Directory of Syndicated Features.

Ernst, Morris L., *The First Freedom,* Macmillan, 1946, pp. 57–124.

Gramling, Oliver, *AP—The Story of News,* Farrar & Rinehart, 1940.

Herzberg, Joseph G. (editor), *Late City Edition,* Henry Holt, 1947, pp. 257–263.

Koenigsburg, M., *King News,* Frederick A. Stokes, 1941.

Lee, Alfred M., *The Daily Newspaper in America,* Macmillan, 1937, pp. 576–607.

McClure, S. S., *My Autobiography,* Frederick A. Stokes, 1912.

McNitt, V. V., "Sam McClure Started Something," *Editor & Publisher,* Vol. 67, July 21, 1934, p. 80.

McRae, M. A., *Forty Years in Newspaperdom,* Coward-McCann, 1924.

Murrell, William, *A History of American Graphic Humor,* Whitney Museum of American Art, 1933.

Neal, Robert M., *Editing the Small City Daily,* Prentice-Hall, 1946, pp. 201–249.

Parton, James, *Caricature and Other Comic Arts,* Harper & Brothers, 1877.

Rosewater, Victor, *The History of Cooperative News Gathering in the United States,* Appleton-Century, 1930.

Shaffer, Laurance F., *Children's Interpretations of Cartoons,* Columbia University Press, 1930.

Stone, Melville E., *Fifty Years a Journalist,* Doubleday, Doran, 1922.

Thorndike, Chuck, *The Secrets of Cartooning,* House of Little Books, 1936.

Thorpe, Merle, *The Coming Newspaper,* Henry Holt, 1915.

United Feature Syndicate, Its Story and Organization, United Feature Syndicate, 1936.

Villard, Oswald G., *Some Newspapers and Newspapermen,* Alfred A. Knopf, 1923.

Waldrop, A. Gayle, *Editor and Editorial Writer,* Rinehart, 1948, pp. 289–309.

10. HOW THE PRESS SEES GOVERNMENT

INTRODUCTION

The relationship between press and government is an unusual one. In its traditional form, the reporting of governmental activities by the media places the press at the very pinnacle of its responsibility as a social institution in a democracy. Without a consistent and accurate dissemination of news about public affairs, the theory of enlightened citizenship loses meaning. But the relationship has another and newer side; one in which the media are not representing and protecting the interests of the public but are dealing as independent business enterprises with government. Increasingly during the twentieth century, the question of how the press sees government has been debated in terms of a twin relationship that clearly reflects the essential dualism of the communications agencies.

The lines of the two relationships do not necessarily cross. A responsible press agency recognizes the vast distinction between the reporting of a political campaign so that the electorate may have guidance and a court test of the Fair Labor Standards Act aimed at determining the applicability of a section of the law to the business operation of a newspaper or radio station.

The possibility exists, of course, that the press will not be able to keep the relationships in sharply divided compartments. It would be very easy for a publisher who has applied to the Federal Communications Commission for a radio broadcasting license to employ the editorial columns of his newspaper to exert pressure on the Commission. Indeed, many critics argue that the treatment of political and legislative news has been cynical, even bitter, ever since the first administration of President Franklin Delano Roosevelt when certain New Deal regulatory laws were declared to be as applicable to the press as to all other business units. Proof of such an interlocking of the relationships, however, cannot be found. Newspaper support of a Republican candidate in an election does not constitute concrete evidence that its only aim is to further its own business profits. Most media owners have a concept of general welfare which, while conservative, is not purely self-seeking.

The reporting of news from political, legislative, and administrative sources always has received the first attention of the press. Such reports have featured the contents of newspapers from the day of the founding of the Boston *News Letter* to the present. They, likewise, have received prominent attention from radio, the news magazines, and the confidential news letters. Their volume and significance increased to a marked degree after the close of the Civil War when all levels of government were forced to make service functions their primary activity. Most political writers today agree that Washington is the news capital of the nation.

Given a strong interest on the part of the media in reporting news about government, what kind of a performance pattern exists?

If we examine news accounts of past activities we see that the element of conflict in news evaluation plays a dominant role. Contests among political leaders and factions before, during, and after elections receive almost exclusive attention. The greater the struggle, the more prominently it is evaluated. Although political conflicts possess undoubted reader interest and are often influential in determining election results, they do not necessarily tell the true story of the continuing programs of parties. Indeed, a party fortunately free from conflict may not find itself in the news until just prior to an election when it announces its slate of candidates. The question emerges as to whether the press is doing the whole job in its coverage of parties if it limits itself to the dramatizing of controversy.

Press attitudes toward news of legislative activities are somewhat comparable. Although a remarkably competent job is performed in the treatment of routine legislative developments, major attention is reserved for dramatic struggles. Sensational speeches of demagogues, meaningless filibusters, committee hearings that bring attacks and counter-attacks, and the strange doings of some legislators are the types of stories dear to the hearts of those who process the news from the national and state capitals. A fist fight between two Congressmen will be recounted on page one of every newspaper in the country. News executives of both newspapers and radio stations defend the often exaggerated prominence given such stories in view of their essential superficiality by citing the old belief that the average citizen is interested in his government only when controversial elements can be detected.

The administrative branch has become an increasingly important issue as the service functions of government have multiplied. Reporters must concern themselves more and more with the work of bureaus and bureau officials. These agencies, in turn, cannot function effectively without the support of public awareness and understanding. If the press faces a truly crucial role in the building and maintaining of public intelligence, it comes at this point. Media attacks on bureaucratic regimentation, governmental meddling, and official propaganda often fail to note the demands for service the citizen levies on his government. Bureau chiefs, at the same time, cannot expect the press to regard their work as forever good, honest, and fair. Bad points must be revealed along with good, and ultimate truth must be the goal.

THE REPORTING OF GOVERNMENT NEWS

—Frederic E. Merwin, a summary written especially for this book. See his "The Reporting of Public Affairs," in *The Annals of the American Academy of Political and Social Science*, Vol. 219, January 1942, pp. 120–126.

THE REPORTING of news about government has been traditionally a great testing gound for assessment of the influence of the press in a democratic nation. This is still true despite the great interest in the manner in which the mass media handle news of science, crime, religion, racial discrimination, agriculture, and other issues which constitute baffling reportorial problems in the Atomic Age.

There is obvious reason for public concern with press treatment of government news. A democratic society can operate on a harmonious basis only if the citizens possess information which will enable them to co-operate and to participate in the functioning of government in an enlightened fashion. Any breakdown in the flow of intelligence through the media to the citizenry constitutes a threat, large or small, to a government which relies for stability on the doctrine that it is of, for, and by the people.

The change in the character of government from that of a police force to a service instrumentality during the last century has greatly magnified the importance of the record the press compiles as it records the multiplicity of legislative and administrative activities which bear on the citizens. The press reports constitute the only basis available to most citizens on which to judge the contemporary course of affairs.

1. *Reporting—the Basic Issue*

The position occupied by the press in reporting government activities has as its outstanding characteristic a freedom which entails a fundamental responsibility. The first amendment to the Federal Constitution, the doctrine of qualified privilege, and a great tradition of a lack of censorship except in periods of utmost emergency afford the press a free hand as it sends its representatives into the halls of government to recapture the story of the state in action.

This requires the press, if it is to justify such a privileged position, to supply an accurate, fair, and adequate report of government to the mass audience which it serves. The main goal must be the truth, even though the truth, as Herbert Agar has pointed out, may be something that men do not wish to hear.

Portraying the activities of government involves three functions for the press: reporting, interpreting, and criticizing.

Now, obviously, the press cannot report *all* government news. And even if it were to do so, the record would be of such proportions as to first amaze and then quickly discourage the public. What the press, therefore, must do is select on a daily, even hourly, basis those events which are to be recorded and reject those which, for one reason or another, cannot be given a place in the flow of news. This is an almost sacred task. Public opinion cannot be formulated unless an event is recorded in recognizable form. There can be no opinion about a rejected event. It is the reporter and his immediate superiors, therefore, who determine what grist shall go into the mill of public thinking.

Selection and rejection are based on rules of guidance, although some editors have argued that intuition (a feeling for news that should be recorded) is sufficient. With few exceptions, the rules are those of news evaluation and reader interest. The two are complementary. A news story has value if it is dramatic, controversial, and possibly unexpected. These values exist because audience response shows that they are the primary ingredients of human interest in external affairs.

While the press deserves great credit for the job it does in reporting government news in a reasonably fair and accurate fashion, doubt exists as to whether proper selection and rejection results from the use of rules which give emotional interests dominance over healthy social intelligence.

The possibility exists that the picture the press presents lacks true meaning because of the stress on the personal attack, a forced resignation, a congressional inquiry, a corrupt act, and an often ridiculous mistake in judgment. While no one argues against the exposure of things that go wrong in public affairs, the fear remains that the picture the public sees of government tends to be superficial because only emotion-tinged highlights are given rapt attention by the communicators.

One aspect of the problem that received scant attention until recent years concerns the capabilities of those who uncover the facts and then describe them in news story form. It is now accepted that the men and women assigned to record the news of a complex, intricate government system must be sufficiently specialized to be able to detect the true facts in the data available on a given event. They must possess a keen sense of public duty.

2. *The Question of Interpretation*

The press cannot claim credit for successful reporting of news of government if it relies on stock accounts of personalities and issues. It must increasingly go below the surface and ferret out the information needed to give the shape of the event proper significance. It must not only tell its audience that an event has occurred but also *why*. The process is one of providing clarification and explanation through interpretation of happenings.

In the years since the close of World War II, the White House, the State Department, and the Pentagon have emerged as the three major sources of news in Washington. In addition, certain new agencies have come into the picture, particularly the Economic Cooperation Administration. These sources have one common characteristic: the events which bring them into the news are not easy to score.

For example, an announcement from the White House of a decision of the President to accept the resignation of a financial adviser can be treated in surface fashion as a spat between two high officials involving failure to clear a public address with the White House before delivery. Actually, such an event is almost invariably representative of some underlying point of policy and if this is not made clear the recorded picture of the event will be out of focus.

The Department of State is considered by some to be a more serious news problem than the White House. The department, as the result of decisions made at conferences held by top leaders during the war, discovered in the postwar period that it would have to deal increasingly with the press on issues of gravest consequence. A policy decision announced by the Secretary of State may have repercussions in a dozen world capitals. Why this should be so and what the ultimate results may prove to be is a question which the department and the correspondents assigned to it must answer if the people are to understand the course of world events.

One of the most difficult problems in the application of the interpretive technique arises out of the understandable tendency of the press corps to let personalities run away with the show. During the fall of 1949, to cite an example, a congressional committee summoned leaders of the armed forces to testify on certain unification policies that had been announced by the defense chief. The testimony quickly featured an inter-service battle with the value of the B-36 during wartime apparently the main issue. Strong statements from the witnesses captured the headlines. The real meaning of the hearing never was brought out in clear fashion.

With some of the best reportorial brains in the country assigned to coverage of government news, it hardly seems presumptuous for the public to expect an integrated picture, based primarily on background data, of the way in which elected and appointed officials discharge the task of public housekeeping.

3. *The Press as a Critic*

Press criticism in the field of public affairs probably represents the single most significant justification of the first amendment to the Constitution. Things do go wrong in government and from earliest Colonial days to the present the press has eagerly accepted the responsibility of pointing out the weak and questionable points in the management of public affairs. All mass media have deemed criticism a duty which must be performed if the citizen is to be assured of the scrutiny of government so implicit in the theory of democracy.

There are aspects of press criticism of government which deserve close examination in terms of influence.

One concerns its extreme breadth. Greeley did not hesitate to advise President Lincoln on the conduct of the Civil War and Hearst bitterly criticized President Wilson's policies in the 1914–17 period. During the second World War, press criticism touched on all matters except those held as closely guarded secrets by the sources. Wars simply highlight the critical function. The press feels no hesitancy at any time in evaluating policies, appointments, administrative decisions, and legislative deliberations, as well as developments in all other fields of public interest.

The breadth of criticism is equalled by the tendency of the press to emphasize the negative. Strongest fire is reserved for developments in public affairs which the media regard as either corrupt, dangerous, or obnoxious. Major press crusades (the high-water marks of criticism) have been waged against personalities and agencies caught far off the path of democratic morality. Those who do the crusading feel, and in many cases rightly, that they are safeguarding the interests of the masses against the few who, either for reasons of personal gain or crass stupidity, seek to soil the processes of representative government. Press vigilance, from their standpoint, is the great bulwark of democracy.

Two tests of criticism must be made by the press.

There is, in the first place, the question of the ultimate value of criticism characterized by a dominantly negative tone. Many observers feel that the feverish attention paid by the press to things wrong in government produces only surface reforms and, more importantly, exerts no lasting influence on the public mind. Certainly, the history of attempts of the press to deal with political phenomena under the popular categories of "good" and "evil" does not offer convincing evidence of the value of the approach. After years as a muckraker, Lincoln Steffens decided that "good" and "evil" were not necessarily significant in understanding political behavior. Far too often the criticism fails to get at the reasons behind the existence of corruption and is merely limited to "what has happened" without any reference to "why did it happen." The dominant interest of the press in things wrong exists only at the expense of what might be a more positive and, at the same time, more expansive critical function. Democracy's ability to act effectively requires support; its positive program may suffer seriously due to the persistent distraction provided by vociferous critics.

Perhaps the greatest desideratum is that criticism be factual. Most difficulty involving adverse press comment can be traced to this factor. While the great newspaper crusades against public wrong-doing have been based on the collection of provable data, there are many instances in which criticism is merely speculation and guesswork. The explanation for this is that criticism often must be formulated at an extremely long distance from the source; the policies of the medium exert a strong influence; the personal views of those who make the criticism are bound to enter the picture; and the high speed schedule followed by both the newspaper and radio make it necessary to render judgments in the space of minutes.

Factual criticism can be achieved by the media only if they are willing to spend the money and take the time to uncover the hidden meanings of events to the degree necessary for a truly judicial evaluation as to their rightness and wrongness. If this can be done, the other problems in criticism will be pretty largely dissipated.

Certainly, no serious student of public affairs would advocate the elimination of press criticism even in time of dire emergency. If properly handled, it represents a great protecting arm for a democratic society.

THE ECLIPSE OF THE PARTISAN PRESS

—George L. Bird, "Newspaper Monopoly and Political Independence," *Journalism Quarterly*, Vol. 17, September 1940, pp. 211–212, 214.

TODAY less than one daily paper in seven calls itself Republican, less than one in six Democratic. Independent Republicans have dropped to 10 per cent, although Independent Democrats have climbed to 11 per cent. Democratic papers have had quite the best of it during the last seven years, due in large part to the flowering of the Democratic party in the two elections of Franklin Delano Roosevelt.

Independent papers have climbed from 778 to 898, or from 41 per cent of the total daily papers to 46 per cent. They control 61 per cent of the circulation. Every state in the Union has at least one Independent newspaper, including Delaware, the kingdom of the duPonts. The only daily in this state is published in Wilmington. Does anyone suppose a paper here could be "independent" in any true sense of that word?

Since 1930 the Democratic papers have dropped from 326 to 307,

Republican papers from 430 to 287, Independent Republican papers from 216 to 195; but Independent Democratic papers have climbed from 139 to 216. Perhaps 30 papers are unclassified. The startling fact is that, out of 1,438 communities publishing newspapers, only 66 have a choice between local papers acknowledging different political allegiance.

In eleven states and the District of Columbia a Republican cannot find a single local paper claiming his own political faith. Three other states, Nevada, Utah, and Virginia, have only one Republican paper apiece, while North Dakota and Oklahoma have but three and Rhode Island two. . . .

The most significant features of the shifting allegiance are that the actual political alignment of a newspaper is not revealed in its new designation, and that the announced independent state is often a new cloak for an old allegiance.

This would be less serious, perhaps, if it were not true that the shift to so-called political independence has been dictated in many, possibly most, cases by expediency, not by principle. In some cases, "independence" is accompanied by a carefully concealed bias which, when it is totalled, assumes the proportion of a definite political allegiance. Sometimes this fact is revealed less by outright championship than by selection and emphasis of the opponent's weaknesses.

For example, in Syracuse, N.Y., the *Herald-Journal* carries in its masthead the announcement of its intention to ignore party politics. Possibly it is not active in party councils. Having read most of the editorials for the last three years, however, I find it fighting on the Republican side so frequently as to see no reason why it should fly the "Independent" flag. And no one who reads the "Independent" Madison, Wis., *Capital Times* would ever call it an Independent. If the Progressive party in that state has had a party organ, it has been this paper. Through the years it has been the chief La Follette newspaper regardless of what ticket a La Follette ran on.

Consider the plight of Folsom Moore, editor as well as managing editor of two papers in Bisbee, Ariz. In the morning apparently he writes Democratic editorials for the *Review*, and in the evening, by some mental legerdemain, writes "independent editorials" for the *Ore*. He is by no means the only publisher in the country capable of performing the feat. Somewhat similar are the abilities of H. C. Ogden of West Virginia, who presides over the Democratic Parkersburg

Sentinel, the Independent Wheeling *News-Register*, the Independent Republican Martinsburg *Journal*, and the Republican Elkins *Inter-Mountain*. He does not, be it noted, have to preside also over an Independent Democratic newspaper. In Fairmont, where he is president of two papers, one Democratic and the other Republican, he has hit upon the solution of having separate editors; but presumably he must give Democratic advice to one and Republican to the other.

In Lewiston, Maine, a Yankee owns the morning Independent *Sun* and the evening Republican *Journal*. . . .

A return to political partisanship is unlikely, unnecessary, and probably undesirable. The present trend, however, is putting pressure on the newspaper to improve the standards and quality of its news and editorials. Perhaps it will have to substitute another vigorous program for its old politics, or its independence will end in the complete indifference of readers to its opinions—if, indeed, that time has not already arrived. Such a program can be found in community betterment, in improving the calibre of the courts, in attention to rural problems, promotion of civil service and similar non-partisan projects.

Political independence must mean exactly that. If the press continues to use this designation as a cloak for political and economic self-interests, the press will steadily drop in public esteem and confidence. Its reporters and its correspondents must do a more scientific and objective job in local, state, national and international reporting and interpretation, or the evil inherent in the growing newspaper monopoly will wreck one of the choicest products of this democracy —a free press.

REPORTING NEWS ABOUT POLITICS

—David Lawrence, "Reporting the Political News at Washington," *The American Political Science Review*, Vol. 22, November 1928, pp. 893–902. Mr. Lawrence is a journalist who has long specialized in news from the national capital.

First of all, let me say that there is no question on which you can develop more controversy than the reporting of political news. Within the profession, within the newspaper business, there is a great deal of controversy, and has been for many years, particularly as to whether political news is fairly reported, impartially reported. I have listened to a good deal of discussion on that point. I have recognized, as have others in the newspaper business, the trend of the times—the so-called decrease in the strength of the editorial page, for instance, and the increase in the amount of material of a semi-editorial flavor printed in the news columns.

The first branch of the topic, namely, reporting political news as it affects our domestic politics, seems to me to require an understanding, first, of the pressure and the difficulties that newspaper men face in handling news of campaigns and, second, some of the pitfalls which they encounter between campaigns.

It is much easier to report political news between campaigns than it is during campaigns. For one thing, your audience is not sensitive between campaigns. Especially just after a campaign has been concluded there is a sort of feeling that the victorious candidate, the newly inaugurated president, the newly introduced congress, should have what we call popularly a square deal—as if, by inference, they did not have a square deal before. Newspaper men call the first few months of a newly elected president's term the "honeymoon period." After a certain time there is less tolerance again: the "honeymoon" is supposed to be over, and generosity of attitude on the part of the press toward the triumphant candidate becomes less apparent. . . .

Newspapers today are all—at least they profess to be—independent. I would like myself to put quotation marks around the word "independent." Every time you send a questionnaire to newspapers listed in the newspaper directory, and ask them for their political affiliations, they invariably reply "independent"; and there is no way to get away from that classification. Some of them, which have been a little more liberal-minded, have chosen the classification "independent Republican" and "independent Democrat"—as if there could be that kind of classification. But, after all, perhaps the best way to classify a newspaper is to find out which presidential candidates it has supported over a period of time; and you can make up your mind whether or not a paper that has never supported any candidate of another party is actually independent.

I mention this because, much as we might not like to admit it, the news content of the newspapers today depends to no small extent on the editorial policies of those papers. This is less true today than it was ten years ago, but the condition still exists. We must recognize the fact that, whether the editor is present or not, the people who select the material for the newspaper each day are conscious of the editorial policies of the publication; and hence a very good thing is frequently relegated to some inside page or the waste-basket if it is favorable to the cause they are opposing, while the meritorious thing about the candidate they are supporting is usually put on the first page and given all the prominence necessary. . . .

We have also the strictly partisan newspapers, which make no pretense of being anything else, which not only print every item of news that supports the candidate in whom they are interested, but which print also the manufactured stuff of his campaign; and there is more of that printed than you can possibly imagine. I do not suppose that the headquarters of our political parties would like to give out the facts and figures on those things. But a good many of us know that a great deal of such manufactured matter is printed, particularly in the small newspapers. What I object to is that it is not labeled. . . . In political campaigns we have that to contend with, and we have also the activities of the various headquarters which are trying to manipulate the natural channels of news—trying to "make news." A good many "stunts" are performed during campaigns purely for publicity purposes. . . .

I have rather held for many years to the belief that the material that is printed between campaigns is the most important part of political news. . . . When the Congress is adjourned there seems to be dissatisfaction on the part of newspapers during a period in which the minority is not represented—a situation with which I have a great deal of sympathy, but which I hardly know how we could correct. Certainly when Congress has adjourned for eight or nine months of the year, and the executive branch of the government is in possession of either the Democratic or the Republican party, all the news that emanates from Washington is about that particular administration. . . . You usually find the same kind of dissatisfaction that nobody is at hand to conduct a crusade and expose the party in office. There is a little of that at all times, but between campaigns unquestionably the party in power gets most of the publicity and benefits immensely. Of course, in a sense, what an administration does, what it is trying to accomplish, is political news between campaigns, and a man may make a wonderful record on a particular activity a year or two after he has been elected. A member of Congress may do something at a time when he is not particularly in the public eye for reelection, and he derives a benefit which is lasting. . . .

The news side of the newspaper is, therefore, the one that I should watch most closely if I were a candidate for office. I believe that the reporting of the activities of government officials in a fair way will have, in its last analysis, more effect on the voter in the making of public opinion than the interpretive articles on some of our editorial pages. . . .

I wish I could say to you that we have in this country an unprejudiced handling of political news, because it would be fine to think that we are practicing impartiality in presenting to the people the information on which they base their judgments; but unfortunately it is not so. The partisan element enters into it very strongly; it enters into it even to the extent that the officials themselves frequently in describing the activities of their offices insert a prejudice which is recognized by the opposite side. You have heard a good deal of criticism from time to time about the use by government officials of their offices to propagandize the particular things in which they are interested and to advertise themselves. . . . I believe that this in itself is not harmful as the tendency to color the news according to the wishes of the newspapers or publications. I am happy to say that the situation in this respect is constantly being improved. But I am telling you no secret, I know, when I tell you that there are in the House of Representatives a good many correspondents who are secretaries to congressmen, who write for their local newspapers, and who necessarily cannot present a very unbiased account of what their employers are doing. . .

Then we have the difficulties with which the press services are faced. Again and again a press service is accused of being partisan, of favoring this candidate or that candidate. I remember that in the campaign of 1912 I was reporting for the Associated Press. I was assigned to go along with Governor Wilson, and there was another Associated Press reporter with President Taft and a third with Colonel Roosevelt, and we used to compare results the morning after to see what the other candidates had obtained in the way of space and the number of words. It was pretty well balanced. The difficulty was that President Taft was not at that time making many trips, and hence there was considerable disappointment in his organization that he was not sharing the wires with Colonel Roosevelt and Governor Wilson, who were out on speech-making tours.

Frequently it is the fault of the candidate, who does not use his opportunities as much as he might; for the most part, the newspaper men engaged in distributing news for the press services are fair and honest and are not chargeable with any of the sins of omission that I have just described. The press services, nevertheless, are accused of bias. Scarcely a campaign goes by but that somebody does not think that it is the avowed purpose of the press associations to advance the cause of some particular candidate. Sometimes it looks that way because several days go by without anything from the other candidate, and it looks as if one candidate has all the space.

Then, too, news breaks at inconvenient times. A world series game occurs on the same day that someone makes a very important speech, and on that occasion that speech must be cut to make way for the details of the game. . . . There is no doubt that the candidate who selects the occasion and opportunity for publicity frequently gets the better of it.

I know something also on the other side of the problem. One day some years ago a certain political treasurer had to make a report to Congress at a time when it was investigating campaign expenditures, and he had one or two uncomfortable facts to disclose. He selected a day during the world series. I believe that the incident was covered in only a couple of paragraphs on inside pages.

The reporting of political news as such will be transcended in the next few years, in my judgment, by the reporting of economic news. That will have a great bearing on our politics. We are talking about tariff revision; we are talking about the financing of foreign countries through private capital; we are talking about farm relief. All are matters of economics. We face large economic problems of flood control, the use of water power, the development of inland waterways, government ownership in one form or another, the power of central government as contrasted with what the obligations and powers of the states ought to be. As the country grows more closely knit, as the telephone, telegraph, radio, air mail, make us a unit, so to speak—certainly a political unit—as we grow more and more homogeneous in our characteristics, these great economic problems will require the best thought that we can bring to bear through an impartial press.

LEGISLATORS AS NEWS SOURCES

—From *The Washington Correspondents,* copyright, 1937, by Leo C. Rosten. By permission of Harcourt, Brace & Company, Inc., pp. 78–83. Mr. Rosten made an on-the-scene survey of the Washington press corps in gathering the material for his book.

HANDOUTS and press conferences offer correspondents a steady supply of routine news. But the correspondent who wishes information of a more revealing nature is obliged to cultivate private news-sources. In this field the value of friendships with senators and representatives is very high. For many years, particularly before the inauguration of White House press conferences, senators were the chief sources of news in the capital. They are still invaluable. Senators are well-informed on the confidential aspects of political life because: (1) they have power over appointments and recommendations; (2) their committees are important incubators of news and news events; (3) senators often initiate action for legislation of interest to their home state or locality; (4) they have their own information machines among political dependents and those whom they have recommended for appointive offices. It is of the highest importance for a special correspondent to cultivate the senators from his state and maintain a friendly liaison with them. Since no correspondent has the time to make a daily canvass of all the agencies, departments, bureaus, and commissions in the capital, congressional figures of importance serve as excellent short cuts to the founts of information.

The special correspondent makes the rounds of his home delegation regularly. . . .

Most newspapermen in the capital develop fairly responsive contacts with from five to fifteen congressional leaders: generally, the legislators from their states and several members of key congressional committees. It is not necessary to court more than a few congressmen; the majority are poor news-sources because they are neither men of public interest nor occupants of important committee posts. But the competent correspondent has an "in" with at least one member of the House ways and means committee, one member of the Senate finance committee, one representative on the House appropriations committee, one on the Senate committee on foreign relations.

It is not difficult for a correspondent to get news from congressmen, however solemnly they may be sworn to secrecy. Newspaper publicity is the legislator's life-line, his most potent method of keeping "the folks back home" alert to his achievements and his stature. The congressman who has aspirations for re-election cannot afford to adopt a cavalier air to the newspaperman who controls the news which his constituents read. Magnus Johnson, former senator from Minnesota, once invaded the Senate press gallery and harangued the correspondents for some of the stories they had been writing. The press corps boycotted him. Stories about Senator Johnson suddenly ceased to appear. The political damage he suffered was inestimable.

The corps' boycott of ex-Senator Thomas Heflin was carried on with equal success after that statesman had indulged in some of his more offensive oratory.

There are professional, social, and personal bonds between legislators and newspapermen. Eleven congressmen are members of the National Press Club, and no less than forty-five have been, or still are, newspapermen. . . . It is natural to expect a common body of interests and experience between such men and the active journalists in the capital, and to find that the former have an understanding of newspaper practices and problems which is gratifying to the latter.

Many congressmen are friendly with certain newspapermen, play poker with them, meet them socially, and do not hesitate to offer them friendly tips. Many congressmen realize that correspondents are an incalculable aid in publicizing a program and bringing facts into prominence. The prominence of Fiorello LaGuardia when he was a representative from New York owed a great deal to the consistent publicity given to him and his work by Ray Tucker. The prestige of such figures as Senators Norris, Wagner, La Follette, and the late Bronson Cutting, or of representatives like Maury Maverick of Texas, owes much to the sympathetic treatment given their activities by correspondents who admire them and find them honest, intelligent, and conscientious public servants.

It is not unknown for Washington correspondents to put ideas into the heads of their political favorites and, sometimes, to put felicitous words into their mouths. A Washington correspondent may type out a statement and ask a statesman if he "would not like to say that for publication." In 1930 a correspondent for the Washington *Post* ran around the Senate getting endorsements for a vigorous personal campaign against the London naval conference.

The late Huey Long was first greeted in the capital with ridicule, but several correspondents were attracted to him and told Long that John J. Raskob and the late Senator Robinson were "selling out" the Democratic party to Wall Street. After several weeks of suggestion, during which Senator Long was impressed by the fact that he had the power to stampede the next Democratic convention, he began to ponder on his political position. Suddenly, to the surprise of everyone, Huey Long made political overtures to Senator Norris and launched a vigorous attack on Senator Robinson's leadership of the party.

Some congressmen feel under a psychological obligation to newspapers which have supported them in election campaigns, and are eager to curry favor with those whose support in future campaigns is uncertain. A congressman knows that papers which helped him can also help to defeat him. It is clear that the loquacity of legislators springs from a rational motivation.

After a secret committee meeting in which seventeen senators participated, two correspondents attempted, on a bet, to discover how many men they could coax into telling what had gone on in the conference. With no particular effort they succeeded in getting the salient facts from thirteen senators within one afternoon.

Congressional "leaks" are common. When President Hoover called in congressional leaders of both parties in June 1931, and received their advance approval for the moratorium he was planning to announce a week later, the story was being telegraphed to newspapers all over the country within a few hours. Mr. Hoover polled many members of Congress by telegram; the news broke more easily because of this.

The alertness of congressmen to favorable publicity for themselves and the programs in which they are interested may be seen in the manner in which congressional committee hearings are conducted. Paul Mallon has pointed out that the modern inquiry is arranged with an eye to providing a "hot story" regularly at noon each day, to give the afternoon papers a striking "lead," and another one late in the afternoon, to give the morning papers a fresh lead. He suggests that investigators are careful not to develop too many important points at once, but gauge their pace so as to hold the public's attention as long as possible.

PUBLICIZING ADMINISTRATIVE ACTIVITIES

—E. Pendleton Herring, *Public Administration and the Public Interest,* McGraw-Hill Book Company, Inc., 1936, pp. 362–367, 373–375. Mr. Herring was a professor of public administration at Harvard University when he wrote this material.

POPULAR GOVERNMENT rests on the assumption that the people are capable of passing a verdict for or against the administration in power. The accuracy of this verdict depends upon the public's knowledge of what the government has done or has failed to do. The judgment of many voters will turn upon some direct experience in dealing with the government. Their special interest in a limited phase of governmental activity may determine their opinion of the whole. The devices for bringing the individual into the governing process are limited, however. Despite the enormous growth of administrative agencies and services, the government is viewed by most people as a thing apart.

Official relations with the "public" turn largely upon the use that is made of the press and the radio. By the public is meant the populace viewed as a great undifferentiated mass. It was to that audience that President Roosevelt directed his fireside talks. Here, likewise, are the millions of newspaper readers who have been so sedulously courted by politicians and officials.

It is no accident that "public relations" have been a matter accorded great consideration during the Roosevelt administration. This problem is intimately linked with administration in the public interest. A government with positive objectives inevitably creates areas of hostility. The regulation of economic enterprises disrupts certain vested interests. The establishment of new services breaks into old habits, often introduces unwanted competition, and frequently incurs the midunderstanding of those to be served. As the government advances into new fields, it must be supported by general approval. This public sanction must more than outweigh the accumulation of petty irritations that official activities arouse among the interests that are dislodged. An administration that undertakes to interpret the general welfare in concrete terms must do two things: It must endeavor to win popular approval for its policies and it must watch the reaction to its proposals. . . .

This relationship between the government and the public in actual practice is narrowed down to contacts between a small group of officials and a small group of newspaper correspondents. Except when the President or other officials speak over the air, the public relations of national administration agencies are little more than the relations between 200 or so of the abler Washington correspondents and 200-odd public relations officials in the federal employ. For the run of routine news this is the picture. It must be modified on occasion to include the direct conferences of journalists with the President and leading administrators, but in the main the view of government presented to the public is the product of official publicity men within the government and the newspapermen stationed in the capital. To the latter governmental problems are all part of "the great game of politics," and it is the brilliant plays, the dodges, the fumbles, and the dramatics of conflict that they regard as most significant. The nature of political news is conceived in much the same terms as events in the world of sports.

Reporting must be a selective process. All the facts in any case can never be presented. Reporting "what really happened" means selecting the elements that seem significant to what the reporter believes is a "full understanding" of any given situation. What the public gets is determined by the subjective hunches of newspapermen as to what they think will titillate the reader's jaded interest. There is in Washington little conscious misrepresentation of fact, but there is the tendency to play up one aspect of certain events and to tone down another. This is natural and even inevitable. Official publicity men recognize this and act accordingly. Necessarily there is a relationship between the general policy of a bureau and the kind of news that is disseminated. Every federal bureau has its staff of experienced publicity men who determine the manner of presentation and the form of news concerning their bureau's activities. . . .

The present system makes for a generally favorable presentation of news concerning the departments. For the newspapermen, the easy course is that of acceptance without further investigation. If a Washington correspondent questions an official statement and wants more information, his questions will be answered. The government bureaus are careful to avoid any appearance of deception or secrecy relating to their activities. In fact, the press representatives are taken into the confidence of officials to an extraordinary degree. This trust is very rarely violated and the success of this relationship is recognized. But it is perhaps more useful to the government than to the press or to the public. To lock up news in a newshawk may disarm the reporter's suspicions, but it does not do the newspaper reader much good. To an extraordinary degree the bureaucracy has taken the newspapermen into its own camp. . . . Newspapermen, however, are not denied access to officials. Information is given out through one official, chiefly because this is a more efficient arrangement. Systematic contacts with the press and the public under the direction of competent and specially designated officers are a necessary and inevitable aspect of administration.

The extent and rapidity of the expansion and multiplication of administrative agencies have made the task of reporting so complicated that the average correspondent cannot cope with the problem. Only news agencies such as the Associated Press are able to designate special reporters to special beats. . . .

The nature of the news is often of such a technical character that it must be interpreted and explained if it is to be reported accurately and understandingly. The increased importance of experts in the government increases the need for publicity experts to interpret the technicians. Administrators well qualified for their special work may be very poorly qualified for dealing with the press. The public relations divisions within the federal bureaus are welcomed by the press, but they are also useful from the purely administrative viewpoint.

Official publicity men promote administrative efficiency by relieving other officials of the task of coping with reporters. Where an interview is sought, the journalist can be sent directly to the appropriate official without wasting the time of others in aimless inquiry. Important officials are available only at prearranged times. Subordinate officials are often frightened into silence by an inquiring reporter or stimulated into making unwise remarks for which the whole bureau is held responsible. Statements of policy, if they are to be authoritative, should come through a responsible source. Otherwise a bureau would find itself in an embarrassment of self-contradictions. The present confusion would be worse confounded if the existing divisions of information and public relations were abolished. . . .

Since the administrative branch is developing systematized and efficient publicity services, since this public-relations work is an inevitable outgrowth of social and technical advances, and since it is essential to efficient administration, it must be seriously reckoned with as a significant governmental development. Its power is great and its purpose generally justified. But its effect is to give the administration a disproportionate amount of influence in the formulation of public opinion. To restore a balance, the views of those in opposition should be brought clearly before the public.

This is a task that cannot be left entirely to those controlling the mediums of communication. They are the mere purveyors of what happens. They can be held to no definite responsibility for disclosing all sides of an issue. The press has not met the need. In fact, it is misleading to talk of the "press" as an entity that can be held responsible for intelligent criticism and leadership. There are thousands of newspapers, large and small, urban and rural, good and bad, according to individual value judgments. The dispatches of Washington correspondents must go through the hands of an editorial staff bound by their owners' policies and their own conceptions as to what is news. The press is a great business for the merchandising of facts, rumors, banalities, and ideals. The problem is one of building up somewhere within the government an opposition bench. What are the possibilities? One way to meet the problem is to organize systematic counter-publicity.

In the publicity division of the minority party is the starting point for developing an agency capable of at least meeting on their own grounds the publicity agencies of the federal administrative offices. Here the needed expert opinion in public relations management could be joined to the essential democratic duty of maintaining an opposition. . . .

The mistakes and abuses of the administration as well as the achievements and triumphs should be called strikingly to general attention. Coordinated criticism might ultimately lead to the presentation of a clear alternative and a constructive program on the part of the opposition. Intelligence and professional skill today characterize the public relations of federal administrative agencies. Before our official publicity work is developed further it is highly desirable that the other side of the picture be presented to the public with something approximating the efficiency with which the administrative branch reports its accomplishments to the press and to the public.

The proviso that there be an active opposition in no way weakens the argument that organized publicity is essential to administration in the public interest. As the federal government shoulders the task of economic recovery and the reform of abuses in the business world, the people must be made to understand what is happening. These responsibilities of government are too complex for the mass of voters to grasp in detail. But the principles must be made clear. Administrators will meet with misunderstanding unless the President and his politically responsible aides explain in clear and simple language the objectives of the administration.

THE PRESS AND THE VOTERS

—James B. Reston, "The Failure of the Press," *Nieman Reports*, Vol. 3, January 1949, p. 17. Mr. Reston writes on national and international affairs for the New York *Times*.

(EDITORS' NOTE. *When Harry S. Truman defeated Thomas E. Dewey in the 1948 presidential election, his victory came as an almost overwhelming surprise to all newspaper readers who had followed election forecasts and public opinion polls published in the press; both had confidently predicted a Dewey victory. The upset prompted Mr. Reston to write the following letter to his employer, the editor of the New York* Times.)

Before we in the newspaper business spend all our time and energy analyzing Governor Dewey's failure in the election, maybe we ought to try to analyze our own failure. For that failure is almost as spectacular as the President's victory, and the quicker we admit it the better off we'll be.

There were certain factors in this election that were known (and discounted) by almost every political reporter. We knew about the tradition that a defeated candidate had never been nominated and elected after his defeat. We knew that the national income was running at a rate of $210 billions a year, that over 61,000,000 persons were employed at unprecedentedly high wages, and that the people had seldom if ever turned against the Administration in power at such a time.

We knew also that this prosperity applied not only to the people in the industrial areas but to the people on the farms as well; we knew that the small towns of the country had, during the war, become more industrialized and therefore more sensitive to the influences of organized labor.

We were, moreover, conscious of the fact that a whole generation had grown up under the strong influences of the Roosevelt era; that there were (and are) more poor people in this country than rich people; that personality is a force in American politics equally as strong as principles; and that the American people have always loved a fighter.

Yet while reporters on the Truman and Dewey campaign trains discussed all these points, each in his own way (including this reporter) was carried away by facts he did not verify, by theories he did not fully examine, and by assumptions he did not or could not check.

In a way our failure was not unlike Mr. Dewey's: we overestimated the tangibles and underestimated the intangibles; we relied too much on techniques of reporting which are no longer foolproof; just as he was too isolated with other politicians, so we were too isolated with other reporters; and we, too, were far too impressed by the tidy statistics of the polls.

What happens when a reporter goes out to "cover" an election?

Usually he does one of two things: he goes on the campaign train or he goes out on his own to the various state capitals. If he goes on the train, he is usually so busy reporting what the great man says that he has no time for anything else. If he goes to the state capital, he usually spends his time interviewing the political managers and the political reporters, all of whom usually get their information from somebody else and place enormous confidence on the so-called scientific polls.

In short, neither on the train nor in the capitals do we spend much time wandering around talking to the people. We tend to assume that somebody else is doing the original reporting in that area, and if the assumptions of the political managers, or the other reporters, or the polls are wrong (as they were in this campaign), then our reports are wrong.

The great intangible of this election was the political influence of the Roosevelt era on the thinking of the nation. It was less dramatic than the antics of Messrs. Wallace and Thurmond, but in the long run it was more important and we didn't give enough weight to it. Consequently we were wrong not only on the election, but, what's worse, on the whole political direction of our time.

REVIEW QUESTIONS AND ASSIGNMENTS

1. What changes have resulted from the way the press sees government as a result of Roosevelt's New Deal and Truman's Fair Deal?

2. Describe the problems faced by a political writer on a daily newspaper. How, for example, can he distinguish between news and propaganda in reporting politics?

3. Interview a politician in your community with the idea of testing him as a news source. The interview might be based on his reaction to several community problems.

4. Write a brief essay summarizing your concept of the responsibility of the press in the American party system.

5. From what you know of news evaluation, how would you explain the charge that the press usually stresses the seemingly superficial actions of legislatures?

6. Do you believe that the prestige of Congress suffers as a result of the manner in which legislative actions are reported?

7. Follow the radio broadcasts of a political commentator for two weeks and write an evaluation of the possible influence of his remarks.

8. Do you think that there are too many "dope stories" published relative to possible congressional activities?

9. Assume that you are the editor of a paper in a city of 100,000 population, and write a summary of the position you would take relative to your paper's handling of legislative news.

10. Would you favor televised broadcasts of sessions of Congress?

11. What would constitute an ideal relationship between the White House and press representatives?

12. How might the press improve its coverage of administrative activities?

13. Do you feel that the press tends to build up political leaders in the minds of the public?

14. What responsibility do you feel the media have in the promotion of better citizenship?

ADDITIONAL REFERENCES

Allen, Robert S., *Our Sovereign State,* Vanguard Press, 1949.

Andrews, Bert, *Washington Witch Hunt,* Random House, 1948.

Catlin, George E. G., "Propaganda as a Function of Democratic Government," in *Propaganda and Dictatorship,* Harwood L. Childs (editor), Princeton University Press, 1936.

Chamberlain, Joseph P., *Legislative Processes,* Appleton-Century, 1936.

Childs, Marquis W., *I Write from Washington,* Harper & Brothers, 1942.

Corey, Herbert, "The Presidents and the Press," *The Saturday Evening Post,* Vol. 204, January 9, 1932, p. 25.

Crawford, Nelson A., *Ethics of Journalism,* F. S. Crofts, 1924.

Dewey, John, *The Public and Its Problems,* Henry Holt, 1927.

Flanders, Ralph E., *The American Century,* Harvard University Press, 1950.

Furman, Bess, *Washington By-Line,* Alfred A. Knopf, 1949.

Garvin, Katharine, *J. L. Garvin: A Memoir,* 1948, William Heinemann, London.

Graves, W. Brooke (editor), *Readings in Public Opinion,* Appleton-Century, 1928.

Hanson, Lawrence, *Government and the Press,* Oxford University Press, 1936.

Kobre, Sidney, *Backgrounding the News,* Twentieth Century Press, 1939.

Laski, Harold J., "The Recovery of Citizenship," *Century,* Vol. 118, July 1929, pp. 257–269.

Lippmann, Walter, *Public Opinion,* Macmillan, 1922.

Milton, George F., "The Responsibility of the Press in a Democracy," *The American Political Science Review,* Vol. 30, August 1936, pp. 681–690.

Mott, Frank Luther, "Newspapers in Presidential Campaigns," *Public Opinion Quarterly,* Vol. 8, 1944, pp. 348–367.

Phillips, Cabell, and others, *Dateline: Washington,* Doubleday, 1949.

Pollard, James E., *The Presidents and the Press,* Macmillan, 1947.

Salmon, Lucy, *The Newspaper and Authority,* Oxford University Press, 1923.

Salter, John T., *Boss Rule,* McGraw-Hill, 1935.

Smith, A. Merriman, *A President Is Many Men,* Harper & Brothers, 1948.

Vance, Earl L., "The News: Fourth Dimension of Education," *Bulletin of the American Association of University Professors,* Vol. 34, Autumn 1948.

Wilson, F. G., *The Elements of Modern Politics,* McGraw-Hill, 1936.

11. THE PRESS AND WORLD INFORMATION

INTRODUCTION

When President Franklin Delano Roosevelt went before the Congress on January 6, 1941, to deliver his annual message on the state of the nation, he looked beyond the then rising tide of Nazi aggression and issued an appeal for a better world in the future. President Roosevelt included in his address a challenge to all nations to labor for the achievement of four essential freedoms. "The first," he declared, "is freedom of speech and expression—everywhere in the world." The others were freedom of worship, freedom from want, and freedom from fear.

The first freedom represents one of the most perplexing problems ever to face both government and press. It is a question of long standing; World War II and its aftermath merely provided another test. The basic question was and is: Can we make the necessary adjustments to permit information to be a truly effective tool in the achievement not only of a lasting peace but also of a secure and orderly world community? The question is in the minds of all men. All admit the desirability of a satisfactory answer. The part the press plays in the drama represents a responsibility of staggering proportions.

During the war years many individuals and groups took steps aimed at the achievement of improvement in the flow of world news once victory and peace were secure. Kent Cooper, general manager of the Associated Press, and Hugh Baillie, president of United Press, asked the government to be mindful of the desirability of world freedom of information, freedom of access to news sources, and equality among correspondents in news transmission when the time came to write peace settlements. The American Society of Newspapers Editors and other press groups agreed. Congress and many state assemblies passed resolutions asking the elimination of all barriers in the interchange of news. Both major parties included supporting planks in their 1944 platforms. The United States Department of State went along and after the close of the war became an active participant in the dissemination of news through its "Voice of America" shortwave broadcasts. Everyone agreed that if the peoples of all nations possessed an accurate picture of unfolding world affairs the likelihood of a World War III would be considerably diminished if not entirely eliminated.

Despite excellent spade work by a number of commissions and committees, the United Nations has found it impossible to agree on a set of principles that might be used as the basis for a workable program of free world news exchange. The General Assembly, meeting at Lake Success, New York, in October of 1949, voted to table a half-completed convention on Freedom of Information because of "deep disagreement" over contents of the pact.

The inability of the United Nations to work out a satisfactory program during its early years was the result of a number of conflicts of such a fundamental nature as to encourage despair among even the most optimistic supporters of the idea of a world press treaty. It may prove helpful to enumerate certain of these conflicts in the form of questions, which must be answered before the problem can be solved:

1. What can be done to eliminate the barriers—control of facilities, censorship, language differences, and varying political beliefs—that still stand as the classic impediments in the exchange of information?

2. How can state-controlled press systems, such as the ones in Russia and her satellites, be made effective partners of systems, such as those of America and Britain, that enjoy great traditions of freedom?

3. Is it possible to project the doctrine of freedom of the press to the world level? The Soviet Union's conception of press freedom is at sharp variance with that of the United States. Who, then, is to define freedom in a manner acceptable to all nations?

4. Will all national press systems be able to agree on a self-policing principle which would be a protection for the world community against tendentious reporting and propaganda?

5. What is the proper role of the American government in the situation? How much control, for example, should the government exercise over the privately-owned and highly competitive news-gathering associations?

6. What can be done to assure greater equality of access to transmission channels?

Meanwhile, until these questions are replaced by solutions, the American press faces the task of reporting and interpreting world affairs with clear and enlightened understanding of the influence of the printed and spoken word on opinion in this country on postwar issues of gravest import. The owners and managers of the media must be cognizant of the fact that any evidence of irresponsible journalism in an Atomic Age may encourage not merely war but chaos.

There is need for the press to demonstrate its ability to take the long-range view, to go behind surface events, to avoid easy confusion of terms, and to present the conflicts of personalities in their true setting.

WORLD-WIDE FREEDOM OF INFORMATION

—Report of the United States Delegates, *United Nations Conference on Freedom of Information*, U. S. Department of State Publication 3150, Government Printing Office, 1948.

(EDITORS' NOTE: *Pursuant to Resolution 74 of the Fifth Session of the Economic and Social Council, the United Nations Conference on Freedom of Information met at the European Headquarters of the United Nations, Geneva, Switzerland, during the period 23 March to 21 April, 1948. The conference, with the Russian bloc of six nations abstaining, adopted the following resolution dealing with the fundamental principles of world-wide freedom of information in the postwar world.*)

WHEREAS Freedom of Information is a fundamental right of the people, and is the touchstone of all the freedoms to which the United Nations is dedicated, without which world peace cannot well be preserved; and

Freedom of information carries the right to gather, transmit, and disseminate news anywhere and everywhere without fetters; and

Freedom of information depends for its validity upon the availability to the people of a diversity of sources of news and of opinion; and

Freedom of information further depends upon the willingness of the press and other agencies of information to employ the privileges derived from the people without abuse, and to accept and comply with the obligations to seek the facts without prejudice and to spread knowledge without malicious intent; and

Freedom of information further depends upon the effective enforcement of recognized responsibilities.

The United Nations Conference on Freedom of Information Resolves, therefore,

1. That everyone shall have the right to freedom of thought and expression: this shall include freedom to hold opinions without interference; and to seek, receive and impart information and ideas by any means and regardless of frontiers;

2. That the right of news personnel to have the widest possible access to the sources of information, to travel unhampered in pursuit thereof, and to transmit copy without unreasonable or discriminatory limitations, should be guaranteed by action on the national and international plane;

3. That the exercise of these rights should be limited only by recognition of and respect for the rights of others, and the protection afforded by law to the freedom, welfare, and security of all;

4. That in order to prevent abuses of freedom of information, governments in so far as they are able should support measures which will help to improve the quality of information and to make a diversity of news and opinion available to the people;

5. That it is the moral obligation of the press and other agencies of information to seek the truth and report the facts, thereby contributing to the solution of the world's problems through the free interchange of information bearing on them, promoting respect for human rights and fundamental freedoms without discrimination, fostering understanding and co-operation between peoples, and helping maintain international peace and security;

6. That this moral obligation, under the spur of public opinion, can be advanced through organizations and associations of journalists and through individual news personnel;

7. That encouragement should be given to the establishment and to the functioning within the territory of a State of one or more nonofficial organizations of persons employed in the collection and dissemination of information to the public, and that such organization or organizations should encourage the fulfillment *inter alia* of the following obligations by all individuals or organizations engaged in the collection and dissemination of information;

(a) To report facts without prejudice and in their proper context and to make comments without malicious intent;

(b) To facilitate the solution of the economic, social and humanitarian problems of the world as a whole through the free interchange of information bearing on such problems;

(c) To help promote respect for human rights and fundamental freedoms without discrimination;

(d) To help maintain international peace and security;

(e) To counteract the spreading of intentionally false or distorted reports which promote hatred or prejudice against States, persons or groups of different race, language, religion or philosophical conviction;

8. That observance of the obligations of the press and other agencies of information, except those of a recognized legal nature, can also be effectively advanced by the people served by these instrumentalities, provided that news and opinion reach them through a diversity of sources and that the people have adequate means of obtaining and promoting a better performance from the press and other agencies of information.

BARRIERS IMPEDING WORLD NEWS FLOW

—Llewellyn White and Robert D. Leigh, *Peoples Speaking to Peoples,* University of Chicago Press, 1946, pp. 64–71. Mr. Leigh served as director and Mr. White as assistant director of the Commission on Freedom of the Press.

WHAT ARE the artificial barriers that impede the flow across national borders of informational raw materials? The shortcomings of the present telecommunications systems have been stressed. Obviously, the most reliable news service in the world cannot reach those who are not reached by cable or wireless; the finest magazines and books and pictures cannot reach those who are not reached by fast plane.

Virtually every nation now forbids foreign radiotelegraph companies the right to maintain their own receiving facilities within its borders. The result is that local companies, usually government owned or controlled, supply reception and internal distribution facilities at whatever rates they can command, with further delays in transmission. Although this situation does not involve multiple address newscasts or shortwave voice broadcasts (except for automatic relay points) and although radiotelephone has worked out relatively satisfactory reciprocal arrangements for international traffic, it is a serious handicap not only to "trunk-line" news transmissions between two points but also to commercial-message traffic. *What is indicated here is a multilateral agreement, binding all nations to permit authorized wireless telegraph and cable companies (and airlines as well) to maintain suitable terminal facilities wherever they are required, subject only to the regulations binding domestic companies, or to maintain nondiscriminatory two-way connections between its own and foreign companies, as has been developed for wireless telephony.* The Bermuda agreements marked a step in this direction.

The need for automatic wireless relay points has been mentioned. These could be obtained through year-to-year leasing of foreign-owned facilities. But wartime experience with this device has shown that long-time control of the relay transmitters by the sender is the only completely satisfactory solution short of the setting-up of international relay points to be operated under the control of an international telecommunications union. Pending the more ideal solution, which does not appear to be immediately realizable, *a sound proposal would seem to involve bilateral treaties giving those nations which require relay points extra-territorial privileges under long-term lease.*

Access at the Source

Meantime, there are other and more serious barriers to the free flow of informational raw materials across national frontiers. Discrimination and censorship are the two broad headings that cover those evils of which foreign correspondents (and natives, too, for that matter) most often complain. What do newspapermen mean by these terms?

In Nazi Germany reporters could not wander about at will, writing of what they saw and felt. Doktor Goebbels and his press section gave them stereotyped handouts, took them on stereotyped trips. The parts of Germany and German-occupied lands that they did not see were the special province not merely of German newsmen but of "reliable" German newsmen. The defeat of Germany brought an end to Goebbels; but correspondents may face precisely the same type of discrimination, in varying degree, for a long time to come in Russia and the Russian "spheres" in Europe and Asia and in Spain, China, various Latin-American countries, Saudi Arabia, and certain parts of the British, French, Belgian, and Netherlands empires.

It is characteristic of the one-party type of government to fear criticism and to make provisions to exclude it, on the pious ground that not all reporters have the mental capacity to criticize fairly. This is the antithesis of the democratic view. Experience in the United States, Canada, the United Kingdom, Australia and New Zealand, France, Belgium, the Netherlands, Denmark, Norway, Sweden, and Switzerland has built up a reassuring body of evidence that unfair critics sooner or later defeat their own purposes. It may be useless to try to convince Russia and the others that this is so. The Russians already have made it clear that they think Americans and Britons are foolish to permit newsmen so much freedom, and they can quote more than one instance of our newsmen's harmful irresponsibility. Reminders from friendly British and American newspapermen that secrecy in itself is likely to breed unwarranted suspicion and give rise to imaginative "news stories" about Russia of the familiar type which, in the twenties and thirties, usually bore Riga datelines apparently do not move the Narkomindell.

This is a problem that will have to be faced and solved. For no news coverage that includes only the "official" versions of events in Russia, Poland, Rumania, Bulgaria, Yugoslavia, Spain, China, Argentina, Iran, Syria and the Lebanon, Palestine, Arabia, Algeria, Tunisia, Morocco, French Equatorial Africa, the Congo, British India, the Malay States, the Netherland Indies, and Indo-China can pretend to the labels "global" or "complete." The problem is not made easier by the fact that everyone knows that the so-called "free-press" countries sometimes preach more zealously than they practice. Britain, for instance, is a conspicuous example of the paradox that distinguishes between the mother-country and its more "backward" dependencies. However much freedom a newspaperman, foreign or native, may enjoy in the British Isles, the moment he sets foot in India he is in another world. The same contrast is noticeable as between metropolitan France and, say, Syria. Even the benevolent and highly democratic Dutch become "security"-minded when a roving newsman debarks at Batavia or Willemstad.

This is not to say that discrimination was never the practice in the mother-countries. In pre-1939 Britain, France, and many another land by tradition devoted to the principle of a free press, it was not uncommon for government officials to show marked preference to a few hand-picked native reporters and even fewer foreigners. The London papers, for instance, felt the pressure of the Chamberlain government during the appeasement period and responded to it to some extent. The Germans made an effort to systematize this practice. Prior to World War I, a Foreign Office press chief named Hammann was permitted to organize a loose affiliation of a few chosen German newspapermen to "interpret" German foreign policy to the German people. The plan does not appear to have been an unqualified success, in part because newspapers which were left out tended to become even more critical and also because the favored few, which happened to include liberal Opposition papers, frequently declined to follow the official line.

The Hammann technique *per se* will not be tolerated by most newspapermen. But favoritism for individuals (and sometimes even for groups) is widely practiced not only by all governments (including our own) but by private corporations and individuals as well. Actually, newspapermen connive at forming such useful contacts. Indeed, one suspects that the clamor against discrimination of this sort is loudest from those who have been outwitted by it. It becomes impressive only when, as in Russia, it affects all foreigners equally and thus becomes an instrument of anti-internationalism. It is less impressive when newspapermen roll the phrase "equal and unhampered access to all" off their tongues; for every newspaperman must know that equal access would reduce every story to a mass press conference or a mimeographed handout.

What newspapermen really want is what Kent Cooper, executive director of A.P., calls "the right to roam the world at will, writing freely of what they see and feel." This is quite a different thing. It means that what they want is an equal opportunity to use their wits to create *unequal* access. Within that rather broad framework, they want assurances that certain areas will not be open habitually to the few and closed to the many; that news-givers will carefully distinguish between timely news breaks and background material and will confine their special favors to the latter field; and that in the case of "hold-for-release" stories the release date will be scrupulously respected. Newsmen are not always sure even of these things, for in essence these things represent a compromise between the ever warring considerations of security and opportunity that beset anyone engaged in highly competitive private industry. Sorely tempted, a New York *Times's* Raymond Daniell will join a pool to receive Army favors; a New York *Herald Tribune's* Theodore Wallen will beseech a Calvin Coolidge to make an "I do not choose to run" news break exclusive; an A.P.'s Edward Kennedy will double-cross his colleagues by breaking a release date. In sum, carte blanche is the maximum that newsmen dream about, equality of opportunity the minimum for which they will settle.

Either is, of course, more difficult of achievement than mere equal access. Both suggest the need for a degree of organized responsibility on the part of newsmen from which they shrink, using the excuse that freedom of the press does not permit of much self-discipline. The apparent paradox has been shrewdly remarked by the Russians; and there is reason to believe that, as long as it persists, it will be a convenient barrier for Moscow to raise against the democracies in the field of international communication. To press for mass interviews and stereotyped handouts, simply because Russia would be more likely to grant such a demand than any other, would be a disservice alike to the correspondents and to their readers. One is tempted to conclude that any deviation from the expressed ultimate goal of "the right to roam the world at will" would lend credence to Moscow's charge that what the newsmen of the democracies are after is simply a chance to make a little more money. A more honorable strategy would appear to be to hold out for the maximum while admonishing the correspondents to grow up to it and, at the same time, frankly recognize that unsettled conditions during the next few years will not be conducive to achievement of the maximum. *This would seem to involve urging a multilateral accord guaranteeing equality of access as between nationals and foreigners*—knowing that the more enterprising in both categories would use that type of equality to get ahead of their fellows.

How, in the meantime, could those who wish to roam the world and write (or photograph) meet the objection of irresponsibility? *One way might be to tighten the foreign correspondents' corps; adopt a code of professional behavior; and require all newsmen, magazine writers, radio people, authors, and photographers who join the corps to observe its code. Appeals from decisions of a government could be taken by the whole corps rather than by an individual, either to the foreign diplomatic corps or to an appropriate unit of the United Nations Economic and Social Council, described later in this report.* A resolute move in this direction might dispose of the contradiction of newsmen asking for group protection while at the same time declining to organize group responsibility.

Censorship

The right to roam the world at will, writing freely, would seem to imply also the right to get what is written to the market. Here we run into another barrier—censorship. Actually, censorship begins at the level of discrimination at the source. But in general usage it is taken to mean the emasculation or total suppression of written and printed matter, pictures and films, and words spoken over a microphone or telephone.

Here, again, the authoritarian powers have been the worst offenders. Before the war, Russia, China, Spain, Portugal, Italy, Germany, Japan, and a number of Latin-American countries openly practiced deletion and suppression. But they did not practice it in the same way. Whereas in Russia correspondents were summoned to discuss cuts and suppressions with the censor who had made them and on occasion were even able to argue him into restoring some of them, in Italy they never knew until they had a chance to check with their home offices from outside what had got through.

More than frank and open censorship itself, newsmen detest the subtler forms. In a sense they have become hardened to a degree of the forthright variety (when a government or corporation official becomes a censor); but the honest, conscientious ones will never become resigned to a mixture of censorship, evasion, intimidation, and deceit. They do not like being visited by police who want to "check their papers." They do not like being beaten up in dark alleys. They do not like having their dispatches lie around in telegraph offices until, like ripe fruit, they have lost all market value. They do not like having their houses searched, their families annoyed or terrorized. They do not like clumsy offers of bribes or subtle hints that they might last longer if they were "more correct." But what they like least of all is being forever in the dark, never knowing what the "rules" are, always wondering when they go to work in the morning what they will be able to "get away with" on that particular day.

What can be done to abolish, or at any rate curb, censorship? *A logical first step might be to press for a multilateral agreement pledging the signatories to keep newsmen informed of the rules by which they expect to operate and to abide by them.* If such an agreement could be reached, the climate might encourage *a second and simultaneous step: agreement to limit censorship wherever and as long as it exists to the open deletion or suppression of dispatches in the presence of the writer.* There is little reason to suppose that Russia, which appears to be the key to any multilateral agreement of this sort, would refuse to adhere to either of these provisions. At a favorable moment Moscow might even subscribe to a *third condition: right of appeal by the writer to the correspondents' corps and through it to the United Nations Economic and Social Council.* Meantime, with the ultimate goal of complete abolition of censorship always before us, we could whittle away at the Russian variety, *either through limited multilateral agreement or through a series of bilateral treaties* —although it must be obvious that the former would almost certainly be interpreted by Russia as a revived manifestation of the *cordon sanitaire.*

Barriers in Distribution

The right to roam and write would seem to imply not only the right to get to the market what is written but also the right to sell it there without unjust discrimination. This brings us to another barrier: insistence on interposing a middleman (usually government-controlled) between the wholesaler (press association, news-picture agency, or feature syndicate) and the retailer (newspaper, magazine, or radio station). A.P., U.P., I.N.S., Reuter, A.M.S.A., and A.F.P. have recently announced that henceforth they will deal only with reputable individual newspapers, magazines, and radio stations or with bona fide associations of reputable newspapers, magazines, and radio stations. Anesta of the Netherlands, the Swedish Tigningarnas Telegrambyraa, and several other European agencies are expected to fall into line with this stern decision, aimed at preventing the reappearance of anything like Havas or the old Reuter. *Except for bilateral pacts, which would have the effect of blessing such arrangements,* it is difficult to see what might be accomplished by formal convention at this time, since, obviously, those who wish to do business in Russia and China will be obliged to deal with government agencies, as A.P. and Reuter are doing. One factor which ought to do much to discourage middleman monopolies is multiple-address newscasting, which will bring uncensored news to the very borders of monopoly-ridden countries—and even enable the more daring publishers there, by listening in, to check what their governments give them against what the rest of the world is getting.

THE ROLE OF GOVERNMENT IN WORLD NEWS

—Arthur W. Macmahon, *The Postwar International Information Program of the United States,* U.S. Department of State Publication 2438, Government Printing Office, 1945, pp. 2–5. Dr. Macmahon, for many years professor of public law at Columbia University, wrote this memorandum while serving as a consultant to the State Department.

THE UNITED STATES GOVERNMENT and specifically the State Department cannot be indifferent to the ways in which our society is portrayed in other countries. The reasons for this concern need only be mentioned. From the standpoint of security, there are the advantages of peace-disposing friendship. At the very least, knowledge about us strengthens the potentialities of alliance. Trade with the United States is helped by an acquaintance with its technology and with its ways of life generally. Granted that eschew what some have called cultural imperialism and properly seek to avoid undue dislocation of the mores of other societies, we would be a decadent people if we did not wish others to know about American standards and techniques—in health, for example—that demonstrably have contributed to human happiness. An outstanding lesson of the last decade is that liberty must believe in itself and that tolerance does not mean indifference.

The concern of the Government is even more pointed. Foreign affairs are relations between peoples, not simply governments. Governmental spokesmen do not address foreign officials only but also the populaces behind them. The overtures of international policies are often items in the press, for example, not diplomatic notes. National spokesmen sometimes speak to other peoples merely by allowing themselves to be overheard when they speak to their own citizens. Sometimes the appeal is more direct and openly avowed.

A collaborative foreign policy, especially, must be open, proclaimed, and popular at home and abroad. The foreign policy of the United States is essentially collaborative. Information about such a policy can be extraterritorial without infringing the rights of other peoples. These facts are the basis of an information policy in both its domestic and overseas phases. Especially in a world of almost instantaneous communicability, foreign policies are formulated and must be viewed in the light of national mores and character. If the policies are to be correctly understood and acted upon in other countries, the peoples of the latter must be aware of the national characteristics that are indispensable to the interpretation of the policies in question.

The United States as a society gains by being truthful about itself in its foreign information. Especially is there need to make other peoples aware of what is broadly characteristic, not exceptional and extreme. The country will be helped by a portrayal of itself which is candid and complete enough to show that, far from being a land of universal wealth and material ease, the United States has problems of poverty and maladjustment. In the past, the picture too often has excited an envy that has been offset only by the extent to which elements in the seeming representation have afforded foreign populations an excuse for despising us as a people.

A candid and reasonably complete national self-portrayal implies certain standards. First, the information must be truthful; it must be balanced, not distorted. Secondly, there must be enough of it sufficiently widely distributed, to convey understanding among the opinion-forming groups in other countries and to an increasing degree among the masses. Third, the information must be conveyed tactfully, for this conditions its effectiveness in securing a reception and its success in promoting attitudes favorable to harmonious international relations.

The peacetime role of the United States Government in striving to attain the foregoing standards of international informational activity should be cautious and limited but positive. It should be cautious and limited for a variety of reasons. The United States does not wish to stimulate competition in foreign governmental publicity. This is true partly because of the relative strength of the private facilities of information based in the United States. In one sense, indeed, the United States would be the gainer if all governments would retire from direct informational activities. But the reasons for avoiding any invitation to intergovernmental competition are deeper, resting upon the ideal of a spontaneous flow of truthful information throughout the world not trammeled or distorted by any self-protective government or group. Until agreements are reached that establish basic standards of fair conduct by governments when they engage in informational activity, increased intergovernmental competition will sharpen nationalistic feeling and, lacking settled standards against which to judge it, will be attended by a progressive worsening of international conduct in this field. The United States would almost certainly be a loser in such intergovernmental competition, being handicapped in this respect by traditions of free enterprise, legislative responsibility, and related factors. We are aware, too, of the value of interested reception that results from a knowledge of the diverse ownership of the media in the United States.

But the role of the United States Government must be positive while it remains cautious and limited. A self-denying attitude on the part of the United States Government will not stop the activities of other governments in the post-war world. The answer to competition is not unilateral disarmament. Nor can the desired international flow of knowledge be secured negatively, merely by agreements about what governments promise not to do. The complications in the way of an all-inclusive international agreement about "freedom of the press" and the like will be examined in the second part of this memorandum. Even if sweeping guarantees can be established, it will not follow automatically that the various private facilities, such as the news agencies, will secure a satisfactorily wide-spread coverage. Such coverage requires cheap and universal communication facilities, suited to news needs, and the incentive to use them. Besides, commercial information services may not supply the background which lends perspective and conduces to a fair understanding of day-to-day episodes.

Broadly stated, the role of the United States Government, being at once limited and positive, must be supplementary and facilitative. The scope of such a role and its organizational implications are found by considering, as to the several media and related institutions, how satisfactory are the conditions for adequate national self-portrayal among all peoples. The analysis includes the institutions (both commercial and non-profit) which are based on the printing press (the publishing industries, the news agencies, and foreign reporting as a profession); wire communications as an adjunct; radio and the methods of recording and reproducing sound; and the camera and the screen (including motion pictures, film strips, and still pictures for the press and for exhibit). As to the coverage in each case, it is necessary to distinguish (1) the adequacy with which knowledge of other peoples is brought to the United States, and (2) the adequacy of the knowledge about the United States that goes abroad, considered both as to its fullness and fairness and as to the completeness of its distribution throughout the world.

This memorandum stresses the outward flow of information from this country. There are reasons for such emphasis. Relatively speaking, the United States imports through the various media more information than is the case with most countries. In addition, other governments are free to establish official information services in the United States and many will continue to avail themselves of such access after the war. The desirability of reciprocity and a two-way flow of international understanding is of course assumed. The reception abroad of information about the United States is helped by a sense in other countries that our people are aware of their life and achievements.

THE PROBLEM IN REPORTING WORLD NEWS

—James B. Reston, "Reporting on Foreign Affairs," *Nieman Reports*, Vol. 3, July 1949, p. 4.

If we in the newspaper business are to raise questions about whether the government and other institutions are meeting the challenge of the time, we should certainly raise the same question about newspapers.

The question we have raised here is whether those who have the responsibility for explaining the foreign policy of the United States are keeping pace with the requirements of what is an unprecedented and even revolutionary foreign policy for America. I have suggested that responsible officials and representatives in the executive and legislative branches of the government have not kept pace. I suggest that the newspapers have not kept pace either.

Again the question is not whether we have made progress but whether we have made adequate progress. Of course, we have made progress in the past decade. The coverage of foreign policy news in the American papers is more detailed, better informed, and in truer perspective than it was in 1939. Like the White House, the Congress and the State Department, however, we too are often the prisoners of old techniques and prejudices, which color our judgment of what is news, and how it should be written and displayed.

The news we have to report and explain these days is not only more important because of America's decisive role in the world, but it is more intricate and many-sided. It does not fit easily into the short news story with the punch lead. It often defies accurate definition in very short space. Very often it rebels against our passion for what is bright and brief.

Nevertheless, we still have a tendency to make this complex modern news conform to our old techniques. It is a natural reaction—space is limited and type will not stretch—but you cannot often make an intricate debate on the European Recovery Program sparkle without distorting the whole picture.

In the past, we in the newspaper business have been satisfied too often with reporting the literal truth instead of the essential truth. It may be literally true to report that "Ten Soviet Yak fighter planes roared into the American airlift corridor today outside of Berlin," but if you do not also report that the corridor is twenty miles wide, that the fighters didn't come near our cargo planes and that the incident was only the eighteenth reported in some 10 months and 200,000 cargo flights into the former German capital, you do not report the essential truth.

The bright, the startling, the bold, the sharp and the clear simple facts may make the most interesting reading; they may be "literally true"; but unfortunately, the material we have to report in this field is not always simple or bright or startling, though it may be vital to men's lives and therefore important and newsworthy.

We have no right, therefore, to twist the mass of facts into forms which are exciting but misleading; to take out of it that portion that conforms to our prejudices, to preserve the shocking or amusing, and leave out the dreary but important qualifications which are necessary to essential truth.

Our preoccupation with what happens today, like our passion for the bold and simple, also often minimizes our value as reporters and recorders of great events. If a detailed study of the economy of Europe or the state of the Federal government is released on a Tuesday afternoon, our tendency is to skim it, summarize it briefly and forget it Tuesday night. Wednesday's news may be a compilation of trivia; it may be far less important than the ill-digested document of Tuesday, but because it happened on Wednesday, we tend to devote all our space to it and abandon the more important question of the day before.

There is another aspect of this today-angle story. It often happens these days that government decisions are taken in private and never reported until some official decides that everything is buttoned up and ready for publication. By that time, however, government commitments may be taken and disclosure cannot lead to objective appraisal by the nation.

Sometimes this is essential, but sometimes it is not. The veto in the United Nations charter was negotiated in private. A commitment was taken by our government to support that veto at the San Francisco conference. By the time an announcement was made about the veto, it was difficult to have an objective debate about it without repudiating the government and embarrassing the President in his conduct of foreign policy.

The time for enterprising reporting in that case was not after the announcement was made but before the commitment was taken. The same thing was true during the negotiations on the text of the North Atlantic Treaty. In that case, Senators Connally and Vandenberg objected in a private meeting with Secretary of State Acheson about making any reference in the treaty to the possibility of using military force against an aggressor. On their objection, the reference was struck out. This fact, however, was ferreted out; a public debate ensued, which indicated that there was considerable opposition to the timid position of the Senators, and in the end, the reference was restored, with their consent.

I am not arguing for less aggressive reporting. Nor am I arguing, believe me, that only the irresponsible can be bright, and that to be accurate you must be dull. I am arguing for a more modern test of what is news; I am arguing for keeping on top of these momentous foreign policy developments while they are developing and not merely after they are announced; for the reporting of ideas as well as the reporting of action; for the explanation of intricate and fundamental issues, even if they have no gee whiz angle.

Good enterprising reporting of ideas on basic issues can in many cases be as important as the reporting of action. The decisive point in many great events comes long before the event happens. It comes in what the diplomats call the "exploratory phase," when influential officials and legislators are making up their minds what they are going to do. The Marshall Plan was a great story in Washington before General Marshall ever heard about it. Few papers, however, paid any attention to it because "it was just an idea." In fact, the idea behind it was all laid out in a speech made by Dean Acheson weeks before General Marshall ever announced the plan at Harvard, and the only paper in the world, to my knowledge, that carried the text of that speech was the *Times* of London.

It will take a conscious effort on the part of those who run newspapers to meet the new responsibilities imposed on us by the new responsibilities of our country. The problem, I suggest, is not that anybody in the business is willfully trying to mislead the public or distort the truth. The problem is that we are busily engaged, like Congressmen, and State Department officials, and even Presidents, in acting the way we have always acted, in using techniques we have always used, without asking whether they are the best techniques for America today.

THE ADVANTAGE ENJOYED BY RADIO

—William Benton, "Shortwave Broadcasting and the News," *Journalism Quarterly,* Vol. 23, June 1946, pp. 157–159. Mr. Benton was an assistant secretary of state and, as such, in charge of the "Voice of America" program when he wrote this article.

THE ABILITY of shortwave to penetrate to the far corners of the earth without regard to national boundaries or other man-made obstacles makes it a potent weapon in the campaign for worldwide freedom of the press. Half the power of a controlled press to do evil is lost whenever the people who read it learn that it is controlled. If it does not jibe with foreign news broadcasts that are truthful and are believed, it cannot completely deceive or corrupt any people. Bad money may drive out good, but corrupt "news" cannot stand against true news if there is a chance for comparison.

American shortwave newscasts are especially effective in this respect, for two reasons. Most of the world knows that in America the collection and dissemination of news is free and untrammeled, and that American newspapers, news agencies, and radio networks record and report world events on an unparalleled scale and with unsurpassed freedom. The second reason is that general respect for the integrity of the American government carries conviction to Voice of America listeners overseas.

Mark Ethridge, publisher of the Louisville *Courier-Journal* and Louisville *Times,* sums it up well. Last fall he traveled throughout the Balkans, as a special representative of the President, to investigate barriers to the free flow of news. He reports that the Balkan peoples listen to American broadcasts and have faith in them. "I have had them, from palace to peasant, tell me about it," Mr. Ethridge said. "One peasant even claimed that the American Government was not putting on the news at the time he wanted it. They believe this news. They believe it beyond any other news in the world . . . first, because they have faith in the American government, and second, because they know that we do not have strategic interests by which news should be measured."[1] . . .

Shortly after Mr. Ethridge returned from his trip, the State Department representative in one of the countries he had visited cabled Washington that editors and other influential persons at his post "were expressing alarm over the possibility that Voice of America broadcasts may be discontinued." He added: "They are widely heard here and many consider them the sole source of objective news."

Only in the United States has shortwave broadcasting ever been in private hands to any extent. The first U. S. shortwave voice broadcast transmitter went on the air in 1934. By December 7, 1941, eleven transmitters were in operation. They were owned by six corporations.[2] . . .

It is estimated that these corporations, now known as "licensees," had spent about $2,500,000 on their shortwave installations and that their annual operating cost was about $1,000,000 as of 1941. Revenues from advertising and other sources returned only a fraction of the operating costs.

The war made an integrated and greatly expanded shortwave system a necessity. In 1942 the government took over all existing transmitters, under lease contracts, and assumed responsibility for programming. NBC and CBS continued to produce some programs of their own, but under government direction. The number of transmitters was tripled, largely by direct expenditure of government funds. In 1945 thirty-nine transmitters were in operation within the country and a dozen more had been installed abroad, primarily as relay sta-

[1] On University of Chicago Round Table broadcast, "Public vs. Private News," February 24, 1946.

[2] National Broadcasting Co., Columbia Broadcasting System, General Electric Co., Crosley Corporation, Westinghouse Electric and Mfg. Corporation, World Wide Broadcasting Foundation, Inc. The Associated Broadcasters, Inc., completed two transmitters in 1942.

tions to pick up and rebroadcast locally the programs of the home transmitters.

During the war all transmitters were operated by and for the government. The OWI shared program time with the Office of Inter-American Affairs, which broadcast to Latin America, and with the Armed Forces Radio Service, which served Army and Navy personnel stationed abroad. A Presidential order terminated OWI and OIAA in June 1945 and transferred their continuing functions to the Department of State. The shortwave operation is now the responsibility of the Department's Office of International Information and Cultural Affairs, which has cut program-hours, number of languages employed, and the size of the operating staff far below their wartime peaks.

Study of a postwar shortwave system began long before the war's end. In November 1943, President Roosevelt wrote James L. Fly, then Chairman of the Federal Communications Commission:

If the principle of freedom to listen is to help in providing the basis for better understanding between the peoples of the world, it seems to me important that we lay the proper foundations now for an effective system of international broadcasting for the future years.

Many technical problems, as well as differences of opinion, were encountered by those—within government and without—who took part in the investigation of this very complex and largely new field. Agreement was reached, however, on a statement of basic policy which was prepared by the Department of State and approved by the Special Committee on Communications in February 1945:

1. Direct short-wave broadcasts originating in the United States should be continued after the war on a daily basis.

2. Facilities, both as to quantity and quality, should in general be as good as those of any other country.

This statement did not face up to the question of who should operate a postwar system—private corporations, the government, or some combination of the two. That is a problem which only Congress can decide.

Whatever form American shortwave broadcasting may take—government, private, or mixed—newscasts will be a major determinant of its audience-appeal. The United States has become the world's most important news center, and the location of UNO headquarters in this country will make it even more so. There is a great hunger throughout the world for news about America, from American sources, collected and presented with the integrity, clarity, and efficiency which are an American tradition. What America has to say on the shortwave will never lack for listeners, especially in those areas which can get little or no American information in other ways.

Will shortwave news broadcasts "compete" with the distribution of news to foreign publications by America's great private news agencies? In other words, will the newspapers of nations reached by American shortwave broadcasts be less interested in buying the news reports of the AP, the UP, and the INS than they would otherwise be? I think not. In fact, I think they will be more interested.

Not many years ago it was widely thought that radio newscasts within this country were a threat to newspaper circulation and to the news agencies. Experience has proved these fears were groundless. News agencies today sell their reports to broadcasting stations as a matter of course, and many of the stations are owned by newspapers.

These domestic developments imply that the loudspeaker does not replace the newspaper in public favor. Indeed, it has been pretty well demonstrated that a news story on the air sharpens the listener's interest in reading about it in his newspaper. There is no reason why the foreign shortwave listener should react differently, and I have heard no evidence that he does. Our shortwave broadcasts will thus develop the foreign market for our wire services, and not the reverse.

The American news agencies, with the wholehearted support and cooperation of their government, are now rapidly expanding their overseas markets and today serve foreign newspapers in numbers that would have seemed impossible a few years ago. Most of the credit for their success undoubtedly goes to the solid reputation the agencies have established for themselves and to the greater importance which news from the United States has in recent years assumed in the eyes of foreign editors and readers.

But I think it is fair to add that the American shortwave radio has done not a little to advance the good repute of news from American sources and to create a greater demand for it.

In a world no longer at war, but not yet at peace, America's radio voice must not be silenced. For it is a powerful and irreplaceable advocate of American principles, not least among which is freedom of the press, freedom to know.

THE PUBLIC AND WORLD NEWS

—O. W. Riegel, "How to Read Foreign News," *Education Against Propaganda, Seventh Yearbook of the National Council for the Social Studies,* edited by Elmer Ellis, 1937, pp. 49–51. Professor Riegel, author of *Mobilizing for Chaos,* is director of the School of Journalism at Washington and Lee University.

THE DISCUSSION leads to the ultimate consumer, the newspaper reader, who is perhaps the most crucial factor in the problem of foreign news. What has been said up to this point mainly concerns the organization and personnel of the machinery of record. . . . In spite of technical, financial, political, and psychological difficulties, the machinery of record is geared to supply American newspapers with a foreign report of high quality and comprehensiveness. Many of the influences will not become drastically effective until political conflicts are further intensified or war breaks out. A fundamental economic dislocation in the American newspaper business, such as the drying up of the present advertising subsidy, might also affect the amount and quality of foreign news radically. But for the moment the intelligent American can, if he reads the better newspapers, and supplements this with the reading of reports of special informational agencies, such as the Foreign Policy, Foreign Affairs, and Editorial Research reports, obtain a more accurate picture of foreign affairs than the citizen of almost any other country.

It may be seriously questioned whether the American newspaper reader is equipped to make adequate use of the foreign news which is, or could be, at his command. Is there sufficient interest in foreign news to justify the extension of foreign coverage, or even the maintenance of the present coverage? How many newspaper readers skip headlines or ignore foreign news entirely? How many readers have an international consciousness which, by any reasonable standard of social values, would justify the publication of extensive news from abroad? How many readers sample foreign news for mere sensationalism, or to feed their own national, class, or racial prejudices or to achieve emotional catharsis without any real social significance? How many are able to discriminate between good reporting and bad, and use their influence to encourage the best services in news, and interpretation? Another explanation of the present extensive reporting of foreign news in many American newspapers is the fact that such reporting adds to the prestige of the newspaper, and is therefore valuable as a form of economic promotion, but scarcely justified by intelligent reader interest in the actual contents of dispatches from abroad.

The primary task for the reader of foreign news, then, is to subject his own temperament and intelligence to the sharpest self-criticism. He must first ask himself whether he reads with critical comprehension. He must then ask whether his reading increases in any real sense his tolerance and appreciation in reference to world situations. If the answers to these self-questionings are positive, he ought to demonstrate his active interest in those whose reports from abroad are most accurate and illuminating. Such an interest on the part of readers would represent a bulwark against many of the unfavorable influences on foreign news which have been mentioned above. As American newspapers are now organized, the reader pays directly only a fraction of the cost of gathering and publishing foreign news. The American reader will prove the genuineness of his appreciation of foreign news when he is willing to share a larger part of the cost of collecting it.

REVIEW QUESTIONS AND ASSIGNMENTS

1. Consider, for the moment, that you are an interested reader of foreign news. What problems do you face in attempting to keep abreast of developments?

2. Do you think your home-town newspaper provides sufficient foreign news to keep its readers intelligently informed?

3. What position do you feel the United Nations should take on the question of world information?

4. Do you agree that the American concept of press freedom could be applied on a world basis?

5. Do you think that a completely free interchange of information would promote the cause of peace?

6. Describe the efforts of the United Nations to deal with the question of the interchange of information.

7. State what you consider to be the arguments for and against peacetime censorship. Do you think that a correspondent is justified in taking all steps to avoid such censorship?

8. Assume that you are the publisher of a Chicago daily and that you are planning to send a correspondent to Germany. Would you send an expert on German affairs or a veteran police reporter?

9. Do you think that the world press might adopt an international policing system to deal with the handling of news?

10. Select an American daily, study its handling of world news for one month, and then write an evaluation.

11. Why should an American press association refuse to furnish its news report to the government for the preparation of news broadcasts to be sent abroad?

12. Outline the role that you feel the United States government should play in the handling of world news.

13. Do you see any solution to the problem of international propaganda?

14. What advantages would result in the field of world information if a universal language existed?

ADDITIONAL REFERENCES

Ackerman, Carl W., "Prelude to War: Controlled Public Opinion," *The Annals of the American Academy of Political and Social Science,* Vol. 192, July 1937, pp. 38–41.

Almond, Gabriel A., *The American People and Foreign Policy,* Harcourt, Brace, 1950.

Birchall, Frederick T., *The Storm Breaks,* Viking Press, 1940.

Brown, Maynard L., "American Public Opinion and Events Leading to the World War, 1912–1914," *Journalism Quarterly,* Vol. 14, March 1937, pp. 23–34.

Butter, Oskar, *La Presse et les relations politiques internationales,* 1934.

Childs, Harwood L., "Public Opinion and Peace," *The Annals of the American Academy of Political and Social Science,* Vol. 192, July 1937, pp. 31–37.

Clark, Keith, *International Communications: The American Attitude,* Columbia University Press, 1931.

Cooper, Kent, *Barriers Down: The Story of the News Agency Epoch,* Farrar & Rinehart, 1942.

Cummings, Arthur J., *The Press and a Changing Civilization,* John Lane, 1936.

Desmond, Robert W., *The Press and World Affairs,* Appleton-Century, 1937.

Gorden, Matthew, *News Is a Weapon,* Alfred A. Knopf, 1942.

Grandin, Thomas, *The Political Use of the Radio, Geneva Studies,* Vol. 10, 1939.

Hale, James H., *Publicity and Diplomacy,* Appleton-Century, 1940.

Harris, Wilson, *The Daily Press,* Cambridge University Press, 1943.

Inkeles, Alex, *Public Opinion in Soviet Russia,* Harvard University Press, 1950.

International Institute of Intellectual Cooperation, *The Educational Role of the Press,* League of Nations, 1934.

Japan Newspaper Publishers' and Editors' Association, *The Japanese Press, Past and Present,* Tokyo, 1949.

Kris, Ernst, and Hans Speier, *German Radio Propaganda,* Oxford University Press, 1944.

Liebert, Herman, "International Communications," *Public Opinion Quarterly,* Vol. 5, June 1941, pp. 295–298.

MacNeil, Neil, *Without Fear or Favor,* Harcourt, Brace, 1940.

Matthews, Herbert L., *The Education of a Correspondent,* Harcourt, Brace, 1946.

May, Mark A., *The Social Psychology of War and Peace,* Yale University Press, 1943.

Morris, Charles, *Signs, Language, and Behavior,* Prentice-Hall, 1946.

Mumford, Lewis, *Values for Survival,* Harcourt, Brace, 1946.

Nafziger, Ralph O., *International News and the Press* (bibliography), H. W. Wilson, 1940.

———, "International News Coverage and Foreign News Communication," *The Annals of the American Academy of Political and Social Science,* Vol. 219, January 1942, pp. 132–138.

Padover, Saul K., *Experiment in Germany,* Duell, Sloan and Pearce, 1946.

Patterson, Ernest M. (editor), "The Press as a Factor in International Relations," *The Annals of the American Academy of Political and Social Science,* Vol. 162, July 1932.

Peterson, H. C., *Propaganda for War,* University of Oklahoma Press, 1939.

Riegel, O. W., *Mobilizing for Chaos,* Yale University Press, 1934.

Seldes, George, *The People Don't Know,* Gaer Associates, 1949.

Thomson, Charles A. H., *Postwar International Information,* Brookings Institution, Washington, 1948.

Tupper, Eleanor, *Japan in American Public Opinion,* Macmillan, 1937.

Ullstein Hermann, *The Rise and Fall of the House of Ullstein,* Simon & Schuster, 1943.

Weber, Karl, *The Swiss Press: An Outline,* Herbert Lang, Berne, 1948.

Wilkerson, Marcus M., *Public Opinion and the Spanish-American War,* Louisiana State University Press, 1932.

Woodward, Julian, *Foreign News in American Morning Newspapers,* Columbia University Press, 1930.

12. THE PRESS AND LAW ENFORCEMENT

INTRODUCTION

THE PRESS has been the object of criticism by social reformers, apologists for various professions that come in contact with criminal activities, and publicity seekers whenever it has printed news of efforts to enforce the law. Critics have held that news of the efforts of police often impeded the apprehending of law breakers, that "trial by newspaper" has been frequent, and that the press has lacked understanding of penal policies. These are but a few among the scores of faults found with newspaper handling of law enforcement. Much of this criticism should have been made of particular newspapers, rather than of the press as a whole. Some of it undoubtedly rests on a substantial basis.

These charges against the press are not new. They are not the outgrowth of current studies, or of a recently awakened social awareness. Such charges have been voiced ever since the newspapers learned that the printing of police news was a short cut to reader interest, mass circulation, and advertising revenue. Criticism reaches almost every point at which the press comes in contact with law breaking, court procedure, and penal policies. However, this chapter will be limited as far as possible to those citations that touch upon alleged interference with the machinery of justice, such as interruption of police work, attacks upon the dignity and work of the court, and failure to understand penal philosophy. Discussion of whether or not the press does encourage law breaking is presented in the next chapter.

In the first article, Gerald cites some difficulties in the working relations between the press and the courts. This type of friction, usually unknown to the public, accounts for some of the reluctance of the press to criticize the courts. Wood and Waite in the second item discuss the nature and amount of crime news, and its influence upon law enforcement.

That officers of the law themselves are often to blame for the misconduct of reporters is brought out by Hutchinson. According to him, newspapermen usually go as far as police and the officials permit. Sutherland, the criminologist, points out that newspapers often carry advance information of police activities. He also charges that such information is sometimes obtained by bribery or threats. Webb cites the benefits of a newspaper crusade against vice and gives some of the rules. Salmon compares the reporter with a detective, but indicates that newsstories are both good and bad. While admitting that the reporter may render aid to the police, she thinks that the press goes too far in discussing pending cases, and that the solution is a more enlightened press.

The student of the press should check local conditions to determine whether those various observations presented above are justified with respect to his own newspaper. It should be remembered that the newspapers are subject to the contempt power of the courts, which may at any time halt improper conduct by the press if they choose.

DIFFICULTIES WITH THE COURTS

—J. Edward Gerald, *The Press and the Constitution 1931–1947,* University of Minnesota Press, 1948, pp. 20–24. Mr. Gerald is professor of journalism at the University of Minnesota.

THE COURTS exercise common-law and statutory powers to punish summarily for disturbances in the courtroom which interfere with the orderly processes of justice.

The newspapers operate in the faith that the constitutional guarantee will protect them in honest and well-founded criticism of public officials, including judges who wield the contempt power.

In the non-metropolitan areas of the country, court and press are often well known to each other. Usually the judge and the editor are acquaintances, sometimes personal friends, sometimes political antagonists.

Political antagonism existing in a city or country town creates a tense situation which sometimes breaks down into an acrimonious exchange of comment. At that moment the judge may wish to extend the contempt power from the walls of his courtroom to his antagonist, wherever he may be found within the jurisdiction. That wish no doubt is as old as the first judge who met criticism where he expected only respect, and the prevailing human factors involved have left their mark on freedom of the press and on orderly administration of justice, perhaps to the benefit of both.

That spats between judge and journalist are fairly common can be demonstrated by a brief review of cases obtaining publicity in *Editor & Publisher* in a brief period of time selected at random.

As 1932 opened, Judge Henry R. Prewitt of Kentucky was presiding over the trial of a miner charged with conspiracy in a murder. Over the objections of the defense, Judge Prewitt permitted the prosecutor to harangue the jury at length, less on the subject of the miner's complicity in the crime, if any, than on the subject of Russia, Communism, and the American home. The trial was taking place in Mount Sterling, a place where the first two were unpopular and the third of the prosecutor's oratorical trinity could be and would be defended by any jury. The defendant, somewhat to his bewilderment, found himself convicted.

The Knoxville (Tennessee) *News-Sentinel* was represented in Judge Prewitt's court by a staff writer who covered the trial in some detail. After the defendant's conviction, the paper criticized the tactics of the prosecution in an editorial which contained the following sentence:

> As long as our courts permit themselves to be a stage for the tirades of political and social prejudice, they will not obtain full confidence of those who believe in even-handed justice.[1]

Judge Prewitt immediately sentenced the reporter for contempt and barred any representative of the *News-Sentinel* from his courtroom. The *News-Sentinel* proved not unequal to Judge Prewitt's challenge, and Newton D. Baker, its attorney, immediately appeared to represent the reporter. In the face of such eminent legal talent Judge Prewitt played the kind of legal game popularly known as the run-around. Forthwith he reconsidered the contempt citation and revoked it. Faced then only with his flat bar of any Knoxville *News-Sentinel* employees from his courtroom, the judge rendered it a nullity by transferring the cases in which the newspaper was interested back to the court whence they had come to him on a change of venue.

The Kentucky statutes, Sections 1291–95, limited contempt cita-

[1] *Editor & Publisher*, Vol. 64, No. 34, January 9, 1932, p. 5.

tions to matter spoken or written in the judge's presence. But Judge Prewitt, in a moment of irritation, probably being himself under the spell of the prosecutor's oratory, struck at a paper printed in another state through its reporter on the scene.[2] And by the time an appellate court could take up the case, the order had been amended sufficiently to save the judge further embarrassment.

J. W. Mapoles, editor of the Hopewell, Virginia, *News,* and Judge Thomas B. Robertson of the Hopewell Corporation Court were well acquainted, and each in his own fashion was dedicated to the upholding of law and order. But when Mapoles wrote a story about a defendant in Judge Robertson's court who was acquitted on a charge of illegal sale of intoxicating liquor, it seemed to so scandalize the court, in the judge's opinion, that only a fine of ten dollars for contempt could atone for the attack. As part of the same proceeding, the police chief was also fined for contempt, though seventeen of the twenty-four lawyers in Hopewell signed a round robin petition asking the judge to acquit him.

Shortly afterward, Mapoles published a letter in his paper which so infuriated Judge Robertson that he demanded the author's name of the editor in a formal appearance in court. The editor preferred not to tell and was sentenced to five days in jail. Before a hearing could be held on Mapoles' application for a writ of habeas corpus, Robertson ordered his release.[3] Nineteen Virginia editors petitioned the General Assembly of the state to impeach Judge Robertson, and a legislative committee investigated his judicial behavior. It reported that the judge was evidently irritated in this instance, but upheld his action at least to the extent of doing nothing more about it.[4]

Editor Howard C. Anderson of Aberdeen, South Dakota, lived in a county where officials had misapplied and misappropriated $250,000 in ten years. When a former county auditor received a six months' suspended jail sentence and a three-hundred-dollar fine on his plea of guilty to third degree forgery charges, Anderson complained editorially of Judge Howard Babcock's leniency. For his temerity in discussing this somewhat notorious public matter, Anderson and two associates were cited for contempt and given their choice of thirty days in jail or vows of perpetual silence. Judge J. H. Bottum heard the

[2] *Editor & Publisher,* Vol. 64, No. 35, January 16, 1932, p. 8.
[3] *Ibid.,* Vol. 66, No. 34, January 9, 1934, p. 7.
[4] *Ibid.,* Vol. 64, No. 43, March 12, 1932, p. 41.

contempt charges and performed for his colleague the chore of meting out punishment.[5]

A jury acquitted a defendant charged with murder in Brooklyn and a reporter for the Brooklyn *Eagle,* Richard W. Thomas, went to question a juror, as his editor had told him to do. The juror said that he and the others voted to acquit because the judge instructed them to do so if there was "any degree of doubt." This was a misrepresentation of the judge's actual charge, which had instructed acquittal if there was "reasonable doubt." The publisher, M. Preston Goodfellow, the managing editor, Harris M. Crist, and the reporter, Thomas, came to court under summons to explain. The judge reserved decision for two weeks and, having disturbed the peace of journalistic minds about as much as the judicial mind had been perturbed, turned them loose.[6]

A grand jury in Greenville, South Carolina, in an official presentment, announced its intention of investigating a sheriff on charges of embezzlement. Judge M. M. Mann banned publication of the presentment or any news based on it, but relented after the newspaper hired attorneys and challenged the rule in the judge's own court.[7] In the meantime the paper had published the story anyway and faced contempt.

The Julian Petroleum Company, with a hundred million dollars' worth of stock in public hands, was declared insolvent. The Los Angeles *Record,* prying into the debris simultaneously with agents of the court, found itself cited in contempt on thirteen counts proposed by a bar association which was on crusade against "trial by newspaper." It took the *Record* two years to prevent the judge who accused it from sitting in his own case. After a total of three years the bar association withdrew the charges. The whole matter seemed to the *Record* to be an experience with duress and censorship encountered in covering the news. To the bar association, of course, it still seemed like trial by newspaper.[8]

[5] *Editor & Publisher,* Vol. 64, No. 39, February 13, 1932, p. 6; No. 40, February 20, 1932, p. 5.

[6] Justice Wiley Rutledge, in *Pennekamp v. Florida,* 328 U.S. 331, 370–71 (1946) diagnosed troubles such as Thomas' as due to inexpertness of the sort to be expected, but not desired, from laymen covering courts. Justice Rutledge's opinion shows that he believes errors in court news reporting rank very high among the many inaccuracies popularly charged to newspapers.

[7] *Editor & Publisher,* Vol. 64, No. 45, March 26, 1932, p. 12.

[8] *Ibid.,* Vol. 65, No. 3, June 4, 1932, p. 8.

One other instance of run-of-the-mine clashes between the newspapers and the courts will suffice to introduce the national policy in such matters as it has been developed by the United States Supreme Court.

A grand jury in Hidalgo County, Texas, indicted two prominent citizens and so reported to Judge R. M. Bounds. C. H. Pease, editor of the *Independent*, looked at the grand jury and found men there he knew well. After reporting the indictment in a news story, he added his opinion: "The general view over Hidalgo County is that these indictments were for political purposes only."

Judge Bounds asked Editor Pease to explain this statement, issued an attachment for contempt and passed sentence of three days in jail and a fine of a hundred dollars. Following legal custom, Judge Bounds waved aside offers to prove the truth of the objectionable statement, applying the old rule of seditious libel—"the greater the truth, the greater the libel"—to interferences with the processes of justice.[9] Ten months later, after Pease had found in his resources wherewithal for lawyers and an appeal, the Texas Court of Criminal Appeals set aside Judge Bounds' attachment, saying that Pease should have been allowed to prove the truth of what he had written.[10] The articles were not contemptuous anyway, said the court. The pendency of this case for ten months amounted to a virtual censorship of the *Independent* with reference to the political aspects of its troubles. The judge, of course, acted in good faith, but the effect would have been the same otherwise.

While the struggle for freedom of the press in England was at its height, cases such as these often resulted in cruel and unusual punishment for the editors involved. No such dangers confronted the American journalists, but the possibility of a court citation is in the minds of editors as they work. The prospect of lawyers' fees and appeal costs causes reiteration in their minds, on such occasions, of the truth of the old adage, "Speech is free but proving it is not." There could be no objection to the power of the courts and to their disposition to use it if such action merely restrained rash and uninformed criticism. But the knowledge that the contempt power could be freely used intimidated even wise editors, and the public interest is not always best served by silence.

[9] *Editor & Publisher*, Vol. 64, No. 52, May 14, 1932, p. 10; Vol. 65, No. 1, May 21, 1932, p. 10.

[10] *Ibid.*, Vol. 65, No. 41, February 25, 1933, p. 11.

NATURE OF CRIME NEWS

—Arthur Evans Wood and John Barker Waite, *Crime and Its Treatment,* American Bock Company, 1941, pp. 216–220. Mr. Wood is professor of sociology and Mr. Waite is professor of criminal law at the University of Michigan.

We may now inquire as to the nature of the influence that flows from that most potent source of public opinion—the newspapers. Much attention has been given to this question by journalists and research students. Obviously, it is one that cannot be answered precisely by statistics. The issue concerns the amount and quality of the crime news in the daily papers, and the effects thereof. Computations may be made of the amount of space devoted to crime news; but as to its quality and effects upon the behavior of readers we can only generalize from outstanding instances.

On the question of the extent of newspaper space devoted to crime news recent studies indicate that it runs from somewhat over 1 per cent to somewhat less than 4 per cent of total news items. Moreover, contrary to the popular view of the matter, there does not seem to be any appreciable difference betwen the extent of such news in recent years and the amount that was published a generation or two ago. It is likely, however, that in recent years there has been a tendency for the newspapers to give the crime news a more favored place on the front page, as though it had special news value. For example, sensational news about Hamtramck, Michigan, is always good stuff for the reporters of the Detroit newspapers; and in one survey it was found that 60 per cent of the Hamtramck news *that made the front page* in the Detroit papers was crime news. No wonder that the citizens of Hamtramck regard the Detroit newspapers as scandalmongers.

We come, then, to the general character of the crime news that is conveyed through the newspapers and its alleged effects on law enforcement and the behavior of people. The indictment against the press on these points has been drawn many times and from numerous sources. First, it is said that the extensive, front-page exploitation of criminal happenings gives the public an exaggerated or distorted sense of the amount of crime. From the papers comes the idea of a "crime wave," implying that there are large fluctuations from time to time in the volume of crime, with a tendency toward an increase in all kinds of offenses. Actually, robberies have apparently been on the decrease in American cities in recent years, while crimes of burglary have remained about the same in number. This is a point that should not be ignored, in spite of the fact that the total volume of crime in the United States is excessive, as compared with other countries, *and always has been so.* In other words, it is possible that the treatment of crime in the newspapers is such as to create a hysterical mood among their readers, as over against a long-range, balanced judgment in the matter. Such an effect is of the essence of sensationalism.

More serious is the accusation that the newspapers are wont to portray the criminal in a semi-heroic role, which leads to sympathy for him, and even adulation, while the offender himself suffers no social degradation. Speaking of three psychopathic sexual criminals, on trial for murder in Detroit, Professor John B. Waite comments as follows on the newspaper handling of the case:

> Yet in reporting even this abhorrent disregard of all the standards of decent conduct which society preaches as "fair play," the tone of the press was less condemnatory of the three murderers than it was of Levine, the enemy who "told" on them. Of course, the crime, the "massacre" was formally reprobated, and the criminals in the abstract were upbraided. But the three men specifically concerned were treated rather as important protagonists in a society drama. The sartorial excellence of their clothing got more space than their cowardliness. All that one front-page item said of them, "see pictures on the back page," was this:
>
> "The three defendants sat without batting an eye in court, Wednesday, while 500 spectators were lined up and searched for weapons. Extra details of police paced the halls and guarded the doorways to prevent any attempt on the life of Sol Levine, star state witness.
>
> "The defendant trio were by far the most expensively and colorfully garbed persons in the room.
>
> "Keywell wore a vivid blue-green suit, brown shirt of softer hue, brown tie and white hose with brown clocks. Milberg chose light green as his motif. His suit was of solid field gray, with tie and hose striking sharper notes."[1]

Such a treatment by the press of the trial of three dangerous men is plainly not conducive to the dignity of the law and its processes. Rather, it plays into what has been termed "the sporting theory of justice," according to which the public is incited to view the process as a contest between the attorneys for the prosecution and defense, in which sympathies are aroused on behalf of the accused quite as

[1] This account, with the excerpt from the Detroit *Free Press,* Oct. 29, 1931, is taken from *Criminal Law in Action,* by John B. Waite, New York, Harcourt, Brace and Company, 1934, pp. 248–249.

much as for the forces of the law. An effect of this sort was unquestionably manifested in the newspapers' treatment of one of the episodes of the notorious Dillinger case. Before his break from jail in Crown Point, Indiana, large pictures were shown of him as he stood encircled by the arm of the prosecutor, with the woman sheriff and other officers standing by as though it were just a family party. For such an outrage the responsibility must be shared by the shameless reporters who invaded the jail with their cameras, and by the idiotic officials who allowed them to do so. On behalf of the reporters it should be said that they were following the orders of their managing editors to get the most sensational stuff available.

More than this, there is much evidence for believing that the newspapers often obstruct the successful operation of the police through the premature publication of plans for the apprehension of offenders. If a gangster is in hiding at a suspected place, the public is promptly informed that the police are about to surround it. If suspicion attaches to certain individuals for a crime for which no arrests have been made, the papers blurt out the names of such persons in time for them to get beyond reach. How is such information secured?—it may be asked. Obviously, from the police and prosecutors themselves. But why do they give it out? It is *because they are afraid to incur the hostility of the press,* which can make or unmake them at election time. We are thus back upon familiar ground, concerning the collusion of politics of a low order, not merely with the criminal elements themselves, but with the operations of the law. The so-called "majesty" of the law appears to be a bit disheveled! It is a sorry picture, and one that cannot be blotted out except by a Gargantuan effort to free the officers of the law from the fear of political disfavor.

The harmful effect of certain types of newspaper publicity was commented upon by Mr. J. Edgar Hoover of the Federal Bureau of Investigation in the following way:

> There was, for instance, in a Mid-West city, the publicity-seeking police officer who could not refrain from supplying a newspaper with the confidential knowledge that plans were being made by Special Agents of the Federal Bureau of Investigation and local officers to apprehend John Dillinger upon his planned return the following day for medical aid. The information was printed, and, of course, John Dillinger did not walk into the trap which had been laid for him by the authorities. Instead, he was able to continue his depredations for several months. Thousands of additional dollars were necessary for his pursuit

and the plunder of armories and banking institutions multiplied from the continued activities of this "mad dog."

In the case of Alvin Karpis, who held the headlines for a brief time, one newspaper could not resist the temptation to "jump the gun" on a tip it had received that Karpis was about to be captured. Karpis was not captured at that time. In the case of "Machine Gun" Kelly, one of the kidnappers of Charles Urschel, plans had been laid to entrap him when, in a Northern city, he picked up a newspaper which emblazoned across the front page the information that "Machine Gun" Kelly was about to be arrested there. It was necessary to chase him several thousand miles farther before the Federal Bureau of Investigation and local officers captured him at Memphis, Tennessee.[2]

It should be said, however, that in connection with the above remarks Mr. Hoover paid his high respects to the press of New York City for the complete silence with which they treated the activities of Federal and local officials in tracking down Bruno Richard Hauptmann by means of the ransom money which he was expending more and more freely.

This interference of the press with the processes of criminal justice extends even into the courts. That sensational cases are tried out in the newspapers is commonplace. Whether the evidence they publish would be really admissible in court is of little concern to them. To protect jurors from considering the news accounts of the trial, and of the circumstances attending the crime, we confine them, *incommunicado*. But the barrage of hypothesis and suspicion has begun its work on the public mind long before the jurors are finally selected. The result is that only jurors who are illiterate or "dumb" could be expected to be without preconceptions as to the guilt of the accused. In the Hauptmann case the newspapers ran riot with the proceedings, bringing down the contempt of European observers for our criminal procedure.

ENFORCEMENT OFFICERS OFTEN TO BLAME

—Paul Hutchinson, "Why Blame It on the Papers?" *Scribner's*, Vol. 99, January 1936, pp. 43–45. Mr. Hutchinson was managing editor of *The Christian Century* when this article was written.

Now it is no purpose of mine to absolve the press from blame for its treatment of crime news. If it were not so obvious that grave abuses

[2] From an address on "Law Enforcement and the Publisher" made by J. Edgar Hoover at the annual dinner of the American Newspaper Publishers Association at New York City, on April 22, 1937. The address was printed and circulated by the Federal Bureau of Investigation of the United States Department of Justice.

exist it would not have been so easy to build up this legend with regard to the malign powers of the newspapers. But there are certain aspects of this situation which seem to be commonly overlooked, yet which in fairness should be borne in mind. For example, it is at least worth remembering that if the press is guilty of exploiting crime and our criminal procedure for its own selfish ends, it is doing no more than everybody else connected with this matter is doing. That, I will admit, is not saying much in behalf of the press, but it nevertheless deserves saying.

More important, however, is the fact that the principal antisocial effects which are alleged to flow out of the papers' handling of crime *could be eliminated tomorrow without passing a new law, holding another convention, or adopting a single additional resolution if the courts really wanted it done.* The plain truth is that if the press is making a scandal of our treatment of crime—and I will not argue to the contrary—it is doing so only to the extent to which our officers of justice are willing, and frequently eager, to have it do so. When I listen to indiscriminate damning of the papers for turning our criminal processes into a circus, I become convinced that it is time for some candid speech. It is a modicum of that which, in the present instance, I desire to offer. . . .

Let us begin at the beginning, when the crime has been committed and the police set out on the criminal's trail. Immediately, we are told, the press does its best to thwart police efforts. All the criminal has to do is to read the papers and he will learn precisely where the net is being spread to catch him and how, therefore, to escape it. Very often this is true. But who gives the reporters their information as to what the police are doing? Sometimes, it must be admitted, the reporters, versed in police methods, make it up. But for every time they do so there are a dozen times when the police themselves come hotfoot with every development, all on the understanding that the newspapers shall give all credit to Captain Doyle of the Twelfth Precinct and Detective Sergeant Pestalozzi of the Homicide Squad and Patrolman O'Flaherty, on whose beat the crime occurred, as the men who are running the criminal to earth. The reporter who uses the tips these cops give him during this phase of the case can go as far as he likes in embroidering the story, but if he fails to play the game—that is, if he fails to see that the captain and the sergeant and the patrolman get the publicity they are after—he might as well turn his talents to the reporting of hotel arrivals or ship news.

Well, the arrest is made and the prosecution takes hold. The prosecuting attorney, or an assistant assigned to the case, meets the press daily, always assuring the reporters that he has "something new" ready for release. This begins with an announcement that the wretch now in jail is unquestionably the guilty party, and details are added to persuade the public that it knows exactly how the crime was committed. The next day there is promise of an impending confession. This confession may continue to impend for three or four days. Finally it comes, and is given to the papers to be printed in full. (Later the confession may not be so much as introduced in the trial; if it is introduced the chances are better than even that it will be thrown out.)

Then follow, during the weeks before the trial, day by day announcements of corroborative evidence unearthed, of "surprise" witnesses uncovered whose testimony will shatter the defense, of sinister facts discovered in the past life of the defendant, and of the thwarting of plans made by the defense to tamper with the jury. After the trial actually starts there is a daily forecast of what the prosecution intends to prove at the next day's session, a daily demonstration of the failure of the defense to establish its case, and a daily summary of the devastating nature of the points scored by the prosecution. The printing of columns of this sort of thing before and during the trial undeniably makes the prospect for even-handed justice considerably less than zero. But where does the public suppose the newspaper gets it? And would there be hell to pay if a paper should refuse to play ball with a district attorney's office by printing such stuff! (Always, of course, being careful that due tribute is paid to the superlative legal talents of "Assistant District Attorney Cecil Sternberg, who is conducting the prosecution under the personal supervision of District Attorney Francis X. Flynn.")

But what is the defense doing all this time while the prosecutor's office is thus using the press to establish the prisoner's guilt in the public mind? Plenty! So far as criminal procedure is concerned, it is safe to say that in the most populous centers of the United States no lawyer can build a criminal practice capable of paying his office rent unless he can demonstrate that he is as proficient a newspaper space-grabber as the late Ivy Lee. The defense lawyer also has his press conferences. In them he asserts, as a matter of routine, that his client's confession has been extracted by third-degree methods; that he has an unbreakable alibi; that almost every day yields another "surprise" witness whose testimony will shatter the prosecution. . . .

Even more important, however, is the attempt to get special reporters assigned to the defendant's side of the case. It is not often, to be sure, that a paper can be induced to order a star sob-sister to move in and live with the defendant's wife, as one of Mr. Hearst's journalistic handmaidens lived with Mrs. Hauptmann at Flemington, but the sentimental gush favoring the defendant which an adept journalist can turn out without going to such lengths is sufficiently familiar to require no description.

The point is that it is as much the desire of the defense as of the prosecutor to try its case in the papers before it ever comes to trial in the courts. And after the trial is under way, the more successful the defense counsel in reducing public opinion to blubbering sentimentalism or cynical indifference, the more roseate his prospects for the future. The net result is that, although the defense is likely to wheedle the papers where the prosecution may try to put on pressure, the end both have in view is the same—publicity for the lawyer.

And the judges? Well, judges differ. But the number is few who do not have a vivid sense of the personal advantage to be gained from presiding at extensively reported trials. Veteran reporters and cameramen could tell amusing tales, if they wanted to, of the lengths to which judges will maneuver to see that the press pictures and the leads in the news stories are devoted to the wisdom of the bench rather than to defense counsel, prosecution, or even defendant.

This is the barest sketch of what lies behind the distortion of criminal procedure of which the press is undoubtedly guilty. It does not begin to make the situation out as bad as it really is. But it should be enough to make clear the basic fact, namely, that at every step in this anti-social process the press is bedeviled *by officers of law and courts* to do precisely what it does do.

THE PRESS HAS ADVERSE EFFECT UPON LAW ENFORCEMENT

—E. H. Sutherland, *Principles of Criminology,* J. B. Lippincott Company, 1947, pp. 187–189. Mr. Sutherland, a distinguished criminologist, is professor of sociology at Indiana University.

NEWSPAPERS frequently carry advance information to the criminals regarding the plans of the police and the prosecutors. During 1933 one of the Chicago newspapers contained an announcement with big headlines that twenty police squads were watching two buildings, the addresses of which were printed in the article, because of information that a notorious criminal who was being hunted used these places as hangouts. The announcement would certainly destroy completely the efficiency of the police work. Such items appear frequently. Though they are sometimes a camouflage of the real plans of the police, they are frequently secured from subordinates by bargains, bribery, or threats. One of the ransom notes in the Peter Levine kidnaping case threatened the death of the child if information were given to police or newspapers. A reporter for a New York City paper secured verification of the kidnaping story by representing himself over the telephone to be an agent of the kidnapers, and his paper printed the story. The dead body of the child was found later. Federal agents have threatened reporters with arrest for obstructing justice in kidnaping cases because the reporters persisted in interfering with the investigations.

The effect of crime news is to throw the public into a panic. Newspapers learned in 1917 that it was dangerous to publish colorful stories about an epidemic of disease and they customarily keep such information entirely out of their columns, especially when a convention or fair is imminent or in progress. They refuse to publish information regarding the financial condition of a bank for fear that a panic which might produce public injury will ensue. The newspapers in England deal with crime news as they do with sickness and financial dangers, that is, quietly and factually. The American newspapers on the other hand, have not realized the dangers of panics of this nature and continue to make the crime stories as colorful as possible. Aside from the effect of colorful crime stories in producing crime and throwing the public into a panic, the newspapers seriously interfere with the course of justice by what has been called "trial by newspaper." Prior to the trial, the reporters present such evidence as they have, which is likely to be partisan information, again and again, until the public accepts the implied verdict of the newspaper and thereafter cannot easily be shaken in its opinion. A fair trial under such circumstances becomes almost impossible, especially in communities where the judges are elected and where they are afraid of arousing public antagonism. It is quite certain that many persons are convicted under such circumstances who are actually innocent, or are punished very severely who would otherwise be given much less severe penalties. The number of cases which attract this detailed and continued attention is probably not large. Any case may be selected for this presentation because some detail is sufficiently striking to make a good story. A man was killed in a drunken brawl; the murderer had previously had a good reputation but was not prominent in any way. The case would probably have passed with the customary procedure as a manslaughter case with imprisonment for, perhaps, three years, except that a reporter happened to learn that the murderer had the nickname "Banjo Ben." That trivial point made a good story of it. It was written up at length and repeated frequently. Consequently this offered an opportunity for the prosecutor to build up publicity for the next election. The offender was convicted of murder and sentenced to prison for one hundred and ninety-nine years. Reporters did everything possible to violate the rules of the court in the Lindbergh kidnaping case. These rules were made in order to secure a dignified and unbiased trial, and the newspapers interfered with justice by their violations. Many members of the bar believe that the reporters should have been severely punished for their behavior, and that this would have been legitimate.

In the spectacular crimes life is made almost unbearable for victims, witnesses, and officials by the reporters. Such persons claim that they have a right to privacy and that their right is invaded. The notorious behavior of reporters in connection with the Lindberghs is an illustration.

CAMPAIGNING FOR BETTER LAW ENFORCEMENT

—Carl C. Webb, "Two Portland Newspapers Join in Vice Crusade," *Journalism Quarterly*, Vol. 25, December 1948, pp. 375, 378–379. Mr. Webb is secretary-manager of the Oregon Newspaper Publishers Association and assistant professor of journalism, University of Oregon.

Leadership of Oregon's two largest newspapers in exposing vice conditions in Portland is an indication that the *Oregonian* and *Oregon Journal* are, in this respect, meeting their responsibilities as common carriers of information and discussion. Their editorials and news coverage over a period of many months played an important part in a campaign resulting in the election of the city's first woman mayor

—a city commissioner who has established a reputation for aggressive and rigid law enforcement. In the same election the state's short-term governor, whose career has been to some extent identified with certain gambling interests, was defeated.

Good journalistic principles were followed by the *Oregonian* throughout its campaign. Fair play is evident from the amount of space and prominence given to replies of the mayor, police officials, and the district attorney. Monotonous repetition was avoided by giving variety to stories and editorials. News stories were objective, without editorial comment. Compared with the committee's basic report, accounts indicated little coloring of the news. At one time three reporters were assigned to the story, and instructions from executives were to stick to the facts. Letters to the editor were well chosen and represented responsible citizens' viewpoints.

In some instances, statements were not attributed to an individual. But this was doubtless because of the anonymity of the committee's report, especially regarding police protection payoffs, and the secrecy of the grand jury investigation. Insofar as possible, the paper seemed to have made every effort to use direct quotations.

From the editorial standpoint, the *Oregonian's* campaign was built around these basic principles:

This is an investigation, not a crusade;
Give readers the facts, and right will prevail;
Grand jury investigations without public support are likely to be "white-wash" affairs;
The grand jury was one of the most effective in years because members were patriotic, intelligent and disinterested;
This inquiry should contribute to an increasingly well-regulated city in the future.

There is little evidence of partisanship. This is best summed up in the *Oregonian's* editorial following the primary election:

> We get no satisfaction out of the defeats suffered by Governor Hall and Mayor Riley. The former would have had our full support if he had been the nominee, and certainly Mayor Riley has contributed much, and soundly, to the upbuilding of Portland. But this is the victor's hour.

While devoting but about half the amount of space used by the *Oregonian* during the campaign, the *Oregon Journal* did lend important emphasis to the committee's report and subsequent developments. Particularly important were the editorials published in the *Journal* prior to the appointment of the City Club committee and throughout the 10 months the investigation was in progress.

Indicative of the attitude of the two newspapers were headlines over stories announcing the committee report. The *Oregonian* said, "Portland Police Protection of Vice, Gambling Charged." The *Oregon Journal* bannered its story, "Riley Wants Grand Jury Quiz."

The *Journal* did not, however, mention the charge of the committee that approximately $60,000 a month was being paid for police protection. It did not believe the committee had sufficient evidence to substantiate this finding.

Comparison of the editorials appearing in both newspapers the day following the release of the report showed more aggressiveness for the vice-cleanup on the part of the *Oregonian,* which upheld the committee by saying:

> Many of the accusations made by the committee are reasonably familiar, by repetitive rumor if not by first hand knowledge, to a considerable number of lawyers, newspapermen and others who brush up against municipal affairs.

The *Oregon Journal's* editorial reiterated most of the previous day's news story and summed up with the statement, "Now let's see what happens."

The *Journal* predicted what was to come in an editorial in its February 21 issue, headed, "The Mayor's Swan Song." In this it referred to his reply to the committee's charges by saying the letter was the most unfortunate utterance that marked Mayor Riley's public career.

All effective campaigns must show some definite results, and this exposé is not an exception. The grand jury did not find any usable evidence of a pay-off system. It did not return indictments. But it did find the Portland police authorities had not evidenced "any effective policy and program for the control or suppression of gambling, prostitution and other vice operations," and it made recommendations to correct the situation.

Most noticeable outcome was the defeat of Portland's chief executive for the past seven years, Mayor Riley, in the primary election by City Commissioner Dorothy McCullough Lee, virtually assuring the city of its first woman mayor in history. Mrs. Lee received 85,567 votes to Mayor Riley's 22,078.

Many citizens concur in the editorial opinion expressed by the

Oregonian that the reform sentiment in Multnomah County was not only responsible for the election of Mrs. Lee but also Senator Douglas McKay, who won the Republican nomination over Governor John H. Hall. . . .

Current reports are that from prior to the primary election in May until July 9, when a special tax levy election was held in Multnomah County, Portland was "closed," but within a few days after the special tax election the gambling places were again operating. One proprietor is said to have commented, "We are now going to make what we can between now and January 1, when the new administration goes into office." Portland expects its reform mayor to clean up the city. And predictions are that the *Oregonian* and *Oregon Journal* will continue their campaigns against vice to keep citizens fully informed and aroused.

NEWSPAPER ACCOUNTS ARE BOTH GOOD AND BAD

—Lucy M. Salmon, *The Newspaper and Authority,* Oxford University Press, 1923, pp. 424–426.

An explanation of this pre-occupation of the press with crime is found in the kinship between the work of the detective in ferreting out wrong-doing and the "nose for news" considered essential in a reporter. Through this characteristic the reporter is often of special service to the police department in its efforts to uncover crime, and the importance of the service has been freely and fully recognized. But in one essential the reporter and the detective radically differ. A crime discovered by a reporter is the achievement of a non-professional, and his occupation demands the immediate publication of all the facts known. The discovery of crime is the profession of a detective, and his occupation demands the concealment of the facts until all can be properly marshalled before the officials authorized to deal with it. The roads of the reporter and of the detective fork at the angle made by the demands of publicity and of concealment.

But while the detective never acts as either prosecutor or judge, the newspaper frequently acts as both, and this opens up another side of the question of the influence of the press on crime. How far should the jurisdiction of the press extend in the trial of persons charged with crime? Many have acknowledged the aid given by journalists in discovering crime, but hold that "they step beyond their province when they undertake to try cases pending in the courts."[1] That cases should be tried out of court by the press has long seemed intolerable to lawyers and judges alike—the "unbridled license of the press in commenting upon and often trying cases in the public print . . . [is] a prolific source of the miscarriage of justice and is most prejudicial to the rights of the defendants charged with crime."[2] The insult is added to injury when the newspaper enterprises in the civil courts are "almost invariably so managed as to convey to the minds of their readers the idea that the decision obtained, if a favorable one, has not come as a result of a just rule of law laid down by a wise and fairminded judge, but has been obtained rather in spite of both law and judges, and wholly because a newspaper of enormous circulation, championing the cause of the people, had wrested the law to its clamorous authority."[3]

The most grave influence that the press has on crime and its punishment is one that again cannot be computed by column space. It is its "systematic and constant efforts to instill into the minds of the ignorant and poor, who constitute the greater part of their readers, the impression that justice is not blind but bought; that the great corporations own the judges, particularly those of the Federal Courts, body and soul; that American institutions are rotten to the core, and that legislative halls and courts of justice exist as instruments of oppression and to preserve the rights of property by denying the rights of man."[4]

The remedies proposed for limiting and correcting this influence of the press have been the extension to all the states of the power, now exercised by the courts of Massachusetts and many other states, of punishing for contempt the authors of newspaper publications prejudicial to fair trials; the enactment of laws similar to those of England prohibiting a newspaper from publishing anything concerning a case that is in the courts other than a *verbatim* report of the proceedings in open court; prohibiting any newspaper from commenting either editorially or otherwise, upon the evidence in judicial pro-

[1] R. Foster, "Trial by Newspaper," *North American Review*, May 1887, Vol. 144, pp. 524–527.

[2] S. Untermeyer, "Evils and Remedies in the Administration of Criminal Law," *The Annals of the American Academy of Political and Social Science*, July 1910.

[3] G. W. Alger, "Sensational Journalism and the Law," *The Atlantic Monthly*, February 1903, Vol. 91, pp. 145–151.

[4] G. W. Alger, *op. cit.*

ceedings until after final judgment; and prohibiting any prosecuting officer from expressing or suggesting for publication an opinion as to the guilt or innocence of a person accused, or from disclosing any of the proceedings of a grand jury, or from publishing or being privy to the publication of any evidence in his possession bearing on any case under his control.

REVIEW QUESTIONS AND ASSIGNMENTS

1. Do you know of, or can you cite, instances in which the press has been of potential material aid to criminals by revealing plans of police?

2. Can you cite instances in which the public has become panic-stricken because of crime reports in the press? If so, was the press justified in handling the situation as it did?

3. Compare several issues of the *Christian Science Monitor* with the same issues of another paper. If the course followed by either of these newspapers were to become standard for the rest of the press, which would best serve the interests of society?

4. If crime conditions are bad in a community, and it is necessary to arouse the public to take action, how should a newspaper proceed to bring about an awakened and active public?

5. If you know of any crime stories handled in an antisocial manner, what were the factors influencing the newspaper's conduct?

6. Can the press be divided into a "yellow" press and a "white" press insofar as the publication of crime news goes? If so, what percentage of the press should be put in each group?

7. If you believe that there is a "yellow" press, how would you characterize its handling of crime news?

8. Discuss the idea that the "yellow" element among the newspapers is to be compared only to the shyster element in the law profession and the quack element in the medical profession.

9. To what extent does the press in your city affect the conduct of the police in their efforts to enforce the law?

10. Do you know of any cases of "trial by newspaper?" If so, discuss the circumstances.

11. What evidence can you show of newspaper failure to understand modern penal policies and theories?

12. Do you know of any cases solved by reporters when police have failed?

13. Look up a famous murder trial, and see in what manner the case has been dealt with by various types of newspapers.

14. Do newspapers aid or hinder the rehabilitation of prisoners who have served their sentences? Justify your answer.

15. Should it be expected of newspapers that they shall have expert knowledge of principles of penology and criminology which they criticize?

ADDITIONAL REFERENCES

Baskette, Floyd K., "Reporting the Webster Case: America's Classic Murder," *Journalism Quarterly,* Vol. 24, September 1947, pp. 250–256.

Bent, Silas, "Newspapermen: Partners in Crime," *Scribner's,* Vol. 88, November 1930, pp. 520–526.

Bliven, Bruce, "The Hall-Press-Mills Case," *The New Republic,* Vol. 49, December 1, 1926, pp. 39–40.

Cole, Virginia Lee, *The Newspaper and Crime,* University of Missouri School of Journalism, 1927.

Crowley-Carroll, Rev. H., "Crime News Pushed to Page Five When Pastor Edited Daily for Week," *Editor & Publisher,* Vol. 60, March 7, 1928, p. 10.

Deland, P. S., "Crime News Deglamorized," *Christian Science Monitor Magazine,* July 12, 1947, p. 3.

Dickey, Carl C., "The Truth About Newspapers," *World's Work,* Vol. 48, September 1924, pp. 503–512.

Fenton, Frances, "The Influence of Newspaper Presentations upon the Growth of Crime and Other Anti-Social Activities," *American Journal of Sociology,* Vol. 16, November 1910, p. 342. (Also published by University of Chicago Press, 1911.)

Frankfurter, Felix, Summary of Report by M. K. Wisehart on "Newspapers and Criminal Justice," in Cleveland Foundation Survey, *Criminal Justice in Cleveland,* 1922.

Godfrey, George H., "Crime News Totals But 1.4 Per Cent of Modern Newspapers, Survey Shows," *Editor & Publisher,* Vol. 61, July 7, 1928, p. 18.

Gottlieb, Lillian, "Radio and Newspaper Reports of the Heirens Murder Case," *Journalism Quarterly,* Vol. 24, June 1947, pp. 97–108.

Harris, Frank, *Presentation of Crime in Newspapers,* Sociological Press, 1932.

Holmes, Joseph L., "Crime and the Press," *Journal of Criminal Law and Criminology,* Vol. 20, May–August 1929, pp. 6–59, 246–293.

Hughes, H. M., "Lindbergh Case: A Study of Human Interest and Politics," *American Journal of Sociology,* Vol. 42, July 1936, pp. 32–54.

Kingsbury, Susan M., and others, *Newspaper and the News,* G. P. Putnam's Sons, 1937.

Kobre, Sidney, *Backgrounding the News,* Twentieth Century Press, 1939, pp. 151–168.

Liebling, A. J., *The Wayward Pressman,* Doubleday, 1947.

Watts, H. M., "The Fourth Estate and Court Procedure as a Public Show," *Journal of Criminal Law and Criminology,* Vol. 19, May 1928, pp. 15–29.

Wilcox, Delos, "The American Newspaper; a Study in Social Psychology," *The Annals of the American Academy of Political and Social Science,* Vol. 16, July 1900, pp. 56–92.

Wilkinson, L. A., "Divine Right of Newspapers," *The North American Review,* Vol. 230, November 1930, pp. 610–616.

Wisehart, M. K., "Newspapers and Criminal Justice," in *Criminal Justice in Cleveland,* Cleveland Foundation, 1922, pp. 515–551.

13. THE PRESS AND LAW BREAKING

INTRODUCTION

THE PRESS is often criticized for standing in the way of law enforcement, but it is certainly quite as true that the same press encourages the enforcement of the law and discourages would-be law breakers. This chapter attempts to show various points of view upon how the press either discourages or encourages respect for law through the amount and kind of crime news it prints. Press influence makes itself felt in a number of different ways. It affects the unstable-minded by picturing crime in glowing terms and thus lending support to whatever interest they may have in breaking the law. It may give information to law breakers and assist them in evading capture. It may encourage contempt of the law in young children by the unsocial character of comic strips and other entertainment offered in its columns. And it may be a hazard to the morals and ethics of the boys employed as street salesmen.

To what degree the influence of the newspaper is felt along the lines mentioned above has by no means been settled. As a matter of fact, many critics hold that publication of news of crime has no ill effects, while others are aroused to the point of anxiety by what they believe they have seen. Among the selections in this chapter are a number that take opposite stands on the questions raised. For the most part they are typical of what is being written upon this subject.

The case against the newspaper is presented by Sutherland. Because it is a thoughtful presentation, it deserves the consideration of students of the press. Readers should examine the newspaper accounts of cases to which Sutherland refers. The citation from Yost is based upon the experience of a lifetime in newspaper editing. He tells why he believes there is a public need for printing of crime news. Wiggins reveals the policies perfected by one modern newspaper to handle crime news in behalf of the public interest.

Some of the adverse influences of crime news upon the criminally minded are explained by Wood and Waite. In contrast, Dewey holds that crime news may act as a vicarious release to such individuals. Salmon states that criminals occasionally seek to escape the consequences of their deeds by placing responsibility upon the press.

These varying points of view indicate, among other things, that considerably more needs to be known about the role of the newspaper in the treatment and causes of crime. It would be well to consider whether the set of rules formulated by the Richmond *News Leader* is a completely satisfactory answer to the handling of crime news.

AMOUNT AND STYLE OF CRIME NEWS QUESTIONED

—E. H. Sutherland, *Principles of Criminology,* J. B. Lippincott Company, 1947, pp. 184–187, 189–191.

THE AMERICAN NEWSPAPERS have been generally and severely criticized for the part they play in relation to crime. The following charges are made against them: First, they promote crime by the constant advertising of crimc, by glorifying the criminal leaders and acting as press agents for them, by a jocular method of presenting crime news which takes away the dignity of the court proceedings, and by providing advance information to the public, including the criminals, regarding the plans of the police and prosecutors. Second, they interfere with justice by "trial by newspaper"and by distortion of news. Third, they produce a public panic in regard to crime which makes consistent and sober procedure difficult. Fourth, they interfere with the right of innocent individuals to decent privacy. Fifth, they become agencies of corruption by the employment of children under morally injurious conditions, of gunmen in circulation wars, and of racketeering reporters.

The desirability of publishing crime news is not here in question. Rather it is the amount and style of the crime news. The English newspapers publish crime news in the form of brief factual statements. The American crime news is much more colorful and detailed, so that the crimes are presented vividly and not distastefully to the reader. Because nothing is said about the millions of persons who lead a consistently law-abiding life, the impression is created that crime is the customary mode of life. Thomas, speaking of the yellow journal, says:

It is a positive agent of vice and crime. The condition of morality, as well as of mental life, in a community depends on the prevailing copies. A people is profoundly influenced by whatever is persistently brought to its attention. A good illustration of this is the fact that an article of commerce—a food, a luxury, a medicine, or a stimulant—can always be sold in immense quantities if it be persistently and largely advertised. In the same way the yellow journal by an advertisement of crime, vice, and vulgarity, on a scale unexampled in commercial advertising, and in a way that amounts to approval and even applause, becomes one of the forces making for immorality.[1]

The effect of this constant presentation of crime news to the public can certainly not be demonstrated in ordinary cases. Presumably the effect in ordinary cases differs only in degree from the effect in the extraordinary cases, such as the following. Not long after the newspapers were filled with vivid stories of the Hickman case in California, Houghteling committed a somewhat similar crime in Michigan and when asked regarding it stated that he could not get the Hickman case out of his mind. Holmes states that an epidemic of similar cases occurred and in some of the other cases the accused persons claimed that the idea was suggested by the Hickman case.[2]

Martin Durkin, with a long record of crimes, including the killing of a policeman, was captured in St. Louis and was being returned to Chicago. The newspapers had been filled with news regarding the case. When Durkin reached the station in Chicago he found flashlights, reporters, moving-picture machines, and an immense crowd to greet him. The crowd was not only interested but was distinctly sympathetic, for they shouted, "We're for you, Marty!" When the motion pictures were shown later in the theatres, the crowds cheered the pictures of Durkin and hissed and booed at those of the police until the Mayor prohibited the showing of the pictures. The situation was definitely dangerous and all the information on which the public had formed its impression had come to it through the newspapers. The newspapers tried to change the public attitudes by writing in disparaging terms about Durkin but the public sympathy could not be changed that easily.[3] Again in 1932 the newspapers created a near-riot. A man was murdered by his wife. The details were of the

[1] W. I. Thomas, "The Psychology of the Yellow Journal," *American Magazine*, Vol. 65, No. 496, March 1908.

[2] Joseph L. Holmes, "Crime and the Press," *Journal of Criminal Law and Criminology*, Vol. 20, No. 258, August 1929.

[3] R. M. Lovett, "Chicago," *New Republic*, Vol. 50, April 20, 1927, pp. 243–246.

usual sordid type, but the striking appearance and mannerisms of the wife gave the reporters an opportunity for a story, and for days the papers were crammed with details. Then the funeral of the murdered man was announced, with the information that the widow would attend the funeral. The streets adjoining the undertaker's chapel were well filled an hour and a half before the hour of the services, and were jammed to capacity a half hour before the time. As the services were about to begin the spectators crashed into the chapel, swarming between the casket and the minister. After some effort sufficient quiet was secured to start the services, but the continued pressure of the crowd outside made it necessary to bring the services to a speedy close. As the services ended a plate-glass window was crashed in by the pressure of the mob, chairs were overturned and the police were helpless. The streets along which the procession was conducted were crowded for many blocks with people filling the sidewalks, the windows, and even the roofs of houses. At the cemetery crowds swarmed over the graves and pushed until those in the front ranks could keep from falling into the open grave only by holding to the coffin. Policemen were shouting and pushing in the effort to keep the spectators back and later to make a path for the widow to start back to jail. If the story of this murder had been confined to the usual factual statement which appears in cases of this kind, there would have been no public interest. The interest which did develop was not based on antagonism against the murder; it was morbid curiosity, created by lurid stories. It served absolutely no useful purposes and could not have occurred in a community in which good taste and morality restrained the newspapers and the public.

Bingay, the editorial director of the Detroit *Free Press,* stated in 1933 that press agents are as useful to criminals as to movie stars or politicians, that the newspapers act without salary as press agents for the criminal leaders, build up their reputations and increase their power with other criminals, with the police and courts, with the politicians and the public. A reporter applied the name "Purple Gang" to a relatively unimportant group in Detroit which up to that time had had no name. The name was used by others, and these gangsters were built up by the label into criminal giants. Their reputation was made by the newspapers. Consequently, when a member of this group went to a business man with a racketeering proposition and announced himself as a member of the Purple Gang, the business man was afraid to kick him out as he might otherwise have done. In Chicago the newspapers announced that Murray Humphries would be the successor to Capone. The successor was by no means determined, but the announcement in the newspapers helped Humphries secure this position as much as a similar announcement would help an aspirant for a political position. Furthermore, the newspaper accounts contribute considerably to the self-esteem of certain criminals, for these professional criminals are generally avid readers of the newspapers. When a newspaper carries the story that a certain criminal is the worst, or the best, or the most dangerous, or some other superlative appellation, it is one of the few consolations this criminal will have, in case of conviction, while he is in prison.

The newspapers, furthermore, are sometimes agencies of corruption. The newspaper circulation war in Chicago, which began in 1900 when two Hearst papers started publication in competition with the other papers and lasted for several years, resulted in the employment of armed guards by both sides, in the killing of more than a score of persons, and the injury of hundreds. Among the guards employed in this war were several persons who later became "public enemies." They had learned that violence, including murder, is safe if one is backed by a strong organization with money and influence. A few editors have been closely associated with gangsters, and several reporters have used their newspaper influence to assist gangsters. This statement by a police official illustrates the corruption of "newsboys" a generation ago:

> I firmly believe that newspapers are responsible for a lot of crime. Out of the newspaper alleys come many gamblers, pimps, sex perverts and a big share of the gangsters. There is no better breeding ground in the world for gangsters than a newspaper alley. Besides that the newspaper circulation department violates every child labor law and statute and many city ordinances that are enforced on other private citizens. They haul their papers through the streets at fifty miles an hour, endangering the life and property of the whole city, but you never hear of one of them being arrested.

The primary reason why the newspapers conduct themselves in this fashion is that they are business concerns, operated for the purpose of profits. Their primary interest is circulation, and public welfare is secondary. The studies of newspaper presentation of crimes, however, provide no evidence that the percentage of space in the papers devoted to crime news has increased or that the emphasis upon crimes has changed.[4]

The newspapers defend their method of presenting crime news, first, on the ground that it is what the public wants. Though there is truth in this argument, it does not take into consideration that the newspapers themselves have to a considerable extent created the wants. At present some of the papers present crime news in the comic strips which are read by the youngest children. Second, they argue that the only way to solve the crime problem is by arousing the inert public and the inert public officials by this means. The difficulty is that action under such circumstances is not likely to be calm and consistent. Expressions of public opposition to crime unquestionably assist in deterring people from crime, but the newspaper expressions are based largely on unusual and extraordinary cases which make good stories. This, however, does not deny the very great contribution that the newspapers make by the factual information regarding crime and regarding official corruption, and by the support of desirable policies. Crime news, as well as other methods of portraying crimes, has been defended on the ground that it satisfies a deep-seated compulsion toward criminality and is thus something like a sublimation of the criminal tendencies. Bar associations have criticized the newspapers for the anti-social behavior which has been described. Recently a joint committee of the bar, the press, and the radio outlined a code of ethics in regard to publicity.[5]

Some of the earlier novels, such as Ainsworth's and Bulwer-Lytton's, glorified criminals. Mayhew offers some evidence of the effect of this from statements of criminals, for many persons desired to be followers of Jack Shepard and the other romantic criminals. In somewhat the same way two generations ago the Jesse James stories and the Diamond Dick novels and others known as "dime novels" thrilled the youth of the country. Though this function has now for the most part been assumed by the motion pictures, the "wood pulp" magazines are continuing it. These magazines, however, are seldom read by the pre-adolescents. The erotic literature in these magazines is perhaps

[4] Frank Harris, *The Presentation of Crime in the Newspapers*, Hanover, 1932.

[5] Paul Bellamy, Stuart Perry, Newton D. Baker, "Cooperation Between Press, Radio, and Bar," *Journal of Criminal Law and Criminology*, Vol. 28, January 1938, pp. 641–656.

the most deleterious because of the continued direction of attention toward sex and the continued presence of sex imagery. There is little evidence that any of this literature is of primary importance in the development of juvenile delinquency, and probably it is not highly important except in occasional cases in adult criminality.[6]

WHY THE PUBLIC NEEDS CRIME NEWS

—Casper S. Yost, *Principles of Journalism,* Appleton-Century Company, 1924, pp. 48–49.

NEWS OF CRIME AND VICE should be printed. It is not only proper to print such news, but it is a public duty to print it. Crime and vice constitute problems with which society must constantly deal. And if it is to deal with them with any degree of effectiveness it must have knowledge of them, of their nature, extent, and the forces and influences behind them. Public opinion is as important a factor in the prevention, suppression, or punishment of crime as in any other field of human activity, but public opinion is never exercised in any field until it is aroused by public events. Crime and vice are menaces to society, and as such must be continuously and actively opposed by the agencies which society creates for its protection. But in the protection of society the law, the courts, and the police must have the public support which can only come from a measure of acquaintance with the facts and conditions with which they have to deal. If the news of this character were suppressed, the people would be deprived of the only general and constant source of knowledge as to such events.

All social progress is dependent upon information. If we do not know there is wrong, how are we to perceive the need of right? If we do not know what is wrong, how are we to know what to attack? If we do not know the extent of wrong, how are we to arouse and array the forces of good? Right is might only when its eyes are open, only when it sees and appraises the power opposed to it, and only when it is urged to action by the knowledge of the danger that confronts it. To suppress the news of evil would be to blind the eyes of right and to deceive it with a sense of security in the face of peril. Evil always flourishes most in the darkness. It grows upon concealment. It fattens under public indifference resulting from ignorance of its activities.

[6] S. Sighele, *Littérature et Criminalité,* Paris, 1908, pp. 165 ff. Sighele maintains that Goethe's *Werther* produced many suicides.

It is essential that the light of publicity be thrown upon it, that its nature, its scope, and its habits be revealed. The publication of evil is a public duty and a public service.

SOME EFFECTS OF CRIME NEWS

—James Russell Wiggins, "The News Is the First Concern of the Press," *Journalism Quarterly*, Vol. 23, March 1946, pp. 24–26.

NEWSPAPERS probably are reproached more for reporting crime news too fully than for reporting it inadequately. Some very substantial arguments have been made against crime news in the press.

(1) It has been contended that crime news increases crime by inviting imitation. Let it be admitted that this does happen. Two young boys in South St. Paul recently attempted an attack on a small girl in a fashion that almost duplicated a crime of the kind just fully reported in the St. Paul newspapers. This risk can be minimized by avoiding the type of story that glamorizes crime, by shunning novel nicknames for criminals, by playing down aspects of criminal acts that make them appear romantic, by emphasizing penalties and convictions, by caution in describing the methods used by criminals. If crime news is to be published at all, however, some risk of imitation must be run; and the public generally must be trusted to emulate good behavior and shrink from examples of bad behavior. The only alternative is to keep people in ignorance of wrongdoing.

(2) It is argued that crime news injures innocent relatives of law violators. Actually, it is the crime that accomplishes this injury and the newspapers that circulate the report only perform more expeditiously (and accurately) a function that word of mouth communication would achieve more slowly.

(3) Crime news is alleged to be a brake on regeneration and reform. It is said to deprive the criminal of an opportunity for a fresh start. Here the general interest must weigh against the individual interest. Crimes that are a matter of public record cannot be wholly concealed from general knowledge. Nor should they be so concealed. It also can be argued that the offender is better off with the knowledge of his crime spread on the record than he would be with its disclosure constantly threatening his new career.

(4) It is contended that crime news offends good taste. I think it

often does. But sometimes it takes such a shock to awaken the community to action against anti-social behavior and the causes of it. The Roscoe Arbuckle case, for example, put into public print some news that offended good taste; but the public reaction caused a thorough clean-up of the whole motion picture industry. The good effects of that clean-up have lasted to this day.

The reasons FOR printing crime news, I believe, far outweigh those against printing it.

(1) "Crime does not pay" is the constantly reiterated injunction of crime stories. The news certainly suggests to even the casual reader that apprehension is usual and punishment inevitable. It is a rare crime story that makes the way of the transgressor look attractive.

(2) Crime news also aids in the apprehension of criminals. News stories and pictures are frequently their undoing. The Shetsky murder trial in Minneapolis in 1945 found the news an aid to the law. News reports and photographs of an escaped convict led to his identification and arrest recently in St. Paul.

(3) Fear of newspaper publicity has a deterrent effect. St. Paul traffic chiefs recently reported that persons arrested for drunken driving are less concerned about penalties than they are about their licenses and getting their names in newspapers. St. Paul courts have found the regular publication of arrests for evading VD treatment an effective aid in causing offenders to continue medical care.

(4) Loss of the "sense of identity" that marks life in a community where the news is well reported would follow suppression of all crime news. The nature of this "sense of identity" and its effect on behavior recently was emphasized by General E. C. Betts, Judge Advocate General of ETO. He attributed crime among American troops to this, among other factors. He pointed out: "This sense of identity is very important. If anyone is among friends or people he knows, and wants their respect, he hesitates before doing anything shameful."

(5) News coverage of the courts and of crime also protects accused persons against the possibility of malfunctioning of law enforcement agencies. Accused persons have a better chance of even-handed justice, of like treatment for like crimes, when the proceedings of the courts are laid before newspaper readers.

In the past seven years the newspapers with which I have been connected have perfected some crime news policies that I believe to be in the public interest. They emphasize consistency—the publication of all crimes in a given category if any are published; the right of the accused to be heard in print as well as in court; the careful treatment of complaints so as not to imply guilt; the full identification of accused or convicted persons.

To make certain of complete coverage the municipal court docket is printed each day.

Convictions for drunkenness are reported in this docket alone unless the person involved has a name that makes news.

Drunken driving convictions are invariably reported with the names of the offender and a proper identification.

Sex crimes are treated without the lurid "love-nest" sort of terminology, and without names of victims of sex attacks.

Juvenile offenders' names are not used unless the crime is a very serious one or the offender is a repeater.

Efforts at self-destruction are reported factually with care to avoid conclusions beyond the facts.

Divorce complaints are not reported in detail and publicity ordinarily is withheld until court action. I will confess that there are some sound arguments for a more exhaustive treatment of divorce news now that the broken home is becoming one of the most serious problems.

Racial identification of persons accused or convicted of crimes is resorted to only where it is an essential element of the story. It seems clear to me that this is the case in race riot accounts or in stories of major crimes in which everything about the accused is a matter of note. I am certain that the use of a racial tag definitely is unwarranted in ordinary misdemeanors in which the use of racial identification tends to encourage, by frequent repetition, reader belief that identified races commit more crimes than others. The Negro people, in particular, justly complain about such identification.

EFFECTS OF SENSATIONALISM

—Arthur Evans Wood and John Barker Waite, *Crime and Its Treatment,* American Book Company, 1941, pp. 220–222.

IF SUCH be some of the general aspects of the treatment of crime news by our American newspapers, we may consider the possible effects of their sensationalism upon the behavior of their readers, especially upon those who are already criminally disposed. These effects are both direct and unconscious. When the young criminal in Shaw's *Natural History of a Delinquent Career* aspires to make the front page, we can see how the papers directly satisfy the criminal's desire for notoriety. Moreover, there are numerous instances of precise imitation of crimes that are exploited in the press. Houghteling, a Michigan child-murderer, was reliably said to have been instigated by the news accounts of the notorious Hickman case in California. In such cases the minute imitation of the details of a reported crime leaves little doubt as to the direct effect of the news account. In too many people the threshold of criminal response to suggestion is low. This is a point that the honorable editors overlook when they claim to "give the people what they want." The wants of people vary from what is most noble to what is most depraved. A public agency is responsible for its selection of tastes to which it caters. The population is afflicted with thousands of nitwits, sexual psychopaths, and otherwise unstable minds, that are ever-ready to be set off to some misdeed by a vivid, overpowering suggestion. Under these conditions, the editors' defense that they "give the people what they want" is fatuous indeed!

Apart from such cases of direct incitement, there is the more remote consideration that the constant reiteration and exaggeration of crime news in the press benumbs our sense of the real offensiveness of crime. Like the massacre from automobiles, it seems so common that we pass it by. "Fourteen dead in this county over the week-end from auto mishaps" (note the word), and "three victims shot by gangsters"—it's all in the day's work so far as any shock to the reader is concerned. The young blood still drives down the highway at eighty miles an hour, ending up at the movie where he sees the gangsters shoot the police. All this is symbolic of the cheapness of life in the United States, a calamitous situation that receives but slight censure in the crime news.

It seems to be otherwise with the press in England. There a newspaper would be severely penalized for tipping off the criminals with accounts of the projected activities of the police; and court procedure is treated with the dignity and respect that is conspicuous by its absence in the habits of the American press. Our papers howl at the suggestion of censorship, but apparently the way is open for some brave judge to cite them for contempt. As Waite says, "American judges have inherently the same powers in controlling the press as those of England, but English judges are not dependent upon the good will of the newspapers for the continuance of pay checks."[1]

It remains, however, to say something for the other side of the picture. Undeniably in some cases the press accounts of crime assist in the apprehension of guilty persons, through the publication of their pictures and probable whereabouts. Conspicuously, in the United States, the New York *Times* publishes substantial articles that deal analytically with various aspects of the crime problem. Curiously enough, Detroit's most sensational newspaper carried on an effective campaign against the restoration of capital punishment in Michigan under a badly drawn mandatory proposal. The virtue of such an achievement, of course, would depend upon one's view of the desirability of the death penalty; but the point is that the discussion was dignified and substantial. Professor E. R. Sunderland of the University of Michigan Law School has told how an English newspaper, single-handed, waged an effective campaign for the reformation of English court and penal procedure in the middle of the last century. When the newspapers in America rise to the opportunity for sponsoring of similar reforms in this country, there will be plenty for them to do. To mold public opinion in constructive ways is their birthright which they can reclaim whenever they are disposed to do so. Of course, the newspapers reflect the mores and cultural standards of the American people. To effect an improvement in these matters is, perhaps, the profounder necessity of the problem of the press in relation to the crime news.

CRIME NEWS AS A VICARIOUS RELEASE

—Ernest A. Dewey, "Crime and the Press," *The Commonweal*, Vol. 15, December 30, 1931, pp. 232–233. Mr. Dewey was a staff member of the Hutchinson (Kansas) *News-Herald* when he wrote this article.

IT MAY be taken as self-evident that the basic social laws are not necessary to protect society against the normal man, for the reason that he is policed by his own intelligence. Laws are equally inoperative against the defective for the reason that, having no control over his emotions, they present no obstacle to an immoral act. The passage of social laws cannot automatically afford him control over himself.

[1] John B. Waite, *Criminal Law in Action*, Harcourt, Brace and Company, 1934, p. 244.

Nor can the suppression of emotional stimuli (considering, for the moment, that crime news is such) nor any other conceivable agency give him that control.

The emphasis on crime news has its parallel in past decades. It is, perhaps, the modern equivalent of the tales of conquest of the plains, of battles wherein "many redskins bit the dust." Previous to that, tales of piracy on the high seas engaged attention with their bloodcurdling details of plank-walkings, looting, and slaughter. Even history, with its lurid pages, has its attraction for the civilized reader with primitive and sadistic impulses. All of these made vivid reading, yet were they charged with promoting crime?

Is there not, after all, a strong possibility that crime news and other such outlets for primitive, sadistic impulses, rather than inflaming the instincts, serve instead to keep many a near-defective within the pale of respectability and the ranks of worthy members of society?

I will venture the assertion that no one was ever corrupted by a newspaper story. I will venture further to assert that anyone who could be corrupted by a newspaper story is not worth saving, and that any effort to save him must inevitably fail. Certainly nothing but a cracked brain could ever be incited to crime, however copiously the news columns may spread the saga of the malefactor. There is a vast difference between finding crime stories interesting or entertaining and being incited to criminality by them. There may be criminals who treasure their press notices, but no intelligent person will argue that they committed their crimes in order to get their names in the paper.

On the other hand, there can be no denial that the printing, emphasizing, even the enthusiastic playing up, of crime news constitutes an attempt, though sometimes indirectly, to apply a needed lash to whip up indignant public opinion, to create public disgust for legal procedure as full of holes as a Swiss cheese, to incite popular demand for a cleaning up of conditions.

THE NEWSPAPER AS A SCAPEGOAT

—Lucy M. Salmon, *The Newspaper and Authority,* Oxford University Press, 1923, pp. 422–423, 426–427.

It is difficult . . . to estimate by the measuring tape the influence of the press on crime—even sample issues of several hundreds of papers may convey an erroneous impression. The contents of the press are not static, but vary with every upheaval of general or local society caused by war, the disturbances of nature, or the derangement of industry and business. The proportions vary on different days of the week—certain classes of advertisements swell to abnormal dimensions Sundays and Mondays, while Saturdays are usually devoted to quite different classes of notices and advertisements. The musical and dramatic seasons as well as art exhibitions, horse shows, and automobile shows all materially affect the relative proportion of news. Any judgment based on specimen copies must be somewhat qualified by these irregular and varying conditions in the columns of the press—an entirely different selection of sample numbers would probably yield entirely different proportions.

It is also true that the results of crime are usually immediate and spectacular, and since the first commandment in the press decalogue is to be the first to publish the news, conjectures and suspicions of crime are amplified and exploited, and thus crime and all its kindred enter the first page at full tide.

Moreover, it must be remembered that misdemeanants and criminals are prone to evade personal responsibility for their acts and that the juvenile offender finds in the press a scapegoat at hand for all his misdeeds. The statements of all transgressors in regard to the moving cause of their transgression must be received with the traditional allowance of salt.

And once more it must be said that crime waves have been noted in all ages and in all countries—long before the appearance of the newspaper, the invention of the headline, or the appearance of criminals' photographs conspicuously displayed in the press. While the existence of crime epidemics has long been recognized, the explanation of them has by no means been satisfactory and there has been far from unanimous agreement in attributing them to the influence of the press.

But when every possible allowance has been made for the inherent limitations of all efforts to measure by mechanical methods an influence so elusive that it cannot be measured by any methods yet devised, it still probably remains true that the influence of the press upon the growth of crime is important. . . .

Much has been made of the influence of the press as an incentive to crime, but comparatively little of the influence exerted in the opposite direction in the prevention of crime and in the positive influence for good. If the yard stick were applied to these phases of the subject and the same mathematical computations were made of the tendencies in the press toward beneficent activities as have been noted of its influence to develop criminal tendencies, the result might be a modification of the judgment so often expressed. The press has undoubtedly often fostered the mob spirit that has led to crimes against society, as lynching. That the stockholders of the San Antonio, Texas, *Express* announced that they would devote one hundred thousand dollars as a reward to persons who should bring to justice any member of a mob guilty of lynching[1] may have been an exceptional action, but the press may justly claim that if it is to be judged by one extreme policy, the opposite must at least be presented. Reporters with "a nose for news" have more than once through the press been able to render genuine service to the cause of justice—in at least one case reporters found that a man long imprisoned for murder was innocent of the crime and he was therefore freed.[2] When a young bank clerk disappeared with three-quarters of a million dollars worth of bonds in his possession, his picture and description were widely distributed through the press and this led to his identification and apprehension—a result that led to public appreciation of the work of the press in giving publicity to a matter of general concern.[3] The press does not print out what is obvious to the normal mind—that crime is crime and that swift punishment is expected to be meted out to the criminal. The daily press more often fails in that is has apparently as yet made little effort to treat anti-social matter from a socially constructive standpoint.

NEWSPAPER RULES FOR THE HANDLING OF CRIME NEWS

—*The Richmond News Leader*, "Regulations of the Richmond (Virginia) *News Leader* for the Handling of News of Crime, Scandal, and Disaster, As Revised March 1, 1935."

1. No crime news to be printed on the front page except (a) local crime news of general interest, and (b) national crime news of the first magnitude, such as major kidnapings or a robbery exceeding $100,000.

[1] New York *Evening Post*, August 14, 1918.

[2] C. E. Grinnell, "Modern Murder Trials and Newspaper," *The Atlantic Monthly*, November 1901, Vol. 88, pp. 662–673.

[3] *Daily Press*, March 9, 1921.

2. Minor crime news, such as that of minor holdups, bank robberies, and violence beyond our circulation territory, is not to be printed at all.

3. In reporting any crime news, other than that relating to an offense of the very first magnitude, no details are to be given of the methods employed by criminals when such details might provoke other crime or incite young men to criminal acts.

4. Never glorify crime or criminals and never publish anything that will make any criminal act appear heroic.

5. News of the juvenile court is not to be printed at all.

6. In cases involving first offenders, where the charge is less than that of a major felony, publication can be withheld by the managing editor when he thinks publication would tend to prevent the first offender from re-establishing himself.

7. The award of local divorces may be printed along with other court news, but no details are to be given. Details of divorces of celebrities may be printed.

8. Local suicides of inconspicuous persons are not to be reported because publication may dispose other unhappy persons to like acts. Brief reports are to be printed of the suicide of persons who are prominent in the news or in those instances where the suicide is spectacular and a matter of general interest. For example, if a person jumps from the top of a high building, that is news which must be printed, but if a poor, overworked woman shuts her kitchen door and turns on the gas, publication of the means of her death will simply humiliate her family without serving any useful social purpose.

9. The *News Leader* is on the side of the law, though it holds no brief for individual officers of the law. In every story of crime, though facts are, of course, to be reported without bias, no touch of sympathy for criminals and no levity in dealing with crime are to be permitted.

10. Disaster news is depressing and unless it is of wide economic or political importance, should not be played up. This does not apply to disasters such as automobile-killings or grade-crossing smashes, which the *News Leader* is endeavoring to reduce.

11. Be sparing of "streamer-heads" on crime and disaster. Unless the news is demonstrably of general interest and important, display it conservatively.

REVIEW QUESTIONS AND ASSIGNMENTS

1. Discuss the statement that it is a public duty to print news of crime.

2. Compare the news and other material about crime in one week's presentation by a local daily newspaper and by radio. Discuss the amount and probable effects.

3. Make a study of a number of news stories that appear to be anti-social and point out what it is that is open to criticism.

4. Discuss the statement that news of crime provides a harmless outlet for some tendencies that otherwise might lead to crime.

5. Does the press provide law breakers with valuable information? Why wouldn't those likely to break the law already have such information?

6. How can the influence of the press on crime be measured? What do you consider the most valuable study on this subject?

7. Do critics of the press arrive at an accurate estimate of the beneficial effects of crime news?

8. Discuss the statement that it is not so much the amount of news that is in question as it is the kind of news.

9. Select some notorious criminal of recent years and, through the use of the New York *Times Index,* make a study of his career in the press.

10. Was there any traceable effect of the Heirens murder case upon the public?

11. If the rules of the Richmond *News Leader* were strictly enforced, what would be the result upon the public?

12. What set of rules would you draw up for handling crime news if you were an editor in charge of a newspaper?

13. What would be the probable results of withholding from the press and radio all news of lawbreaking?

14. Make a study of the influence of street selling upon local newsboys. What do the child welfare officials and others say upon the dangers of this trade for children?

15. What has been the record of the American press upon the Child Labor Amendment?

16. Make inquiry of a group of mothers of the effect of the comics upon their children. What antisocial activities have grown out of reading the comics?

17. Make a study of some such comic-strip character as Dick Tracy, Little Orphan Annie, or Brick Bradford, and set forth the extent to which they break or show disrespect for the law and the mores.

ADDITIONAL REFERENCES

Anonymous, "Fascism in the Funnies," *The New Republic,* Vol. 84, September 18, 1935, p. 147.

———, "The Press and College Athletics," Carnegie Foundation for the Advancement of Teaching, Bulletin No. 23, 1929, pp. 266–290.

———, "Trial By Reporters," *Time,* Vol. 27, April 6, 1936, p. 32.

Baskette, Floyd K., "Reporting the Webster Case," *Journalism Quarterly,* Vol. 24, September 1947, pp. 250–256.

Bergengren, Ralph, "Humor of the Colored Supplement," in *The Profession of Journalism,* Willard G. Bleyer (editor), Atlantic Monthly Press, 1918, pp. 233–242.

Bird, George L., "Newspaper Attitudes in Law Breaking," *Journalism Quarterly,* Vol. 15, June 1938, pp. 149–158.

Brasol, Boris L., *The Elements of Crime,* Oxford University Press, 1927, pp. 170–172.

The Commission on Freedom of the Press, *A Free and Responsible Press,* University of Chicago Press, 1947, pp. 54–56.

Crawford, Nelson A., *Ethics of Journalism,* Alfred A. Knopf, 1924, pp. 114–120.

Flint, L. N., *The Conscience of the Newspaper,* Appleton-Century, 1925.

Gottlieb, Lillian, "Radio and Newspaper Reports of the Heirens Murder Case," *Journalism Quarterly,* Vol. 24, June 1947, pp. 97–108.

Graves, W. Brooke (editor), *Readings in Public Opinion,* Appleton-Century, 1928, pp. 1090–1093.

Healy, William, *Individual Delinquent,* Little, Brown, 1915, pp. 58, 301–304.

Highfill, Robert, "The Effects of News of Crime and Scandal upon Public Opinion," *Journal of Criminal Law and Criminology,* Vol. 17, May 1926, pp. 40–103.

Hoover, J. Edgar, "His Article Misinterpreted, J. Edgar Hoover Declares," *Editor & Publisher,* Vol. 71, August 27, 1938, p. 7.

Hughes, H. M., "Lindbergh Case: A Study in Human Interest and Politics," *American Journal of Sociology,* Vol. 42, July 1936, pp. 32–54.

Hutchinson, Paul, "Why Blame It on the Papers?" *Scribner's,* Vol. 99, January 1936, pp. 43–47.

Liebling, A. J., *The Wayward Pressman,* Doubleday, 1947, pp. 243–251.

Lippmann, Walter, *A Preface to Morals,* Macmillan, 1929, Chapters 11, 12, 13.

Merz, Charles, *The Great American Bandwagon,* John Day, 1928, pp. 71–91, 215–233.

Moley, Raymond, *Politics and Criminal Prosecution,* Minton, Balch, 1929, pp. 221–238.

Pennekamp, John D., "Press Cooperation with G-Men Refutes 'Death in Headlines,'" *Editor & Publisher,* Vol. 71, August 13, 1938, pp. 5, 23.

———, "John Pennekamp Replies to *Collier's* President," *Editor & Publisher,* Vol. 71, August 27, 1938, p. 26.

Radder, N. J., *Newspapers in Community Service,* McGraw-Hill, 1926, pp. 190–194.

Reynolds, Quentin, "Death in the Headlines," *Collier's,* Vol. 102, August 13, 1938, p. 10.

Van Waters, Miriam, *Youth in Conflict,* New Republic, 1925, pp. 23, 136, 144–145, 165, 275.

Wisehart, M. K., "Newspapers and Criminal Justice," in *Criminal Justice in Cleveland*, Cleveland Foundation, 1922, pp. 515–551.

14. THE PRESS AND SPECIALIZED FIELDS
(*Labor, Science, and Business*)

INTRODUCTION

THUS FAR we have examined the performance of the press in connection with four great sources of news: government, international affairs, law enforcement, and law breaking. We turn in this chapter to a consideration of press treatment of news developments in three other fields of public affairs: labor, science, and business. All represent continuing and often controversial problems for newsmen.

Press coverage of labor affairs has attracted increasing attention in recent years. Several factors are responsible: (1) the increased tempo of the labor movement as the result of legislation such as the Taft-Hartley Act, passed on both the national and the state levels of government; (2) the extremely active program of the C.I.O. involving not only unionization drives but also political activity; (3) internal upheavals resulting from the influence of Communists in the labor movement; and (4) the rise of labor organizations seeking to attract members among the employees of the media.

Media handling of labor news receives close attention from those who watch the unfolding communications record because it is another instance of the somewhat paradoxical dualism of the press: the instrumentality to which the public looks for information about labor developments is itself a great employer of labor. (One of the most prolonged strikes of the early postwar period involved the International Typographical Union and the daily newspapers of Chicago.) This forces newsmen to adopt strict safeguards to make certain that the labor news that reaches the public is fair and accurate.

Labor controversy in its many different forms (strikes and threatened strikes, government intervention, jurisdictional conflicts, and internal bickering) provides the major test for the media. The element of conflict means that the occurrence will be accorded a top news position. Indeed, many labor leaders complain that the only news the public ever sees about unions is that based on strikes. The tendency of the press to stress the controversial is complicated by the difficulty of reporting labor warfare in a purely objective and accurate manner.

Media dissemination of emotion-tinged exchanges of charges between management and labor often actually obscures the real issues, because it is almost impossible for the press to satisfy the needs of the public without antagonizing the parties in conflict.

News stories about science offer another kind of difficulty. Although occasionally there is controversy about conflicting scientific theories, the real problem for the press is to present scientific developments in an accurate and significant fashion.

For many years, editors were interested in science news only when it appeared in a form that would make it possible to fit it into the pattern of news evaluation. Reporters assigned to cover gatherings of scientists or to abstract scientific papers searched high and low for aspects that they felt would attract the emotional interests of the public. The result was a succession of stories and features detailing the unusual, the dramatic, and the weird. In many instances, pure quackery was dignified in the news columns. There was no problem about quantity, but quality was a serious issue.

There has been a decided change in recent years. Watson Davis, long head of Science Service, estimates that it began in 1921, the year when his organization pioneered a serious effort to report news of science. World War II was possibly a much greater influence. The announcement of the use of the atom bomb against Japan was merely the climax of a number of developments that made it painfully evident in the news rooms that science would have to be reported from an entirely new angle. The result was the slow emergence of the science specialist and new modes of treatment of his subject by the media.

Serious problems remain with respect to the handling of science news. Probably no other type of news requires so much intelligent and friendly co-operation on the part of the man who is the source. Yet in many instances he finds it impossible to speak and write so that the journalist can quickly comprehend. Even if there were no problem of source, the media would still face the expensive and prolonged task of developing specialists who could write science news in a style certain to draw public attention and interest.

There is almost unanimous agreement among journalists that news about business and finance has had increasing popular acceptance ever since the Wall Street crash of 1929.

In some ways, the treatment of economic developments by the press has been like the treatment of science. For years, all business news was confined to the financial pages except that dealing with some such dramatic development as the exposure of a corrupt act. The impact of the New Deal on public thinking may have been the spark that ignited the change. In an event, the content of the media shows increasing page-one news emphasis on many different types of economic developments.

Once more, as in the case of science, the reporting of business and financial news places responsibility on the press to see that what is recorded is the real picture and not just one superficial aspect. Likewise, the media must recognize that as private business enterprises they face constant surveillance of the way they report occurrences involving the policies, the ethics, and the accomplishments and failures of their fellow entrepreneurs.

LABOR NEWS IS PAGE-ONE MATERIAL

—Louis Stark, "The Press and Labor News," in *The Press in the Contemporary Scene, The Annals of the American Academy of Political and Social Science,* Vol. 219, January 1942, pp. 109–113. Mr. Stark specializes in the reporting of labor news for the New York *Times.*

LABOR as news deserving of extended treatment may be said to have begun to make a dent on editors about 1917, when President Wilson addressed the convention of the American Federation of Labor. Labor's co-operation in the war effort had been received with satisfaction by the President, who emphasized his feeling of gratitude by a speech to the delegates, the first time that a Chief Executive of the Nation had addressed this annual gathering.

During the war, labor was big news, for the activity of the War Labor Board in dealing with strikes and labor disputes made good copy. Labor unions grew rapidly for a time, and news of their activities and aspirations found their way into the daily press.

The training or hiring of labor specialists on the daily newspapers dates from those World War days. The postwar decade saw writers with special labor and economic training on a score of newspapers, including the New York *Times,* the New York *World,* the New York

Herald Tribune, the Chicago *Daily News,* the Chicago *Tribune,* and dailies in Boston, Philadelphia, St. Louis, San Francisco, and Seattle.

Despite the growing interest of a handful of newspapers in labor coverage, most newspapers in the early twenties relied upon their general work staff to handle the news of the labor unions.

News-gathering agencies depended in considerable measure on local "string" correspondents in smaller cities for reports on strikes and labor news. Sometimes these part-time men, holding full-time jobs on local newspapers owned or dominated by local business interests, permitted the employer point of view to color their dispatches. Thus, the first impression that the world might get of an important strike, for example, would be the version retransmitted by the press association from the initial report sent out by its part-time man in the locality where the event occurred.

In recent years, however, press associations are careful to send their own staff men to out-of-the-way localities for labor news, just as they do for any other kind of news.

The year 1922 was an important one in the postwar deflationary period. Besides a national coal strike, there was a nationwide shopmen's strike on the railroads. Labor everywhere was stirring and opposing wage reductions and open-shop drives. There was an enormous amount of labor news available, and the newspapers gave more attention to this phase of the American scene.

Gradually specialists were hired or trained to handle the labor coverage. The Associated Press took on a young man whose father had been an officer of the carpenters' union in Michigan, and who had some labor background. Other newspapers followed suit, and in a few years the field of labor news was cultivated more assiduously than it had ever been. However, it was not until the passage of the National Industrial Recovery Act that newspapers began to go behind the surface events and strike situations for more serious interpretations of the aims of labor and its views and policies.

The N.I.R.A. contained a section, 7-a, which guaranteed employees the right of collective bargaining without the coercion of employers, through their own freely chosen representatives. Depression-bound unions took advantage of this guarantee and began to revive. Employees in hitherto unorganized industries, particularly in steel, automobiles, rubber, glass, and aluminum, also showed interest in Section 7-a, and they too began to form unions. Simultaneously many employers who had successfully warded off organizational attempts by their employees began counteroffensives to discourage independent unionism. They subsidized the formation of employee representation groups, ostensibly independent plant associations but in reality controlled by management.

Conflict is news, and the story of the unionization attempts of the N.I.R.A. days was chronicled at length and served to stimulate increasing public interest in problems of labor and labor organization.

Under the N.I.R.A., codes of fair competition were formulated for approval of the administration of the act. One of the requirements for any code was that it should contain the language of Section 7-a. Some employing groups sought to modify or weaken this provision, others tried to insert other provisions in the codes to nullify the labor provision. Naturally, the unions fought all such attempts. There were open hearings at which these dissenting views were expressed, and these too served to educate the public to problems of unionism and labor organization.

Invalidation of the N.I.R.A. by the Supreme Court in 1934 was the focal point for agitation by unions for a new law to insure more adequate protection of labor in its right of self-organization. Under the Recovery Act the maximum punishment that might be meted out to those employers who violated the labor provision was deprivation of the Blue Eagle, symbol of compliance. The law gave no real enforcement power to the administrator, and reference of a labor violation case to the slow and tortuous processes of the Department of Justice was of little avail.

As a result of labor pressure and with the assistance of the Roosevelt Administration, Congress in 1935 passed the Wagner Act, or National Labor Relations Act, which not only embodied Section 7-a of the N.I.R.A. but also noted specific unfair practices which were forbidden. For an employer to engage in such practices—coercion of employees or discrimination against union members—would mean that he would be summoned before the National Labor Relations Board, and if found guilty he would be called upon to restore jobs to those who had been victimized. . . .

Over night the developments in connection with the Wagner Act and the National Labor Relations Board became front-page news. The act was attacked in the courts as unconstitutional. Scores of injunctions were issued against the National Labor Relations Board, some even preventing the board from holding hearings on complaints. Employees, encouraged by what they felt to be a new Magna

Charta, made unprecedented attempts to organize into unions. There were strikes and threats of strikes.

Through the city rooms of the newspapers these events flowed in a steady stream. It was like a Niagara of news, for the Wagner Act had released energies that had long been repressed. However, it was soon apparent that something had to be done about the new source of news. The labor act, with its technical provisions, and the legal arguments raging about collective bargaining, called for a more adequate handling than the newspapers had previously accorded labor news. As a result, many newspapers trained men to do this work, and labor reporting took a big step forward. Labor specialists were developed by the press associations, and the quality of labor news gathering improved tremendously. In cities with a one-industry aspect, such as Akron in rubber and Detroit in automobiles, the labor news writers even tended to specialize in labor news of a single industry. This was a natural development. . . .

By the time the Committee for Industrial Organization was formed by John L. Lewis and his associates in 1935 there was a large public ready to devour all the news that the papers could supply on labor's aims.

To the craft-versus-industrial-union struggle between the Committee for Industrial Organization and the American Federation of Labor may be attributed an important part in the breakdown of the remaining apathy of some newspapers against publishing news of labor. I am not discussing the fair or unfair attitudes of some newspapers toward the Lewis-led movement, but I wish to make the point that they found that this controversy was news and had to be published. Imperfect as the handling of labor news may still be in some cases, nevertheless the quantity of such news which is published has vastly increased. On the whole, one may say that the quality also has enormously improved.

Today, many metropolitan papers dispatch their labor reporters to all parts of the country to cover labor conventions, strikes, and other events of labor-management significance. . . .

The future is unlikely to see any diminution in the news value of labor. So long as freedom of the press in the United States remains one of the Four Freedoms, and democratic institutions prevail, the men and women who work in the Nation's mines, mills, and factories and join unions of their own choosing will make front-page news, because their organizations are participating more and more in vital decisions of national policy.

PROBLEMS IN REPORTING LABOR NEWS

—Frederic E. Merwin, a summary written especially for this volume.

For many years the chief issues in the attitude of the press toward news about organized labor were: (1) the possible encouragement or at least acceptance of the use of violence to end labor disputes, and (2) direct or indirect interference on the side of management in controversies over organizing, recognition, wages, and working conditions.

Today, these issues have pretty largely disappeared. There has been an acceptance on the part of the press that labor unions are here to stay, that violence benefits neither side, and that the public expects a policy of neutrality to be followed. This has resulted in a maturing of press attitudes toward unions and their leaders although the record is still not spotless. Leaders of the media realize, among other things, that as major employers of labor they hardly dare permit bias and unfairness to color their reports and comments on news involving the working men and women of the nation.

This improvement in the record of the press probably came none too soon, because the postwar years produced a tremendous increase in the amount of space devoted to labor news. Numerous developments were responsible. The rounds of wage increases demanded by the unions to help members cope with the postwar inflationary spiral brought many strikes and threats of strikes. The nationwide railroad strike in 1946, the repeated walkouts ordered by John L. Lewis against coal mine operators, and C.I.O. battles with both steel and automobile manufacturers made front page news of dramatic proportions. Labor's efforts to purge itself of communistic elements captured the leads on many stories dealing with labor meetings. The pension demands of Philip Murray, leader of the C.I.O., produced numerous repercussions, including a costly steel strike in 1949. Labor entered politics formally through the Political Action Committee of the C.I.O., a development which had to be closely watched by the political writers. Congress stepped into the picture with the Taft-Hartley labor regulation act, destined to have its first test in a strike involving Chicago newspapers and the International Typographical

Union. Washington was a focal conciliation point and correspondents there found themselves writing ever-increasing amounts of copy based on labor.

These issues presented many grave coverage problems for the media.

1. Evaluation of the forces and issues in conflict was one. As Louis Stark points out in the preceding selection, there is news in any labor controversy. But news emphasis on the controversy's immediate manifestations, for example, police enforcing a picketing rule, may obscure the basic realities with a consequent damage to labor's reputation. Likewise, the great importance given conflict tends to keep labor from public view until either a strike or the threat of a strike exists. This means that the average citizen sees little about labor except a succession of incidents in which union leaders are threatening the economic status quo as a means of enforcing their demands. The situation has made the term "labor leader" almost synonymous with "strike leader." It causes labor leaders to complain frequently, and often bitterly, about what they term the failure of the press to give the public "the whole picture" of unions and their programs.

2. Explanation shares a place in the picture. The problem can be stated in this fashion: In any given labor controversy do the media give the public an accurate and meaningful explanation of the basic issues? Many students of the subject think not. They argue that the reports disseminated by the media usually show labor in opposition to the general welfare as well as management without any reference to what might be called the "justice" of a union's demands. The Nieman Fellows, in discussing press coverage of the 1946 railroad strike, stressed the point that while a tremendous job of reporting was achieved (on one day the New York *Times* carried 39 columns), "the most important detail was missing: what was the strike about? Some papers mentioned vaguely at the tag end of their stories that the railroadmen had demanded certain changes in the 'rules.' What were the 'rules?' It was left a tantalizing puzzle; most readers did not find out until the end of the strike."[1] The postwar years have witnessed an amazing increase in demands from certain members of the working press for a journalism that would accurately and fairly clarify great

[1] *Your Newspaper: Blueprint for a Better Press,* Leon Svirsky (editor), Macmillan, 1947, p. 60.

public issues. Labor certainly was one field in which this was needed.

3. Personalities make news and in so doing they occasionally either obscure or distort the picture of the events that involve them. John L. Lewis became an almost legendary labor figure in the years following World War II. Everything that he did and said carried a tone of defiance and belligerence and made excellent copy for a name-hungry press. Men like Walter Reuther of the U.A.W., and David Dubinsky of the Garment Workers learned how quickly a name can capture a headline and dominate a news story, particularly at a time of controversy. Just as the tendency to stress conflict can distort the news picture, the ease with which the press can magnify a personality tends to produce distortion. In the coverage of John L. Lewis, the real aims and aspirations of the United Mine Workers tended to fade from public view as the media concentrated attention on the defiant Mr. Lewis battling both the mine owners and the U. S. Government. The same thing occurred in the long internal war waged by Mr. Reuther and R. J. Thomas for control of the auto workers' union. The problem for the press still is to discover some means of keeping names and complex issues on a somewhat even keel.

4. Communism in the unions proved a serious postwar factor and was linked to the much broader issue of relations between this country and Russia. The Taft-Hartley act required labor leaders to file affidavits attesting lack of membership in the Communist Party; and in November, 1949, the C.I.O. went so far as to expel the electrical workers from membership because of radical leanings. The media found the situation difficult to report largely because of their own practices and the power enjoyed by the source. When one labor leader labelled an opponent as a Communist the press printed the charge as objective news. The same thing happened when a group of union officials blamed internal friction on agitation by the "Red element." The press also carried to the public the charge that Communists in the ranks of labor were taking orders from the Kremlin. There was little the press could do to meet the demands of those who called for "the true picture" of communism in labor. If a reputable labor leader called a union official a Communist, the charge, true or untrue, made news by all standards of press performance. Some relief might have been found through background interpretation, but not enough to dim the lustre of the page-one headline.

5. Sources constitute still another irritating problem in collecting news about labor. During the course of a strike, both management and the union may refuse to deal with representatives of the media for different reasons. Likewise, in many labor disputes one side may flood the press with news releases, texts of speeches, and policy announcements while the other side persists in saying nothing beyond a terse "no comment." Still a third possibility exists, one in which both parties take vigorous steps to bring their stands to the public with a resulting welter of confused and conflicting statements, many of them sheer propaganda. There has been a tendency on the part of labor in recent years to aggressively seek a "good press" when conflict emerges, but much still remains to be done by both sides in bringing the issue to the public.

The source is also a problem in the handling of what we can call routine or peaceful labor news. Many labor leaders, often suspicious of the press, make little or no effort to report their continuing activities except through their own publications. Management sees no reason to include labor in its publicity program. And the press, bound by its system of news values, turns to the situation only when drama appears.

A third aspect of the problem of source concerns an internal issue for the press, namely, the coverage it often receives from local correspondents, or stringers, on a labor development. These men report a great deal of localized news, and the way in which they see and report happenings later becomes a part of the national news flow. In some cases, these correspondents are not qualified to report a complex labor strife; in others, for one reason or another, they seem to have cause to inject prejudice into what they write.

SCIENCE IN THE NEWS

—William L. Laurence, "How to Know Nothing About Everything," *The Saturday Review of Literature*, Vol. 32, March 5, 1949, pp. 9–10, 36–37. Mr. Laurence writes news about science for the New York *Times*.

SINCE Hiroshima there is no longer an editor anywhere who does not believe in atoms. In fact, judging by some of the stuff that gets into print, editors have become almost too gullible. (Along with the general public, for example, most of them are still ready to believe, despite universal scientific assurances to the contrary, that the explosion of an atomic bomb presents the danger of starting a chain reaction in the atmosphere.) Nor do they shudder any more at the mention of cosmic rays, once you make it clear in the lead paragraphs that they hold an important key to the forces within the atom. They have developed a wholesome respect for neutrons, both the slow and fast varieties, and take protons, deuterons, and alpha particles, gamma rays and beta rays, even mesons, in their stride. If there is any grumbling, it is on the part of the hapless copy reader who cannot fit in such outlandish words as synchrotron, synchro-cyclotron, or linear accelerator into his headline, but no doubt he will learn to abbreviate them just as he learned to shorten sodium sulfathiazole, sulfapyridine, sulfanilamide, etc., into the now familiar "sulfa" drugs.

Nevertheless, the problem of educating the editor to the importance of science news, and to the fact that science news is the most significant news of our times, shaping and profoundly affecting all other events filling the pages of our newspapers, still largely remains. The relative amount of space devoted to science news, as compared with other subjects, such as politics, business, finance, and sports, is still very small. This can hardly be blamed entirely upon the editor, who judges news by what he believes his readers are most interested in. If his readers are more interested in baseball than in nuclear physics or the quantum theory, who is he to force an unwanted pill down their throats? After all, the editor, himself likely as not an ardent baseball fan, wants to produce a newspaper with the most interesting reading matter for the majority of his readers, the circle of which he aims not only to hold but to increase. "Quantum theory, did you say? Sorry, we are very tight on space tonight. Forget about it!"

Here is where one of the major problems of the science reporter comes in. He not only has to have at least an elementary understanding of what the quantum theory and similar abstruse subjects are all about; he must be able to translate the jargon of the scientists into ordinary language understandable to the layman. But mere translation is not enough. The translation must not only be accurate as to the facts, it must also be told in a manner to arouse the interest of the reader. It must, in other words, compete with the average run of news of the day and claim attention on its own merits as a news story. Furthermore, he must be prepared to do it under the pressure of the deadline.

Of course, not all science stories deal with relativity or the quantum. In fact, most science reporters shy away from these and similar highly abstruse subjects, not only because their own understanding of them is hazy, to say the least, but because they also know the reader resistance against them is too great at present to be overcome without the greatest difficulty. As a result some of the most fascinating explorations into the nature of the cosmos go largely unrecorded in our daily press and are only rarely touched upon in popular periodicals and other literature accessible to the average reader. yet the quantum and relativity theories have profoundly affected the lives of everyone now living and will play an even more important role in the lives of future generations for the very simple reason, realized even today by only a small minority, that these two theories not only brought about the greatest intellectual revolution in modern times, if not in all recorded history, but also were responsible for the advent of the atomic age.

Be that as it may, the average newspaper editor and science reporter is satisfied to deal with more practical subjects, of more immediate and direct interest to the daily lives of the average newspaper reader—new atom-smashing machines, new telescopes, new chemicals, new drugs, new hormones and vitamins, new approaches to the treatment of disease, animal experiments on nutrition, the results of research on cancer, heart disease, high blood pressure, and many other ills that plague mankind, and the latest advances in physiology, biology, chemistry, nuclear physics, astronomy, zoology, botany, etc., not to mention the many specialties in which most of the major branches are now being subdivided.

It can be seen from this enumeration that the science reporter is confronted with the impossible task of having at least a smattering of knowledge, or rather, of ignorance, over the entire range of the physical and biological sciences and the splinter groups that have grown, and are still growing, out of them. It is by now a truism that a specialist is one who knows "more and more about less and less until he knows everything about nothing." The science reporter, on the other hand, is the exact opposite. He knows, or presumes to know, less and less about more and more until he knows nothing about everything. These two extremes, and the points in between, illustrate the dilemma of both the scientist and the popularizer of science. Whereas on the one hand the field of the scientist becomes narrower and narrower, until there is hardly any contact between specialists even in the same general field, the field of the science reporter at the same time becomes correspondingly wider and wider. Within the last few years, to cite but a few examples, the specialists of virology (study of viruses), enzymology, cytology, cytogenetics, and protein chemistry were born as independent subdivisions of bacteriology, biochemistry, and genetics. Their importance may be gauged by the fact that virology may hold the answer to the cure of prevention of infantile paralysis and any other serious virus diseases, not to mention the common cold, while any one of the others, singly or in combination, may provide the key to the cure or prevention of cancer, and to some of the basic processes of life.

Obviously the science reporter cannot be a walking encyclopedia. He must have, of course, to start with a general elementary knowledge of physics, chemistry, and biology, obtained through elementary courses in college and supplemented by reading authoritative books on the subject. With this start, his job is very much like the job of any other good reporter in other fields, such as politics, finance, and business, namely, to have a thorough familiarity with the authentic sources of the news and to establish intimate and mutually trustworthy contacts with these sources. The main difference here is that the sources and the contacts are by necessity much more widely scattered than they are in other fields. More important still, the possessors of the first-hand knowledge are generally not very articulate in conveying what they know to the non-expert in simple terminology. . . .

. . . Probably the major sources of science news are the reports on research presented at the annual or semi-annual conventions of the major national scientific societies, such as the American Chemical Society, the National Academy of Sciences, the American Physical Society, the Federation of Experimental Biologists, and many others. A few of these, notably the American Chemical Society, maintain an excellent news service which provides abstracts and frequently full texts of most of the important papers presented at the meeting. Others provide a service that is very sketchy or none at all. The latter present the science reporter with a major headache. Scientific meetings are no longer the simple gatherings they used to be. They have literally become many-ringed circuses performing simultaneously in different arenas, depending on the number of sections in which the program is divided. As many as a thousand individual reports, for example, are presented at the annual winter meeting of the American Association for the Advancement of Science in a period of five days, and this in addition to several hundred scientific exhibits, scores of which may represent work of outstanding importance. The same is true to a lesser extent with other national scientific meetings. Confronted with the ever-present problem of space limitations, not to mention the even greater problem of time, the science reporter must practice selectivity to the utmost of his ability, experience, and judgment, always haunted by the doubt that he may have missed something of high significance and by the worry of being scooped by his rival newspaper. . . .

Superficially it may appear that outstanding scientific discoveries are in themselves so self-evident as to hit anyone with ordinary common sense square in the eye. Take, for example, the discovery of penicillin. In retrospect that would seem to be a natural for any reporter—a miracle drug, if there ever was one. That, however, is true only in retrospect. The first paper on penicillin ever to be presented in this country was a short ten-minute preliminary report given before a meeting of a small select medical society (the Association of American Physicians) early in May 1941. It reported largely on experiments on mice and on only three or four human patients. The total quantity of penicillin available then was a few milligrams, just enough to carry on more experiments with mice. The outlook for its large-scale production in the near future, if ever, was practically nil.

This kind of situation always confronts me with a formidable problem. Mice aren't men, and a few preliminary experiments on mice, as all scientists will tell you, are far from justifying any conclusion that the results will also be similar in humans. Emphasizing this fact in the newspaper report seems to be useless, for the desperate human patient dying of some incurable disease, or his family, flatly refuses to accept any such explanation. In the case of penicillin, and indeed in the case of most new drugs, the problem is further complicated by the unavailability of the material. If one has a conscience—and I confess to having one—one cannot help but visualize in his mind's eye, as he sits by his typewriter dashing off his report on preliminary results gained largely in animal experiments, the thousands of victims of a particular disease, and the families of the victims, in whose hearts he will kindle a spark of false hope. It does not do the patient dying of a terrible infectious disease, or his family, or his physician, any good to read one day in the newspaper that a new drug, or a new method, had been developed that cures mice of his particular affliction, but is, alas, still unavailable for him. This conflict between one's obligation to the public as a disseminator of information, on the one hand, and one's conscience as a human being not to inflict unnecessary suffering on helpless human beings already sorely afflicted, and most of them doomed to die, becomes particularly acute in reporting any developments in the field of cancer research. Speaking again for myself, I try my best to resolve this dichotomy by sticking scrupulously to facts and emphasizing to the utmost that the report in question is not yet, and may never be, applicable to human disease.

The story of penicillin may also serve as a striking illustration of what is to my mind the principal function of the science writer and the service he can perform for contemporary civilization. It is the reduction of the lag between discovery and application, with all that this implies for modern society and for the future of man.

Penicillin was originally discovered by Dr. (now Sir) Alexander Fleming of London in 1928, but the report on it in a British biological journal collected dust for more than a dozen years, and, for all we know, would still have been collecting dust were it not for the urgent need for such an anti-bacterial substance brought about by the most cataclysmic war in history. I shall never forget the remarks of Sir Alexander on one of the numerous occasions when he acknowledged an honor bestowed on him for his epoch-making discovery. "On such occasions," he remarked rather wistfully, "I cannot help thinking of the thousands now dead who would still be alive had interest in penicillin been aroused when I first discovered it in 1928."

The science writer is, of course, not alone to bear the responsibility for "the thousands now dead." Nevertheless, he must accept a large share of the blame. Had the newspapers reported on penicillin when it was first discovered, who knows but that somebody, somewhere, might have become sufficiently interested to carry on further work on it and thus make it available years before World War II? Possibly Sir Alexander himself must accept a share of the blame for not calling it to the attention of some responsible British newspaperman. But this would have been contrary to the rather rigid code of the scientists. Happily, the rigidity of this code is being relaxed somewhat, and as the science writer grows to recognize more fully his responsibility to society and convinces scientists of this sense of responsibility on his part, the more cordial will become the relations between scientists and science writers and the greater the promise for the reduction of the lag between discovery and application.

Science writing is still in its infancy. It has developed largely during the past twenty years in a helter-skelter fashion. The time has long been ripe for our universities and schools of journalism to make science writing an important part of their curriculum. An enlightened and consecrated corps of science writers can play a highly important role in a democratic society in bringing science—and its vast social implications—closer to the people and the people closer to science, with inestimable benefits to both. The well-trained and socially-conscious science writer could serve as the true descendant of Prometheus, bringing down the fire from the scientific Olympus to the people in the valley below with the full consent and cooperation of the Olympians.

THE SPECIAL PROBLEM OF MEDICINE

—Lester Grant, "Enzymes and Headlines," *Nieman Reports*, Vol. 2, January 1948, pp. 6–7. Mr. Grant specializes in reporting medicine and science for the New York *Herald Tribune*. He wrote this article while on a Nieman Fellowship at Harvard.

(EDITORS' NOTE: *In 1947, Mr. Grant and Joseph G. Herzberg, city editor of the New York* Herald Tribune, *prepared an extensive memorandum on problems in the reporting of news about medicine and forwarded it to the New York Academy of Medicine. The following is a summary of the memorandum's major points.*)

1. *Medical ethics.* Some doctors protest vigorously (some protest too much) about the use of their names in stories, particularly the constant repetition of the name through the story, on the grounds that this amounts to personal glorification and such usage can become a device whereby charlatans promote their own trade. Many doctors would prefer to remain anonymous—or say they would—as far as newspaper stories are concerned.

This is really a dangerous line of thinking, for a doctor's name in a story is some protection for the public, is at least a check against careless reporting. Without having to worry about where he got his information, the reporter might be led to the following fantasy: "A cure for cancer has been discovered, it was learned last night. This cure involves the drinking of a quart of water a day, elimination of pepper from the diet, and strict bed rest for nineteen years." If a doctor protested against the spreading of such nonsense and demanded to know the source of information, the writer might stand on his professional ethics, so called, and refuse to give the name of his informant. Such hyperbole may seem out of reach, even of some of the less responsible newspapers, but one has only to track down the sources of some of those "reliable" reports coming from "well informed spokesmen" to appreciate the risk of doing this sort of thing in science stories.

If it is an aggravation for a doctor to find his name mentioned in every paragraph of a newspaper story, then perhaps the simplest thing to do is to mention it once and let it go at that. The point is not that the reporter necessarily wants to use the doctor's name, but the story, in most cases, lacks authority without it.

2. *Bibliography*. The failure of newspapers to distribute credit, where credit is due, is one of the most frequent complaints which doctors—and scientists in general—level at the press. (In one case, the doctor complains because his name is in the story; in another he complains because there aren't enough names in the story.) The scientist argues that since his own work is bound up with the work of his predecessors, and since this is a point he usually underscores in any report of his work, it is reasonable to expect the newspaper account to credit the source of his ideas.

Some scientists are so insistent on this that one gets the impression that any mention of, say, oxygen should be traced back to the discoveries of Priestley and Scheele. It wouldn't take much of this sort of thing to make the newspapers read like text books, which is what some scientists would prefer. It is interesting, however, that even a casual mention in a story of where the doctor got his ideas, or the fact that he drew on "previous experiments of a similar nature conducted by So-and-So at such-and-such a place" makes the doctor infinitely more willing to discuss his work and explain his objectives. It also adds more words to a story and more type to the overset galleys. Yet, perhaps if this sort of thing can be done briefly and simply, it will serve a useful purpose. But one cannot hope to write a definitive history of science in every half-column account of a medical development.

3. *Qualification and accuracy.* Doctors argue that newspapers too frequently fail to make a distinction between a treatment and a cure and point—justifiably—to the confusion wrought by popular accounts of the effectiveness of streptomycin in the treatment of tuberculosis, just to name one example. Thousands of persons die annually of tuberculosis and perhaps other thousands wonder why this is so in the light of the new drugs. With faintly concealed exasperation, the doctor wonders why the science writer can't follow some such simple procedure as this: Having stated that the drug will work—or may work—under certain conditions, then state that it will not work—or may not work—under others; state the second point quickly—and high in the story—so that there will be no chance for confusion in the reader's mind. In many ways, such an argument is unanswerable and the only defense for the press is, again, that among the more responsible science writers, such a procedure is generally followed.

4. *The Doctor's Part.* Whether the doctor approves or not, or thinks that the trend is good or bad, the fact is that newspapers are carrying medical stories in increasing volume. Therefore, it would appear to a reporter that the question facing the doctor is not how to keep medicine out of the newspaper but how to get it in so that it makes sense and conforms to reasonable standards of accuracy. This is such an elementary point to the reporter that he finds himself completely confounded by either the indifference or the open hostility of some members of the medical profession.

The doctor is likely to assert that if he gives the reporter the story, the reporter will probably get it wrong; or, if the reporter does write it accurately, the doctor's colleagues will frown on the publicity. Such a disastrous generalization can only lead one to the conclusion that while newspapermen may need considerable education in science, the medical profession needs at least as much briefing in public relations.

Many doctors complain that newspapers spend too much of their time and precious white space discussing seven-day medical wonders which turn out either to be failures on the eighth day or to be a considerable distance from acceptable treatment. There is evidence to support such an assertion (reports on the use of nitrogen mustard in the treatment of cancer were overplayed, to cite one case in point), but the doctor also bears some responsibility here. Many doctors, in venting their spleen on newspaper coverage of medical matters, complain that the newspapers leap at superficial, spectacular, unproved techniques instead of confining themselves to accounts of sound, proved developments. When this happens, this writer usually asks the doctor exactly what he means and in most cases it turns out that he does not know what he means. What he probably means is that the reported ulcer cure (even though it may have been reported accurately) does not work. Yet the doctor himself may have listened as eagerly as the writer to the account of the new development. It would appear, then, that one of the things the doctor is complaining about is irresponsible doctors, not necessarily irresponsible reporters.

If this judgment makes no sense, then the alternative is clear: medical writing should be confined, if it is to appear anywhere, to the medical journals and should never be touched by the popular publications. This is a rather simple way out of the problem and one that would save responsible newspapers considerable trouble and expense. If on this basis, doctors think they can educate the public about medicine and science, as some newspapers are doing, or can raise millions of dollars for medical research, hospitals and other facilities, or can counteract the vicious propaganda of the anti-vivisectionists, or stress the necessity of vaccination in certain situations, then the doctors know an important secret about public relations which they have not yet let the newspapers in on.

When one circulates among scientists today, one is struck by a remarkable change in the thinking of scientists about newspapers and popularizations of science. For reasons which are not quite clear, scientists appear much more willing today to discuss their work and the impact of science on the community than they were, say, ten years ago. One cannot be sure that the turmoil attending the discovery of the atom bomb—with all of its terrible implications for the future—is solely responsible for this apparent change. Whatever the reason for the scientist's seeming increasing willingness to talk to reporters, the result is that newspapers are carrying more science stories than ever before. It is true that many of these stories are overdrawn, distorted, occasionally inaccurate (even by the loosest definition of accuracy), contain errors of omission and too frequently explain that a new development has certain possibilities without also explaining that it has certain limitations. Yet some of the science writing—and an increasing amount of it—in newspapers and magazines is of high quality: interesting, clear, accurate. Many scientists are willing to concede this point. And one reason it is so is because the scientists have made themselves more accessible. This is particularly true in the fields of chemistry and physics, not quite so true in the field of medicine. If the atom bomb has helped to accomplish this, perhaps it has served at least one useful purpose.

FINANCIAL NEWS DIFFICULT TO REPORT

—Frederick W. Jones, "Sources of Information and Advice," in *The Security Markets,* Twentieth Century Fund, Inc., 1935, pp. 624–629. Mr. Jones was a member of the special staff of the Twentieth Century Fund that compiled the report from which this extract is taken.

THIS IS hardly the place for an extended appraisal of American newspaper traditions or practices in general. It is, however, very much to the point to call attention to the fact that financial problems, policies, and developments do not lend themselves well to the newspaper type of treatment. The choice of news items and the treatment of them on the basis of the man biting the dog rather than of the dog biting the man, may be conducive to the production of an entertaining newspaper. But the larger part of the significant financial news from day to day is essentially routine and undramatic. It is, moreover, likely to be technical, complex, and often incomprehensible. The omission of news items for such reason, or the attempt to make them appear dramatic or to oversimplify them can hardly fail to lead to misunderstanding, erroneous impressions, immature and rashly drawn conclusions and actions by both speculators and investors. Moreover, when the dramatization, the selection, and the interpretation is effected by persons far more carefully prepared for the popularization of information than for a clear and accurate understanding and presentation of the material, the hazards are obviously increased.

In still another respect the traditional operating policies of the American press have unfortunate results when applied to financial and industrial materials. These materials are often made to order for those who wish to convey certain impressions to the general public. Both in Washington and in Wall Street organizations exist for preparing ready-made, predigested stories of economic and financial events and conditions. Skilled newspaper writers, well acquainted with the requirements of the editors, man these organizations and regularly proceed either by word of mouth or in written form to hand the reporter his story largely prepared in advance. It usually makes a good story. It is printed in essentially the form in which it has been prepared, partly because the cost of producing a newspaper is greatly reduced in this way, and also, one is forced to believe, because in a great many instances the staff of the newspaper is not sufficiently versed in the matter in hand to detect its shortcomings. It would, moreover, usually be difficult to prepare a better story, as judged by accepted newspaper standards, and the omission of the "debunking" of it by any one newspaper would leave the publication in an awkward position in comparison with its competitors which are certain to carry it and perhaps feature it. The fact is that a sane and realistic treatment of such items would often rob them of drama and preclude great simplicity of presentation. It would then provide the reader with a much truer picture of the situation, but might not entertain him as well or attract him as effectively to the newspaper in question. The question seems here to be whether the speculator and the investor want to be entertained and excited, or really informed.

This general journalistic theory and practice is at bottom responsible for the abuses growing out of what are generally known in this country as "press conferences." Much of what is inferior in the presentation of financial news is the outgrowth of the press conference, the most conspicuous examples of which are those attended by Washington reporters. Those conferences in which the official granting them expects to be directly quoted, are relatively unobjectionable. Many conferences, however, are held for the purpose of furnishing the writers "background information" with the understanding that the official granting the audience is not to be quoted nor to be made responsible for what is published.[1] The opportunity thus presented for the exploitation of an uncritical reportorial press staff for the purpose of disseminating financial propaganda is too obvious to need explanation. So convenient an instrument, of course, has not been overlooked by the financial community. The most conspicuous use of

[1] Conventional phrases used in attributing the statements to some unnamed source have in many cases become so standardized that experienced newspaper men are able to "spot" the story growing out of these conferences. But the rank and file of the public cannot understand the facts of the situation nearly so well; and in any case, the official instigating the story can usually in no way be held responsible for it.

it in New York City in the past has been by the Federal Reserve Bank of New York. Here such conferences have for years been a daily feature in the life of financial reporters for the metropolitan press. The general public, perhaps, has never suspected that the opinions of "well-informed bankers," or the private comment heard in "important financial quarters," was often in reality but the personal opinion or the personal statement of one officer of the Federal Reserve Bank of New York. Yet such is the fact.

The discussion so far has concerned itself with the presentation of individual news items. There is another, and from our point of view highly important, section of the daily newspapers which clearly shows the impress of the same set of factors—the daily reports of the speculative markets themselves, particularly, of course, the stock market. These articles, too, must be bright, dramatic and, relatively speaking, superficial. Otherwise, it is thought, and perhaps correctly, that they would not be read. As in the presentation of news, the value of these reports is thus lowered from the point of view of those who wish real light upon investment and speculative situations. The reports suffer also from other defects. They are, with few exceptions, written by men who are governed in their comments and appraisals by the speculator's interest in the security markets. Few of these writers give evidence of much knowledge or consideration of the stock market as a place in which the investor may be greatly interested. The usual daily stock market review either ignores the bond market or else mentions it only as one of the factors governing the action and the trend of the stock list. In view of traditional American ways of thought in reference to such matters, all this is doubtless natural enough, even perhaps inevitable, but the full significance of it and its effect upon the public in helping to keep the speculative spirit alive, ought not to be overlooked for that reason.

There is still another factor that needs careful consideration at this point. The usual writer of stock market reviews is not merely of one mind with the speculative public. Through constant and long-continued direct contact with the speculatively inclined elements of the financial world, he is also likely to have become possessed of almost no other viewpoint, so far as the stock market is concerned. Moreover, during the boom period ending in 1929 and at times since that date, the pool managers and the manipulators have more often than not had relatively complete control of the stock market. They have been the most active, the most vociferous and, from the speculative point of view, the best source of information about short-term price movements. The existence of pool activity in particular stocks, or the prospect of early activity of this sort, became, and still is, important news to the stock market reporter, the more so if he is inclined, as most of them are, to undertake direct or implied predictions. More than one of these writers have been and still are more or less regular speculators on a small scale on their own account. This daily living in the atmosphere of excited speculative operations, this partial identification of personal interests with that of current speculation, and this constant and relatively intimate contact with the most speculative elements in the financial community can hardly fail to leave its impress upon the articles of the daily stock market report writer. The whole country in recent years has obviously been suffering from a sort of stock-gambling mania, and probably is still quite susceptible to the malady. The stock market leader writer is simply one of the victims, but he is also an active carrier of the disease and an aggravating element in its presence. Whether or not the newspaper publisher can reasonably be expected to feel obligated to do more than to give his readers what they most want and will pay the most for, is a question concerning which opinions may and do differ. Whether there is any effective remedy that can be applied from the outside, is another story. The effort here has been merely to set forth the facts.

A practice, somewhat less indulged in at the present time than in the active years of the late twenties, is closely associated with the daily report of the stock market itself. This is the publication of a column of "Wall Street gossip," or comment, based upon reports of one sort or another in current circulation. These columns have various and sundry titles such as "*On dit,*" "It is said," etc., but they are all to the same general effect. They are devoted to the voluminous gossip current in the financial district, which is too indefinite, or not sufficiently verifiable, to print as actual news. Such columns obviously can easily be made the vehicles for the reports, vague and often even groundless, that manipulative groups purposely put into circulation to serve their own ends at the expense of the general public. In the past they have often served just such a purpose, whether or not by specific intentions of the editors or writers.[2]

[2] In some instances, they have been consciously used by writers subsidized by the manipulators. This fact has been well established in some cases by the investigations of the Committee on Banking and Currency of the United States Senate.

These chatter columns can, of course, be so written and so presented as to be relatively harmless, possibly, on occasion, even helpful, but, unfortunately, in the past they have often not been so edited. To make the matter worse, perhaps the most extensive broadcasting of financial gossip has been by publications with the largest number of readers of those classes in the population most likely to snap at the bait held out. The regular publication of brokerage comment is perhaps to be placed in the same general classification, although here the appeal is somewhat different, consisting for the most part of vaguely expressed[3] opinion that this, that or the other course of action by the reader is thought to be desirable and probably profitable at the time of writing. Here the objection is primarily the same as that which must be registered against all other forms of solicitation of margin business.

In bringing this section to a close it is well again to disavow any effort to present a critique of the American press in general. Such an appraisal would lead far beyond the province of this study. The undertaking here has been merely to look with dispassionate and realistic eyes at the press of the United States as a servant of the investor and the speculator. Judged by their worldwide coverage of outstanding and spectacular events, several of the leading daily and periodical publications of the United States are probably without superiors in the world. As purveyors of solid, useful, well-presented information concerning subjects of real import to holders of securities, and as constructive leaders of financial thought, even the best of the American dailies are inferior to such outstanding newspapers of Europe as the Manchester *Guardian,* the London *Times* and the *Frankfurter Zeitung.* This inferiority appears to be due fundamentally to the belief prevailing in this country that it is first of all the function of the press to entertain, to divert and to attract readers, and only secondarily to inform and really to enlighten them. The second cause —staffs better trained in making newspapers and magazines readable than in informing the public and guiding popular thought on financial subjects—is probably a corollary to the first. It is, of course, conceded that many of the topics about which the press is called

[3] Of course brokerage house comment on occasion becomes more pointed and in the past has often been designed to sell specific securities in which the firm had an interest. But the "comments" here referred to are of another variety.

upon to write are controversial and that even thoroughly trained economists differ at many points concerning them. It is further admitted that many of them are affected with a national and international political interest, which naturally tends further to influence individual judgments in respect to purely economic questions. None of this, however, nor all of it combined, offers, or can offer, any valid excuse for a large part of the ineptitude, the ignorance, the buncombe and the shillyshallying that characterizes so much of the economic and the financial matter appearing in the press of this country.

REVIEW QUESTIONS AND ASSIGNMENTS

1. Outline the major difficulties faced by the press in its attempt to provide an accurate and honest report of labor activities.

2. Compare newspaper and radio coverage of a current labor controversy.

3. Prepare an analysis of the editorials on a labor strike in ten newspapers published in your state.

4. Interview a labor leader in your community and write a description of his attitude toward the press.

5. Write a short paper detailing the impact of the Taft-Hartley Act on the press.

6. Study references to the union in a labor controversy in a selected newspaper or radio station and point out favorable and unfavorable words and phrases.

7. Discuss the proposal that organized labor should subsidize a national labor daily.

8. Study the coverage of science news in your home town newspaper for one month and outline strong and weak points.

9. What steps would you take as a managing editor to improve the reporting of science news?

10. What suggestions do you feel might be made to the leaders of science that would insure more satisfactory press coverage of their work?

11. What duty does the press owe its public in the reporting of financial news?

12. Prepare a list of the types of business news that you feel attract considerable reader interest.

13. What steps might the press take to improve its recording of business and financial news?

14. What would be your policy concerning business news if you were the editor of a daily in a mid-western city with a population of 25,000?

ADDITIONAL REFERENCES

Labor

Ameringer, Oscar, *If You Don't Weaken,* Henry Holt, 1940.

Bush, Chilton, *Newspaper Reporting of Public Affairs,* Appleton-Century, 1940, pp. 404–419.

Faulkner, Harold U., *Labor in America,* Harper & Brothers, 1944.

Gregory, Charles O., *Labor and the Law,* W. W. Norton, 1946.

Harris, Herbert, *American Labor,* Yale University Press, 1939.

Hartley, Fred A., *Our New National Labor Policy,* Funk & Wagnalls, 1948.

Holt, Hamilton, *Commercialism and Journalism,* Houghton Mifflin, 1909.

Howe, Irving and B. J. Widick, *The U.A.W. and Walter Reuther,* Random House, 1949.

Interchurch World Movement, *Report on the Steel Strike of 1919,* Harcourt, Brace, 1922.

Lee, Alfred M., *The Daily Newspaper in America,* Macmillan, 1937.

Leech, Harper, and John C. Carroll, *What's the News?* Covici Friede, 1926, pp. 93–117.

Lundberg, Ferdinand, *Imperial Hearst,* Equinox Cooperative Press, 1936.

Miller, Glenn W., *American Labor and the Government,* Prentice-Hall, 1948.

Seldes, George, *Lords of the Press,* Julian Messner, 1938.

Sinclair, Upton, *The Brass Check,* published by the author, 1929.

Wechsler, James A., *Labor Baron, a Portrait of John L. Lewis,* W. Morrow, 1944.

Werne, Benjamin, *The Law of Labor Relations,* Macmillan, 1949.

Science

Bryson, Lyman, *Science and Freedom,* Columbia University Press, 1947.

Davis, Watson, "Science and the Press," *The Annals of the American Academy of Political and Social Science,* Vol. 219, January 1942, pp. 100–106.

Friedwald, Eugene M., *Man's Last Choice,* Viking Press, 1947.

Herzberg, Joseph G. (editor), *Late City Edition,* Henry Holt, 1947, pp. 101–108.

Kaempffert, Waldemar B., *Science Today and Tomorrow,* Viking Press, 1939.

Krieghbaum, Hillier, *American Newspaper Reporting of Science News,* Kansas State College, 1941.

———, "The Background and Training of Science Writers," *Journalism Quarterly,* Vol. 17, March 1940, pp. 15–18.

Laurence, William L., "The Bomb and the Press," *The Saturday Review of Literature,* Vol. 31, September 18, 1948, p. 10.

Nieman Fellows, "Science in the Press," *Nieman Reports,* Vol. 1, April 1947, pp. 11–12.

Business

Elfenbein, Julian, *Business Journalism: Its Function and Future* (revised), Harper & Brothers, 1947.

Forrest, John G., *Financial News,* published by the New York *Times,* 1937.

Hall, S. Roland, *Business Writing,* McGraw-Hill, 1924.

Noyes, Alexander D., *The Market Place,* Little, Brown, 1938.

Nystrom, Paul H., *Marketing Handbook,* Ronald Press, 1948.

Plackard, Dwight H., *Blueprint for Public Relations,* McGraw-Hill, 1947.

Robertson, Nathan, "The Newspapers' Blind Spot," *Nieman Reports,* Vol. 2, June 1949, p. 20.

Wright, J. Handly, and Byron H. Christian, *Public Relations in Management,* McGraw-Hill, 1949.

Zack, Albert C., "A Study in Ethics," *The Guild Reporter,* Vol. 15, June 25, 1948, p. 6.

15. THE INFLUENCE OF EDITORIAL COMMENT

INTRODUCTION

EDITORIAL COMMENT and criticism offer the newspaper and other media an opportunity to enlarge greatly the scope of their influence on public opinion. The editorial, whether merely explanatory or sharply controversial, is a most significant part of the relationship between the press and its public. It is a powerful weapon for journalists to use in discharging their self-assumed responsibility for adjudicating those issues on which the public is deemed to need special guidance.

Editorial influence came into its own at the hands of the personal journalists of the nineteenth century, when editors like E. L. Godkin, Horace Greeley, Henry W. Grady, Samuel Bowles, and Henry Watterson pioneered a glorious trail in American journalism. These men were better known than their newspapers; their personal opinions often meant the success or failure of their publishing enterprises. They regarded all fields of man's activity as proper subjects on which to editorialize.

The sweeping change in the character of the American press, produced by the economic and technological developments that came late in the nineteenth century, brought about the eclipse of the personal journalist. The newspaper, like other business enterprises, was transformed into a highly complex corporate structure, the expenses of which could be met only through high and sustained advertising and circulation income. Management emerged as the dominant factor in internal operations and the extremely personal, often controversial, and occasionally vitriolic editorial gave way to a more judicial type of commentary. When radio and the news magazines entered the communications picture they quickly adapted themselves to the new pattern.

Contemporary editorial writers reflect this transformation to a marked extent. While "name" contributors are common in other departments of a newspaper, including the editorial page itself, the molders of opinion offer their thoughts to the public in a completely anonymous fashion. They speak simply in the name of the publication. The same fate befalls those who write editorials for magazines like *Collier's* and *The Saturday Evening Post.*

The situation, however, offers certain compensating elements. The hired editorial writers are expected to prepare comments that will reflect the authority and dignity of the publication; this obligation forces them to accord each subject a judicious and logical review. In the editorials that result, authenticity is clearly evident. There is also evidence of a strong reliance on background knowledge. The trivial is avoided unless the subject lends itself to the so-called human-interest treatment.

Whether such gains offset the losses resulting from the disappearance of the personal element is a serious and much-debated question for students of press influence. Those who think they do cite the modern commentary as a great guiding influence to which responsible members of the public can turn as they seek to solve the baffling problems of a complex civilization. The same group argues that even though editorial readership may not be high, nevertheless those who do read a paper's opinions are the most influential thinkers in their communities.

The negative side, which occasionally goes to the extreme of urging abolition of editorials, asserts that readership surveys show there is not enough audience interest in the editorial to permit the press to claim much influence for it. Data to support this view can be found in the records of a number of presidential elections, as well as those of purely local ballot contests. Where opinions are sharply divided concerning candidates and issues, the press has no assurance that the stand it takes editorially will prove acceptable to a majority of the voters. Front page headlines and pictures create much more influence than the editorial, and if the news record favors one candidate he can disregard policy pronouncements appearing on the inside of the paper.

Many reforms intended to increase readership of editorials have been tried and suggested. The most successful ones involve the use of typographic variations designed to capture attention. There is increasing interest in the use of illustrations. It would seem, however, that no matter how many innovations may be introduced, the final determinant will continue to be not how the editorial looks in type but what the editorial says.

The role of the newspaper columnists and certain radio commentators in editorial influence has increased considerably in recent years. These men, specialists who speak with the voice of authority, offer the public a syndicated version of the personal journalism of the nineteenth century. The very success of the columnists, however, serves to diminish rather than increase the possibility that the press will give more serious attention to the way it handles the opinion function on a local basis.

FOUR SIGNIFICANT TRENDS IN EDITORIALS

—Charles Merz, "The Editorial Page," in *The Press in the Contemporary Scene, The Annals of the American Academy of Political and Social Science,* Vol. 219, January 1942, pp. 140–144. Mr. Merz is the editor of the New York *Times.*

. . . WHERE it is possible to detect signs of life and movement, and to say that the editorial page is not simply standing still and giving off faint echoes of the past, certain definite trends can be distinguished. I find four such trends significant enough to be worth reporting.

The first trend is toward *interpretation.*

In descending from Olympus the editor has not really lost either his function or his opportunity. It is still his business to try to do in print for the whole body of his readers what every one of these readers does for himself or is supposed to do for himself; and that is to look out upon the world as pictured in the news columns and try to understand it and, where the news calls for action, to determine the best course of action. Every reader does that, more or less. The editorial page strives to help him.

That the editorial page has many new competitors in this field—columnists, radio news-commentators, news magazines, and so forth—ought not to be discouraging. There is plenty of work for all hands. For we are all living, and have been living for a decade, in one immense continuing crisis which has included the greatest of all depressions and the most decisive of all wars; and it is more than possible that all the interpretation that can be supplied by all the interpreters will still fall short of providing wise solutions of the enormous problems we face now and are certain to face in future. The newspaper editor ought to be willing to roll up his sleeves and pitch in eagerly, welcoming all new competition. He has his own advantages in the situation. As against the columnist, he has the advantage of being able to publish material which gains strength and variety from the experience and knowledge of a whole group of men. As against the radio, he can talk to his readers at their own convenience, and not merely catch only that part of his potential audience which happens to be listening at a particular hour of the day. He ought to make the most of these advantages.

If he is alive to his responsibility, the editor studies the news more carefully than any possible reader of his paper. He puts together items that are seemingly not linked, and looks for trends that are not always evident on the face of the day's news. He reads a good many books, talks with as many informed people as he can, uses his personal contacts for enlightenment. He tries to equip himself to interpret the news just as an architect equips himself to interpret buildings, a physician to interpret what he sees under a microscope in a blood smear. He takes it as his duty to tell his readers what, in his opinion, the news signifies. He tries to keep his prejudices out of this process as much as he can, but he makes it plain that he is interpreting news on the editorial page because the element of belief enters into the interpretation and because he cannot conscientiously inject that element into a news story. If he is equally conscientious in the handling of his own page, he weighs the evidence fairly and puts before his readers the facts that have formed his own opinions, so that the same facts will be at their service when they form their opinions. To the extent that he succeeds in clarifying any given situation, he helps to create the conditions in which self-government can function successfully.

He does not always succeed, even within the limited scope of his own opportunity. But he tries in a large enough number of cases to establish a pattern of effort. Where Mr. Greeley thundered, Mr. Greeley's successor is forced by the circumstances of his own generation to try to create some light.

The trend toward intelligent interpretation of the news is the first trend of the times that can readily be identified.

The second trend is toward *specialization.*

It is a natural corollary of the first. Since the emphasis of the modern editorial page is increasingly on interpretation of the news, and since the news itself grows more complex, it is inevitable that more people with special knowledge and experience should be recruited for the writing of editorials.

There may have been a time when the editorial staff of a metropolitan newspaper consisted of a few elderly gentlemen who lived in an ivory tower and wrote from force of habit about events which occurred at a great distance from their placid lives. But that picture, if ever true, has ceased to be an accurate portrait of most editorial offices. Today the trend runs strongly toward specialization, toward utilizing the particular abilities of men who have firsthand information gathered on the spot, toward creating an editorial page out of the aggregate experience of the whole staff of the organization.

As evidence of this trend I can cite a case with which I am familiar. The editorial staff of the New York *Times* consists of ten writers who contribute regularly to the editorial page. But this does not mean either that the editorial page is written by these ten alone, or that these ten spend all their time writing editorials. Practically without exception, they write also for other departments of the paper—the Magazine section, the Sunday book review, the news-of-the-week review. This writing takes them away from the editorial page for considerable periods. It leads them into special research. It takes them out of the ivory tower. It gives them special assignments in the field, handling such material as the progress of national defense, the question of priorities, the problems of taxation, the operation of farm laws and labor legislation, the shift of American opinion in different sections of the country on issues of foreign policy.

But this description does not even begin to suggest the extent to which *Times* editorials are the product of the specialized training and experience of the whole organization. The editorial page is not written merely by the ten regular contributors. It is written also by a large number of men and women in other departments of the paper whose special knowledge and experience in some particular field gives them a right to be consulted in the shaping of editorial policy, and from whose special knowledge and experience the editorial page can profit. How far the *Times* has gone in this direction may be measured by the fact that during the past year it has published editorials written by no fewer than fifty-three members of its staff. . . .

What is evolving here is a genuinely co-operative editorial page, built on the experience of the whole organization. The *Times* may have experimented more in this direction than most other newspapers, since it has a larger-than-average staff to draw upon. But the trend toward specialization—and accordingly toward the co-operative editorial page that is the result of specialization—is a general trend, arising from the very nature of the problem of interpreting many kinds of news.

This seems to me to be the second noteworthy trend in the evolution of the modern editorial page.

The third trend is toward *independence.*

This is a big word. But it describes the unmistakable drift of the editorial page away from its old habit of political and economic and social "regularity."

There are plenty of stalwarts left, but the habit of orthodoxy is weakening visibly. It is no longer a journalistic sensation when a "Democratic" newspaper bolts a Democratic candidate or a "Republican" newspaper attacks the Republicans in Congress. Issues cross party lines, and the editorial page pursues them. On all the important issues of the day—foreign policy, national defense, taxation, regulation of the markets, social reform, and labor legislation—there is less sheer partisan regularity than there has ever been at any other time in the whole history of the press. Labels have lost their meaning. It is a common experience to find two newspapers of the same political faith disagreeing with each other's arguments. New ideas, and proposals unorthodox enough to be called radical, have a way of turning up in conservative circles. The letter columns which share the page with editorial comment have themselves acquired a larger measure of independence, with less emphasis on the correspondent who politely echoes the editor's own opinions, and more space given to the critic and the dissenter.

All this would have astonished and dismayed the older editors who beat down opposition with a club and stuck to a party "line" through thick and thin. But the new trend toward independence of "lines" is a natural product of the times. It is the consequence of influences which have already figured in this discussion: of the increasingly complex character of the news itself; of the fact that the editorial page now spends more and more of its time trying to understand this news and interpret it; and of the further fact that more and more of this work of interpretation is done by specialists whose only interest is to reach a sound conclusion.

This is not to say that the editorial page has lost its convictions in the process of becoming more impartial. It is quite proper, and in fact in the nature of things, that an editorial page should have its basic body of doctrines and loyalties, just as it is natural that a man should have his own beliefs. Moreover, a good page values consistency. It does not wish to defend one set of principles on one subject and a conflicting set on another subject.

But a good page, while it values consistency, does not make a fetish of it. And since the editorial page no longer claims to be written on Olympus by men who are omniscient, it can afford to alter its position when facts or changes in conditions show it to be wrong.

To the degree that his philosophy makes him wish that one kind of thing will happen and another kind of thing will not happen, an editor necessarily goes beyond interpretation and takes to open advocacy of action. He finds himself urging support of one policy as against another. This is to say that he appeals to the moral nature of his readers as well as to the intellectual nature. He tries to make them see the good or bad results, from his point of view, of the things that they, individually or collectively, are doing or not doing. He sometimes praises and sometimes blames.

By what authority may he do this?

At this point I think that we can note one further trend in the evolution of the editorial page. This is the necessary assumption of a larger measure of *responsibility*.

Certainly the editor's right to admonish his readers no longer derives from the fact that he owns a newspaper or has been employed to speak on behalf of the owner of a newspaper. The era of the self-assumed and wholly irresponsible authority of the old owner-editor is ended. A kind of democratic process now enters into what the editor says. He cannot afford to let himself be cajoled or bullied by groups among his readers, yet every day he must submit himself to their electoral franchise. His opinions may be loftier than their actions, or even than his own actions. He may inculcate unselfishness in a selfish world, tolerance in a prejudiced world. But if he outrages his readers' sense of what is fair, right, and reasonable, he will hear from them. Some of them will complain directly. Some of them will stop reading his newspaper. Some of them will continue to read the newspaper but skip the editorial page—and the editor has means today of knowing when this happens, even though he lacked the intuition to realize it.

He finds that he is limited in what he may do. He must not fall behind his constituency's moral or intellectual standards. He must not get so far ahead of them that his constituency will not understand him. But he can, if he is a good editor, sensitive to popular currents, keep a good step or two in front of the procession. He can set himself against the trend of the moment when he thinks that trend is wrong. He can do his best to precipitate discussion in a democracy. Only by following his conscience and his best judgment can he have or deserve influence.

He can, of course, gain some following by expressing the prejudices or the foolishnesses of a large body of readers. Examples of this kind of editorializing are still easy to find. He does not gain respect in this way. He does not even gain influence, for he is simply exploiting states of mind and emotion that already exist.

In the long run, the editorial page, like the rest of the newspaper, is what a majority of its readers are willing to have it be. It can contain much that they do not demand, but nothing that they will not accept. It can appeal to the best side of their natures, and do this successfully, but it cannot appeal to a side that does not exist.

EDITORIAL SHOULD GUIDE PUBLIC'S THINKING

—Robert J. Blakely, "The Responsibilities of an Editor," in *Communications in Modern Society*, Wilbur Schramm (editor), University of Illinois Press, 1948, pp. 235–237. Mr. Blakely was an editorial writer for the now extinct St. Louis (Missouri) *Star-Times* when he wrote this article.

When it is realized that the press's responsibility is to the democratic process, then several prevalent conceptions of the editorial page become inadequate or even wrong. The editor's primary concern should not be with the reader's *opinions* but with his *process of thought.* Does the reader know the essential facts concerning events? Is he familiar with the issues and the arguments? Is he continually growing more respectful of reason and more suspicious of appeals to passion? Is he growing less dogmatic and more tolerant? Is he being helped to apply sound tests of logic and authority? These are the concerns of the editor, not attempts to support or oppose a party or class, not a pride in always having the answers, always being trenchant, always being "right." The editor ceases to be an advocate and becomes a teacher. This conception of the editorial page does not preclude occasional "crusades" and vigorous "stands." He who is for the free and rational debate of public issues must do battle in the service of the environment in which this kind of debate can be conducted. But the day when the editor was supposed to be Moses bringing down the tablets from Sinai has passed—and happily so. Incidentally, when an editor has been wrong or when a newspaper has a direct institutional interest in an issue, a frank admission on the part of the editor would probably build more prestige than it would destroy—after the shock had died away.

An editorial page should be a people's university. A large part of its energy should be engaged in the basic education of its readers. For illustration I give four examples. First, China. Many Americans know that eggs stand on end in China on New Year's Day, but few Americans are sensitively following the vast drama which is being played in the Asiatic theater. Second, science. Not enough Americans know the basic facts of science, but even fewer understand the methods by which science makes its discoveries, the significance of the methods of science for society, the impact of science upon their daily lives and the importance of sound national policy respecting science. Third, the Marshall Plan. The American people are told that the peace and prosperity of the world depend upon the United States' helping to reconstruct Europe. This sounds all too familiar. They were told the same things about aid to Britain, about Lend-Lease, about UNRRA, and about the British loan, yet we still have not secured peace and prosperity. Were the other appeals false? Is this one false? If not, why not? Why are we continually being asked to do more? Fourth, how to read a newspaper. Most readers do not understand the limitations of headlines and "lead" paragraphs, the importance of sources, the differences between a story's saying that something is so and its saying that somebody else says it is so. This job of basic education and current information can be tackled in a number of ways—editorials, editorial features, "trained seal" columnists, and miscellaneous material such as digests, excerpts, reprints and the like.

A major portion of an editorial page or section ought to be given "letters to the editor." Rigid requirements concerning "expertness," the social standing of the writer, literary excellence and the point of view should not stand in the way. A part of the democratic process is the distillation of relatively simple moral and common-sense issues out of complex and technical issues. The people must not be expected merely to observe this distillation. They must take part in it. "The people's forum" is a vital part of that process. It is a substitute for the opportunity to start one's own newspaper, which has now disappeared for all except a few. Over the years real contributions to sound discussion are made by lay readers. Even those which are foolish or ill-tempered serve the valuable purpose of "letting off steam." Professional newspapermen should not have a monopoly on the right to be trivial, wrong, stupid, hysterical and vulgar in print.

A word about the problem of the functioning of an editorial page staff. How can an institutional point of view be harmonized with the existence of a number of individuals? There seem to be three approaches to this problem. The first is to get "mouthpieces." Remember Henry Morgan's crack, "An editorial writer should have an open mind—so that it can be filled by the publisher" (or editor.) I can't believe that an honest editorial page can be run on this basis. The second is to get from a number of highly individual persons the "lowest common denominator" of their agreement and effort. This is all too often the result. The third is to assemble a group whose members have the same broad *general* philosophy and to have a broadly hospital editorial policy. This, I think, is the best solution. An individual can give his best. When the individual's expression is accepted as the newspaper's policy, he can be sincerely articulate; when it is not he can be honorably silent. Most of the time all members are working on the basic job of education and information to which they are all devoted.

THE WRITER AND EDITORIAL QUALITY

—Roscoe Ellard, "How to Read Editorials," *Education Against Propaganda, Seventh Yearbook of the National Council for the Social Studies*, edited by Elmer Ellis, 1937, pp. 53–56, 60–61. Professor Ellard is a member of the faculty of the Graduate School of Journalism, Columbia University.

WHEN ANY good worker could choose between half a dozen jobs, the man of the street read of burglaries and a distant war in terms he could understand. He supposed the effect of foreign exchange was as remote from his pay envelope as Betelguese. Today he is out of a job and reads that "sudden tightening of the rediscount rate caused it." He feels an emotion that through history has caused private hatred and public war: loss of support, insecurity, personal fear.

So the average reader goes feverishly to editorials to discover what it means so he can get to sleep at night. He turns to the editorial page to ease the physical weariness of mental confusion—and to articulate his indignation.

And it is doubtful that major news in our lifetime will ever again be simple. The mind seeks order in the things that vitally concern it; and there is little order in a day's news. Editorial pages, therefore, are no longer caviar to the general; they are butter and eggs, according to sixty-five editors in a survey of leading American dailies. To meet this problem, we find two extremes of editorial capacity, with varying degrees between them.

At one extreme, the understaffed newspaper expects one or two editorial writers to fill from two to three columns a day from six to seven days a week. Of sixty-five large dailies recently studied, nineteen had one editorial writer; twenty-five had two; five had three; eight had four; seven had from five to seven working full time on from one and a half to never more than two 17-em columns. One paper reported that it had "one-half of an editorial writer," explaining that their Janus spent half of his time at other duties. And there you have a pretty good index of newspaper editorial quality.

Of these sixty-five strong newspapers, fifteen employ from four to seven men to write half a column or less of editorial comment a day. This affords a certain specialization, reasonable weighing of facts, and revised editing. Good editorials come from 90 per cent analysis and 10 per cent composition; they never come from tired minds. On well-staffed editorial pages, cases before the Supreme Court, important bills before Congress, international crises, are studied for weeks before particular news occurs to make comment timely. Frequently an editorial writer spends from two days to a week preparing a half-column editorial. . . .

The principal reason why the best editorial pages are worth reading is because their writers make a business of informing themselves about the background and integration of the news. Few editorial writers on important papers are under 40 years of age; most of them are between 50 and 60. Practically never does a newspaperman become an editorial writer until years of reporting have prepared him to interpret particular fields. Editors consider a knowledge of social science indispensable. Irving Brant, chief editorial writer of the St. Louis *Star-Times,* recently published a book on money, another on the Constitution; scholars rank both as "brilliant and authentic." Commentators' contacts with important men and affairs help to give them a practical, unacademic view.

Editorial sources of information, besides including men in key positions, embrace newspaper reference libraries situated a few steps from the editorial desk. Journalists do not depend on public libraries, because general collections of books cannot contain the current documents and constantly replenished clippings which daily publications require. The extent to which newspapers go to afford their writers reference material can be gleaned from the fact that the library of the Philadelphia *Public Ledger* was appraised at $2,000,000, that of the Boston *Globe* at $1,000,000, and in newspaper sales of smaller papers the reference departments have frequently been listed at more than $500,000. . . .

It is not essential—or possible—that editorials should reveal the "ultimate truth." No one knows the ultimate truth about current history; and truth is always truth from a point of view. What does matter is that editorials should tersely, intelligibly, and as authentically as time permits, define and explain the news with the principal purpose of inducing large numbers to think—not to think occasionally, but to think habitually, day after day, about the public affairs that surround them.

Editorials should not consist of unsupported opinion; they have substance only when specific data and logic are supplied. The best practice today is not to tell readers paternally what to think, but to give them light with which to see and stimulus to reflect. To accomplish this requires an unusual ability to make commentative writing widely interesting; and interest cannot be aroused without humanization and clarity. Editorial pages which circulate among hundreds of thousands of all sorts and conditions of men cannot be "confidential communications" comprehensible only to those possessing technical vocabularies and extensive background. . . .

Every editorial, it seems to me, should answer an inevitable question and evoke an exclamation. A reader begins an editorial with the unformulated query, "What's this to me?" A writer should make the answer unobtrusively clear. On finishing the editorial, a reader should be stirred to think, "Now there's an idea, isn't it!" Peter Hamilton of the *Wall Street Journal* once asked, "Are editorials worth reading?" and *Editor & Publisher* aptly answered, "Yes, when they are worth reading."

Thus we see that a critical reader needs first to understand that good, bad, and indifferent editorials make up American journalistic opinion. Fortunately, one cannot read it all. If we know the earmarks of an authentic editorial page, we can read it and one or two of its peers; for newspaper comment in a particular journal is reasonably even in quality. It is the product of a fairly permanent staff and a fairly constant source of information.

A critical reader should next understand that editorials today are written chiefly to define and explain, to provoke thought by supplying light and interest and broadly usable material. Comments seldom attempt to tell people what to think or to assume omniscience. Frequently they state a conclusion and suggest a definite program not as paternalism, but as an aid to interest and to concrete reflection.

Editorials often result from conference and from several contributory minds. Editorials may define by setting forth a geographical setting, an historical background, by identifying and classifying conflicting forces, by delineating involved issues, or by outlining movements and groups. They may explain by analyzing unapparent causes, by interpreting national policies, by assessing personal motives, or by setting forth the effect of an event, dangerous as an irresponsible functioning of these last two methods may be. They may debate a contrary position in a polemic issue, or they may merely entertain as a condiment for the page. For the most part, however, editorials seriously attempt to throw light on obscure news.

THE EDITORIAL WRITER'S CODE

—Robert U. Brown, "Editorial Writers Adopt Basic Code of Principles," *Editor & Publisher*, Vol. 82, October 29, 1949, p. 7. Mr. Brown is editor of *Editor & Publisher.*

(Editors' Note: *The National Conference of Editorial Writers, organized in 1947, adopted the first Code of Principles ever outlined by U. S. editorial writers at its convention in October, 1949. In announcing the Code, the editorial writers said that they planned to "assume, year by year, the large share of moral responsibility for the integrity of a free press in a democratic society that goes with editorial writing and editiorial page editorship.*")

THE BASIC CODE of principles follow:

Journalism in general, editorial writing in particular, is more than another way of making money. It is a profession devoted to the public welfare and to public service. The chief duty of its practitioners is to provide the information and guidance toward sound judgments which are essential to the healthy functioning of a democracy. Therefore the editorial writer owes it to his integrity and that of his profession to observe the following injunctions:

1. The editorial writer should present facts honestly and fully. It is dishonest and unworthy of him to base an editorial on half-truth. He should never consciously mislead a reader, distort a situation, or place any person in a false light.

2. The editorial writer should draw objective conclusions from the stated facts, basing them upon the weight of evidence and upon his considered concept of the greatest good.

3. The editorial writer should never be motivated by personal interest, nor use his influence to seek special favors for himself or for others. He should hold himself above any possible taint of corruption, whatever its source.

4. The editorial writer should realize that he is not infallible. Therefore, so far as it is in his power, he should give a voice to those who disagree with him—in a public letters column and by other suitable devices.

5. The editorial writer should regularly review his own conclusions in the light of all obtainable information. He should never hesitate to correct them should he find them to be based on previous misconceptions.

6. The editorial writer should have the courage of well-founded conviction and a democratic philosophy of life. He should never write or publish anything that goes against his conscience. Many editorial pages are the products of more than one mind, however, and sound collective judgment can be achieved only through sound individual judgments. Therefore, thoughtful individual opinions should be respected.

7. The editorial writer should support his colleagues in their ad-

herence to the highest standards of professional integrity. His reputation is their reputation, and theirs is his.

THE USE OF PICTURES AS EDITORIALS

—John W. LaRue, "Crusading With Pictures," in *Problems of Journalism,* Proceedings of the American Society of Newspaper Editors, Washington, 1941, pp. 133–135. Mr. LaRue was a member of the editorial staff of the Cincinnati (Ohio) *Enquirer* at the time he made this address.

EDITORIALS didn't always have to be in print. We put editorials into pictures. It might be hard, in print, to convince 65 per cent of a voting populace that, according to our surveys, reads editorials up to only 12 per cent. Probably some of these surveys are not quite truthful, but something like 75 per cent really do look at pictures.

Pictures can't be contradicted. You can use them with short texts in large type, and knock your readers' eyes out. You'll get results. . . .

So here are the elements. We have a river pool full of sewage, a water intake for three cities totaling 700,000 people, a proposed bond issue, and a state law requiring a 65 per cent vote on a municipal bond issue.

That 65 per cent is the killing item. But we thought that in a matter that is more vital to people than bread, we could beat it, although mere editorial endorsement had failed before. So we used pictures—and they were pretty horrible pictures. We frequently debated whether it was quite nice to put such pictures before Mr. Citizen at his breakfast and, alas, his morning glass of water.

I have some of these pages with me, not very many, but enough to show the general use of them. We used the scummiest pictures we could find; pictures of the filthiest sewers nearest to the city water works; pictures that almost had a stench; micro pictures of horrible little monsters found among the deadly bugs in the river. And we kept repeating, in page-one editorials calling attention to the pictures, that "this is what you drink."

I will always believe that that campaign, aided manfully by all the newspapers up and down the river, has won a victory for clean water that will free from their own folly the 20,000,000 of the Ohio River watershed.

The bond issue? I don't remember the vote. It was close to three to one.

There were other bond issues. I will take notice only of those that are partially illustrated by the pages that I have with me. School bonds, for instance. Children are like the poor: we always seem to have more and more of them with us; and they all seem to have a perfect passion for going to school, which we will all recognize as another sign of changing times. In any event, the city school system which everyone had been complacently criticizing as the country's most extravagant, was suddenly found to be short of teachers and housing, and stoves, and facilities of every kind. And while you should always listen twice to the complaints of an educator—the second time with your bad ear—the schools really needed help.

So we tried the same technique. And again it worked. The school bonds, in addition to an extra tax levy, went over with a wide margin to spare over the 65 per cent. After all, you can make a very convincing case with pictures of kiddies with bare legs hovering in the cold of an auxiliary shack. Of course, they might not have had to have bare legs, but that seems to be a part of modern education.

Then there was the necessity of saving a hospital—and I mean it was a necessity. It was, and, fortunately, still is, operated by the Sisters of a Catholic charity, in what might be called the darker areas of downtown Cincinnati. But it was still a great and invaluable institution, and without money. It was about to close; it needed new equipment; the marvelous work it did with West End children was about to die. Well, everybody got behind St. Mary's Hospital, but after the known influence of picture editorials in other ventures, I always feel that they were most instrumental. I have two of a series here.

In the last two or three years we have consistently used editorial picture pages to further or to support what we think are good things.

In connection with a great many of them we have used editorials in large type on page one, not so much as editorials but as an index to where the pictures are.

We have had some rather fervid arguments here about the decline in power of the editorial. We have wondered vocally if we weren't all slipping from those magnificent days when a vociferous editor—a Greeley, a Dana, a Watterson—swept all before him. Certain among us here cried in their beer because the nearly combined efforts of every great newspaper north of the Ohio River and Texas couldn't defeat one man. Ostensibly we hated him so much. Of course, now most of us are supporting him.

I don't think we should worry about the decline of the editorial. It's probably a little more popular now than before the war—this war, I mean. And it's interesting to note that the strictly technical editors who bewail the loss of editorial prestige, and say that the columnists have taken it all away from them, never reflect that those old and great editors were the influential columnists of their day. They didn't sign their columns but everyone knew who wrote them. You expect more of a man than you expect of so many lines of type. But regardless of what you expect from a picture, it's there before you, and it can't be denied.

Naturally, we have kept the editorial use of the picture page absolutely precise; no politics; never publicity. You can't abuse a great power; and if you'll use it you'll be surprised how strong it is.

WHAT ABOUT THE COLUMNISTS?

—Arthur Robb, "Shop Talk at Thirty," *Editor & Publisher*, Vol. 73, April 20, 1940, p. 80. Mr. Robb was for many years editor of *Editor & Publisher.*

WHAT ABOUT the columnists? Is the ever-growing list serving to bring newspapers into disrepute? We are asked these questions by a newspaperman, with 40 years of modest success to his credit in advertising, circulation, and administrative posts. "I have never worked as a reporter or editor," he goes on, "but I have always had the highest regard for editorial people because of their adherence to ethical standards. I have no personal knowledge of any reporter worthy of the name violating a confidence. And I do not believe any reporter or editor of the average newspaper could get by with the lack of restraint shown by the average columnist. I do not believe any newspaper would keep a reporter or editor who was as careless with truth, who dealt with rumor and personal antipathies as many of the columnists do. I don't believe the average columnist represents the best side of the newspaper, or that he is bound by the same standards as the men who have contributed to making the American newspaper an essential part of community life.

"I do think that lack of editorial supervision over the utterances of columnists who are credited as representative of the newspapers' editorial side is responsible for mounting suspicions by readers that the truth is not necessarily a consideration in producing the average newspaper."

Well, there are columnists and columnists. A few of them deserve the harsh words our friend applies to them. We think so, anyway. Many more are just as sincere and just as honest and as ethical in their writing as any newspaperman who ever lived. We don't suppose there is any columnist on the American scene who could be accurately called the "average," and there is no newspaper which can be called "average." Some columnists are genuine ornaments to the newspaper profession. Others are allowed to call themselves newspapermen mainly because their unconventional technique produces provable circulation. They are the strip-tease part of the newspaper vaudeville show, known to their columnar contemporaies by various uncomplimentary titles. They are, however, in the newspaper picture because the public reads them, whether it believes them or not. We can testify, from repeated experiences, that many of the "exclusives" claimed by these prophetic gentry remain "exclusive," and we'll agree with our advertising friend that no reporter or editor could get by with as low a batting average as some of the better known gossipers own.

We have never considered the night club gossip columns as having solid asset value. Some are better than others in respect for privacy and in accuracy of reporting; none of them particularly add to the public's esteem for newspapers and newspapermen.

We can't make any blanket decision on the political columns. Some of them are excellent and carry out scrupulously their assignment of interpreting the news fairly and temperately. We can name half a dozen who would be certain of a place in any paper under our direction. Not every day, possibly. Their job is to bring something to the reader by virtue of their familiarity with political trends and the people who make and guide those trends. The people we have in mind come through often enough to merit the confidence of both editors and readers. There are only a few whose work is prejudiced, propagandist, or just plain reckless, and newspaper people know who they are.

The last word, of course, rests with the editor—and we suspect that one of the major troubles with the columns is that in too many offices they do not receive the meticulous attention that is given to home-produced stuff. Some papers we have read seem to toss the stuff into its allotted page, and then edit it in type for space rather than for policy or sense. You can get some curious results that way. We do not believe that any editor has the right to change the signed opinions of another man either for space or for policy; corrections for space should not be made hit-and-run as the page is being locked up and they should be made carefully to conserve the writer's meaning. If the editor believes that a column is offensive or that it violates fundamental policies of the paper, we maintain that he has the full right to leave it out.

The political column has a place of tremendous importance. It ought to give the reader information that the home-town editor cannot produce from his resources. It might also be selected with good reason to give the reader another viewpoint than that of the editorial page—but emphatically, we have always maintained that no column should be a substitute for the newspaper's own leadership and guidance of home-town opinion. Columns may supplement or complement that newspaper function, but they cannot perform it for a healthy newspaper.

We might also observe that columns have been selected occasionally for their alleged circulation value—the so-called big name appeal. The column thereupon becomes an investment, a slug of type which the staff believes must be used, regardless of whether it is sense or tripe. That doesn't happen very often and it doesn't happen at all in an office where the editor is conscious of his responsibility, and has the responsibility for buying and keeping features. Regardless of salesmen's claims, the test of any column is the same as that for any other news and comment—is it true?, is it interesting?, is it a fair presentation of its subject? "Keyhole" and "gents room" journalism (which Joe Williams considers a libel on gents' rooms) can't have a permanent place at all in columns dealing with national policies and personages. The line is thin between smart reporting and scandal-peddling, but good reporters know where it is and don't cross it.

COLUMNISTS AND EDITORIAL RESPONSIBILITY

—Marvin H. Creager, address before the American Society of Newspaper Editors, *Problems of Journalism,* Proceedings of the 17th Annual Convention of the American Society of Newspaper Editors, 1939, pp. 29–32. Mr. Creager was president of the Milwaukee (Wisconsin) *Journal* when he made this address.

In the remarks that I am going to make I think perhaps that I should explain that this isn't an attack on columnists. I am not going to take up the line of Mr. Ickes, who referred to them as "calumnists." I think they are pretty smart people. In fact, I think that is perhaps the one thing that we have to watch. I am not here to blame them in the least, or to criticize them in the least. If they can get out a column that they can sell to from 50 to 300 papers, I think they are pretty smart people, and if they can find the buyers, O.K., but, it is a matter of *caveat emptor*, as President White said, the buyer ought to look over this product.

Information as to the number of subscribers to each of these columns is available from some of the syndicates which merchandise the writings, and according to those figures the highest circulated column has 318 newspapers, the next highest is 174, and altogether there are six that have 100 subscribers or more, according to the figures of the syndicates. In one or two cases the number of subscribers was withheld by the syndicate.

Among the newspapers buying from several to a dozen each of these columns are many of the most widely known of the American newspapers, and I enjoy the privilege of acquaintance with several very able editors who consider those columns of the highest importance to their newspapers.

There can be no question as to the ability and probity and skill of the authors of these columns as a whole. They turn out highly readable and interesting material. They write columns that glitter, but their success, especially their financial success, depends upon the number of newspapers that buy their wares. They are writing something to sell and their audience changes with the vicissitudes of the syndicate business, over which they have little control.

With this number of column writers so widely used throughout the country, it would seem obvious that the "obligations" of interpretation are being widely farmed out, and they are being farmed out to writers whose prosperity depends upon the salability of their writings. How generally these columns are being substituted for individual editorial work by newspapers, I do not know, but my impression is that it is being done extensively. And so arises the question as to whether American editors are shirking their responsibility.

I think they are in many cases. Doubtless there is an economical factor in the situation. These columns are not inexpensive, especially if competitive papers in the same town want the same column, but even so they do not cost as much as a competent and adequate staff of editorial writers. Not only that, but their output has professional polish, often luster, and is likely to be more attractive than the home-made product.

But granting all that, the newspaper that accents and depends upon the interpretation of important events by persons with whom it is not in touch and over whom it has no control is to that extent, shirking the "obligations" quoted in our text. Not that a newspaper should control interpretation to the extent of dictating everything that is printed, but it must be responsible for what is printed and to be responsible it must know the circumstances under which it was written and understand the background for it.

There is the old editor that Kin Hubbard told about. He said he just came from the poorhouse, where he went to visit an old editor friend of his who tried to please everybody. Some editors evidently wish to please everybody, believing they achieve that end by printing columns representing various schools of thought and then preen themselves on their fairness. That plan does not appeal to me as fulfilling a newspaper's "obligations" as interpreter. A newspaper should have ideas of its own and express them without the help of syndicated writers who at the same time are expressing opinions for from 50 to several hundred other newspapers over the country.

Some newspapers edit these columns although it is my impression that comparatively few do so unless it be to cut them down occasionally to meet space conditions. A newspaper in my home town made bold to edit one of its syndicate columns a few weeks ago and was bitterly assailed by another newspaper for violating freedom of the press. So a sort of sanctity seems to be growing up around these columns. Mere editors are not supposed to meddle with them but to take them and like them. I don't mean to imply that I think that is the general feeling, but I have heard that there are columns sold with the understanding that they be not edited.

I think we are all agreed that the important thing is to inform the reading public rather than confuse it. The real information on public affairs is contained in the day-by-day news properly prepared and presented. The public is sufficiently intelligent to follow this news if it is intelligibly presented and to draw their own conclusions from it. The trouble is to get them to read it. I submit that often columns of comment are in effect predigested versions of the news, easy for the reader to take and tending to wean him away from the news columns which he ought to be reading.

I have had an opportunity to note the effect of these columns on the readers of newspapers in a typical American industrial city. Practically all of the top-flight columns are printed in the newspapers there, and those columns are widely quoted. One hears on every side about what this column writer and that column writer said. But it is always the columnist and never the newspaper which printed the column that is quoted. The editorials in the newspapers using these columns are so seldom mentioned that one wonders if the columnists haven't stolen all the thunder from the paper. And still we inquire what has become of newspaper influence. I think they still have influence and plenty of it, but I don't believe the columns add any to that influence and I don't think the newspaper that surrenders its "obligations" to any outsider can expect to hold its influence unimpaired.

I am willing for the sake of argument to grant that these columns have wide reading. The fact that they have wide reading is one of the main reasons why I am inclined to view them with alarm. But I wonder if editors are not sometimes somewhat deceived as to the number of readers they have. A somewhat desultory survey in the community mentioned before indicates that the run-of-mine readers are not particularly up on columnists; in fact, several of the burghers were under the impression that one of the most profound commentators was a sports writer. Furthermore, in that same community one newspaper which has never printed more than one column, and that so nearly as possible a factual column, has improved its circulation situation in comparison with competitive newspapers which have carried them all or practically all.

I am not sufficiently familiar with these columns to attempt a criticism of their contents. I think they, for the most part, represent the highest grade of public writing. It seems to me that sometimes I have noticed a little inclination toward mutual back scratching. Within the last few weeks I have seen one column devoted to an explanation to the Irish readers of what the columnist had meant in a recent reference to that nationality in his writing. Another columnist used one day's space to repeat what the same writer had said a year ago and to add, in effect, "I told you so." But that is all human enough.

There is another phase of the situation that I think may be worth mentioning. American journalism always has attracted to its ranks many brilliant and ambitious young men and women. It is, of course, the ambition of these young men and women to become wielders of influence through their writings. They are all set to make the rafters ring and, Lord bless them, I admire their enthusiasm. But what chance have these youngsters to achieve their ambition if they must work in a journalism in which the editorial functions are largely purchased from syndicates? Years ago a fledgling journalist out of Emporia wrote a piece entitled "What's the Matter with Kansas?" It got into newspapers all over the country and William Allen White was made. Of course he has been improving every one of the forty or more years since then, but that piece put him on the map. I am just wondering how many papers would use a piece like that by a boy unknown to fame in competition with widely promoted readymade columns that many papers feel must be used every day whether they say anything or not. Among the duties of the newspapers of America is the perpetuation of American journalism. It can't be perpetuated if ambitious youngsters cannot see in it some chance for individuality. The recent activities of the Guild have tended toward leveling off individuality. Further influences toward that end can only have unhappy results on the future influence of American newspapers.

And so, in so far as editors are permitting mailorder columns to usurp the functions of their own editorials, I believe that they are shirking a solemn duty and "obligation" and are sacrificing their influence in their communities. True, the ready-made product may be smoother and more attractive. Mother's pie is often not so beautiful as the one painted on the bakery wagon, but you do know what is in it and how it got there.

REVIEW QUESTIONS AND ASSIGNMENTS

1. Do you feel that a Horace Greeley would be a beneficial influence today?

2. Why wasn't the modern newspaper able to retain the practices of the personal journalist of the nineteenth century?

3. How would you summarize the strong and weak points of the present-day editorial from a standpoint of influence?

4. Do you feel the modern newspaper lacks personality because it prohibits bitterly controversial editorials?

5. Do you favor the use of the editorial approach by radio?

6. Study the style and content of editorials over a period of two weeks, in five selected newspapers. What are your conclusions?

7. Do you detect any use of editorial expressions in the broadcasts of radio commentators? Cite illustrations and discuss.

8. If you were an editorial writer on a newspaper in a town of 50,000 population in the Middle West, what would be your editorial philosophy?

9. Carry out the same discussion as in Question 8 for a weekly paper in a county-seat village with a population of 3,000.

10. Do you see anything either dangerous or pernicious in buying editorials from a syndicate and reproducing them as though they had been written in the office of the newspaper?

11. Interview an editorial writer for the answer to the questions about editorial influence that strike you as most pertinent.

12. Evaluate the criticisms and defenses uttered on editorial influence following a selected presidential election.

13. Study the writings of a columnist and write an evaluation of the style and structure employed.

14. Would you favor the use of signed columns as a replacement for editorials?

ADDITIONAL REFERENCES

Abbott, Willis J., *Watching the World Go By,* Little, Brown, 1933.

Allen, Eric W., "Economic Changes and Editorial Influence," *Journalism Quarterly,* Vol. 8, September 1931, pp. 354–359.

Baehr, Harry W., Jr., *The New York* Tribune *Since the Civil War,* Dodd, Mead, 1936, pp. 3–21.

Bingay, Malcolm W., *Of Me I Sing,* Bobbs-Merrill, 1949.

Bleyer, Willard G., *Main Currents in the History of American Journalism,* Houghton Mifflin, 1927.

Bush, Chilton R., *Editorial Thinking and Writing,* Appleton-Century, 1932.

Carlson, Oliver, *Brisbane,* Stackpole Sons, 1937.

Dana, Charles, *The Art of Newspaper Making,* Appleton-Century, 1895.

Davis, Elmer, *History of the New York* Times, the New York *Times,* 1921.

Doob, Leonard W., *Propaganda, Its Psychology and Technique,* Henry Holt, 1935, pp. 333–339.

Ferril, Thomas H., *I Hate Thursday,* Harper & Brothers, 1946.

Fisher, Charles, *The Columnists,* Howell, Soskin, 1944.

Foster, Charles R., Jr., *Editorial Treatment of Education in the American Press,* Harvard University Press, 1938.

Graves, W. Brooke (editor), *Readings in Public Opinion,* Appleton-Century, 1928.

Gross, Rebecca F., "Editorials–Whether, Why and Whither," *Nieman Reports,* Vol. 2, July 1948, pp. 16–18.

Hale, William Harlan, *Horace Greeley: Voice of the People,* Harper & Brothers, 1950.

Harlow, Rex F., *The Daily Newspaper and Higher Education,* Stanford University Press, 1938.

Hearn, Lafcadio, *Editorials,* Houghton Mifflin, 1926.

Hearst, William Randolph, *Selections From the Writings of William Randolph Hearst,* published privately, San Francisco, 1948.

Heaton, John L., *Cobb of the* World, E. P. Dutton, 1924.

Hooker, Richard, *The Story of An Independent Newspaper,* Macmillan, 1924.

Howe, Quincy, *The News and How to Understand It,* Simon & Schuster, 1940.

Johnson, Walter, *William Allen White's America,* Henry Holt, 1947.

Krock, Arthur, *The Editorials of Henry Watterson,* Doubleday, Doran, 1923.

Lundberg, Ferdinand, *Imperial Hearst,* Equinox Cooperative Press, 1936.

McKelway, St. Clair, *Gossip: The Life and Times of Walter Winchell,* Viking Press, 1940.

Mencken, H. L., *The Days of H. L. Mencken,* Alfred A. Knopf, 1947.

Miller, Lee G., *The Story of Ernie Pyle,* Viking Press, 1950.

Mills, William H., *The Manchester* Guardian, Henry Holt. 1922.

Mitchell, E. P., *Memoirs of an Editor,* Charles Scribner's Sons, 1924.

Nevins, Allan, *American Press Opinion,* D. C. Heath, 1928.

Rogers, James E., *The American Newspaper,* University of Chicago Press, 1909.

Salmon, Lucy M., *The Newspaper and the Historian,* Oxford University Press, 1923, pp. 271–277.

Seitz, D. C., *Horace Greeley,* Bobbs-Merrill, 1926.

———, *Joseph Pulitzer,* Garden City, 1924.

Svirsky, Leon (editor), *Your Newspaper: Blueprint for a Better Press,* Macmillan, 1947, pp. 143–151.

Waldrop, A. Gayle, *Editor and Editorial Writer,* Rinehart, 1948.

Weingast, David Elliott, *Walter Lippmann: A Study in Personal Journalism,* Rutgers University Press, 1949.

White, William Allen, *The Autobiography of William Allen White,* Macmillan, 1946.

16. THE CRUSADING NEWSPAPER

INTRODUCTION

NEWSPAPERS have been as proud of their "crusades" during the past fifty years as of almost any other activity. The campaigns against vice, erring politicians, the law's delays, iniquities of the public utilities, and scores of other ills have brought much self-satisfaction to the press and have been used as the indirect answer to a great deal of the criticism directed against it. Most newspapermen admit that a great deal of truth is contained in the criticisms of the press. In fact, the newspaperman is generally on the defensive against himself as well as against the critical public. Whenever any such criticism has grown too severe, he has been inclined to seek shelter by turning to the brilliant feats of numerous papers scattered about the country. In them he finds a partial justification for the press and his presence therein.

But it may not have occurred to many newspapermen that one of the great abuses of the press is to be found in the crusade itself. The facts that some campaigns undertaken in the name of public morality are actually drives for circulation and advertising revenues, that many campaigns leave the public more befuddled and more ignorant of true conditions than before the campaign opened, and that reforms apparently accomplished are often swept out with the first contrary political breeze have not received the publicity in the newspaper columns that a complete exposition of affairs demands. In fact, it is difficult outside the newspaper office to distinguish between the crusades undertaken wholeheartedly for public benefit and those begun for personal gains alone.

It may be true, however, that newspaper crusaders belong to a vanishing era. At least Gorman indicates in the first citation that this may be the case. But for the still hopeful reformer he has some excellent advice on how to conduct a crusade. Some of the pitfalls of crusading are pointed out by Linford in his tale of battling for civic improvement in a small town.

Many writers (including Eric W. Allen) who have studied the

problems of these campaigns have decided that there are virtues in the use of other types of reform influence. Yet some glorious records of achievement have been set by the crusaders; Bleyer describes one of these in his account of Nelson of the Kansas City *Star*. However, several decades ago Lincoln Steffens gave a different picture of crusading that should not be forgotten. The last citation is from Silas Bent's *Newspaper Crusaders,* the best work yet done on this subject.

ARE CRUSADERS DYING OUT?

—Mike Gorman, "The Anatomy of the Crusading Reporter," *Nieman Reports,* Vol. 3, April 1949, pp. 5–6. Mr. Gorman is a staff member of the Oklahoma City *Daily Oklahoman.*

THERE WAS a time in American journalism when the so-called crusading reporter—the newspaper writer who continually looked under rocks and yelled to the high heavens about what he found there—enjoyed a rather exalted status among both his colleagues and the general public.

As one of the members of what a friend of mine has chosen to call a dying breed, which he claims will soon be as extinct as the bison and the five-cent cigar, I have tasted both the bitterness of the gall and the sweetness of the adversity.

I am alarmed at the number of crusaders who are deserting the profession each year. Recently, I talked with a prominent magazine writer who had been quite a newspaper crusader in his day. I was annoyed when he placed the average life-time of a crusader in modern journalism at five years. I asked him how he arrived at his precise mortality figure.

"Very simply," he replied. "Any crusading reporter worth a damn will burn himself out in five years. If he is bucking the status quo, his guts get worn out being punctured on the firing line. If he doesn't get worn out this way, he packs it in because he gets sick and tired of the righteous snipers—the respectable delegations calling on the publisher and telling him the reporter's writings are inspired by the devil himself."

He had something there. There really were few obvious satisfactions. The little money one got certainly wasn't one of them. If you looked for a substitute for Mammon in the form of personal prestige in the profession, you were looking up a blind alley. The hot rocks on the paper—the policy men—were the reporters who handled the big runs like the state capitol, city hall, the courthouse, etc. The crusader, who had an amorphous run which he usually built up himself, sat off in a corner and ranked in importance with the garden editor or the guy who wrote the fishing column. His colleagues, "realists" who hung a cigaret from their lips and met each deadline with unfailing monotony and an equally unfailing lack of imagination, took a dim view of a reporter who got emotionally excited about human welfare and the stinking state of the present world.

Above all, there was the constant pressure of that mechanized giant—the modern newspaper. Everything was as appallingly efficient as the factory in Charlie Chaplin's "Modern Times"; the wire services clacking away, the copy kids racing to the chute with the latest two-paragraph bulletin, the constant key-pounding of the constant reporters. You got the impression there just wasn't time for the probing, the digging research the crusading reporter must do. Many a time I have sat in my corner of the city room feeling very sinful and useless instead of whacking the black, mechanical beast in front of me.

But despite the number who are deserting crusading for a normal life, there are, thank Jehovah, a goodly number who stick to it because of its tremendous fascination and its soul-satisfying rewards. Those who have made a moderate success of it deserve a little analysis as to what makes them tick.

I think the first requisite of a successful crusading reporter is a strong sense of personal indignation. It is this, more than anything else, which refuses to let him cover the surface side of a story and walk away from it then and there. It gnaws at him, pushing him further and further into it until he comes out with some solid answers.

Closely allied to it is the role of crusading reporter as citizen. I have never known where the reporter stopped and the citizen started, or vice-versa. All of it is rolled up in a 24-hour a day job into which one plunges with both feet, the full quota of glandular juices and a lot of what for want of a better word I call "heart."

In a recent issue of *Nieman Reports*, Walter H. Waggoner hit on it when he talked about the arbitrary dichotomy between the ethics of a newspaper and the ethics of society. In the same sense, a thinking, ethical citizen cannot transform himself, from deadline to deadline, into an unthinking, amoral reporter. Too many reporters today, however, are attempting this damaging schizophrenia. They put on a pair of blinders, grind out their copy with a spiritual satisfaction equivalent to that of a garment worker cutting a suit, and then head for home to listen to "Stop the Music."

Above all, the crusading reporter must keep pounding away until he has aroused the public. Too many newspapers start off with a Hollywood-trumpeted exposé—complete with promotional ads and pictures of their star reporter—then fold as soon as the original series appears. In the field of exposing conditions in mental hospitals, a number of papers in the last two or three years have done the first brave splash, then quit cold and later wondered why the public didn't rise up on its hind-legs and do something about it.

The opening blast, I have learned from bitter experience, is merely five per cent of the battle. It's the follow-through—the constant pounding away over a period of months, even years—that gets the job done. In the same way the advertising huckster makes you like that soap, love that soap, finally buy that soap, the reporter has to make the reader like the idea, get indignant about the idea, and then get off his posterior and do something about the idea.

And this involves a lot more than just straight reporting. First of all, it means battling for your stories with the desk, fighting to get them in and played properly. It means writing editorials, moving in on the sacred preserves of the umbilicus-contemplaters because you have something to say and you insist it get into print.

It means checking your stories constantly for public reaction. In the crusading business, the reaction is the Alpha and the Omega. It isn't the idea *per se* which fascinates so much; it's the idea when it hits a person, then gets hold of him and makes him move into action.

It means getting out and exerting personal pressure on people. I have a vivid recollection of the hectic period after my original series of articles on Oklahoma's mental hospitals appeared in 1946. The phone rang off the wall, letters poured in, streams of people called at the newspaper office. All of them were indignant about the conditions, and all of them asked me: "What Can We Do?"

I had no ready answer then. For a month or so, I stalled them off with the old bromide about writing their legislators. Trying to convince myself, I argued with my wife, a veteran newspaperwoman, that I had done my part of the job.

"You have aroused these people," she told me. "If there is no organization in the state to channel that arousement, you go out and build one."

I have learned, in the three years since then, how to answer that "What Can We Do." You've got to be ready to give them a series of specifics. Write up and distribute outlines of the bills you are proposing, tell the people what organizations to get active in, tell them the specific legislators who will control the destiny of the bills. That initial arousement is the most precious thing in the world; when it wears off, you're licked.

It means moving out and speaking to every organization and civic club that will listen to you. If you're a poor speaker, as I was, no matter. You've got a tough package to sell and you've got to get out and sell it. And it means more than just haranguing the good Rotarians or Shriners—it means giving them a set of specifics, telling them exactly what you think their organizations can do, and then putting them on the spot as to whether or not they'll do it.

It means, finally, judging the battle in terms of the pay-off. A crusade which merely arouses the emotions of people but does not induce, or seduce, them into action is a misnomer, a travesty.

And now back to my magazine friend who quit newspapering because there weren't enough satisfactions in the crusading business, because he got sick of the sleepless nights, the constant snipings, the ever-present nervous tensions.

I say to him there is no greater satisfaction on earth than seeing a great mass of people, fired up by an idea, tearing up the pea-patch to get that idea across. A million dollars and a thousand loving cups couldn't put a down payment on that kind of satisfaction.

I quote to him a passage from Charles W. Ferguson's brilliant book, *A Little Democracy is a Dangerous Thing*, which spells out both the dilemma of our present day and the corollary faith of the crusading reporter who wants to turn the tide.

"The depressing consequence to be seen on every hand is that the business of the world is being carried on in the candle power of the executive minds rather than with the immense power that might well be generated by the dynamos of democratic action."

That faith in the people, that abiding, unswerving belief in their goodness of intent and action when they fully grasp an idea—this is the faith that moves mountains, and crusading reporters, too. When that faith is lost, then it is time to get out—but not before.

Finally, there goes along with that faith a great pride in his profession as a newspaperman and in the function of a newspaper in the community. He feels himself a responsible cog in a responsible enterprise. In closing, I can do no better than quote the definition of a newspaperman which the late John H. Sorrels gave to E. W. (Ted) Scripps when the latter was a Stanford student wondering whether he ought to go into journalism.

"Journalism is a profession for gentlemen. I suppose there are different definitions for a gentleman. But breaking the word apart, it would seem that a gentleman is a man of compassion and tolerance; a man of honor, bound by something inside himself, to a cause of selflessness. He is a man who considers it his obligation to protect and defend the weak; to give utterance for those who are inarticulate. He would consider that whatever strength and power he has are endowments, not to be used primarily for his own gain, but for which he is merely custodian, and must use for the general welfare."

CRUSADING IN A SMALL TOWN

—Ernest Linford, "Crusading in a Small Town," *Nieman Reports,* Vol. 1, February 1947, pp. 7–8, 10. Mr. Linford is editor of the Laramie (Wyoming) *Republican-Boomerang.*

SEVENTEEN YEARS in small town newspapering, twelve as an editor, have taught me that success is sometimes more troublesome than failure, journalistically speaking. Professional and personal jealousies often take the edge off satisfaction of a job well done. I have learned through experience, at the end of a campaign, to bow out in favor of the Chamber of Commerce and other civic organizations which keep the ball rolling; to lie low while others take the bow; to compliment public officials.

At the end of a successful campaign a newspaper editor often learns that his work is just beginning to get tough, that he has a responsibility to guard and defend the new project, to protect it from attacks and death by lethargy. When the newness wears off a program comes up against hard realities.

In 1942 my newspaper brought to a climax a spirited campaign for council-manager government. Laramie citizens voted in the first city manager setup in Wyoming. Many factors contributed to the success of the drive. The old mayor-council (second class city plan) had become outmoded, unwieldy and illegal. The outgoing city administration, locked in bitter rows, was unpopular and some members were under suspicion. The town had outgrown its ancient charter. We hit while the iron was hot and helped convince the voters that they should not only turn the rascals out but bring in an entirely new setup.

But the sponsors of the radical change, including the editorial writer, were not prepared for such sudden success! When the council-manager system was voted in we found ourselves in a dilemma. The state statute governing the system was full of bugs. Nobody had had any experience with the new plan. The constitution forbade hiring anybody outside of the state and the state had no city managers.

Our No. 1 problem was to buck the machine which had picked mayors and councilmen for years and to institute a council of non-partisan business men. Since the city treasury was sadly in the red, it was thought best to get as many business men on the council as possible. We were successful but not without a great deal of finagling which would put the old party ward heelers to shame.

By this time the "rugged individualists" had awakened and a belated campaign of sniping at the new form of government was begun. Court action challenging it was threatened. Some of the town's notorious "pillars of the good society," fearing loss of power, joined malcontents and chronic beefers in a campaign of sabotage. They succeeded once in getting sufficient signers to petitions for a kind of recall reconsideration of the issue at the polls, but no statutory provision could be found outlining "Where to go from here." The undercurrents still continue but meantime Laramie has come out of the red financially, established some municipal improvements and has a better than average city government.

No editor loves the defensive tack, but we joined forces with others interested to watch over the new baby, change its pants and its formula and, on occasion, walk the floor with it. A main bulwark was a citizens committee for good government, similar to the Cincinnati plan, where top-flight business and professional men were sought out and persuaded to run for the council.

The paper vigorously campaigned for these hand-picked candidates and fought the nominees of the opposition, which tried to join up and get control of the council as a means of junking the setup. We elected our men at each succeeding election.

A national city officials' magazine gave the *Republican-Boomerang* credit for securing the new government setup, but nobody knows better than the editor that it took more than a newspaper campaign. You can't shove a proposition down the throats of the people unless they are ready for it. You can help to make them ready but you must not move too rapidly. In most of our successful campaigns we worked hand in hand with civic organizations and in some cases have had the impetus appear to come from outside sources.

Our campaign for better government started five years before there was any hint of success. We published stories on government of other towns. We ran series of articles on plans available under Wyoming law and discussed their merits and faults. When the time seemed propitious the editor took the project to the Lions club, whose civic betterment committee he headed. We held a number of panels, discussing municipal governmental problems and climaxed the series with the organizing of a Lions club study committee. The Chamber of Commerce, which often coordinates the work of civic groups of the community, then absorbed the committee, adding other members. After several months of investigation the commission presented a report at a well-publicized mass meeting. The body recommended the council-manager form of government for which we had been thumping for a long time.

The recommendation was placed on the ballot at the general election that fall and then we went to town with our campaign, which from all indications was eminently successful. . . .

Years of crusading have convinced me that the small town newspaper's leadership should not be too obvious to the reader. And when a campaign is won, silence or passing the credit to others is a good way to insure success in the next campaign.

One of our main handicaps today is the suspicion on the part of a number of citizens that the newspaper is trying to "boss" the town. Needless to say, we haven't always been bosom buddies of some mayors, city managers, and Chamber of Commerce officials, although we all had essentially the same aims.

We have found it effective to stir up the populace, to point with alarm, to indulge in torrid name-calling if necessary to get action, to make a big fuss until the community is well aroused, then retire to the bleachers and let the committee of citizens which has been appointed complete the job.

An editor has to keep in mind the long-term project, the campaigns which cannot be won in a few months or years—the drive that is never entirely won. His responsibility is to jog the community conscience, to keep ever vigilant, to do all possible to make honesty and responsibility the thing. If the would-be political boss knows that the press will fight him if he turns dishonest or does something which is not for community benefit, he will be more cautious at least.

It would be more comfortable to sit on the moon, and raise hell in complete objectivity when hell-raising was indicated. But the editor who plans to live in the community the rest of his life has to think of the long-time results and his future effectiveness.

It is a hard job to trample on the toes of a fellow-citizen in the editorial column and meet him socially that evening or the next. Small town citizens take their editorial column seriously. It takes courage to jump on the police department—even demand that the chief be fired—and go around the next day in search of news.

CRUSADING OR GENTLER METHODS?

—Eric W. Allen, "The Newspaper and Community Leadership," *The Press in the Contemporary Scene, The Annals of the American Academy of Political and Social Science,* Vol. 219, January 1942, pp. 28–29.

LET US become more personal to see how the process operates. Here is an editor-publisher, let us say, in his late sixties. As he looks back, he is conscious that he is not quite the same kind of an editor as when he was young, nor is his job quite the same. He is still proud of his reputation as a "fighting-editor," but his all-out fights seem to belong rather to the remote past. He remembers when he cleaned out gambling houses and resorts in a bitter campaign that for a while cost him advertising, but brought him, along with threats to his safety, an increase in circulation. Years later, too, he caused the recall of a mayor, effecting a permanent change in the way his city is run. It has been a lifelong job to watch city politics and to help maintain honest and efficient city government.

There are many other memories that bring a satisfying glow of pride—how once he braved contempt of court and a boycott to force a Federal judge before the Senate for impeachment. For a whole generation he believes he has made it easier for good men to rise to leadership and harder for the itching palm and the "stuffed shirt." . . .

In retrospect he recalls many things he has accomplished by gentler, gradual methods. His gains have not all come through fighting. His paper has always given music and musicians more space and more discriminating praise and blame than his colleagues thought the subject worth. But now his city is a musical center—famed for orchestras and bands, good music in schools and parks, large and quiet audiences at concerts. He thinks he played a vital part in that.

He takes some credit for the healthy condition of the playgrounds and outlying camps, the excellent organization of the Boy Scouts, the vocational school, and the local scholarship fund for able youngsters.

NELSON, THE CRUSADING EDITOR

—Willard G. Bleyer, *Main Currents in the History of American Journalism.* Used by permission of, and arrangement with, the publishers, Houghton Mifflin Company, 1927, pp. 311–313.

AGAINST FRAUD in city and county elections and corruption in municipal government, the [Kansas City] *Star* from the beginning took a firm stand. It exposed and denounced those responsible for dishonesty in elections; it offered rewards for the conviction of election crooks; it employed detectives to watch for fraud on election days. It waged unrelenting warfare against gang rule and against the protection of gambling and vice. When many years later the commission form of municipal government seemed to offer a remedy for some of these evils, Nelson sent reporters to investigate this form of government in cities where it was being tried. To make the information thus secured available for municipalities interested in better government, the *Star* published a pamphlet on the commission plan, for free distribution anywhere in the country. It also encouraged members of its staff to speak on the subject wherever municipalities in its territory were considering the commission plan. With the aid of the *Star,* Kansas City, Kansas, adopted this type of government.

Early in its career, the *Star* began a long fight against monopoly in street railway transportation, and against the granting of long-term franchises without adequate return to the city. In 1882 it succeeded in securing a franchise for a new company that later constructed the cable system as a rival to mule-drawn street cars. Two years later, it prevented a thirty-year extension of the franchise of the old company, by arousing sufficient public sentiment against it to induce the mayor to veto the proposed grant after it had been passed by the city council. To the end of Nelson's life, the *Star* kept up the struggle to protect the city against the traction interests.

Within its first year the *Star* began a campaign for city parks. Eventually a remarkable system of parks and boulevards was secured, which may be said to be Nelson's greatest achievement. In the face of apathy on the part of the average citizen, and of opposition from men of wealth who objected to increased taxation, the *Star* carried on a fifteen-year campaign before the first public park was secured. Organized opposition not only denounced the proposed park system as needless extravagance, "confiscation," and "robbery," but carried the fight against it into the courts. These enemies of parks were dubbed by the *Star* the "Hammer and Padlock Club," because they sought to destroy the project and to protect their own pockets. "Of all the measures for which the *Star* labored," wrote Nelson after the struggle was over, "the one most despairingly blocked by this spirit of benighted non-comprehension was the project of parks."[1] Not satisfied with urging a park system for Kansas City, Nelson published and distributed pamphlets showing the advantages of public parks for smaller communities in the territory served by the *Star*.

While carrying on the campaign for a park system, Nelson also advocated the development of boulevards bordered by shade trees. He experimented with various kinds of trees to determine which were best suited to the soil and climate. He had trees grown in his own nurseries and then transplanted to permanent locations along the boulevards. Similar tests were made under his direction to find out the grasses, shrubs, and flowers most suitable for beautifying streets, parks, and lawns.

The interest in building that he had acquired as a contractor in Indiana continued throughout his life. Through the columns of the *Star* he encouraged the erection of substantial, attractive, moderate-priced homes, particularly in the residential sections that were being opened up along the new boulevards in outlying parts of the city. By building his own home on a site some two miles from the city limits, in what was then an undeveloped section, he set an example for others and showed his faith in the future growth of the city. In the construction of his home he demonstrated the possibility of using effectively the then neglected native limestone. That Kansas City came to be known as a "city of beautiful homes," was a source of great pride to Nelson.

For five years, beginning in 1893, he urged through the *Star* the desirability of a municipal auditorium for Kansas City, and one was finally erected. When, within a year after the completion of the auditorium, it was destroyed by fire, he launched another campaign to have it rebuilt in time for the Democratic National Convention of

[1] *William Rockhill Nelson,* Riverside Press, Cambridge, 1915, p. 36.

1900, the first convention of its kind to be held in Kansas City. The *Star* was likewise instrumental in bringing about the construction of viaducts to connect the city with Kansas City, Kansas. All these campaigns were carried out in accordance with Nelson's belief that it is the function of a newspaper to bring about all forms of civic improvement. "Anybody can print news," he declared, "but the *Star* tries to build things up. That is what a newspaper is for."[2]

HOW THE CRUSADER CREATES "CRIME WAVES"

—From *The Autobiography of Lincoln Steffens,* copyright, 1931, by Harcourt, Brace & Company, Inc., pp. 285–291. Mr. Steffens was famous for his autobiography and for his investigations as a newspaper reporter.

EVERY NOW AND THEN there occurs the phenomenon called a crime wave. New York has such waves periodically; other cities have them; and they sweep over the public and nearly drown the lawyers, judges, preachers, and other leading citizens who feel that they must explain and cure these extraordinary outbreaks of lawlessness. Their diagnoses and their remedies are always the same: the disease is lawlessness; the cure is more law, more arrests, swifter trials, and harsher penalties. . . .

I enjoy crime waves. I made one once; Jake Riis helped; many reporters joined in the uplift of the rising tide of crime; and T. R. stopped it. I feel that I know something the wise men do not know about crime waves and so get a certain sense of happy superiority out of reading editorials, sermons, speeches, and learned theses on my specialty. . . .

It was indeed one of the worst crime waves I ever witnessed, and the explanations were embarrassing to the reform police board, which my paper and my friends were supporting, in their difficult reform work. The opposition papers, Tammany, and the unreformed police officers rejoiced in the outbreak of crime, which showed that the reformed police and especially the new detective service could not deal with criminals in a city like New York. This criticism had a point which pricked the conscience even of Roosevelt himself. He had got rid of Superintendent Byrnes, the most famous of New York's detectives, removed Byrnes's self-trained inspector, and put in a captain who would have no dealings with professional criminals. The old system was built upon the understood relations of the crooks and the

[2] Julian Street, *Abroad at Home,* New York, p. 304.

detective bureau. Certain selected criminals in each class, pickpockets, sneak thieves, burglars, etc., were allowed to operate within reason; the field was divided among them by groups, each of which had a monopoly. In return for the paid-for privilege the groups were to defend their monopoly from outsiders, report the arrival in town of strangers from other cities, and upon demand furnish information (not evidence) to the detectives and return stolen goods. This was called regulation and control, and it worked pretty well; more to the glory of the police, who could perform "miracles of efficiency" when the victim of a robbery was worth serving, but of course it did not stop stealing; it protected only citizens with pull, power, or privilege. There were many crimes done within and without the system, which depended for public sufferance on the suppression of the news, as any detective system does. . . .

Roosevelt's chief of detectives was appointed because he hated the old system, held it to be useless, and declared that he had a better way of dealing with the crooks. He asked leave to run the old crooks out of town, to watch for and arrest at the railroad stations new and known arrivals and to drive them away by threats of holding them as fugitives from justice until he could obtain evidence against them from the cities where they had been working. This method was succeeding so well that Commissioner Parker, who was watching it, was satisfied with the progress made, and T. R. believed all was well till the crime wave rose and frightened him. He suspected Parker anyhow; the detective chief was Parker's choice, and the outbreak of crimes all over the city so alarmed him that he was almost persuaded that the opposition was right in its criticism: that the police reformers, knowing nothing of crime, criminals, and police work, technically, had blundered in changing the system, the good old Byrnes method of handling this, the real business of the police; not to interfere with business and sport, but to catch and punish housebreakers and other law breakers. He called a secret meeting of the police board and was making one of his picturesque harangues when Commissioner Parker interrupted him.

"Mr. President, you can stop this crime wave whenever you want to."

"I! How?"

"Call off your friends Riis and Steffens. They started it, and—they're sick of it. They'll be glad to quit if you'll ask them to." . . .

T. R. adjourned the meeting, sent for Riis and me, and bang!

"What's this I hear? You two and this crime wave? Getting us into trouble? You? I'd never have believed it. You?" Up and down his room he strode. Betrayed he was, and by us whom he had trusted. Who, then, could be trusted? And for what? Why had we done it? Why? . . .

Riis told him about it, how I got him called down by printing a beat, and how he had to get even. And did. "I beat the pot out of you," he boasted to me, his pride reviving. "And I can go right on doing it. I can get not one or two crimes a day; if I must I can get half a dozen, a dozen. I can get all there are every day." . . .

Thus the crime wave was ended to the satisfaction of all. T. R. took pleasure in telling Parker that he had deleted, not only the cause, but the source of the wave, which was in Parker's department. He would not say what it was; sufficed that it was closed for ever. Parker had to resolve that mystery by learning from the chief of detectives that the President had ordered the daily crime file removed from the public to his inner office—forever. . . . When Riis and I ceased reporting robberies the poker combine resumed their game, and the morning newspapers discovered the fickle public were "sick of crime" and wanted something else. The monthly magazines and the scientific quarterlies had some belated, heavy, incorrect analyses of the periodicity of lawlessness; they had no way to account for it then. The criminals could work o' nights, honest citizens could sleep, and judges could afford to be more just.

CRUSADING, A NEGLECTED STORY

—Silas Bent, *Newspaper Crusaders*, McGraw-Hill, 1939, pp. 3–4. Mr. Bent has long been noted for his critical appraisals of contemporary American press affairs.

IT IS SINGULAR that newspapers, seldom bashful about their virtues, have made so little to-do about their achievements in crusading. As champions of reforms, as defenders of individuals, as protagonists of their communities, they have exercised influences, I venture to believe, quite as important as the transmission of information and the expression of opinion.

Yet this has been written only in fragmentary form. Historians of daily journals, biographers of newspaper publishers and editors, and occasionally an instructor in a school of journalism have dealt with it in particular, sometimes in its larger aspects, but not sweepingly. A treatment at once minute and comprehensive, indeed, is impossible within the scope of a single volume, such is the wealth of material available. What is presented here must attempt a representative selection.

More than once a newspaper, at the conclusion of a successful campaign, has preened itself or has paid tribute to a fellow; by and large our most articulate institution, sometimes almost as vainglorious as politics (God save the mark!) has been surprisingly reticent about one of its primary responsibilities. Yet it has recognized crusading as a natural function and as a responsibility, and has discharged it for the most part admirably, sometimes at severe sacrifice. That there has been default in certain areas none can deny, but the account balances heavily to the credit of the press and to the benefit of the public.

Here lies the best argument for newspaper freedom not only from governmental interference but from the coercion of a capitalist economy. The history of our press since Colonial days is shot through with the struggle for unrestricted critical activity and the right to crusade. Every crusade implies, to be sure, the expression of opinion or of an attitude, but it involves more than that. It means also a willingness to fight if need be. It means, according to my dictionary, "to contend zealously against any evil, or on behalf of any reform."

To contend zealously must mean surely to struggle with ardent devotion. The zeal which fires a crusading editor may bring him to the boiling point of fanaticism, and has done it time and again. None who has undertaken a campaign in the certainty that it would entail loss of circulation and advertising, perhaps permanently, but was a fanatic, just on the sunny side of lunacy. Skeptics who deny that campaigns are ever undertaken for other than sordid motives may disabuse their minds by examining the record. If newspapers have faced actual losses in the discharge of their duties as public servants, then they have an unmistakable claim to the guaranty of the First Amendment.

REVIEW QUESTIONS AND ASSIGNMENTS

1. What evidence is there that newspaper crusades are dying out?

2. Is a newspaper justified in crusading against admitted social ills when its motives are purely selfish?

3. Is the chief appeal in any crusade to the "unthinking voter"? If so, what justification may be offered?

4. Why does the public lose interest in reform as soon as one man is put behind the bars, or another is put into office?

5. What are some of the "rules" for making a crusade successful?

6. What lengths of time have been required for success in the campaigns cited in this chapter?

7. Is the crusade that ends in legal reform likely to endure longer or not so long as that which puts a new set of officials into office?

8. Does the experience of the Kansas City *Star,* which has crusaded throughout its history, indicate that a crusading newspaper can retain the respect and affection of the general public? Or does the public tend to forget the battle won for it by the newspaper?

9. In what sense was Lincoln Steffens a "crusader"? Discuss the ethical conduct in this crime wave.

10. What are the substitutes, if any, for newspaper crusades so far as the newspaper is concerned?

ADDITIONAL REFERENCES

Anonymous, "Chicago *Tribune* Saved City $1,700,000 by Exposing Political Conspiracy," *Editor & Publisher,* Vol. 61, June 23, 1928, p. 3.

———, "Amazing Chapter of Violence Climaxes War of Louisiana Press and Governor," *Editor & Publisher,* Vol. 63, September 13, 1930, p. 15.

———, "Crusading New Jersey Publisher and Family Get Death Threat," *Editor & Publisher,* Vol. 62, March 15, 1930, p. 10.

———, "Dailies Fighting the Public's Battles," *Editor & Publisher,* Vol. 61, March 9, 1929, p. 9.

———, "Daily Forced Lawyers to Clean House," *Editor & Publisher,* Vol. 62, May 18, 1929.

———, "Minneapolis Editor Shot by Gunmen," *Editor & Publisher,* Vol. 60, October 1, 1927.

———, "Oklahoma Chief Justice Threatens Life of Carl Magee," *Editor & Publisher,* Vol. 61, July 14, 1928, p. 22.

———, "Scranton Dailies Smash Gambling Ring," *Editor & Publisher,* Vol. 62, February 1, 1930, p. 7.

———, "Scranton *Sun* Accepts Bombers' Challenge," *Editor & Publisher,* Vol. 60, January 7, 1928, p. 5.

———, "Stood His Ground," *Editor & Publisher,* Vol. 59, April 16, 1927.

———, "Two Editors Behind Stephenson Political Exposé in Indiana," *Editor & Publisher,* Vol. 60, July 16, 1927, p. 6.

———, "U. S. Press, Attacking Civic Problems, Active as Community Builders," *Editor & Publisher,* Vol. 61, March 2, 1929, p. 6.

Atwood, M. V., *The Country Newspaper,* A. C. McClurg, 1923, pp. 61–62.

Campbell, J. Hart, "How Don King Caused Sinclair Mistrial," *Editor & Publisher,* Vol. 60, November 12, 1927, p. 7.

Flint, L. N., *The Conscience of the Newspaper,* Appleton-Century, 1925, pp. 335–336.

Howey, Walter, *Fighting Editors,* David McKay, 1948.

Kansas City Star Staff, *William Rockhill Nelson,* Riverside Press, 1915, Chapters 3, 7.

Mencken, H. L., "Newspaper Morals," *The Atlantic Monthly,* Vol. 113, March 1914, pp. 289–293.

Miner, Herve W., "Mellett's Successor Avenged Slain Editor," *Editor & Publisher,* Vol. 59, January 1, 1927, p. 5.

Mott, F. L., *Headlining America,* Houghton Mifflin, 1937, pp. 229–244.

Muir, Florabel, *Headline Happy,* Henry Holt, 1950.

Older, Fremont, *My Own Story,* Macmillan, 1926.

Overmyer, Richard P., "Newsboys Arrested, Their Papers Seized by Muncie Judge, Attacked by Dale," *Editor & Publisher,* February 26, 1927, p. 4.

Perry, John W., "No More Crusades, Publisher Decrees," *Editor & Publisher,* October 11, 1930, p. 9.

Pulitzer, Ralph, "Newspaper Morals: A Reply," *The Atlantic Monthly,* Vol. 113, June 1914, pp. 773–775.

Radder, N. J., *Newspapers in Community Service,* McGraw-Hill, 1926, Chapters 5, 7.

Schlesinger, Arthur M., *The American as Reformer,* Harvard University Press, 1950.

Schuyler, Philip, "Crusading Daily Fights the Law Delays," *Editor & Publisher,* May 19, 1928, p. 7.

Sinclair, Upton, *The Brass Check,* Boni, 1936, pp. 235–236.

Webb, Carl C., "Two Portland Newspapers Join in Vice Crusade," *Journalism Quarterly,* Vol. 25, December 1948, p. 375.

17. THE COMMUNITY PRESS: THE INTIMATE PRESS

INTRODUCTION

THERE IS an old saying that members of the working press in metropolitan centers dream of the day when they will have saved enough money to buy a community newspaper. Behind the saying is the belief that owning and editing a small paper would let the newsman enjoy a journalistic heaven not open to those who perform one isolated function at a weekly salary on the staff of a large daily.

Those who publish and edit community newspapers lend some support to this view but they are quick to point out that the problems they must face and solve prevent "small-town journalism" from even approaching the bed of roses so frequently pictured by their brethren on the metropolitan press.

The community press, a term applicable to the small-town daily as well as urban and rural weeklies, does enjoy an intimacy with its public which the large dailies cannot duplicate. The editors in hundreds of small communities across the country are true personal journalists. They are leaders in civic affairs, sources of friendly advice and comments, and contemporary historians of the thousand and one dramas in the daily lives of their fellow townsmen.

There is another side to the picture, however, one which takes much of the romantic charm out of community journalism except for a relatively few dominant publications.

The spectre of economic insolvency bothers many small-town publishers. Costs are high and relatively little national advertising comes their way; as a result, they are forced to rely on strictly local sources of revenue. And these sources may devote part of their advertising budgets to space in neighboring dailies. The community publisher, therefore, must seek to develop what amounts almost to an *esprit de corps* among his merchants on behalf of the paper. A common means of partly solving the problem is operating a job printing plant. But the failure in many cases to achieve a satisfactory operating income makes it necessary to keep staffs below minimum needs and to fall behind on such items as machinery replacement; these practices, inevitably, damage the quality of the paper.

A comparison of the content of the well-edited community newspaper of today with that of 100 years ago shows considerable improvement. The nineteenth-century community editor fed his readers a steady diet of stories, essays, travel sketches, sermons, and medical advice. He clipped much of this material from the inside pages of city newspapers. He had no appreciation of his community as a news source. Today, the alert community editor runs column after column of straight news, much of it about the men, women, and children in his community. All news to him is local. The new policy undoubtedly is a major factor in the high readership scores of weeklies that have had their readers surveyed.

The influence exerted by the community newspaper tends to be the product of the personality of the owner-editor. It is always possible for a William Allen White to emerge as a great force in his community and state as a result of what he says in the columns of his paper. The nation is dotted with towns in which an editor's influence can be seen in almost every worthwhile undertaking. On the other hand, the owner-editor can just as easily devote all of his attention to his property as a somewhat hazardous business enterprise. This results in a publication strictly neutral, strictly safe, and strictly colorless.

One major advantage enjoyed by almost all small newspapers is a monopoly on news in their communities. Neighboring dailies haven't the space to permit complete coverage of the many communities in their circulation areas. Radio stations are even more limited, although the emergence of FM outlets in smaller cities has partly altered this situation. By and large, this monopoly obligates the paper to cover its community fairly and completely.

The negative view of the country editor's role is presented by Turner in the first reading. An answer to this presentation was made by Waring, whose reply is also cited. The status of editorials and editorial features in Minnesota is revealed in an article by Duncan; Barnhart uncovers a broad picture of the editor's methods of work. That the country editor is evolving with the times is related by Crawford in "The Modern Country Editor." Hough points out some of the economic problems that face the editor.

ALL IS NOT GLAMOROUS IN COUNTRY FIELD

—Fitzhugh Turner, "The Country Weekly Dream," *Nieman Reports*, Vol. 2, October 1948, pp. 4–5. Mr. Turner, a former weekly editor, is now on the staff of the New York *Herald Tribune.*

To THIS REPORTER, an old country weekly man himself, it has seemed that everybody he meets is a prospective country editor. Anyone with ordinary acquaintanceship in the writing trades knows editors, advertising men, magazine executives, publicity people and printers, not to mention individuals in fields from selling to soldiering, who assert that their aim in life if "to settle down some day and run my own little newspaper."

Why, Heaven knows.

The country editor legend paints a pretty picture, granted. Small towns look good from the city. The rich rural life has great appeal, especially to those who aren't living in it. But the country weekly dream is beyond these things; it can be explained only on grounds of A) wishful thinking and B) ignorance. The man who says he wants to be a country editor rarely has a clear idea of what a country editor must be, and the country weekly he thinks he'll run has infrequent existence in real life.

Your would-be editor thinks of his newspaper office, chances are, as a charmingly quaint old establishment in a pleasant side street of some shady village, with himself occupying the chair at the battered rolltop desk, exchanging remarks about weather and crops with old-timers, dispensing homely wisdom to the young, and confounding, on occasion, the local squire. Either that or he pictures a perfect newspaper on a small scale, complete with tiny but modern plant, utilizing scores of ideas he has picked up in the big time, the drudgery being handled by a small but capable staff. All this with plenty of time of his own for hunting or fishing and very possibly a bit of farming on the side.

Well, pleasant villages are rare and each has its own newspaper now with a waiting list of buyers. Equally important, there is the money question. Ideal newspapers, city or country, have a way of losing money, and rolltop desks don't of themselves pay dividends. Only the wealthy can go in for publishing on a losing scale; an unprofitable weekly is notorious for its ability to drain large sums down the hatch.

What is a country weekly anyway? Putting aside the wistful notions of the would-be publisher in the city, the country weekly as it now exists is very much the same kind of institution as a metropolitan daily. True, it is often mailed to its readers rather than delivered by carrier or sold on the streets. It has, however, a front page, an editorial page, a society column, sports coverage perhaps, and, of course, advertisements. The usual issue contains eight pages, but it may run down to six or four or up to twelve or twenty, depending on the location and the capability of the owner. It is set up in type, made up and printed just as is the daily, although usually it is turned out by a flatbed press. In its community, it occupies the same position as does the daily, and fulfills very much the same function.

The similarities are obvious. The dissimilarities are more important. The country weekly, by its nature, can be concerned with only one kind of news—local. It may run a "canned" roundup column of world news and national affairs, but its front page is devoted to community happenings, doings of the volunteer fire department, schools and civic clubs, local merchants and local politicians, and churches. To its credit, crime and police news is played down, the wealth of small town scandal ignored entirely. The quality of the writing, speaking generally, is bad, the news very probably flavored with the opinion of the editor. Obituaries, which are important, are of a stereotyped complimentary nature for heel or hero alike, the old-fashioned "he was beloved by all who knew him" still being a good phrase or considered so.

Editorial opinion, displayed widely in the news columns, is feeble on the editorial page, likely to run to such subjects as "Why We Like Our Town," "Be Patriotic—Shop at Home," or "Go to Church This Sunday." The exception is in politics, which sometimes brings more controversial writing into print, or it may lie in the not infrequent issue which finds the influential elements of the community on one side of the question and no one the editor fears on the other. Even political opinion is more often based on the editor's personal business connections than the public interest. Many a weekly owes its existence to the factionalism of local politics, and many a politician lies in the background as the man who holds the mortgage on the local gazette.

We are talking here, it should be pointed out, in terms of the typical and average. There have been and are country editors of character and courage who have published newspapers of character and courage. There have been enough of them to account for the man-at-the-rolltop-desk legend. But as is usual in such cases, the legend in turn has accounted for the imitators, whose only qualification has been possession of a rolltop desk.

Over the country, weeklies run the gamut in quality, prestige and competence. In New England, New York State, parts of California and scattered elsewhere, mainly in areas of prosperity, there are important rural newspapers. They are in the vast minority. The others, and there are thousands of them, reflect the typical present day small town publisher. Far from the legendary shirtsleeved philosopher, he is a conservatively dressed man of careful habits, occupant of one of the good houses in town, a figure you might mistake for a druggist or the cashier of the bank. His appearance, his thinking and his conversation reflect the element in which he is steeped and to which he owes his existence, the retail trade of his community. Consequently he and his newspaper most often are found stooging, purposedly or not, for the merchant-lawyer-banker clique which runs the average small town. He is backward in his mental processes, insular in his opinions, limited in his horizon, and, of course, by no means can he be a good newspaper man. He couldn't afford to be if he knew how.

This may be a bad situation. It is not, of course, unique to country weeklies. Those daily newspapers which lack independence are in that fix for similar reasons. There is little real difference between domination of a metropolitan editorial department by the advertising manager and domination of a country editor by his own pocketbook.

The usual country weekly, it is well known, is very much a one-man proposition. The editor owns and bosses the establishment, makes the decisions, spends the money, sets the policy and possibly some of the type. He himself solicits the advertising, writes the principal news stories, composes the editorials.

He has an assistant, a girl who handles the all important personal notices, answers the telephone, keeps track of subscriptions, reads proof and otherwise does the office dirty work. If it is a well-run business, there may be another girl to keep the books and help out. The rest of the staff consists of one, two or three printers.

The editor's work week is sixty or seventy hours. His return after he has met the power bill, the rent, the installment on his machinery, the paper bill and the payroll is possibly enough to support him, but certainly not enough to make him independent. A monthly net income of $300 or $400 is considered highly satisfactory by many weekly newspaper proprietors. Weeklies, the fact is, just don't make money. Advertising sells as low as twenty-five cents a column inch, or a fourth the rate of even a tiny daily. An average weekly of eight pages may gross up to $350 an issue on advertising, but the payroll and paper bill will account for this sum with ease. The profit, it develops, must come from job printing.

As a business printing is respectable, interesting and reasonably remunerative. Small shops can produce work of high merit, if the printers have time, equipment and skill. But few men can be commercial printers and newspaper editors at the same time with much success. It requires a business man to make a successful printer. Business men, on the whole, make poor editors. As a result, your country editor is weak in the qualifications that make for good newspapers. His sense of responsibility to his readers is subordinated to the interests of his business. To cite a common situation, he cannot afford to offend the politicians who make up the local government, since the local government is a good customer for printed forms. Handling the news to the satisfaction of the men who constitute his advertisers and printing customers occurs to him as the normal method, surely the least troublesome. Editorial policy thus consists of preservation of the status quo and resistance of the new, foreign, or unfamiliar. Ask him to write a fair news story and fight it out in the editorial column, to print both sides of the question or to try for objectivity and he thinks you're advancing a radical idea. From the professional viewpoint, he may not even know what you're talking about.

Although most Americans can, if they wish, read a daily newspaper, more than half of them read weeklies alone, or weeklies along with dailies. Surveys again and again demonstrate that weeklies are read many times more thoroughly than dailies. The most reasonable theory here is that weeklies are full of names their readers recognize and subjects familiar to them. Smalltown readers are avid for news of their neighbors, and seem to like to see it in print even when they've known the details for days. A daily newsman recognizes this same trait in the fact that among city folk, those who saw the game or the show are the most eager readers of, for instance, a football story or a theatre criticism.

There are, in the nation, some 1,872 daily newspapers. Weeklies, by contrast, total 10,050, but the smaller circulations of weeklies give each medium, in the aggregate, about the same number of readers. Thus weeklies should play as important a role in shaping public opinion as dailies. Weeklies, as much so as dailies, ought to be published by men with strong feeling for the responsibility of the press to all the people of the community and the country. On the whole, they are not.

Even your least responsible editor, let me hasten to say, does fill a need in his town. During the war he promoted government bonds, fat salvage, paper collection and all the other patriotic activities. If he condemned inflation in one breath and urged higher prices for the local product in the other, well, he was in numerous company there. War or peace, he covers the news after a fashion and contributes at least something to his community, if only the label of "The Nicest Small Town in the World" or "The Largest Spinach Center in Southwestern Gooch County." While things go smoothly, as an editor he may be almost adequate. When the going grows rough and the situation calls for truth, courage and fair play, chances are he's in there pussy-footing with all his might, or else fighting for localism, special interest and reaction.

Unfortunately, the kind of men who are in office as country editors seem to be the only kind of men who can make a go of country publishing. This single fact is the greatest discouragement of many to the competent fellow with notions of publishing a weekly newspaper of high standards. Next greatest, of course, is the low financial return for the hard work involved. The city man who is looking for ease will do better in his office with his five-day week and his annual vacation than he will in the country working all hours six or seven days a week every week of the year.

Entering the field, if he chooses to do so in the face of every difficulty, the newcomer will find it necessary to make many concessions. Because, in the usual small town, "no outsider is going to come in here and tell us how to run our business," he can't afford at first to expose a public scandal or kick out a bad official. Paradoxically, he'll find himself an ex officio leading citizen, and he'll find it impossible to hold himself personally aloof from the petty day-to-day quarrels that arise. He'll be expected, almost required, to take sides in everything, to be a partisan in person at the same time he is trying to be a non-partisan reporter in print.

Incidentally, he'll have to learn to avoid the term "country weekly," an expression offensive to the men who publish country weeklies. He'll be publishing, he'll find out, a "country paper," a "community newspaper," or, at least, a "weekly newspaper."

He'll be expected as a matter of course to join the local civic organizations, to be active in them and enjoy them. He must be careful in his friends to choose them from the "right" people. He must watch his conduct and keep it good, gray and unexciting. He must attend the proper funerals, and take part in the chicken suppers and the bazaars and the benefits and the interminable meetings.

Particularly must he observe the rules for the first few years, since for that length of time or more he will be regarded as a "newcomer," and will be watched carefully and with suspicion.

If he does everything right, if, as an editor friend of mine puts it, the town comes "to like the way he shines his shoes," and more important, if he himself learns to enjoy small town life, he will be accepted eventually as a real member of his community. If he is a rarely talented man or even one of those infrequent individualists who can get away with individualism, he may make something better of it. Otherwise he and his paper inevitably will settle down to become the tired and mediocre voice of the unimportant local interests of his particular unimportant locality.

COUNTRY FIELD OFFERS OPPORTUNITIES

—Houstoun Waring, "The Country Weekly Dream Is Real," *Nieman Reports*, Vol. 3, January 1949, pp. 4–5. Mr. Waring is editor of the Littleton (Colorado) *Independent.*

THE WEEKLY NEWSPAPER in the small town is seldom found outside the English-speaking world. It has played a role in the democracy of these countries which seems to have been ignored by Fitzhugh Turner when he exploded "The Country Weekly Dream" in the last *Nieman Reports.*

First of all, let us look at some of Mr. Turner's statements.

"Ideal newspapers, city or country," he says, "have a way of losing money, and rolltop desks don't of themselves pay dividends."

We have tried to operate an "ideal" newspaper. We have butchered all the sacred cows. We have published items in the forty categories of news generally omitted from the metropolitan press. We have had sixteen competitors come into our town and start newspapers. We have trod on shoes and on beliefs not usually touched. We have never tied up with a political party as a party organ. Yet many's the year we have declared dividends. . . .

Weeklies, one old rule of thumb advises, should sell for five times the net earnings. This means 20 per cent dividends, a high yield for money these days. Wall Street should be interested. Yet fortunately for society, weeklies don't easily admit of absentee or chain ownership. There are a few small chains, but most of the 10,000 country papers in America are owned by the men who operate them, and their voice is the voice of the community.

Mr. Turner writes that small papers are mainly published by men with printing and business knowledge. "Business men, on the whole, make poor editors," he declares. I agree. On the other hand, his big city friends who are successful reporters, magazine writers, and managing editors want to be country editors without any demonstrated business acumen. This is the dilemma. We have high hopes when writers start a publication like '48 and then, when the venture fails, we are jerked back to the realization that publishing is a business.

For twenty years I have tried to get journalism graduates with a liberal arts training to enter the small-town field. Most such graduates either lack the small capital needed or are not interested in anything except the daily press. I know a few who are good editors and businessmen, and they are serving their communities well. They are also bringing their families in more than the $300 or $400 a month Mr. Turner scorns.

That brings us to the question of what gives satisfaction to a man. If he needs two Buicks and wants to send his sons off to private schools, he should work for an advertising agency or be a public relations counselor for a business establishment. On the other hand, if he is content with a Ford and a six-room house, with the public high school and the state university, he may choose the ministry, education, or the country weekly. He may work more than forty hours a week, but if it is work that counts in other people's lives he will be happy. As Granville Hicks has said in his book, *Small Town,* people have an inborn desire to control their environment. The country editors, like all folks in the rural areas of America, have this feeling of shaping their destiny.

Mr. Turner contends that weeklies, having the same aggregate circulation as dailies, should play as important a role in forming public opinion. Reading this statement after the Truman victory brings a chuckle, as only 10% of the daily circulation backed the president. Actually, it is hard to gauge the effect of newspapers, but it is not hard to learn their circulations. Dailies, as a matter of fact, have a circulation three times as great as the weeklies, and that circulation has its impact on the reader six or seven times a week instead of once. But page for page, advertising readership studies indicate that the weekly has three times the effectiveness. Whether its influence is of a better or poorer quality, we cannot judge. Certainly, there is plenty of room for improved editorial direction in both the fields. That is why we must try to teach old dogs new tricks by means of American Press Institutes, Nieman Foundations, and Hutchins Commissions.

There is nothing wrong with the country weekly that good men can't cure. The state press associations, with their field managers, have placed country editors on their feet financially in the last quarter century. With this independence, more and more weeklies have been weaned from the political parties that once controlled them. The same forces that might control the daily press cannot control the weeklies, and vice versa. This is all to the good and it is a further safeguard to our democracy.

The small-town editor knows what the masses of unorganized Americans are thinking, and he puts these thoughts into words. His editorials may not have the style of the metropolitan daily, but they carry weight in Washington when the congressman opens his mail. And they are not bad. In a ten-year period, when I offered a trophy for the best editorials, the weeklies nearly always won over the dailies. This judgment was reached each year by an entirely different set of intelligent men and women from various walks of life.

The country weekly dream is real. I wish more capable young men were dreaming it. It is no job to retire into.

EDITORIALS NOT "ON WAY OUT"

—Charles T. Duncan, "Editorials Not 'On Way Out' Among Minnesota Weeklies," *Journalism Quarterly*, Vol. 26, March 1949, pp. 57–58. Mr. Duncan teaches journalism at the University of Oregon.

If the weeklies of Minnesota can be regarded as being reasonably indicative of the general trend, it would appear that the editorial function still flourishes.

Editorials and editorial features are carried regularly by more than three-fourths of the state's 389 weekly newspapers, it was found in a survey. Approximately 77 per cent of the Minnesota newspapers habitually run the conventional-type editorials, editorial columns, or both, according to information supplied by 236 editors to the writer. Supplemental data were gathered by direct inspection of those papers whose editors did not respond to the questionnaire.[1]

Other conclusions, also drawn from the 236 replies, include these observations:

1. Minnesota weeklies today place greater emphasis on editorials and editorial page content than at any time in the 20-year period covered by the survey. This is indicated by the answers to questions on editorial activity in 1928, 1938, 1943, and 1947, as well as in 1948.
2. Nine out of 10 of the 236 editors feel that editorial writing serves a good purpose and that small-town newspapers "should run editorials."
3. More than half (55.3) per cent of the editors conduct a personally written column.
4. A slightly smaller percentage (53.3) run columns written by others than themselves.
5. More than two-thirds (67.7 per cent) believe there is a greater reader interest in columns than in the standard editorials.
6. Following a noticeable decline during the war, these 236 newspapers are now back to pre-war (1938) standards of editorial activity.
7. With editors who believe in "taking sides" on issues, local politics is the topic most likely to be avoided. Issues of non-political local nature, however, are most popular.

COUNTRY PRESS IS AN INTIMATE PRESS

—Thomas F. Barnhart, *Weekly Newspaper Management,* Appleton-Century, 1936, pp. 3–7. Mr. Barnhart is professor of journalism at the University of Minnesota.

MORE THAN ten thousand weekly newspapers are published in this country today. Obviously this great group of papers exerts immeasurable influence in the lives of millions of people in the smaller cities, towns, and rural districts. Each publication provides its community with a localized expression of the nation's common ideals and purposes. As an ethical force and binding power in the community, the weekly press ranks with the school and the church. It serves as a

[1] This study of editorial activity and trends was conducted under a grant from the University of Minnesota's Graduate School.

welding unit for the educational, religious, political, social, and economic life of its community.

The weekly newspaper is unique for the manner in which it touches intimately the lives of its readers. The reasons for its acceptance and widespread popularity are fourfold.

First, the weekly newspaper editor wins attention and goodwill for his paper by "keeping up the home lick" in the news. Accustomed to the use of subjects close to home, he has a sensitive ear for news of the commonplace. He writes of man's everyday experiences.

Frequently items strike an intimate chord for the reader. They announce the birth of a child, describe the wedding of a cousin, tell of a friend's illness, or perhaps report the death of a loved one. It is this close association with the affairs of intimate interest, with the moments of anguish and happiness in life, that has earned for the weekly newspaper a traditional place in the homes of small-town and rural America. It is recognized as a sympathetic friend. It has created for itself a place of sentimental value.

For his main news content, the weekly editor turns to such necessary institutions as schools, churches, local government, business, political parties, and civic, patriotic, fraternal, and social organizations and clubs. Through accurate, constructively fashioned accounts of the relationships of these institutions and organizations to the community, he records the interesting and important events in the organized life of the groups and he covers also the activities of individual members.

Unexpected happenings make up another large classification of news stories. This group includes accounts of such occurrences as fires, farm accidents, automobile wrecks, explosions, floods, storms, and disasters, and news of crimes and misdemeanors, which are minimized. First offenders are not always mentioned by name. Convicted law breakers, if local persons, are dealt with kindly, and they are given every possible assistance in their efforts to reinstate themselves in society.

For news of the neighborhood family and its activities, the editor turns to the gathering of "personals," or news briefs of visits, visitors, travels, and social events. The personal item, like the at-home activities of the farmer and his family reported in the country correspondence columns, depends upon the name of a person for its importance.

Another common type of news in the weekly press is the local item.

Its use is confined largely to facts about an event or condition in the community, such as the erection of snowfences, the shipment of a load of horses, the condition of the roads, or the amount of rain or snowfall in the area.

The editor usually confines himself to his field—the trade area of the town of publication. He concerns himself primarily with the constructive side of community activities, reporting significant and insignificant news reliably, fairly, and interestingly. He turns out a paper which mirrors the lives of small-town and rural folk. His paper thrives because of the curiosity of its readers, which may be explained as desire to know more about the lives of neighbors and friends. In short, it is the "home paper."

The second factor contributing to the reader's intense interest is that editorially, too, it is natural for the weekly editor to confine himself largely to his own immediate neighborhood. Or, in scanning the national or state scene, he may seek a local application of a problem of wider significance. Usually earnest, moderate, and measured, he knows that his readers are interested chiefly in the happenings close at hand, so he interprets and comments on these events in the friendly, straight-forward, and sympathetic manner one would expect to find in a letter from home. Bias and partisanship are comparatively rare. Experience has taught him that the allegiance of his community is won by adopting a sincerely interested, sober, natural approach when he is writing about the problems of his own people.

The editor's third means of winning and sustaining interest and influence is the use of feature material, a third classification of content which has pushed its way to a place of prominence during the last four decades. The reader's interests are not entirely satisfied by the news and editorial columns. Thus, to capture the whole-hearted acceptance of every member of the family and to augment the news and editorial content, the editor has added lures in the form of reader-interest features for all age groups. He has sought continued stories, accounts of the bizarre and the unusual, historical anecdotes, humor columns, comic strips, cartoons, games, puzzles, and other matters intended to satisfy his readers' desires for adventure, romance, pathos, amusement, humor, and hobbies. While many such features are prepared locally, most editors rely upon the creations of syndicate organizations.

In addition to its historic functions of informing, instructing, and entertaining the reader, the weekly newspaper has long been active in a program of leadership for projects for community betterment. Herein lies the fourth means of developing interest. This field of activity, very significant in recent years, touches upon almost every conceivable range of service required by mankind. Here it is that the weekly press has been unstinted in its performance of good deeds in the interests of government, both national and local. Likewise business, schools, churches, charitable and welfare institutions, and the civic and patriotic organizations and clubs in the community place heavy burdens of responsibility on the shoulders of the editor.

Every community problem makes it necessary for the editor to devote time and attention, and, usually, newspaper space to some worthwhile community institution, or even to save it. One week it may be a local industry that requires his aid; the next week, the schools or the band concert fund, or the Red Cross, or the Boy Scouts, or local reemployment projects, or farm relief. And it is extremely likely that he will be expected to aid in the solution of many of the endless flow of problems of the community. Some require two-fisted leadership; others need only cooperative effort and organization. All require time from the day of the busy editor. He is expected to give his attention freely to all. Moreover, his opinion is sought on topics ranging from those important enough to merit discussion throughout the county to those treated casually in conversations on the sidewalk in front of the post-office.

There is no end to opportunity for community leadership. The immensity of the field offered by our complex social structure is inviting to many editors, not only from the standpoint of possibility for achievement, but also in the satisfaction that inherently must come to those privileged to render useful service to their fellow men. In its leadership efforts, the weekly newspaper has demonstrated that it has somthing to offer of practical benefit to its community. It is the leader, mouthpiece, and historian.

The position of the country weekly newspaper is that of a pulsing, throbbing institution which reaches to the grass roots of the community social structure reflecting its life, customs, and civilization. In an oft-repeated eulogy, "The Country Newspaper," John H. Casey, professor of journalism at the University of Oklahoma, stresses the necessity, character, and influence of the country weekly in these words:

Without its newspaper the small-town American community would be like a school without a teacher or a church without a pastor. In the aggregate, the country newspaper determines the outcome of more elections, exerts a greater influence for constructive community progress, is read longer by more members of the family, and constitutes, with its millions of circulation and quadrupled millions of readers, a better advertising medium than any other group of newspapers or periodical publications.

When properly conducted, its cultivates so intensively its home news field that city dailies, farm journals, and general magazines circulating in the same territory become only secondary influences.

Through service to its community, the country newspaper will not merely survive; it will continue to flourish as the most representative, most distinctive, most wholesome type of journalism America has produced.

THE MODERN COUNTRY EDITOR

—Bruce Crawford, "A New Type of Country Editor Emerges," *The New York Times,* September 22, 1935. (Magazine section of Sunday edition.) Mr. Crawford, a free-lance writer, was formerly editor of *Crawford's Weekly,* Norton, Virginia.

CHANGE has come over the country weekly newspaper as change has come over the country itself. Only in most backward counties may be found the old weekly, the four-page fleabitten sheet, loudly political, whose editor is also postmaster.

The modern weekly is a community paper. Its editor is not only a writer but a business man who has cast his lot with his fellow-citizens. He wants business from all of them and therefore wishes to see all of them succeed, whereas the old country editor staked everything on the fortunes of his political party and insulted those of his customers who were outside of his party.

The country editor of today, if he has his territory all to himself, does a thriving business. Modern advertising has enabled him to enlarge his paper. He has installed more productive machinery, a typesetting machine, and in some instances a press that prints newsprint from rolls. His weekly has departments to serve all interests in the community. He is editor not in the colorful sense of the old days but in a managerial sense. He may not express his own opinions on all occasions, but by stimulating issues he induces his readers to say a lot—and then he acts as chairman.

Instead of being a politician, he is conspicuous as a reporter at all political meetings, thereby drawing business from both parties. With a tolerance not characteristic of the old-time editor, he believes in at least two parties.

He may teach in the Sunday school, direct Boy Scout work, belong to the Kiwanis club, and talk in the high-school lecture series on the meaning of success. He does not affect a goatee or a cane, although he may be seen quite often in golf clothes.

Unlike his colorful predecessor, he keeps books and is careful about his credit rating. Perhaps he owes a batch of notes for new equipment or for having brought out his competitor, but he budgets his business. He manages to meet payments, payroll, supply bills, and taxes while enjoying a modern home, an automobile, and luxuries of sundry kinds. Only in rare instances is he a throwback who goes colorful, waxes foolishly independent, and fights his customers. He is primarily a business man.

This not to say that the country editor of today is a spineless individual, knee-bent to the key men of the community. But he does exercise a certain caution. He may weigh the costs of taking sides or of being indifferent. Not always is he as brave as the "militant" editor who hopes to be caught up into a career. He takes as forthright a stand on public issues as he can without wrecking his business. He knows that courage on most questions pays in the long run, if only in prestige, but he does not care to break his back and be a permanent sacrifice.

As a rule he is independent enough to attack local and state officeholders or advocate town improvements of a kind that might deprive an advertiser of revenues. But he considers long before going to the mat with the banker or the industrial leader who controls payrolls. And rare is the editor who defends labor trying to unionize.

About most issues the country editor can be more outspoken today than he could fifteen or twenty years ago. This may be due to the general bewilderment about morality, religion, education, and uncertainties in the economic life. A few years ago the little editor was crazy who stepped forward to combat the Ku Klux Klan. Today no editor is afraid to take a crack at the Klan.

Nor is the editor nowadays tender toward the "political parsons." He is too modern to countenance the Sunday blue laws. He does not revere, though he may respect, the moneybags. While for a time he didn't dare question the New Deal, he shows increasing temerity in tossing brickbats in the direction of Washington when he sees something there he doesn't like—even though he is a Democrat.

In many public movements he heads the procession after seeing which way it is going; maybe he is too busy balancing his own budget to keep up with fiscal problems of the state and nation, and rather than be left behind he joins the herd. On the whole, he knows there is safety today in frank criticism so long as ideas are being turned over and over in the intellectual concrete mixer and are not ready for pouring and setting.

In these critical times there is real opportunity for the country editor who is alive to the needs of the hour, and courageous—for the country weekly with convictions and character. This opportunity is greater notwithstanding the coverage of most communities by city dailies taking advantage of modern means of communication and transportation.

This type of editor is helping to prepare his readers in the small town and rural section for the effects of world change on their environment and their lives. By printing local news and interpretations of national and international events for the remote resident who may not take a daily paper, he helps to keep his readers in contact with one another and with mankind the world over.

Like the schoolmaster or the preacher, the country editor has peculiar trials and tribulations. However aware and on the jump he may be, he can never satisfy everybody. He may dutifully mention all of John Doe's achievements, including the latest baby, and then overlook his new car. If John's subscription has fallen due, he may not renew.

If the Town Council can balance its budget and at the same time repair only one of the streets that are worn out, it would be thoughtless of the editor to recommend any particular street for reconstruction. But a rushed editor sometimes is thoughtless. And the postman may prove it to him by bringing back a stack of papers marked "refused" from outraged sectors of the town.

Not many country editors dare condemn a lynching other than in a perfunctory manner. Let an editor call for an investigation of a local mobbing, with a view to conviction and prosecution, and he is likely to find himself lynched by the petition method. He may receive dozens of cancellations from subscribers, who explain nothing. Nor will he get much cooperation from law-enforcement officers. A politician can be "mobbed" by the covert petition, just as an editor can.

It is expecting too much for a lone editor to stand out in a fight on a lynching mob in his own bailiwick. The repercussions can be disastrous. Editors in their state press associations have yet to agree to hold up one another's hands in war on the mob spirit, to join in helping the colleague willing to fight the issue of a particular lynching to a finish. Sherwood Anderson, himself a country editor for a time, thinks that "twenty to thirty live and up-to-date country weeklies in any Southern State could eliminate lynchings."

There are many responsibilities which eat into the country editor's leisure moments and keep him from forgetting that he belongs to 2,000 or 3,000 subscribers. If he had a staff, he could assign some of his work and spend an evening at home without dread of interruption or sense of dereliction. But, unless he has an exceptionally prosperous weekly, he doesn't employ a reporter or an "ad" man. He must always keep the community's agenda in his own mind.

There's that plagued home-talent play to cover tonight! He must write a favorable word about each character in the cast or proud parents and admirers will be sore. Then to think that the female promoter of the play is an outsider, taking half the proceeds away from the community and also ruining his week's advertising quota by selling the merchants "ads" on the program!

And there's the Town Council meeting tonight. After urging the council to complete the community swimming pool . . . how can he consistently stay away?

He must also try to get the news about a meeting of the Red Cross committee (of which, of course, he is a member), and about the drug store merger, the new works relief director, the two stop-and-go lights operating in his town tonight for the first time, the condition of a patient hurt yesterday in a car wreck, and the results of the bowling tournament.

All the while he is gnawed by the consciousness that he should have got So-and-So's advertising copy instead of putting it off till tomorrow, when he must get newsprint out of the depot for this week's issue, act as pallbearer for an old subscriber, and collect a printing bill from that fly-by-night who, blindfolded, is going to drive a new model car down Main Street for a local dealer.

But if the editorship of the country weekly has its worries, it has its humorous incident and its satisfaction, too. The routine may be relieved by a near tragedy turned into comedy, as in the case of the Virginia editor who one day was confronted by the political boss he had said the worst things about. The editor looked up from his desk when the politician, a tremendous man, introduced himself.

"You really ought to know me, much as you have written me up," said the politician, grimly.

The newspaper man raked some pencils and copy paper into a drawer and pulled out two things—a pistol and a bottle of whisky. Placing both on top of the desk, he stood up and, with beaming politeness, said: "Will the visitor take his choice?"

The editor lived on.

There was the editor who apologized to the City Councilmen for publishing one week that "half of the town council are idiots." They resented the comment and demanded an apology. Next week the editor stated that he wished to make a correction. "Half of the town council are not idiots."

It is amusing and a bit pathetic to have a reader, who lives "on the other side of the tracks," assume that all items, including personal mentions, are paid for and offer a scrawled item like "Mr. Jim Hunsucker and wife went to Big Stone Gap last week to visit their daughter," adding: "What's the charge for printing that?" But it is gratifying to the editor when subscribers from the rural section come in and pay up with potatoes, apples, chickens, corn liquor. They always give good measure.

It is fun to print the week's issue and then steal around to see how it takes. The editor who loves his work is human enough to want it to "make an imprint." After writing an unsolicited puff of a regular reader, the editor will make it a point to bump into that reader soon after.

It pleases the country editor to have his writing mentioned or quoted in meetings. His annual editorial on General Lee may be praised by the local chapter of the United Daughters of the Confederacy. Road boosters order a thousand extra copies of his editorial, "Finish Route 23," and he feels more important. And if the city dailies reprint his stuff he is glad that his wagon is hitched at last to the great world of ideas.

In such a mood he allows himself the luxury of some high audacity, like starting a crusade for a town-owned power plant.

The editor feels a solicitude for the welfare of his community and pride in the part he plays. It feeds his self-esteem to have citizens coming into his printshop to enlist his cooperation in projects and undertakings. If it is not a lawn and garden contest, a program of sanitation and beautification, or a community playground, it is a bake sale.

When all is said and done, the editor takes his responsibility seriously. He knows that his weekly reflects the life of his community, the struggles, hopes, achievements, happiness, births, and deaths of his people. More than reflecting, the paper helps to coordinate the work of all civic organizations.

His weekly may not be making a lot of money, but he feels that it has the confidence and good-will of its public. He imagines himself being awarded stars in his crown if not always "bucks" in the bank. And what is a bank balance, anyway, lying up there and doing no good, compared to a community park publicized into a reality, a back alley cleaned up, a new fire siren on the City Hall, historical markers at the approaches of the town, and encomiums from the Kiwanis toastmaster on ladies' night?

THE COUNTRY WEEKLY IS DIFFERENT

—From *Country Editor* by Henry Hough, copyright, 1940, reprinted by permission of Doubleday, Doran & Co., Inc., pp. 292–293. Mr. Hough is editor of the *Vineyard Gazette* on Martha's Vineyard.

COUNTRY newspapers never were edited in an ivory tower or a laboratory. They are published in real life, in towns which are to be represented and served. It is pleasant to have a nice looking paper, and at times we have been somewhat proud of the *Gazette*, but we never excluded advertising from the first page, because to have done so would have been to impair the honest function of the paper.

The front page rule is, obviously, an excellent one for dailies, although a great many of them violate it without inviting condemnation from the professors. They have a great number of pages, and they can departmentalize their news, classify their advertising as much as they choose, and make provision for all contingencies. It is unfortunate that advertising on a front page does not look citified, but the professors should remember that it is, at least, functional. (They are the ones who want to see a citified front page; we don't care.)

Country publishers are being advised, also, to be good business men, which is exactly what they ought not to be. "Know your costs," say the professors. It is a mighty dangerous thing, sometimes, to know your costs in the newspaper business. Other enterprises are continually studying their own operations with the absorption of a mechanized Narcissus, and it would not be surprising tomorrow if the electric companies announced they had found they were losing money on the reading of meters, and would have to charge a dollar and a half in the future for every meter read. Or if the banks declared that they were running into the hole on deposit slips, and would have to collect a cent and a half for every deposit slip used. In cases like these the public utility commissions and the banking associations would doubtless see that the necessary additional charges were passed on to the public, but in the instance of a country newspaper there would be no way to collect an extra amount. The tendency would be to trim and cut the newspaper, and every bit of trimming and cutting would sadly deface the character and quality of the paper. This must be the case always, because the only things upon which money can possibly be saved in a well-run newspaper office are those which are important from a professional point of view.

Leaning over pages of figures is not a natural pose for a newspaperman, and the professors should be ashamed of trying to force him into it. Anyway, if the newspaper keeps its bills paid from month to month, everyone in the shop will know the costs well enough. A job printer may need to sit up nights with a ledger and little pots of red and black ink, but not a newspaperman.

REVIEW QUESTIONS AND ASSIGNMENTS

1. What is the answer to attempted boycotts by influential advertisers in community newspapers?

2. Discuss the proposition of abandoning the editorial page for editorializing in the news columns.

3. Discuss the statement that the small-town editor is usually the most influential citizen.

4. Discuss the theory that editors should not attempt to mold public opinion in the small-town and rural areas.

5. Does the small-town paper justify its existence merely on its record as a historical document and an advertising medium?

6. Discuss Turner's statement that community editors usually "play ball" with local business interests.

7. How does the country weekly exert political influence?

8. What is the relative power of the country weekly and the metropolitan paper over the individual subscriber?

9. If the community paper must specialize in the local field to exist, what broadening influence will its readers lose?

10. Is there danger of small-town papers becoming too provincial? What compensating influences are there in the community for a too-localized newspaper?

11. How can the newspaper interpret the community to itself?

12. Discuss the role of the newspaper as a community institution.

13. How is the influence of metropolitan competition changing the content and character of community dailies and country weeklies?

14. Should the editor take part in community politics as a candidate for office?

15. In what respect should the country weekly imitate the physical makeup of metropolitan dailies?

ADDITIONAL REFERENCES

Allen, Charles L., *Country Journalism,* Thomas Nelson, 1928, Chapter 2.

Anonymous, "Empire Saga," *Time,* Vol. 41, February 22, 1943, p. 53.

———, "Small Papers Read More Closely, Stanford University Study Shows," *Editor & Publisher,* Vol. 78, July 14, 1945, p. 12.

———, "Small Town Journalism Reported on Upsurge," *Editor & Publisher,* Vol. 80, May 17, 1947, p. 24.

Barnhart, Thomas F., *The Weekly Newspaper: A Bibliography—1925–1941,* Burgess, Minneapolis, 1941.

Bing, Phil C., *The Country Weekly,* Appleton-Century, 1920.

Clark, Thomas D., *The Rural Press and the New South,* Louisiana State University Press, 1948.

Ernst, Morris L., *The First Freedom,* Macmillan, 1946, pp. 102–112.

Harris, E. P., and F. H. Hooke, *The Community Newspaper,* Appleton-Century, 1923, Chapter 20.

Haworth, Peter, "Country Weekly's Place in the Helicopter World," *National Publisher,* Vol. 26, August 1945, p. 6.

Irwin, T. S., "Small Dailies Produce Some Big Promotions," *Editor & Publisher,* Vol. 78, March 24, 1945, p. 48.

Lyons, L. M., "Press and Its Critics," *Atlantic Monthly,* Vol. 180, July 1947, pp. 115–116.

Meredith, Charles M., *The Country Weekly,* Bruce Humphries, 1937.

Neal, Robert M., *Editing the Small City Daily,* Prentice-Hall, 1946.

Northbridge, George, "Reliance on Local News Shown in Chester, Pa.," *Editor & Publisher,* Vol. 76, February 27, 1943, p. 9.

Rogers, Charles E., *Journalistic Vocations,* Appleton-Century, 1937, Chapters 4, 6.

———, "The Role of the Weekly Newspaper," *The Annals of the American Academy of Political and Social Science,* Vol. 219, January 1942, pp. 151–157.

Salmon, Lucy M., *The Newspaper and the Historian,* Oxford University Press, 1923, pp. 486–487.

Smith, J. Garland, "Small Town Editor Knows His People," *Quill,* Vol. 35, March 1947, p. 10.

Willey, Malcolm M., *The Country Newspaper,* University of North Carolina Press, 1926, Chapter 9.

——— (with W. Weinfield), "The Country Weekly and the Emergence of 'One-Newspaper Places,'" *Journalism Quarterly,* Vol. 11, September 1934, pp. 246–257.

18. RELIABILITY OF THE PRESS

INTRODUCTION

Can you believe what you read in the newspapers? A body of criticism, too huge to have been missed by the least erudite reader, has slowly accumulated through the years against the press for its inaccuracy, until it has become "the thing to do" to say that you can't believe what you read in the newspapers. This statement can be lightly tossed off, and it is usually popular wherever it is made, because it makes both speaker and listener feel superior to the men and women who publish those same newspapers.

But can you believe what you read in the newspapers? This chapter attempts to answer a portion of that question. In the chapter on suppression another phase of the question was handled, and still other portions have been treated elsewhere, because that question at a stroke lays bare the heart of the biggest problem concerned with the press. Hence, it is the accuracy of the facts as gathered by the newspapers themselves that is brought up for questioning here.

One of the best efforts to appraise newspaper accuracy and to relate it to objective truth is that of Walter Lippmann, who points out that many newspaper errors arise from the fact that few objective standards for truth and accuracy of reports exist. He holds that the press is not constituted to furnish from one edition to the next the exact knowledge needed by public opinion.

One of the noteworthy critics of the press, Bruce Bliven, has summed up his long study of the American press. The article, quoted in full, will prove a revelation to those who have known his previous bitter articles. Events abroad have brought about a better appreciation of newspapers in this country, and some critics, like Bliven, have changed their stand.

The most thorough study of the American newspaper has been made by Salmon. An excerpt on newspaper reliability from an address by one of the country's outstanding university administrators is included. Tolley finds that the picture of events presented by the press on the most vital subjects is sometimes insufficient to permit the people to form adequate judgment. Lyons backs up the criticism as he calls attention to how badly the press erred in reporting the presidential campaign of Truman and Dewey.

Among the very few efforts to measure precisely the accuracy of newspaper reports is the citation from Charnley. This is only a beginning step; but it deserves careful scrutiny, since it indicates the basis for much public distrust of the press. Additional studies in this area might well be more fruitful than many now made of reader interest and readability. Another effort at a scientific study of newspaper reporting is the citation from *The Nation,* based upon an analysis by the Bureau of Applied Social Research. These interesting findings should be checked against the reader's own impressions or observations of a presidential campaign.

THE PRESS AND OBJECTIVE STANDARDS OF TRUTH

—From Walter Lippmann, *Public Opinion,* 1922. By permission of The Macmillan Company, publishers, pp. 358–361.

As WE BEGIN to make more and more exact studies of the press, much will depend upon the hypothesis we hold. If we assume with Mr. Sinclair, and most of his opponents, that news and truth are two words for the same thing, we shall, I believe, arrive nowhere. We shall prove that on this point the newspaper lied. We shall prove that on that point Mr. Sinclair's account lied. We shall demonstrate that Mr. Sinclair lied when he said that somebody lied, and that somebody lied when he said that Mr. Sinclair lied. We shall vent our feelings but we shall vent them into air.

The hypothesis which seems to me the most fertile is that news and truth are not the same thing, and must be clearly distinguished. The function of news is to signalize an event, the function of truth is to bring to light the hidden facts, to set them into relation with each other, and make a picture of reality on which men can act. Only at those points where social conditions take a recognizable and measurable shape do the body of truth and the body of news coincide. That is a comparatively small part of the whole field of human interest. In this sector, and only in this sector, the tests of the news are sufficiently exact to make the charges of perversion or suppression more than partisan judgment. There is no defense, no extenuation, no excuse whatever, for stating six times that Lenin is dead, when the only information the paper possesses is a report that he is dead from a source repeatedly shown to be unreliable. The news, in that instance, is not "Lenin Dead" but "Helsingfors Says Lenin Is Dead." And a newspaper can be asked to take the responsibility of not making Lenin more dead than the source of the news is reliable; if there is one subject on which editors are most responsible it is in their judgment of the reliability of the source. But when it comes to dealing, for example, with stories of what the Russian people want, no such test exists.

The absence of these exact tests accounts, I think, for the character of the profession, as no other explanation does. There is a very small body of exact knowledge, which it requires no outstanding ability or training to deal with. The rest is in the journalist's own discretion. Once he departs from the region where it is definitely recorded at the County Clerk's office that John Smith has gone into bankruptcy, all fixed standards disappear. The story of why John Smith failed, his human frailties, the analysis of the economic conditions on which he was shipwrecked, all of this can be told in a hundred different ways. There is no discipline in applied psychology, as there is a discipline in medicine, engineering, or even law, which has authority to direct the journalist's mind when he passes from the news to the vague realm of truth. There are no canons to direct his own mind, and no canons that coerce the reader's judgment or the publisher's. His version of the truth is only his version. How can he demonstrate the truth as he sees it? How can he demonstrate it, any more than Mr. Sinclair Lewis can demonstrate that he has told the whole truth about Main Street. And the more he understands his own weaknesses, the more ready he is to admit that where there is no objective test, his own opinion is in some vital measure constructed out of his own stereotypes, according to his own code, and by the urgency of his own interest. He knows that he is seeing the world through subjective lenses. He cannot deny that he too is, as Shelley remarked, a dome of many-colored glass which stains the white radiance of eternity.

And by this knowledge his assurance is tempered. He may have all kinds of moral courage, and sometimes has, but he lacks that sustaining conviction of a certain technic which finally freed the physical sciences from theological control. It was the gradual development of an irrefragable method that gave the physicist his intellectual freedom as against all the powers of the world. His proofs were so clear, his evidence so sharply superior to tradition, that he broke away finally from all control. But the journalist has no such support in his own conscience or in fact. The control exercised over him by the opinions of his employers and his readers, is not the control of truth by prejudice, but one of opinion by another opinion that is not demonstrably less true. . . .

The task of deflating these controversies, and reducing them to a point where they can be reported as news, is not a task which the reporter can perform. It is possible and necessary for journalists to bring home to people the uncertain character of the truth on which their opinions are founded, and by criticism and agitation to prod social science into making more usable formulations of social facts, and to prod statesmen into establishing more visible institutions. The press, in other words, can fight for the extension of reportable truth. But as social truth is organized to-day, the press is not constituted to furnish from one edition to the next the amount of knowledge which the democratic theory of public opinion demands. This is not due to the Brass Check, as the quality of news in radical papers shows, but to the fact that the press deals with a society in which the governing forces are so imperfectly recorded. The theory that the press can itself record those forces is false. It can normally record only what has been recorded for it by the working of institutions. Everything else is argument and opinion, and fluctuates with the vicissitudes, the self-consciousness, and the courage of the human mind.

AN APPRAISAL OF THE AMERICAN PRESS

—Bruce Bliven, "Balance Sheet of American Journalism," *The New Republic*, Vol. 104, March 10, 1941, pp. 331–334. Mr. Bliven long was a member of the staff of *The New Republic* and is an experienced newspaperman.

How does the American newspaper look, viewed as objectively as human frailty permits. . . . For the sake of brevity, let me express my points in the form of a series of perhaps dogmatic statements, accompanied by brief supporting data.

1. The American Press Is the Best in the World Today

Our journalism has plenty of faults, and I shall devote the rest of this essay to pointing them out. But with all its weaknesses, no one familiar with newspapers around the world will dispute the statement above. In the totalitarian countries, the lamp of journalism was long ago dropped into the cesspool and extinguished. At least two-thirds of the world's population have no access to newspapers which make any pretense of telling the truth.

In Latin America and Switzerland there are a few fine papers, but only a few. British journalism has a great history. . . . Moreover, in the past many too-modest Americans have had the habit of looking only at the best British journals, the Manchester *Guardian,* the London *Times,* the London *News Chronicle,* and ignoring the mass of mediocre provincial sheets. It is just as misleading to compare America's vulgar tabloids with the Manchester *Guardian* as it would be to compare the New York *Times* with the *British News of the World.*

2. The American Press on the Whole Is Improving

Those who talk about the good old days of journalism are usually people who have either forgotten what those days were like, or never really knew. Most of the great editors of a century ago wouldn't last five minutes on a self-respecting paper of today. They vilified their opponents in seeming total disrespect for the libel laws; they left out important news whenever they felt like it; they were primarily propagandists. These faults persisted for a long time; even in the last few decades journalism has greatly improved.

Several things have united to bring this about. The sharp criticisms of men like Upton Sinclair, George Seldes, and Ferdinand Lundberg have been fiercely resisted and repudiated by American journalism, but it has then proceeded to remedy some at least of the faults charged, whose existence it denied. Ethical standards are higher and have been helped by the conscious efforts of many editors to improve them.

Whether schools of journalism are worth while is a moot point; but certainly a newspaperman who is a college graduate, even though he has had no technical training, is almost always a better journalist than one who is not. In the last quarter-century, the proportion of college men on newspaper staffs has risen from a small minority to an overwhelming majority. The average reporter or editor today knows a great deal more about a wide variety of subjects than did his confrères at the turn of the century. What is more, he is not afraid to print what he knows. The reading public has either become more highbrow or else the press has discovered that the higher brows were there all the time. (I suspect that the latter is true.)

The proportion of heavy drinkers in newspaper work has greatly decreased, and this is a decided benefit. The old-time wandering reporter was only too often a badly dressed dipsomaniac who either had no family or should have had none, whose boast it was that he had been fired successively off every paper from Portland to Portland. While there are still traces of him around, today the more typical picture is a hard-working man with a wife and one child who is buying a home from the FHA and a Dodge or an Oldsmobile from a limited-dividend finance company.

The American Newspaper Guild, these past few years, has done a great deal to increase the self-respect of the individual newspaperman. Whatever you or Westbrook Pegler may think about the Communist sympathies of some of the Guild's leaders, in the average shop the Guild has helped to put hair on the chests of the boys. The Guildsman knows that he can no longer be fired at the whim of the boss or because he refuses to do anybody's dirty work. If journalism ever approaches the ethical standards of such professions as law and medicine, the Guild or some similar organization will play a great part in the transformation.

3. Censorship by Publishers Is Worse Than That by Advertisers

People who read muckraking books about journalism often get an exaggerated idea of the importance of advertiser dictation. It does exist and it is important; newspapers have many times in the past killed a story to which their advertisers might object and no doubt they will continue to do so; but there are still more serious evils of which the lay public is hardly conscious at all. Usually the advertiser doesn't need to exert any influence, because the publisher, who has the control, is himself very much the same kind of fellow as the advertiser, with the same ideas and inhibitions. Usually he tries to make the sort of paper the advertiser will take because it is the kind of paper he himself admires. In fact:

4. Newspapers Are Edited by Business Men

The great change in journalism in our big cities in the past hundred years has been the virtual disappearance of the owner-editor. A century ago the owner did his own editing, or most of it. With all their faults, mentioned above, Dana, Greeley, Bennett wrote many of their own editorials, even did reporting. The readers knew that what they said they believed. Today a big-city newspaper is a tremendous financial enterprise, with an investment of millions. It has drifted into the hands of money-minded men who are interested in profits, whereas the editorial-minded men are usually interested in trying to influence their city, state, and nation in what they consider the right direction. Many of these publishers—not all, certainly—are hard-boiled, ruthless individuals. While they take no part in the normal editorial work from day to day, they insist that their ideas shall prevail in all cases of important controversial issues.

This is strikingly exemplified during a national political campaign. Both in 1936 and 1940, informal polls showed that something like 90 per cent of the editorial staff of the New York *Herald Tribune* was in favor of President Roosevelt; nevertheless the paper itself went with the minute minority which happened to include the publisher, and supported Landon in '36 and Willkie in '40. I strongly doubt whether more than a small proportion of the Chicago *Tribune's* staff agrees with the violent isolationism and hostility to the New Deal of Colonel Robert McCormick; yet even if 100 per cent of them disagreed with him, the paper would doubtless continue in its course. William Randolph Hearst has repeatedly swung his mighty journalistic batteries from one side to the other of some public question according to his own whim, and all his thousands of editors have hastily reversed their coats. Similar conditions prevail on hundreds of other papers.

5. *Monopoly Is a Grave Danger in the Press*

Fifteen years ago many people were concerned about the onward march of chain journalism, one man or one corporation buying up successive newspapers all over the country. It looked as though this process might continue indefinitely until we had only a few gigantic newspaper trusts. Since then, for various reasons, the trend toward consolidation seems to have halted. The chain papers today are only a small minority of the total number; but since they are usually the largest and strongest journals, with tremendous circulations, their influence far exceeds their numerical strength.

Chain journalism has its good points as well as bad. Twenty papers can share among them the salaries of Washington correspondents, or syndicated columnists, whom no one of them could afford. If the local advertisers in a single town should gang up on the editor, as sometimes happens, the chain can pour in it resources and win a fight that would otherwise have been lost in the first round. But against this must be weighed very serious evils. The accumulation of power in the hands of one man or group is tremendous. The three most important personalities in chain journalism at present are W. R. Hearst, Roy Howard, and Frank Gannett. I happen to disagree violently with all three of these gentlemen on a majority of their most important policies and, with some of them, I strongly disapprove of their way of doing business. But even if I thought they were right in everything they say, and considered them as impeccable as Shadrach, Meshach, and Abednego, I should still feel that they wield more power than is safe in a democracy. . . .

6. There Is a Dangerous Tendency Toward Standardized and Syndicated Material

Within the past few years an extraordinary development has been seen toward amusement features and away from the news, not only in evening papers, the traditional home of this sort of thing, but morning papers as well. The so-called comic strips, which are no longer comic at all but are sensational serial stories of melodrama or fantasy, have proliferated like a colchicine-treated vegetable. Instead of three or four columns of these strips per day, three or four pages have become more nearly normal. As for the columnists, they have come trooping out of Pandora's box. The editors tacitly admit the weakness of their own writing by hiring Lippmann, Pegler, or Miss Thompson. The news columns are remorselessly whittled down to make space for an ever increasing proportion of such feature material.

This situation, again, has its good as well as its bad side. The leading columnists have become such on their merits; when a paper in Flagstaff, Arizona, presents half a dozen of them, it is giving a better service than could be performed by any six Flagstaffians sitting down at their typewriters each day at 9 A. M. The columnist gains some freedom, because no one editor can dictate what he shall say.

Yet there are disadvantages too. Standardized journalism has lost much of its local flavor. Ride across the country by train, buy the local paper at each stop, tear off the logotype containing its name, and you will be hard pressed to tell one from another. With local news so minimized and routinized, the papers lose some of their initiative; local crusades become scarcer than before. The syndicated columnist, because of the very fact that he is appearing in three or four hundred papers, is under temptation to pull his punch, not to say anything startling or upsetting. If he suddenly changed his mind on some important question it might cost him many clients and a lot of money.

7. *The Middle Class Is Overrepresented in the Press*

American newspapers on the whole speak for the middle class and not for the workers of the country. The newspapers which represent the middle-class point of view circulate approximately 40,000,000 copies a day. All labor journals, whether daily, weekly, or monthly, have a combined circulation of perhaps 8,000,000, and this figure is less impressive than it seems, because there is heavy duplication. Many so-called labor papers are in fact house organs for some radical sect and nobody except the members would touch them with sugar tongs.

I am aware of the answer that will be made to this comment. I shall be told that in America the workers think like the middle class, that they don't want to read special papers giving their own point of view. There is some truth in this, but not the whole truth. It is a fact that most workers prefer a good middle-class paper rather than a bad labor one. The American worker does have some traits in common with the middle class, though these are not necessarily incompatible with being a good trade-union man. He is sometimes taken in by the spurious expressions of friendship that are found, for instance, in the Hearst press. And yet there is a real and dangerous situation in which many thousands of workingmen feel that the press as a whole is hostile to them, will not tell their story fairly, gives disproportionate space and emphasis to the employer's side in every dispute.

8. *Journalists and Papers Get Old, Fat and Timid*

It seems to be a normal part of biological history (at least in our civilization) for the individual to grow more conservative and timid with age. While there are plenty of conspicuous exceptions, most men, as their knee joints begin to creak, lose their crusading zeal to make the world over and begin to look instead for a pleasantly padded corner in which to spend their declining years with a maximum of security and peace. This has happened to innumerable journalists, and it will continue. Unfortunately, the policy-making jobs on most papers are in the hands of men who have reached this stage of life.

Journals, too, grow old and suffer from the diseases of advancing age. Some of our stodgiest Tory papers of today, which earn vast profits by grinding out unsalted pap for masses of apathetic readers, began life as crusading journals of young men who had little to lose from speaking out. In the old days this Toryism did not matter greatly because you could be sure that somewhere a pink-cheeked young William Allen White, with a shirt-tail full of type, would come along and launch a new, fighting paper.

But unhappily this is no longer true. Very few newspapers are started any more, and especially in the big cities where the investment is so enormous. The result has been an important trend toward monopolistic or semimonopolistic conditions. More and more communities have only one newspaper, or only two, one in the morning and one in the afternoon. Where there are two, they tend to be under common ownership and common editorial direction. An increasing proportion of our population is no longer able even to choose the lesser of two journalistic evils. In such circumstances, if you don't like the views of the publisher in your community, you can only buy a radio; and the radio is certainly no substitute for journalism.

9. *In Technology There Is Hope*

Among other things that this country needs, it requires newspapers with a far smaller capital investment, so that genuine competition will more easily be possible. Here again, the argument can cut both ways. Advertising in large quantities has its dangers, but a paper on a shoestring is also subject to secret, corrupt control of a different sort. For the past half-century the most venal journalism in the world was probably that of Paris, where advertising in the American sense is little understood or practiced. In this country the shoestring paper is saved, in most cases, only because it is not published primarily as a moneymaking enterprise but to represent the ideas of some special group in the community. I should like to see a proliferation of such papers, not as substitutes for orthodox journalism but as supplements and gadflies to it, publishing the news it is afraid to print, delving into special fields of limited interest. The liberal magazines such as . . . *The Nation*, and *The New Republic* already perform something of this function. Technological advance is likely to bring down the cost of newspapers materially in the next few years. There is a machine which sets type simultaneously in a thousand offices while only one man operates a central keyboard. The self-justifying typewriter, which produces lines of equal length, makes it possible to print from photographed plates without setting any type at all. Greatly improved techniques for transmitting pictures by wire make it feasible to prepare a newspaper in New York each night and print separate editions next morning in any number of cities all over the country. The radio printer will produce a complete paper overnight in your own home at nominal cost. New printing presses are marvels of speed and economy. Quite possibly through these devices we may soon begin to break the iron grip of big, monopolistic newspapers.

10. We Get About What We Deserve

It is wrong to single out journalism as though it were materially inferior to other things in our civilization. Newspapers are not so cowardly as the radio, not so money-minded as the movies, no more servile to community sentiment than are the church and the school. I have heard dozens of plans brought forward for creating Utopian newspapers, but I doubt strongly whether it is possible to bring any one aspect of our society far out ahead of the others. There are certain bad spots which need to be remedied at once, without waiting for the slow march of civilization; but in the main, newspapers will get better as the country gets better, as our people realize the importance of an accurate, impartial, and complete reporting of the news, and insist on having it.

AREAS OF NEWSPAPER RELIABILITY

—Lucy M. Salmon, *The Newspaper and the Historian,* Oxford University Press, 1923, pp. 75–80, 83–84.

THESE FEDERAL and state provisions that guarantee freedom of the press throughout the country have their counterpart in laws restraining the press from printing false or malicious statements. It must be assumed not only that the press as a whole wishes to publish only trustworthy information, but that even the most sensational member of it hesitates to incur the notoriety and the expense involved in becoming the defendant in a suit of libel, yet these laws are necessary to afford an effective guarantee that all possible care has been taken not to make statements that are wilfully untrue. Libel laws, however, carry with them no guarantee of the wisdom of printing articles that may be true in themselves, but nevertheless may convey a wrong impression. The historian may be reasonably sure of the truth of what he reads but he has no assurance that he has read the whole truth, or that the truth printed is in fair proportion to the truth not printed. . . .

The federal government not only gives certain guarantees through its Constitution and its laws, but it becomes itself responsible for the authoritativeness of no small or unimportant part of what appears on the pages of the press. The weather reports and forecasts, the times of sun and moon and tides, the arrival and departure of domestic and foreign mails, shipping news, regulations affecting the army and navy, the time and place for holding examinations for the federal civil service, the calendars of federal courts and summaries of court decisions, the names of persons admitted to practice in these courts, signed proclamations of the chief federal executive, reports of the regular federal administrative departments as well as those appointed for times of emergencies, and a mass of official announcements and reports are made with the sanction and approval of the federal government.

In a similar way the state governments are directly or indirectly responsible for the publication of state laws, proclamations of governors, the calendars of state courts, the notices of the incorporation of stock companies, election notices, change of personal name, reports of state bureaus or commissions charged with the oversight of state educational, charitable, reformatory, and penal institutions, and with the direction of all efforts to conserve food and fuel, and for other large classes of legal and public matters.

County, town, and municipal governments are responsible for calendars of cases arising in criminal, civil, and surrogates' courts; for all notices concerning the administration of the estates of deceased persons, for notices concerning recorded transfers of property, recorded, satisfied, and assigned mortgages, and mechanics' liens; for the publication of permits for new buildings and the alteration of old ones; for notices of bankruptcies and business reverses and of the sale of property for unpaid taxes; for notices of bids for city contracts and of assessments for pavements and for water and sewerage improvements; announcements of permanent and temporary assignments in the police department, as also the transfers, leaves of absence, fines, reprimands, and dismissals of charges in the department, and similar notices concerning the fire department, when this is under civic control; and for all legal advertisements that concern the local government. . . .

The newspaper on its part stands ready to assume much more responsibility than is formally demanded by the law. If it does not actually print, it is at all times ready to give the name of the person in charge of the various special departments demanded by its readers, or engaged to increase its circulation.

Much space is given in the press to the letters of regular correspondents concerning foreign and domestic affairs. These are as a rule signed with the name of the writer, or with his initials and thus easily identified. The larger papers have their columns or pages for games, sporting news, and athletic contests, and these are in charge of an editor usually named. The art editor, the musical and dramatic critic, and the literary editor often sign their names or initials to their contributions, and thus indicate their willingness to assume the responsibility for their part of the newspaper.

The newspaper makes its own regulations for its own protection as well as for that of its readers. The occasional correspondent must give his name and address, "not necessarily for publication but as a guarantee of good faith," and this regulation is frequently re-enforced by the statement that the paper will pay no attention to anonymous communications. In large cities, all notices of marriages and of deaths must be accompanied by the name and address of the sender, although no regulation seems to have been devised that will prevent a person from sending a false notice of his own marriage. . . .

There is a somewhat general assumption that the main object of a paper is to hoodwink the public, yet even a cursory examination must show that the newspaper and other periodicals give their own explicit guarantees that they have used every known means to guarantee the reliability and the authoritativeness of the definite statements made by them, in the ways that have been enumerated, and that they are to the best of their knowledge true and unimpeachable.

The newspaper as a business enterprise offers certain guarantees through the information it publishes concerning itself. It often prints facts concerning its own history, such as the year when it was established, its press ancestors, consolidations, and consequent change of name, and this pride in ancestry or of a long and honorable journalistic career has a tonic effect. It states its membership in one or more of the great co-operative news-supplying associations, such as the Associated Press, the United Press, the New York Associated Dailies, or that it has received the news service of the New York *Sun*, or of the International News Service, thus guaranteeing a far-reaching collection of news and availing itself of the guarantee afforded by these great organizations. . . .

The church in its various branches becomes responsible for the official announcements of its religious services, for information in regard to the increase or decrease in its membership, for facts concerning its missionary and charitable undertakings, and for the published programmes of its stated local, state, and national meetings.

Educational authorities are responsible for official information in regard to school buildings, school organization, school curricula, and all extra-school activities carried on under their auspices, such as playgrounds and school gardens; for official statements concerning expenditures needed for school buildings, salaries, and general operating expenses; and for the names of persons appointed to the teaching staff.

Public and private hospitals publish the vital statistics that come under their jurisdiction, and boards of health and health officers are in their turn responsible for other information in regard to health conditions.

These are but suggestions of the large number of responsible organizations and individuals that in effect guarantee the authoritativeness of much that is published by the press. The material thus guaranteed by the nature of its source does not lie in the field generally denominated "news," nor is it in the assignments given reporters, nor is it found in editorial columns, nor does it lend itself always to the writing of a "story." Nevertheless, this guaranteed material forms a large part of every newspaper and it can easily be separated from other parts where the guarantee is less in evidence. It is also obvious that while the greater part, if not all, of the newspaper that has behind it an absolute guarantee cannot in any sense be considered *news,* yet its inherent value in reconstructing the past may be far greater than the published news of the hour.

It is thus evident that the newspaper always contains certain features permanent as regards the source from which they are derived. The superficial details may vary, but the source remains the same, and hence the responsibility is a constant one. These permanent elements are those furnished by federal, state, county, town, and municipal governments; by other official organizations of a public or private character; by business associations whose credit in the eye of the public depends on their contributing to the press only absolutely trustworthy information; and by many elements of the newspaper itself considered as a business enterprise.

The responsibility of these permanent features of the newspaper is thus readily recognized and it becomes as absolute as lies within the range of human responsibility. Error may be found in these portions of the newspaper—permanent as to their source and as to their responsibility—but every possible precaution to avoid them has been taken by their guarantors. The student of history may accept at its face value this permanent element in the press and be assured that in so doing he has not been led into avoidable inaccuracies of statement. The errancy of the press, if such there be, must lie elsewhere.

NEWSPAPERS REVEAL BUT PART OF THE FACTS

—William P. Tolley, "Newspapers Reveal But Part of the Facts," *Syracuse University School of Journalism Publications,* Series 2, No. 7, September 1948, pp. 17–21. Dr. Tolley is Chancellor of Syracuse University.

I DO NOT want to minimize the difficulties experienced by the newspapers themselves in finding out the truth. The fact remains that despite their freedom, they either do not get the truth or do not succeed in telling it to the American people.

Such a thesis requires documentation. For that, let us first go back to the tense, critical months immediately preceding entry of the United States into World War II. You recall the issues of the day. Was lend-lease an act short of war? Was the United States Navy actually convoying? Had we begun a shooting war with the Germans?

Never had the press, except in actual warfare, faced a more difficult task in finding the facts and learning the truth. Most of the action that was developing the critical news of the day took place at sea or in distant lands. News of it sifted back to the country only after a bureaucratic screening by War, Navy, and State departments. Soon the Navy demanded voluntary newspaper censorship of news concerning its operations.

Occasionally, by chance, a bit of news from the Atlantic front slipped through to the press from an unofficial source. If the story conflicted with the "no war" plank on which President Roosevelt had won his third-term election, high officials branded the dispatch as a lie.

Charles A. Beard in his *President Roosevelt and the Coming of the War of 1941,* the final contribution of a brilliant historian, has traced the struggle of these months between so-called isolationist and interventionist groups in America. He documents the fact that while proclaiming a policy of peace and denying warlike acts on the part of the United States, the administration at Washington was pursuing a policy carefully calculated to carry the country into war—carefully conceived to cause the United States to be attacked.

When his Atlantic policy finally resulted in shooting, the President promptly announced that the American destroyers had been attacked. He seemed then to have set the stage for our entry into the war. However, an immediate senate investigation of the shooting in the Atlantic raised so many doubts as to who was attacked and who was the attacker, that the incidents failed to stir the war spirit essential to support of a declaration.

Soon the complicated moves in our diplomacy with Japan were stepped up rapidly. At Pearl Harbor, the Japs obliged the Roosevelt administration by leaving no question that the United States had been attacked. We did not have to get into the war—we were in it.

Dr. Beard's carefully documented volume makes it evident that between the beginning of lend-lease discussions and Pearl Harbor the public never learned the truth. Dr. Beard makes no accusations against the press of this period. It was accurately reporting the statements of the president and his cabinet. It displayed remarkable enterprise in the publication of occasional accounts of the warlike acts in which the Roosevelt administration was engaged.

In a footnote, however, Dr. Beard does point out the fact that although the publisher of the New York *Times* subsequently declared that "we had gone into the war when we made the lend-lease declaration," the *Times* in its editorial on the lend-lease act failed to characterize it as a war-like act.

. . . If the newspaper editors saw (what was going on)—and I personally doubt if they did—they certainly didn't inform the American people. In general, the newspapers failed to tell the American people the score of any inning of the war preparations game. We were led by the nose toward war almost as easily as would have been the case if we had had a government controlled press.

The second illustration is the story of losing the peace. The Bullitt articles in *Life* magazine do not tell us very much that we should not already have known. Yet this is a view of the case quite new to the American public. Not always, but at times, the people of the United States have been poorly informed about foreign affairs. Not until long afterward do we learn the enormity of the blunders of our own Government.

The third illustration is our preparations for World War III. One would get the idea by reading the newspapers that America is a big, easy-going, friendly fellow full of good-will toward his neighbors, as patient as Job, and anxious for peace at almost any cost. One also gets the picture of Russia as a colossus itching for a fight and dead set to conquer the world. The American public is told that only the Marshall Plan will save Europe from Communism and that if Europe should go Communistic, we could not survive as a free country. It may be that this is all true. Perhaps our State Department has made no errors. Perhaps the enemy is even worse than he is now painted. . . .

Or take the story of our flirtations with the rightist totalitarians like Peron and Franco, and from time to time with rightest groups in France, Italy, and Greece. Politics makes strange bedfellows, and we have been playing politics in a big way on the world scene. The American public, however, does not seem fully aware that we have returned to an era of power politics. All the public is allowed to see is a knight in shining armor.

What I am trying to say is that, while we have a free press, the American public is still not adequately informed. This is a tragedy. It suggests that we are all beginning to walk the goose step and to chant the national party line. We seem hell-bent for war; our factories are getting ready, our armed forces are getting ready, and the newspapers are getting us ready.

When a slave state wins a war, it really wins something. When a democracy wins a war, it wins nothing but time. If we go to war with Russia, it may well prove not only the final débacle of democracy but of western culture as we know it. One of the most striking pictures of the New Testament is that of the Gadarene swine rushing at full speed over the precipice to their destruction in the sea. That seems to be the picture of the world at the present time.

In general, Americans are better informed about domestic affairs than about foreign policy or news from abroad. Yet there is plenty of distortion of news even on the domestic scene. The suppression or toning down of news hostile to business, religious, or political interests is an old story, but the role of public relations counsel is a new factor. His skill in presenting his version of the news makes it increasingly difficult for the reading public to get the plain unvarnished truth. . . .

The basic reason, however, for the shortcomings of the press in the matter of truth has been ably discussed by Walter Lippmann. Accurate reporting is not the solution for our difficulties. An accurate report of a lying official statement is still not the truth.

The chief reason why we fall so short of truth is that our vaunted freedom of the press is a one-way freedom. Legally and historically, freedom of the press in America means merely freedom to publish without prior censorship. In other words, the freedom of the American press is a freedom of expression only. It does not have an equal freedom in access to the truth. Obviously the truth that comes out of the American press can be no greater or more certain than the truth that goes into it.

So long as we have existing censorship at the source of all types of important news, the newspaper will not be able to give the public the truth. Government bureaucrats and the public relations operatives of business have established a quarantine on truth through which the press is able to break only on occasion.

If the American press today seems to tend to follow a sort of national party line in its treatment of critical issues, it is because news of government is so greatly regimented at its source. If editors all receive the same information carefully tailored by propagandists to point to particular conclusions, it is little wonder that independent editorial thought and leadership is difficult to attain. Its raw materials are lacking. If we are to have more truth in our newspapers, we must have freedom of access to the news, as well as freedom of expression of the news. We must lift the quarantine on truth.

I for one do not blame the editors. I do not blame the reporters. I do not blame the publishers. All are doing the best they can—and their best is very good indeed, all things considered. But the problem remains. The citizens of America are not getting the truth. And I am inclined to think that they will not get it until the powers of the press are much wider than they now are. Truth should not be muzzled at its source. . . .

THE PRESS AND ELECTIONS

—Louis M. Lyons, "The Press and the Election," *Nieman Reports*, Vol. 3, January 1949, p. 16. Mr. Lyons is curator of the Nieman Foundation at Harvard.

THE MOST conscientious American newspapermen realize that the position of the press with the public must have fallen far with their complete misreading of the (1948) election. It will take a chastened and informed effort to restore it. In very few spots is there any evidence of such an effort or even a recognition of its need.

The newspapers were further wrong than most want to admit. "We were wrong," as James B. Reston of the New York *Times* wrote in a letter to his own paper, "not only in the election but on the whole political direction of our times!" That's it. For sixteen years most of the big city papers had voted (editorially) on the opposite side from most of their readers. Now . . . the gap had widened until they were completely out of touch with the minds of the readers. Walter Lippmann once told a Nieman seminar that it was the task of a political columnist to write of events in such a way that his readers would not be too surprised by the development of the news. But the columnists led their readers into utter surprise in November.

"A little careful reporting and a little less guessing," as Carroll Kilpatrick said in the San Francisco *Chronicle*, "might have resulted in a more honest picture." The newspapers tend to shrug it off as a muff by the pollsters. But it was far more than that. Anyway the polls had become practically a property of the newspapers. They built them up and ran them as their own features. Nobody ever asked the newspapers to go into the business of prediction. Their business is reporting. In overreaching themselves to see the future they failed in their primary function of reporting. They were discounting the election and discussing what was to come after. A Presidential election is too momentous an event ever to be discounted or anticipated. It stretches the journalistic curse of predating, of anticipating events, to the breaking point. And a good thing it broke down with such a crash as to discredit it. The reporters have a right to be indignant. For it was their function their papers forfeited to the crystal gazers.

The political reporters, many of them, as Mr. Reston indicates, had many reasons to doubt the certainty of the polls. But they failed to express their doubts, partly, as he explains, by their intoxication with the accepted certainty; but partly, one may suspect, because they doubted that their papers would welcome a dissenting report.

The polls, as newspapermen well know, were never entitled to the legend of invincibility the newspapers had built up for them. Their errors in earlier elections were wide enough to have defeated their prediction in a close election. But their errors of detail were washed out in the Roosevelt sweeps.

Their huge error this time may prove to be largely in their bad guess as to the size of the vote. But why do they predict the size of the vote and "weight" their predictions by their guesses as to which party will be most effective in getting its voters out? That is a political, not a statistical problem, and political reporters are much better fixed to estimate it than the pollers. Indeed if the pollers had presented in their polls just what their samples showed without "weighting" them by their guesses about the capacity of the machines to get voters to the polls, then the political reporters might have used the polls as raw material to make much better guesses than were made.

If there is to be any future of Presidential polls, that would seem to be its limit: to present the actual state of opinion as they measure it, and leave the rest to the parties and the political writers. In the average performance of the polls, the New York *Times* reported, the estimate of the Truman vote was off by 18 per cent, of the Dewey vote by over 10 per cent, of the Wallace vote by nearly 40 per cent, the Dixiecrat vote by 33 per cent. Dixiecrats were expected to sweep so widely as to threaten Truman in Virginia, Tennessee, and Texas. Actually they had no effect outside the states where the electoral slate was shanghaied before the nominations. Massachusetts was unanimously put in the Republican column and it went Democratic by 390,000 votes (for governor), a 240,000 margin for Truman. Here the polls evidently ignored utterly the increased registration in the Democratic cities and the widely published reports that Church and Labor were working overtime to get out their maximum vote (for certain local referenda) that was bound to be overwhelmingly Democratic. Yet the very Boston papers that were keenly aware of this heavy factor were publishing their own local polls that predicted Massachusetts to go Republican.

The New York *Times* the Sunday before election presented forecasts for every state and gave Dewey 345 electoral votes. The Sunday after election the *Times* analyzed its failure under the head "Our Forecast: What Was Wrong?" This was an honest job. It finds "One fact emerges more clearly than any other. It is that the polls colored the thinking of the 'experts' all down the line." The *Times* had been printing the polls. When it asked its far-flung correspondents for their views, they gave back just what they had read in the *Times*. As one correspondent confessed, "they simply let Gallup do their thinking for them."

A TEST OF NEWSPAPER ACCURACY

—Mitchell V. Charnley, "A Study of Newspaper Accuracy," *Journalism Quarterly*, Vol. 13, December 1936, pp. 394–401. Mr. Charnley is professor of journalism at the University of Minnesota.

THE STUDY here described was undertaken with the hope, first, of developing a practicable technique for ascertaining the actual amount of error in factual reporting, and, second, of learning the kinds of error common in reporting, their frequency and their source or agent. It is my belief that, on the basis of such knowledge, newspapers may make effective progress toward greater elimination of error than is possible when guesses and rules-of-thumb are the only guides.

It was first decided to check the accuracy only of stories that might be considered wholly objective. Obviously some newspaper writing —interpretative stories, many feature stories, stories that depend on point of view or expert opinion—is unsuitable for such a survey. Four categories of stories suitable for the study were set up:

1. Simple "straight news" stories—announcements, short meeting stories, short advance stories, simple accident and police stories and so forth.

2. Longer "straight news" stories that are distinctly factual—stories on drives and campaigns, business meetings, community celebrations, holiday parades and the like.

3. Speech stories, when they could be submitted to the speakers for checking.

4. "News interviews," when they could be submitted to the persons interviewed for checking.

This listing excluded sports stories, "color" stories, stories coming from several sources, most human interest stories, critical or commentative stories—any stories in which there was any visible subjectivity. Also excluded were all stories which could not be readily checked by the original source of information. . . .

One thousand stories were sent out; 591, almost 60 per cent, came back. This return was adequately representative of the whole group sent out. Many of the 591 brought with them letters—some of commendation for the effort, more of criticism for newspaper practice. Such criticisms were more interesting than helpful. Many, such as that declaring an accurate advance story to be unsuitable for the survey's purpose, since "obviously nothing had happened" before the occurrence of the event forecast in the story, showed a thorough-going misunderstanding of the newspaper problem.

. . . A few more than half of all the stories returned–319 of 591, or 54 per cent–were entirely accurate. Paper A made an accuracy score of 52 per cent; Paper B 53 per cent; and Paper C 57 per cent. The over-all accuracy score, 54 per cent, was the same as that for all stories in Group One; but the three papers varied from 51 per cent to 60 per cent among themselves on stories of this class. Wider variations showed up in the other three groups; but these percentages are not as reliable as those for Group One, since the number of stories checked is in all cases so much smaller.

. . . Setting the total number of errors against the total number of stories returned, shows an expectancy of about three errors in every four stories. . . . A comparison of total number of errors to total number of inaccurate stories shows 1.67 errors per inaccurate story–five errors in three stories.

. . . Three varieties of errors occurred frequently, and of these the "error in meaning" was most common. This is, of course, a commentary on the skill and understanding–or lack of them–of the news writers who handled the stories. Perhaps this finding will not surprise any student of news writing. To me it seems that the figure should not be taken at face value, however. The individuals who checked the stories often knew more about the facts involved than any reporter would care to tell his readers, and such individuals might declare stories to be deficient in meaning merely because they did not present every fact, no matter how trivial.

That 66 of the 455 errors–14.5 per cent–had been committed in previous stories seems also significant.

Two further analyses of the data are of especial interest. One shows that, of 74 stories which appeared in two or all three papers (that is, stories based on the same news impulses), 33 were correct in each publication; 18 were correct in two publications, wrong in the third; and 23 were in error in all papers that used them. Of the last group, 18 presented identical errors, which would indicate either that the stories had been lifted by one paper from another without checking, or that the sources of information had been in error in providing data.

. . . Of 118 stories handled by reporters, only 40–34 per cent–

were correct. But of 98 stories the information for which was actively presented to newspapers by "original sources," 62—63 per cent—were correct.

Many other tabulations and comparisons are possible, but these seem the more important ones.

Only two conclusions seem justified by the data from this comparatively limited survey: That about half—perhaps more than half—of the simple factual news stories appearing in daily papers is completely free from error; and that errors occurring most frequently are those in meaning, in names and in titles. It would be unsafe to assume, for example, that speech and interview stories are less likely to be accurate than "straight news." . . . The number of samples is too limited to justify any such assumption.

And it would certainly be unsound to assert that . . . more news should come from "original sources" and less through the hands of reporters. The figures show that most of the accurate news in the stories included in the table came from "original sources" and most of the errors occurred in stories handled throughout by reporters. But a factor untouched by such a survey as this is of major importance: That news furnished direct to the papers by interested persons and declared accurate by them is precisely what they want the public to know, whereas news presented by reporters is much more likely to be what the reporters believe will interest or affect the public. That reporters must be more accurate is another problem.

BIAS IN THE NEWS

—Anonymous, "Front-Page Bias in Newspapers," A Study by the Bureau of Applied Social Research, Columbia University, *The Nation,* Vol. 159, September 23, 1944, p. 348.

CONTRARY to the press's theory that it reports the news "straight, without reference to editorial opinions," a study conducted by this bureau shows that Roosevelt and Dewey papers differ sharply in the content of their front pages. They devote almost exactly the same proportion of their front pages to the campaign, but they choose somewhat different subjects and often "angle" the news.

More than half the stories in the Roosevelt papers were pro-Roosevelt; almost half of those in the Dewey papers favored the Republicans. In each group the content of about one in every five stories was favorable to the opposition. Three of every ten campaign stories on the front pages of the Roosevelt papers were neutral in content; between three and four of every ten were neutral in the Dewey papers. Both groups were even more partisan in terms of space, than in terms of number of stories. Thus 56 per cent of the 2,089 column inches given to the campaign in the Roosevelt papers was pro-Roosevelt or anti-Dewey material; 51 per cent of the 2,289 campaign inches in papers for Dewey favored him. About one fourth of the space in Roosevelt papers was neutral; 16 per cent was unfavorable to the Administration. Dewey papers gave a little more space to neutral and 18 per cent to pro-Administration items.

If both groups of papers used the same material, they frequently showed their editorial preferences in their headlines and in the sections they cut or kept. Thus the Cleveland *Plain Dealer* (pro-Dewey) headlined an A.P. story "Peace 'Say' Seen for Smaller Fry," while the pro-Administration Richmond *Times-Dispatch* captioned it "Dewey Fear Is Groundless Hull Asserts." The two papers ran precisely the same story until, at the very end, the *Plain Dealer,* after quoting Senator Connally (Dem.), added a pro-Dewey quotation from Senator Vandenberg (Rep.); the *Times-Dispatch* quoted only Connally, and closed with a favorable reference to Hull's conference omitted by the *Plain Dealer.*

Our study was based on an analysis of seven Roosevelt and seven Dewey papers. Since differences in news coverage might be due to differences in the news available to the two groups, the papers chosen were matched in terms of their circulation, the regions in which they were published, and the time of appearance. As typical pro-Roosevelt papers the Chicago *Sun,* the Louisville *Courier-Journal,* the Philadelphia *Record,* the Atlanta *Constitution,* the Richmond *Times-Dispatch,* the New York *Post,* and the St. Louis *Post-Dispatch* were used. Matched with these were the pro-Dewey Chicago *Tribune,* the Cleveland *Plain Dealer,* the Philadelphia *Inquirer,* the Washington *Times-Herald,* the Baltimore *Sun,* the Washington *Daily News,* and the Kansas City *Star.* All fourteen papers were read from August 16 through August 26, excepting Sunday, August 20, when the full sample was not available. Only the front pages were analyzed, since these presumably contain the material which editors and publishers want to call to the attention of their readers.

Of a total of 969 stories in the Dewey papers, 119 were devoted to the campaign. In the Roosevelt papers 105 of 865 stories dealt with the candidates and their activities or other political news. Thus in each group about 12 per cent of the front-page material was on the coming election. In terms of inches Dewey papers gave slightly more space to the campaign than did Roosevelt papers (9.4 as against 8.7 per cent).

The major news breaks in the ten-day period covered were Republican and Democratic reactions to the Dumbarton Oaks Conference, the controversy in the War Production Board over Nelson's assignment to China and Wilson's resignation, and stories about Pearl Harbor, army censorship, labor's role in the campaign, and reconversion. The development of Republican foreign policy received very different emphasis in the two groups of papers. Dewey papers devoted four times as much space to the Dulles-Hull conference as the Roosevelt supporters (447 to 124 column inches). But the conference between Willkie and Dulles was given almost twice as much space in pro-Administration as in pro-Republican papers (101 to 61 column inches)—because Willkie's agreement to meet with Dulles was accompanied by a rebuff to Dewey.

In general, then, the study shows clearly that editorial preferences influence the selection and treatment of campaign news. And since a large majority of papers are anti-Administration, the greater part of the news to which the public is exposed has that slant.

REVIEW QUESTIONS AND ASSIGNMENTS

1. What contribution can a code of ethics make to the press when there are no provisions for enforcement?

2. Are the newspapers conservative because their advertisers are, or because they believe in conservatism as a principle?

3. Does the press mirror the opinions of advertisers any more than they are mirrored by the pulpit and platform?

4. What are the real dangers from the press according to Lippmann? What would you suggest to combat them?

5. What examples of unethical conduct have you observed in the press handling of crime reports?

6. Can you cite any examples of faking in the press? Of what significance were they? How do you think they arose?

7. Discuss the statement that, if society provided more objective records of its activities, the press would thereby be improved.

8. What exact tests could be made for determining the accuracy of the press?

9. Discuss the merits of giving the reading public what it wants.

10. What do you think of the statement that it is the newspaper's duty to educate its readers to want something better in reading matter?

11. What are the reasons, other than suppression, why stories fail to appear in the press?

12. Discuss the statement that part of the press influence is due to the bias readers bring to it.

13. What has speed of newspaper production to do with ethics? Is this likely to be affected by competition with the radio? If so, in what way?

14. Discuss the idea that a reporter should write his own headlines, rather than the copy reader.

15. Is there any evidence of a widespread conspiracy by the press in any field of reporting or are the faults individual?

16. What evidences are there that the ethical standards of the press are changing?

17. What forces exist in the public to prevent biased reporting of situations upon which opinion is divided?

18. What evidence is there that the newspapers have themselves broken the law?

ADDITIONAL REFERENCES

Anonymous, "The Ethics of the Professions and of Business," *The Annals of the American Academy of Political and Social Science,* Vol. 101, May 1922.

Bent, Silas, *Ballyhoo,* Liveright, 1927, pp. 150–180.

———, "Scarlet Journalism," *Scribner's,* Vol. 84, November 1928, p. 563.

Bliven, Bruce, "Newspaper Morals," *The New Republic,* Vol. 35, May 30, 1923, pp. 17–19.

Brucker, Herbert, *Freedom of Information,* Macmillan, 1949, pp. 49–70, 149–168.

Cole, Virginia Lee, *The Newspaper and Crime,* University of Missouri School of Journalism, 1927.

The Commission on Freedom of the Press, *A Free and Responsible Press,* University of Chicago Press, 1947, pp. 21–23, 52–68.

Crawford, N. A., *The Ethics of Journalism,* Alfred A. Knopf, 1924.

Dickinson, B. S., *The Newspaper and Labor,* University of Illinois, 1931.

Doob, Leonard W., *Public Opinion and Propaganda,* Henry Holt, 1948, pp. 21–23, 52–68.

Flint, L. N., *The Conscience of the Newspaper,* Appleton-Century, 1925, pp. 427–461.

Gilman, Mildred, "Truth Behind the News," *American Mercury,* Vol. 29, June 1933, pp. 139–146.

Graves, W. Brooke (editor), *Readings in Public Opinion,* Appleton-Century, 1928, pp. 306–311, 328–330.

Henning, A. F., *Ethics and Practices in Journalism,* Ray Long and Richard R. Smith, 1932.

Hocking, William Ernest, *Freedom of the Press,* University of Chicago Press, 1947, pp. 107–108, 148–149.

Hutchinson, Paul, "The Aurora Killing," *Christian Century,* May 15, 1929.

Kingsbury, Susan M., *et al., Newspapers and the News,* G. P. Putnam's Sons, 1937, pp. 211–212.

Lahey, Thomas A., *Morals of Newspaper Making,* Notre Dame University, 1924.

Lehman, H. C., and P. A. Witty, "Ethics and the Press," *International Journal of Ethics,* Vol. 38, January 1928, pp. 191–203.

Liebling, A. J., "The Whole Story," *New Yorker,* Vol. 24, November 13, 1948, pp. 122–131.

Lippmann, Walter, and Charles Merz, "A Test of the News," *The New Republic,* Vol. 23, supplement to issue of August 4, 1920.

Seldes, George, *Freedom of the Press,* Bobbs-Merrill, 1935, pp. 21–22, 49.

Svirsky, Leon (editor), *Your Newspaper: Blueprint for a Better Press,* Macmillan, 1947, pp. 75–102, 165–168.

Swanson, Charles E., "Readability and Readership," *Journalism Quarterly,* Vol. 25, December 1948, pp. 339–343.

Warren, Carl, *Modern Newspaper Reporting,* Harper & Brothers, 1934, pp. 267–282.

Wisehart, M. K., *Public Opinion and the Steel Strike,* supplementary volume to Interchurch World Movement Report on the 1919 Steel Strike, Harcourt, Brace, 1920, pp. 87–162.

Yost, Casper S., *The Principles of Journalism,* Appleton-Century, 1924, Chapter 14.

PART THREE

THE PRESS, A PRODUCT OF MANY FORCES

19. THE PRESS AND PROFITS

INTRODUCTION

THE FACT that nearly all newspapers are operated for profit is calculated to exert influence in several directions. It must affect their attitude toward other profit-making businesses; it must affect their attitude toward an economic system under which expected profits are the prime business motive, as well as their attitude toward other economic systems that offer a threat to that system; and it must affect the conduct of their financial dealings with subscribers, advertisers, paper and ink manufacturers, and many others.

But it should not be thought that the business interests of the press are all on the debit side of the ledger—quite the contrary. Even the most severe critics of the press cite definite benefits. Whether or not the press could exist on a profitless basis is another question. At least efforts to conduct newspapers without profit have uniformly failed, and it is certainly true that a shift to such a system would mean the end of most newspapers, and probably the end of a free press.

The growth of the press as big business is in step with similar shifts throughout the American economic scene. Any institution will naturally reflect the conditions that produce it. Most of the adverse criticism of the press has become standardized. So has the defense. Morris Ernst presents some of the dangers seen by a considerable body of critics. Johnson tempers the Ernst arguments with a slightly different point of view on the effects of monopoly. The student will recognize that much of the difference between the two men is a matter only of degree.

Probably all newspapermen recognize that the press taken as a whole has become "big business." Poynter takes the position that profitable newspapers are a safeguard of press freedom, but he finds fault with them for being unprogressive on the mechanical and business sides. Some critics hold that competition between local newspapers is good because it increases the accuracy of the press. Blakely shows that this contention is often untrue. Some examples of how the "big business" bias causes the press to ally itself with other "big businesses" are cited by the Hutchins Commission.

The very real financial difficulties of the press are illustrated in the citation from the *Wall Street Journal*. The entire article is worthy of a careful reading. What is true of the papers mentioned in the article is true of newspapers throughout the country.

THE TENDENCY TOWARD MONOPOLY

—Morris L. Ernst, *The First Freedom*, pp. 68–71. Copyright 1946 by Mr. Ernst. Used with the permission of The Macmillan Company.

ONE OF THE UGLIEST impacts of the decimation of our daily press is found in the number of towns formerly with several dailies which now have been reduced to only one. These one-paper towns are now the overwhelming majority of communities which have any daily papers. This is very important in terms of community living. How easy is it, for example, to press for local reforms in a town where the only paper supports the local administration? How do you elect a mayor, a new school board, or debate the problem of parks and playgrounds? What price democracy in such an area? It is no answer to say, "Turn on the radio." We shall see later how the radio and press by joint operations still further tighten the bottleneck.

The best of newspapers reflect the publisher's opinions. A great editor, E. W. Scripps, once said: "Humanity is vulgar; so we must be vulgar. . . . It is passionate, therefore, the blood that runs in our veins and in our newspapers must be warm." His successor, Roy Howard, in 1912 declared, "I do not subscribe to the general idea that news and opinion are two different and easily separated elements." With consistency he asks for *his* kind of bias in *his* papers.

Under our philosophy of a free press each publisher has a right to be wrongheaded and even malicious. That is our creed—and we are safe adhering thereto as long as there are enough different wrongheadednesses in the market.

That is as it should be. But suppose you live in a single-paper town and you want to get across to your fellow-citizens a set of ideas different from those of the newspaper owner. How do you go about it, in these days when handbills and soap-boxes are less than effective means of communication? "Go hire a hall" is no longer a sensible answer.

Democracy grows on local vitality. The democratic strength of a nation is truly no greater than the sum of the democratic strength of the innumerable local communities. To the extent that cities and towns are dominated by single instruments of opinion, we invite further concentration of national power and national action. A grassroots democracy lives mainly on grassroot mental soil—local debate, local concern, local conflicts of thought. There is no healthy national debate that does not stem from innumerable strong local debates.

The total number of one-paper or singleton towns, as opposed to those with a diversity of papers, has *doubled* in the period from 1910 to 1939. While population increased by 43 per cent in these years, the number of towns with only one newspaper also grew by 43 per cent. We are traveling fast in the wrong direction. This threatening trend takes on a much blacker hue if one looks not only at the decline of newspapers but at the chain newspaper situation. Moreover, newspaper ownership is far less than the number of newspapers. There are at most only 1,300 newspaper owners today. Ten entire states have no cities with newspaper competition.

Only one state, New Mexico, had greater newspaper diversity in 1939 than in 1910. In 1910 there was only one town with more than one paper. In 1939 there were four such towns. Actually, since the total number of towns having any daily papers had doubled (population increase of 62 per cent), there was only an over-all increase of 10 per cent in diversity for the state.

On the dark side of the ledger, to cite one striking example from many, there is Nevada, which started out in 1910 with 86 per cent of its towns having newspaper diversity. By 1939 not a single city could boast two dailies.

There are interesting sectional variations which are difficult to explain. It can be generally stated that industrial areas show a much higher rate of disappearance of dailies than do agricultural areas. In the large cities with metropolitan papers, replacement is much more costly and, therefore, improbable.

The greatest rise in number of singleton towns (as opposed to multinewspaper towns) occurred in the North Central states, which had an increase of 144 per cent. Percentages of increase in one-paper towns for the rest of the country are as follows: Pacific Coast, 129 per cent; North Atlantic, 90 per cent; Western, 86 per cent; South Atlantic, 80 per cent; South Central, 46 per cent.

If the proportion of towns with more than one paper had stayed the same in 1939 as it was in 1910, there would be 987 towns with more than one paper. Instead we find only 203. This is a loss of 784 towns, areas which, on the assumption of 1910 actual diversity of daily newspaper competition, now find themselves with a monopoly. That loss does not even take into account the literate population increase which would justify exceeding the 1910 level of diversity.

There is one important economic explanation for the startling increase in the number of cities which dropped from two papers to one. In many of these towns there was a morning paper published by one publisher and a separate, unallied evening paper. It was often more practical, since the cost of equipment was so high, to print both papers at the same plant, even though separate staffs were sometimes maintained. In very many cases this process resulted, sooner or later, in one of the publishers buying out the other. The result was a morning and evening edition of the same paper, or where this seemed unfeasible, only one edition.

It is often said that to urge many more newspapers is unwise, on the theory that this results in economic instability which in turn produces a corrupt press, like the French press before the war. It is true that a newspaper on the edge of bankruptcy might be more easily corrupted than a solvent paper. But today there is no way of judging how many papers could be supported by a local economy. In the first place, under present laws economic restrictions existing by newspaper contracts make it so difficult to start a new paper that a test cannot be made. Secondly, a local economy does not carry the whole burden of supporting its papers. The cost of the American newspaper is increasingly borne through advertising by the purchase of other commodities, like soap and automobiles. This national advertising cost is scattered to consumers all over the country. But one fact is apparent—concentration of newspaper ownership has little relationship to the economic income of a community. The main economic impact of multiple local ownership of papers is to compel combination insertion of advertisements, whether wanted or not, in all the papers of the combine.

NEWSPAPERS MUST MAKE A PROFIT

—Gerald W. Johnson, "Great Newspapers, If Any," *Harper's Magazine,* Vol. 196, June 1948, pp. 541–543. Mr. Johnson was for many years one of the editors of the Baltimore (Maryland) *Sun.*

FOR THE NEWSPAPER itself is contradictory, which is one way of saying that it is a very human enterprise. The newspaper is a social force.

That is indubitable. It is also a manufactory. That is just as certainly true. Like the school, it purveys information, but its information, unlike that of the school, must be fresh, which is to say, it handles a product that deteriorates with unparalleled speed. The very conditions of its existence, therefore, are impossible of perfect fulfillment; for information to be sound must be true, and to be fresh must be disseminated at high speed. But in the process of learning and informing others, high speed and perfect accuracy are incompatible. It follows, therefore, that, judged by the ideal standard, all newspapers are bad newspapers and can't be anything else.

The tendency of investigators, however, is to overlook the necessary conditions of the newspaper's existence and to measure its distance from the ideal standard absolutely. Many of them would eliminate, for example, the newspaper's status as a profit-making enterprise. The necessity of showing an operating profit every year, they assert, inhibits any real freedom and only a newspaper subsidized, either by the government or by private funds, can enjoy liberty. . . .

A man who cannot stand on his own feet, or a newspaper that cannot pay its own bills, enjoys freedom only on sufferance. If its unearned funds are cut off, its merit will not save it. Hence in a capitalistic economy the ability to make a profit, or at least to stay in the black, is one of the indispensable elements of a great newspaper. For this reason I cannot agree with those who lament the extinction of the New York *World* as the destruction of a truly great newspaper. It had been great, without doubt, and it remained brilliant and useful; but when its books went into the red, it lost one of the essential requirements of real newspaper greatness. The same consideration applies to *PM* and the Chicago *Sun.* They have never been more than hopeful experiments. They are not truly great newspapers.

Unfortunately, this same factor, essential to greatness, is quite capable of destroying greatness in a public journal. It is another illustration of the intense humanity of the newspaper, for it is emphatically true of a man. One of the most dismal facts of life in the United States of America is that here very few men indeed have a million dollars, but many a million dollars has a man. If it is impossible for a newspaper to be free without a bank account acquired by its own efforts, it is only just possible for it to be free *from* that bank account after it has been acquired.

Within the past generation the newspaper has become Big Business and, because of its size, it has acquired, except in a very few places, the characteristics of a natural monopoly. The annual expenditures of such a newspaper as, for instance, the Baltimore *Sun*, published not in the largest but the seventh city, run into eight figures. Disregarding national advertising and some other minor sources of revenue, expenditures of a newspaper are a charge upon the business activity of its city of publication. Few cities of less than two or three million people have business enough to support more than one really first-class newspaper. Washington, whose business is politics that involves the revenues of the whole country, is the only conspicuous exception. Outside of New York, Chicago, and perhaps Philadelphia, American cities cannot afford two ten-million-dollar newspapers any more than they can afford two telephone companies, or two water-supply systems.

But Big Business in the nature of the case involves big profits. Newspaper proprietors—not newspaper editors who are, as a rule, hired men—are tycoons of the first order. Inevitably they tend to associate for the most part with other tycoons and to acquire the mental and emotional attitudes of other millionaires; and it is an unusual millionaire who is not to some extent the bond-slave of his own money.

There are few things in this vale of tears more jittery than a million dollars, and the man who is owned by a million dollars inevitably shivers like an aspen leaf. The notion that it is advertisers that newspaper proprietors fear is usually a misconception; normally, the advertisers fear the newspaper more than it does them, for a well-established newspaper, dominating its field, can heavily damage, perhaps wreck a department store, theater, or hotel simply by excluding its advertising and its name from the news columns. What newspaper proprietors fear is what all men fear, namely, the condemnation of public opinion; but the public opinion that presses most intimately upon the owner of a big newspaper is the opinion of big business men, not of the man in the street. . . .

Considering the environment in which they live and the pressure to which it subjects them, the marvel is not that American newspaper proprietors are so conservative but rather that they are not all reactionaries. It is much easier to be a howling Communist in Greenwich Village than it is to be even a Cleveland Democrat in the stately midtown clubs, yet respectable numbers of American newspaper owners manage it.

For one thing some of them, but not all, have gained some, but not an adequate, conception of the responsibility that is irremovably attached to a monopoly position. Every respectable newspaper in the country now acknowledges its duty to print the news, even when the news is unfavorable or possibly ruinous to the policy it advocates. Republican newspapers published full accounts of the conviction of Albert B. Fall, even though that case was damaging to the Republican party; Democratic newspapers recorded the conviction of Andrew J. May, although that news certainly did not help the party. Sometimes newspapers bury unfavorable items in the back pages, but they print them, and really big stuff usually goes on the front page, although the newspaper may regret bitterly the necessity of having to print such news.

But the notion that opinions, also, are news is one that is by no means universally accepted. Many newspapers regard it as no part of their duty to present their readers with a summary of all shades of opinion, even when they hold a monopoly position in their towns. A conservative paper that reported faithfully the election of Wallace's candidate in the Bronx may have never printed a line of the argument by which that candidate won the election. Such a paper's readers therefore know that the man was elected but, as far as their paper is concerned, they have never been told why he was elected. They are not well informed and the paper is not accepting the duty that lies upon every monopoly, whether of goods or of services, to serve all classes of its constituency without favoritism.

I would not imply that it is the duty of a newspaper to open its editorial columns to opinions it deems false and pernicious. The editorial page is admittedly the place for the paper's own opinion, and no other. But in a one-newspaper town it is clearly the duty of the paper holding the monopoly to make room somewhere for the presentation of opinions challenging its own. Many newspapers today contrive this by carrying signed columns expressing opinions differing from, and sometimes flatly contradicting, those on its editorial page. This policy is doubly creditable, first, because it serves the constituency fairly, and, second, because it is sometimes distasteful to the paper. Not infrequently the signed columns are so much better written than the editorial page that they show it up rather dreadfully, and in that case it takes courage to continue them.

SELF-SUPPORT AND PRESS FREEDOM

—Nelson P. Poynter, "The Economic Problems of the Press and the Changing Newspaper," *The Press in the Contemporary Scene, The Annals of the American Academy of Political and Social Science,* Vol. 219, January 1942, pp. 82–85. Mr. Poynter is editor of the St. Petersburg (Florida) *Times.*

DEMOCRACY'S keystone is a free press—free, authentic, untainted information about democracy's progress, its public servants, its government.

To be free, the press must be self-supporting, yielding a good living or profit to those who are operating this quasi branch of government, this fourth check on the integrity, efficiency, and effectiveness of a self-governed people.

The modern American newspaper economy is the result of our industrial system of mass production and mass distribution, but it is out of kelter with the very system of which it is a part and which it helps to support. A man from Mars would have trouble making sense out of the two. He would find that the newspaper manufacturer sells his product at a loss in most cases, and lies awake at night dreaming up new and spectacular schemes to sell more units of his product at a loss. He then turns around with a Robin Hood type of economic justice, and through advertising seeks to recoup these losses.

Likewise, the American press has been timid about finding new and cheaper ways of editing and publishing its products. Radio has relieved the press of much of the urgency of multiple editions, large, wasteful headlines, duplication of text. Apply your pencil to almost any newspaper that comes to hand, and you will find that the same amount of information and fact can be conveyed to you in a fraction of the space presently taken.

The American press is undergoing a change. It must adapt itself or die. This frightens many publishers and employees of the press. They cannot see that our changing economy offers real freedom to the press. Actually it can be better, more free and profitable. It is up to editors, owners, and business managers to determine whether they are engaged in a dwindling industry.

A seeming dilemma exists in the American free press. To be free, it must be independent and profitable. To be profitable, the present press must have a big volume of advertising. Advertising is diminishing while "fixed charges" of the American press are increasing. Many argue that this will undermine profits, independence, and freedom. We think this may be an opportunity instead of a disaster, an opportunity to get down to the fundamentals and realities regarding the relationship of the press to its people.

To serve the people best, the press must have a sense of responsibility. Profit breeds this sense, and therefore it is desirable from the standpoint of the people that the press be profitable. Certain economic trends, certain industrial and social changes jeopardize the profits of the American press. Some of these changes are due to the inflexibility, shortsightedness, and stupidity of the American publisher. Other inexorable trends, over which he has no control, will force changes or kill profits, force further consolidations of newspapers. Thus we shall have fewer newspapers covering wider areas. Only by imaginative operation of the press that survives this drift, an operation freed from conventional practices, can publishers get back on the comfortable profit basis that will breed a proper sense of responsibility to the public.

While the press *can* be more adaptable than most commercial enterprises, the brutal fact remains that profit has diminished. Radio and other publications have forged ahead and decreased the relative importance of the press.

The press has not taken advantage of its potential adaptability. It has not adequately met the challenge of new and aggressive competition.

E. W. Scripps founded the penny press more than sixty years ago with the revolutionary idea in publishing that a workman getting a dollar a day could pay 1 per cent of his income for a newspaper. He touched a new consumer market. Publishers had been snobbish in their ideas of markets. There is no law to guarantee it, but during the ups and downs of the business cycle the American press has taken approximately 1 per cent of the national income.

The ratio of advertising and circulation revenues has changed with an expanding economy, but the percentage of the total "take" of the press from the national income is dwindling.

If the press is vital enough to the lives of its readers, if it is valuable enough as a check and balance—a super-auditor of our self-government—it is certainly worth 1 per cent of our income.

It takes an unbelievable amount of capital to start a standard, omnibus newspaper in an area where present publishers are doing even a moderately good job. The writer knows of a small field in a southern state where a wealthy family through pique started a new paper. It cost $250,000 to find out they could not lick even an ordinary newspaper. Aside from the spectacular success of the New York *Daily News,* there have been virtually no newspapers starting from scratch in the last twenty years that have achieved profits without mergers or other extenuating circumstances.

The cost of capital equipment is not too important a factor in this, but it is enough to discourage casual experiment. This has helped to breed complacency in the press. It has been content to merchandise a Model T in an aerodynamic age. The press has not showed mechanical improvement comparable to most other industries during the past twenty years. It has shied away from color, from new printing processes, new engraving techniques. Newsprint, its basic raw material, has not showed marked improvement. Bold technical imagination does not flourish in a dwindling industry.

A few publishers have toyed with the idea of offset printing as a possible answer to a better product and better pictures with declining revenues, but aside from this experimental venture—which has not yet proved itself—little has been done to keep up with the times. There are exceptions. There are, to be sure, some farsighted and imaginative editors who are willing to strike out in behalf of a more up-to-date press. Here and there are enterprising publishers, business managers, and mechanical superintendents, but no significant portion of the newspaper press has marched forward with vision and determination to test every possible means of improving itself.

Today's press is a composite, omnibus vehicle carrying a variety of loads. Its primary function is to serve the wants of the people for the latest news. It has a merchandising function in our industrial society —advertising. Many of the early publishers resisted advertising and placed all kinds of restrictions around the size of the advertising they would carry. Thus the original concept of advertising was that it should be high in cost. This concept is sound if the publisher resolves to depend on reader revenue. It is unsound if he is going to let advertising carry most of the load.

The press became the foremost merchandising vehicle for distribution under the "high rate" concept. Circulation was at a premium. This led to the addition of a third function—numerous entertainment features to attract circulation. Then ensued wasteful circulation methods to stimulate circulation. World War I taught manufacturers mass selling. Advertising boomed and became the dominant factor in the economy of the press.

The depression of the thirties forced newspapers to reduce circulation expense and increase circulation revenues, but advertising revenue is still more than twice as great as circulation revenue in most of the press. The writer recently examined more than a hundred operating statements of American daily newspapers functioning in areas ranging from small cities to metropolitan centers. Only one of them took 40 per cent of its revenue from the reader. Most of them averaged less than 30 per cent; many were near 20 per cent. It is evident that readers should and *must* contribute a greater share than they now do to meeting newspaper costs of production and revenue.

The depression leveled a devastating blow at newspaper advertising. The press awoke to find new and lusty competitors, children of the bleak days when advertisers sought new and/or more economical means of carrying their merchandising story to the public. Radio, picture publications, shopping news, and throwaways flowered during the lean years.

While advertising revenue diminished or stood still, expenses rose in the newspaper business. The readers demanded better papers. The movies and radio created new interests and curiosities that the press was obliged to recognize and exploit. Public affairs necessitated and forced better coverage and reporting. Picture techniques demanded new skills and expense. Long hours had been a custom in a business where forty hours a week is now standard. As in other businesses, taxes increased.

Less visible forces also operated to make the business of newspaper publishing more difficult. Its influence was diminishing because its readers had more time to read other publications, listen to the radio, and enlarge their social contacts. Newspaper circulation was not affected, but the relative importance of newspapers was affected. Gradually some newspapers attempted to meet this challenge. Publishers went through an era of "streamlining" which consisted in most shops of buying some new type and dumping the same old stuff into the paper. The bolder spirits recognized that editorial techniques and values had to be reappraised, and undertook experiments to recapture the interest and the confidence of the reader. Enterprising business managers undertook to reappraise their efforts and meet diminishing advertising revenues and rising costs by heroic elimination of wasteful methods of distribution.

This process in the business office has only begun. One of the outstanding moves which has passed the experimental stage is the organization of a single printing establishment to publish two or more newspapers and yet leave ownership and editorial autonomy to separate publishers. The formula varies, but in cases like Albuquerque, El Paso, Evansville, and Nashville, all circulation and advertising revenues go into a common pool. All expenses except editorial expenses are paid from this pool, and the surplus is distributed between the publishers of the rival newspapers according to a previously negotiated ratio. This formula has made profits for the owners, but has not resulted in marked improvement of the editorial products.

In larger cities the newspaper trend has been death or consolidation. Publisher agreements have eliminated some waste in distribution and increased prices to the reader, but no bold, original plans have come forward to improve the basic editorial products. Some waste has been reduced by publishing fewer editions, but no great effort has been made to re-evaluate the news and features and supplements. Circulation rates in metropolitan centers remain low as a whole, while the papers remain bulky with little-read features.

COMPETITION DOES NOT RAISE QUALITY

—Robert J. Blakely, "The Responsibilities of an Editor," *Communications in Modern Society,* Wilbur Schramm (editor), University of Illinois Press, 1948, pp. 225–226.

Several current developments heighten the editor's responsibility. One is the trend toward concentration of ownership of the press, toward the consolidation of newspapers, and toward greater capital requirements for entering the field. True, the disappearance of competition between newspapers in particular cities is somewhat compensated for by the appearance of competition on larger scales and of other kinds: between large newspapers whose territories overlap, between large newspapers and smaller newspapers within their territories, and between newspapers and radio stations. However, this at best is only a partial compensation, because newspapers are tending to become standardized and because newspapers and radio stations use the same or similar services.

At this point we may consider the problem of newspaper monopoly. If the choice were between having one good newspaper and more than one good newspaper in a community, who would prefer one? But often this is not the choice. A quick survey of the nation's newspapers reveals every possible combination: one city with competition and no good newspaper; another with competition and one good newspaper; a third with competition and more than one good newspaper; a fourth with no competition and a good newspaper; a fifth with no competition and no good newspaper. I can see little relationship between the quality of a newspaper and the amount of competition which it faces. Competition when the community cannot support more than one newspaper creates financial shakiness, which does not make a newspaper either good or free. In other situations newspapers seem to compete in cheapness and sensationalism. These comments are no argument for a monopoly situation. The point is that in newspapering, as in many other fields of our economy, the trend is toward concentration. This trend is deep-rooted in the requirements of technology. We don't need just *more* newspapers; we need more *good* newspapers. Whether or not a newspaper is good seems to have less to do with external competition than with internal integrity. When one says this, however, one is saying that the obligation of an institution in a monopoly situation is greater than in a competitive situation. A monopoly newspaper must provide its own competition, set its own standards, create its own requirements and compulsions.

THE PRESS AS BIG BUSINESS

—Commission on Freedom of the Press, *A Free and Responsible Press,* University of Chicago Press, 1947, pp. 59–62.

As William Allen White put it: "Too often the publisher of an American newspaper has made his money in some other calling than journalism. He is a rich man seeking power and prestige. He has the country club complex. The business manager of this absentee owner quickly is afflicted with the country club point of view. Soon the managing editor's wife nags him into it. And they all get the unconscious arrogance of conscious wealth. Therefore it is hard to get a modern American newspaper to go the distance necessary to print all the news about many topics." In the last thirty years, in Mr. White's opinion, newspapers "have veered from their traditional position as leaders of public opinion to mere peddlers and purveyors of news . . .

the newspapers have become commercial enterprises and hence fall into the current which is merging commercial enterprises along mercantile lines."

The same point is made with equal force by another distinguished editor, Virginius Dabney of the Richmond *Times-Dispatch* writing in the *Saturday Review of Literature*: "Today newspapers are Big Business, and they are run in that tradition. The publisher, who often knows little about the editorial side of the operation, usually is one of the leading business men in his community, and his editorial page, under normal circumstances, strongly reflects that point of view. Sometimes he gives his editor a free hand but far oftener he does not. He looks upon the paper primarily as a 'property' rather than as an instrument for public service." The typical American publisher, Mr. Dabney continues, "considers the important part of the paper to be the business management, and is convinced that so long as high salaries and lavish expenditures are made available to that management, the editorial department can drag along under a schedule of too much work and too little pay. Of course, such a publisher sees that the editorials in his paper are 'sound,' which is to say that they conform to his own weird views of society, and are largely unreadable."

Neither indictment is of universal application nor was it intended by its author to be so. There are, as Mr. Dabney says, "brilliant and honorable exceptions." But another highly respected editor, Erwin D. Canham of the *Christian Science Monitor*, thinks upper-bracket ownership and its big-business character important enough to stand at the head of his list of the "short-comings of today's American newspapers."

The published charges of distortion in the press resulting from the bias of its owners fall into the categories that might be expected. In 1935 the American Newspaper Publishers Association condemned the proposed Child Labor Amendment. The A.N.P.A. action with regard to the child labor provision of N.R.A. was characterized by the St. Louis *Star-Times* as "a disgrace to the newspaper industry." Bias is claimed against consumer co-operatives, against food and drug regulation, against Federal Trade Commission orders designed to suppress fraudulent advertising, and against F.C.C. regulations affecting newspaper-owned broadcasting stations. Other claims involve affiliations with suppliers of raw paper stock and their affiliations with electric power companies. Still others arise from the ownership of outside businesses by the owners of the press. Many people believe that the press is biased in matters of national fiscal policy.

FINANCIAL PROBLEMS OF METROPOLITAN DAILIES

—J. Howard Rutledge, "Newspaper Income Lags Behind Soaring Costs," *Wall Street Journal,* February 14, 1949. Mr. Rutledge is a staff writer on the *Wall Street Journal.*

A JOURNALISTIC "sob sister" could dig up a story in her boss' office these days.

Soaring costs, which killed the fledgling *Star* on January 28, are creeping up on the eight other big dailies of America's greatest newspaper arena, New York City. Even the best money-makers—the *Times* and the *Daily News*—agree expenses are going up faster than income. So, for that matter, do many other publishers 'round the country; this is one chapter in a national story.

Newspaper economics are a special type. Consider the three cents the reader pays for the bulky morning *Times.* Distribution costs more than a penny; the half-pound of paper in the average copy costs 2½ cents. On top of that comes all the expense of gathering news and printing it. Nickel prices charged by most other dailies still make a small dent in total costs.

Advertising accounts for the major share of a newspaper's revenue. And advertising is showing definite signs of leveling off after a post-war rise to a new record last year—nearly 6% over 1947 for New York's major papers.

Publishers have been paying $4 a ton more for newsprint since last summer. Apply this to the tabloid *News* and the new price of $100 a ton adds up to a $20 million annual paper bill. This newspaper consumes 200,000 tons of paper a year in serving over two million daily and nearly four and a half million Sunday readers.

Premium prices for newsprint are slipping now, however.

Telegraph wires crackle with newsprint offers to newspapers at as low as $125 or $130 a ton, a full $30 below the premium prices of six months back. The contract price in New York City is $100 a ton.

Printing presses are wearing out under the daily grinding of war and early post-war years when replacements weren't available. Now, publishers find new presses cost over 70% more than before the war. The *Herald Tribune* recently tossed $2,500,000 into re-outfitting an entirely new pressroom.

But advancing payrolls for their 15,000 employes have run up the bill most for the big New York City publishers—and in this area a number are now cutting down.

The members of the metropolis' 10 big newspaper unions are the best paid in the world. Since before the war they have tacked on an average of 70% to their hourly wages, most of it through three "rounds" of post-war negotiations. . . .

How profitable are New York City newspapers?

A New York *Times* official states: "The *Times* has never been in the red under the present ownership." This ownership dates back to 1896 when the late Adolph S. Ochs bought the property for $75,000. The *Times* doesn't disclose what it's worth now, but it's one of the most valuable newspaper properties in the world—and the most expensive to operate.

The *Times* has over 3,500 employes. Publisher Arthur Hays Sulzberger once disclosed the payroll for 1944 was $170,000 a week for 2,500 it then employed—the dollar figure is now believed to be more than doubled. Mr. Sulzberger also indicated the *Times* had an income that year of over $21 million, and that has probably doubled, too.

Mrs. Reid, publisher of the *Herald Tribune,* owned by her family, asserts her newspaper "made some money last year." Publisher Flynn of the *News* declares: "Profits in 1948 approximated what we could consider a reasonable pre-war figure."

The *Post Home News* conceded that it lost money last year; so did one other paper which refused to be identified. The three other publishers among the big eight questioned refused to discuss profits.

It's the advertising dollars that determine whether a newspaper property is profitable—and evidence of a leveling off has publishers on edge.

Newspapers measure advertising in terms of lines one column wide, set in small "agate" type. Tabloid pages have 1,000 lines; full-size journals usually run 2,400 lines to the page.

This January, linage for the eight dailies totaled 11.8 million, up 12% from the comparable 1948 month. But the figures include a joker.

There were five Sundays—one more than last year. And Sunday is the biggest advertising day.

The *Times* figures that, leaving aside the extra Sunday and the fact that it has two special turn-of-the-year business sections, it showed only a "slight gain" in a day-to-day comparison with 1948. The *Tribune*, on this basis, just about held its own.

The *World-Telegram* and *Sun*, afternoon papers which don't have Sunday editions, were both down in linage from January 1948. For the *Telegram*, the descent was a mild 2%, for the *Sun* a sizeable 9%. Most papers agreed retail linage was slipping.

THE NEWSPAPER, A MANY-SIDED BUSINESS

—Kenneth E. Olson, a note written especially for this book. Mr. Olson is dean of the Medill School of Journalism at Northwestern University.

A NEWSPAPER is many things. It has been defined as "a medium of information conducted for profit," but only the most callous will accept that definition. Every responsible publisher and editor recognizes that the right to operate such a medium of information carries social responsibilities with it. No newspaper can long endure without a sense of its public obligations, any more than it can endure without competent business management.

One division of the newspaper has all the attributes and social responsibilities of a profession. It must be the chronicler and interpreter of current history; it must provide the electorate with facts upon which sound public opinion can be based; it must furnish that check upon government which no constitution has been able to provide.

Another division is in reality a highly organized advertising agency; but it is more than an agency. Not only does it create advertising, but also through distribution of widely circulated advertisements it fosters business and commerce and keeps the wheels of industry turning.

Still a third division involves everything that goes with running a streamlined manufacturing plant. Newspapers are engaged in merchandising news; they buy raw white paper and transform it into a printed product with incredible speed. And all of this would be of little avail if it were not for still a fourth division, which is in effect a highly organized sales, distributing, and marketing organization.

None of these four could function if it were not for still a fifth division, which through wise management provides the wherewithal to keep the presses turning, to buy the raw materials, to meet its obligations to its employees on payday, to retire its debts, and to safeguard the claims of its investors.

Thus the public responsibilities of the first division can be performed only if the other four divisions also play their parts.

When the founders of our republic started their modest experiment in democracy in a world still ruled by autocrats, they knew full well that the success of their government depended upon an intelligent electorate. That was in a day when educational opportunities were limited and when slow and meager transportation and communication facilities made it difficult for the young government to keep its people informed. These founders had had proof that Americans would fight for their right once they knew their interests, but first they had to be kept informed. This duty they turned over to the newspapers of the young nation, making them, in fact, if not in name, copartners with the legislative, executive, and judicial divisions of the government.

Thus from the very beginning of our nation, the function of our press has been to give the people accurate and adequate information on what their governments, national, state, and local, were doing on the political, economic, and social problems that might affect them, on developments in arts and sciences, in education, and in business, to the end that we might have an informed and intelligent electorate. This meant that our newspapers must try to get as wide a distribution as possible. But it costs money to produce newspapers. If readers were to be asked to pay what it actually costs to provide their newspapers, there would in all likelihood be few subscribers.

Analysis of the 1947 operating costs for one small Illinois daily paper disclosed that it cost the publishers $29.71 to provide each of their subscribers the 304 issues they had published during the year. Subscribers paid 23 cents a week for the paper delivered to their doors, but the publisher netted only $9.06 a year per subscriber. How many subscribers would this paper have had, though, if it had attempted to charge even $25 a year? Newspaper readers simply have not been educated to pay a fair price for the most inexpensive product they buy each day.

Perhaps readers should be charged more, but long ago the policy grew up of charging readers only a nominal amount so that the newspaper could reach as many readers as possible. Because our newspapers have been able to reach almost every family in the nation and because they have been free to print the truth, the citizens of our country know more of what their government and other governments are doing than do the people of any other nation in the world.

But if income from newspaper circulation can be relied upon to furnish only a fourth, or at most a third, of the operating costs, other income sources must make up the deficit. If the newspaper is going to stay in business, there must be money coming to meet payrolls on Saturday noon, to pay for newsprint, ink, metal, mats, pictures, syndicate and wire services, and all the other things it takes to put out a newspaper, not to mention light, power, heat, taxes, insurance, interest, and everything that goes with the overhead costs of doing business.

Part of the $19.65 deficit on each subscriber of the little paper cited above was made up by receipts from sales of commercial printing. A far larger part came from the sale of newspaper white space for advertising. Though advertisers may pay from 50 to 70 per cent of the cost of putting out this newspaper, they are in turn provided with the most inexpensive and effective advertising medium they could have.

The local merchant, in order to stay in business, must draw customers from every corner of his trade area. If he used the cheapest form of direct-mail advertising, the penny postcard, it would cost him $100 in postage alone to send out a meager announcement to 10,000 families, many of whom would greet it as "just another piece of advertising." But for one third of what it would cost him to buy, print, address, and mail 10,000 postcards, this merchant can buy a good-sized advertisement in his local 10,000-circulation newspaper, an advertisement that will give him an opportunity to display and describe his merchandise effectively and that will be surrounded with interesting news and feature matter, to which these readers turn eagerly every evening. His message, moreover, will come into these 10,000 homes not as an intruder but as part of the business news in a family newspaper, which these readers accept into their homes as a welcome guest every day.

Thus we have developed in our American system of newspaper economics a plan that has worked well for everyone. It has provided the advertiser with his most inexpensive medium. It has made it possible for every family to have a newspaper at a very nominal cost. From the standpoint of government and the functioning of our democracy it has made possible a wider distribution of information to every citizen than the founders of our republic ever could have foreseen.

Since the war the editors of the resistance press, who gave France its first honest press in generations, have been determined not to permit the postwar press to be of disservice to its people. In spite of difficulties, the better papers have been able to achieve that financial independence which means political independence. Only a few of the weaker papers are beholden to party treasuries. But in the countries behind the Iron Curtain, newspapers have had no alternative but to accept government subsidy and government control. They are now only the mouthpieces of their Communist masters.

Of the three systems, most Americans will prefer their own, for the American system has made it possible for newspapers to be financially independent. Only when newspapers are financially independent can they also be editorially independent.

REVIEW QUESTIONS AND ASSIGNMENTS

1. Why does the Chicago *Tribune* call itself the "World's Greatest Newspaper"?

2. What rank does the press have among national industries?

3. How has the newspaper been affected by such aspects of modern big business as mass production, consolidation, and chain ownership?

4. To what extent is the American press under monopolistic control?

5. What are the dangers to democracy arising from monopolistic control of the press?

6. Discuss the statement that newspaper readers have little or no choice of a local daily.

7. If abuse of power grows out of monopolistic control of the press, what system of regulation would you suggest?

8. To what extent should the press be permitted to follow the doctrines of *laissez-faire* and *caveat emptor*?

9. Is monopolistic control of the press increasing or decreasing?

10. Which is more important to the press, the business side or the editorial side?

11. Does the press give a fair presentation of the weaknesses of capitalism?

12. To what extent is news printed only that it may carry a given amount of advertising?

13. Does the fact that only the propertied class can own newspapers affect the attitude of the press toward the classes?

14. How has the press reported news of economic systems that differ from the American system?

15. How can the public be kept informed of the interests that own and control certain newspapers, so that it can be on its guard against bias, coloration, and propaganda?

ADDITIONAL REFERENCES

Allen, Charles L., "The Press and Advertising," *The Annals of the American Academy of Political and Social Science,* Vol. 219, January 1942, pp. 86–92.

Anderson, N., and E. C. Lindeman, *Urban Sociology* (index), F. S.Crofts, 1928.

Benn, Ernest, *Confessions of a Capitalist,* published by the author, 1932, Chapter 7.

Bird, George L., "Newspaper Monopoly and Political Independence," *Journalism Quarterly,* Vol. 17, September 1940, pp. 207–214.

Bleyer, Willard G., *Main Currents in the History of American Journalism,* Houghton Mifflin, 1927, Chapter 16.

Borden, Neil H., *The Economic Effects of Advertising,* Richard D. Irwin, 1942.

———, Malcolm D. Taylor, and Howard T. Hoode, *Revenues and Expenses of Newspaper Publishers in 1941,* Harvard University Press, 1941.

Brown, Robert U., "186 Dailies 'Lost' Since '29 Were Under 5,000 Class," *Editor & Publisher,* Vol. 80, January 4, 1947, p. 7.

Brucker, Herbert, *Freedom of Information,* Macmillan, 1949, pp. 72–73.

Crawford, N. A., *The Ethics of Journalism,* Alfred A. Knopf, 1924, Chapter 1.

Doob, Leonard W., *Public Opinion and Propaganda,* Henry Holt, 1948, pp. 428–429.

Emery, Edwin, *History of the American Newspaper Publishers Association,* University of Minnesota Press, 1950.

Harding, T. Swann, *The Degradation of Science,* Farrar & Rinehart, 1931, pp. 83–89.

Kinter, Charles V., "Effect of Differences of Income on Newspaper Circulation," *Journalism Quarterly,* Vol. 22, September 1945, pp. 225–230.

Lasseter, Robert, "No Other Allegiance," *Nieman Reports,* Vol. 1, July 1947, pp. 1–5.

Lee, Alfred M., *The Daily Newspaper in America,* Macmillan, 1937, Chapters 7, 8.

Lippmann, Walter, *Public Opinion,* Macmillan, 1922, pp. 335–337.

Lynd, R. S., and Helen Merrill Lynd, *Middletown,* Harcourt, Brace, 1929, pp. 474–477.

Mergenthaler Linotype Company, *A Survey of Daily Newspapers,* December 1943.

Mott, Frank L., *American Journalism,* Macmillan, 1950.

Nixon, Raymond B., "Concentration and Absenteeism in Daily Newspaper Ownership," *Journalism Quarterly,* Vol. 23, June 1945, pp. 97–114.

———, "Implications of the Decreasing Number of Competitive Newspapers," in *Communications in Modern Society,* Wilbur Schramm (editor), University of Illinois Press, 1948.

Pollard, James E., *Principles of Newspaper Management,* McGraw-Hill, 1937, Chapter 14.

Seldes, George, *One Thousand Americans,* Boni & Gaer, 1947, pp. 12–14, 81–90.

Villard, Oswald Garrison, *The Disappearing Daily,* Alfred A. Knopf, 1944.

———, *Some Newspapers and Newspapermen,* Alfred A. Knopf, 1923, pp. 163–167.

Waymack, W. W., "America's No. 1 Public Utility," *Saturday Review of Literature,* Vol. 29, November 23, 1946, pp. 9–10.

Wisehart, M. K., *Public Opinion and the Steel Strike,* supplementary volume to Interchurch World Movement Report on the Steel Strike of 1919, Harcourt, Brace, 1921, pp. 87–162.

20. CHAIN OWNERSHIP AND PRESS INFLUENCE

INTRODUCTION

ECONOMIC CHANGES during the last century have strongly influenced ownership and management practices in the operation of the channels of communication.

What was perhaps one of the most significant developments took place late in the nineteenth century with the advent of Big Business—the centralized ownership of business units on a nationwide, even worldwide, scale.

Concentration of ownership quickly spread to the newspaper industry when publishers like E. W. Scripps and William Randolph Hearst found it feasible to add one newspaper to another and form a chain of properties under the control of a central headquarters staff. These men merely adapted to the newspaper a form of ownership that was proving successful in many other fields of business: grocery, drug, dry goods, gasoline, and banking, to name just a few.

Along with concentration of ownership through the chain came related changes in the pattern of control of the media. What is now known as absenteeism, that is, ownership of a newpaper and/or radio station by an individual who does not reside in the community the media serve, has been a development that has played hob with traditional concepts of the position of the publisher in his community. Of equal social importance has been the emergence of an increasing number of communities in which all communication channels, usually the newspaper and radio station, are either owned or controlled by one individual. The situation has received the attention of both Congress and the Federal Communications Commission.

Central operation of two or more newspapers has been found feasible under almost all circumstances. There are national, regional, state, and county chains of both daily and weekly newspapers. The management of the chains enjoys many advantages. Single-office control over business and editorial policies permits a small number of executives to direct effectively widely scattered properties. There are also gains in centralized handling of national advertising, equipment purchases, supplies, labor negotiations, and legal services. The financial resources of the chains undoubtedly permit publications of better quality than would be possible if the same properties were under individual local control.

Despite these business advantages, many serious questions have plagued the owners of the chains ever since the first one made its appearance.

Most critics of chain publishing maintain that the position of a newspaper in its community is vastly different from that of a grocery or drug store. They cite the often repeated claim of the press that it enjoys a remarkable degree of intimacy with the public and ask how the audience served by a daily in El Paso, Texas, can feel a very close connection with owners who live and work in New York City.

The owners of the chains, particularly those on a national basis, have acted energetically to assure local personal influence in the operation of individual units. It is a common practice to have the top executive on the local staff use the title "publisher." Most chains grant a great deal of autonomy to local staffs except on questions involving strong central office policy directives. Many chain daily publishers and editors occupy significant civic positions in their communities and to the extent that this occurs the aggravations of remote ownership tend to be diminished.

Another serious problem exists in the power the owners of the chains possess to formulate news and editorial policies with extremely widespread effects on the public. The personal likes and dislikes of Mr. Hearst are known not only by his readers in California but by broad publics in Hearst cities across the continent. There is top news value in an announcement by Scripps-Howard that it will support a given candidate in a national election.

Such power leads to two questions: (1) Should one man be allowed to employ a chain of newspapers to crusade for an objective based on nothing more than a personal whim; and, if so, (2) what steps might be taken within the meaning of the first amendment to the Constitution to assure the public that the editorial policies of any chain will follow a responsible and enlightened course?

These are not easy questions to answer. Only the fact that the average chain is operated in a responsible fashion keeps such issues from becoming pressing public concerns.

Standardization plays a significant part in chain journalism. Many social implications result from the use by a group of newspapers of the same editorials, columns, features, special news stories, and even type faces. Such uniformity must weigh heavily on the initiative and imagination of individual staff members. Its impact on the thought processes of the many different publics served by the chain is probably a consequence of even deeper significance.

CHAIN AND ABSENTEE OWNERSHIP

—Raymond B. Nixon, "Concentration and Absenteeism in Daily Newspaper Ownership," *Journalism Quarterly,* Vol. 22, June 1945, pp. 105–110. Dr. Nixon was editor of the *Journalism Quarterly* and director of the Emory University Division of Journalism at the time he did this study.

ALTHOUGH the term "newspaper chain" means simply two or more newspapers in different cities with the same ownership or control, most critics seem to imply that chain ownership is the same as absentee ownership. For example, it has been said that the chain "applies national formulae to local situations to which they are never quite adequate," and that the chain "changes the character of the newspaper . . . to a purely commercial organization and instrumentality. . . ."[1]

Yet the home paper of a chain may be just as much a part of the community as if its owner had no papers elsewhere. Conversely, a paper may have no connection with a chain and still have an owner, either resident or absentee, whose only interest is "purely commercial." . . .

The rule is that, irrespective of the amount of local autonomy which may exist, a paper is classified as "absentee-owned" whenever the ultimate ownership or control appears beyond any reasonable doubt to lie outside the city of publication.[2]

On the basis of this definition, 297 or 17 per cent of the English-language dailies of general circulation in the United States as of March 1, 1945, are absentee-owned. The circulation of these paper is 12,755,791 or 27.7 per cent of the total circulation. On Sundays the

[1] Quoted by Curtis D. MacDougall, *Newsroom Problems and Policies,* The Macmillan Company, 1941, pp. 16–17.

[2] Dr. Nixon offers some later interpretations of his findings in his chapter "Implications of the Decreasing Numbers of Competitive Newspapers," in *Communications in Modern Society,* Wilbur Schramm (editor), University of Illinois Press, 1948, pp. 43–57.

relative number of absentee-owned papers is 25.2 per cent, while the relative circulation is 31.5 per cent.

The total number of all chain dailies as of March 1, 1945, is 370 (21.2 per cent of the total). This figure is obtained by subtracting 16 individual ownerships from the number of absentee-owned papers and adding the 89 "home-papers" of the various chains. In contrast, the number of chain dailies identified by William Weinfeld for 1935 was 328 or 16.8 per cent of the total number of papers in that year. On Sundays the relative number of chain papers is now 32.9 per cent as compared with 25.3 per cent in 1935, while the total circulation today is 53.8 per cent as compared with 52.4 per cent ten years ago.[3]

In spite of this slight increase during the last ten years, relative chain circulation is still below its 1930 peak of 43.4 per cent daily and 54.1 per cent Sunday. In fact, the proportion of chain circulation to total circulation has remained at almost exactly the same point for the last fifteen years. The number of chain papers has increased, but the average circulation has decreased.

The average chain also has grown smaller in number of papers. Weinfeld in 1935 listed 63 chains with an average of 5.1 papers each, while the tabulation for 1945 shows 76 chains with an average of 4.8 papers each. Of the 52 chains which are on both lists, 16 have grown smaller, losing an average of 2.8 papers each; 13 have grown larger, gaining an average of 2.4 papers each; and 23 have remained the same size.

A comparison of the 1935 and 1945 lists reveals likewise that there has been a tendency away from large national chains toward state and regional chains, or chains of only a few large papers. At present 44 of the 76 chains (57.8 per cent) are confined to one state, and 255 (67.6 per cent) of the 370 chain dailies are located in the state in which their ownership is located.

Although none of the earlier studies of chains has divided papers on this basis, some further comparisons are possible. For example, the two national chains which in 1935 were largest in number of dailies have both declined, Hearst from 26 to 17 papers and Scripps-Howard from 23 to 18. The Frank E. Gannett chain, which was the

[3] In the first edition of this study of the press somewhat comparable data on the chain newspaper were presented through an article written by William Weinfeld entitled "The Growth of Daily Newspaper Chains in the United States: 1923, 1926–1935." It was published in the *Journalism Quarterly*, Vol. 13, December 1936, pp. 368–375.

third largest in 1935, has grown from 16 to 17 papers (14 in New York, two in adjoining states, only one at any distance). These are highly concentrated in location and enjoy a large degree of local autonomy.

Hearst, McCormick-Patterson and Scripps-Howard still lead in total daily circulation, in the order named, but Hearst has lost ground and Scripps-Howard has gained only slightly. The chain which has gained the most in circulation, McCormick-Patterson, is concentrated entirely in two cities and has one of its two owners as resident publisher in each city.[4]

The implications of all this are clear: daily chain ownership has been becoming morc *intensive* and less *extensive* in its concentration. Indeed, when one encounters a situation like that of the Marlboro-Hudson (Mass.) chain, where the two papers are located in cities only five miles apart and sell their advertising only in combination, it is almost a toss-up as to whether it should be classified as a chain or as a local combination.

It remains to be determined whether the more extensive national chains have declined because they had reached that still unknown point at which the advantages of chain operation fail to compensate for the disadvantages of absentee ownership. Perhaps the owners merely have been too busy looking after their present properties during these years of depression and war to give much thought to expansion. The chains experienced their greatest growth after World War I and may expand similarly after World War II. The time seems to have passed, however, when a Hearst would seek to further his presidential ambitions through personally directed papers located in every section of the country. Present-day conditions seem to favor a more intensive type of ownership concentration, in which absenteeism is less of a factor.[5]

[4] The McCormick-Patterson picture changed somewhat when Captain Joseph M. Patterson, publisher of the New York *Daily News*, a tremendously successful morning tabloid, died on May 26, 1946. The surviving owners of the *Daily News*, particularly Colonel Robert R. McCormick, publisher of the Chicago *Tribune*, named F. M. Flynn president of the News Syndicate Company, Inc., and general manager of the *Daily News*. Richard W. Clarke was appointed executive editor with the hope that he could continue the philosophy of journalism developed and (from a circulation standpoint) perfected by Captain Patterson. —The Editors.

[5] The postwar years brought no appreciable increase in the number of chain dailies. In fact, one of the chains listed by Dr. Nixon in 1945, that of J. David

IS THE CHAIN NEWSPAPER A MENACE?

—Col. Frank Knox, address delivered at the Seventh Annual Meeting of the American Society of Newspaper Editors, 1929. Reprinted in *Problems of Journalism,* 1929, pp. 103–110. The late Colonel Knox was well known both as a publisher and as Secretary of the Navy in World War II.

PRESIDENT of the American Society of Newspaper Editors, fellow newspapermen: I have been asked to answer the question, "Is the Chain a Menace to American Journalism?" I will try to do so to the best of my ability, but I do criticize the use of the word "chain," "Chain" implies something binding, a degree of inflexibility—something a man can't get away from, but if there is any one thing a chain of newspapers possess, it is elasticity. And I do not believe there is any class of men who can appreciate this fact better than a body of editors. Take a single newspaper, with its publisher issuing instructions to his editor. If the editor listens to or reads them that is a big point gained by the publication. If he pays any attention to them, it is a miracle. As a rule, the editor goes blithely on his way, printing the "Thing as he sees it for the God of Things as They Are," happily indifferent to any appeal for economy in space or expenditure and ignoring all hints as to the desirability of getting out or staying out of "the red." He just goes ahead and gets out a good newspaper. Now, multiply your editorial room by, say, twenty-eight and the distance from your publisher by several thousand miles, and you will see why the word "chain" does not particularly impress me when applied to a group of newspapers.

Still, since I am to speak on group, or, if you will, "chain," newspapers, I do not know that I could have wished for a more suitable place than here—here in Washington, the head of the greatest and happiest example of the chain or group system the world has ever seen. Here, at the central office of a group of units gathered together for mutual benefit and protection and held together by the economic laws that pay big returns for unity and cooperation.

Nor could I have chosen a better time than now, when this nation is presided over by one whose life has been devoted to the very things that are aimed at by newspaper combinations—greater efficiency, increased production with less waste, a higher grade of product, giving

---

Stern, who owned the Philadelphia *Record* and the Camden (New Jersey) *Courier* and *Post,* disappeared when Mr. Stern sold his properties.—The Editors.

people more of what they want and should have and at less cost, speeding up the wheels of commerce and progress—in short, helping to make this country, day by day and year by year, a better and happier place in which to live.

Now to our question, "Is the Chain a Menace to American Journalism?" Let me ask another question: "What do you mean by journalism?" If you mean the journalism of other days, the days when editors went at it hammer and tongs in the morning and then drank mint juleps together or shot at each other in the afternoon, the answer is "Yes." Rather, it was, for that era of journalism is a thing of the past. If you mean by journalism anything that is not businesslike, efficient, and in keeping with the demand of the present day, the answer is "Yes." In either case, it is an autopsy, not a diagnosis we are holding. For old-time journalism, picturesque as it was and suited to its day as it was, has passed, as have the stagecoach and the shoemaker. One might as well ask, "Are express trains and automobiles a menace to transportation; are shoe factories a menace to shoemaking?"

In fact, I must confess that "journalism" itself is a word I seldom hear outside of colleges of journalism. As a rule, I find that even the graduates of these excellent institutions cease to be journalists very early in their careers, and either become good newspaper men or go into some other line of business.

So, to avoid the vagueness of the term "journalism" let me revamp the question in order that we may all be considering the same problem, no matter what results we obtain. Let us translate the question to this: "Is the 'chain' (or group) a menace to the highest development of American newspapers—a hindrance to the service they should render their readers, their communities, and the nation?"

To this question I unqualifiedly answer, "No." This audience alone is a sufficient answer to the question. Newspaper chains have been in existence many years, and I do not believe that the newspapers of the country, chained or unchained, ever had better editors than they have today, were ever edited more intelligently and conscientiously than now.

The development of chain or group newspapers was as necessary and as inevitable in our economic change and growth as chain stores, chain hotels, great railroad systems, branch banks, big factories, and other great combinations were inevitable. Whether we like them or not, these things are here as a part of our social, commercial, financial, and manufacturing evolution. One might as well argue against the law of gravitation or the law of supply and demand. Group newspapers are simply the result of the latter law, and have been gradually brought about by the demand for more, better, and more varied newspaper content, a more complete coverage of news, and quicker distribution. This demand, with the increasing cost of labor and material, and narrowing profits, called for highly systematized organization and methods. The old, easy-going, slip-shod, wasteful days of newspaper-making disappeared years ago, and in their place has come the necessity for the same degree of specialized effort as is required by any other great and successful business.

So, while it is not true that everything that is is right, it can safely be taken for granted that whatever is absolutely necessary to meet changing conditions and fill growing demands must be held to be for the best.

And conditions have changed and they have made the chain newspaper a necessity in our economic life—a social, financial, commercial, and industrial necessity. Nor were these new conditions made or the necessity created by the publisher. The pressure came from outside; the demand was made by the two classes of newspaper patrons, the reader and the advertiser.

The reader had changed in his mental habits; his appetite had grown. There was a time when a newspaper reader was content with what the staff of one newspaper could give him in news, editorials, pictures, humor, poetry, art—everything. He was satisfied with its policies and politics and probably bought his newspaper entirely on account of them. He swore by his own paper and swore at all others. His reading was table d'hôte rather than à la carte, and he bolted his meals of newspaper columns.

Gradually, however, his appetite grew, and he became less easy to suit. The elimination, or at least the slurring, of party lines helped to bring this about. The new generation of readers wanted to be served with the best and it wanted to be able to pick and choose. It wanted to know, not only what a few people did and thought in a few places, but what everybody did or thought in a great number of places. It demanded the latest and best in news, art, humor—everything. It wanted pictures of everyone and everything taken on the spot, and it wanted them right away. It was insatiable in its demands, reckless of salaries, of telegraph and cable tolls. It would have ruined an individual newspaper, relying on its own resources only, in a day. But there was a way out, and that way was through the grouping together of newspapers. Properly apportioning vastly increasing expenditures among these, pro-rating salaries and tolls, each newspaper might, without losing its individuality or becoming less of a local institution, still give its readers the best the world afforded in every line that makes a newspaper attractive. So much for one urge that brought about the chain newspaper.

The other was from the advertiser. Production was increasing in tremendous volume. Distribution and consumption must keep pace with it. The advertiser became a serious student of merchandising problems. He looked over his charts and sales records and found that he was doing too much advertising with too meager results. He planted plentifully enough, but he seemed to be reaping his grain with a scythe. What he demanded for gathering in his crops was a McCormick harvester. If there were three newspapers, with three different brands of political opinions, in a town, he must advertise in all three newspapers to reach his potential customers. If there were three newspapers appealing to three different grades of income, one, say, to the man with one automobile, one to the man with two, and one to the man with three, he must advertise in all of the three newspapers. This, he felt, was an economic waste. Worst of all, it was an economic waste that hurt him. He had discovered that buying was done, not by strata of readers but by cross-sections. He had found that, to keep his factory going or his store filled with customers, he must slice, not skim. In other words, he had discovered that, to reach all the customers or customers he wanted to reach he must find newspapers that appealed to all classes.

He discovered also another important fact: namely, that the feminine voice has the final say, as perhaps in other matters, in the buying of about 80 per cent of things sold—whether it be a house or a hat, a limousine or a man's necktie. So, to reach the lady of the house, he demanded that the newspaper for his purpose should contain, not only news and editorials, stock market reports, and a sports section, but a page or two in regard to matters dear to the feminine heart. In a word, he was as preposterous in his demands as the reader had been, but his demands must be met, for, as the years had passed, the newspapers of the nation had gradually taken on their shoulders a tremendous responsibility, no less a task than that of keeping the business of America running in smooth channels from factory to merchant, from the merchant to the home. The daily newspaper had not only become a great business itself, but it had underwritten all other businesses. It had become a great cog that must never stop or slip or slow down.

The advertiser's demands must be met and, as in meeting the demands of the reader, there was but one answer, the group newspaper. The group newspaper, because no individual newspaper could carry this burden alone.

May I interpolate here a distinction. I don't necessarily mean a group owned by one man or a group owned by a single corporation, but in a wider sense, all of us practically are tending toward that idea, because where we find ourselves incapable, because of our limited resources, to carry on a certain type of activity out of our own means, we all join together with others to accomplish that purpose.

Now, when I have spoken of changing conditions and increasing demands, and said the answer was the "group newspaper," I would not have you think that I am merely making out a case for the largest of these groups, the one with which I happen to be connected. On the contrary, I am simply reviewing newspaper conditions as they exist today. Mr. Hearst, with that vision and intuition without which no publisher can be a great publisher, may perhaps have foreseen the coming change earlier than others. He may have known what readers and advertisers would want before they knew it themselves and met their demands in advance, but, leaving out the Hearst group, leaving out the Scripps-Howard group, leaving out, in fact, all actual groups or chains, the group principle is dominant today among American newspapers. So true is this that the question, "Is the chain a menace?" almost resolves itself into the question, "Are American newspapers a menace?" for there are practically none of them that have not recognized and accepted the chain idea in one way or another. . . .

In addition to the fact that chain newspapers are an economic necessity and were inevitable, in addition to the fact that the basic idea of the group seems to have been almost unanimously accepted and endorsed, the experience of over a quarter of a century would seem to answer any question as to the menace of the newspaper chain. During that time, chain newspapers have been steadily gaining. Within that period, we have gone through a great war, since then we have passed through trying years of reconstruction and readjustment. Only last fall we had a rather hotly contested election; for months the country and the stock-markets have been indulging in some high and lofty financial gymnastics. Through it all, the pulse of the newspapers has beaten steadily. If there is a menace, it would seem to me that it has had plenty of time to get into action.

No, I see no danger in the newspaper chain. On the contrary, I see many merits, great actual value to communities, to states, and to the nation.

Probably one of the greatest merits of the chain is that it gives greater independence, additional liberty of action, to each newspaper belonging to it. This may seem paradoxical, but it is not. Many an individual newspaper has gone into a local fight—perhaps against crooked politics, against graft, against crime, or in behalf of some needed reform or city or state improvements—and, for lack of resources, has been driven from the field, perhaps annihilated. To a newspaper belonging to a strong group, there is little danger of this. Reserve forces, both financial and in personnel, can be called on until the battle is over and the paper has tided over its strain.

Not only that, but a chain newspaper can in another way often render its city and state valuable service from the fact that it is a part of a chain. Let me illustrate. A few years ago, Atlanta started a campaign designed to draw business and capital to that city. Our newspaper there not only entered actively into the campaign, but called on its sister newspapers for editorial assistance, which was cheerfully given. The Hearst newspapers "boomed" Atlanta. They insisted on putting it "on the map." Now, how much they had to do with the success of the campaign, I do not know, but I do know that the campaign was a success and that, as a result, 410 new concerns came to Atlanta and increased the city's payrolls by $20,000,000. There can be no menace in work of that kind, and I could give innumerable instances of the same nature.

Nor are the benefits of such cooperation among newspapers merely local and temporary. Their most beneficial result is in awakening the permanent interest of thousands of readers in one part of the country in the welfare of other and, possibly, far-distant cities and states. They tend to draw the nation closer together, to do away with sectionalism, to make the United States, more truly than ever, the *United* States.

So far, I have tried to answer the question you have asked me by stating facts that are open to anyone. May I, in all sincerity and earnestness, add a personal word? For over a year I have been the General Manager of the largest group of personally owned newspapers in the world. I have seen no menace in that chain. In other words, I have never received an order or a request from my Chief that, as a publisher and a good citizen, I would not be glad to put into effect on a newspaper of my own.

In closing, let me repeat the question—"Is the chain a menace?" Is it a menace, not only to journalism, but to our nation, our traditions, our ideals, and our institutions? It is not. Not a chain binding newspapers together. I have no fear of that.

The only chain that can menace our institutions or our ideals is any chain that might possibly bind a newspaper to sordid interests, to selfish and un-American ambitions, to corrupt and dangerous political machinations, and I have no fear of that chain either. For I do not believe that, in spite of something they may have lost in picturesqueness and personality, the newspapers of our country, whether in groups or individually owned, were ever better, ever more honest, ever truer to themselves and to their readers, ever more adequately doing their part in the business of a great nation, ever more earnestly and conscientiously trying to lead that nation on to its high destiny.

OUTSIDE INFLUENCES IN THE DEVELOPMENT OF THE CHAIN

—William P. Beazell, "Tomorrow's Newspaper," *The Atlantic Monthly,* Vol. 146, July 1930, pp. 26–29. The author, veteran journalist and essayist, was day managing editor of the New York *World* from 1921 to 1930.

THIS SPREAD of mergers and of chains among newspapers has been only in part a matter of choice; to a far greater degree it has been the result of outside influences. Extraordinary changes are being wrought in our whole economic structure. The evidences of this are on every hand, and of the profound effects they are having on our everyday lives. Not even in the "trust years" at the turn of the century were mergers so much the order as they are to-day. They are going forward swiftly in industry and even more swiftly outside industry. What is happening in banking may be cited as a single vivid example. Last year 799 banks were absorbed by others. Steadily banking control is being concentrated—1 per cent of the banks now hold 75 per cent of the country's deposits. Relentlessly the number of banks is being cut down—in the last seven years it has been reduced 20 per cent. (In this reduction, it must be made plain, mergers have been but one factor; the trend is the point I seek to emphasize.)

Closely allied to mergers is the chain store, and again banking may be cited as an illustration of its growth. To-day there are 272 banking chains in the United States with thirteen billions of resources. In trade (where, of course, the chain has had its greatest expansion) there is now, quite literally, nothing that cannot be bought in a chain store, and there are communities where nothing can be bought outside one. J. C. Penny reckons that 15 per cent of the retail trade of the country is done at chain stores; one grocery chain did more than a billion dollars' worth of business in 1929. Installment buying has become an equal factor in these economic changes. No one can say what its volume is, but it may be guessed from its dominance in our greatest industry—more than half the automobiles sold are sold on deferred payments. These things mean mass production, centralization of control, and standardization of products and policies—powerful factors, each of them, in social no less than industrial and mercantile organization.

It was inevitable that the newspaper should have been affected by this development—it touches upon and is touched by too many aspects of business to have escaped so pervasive an influence. Two interior factors hastened the yielding of the newspaper to this influence. One was the great increase in the cost of production—wages, materials, equipment—in the years following the war. As soundly informed an executive as I know declares that this cost has risen to a point where a variation of 10 per cent in volume of advertising would turn profit into loss for four papers out of five. Compactness of organization and concentration of competition are obvious objectives under such a condition. The second factor was the advertiser. Advertising has become, too, as fixed a charge as rent or payroll, and like these must justify itself. Just as he found one store and one force of employees sufficient for serving all classes of his patronage, the merchant began to wish for a single medium of announcement. Having wished, he began to demand, and having demanded, he began, in many instances, to lend actual aid toward the consolidation of the agencies of appeal. Few negotiations toward merger, or even toward the advent of chain ownership, have been carried beyond the preliminary stages without consultation with the principal advertisers of the community. On the whole the change has been to the satisfaction of the advertiser. It is not always that he finds himself spending less money, but he is getting better returns.

Now and then he has been rather painfully hoist with his own petard; under consolidation, rates have been raised to a point where he himself, in turn, has risen—in rebellion. Such strikes of advertisers resulted in Cleveland and Dayton in the establishment of "shoppers dailies" carrying nothing but advertising and, in a final stage, neighborhood announcements. Less elaborately organized strikes have been carried on in other cities. It is significant that victory—not always complete, but definite nevertheless—has rested with the newspapers.

The newspaper has proved especially plastic to two, at least, of the major elements of this trend toward mergers and chain ownership. Mass production is not yet feasible for newspapers; news must come molten from the crucible of events, and communities are too self-contained and distances in the United States are too great. Centralization of control, however, fits snugly into the newspaper scheme, and standardization has become a dominating trait of the newspaper of today.

Never were newspapers cut so true to a single pattern as they are now. They compete no longer in content, but only in form, and in form there is coming a curious similarity among them. In scores of cities one newspaper differs from another only in the head letter it uses. Features and illustrations will be the same, in kind at least, and not only will the news be the same, but, by the time the last edition has come from the press, the same "stories" will have been chosen for display and the same themes and incidents for emphasis in the headlines. . . .

Chain ownership, too, lends a strong hand to standardization. To a peculiar degree the newspaper still reflects the personality of its ownership. Sometimes the reflection is physical—a Hearst newspaper may be recognized as far as you can see it, no matter what city it is published in. Sometimes it is a manifestation of policy, as in the Scripps-Howard support of the candidacy of Herbert Hoover regardless of the preferences of individual clienteles.

We have, then, one reflection not in a single newspaper or a single community, but in five or ten or twenty-five. There are shortcomings other than monotony in the standardized newspaper. Often it lacks the outward and inward evidences of individuality—of its own individuality, at least. Often it lacks vigor and initiative, and sometimes the courage that is born of competitive need. Nevertheless, the newspaper of today, standardized or not, is a good newspaper. Factor for factor in its content, newspaper quality was never so high as it is today. The gathering of news has been brought to a magical perfection of scope and detail. Authority in presentation and interpretation is at the highest point that has ever been reached. The syndicate, and the news service, as they function nowadays, can furnish for a hundred newspapers material that in excellence and importance would be beyond the reach of any one newspaper, except, perhaps, a few of the greatest of them all. In every sense of the word the newspaper of today is the best bargain any man can buy. Regarded as a manufactured product alone, it sells for less than half the cost of turning it out.

EDITORIAL POWER OF THE CHAINS

—Oswald Garrison Villard, "The Chain Daily," *The Nation*, Vol. 130, May 21, 1930, pp. 596–597.

IF THERE IS as yet no deliberate planning of newspaper chains to control opinion there is no reason why this could not be undertaken. It is already quite in the power of rich men to buy all the dailies in the small states—there are only three in Delaware, six in Wyoming, five in Idaho, twenty-two in Alabama, and thirty-six in Washington. Henry Ford could long ago have purchased the sixty dailies in Michigan with the exception of the very rich Detroit *News*, with but a portion of one year's income. Since there are forty-eight towns and cities in Michigan which possess only one daily journal apiece, despite the theory that this is a government by two political parties, the opportunity must be pretty obvious to those with political ambitions. The purchase of the California chain of Colonel Copley was attributed by some to a desire to control public opinion in southern California in favor of the power interests, but this was denied by his employees. The relative worth of the chain, and whether it is a gain or a menace, will depend upon the personal equation, the character and the aims of the owners.

So far it is impossible to say that any one chain has been used for specific anti-social or reactionary propaganda, if we omit the Hearst dailies. The Scripps-Howard newspapers are usually liberal, and most friendly to reform movements. It is a pity that their reporting is sometimes poor, their makeup and typography wretched. They sorely lack high standards in these respects, but their answer is the old one—"we must stoop to get circulations in order to put our ideas over." Even the New York *Telegram* lacks typographical distinction and is messy; yet the New York *Times* has made its great success while adhering to typographical dignity and taste, with the *Herald Tribune* following its example. None of the chains, again excepting Hearst, strive for typographical uniformity. It would be welcome if a format of beauty and distinction were to be adopted by one of them; but those two qualities have largely disappeared from the American press.

By using the new technique of getting the public to advance some of the money while the promoter himself holds control there is no reason whatever why we may not see a chain of one hundred dailies controlled by one man. Theoretically at least; whether this would work out well practically is doubted by many. Yet the steady progress of the Scripps-Howard syndicate, despite certain weak members, would seem to prove this is no more impossible than the creation by one owner of a group of five hundred grocery or five-and-ten-cent stores. I can see no valid reasons why we should not have much larger chains and, I believe, we shall see them when those having great stakes in the present economic system are sufficiently enriched or sufficiently frightened by the specter of radicalism to seek more directly to control public opinion. Here is where the danger lies. In this connection the action of the International Paper and Power Company in buying its way into a number of dailies in 1928 and 1929, and lending much money to newspaper owners, including Mr. Gannett, is highly suggestive. The purpose of this new policy, the president of the company said in his own defense, was simply to assure to the company steady customers for its paper. But the outcry within the press and the disapproval of the public were so great that he was speedily compelled to change his mind about the advisability of this policy and to get out of the newspaper business. Similarly persistent and at times successful efforts by the power lobbyists to get their hooks into daily newspapers are a warning of a tendency that must be guarded against if the press is not to become a creature of the great capitalists. It is, heaven knows, today sufficiently in the clutch of the forces which make for reaction and the support of the *status quo.*

Again, the question of absentee ownership sometimes plays a considerable part in the development of the chain. Some of the smaller communities resent the control of their dailies by men living elsewhere. This is not, however, a universal feeling. There might, however, well be dissatisfaction in Pittsburgh, where all three of the dailies remaining in a city which had seven morning and evening newspapers only a few years ago are now owned by capitalists residing elsewhere—the Scripps-Howard Syndicate, Hearst, and Paul Block. At bottom the owners of the Hearst and Block Pittsburgh newspapers have no more direct interest in the city than have the owners of chain cigar stores. It is true that there are always editorial writers to deal with local problems; that the staffs are still largely made up of local men. The owners of the Scripps-Howard papers make every effort to tie up their editors with the local interests of the cities in which their papers are situated. Local autonomy is the watchword and it is generally lived up to, except in national affairs. The local Scripps-Howard editor is given help to buy an interest in the paper and is expected to spend the rest of his life in its service. He is constantly urged to "know your town" and "feel its pulse." Scripps-Howard editors are, however, freely transferred from one city to another. It still seems impossible that there should be quite the same relationship of the daily to its community that exists when the paper is owned by a local man known to all his fellow-citizens, to be seen at local gatherings, and to be held directly accountable to local opinions and desires. It would seem as though no community of the size of Pittsburgh could rest happy under such conditions. They seem to me intolerable.

On the other hand, defenders of the chain allege that there is a certain advantage in this freedom of a chain editor from local entanglements—social, business, and financial. While it was always Mr. Scripps' idea that his editors might purchase stock in the papers they were serving he rigidly ruled that they should not invest their savings in other enterprises which would interfere with their complete freedom of opinion and action. He wished them to be exclusively and only newspapermen. Another view is expressed by Eugene A. Howe of the Howe Newspapers (chiefly located in Texas, where the chain idea is being developed most rapidly and successfully). "I think," he states, "that it doesn't matter who owns a newspaper as long as it is operated vigorously and honestly. The average reader doesn't bother about the paper's masthead. Give him a judicious selection of news and features, give him a good newspaper, and he is satisfied. And the paper usually will be a profitable investment. We are still experimenting in Texas, but we feel we are going a long way in establishing group dailies."

There remains, however, the question of the editorial opinions of a chain of newspapers. Here we have three distinct policies. The Scripps-Howard dailies, while free to deal with local issues, all conform to the national editorial opinions formulated by chief editorial writers, or, as in the case of their support of Herbert Hoover for the Presidency (which they are presumed to be repenting in sackcloth and ashes), as a result of an editorial convention and a free vote of all the editors. Mr. Hearst's editors reflect his own contradictory and changing views and personal whims. Frank Gannett, however, does not alter the political policies of the papers he purchases. Thus the Hartford, Connecticut, *Times* remains Democratic, and the Brooklyn *Eagle* independent Democratic, while most of the others are Republican. Mr. Gannett is a convinced and sincere dry; it will be interesting to see if it will be possible for him to allow some of his papers to take the opposite viewpoint if the question of prohibition becomes still more acute. His policy seems to me entirely ethical and quite defensible. It is certainly unusual for an owner to grant to his editors the complete freedom of opinion and expression which Mr. Gannett permits. . . .

It cannot be maintained that the chain development is a healthy one from the point of view of the general public. Any tendency which makes toward restriction, standardization, or the concentrating of editorial power in one hand is to be watched with concern. For the ideal journalistic state of a republic, especially where the two-party system prevails, is one in which papers may easily be created by single individuals, as Horace Greeley established the *Tribune* and Alexander Hamilton's friends the New York *Evening Post*, to rise and disappear if need be. If the coordination of the press with the current urge for larger and larger combinations is inevitable, it is regrettable if only because this makes it additionally harder for the man of small fortune to start a daily and compete successfully for public support. That this chain development is an international phenomenon does not alter the situation.

REVIEW QUESTIONS AND ASSIGNMENTS

1. What trends do you see in the economic history of America during the last 50 years that help to explain the rise of the chain daily?

2. Can you offer any explanations for the failure of new press chains to appear in recent years?

3. Do you feel that absentee ownership of a single newspaper is more of a problem than chain ownership?

4. Do you agree that a chain of newspapers should not be allowed to own radio stations? Why?

5. Study the personnel procedures of a selected chain and relate the results to the claim that employment insecurity is inevitable in chain ownership.

6. If you were the owner of a chain of newspapers how much control would you exercise over individual units in the group?

7. Study the life of any one chain publisher in this country and outline his principles of journalism.

8. Discuss the often-repeated charge that chain publishing has added alarmingly to the standardization of the press.

9. Do you think that the personnel of a chain daily is likely to lose initiative and spirit as a result of absentee ownership?

10. Prepare a list of questions summarizing the five or six major charges against chain papers and submit the list to the editors of 10 or 12 papers owned by at least three different chains. Discuss their replies.

11. Discuss the proposition that one man should not be allowed to acquire and publish a group of newspapers.

12. What do you think of the business merger of competing newspapers without any combination of editorial departments?

13. What differences and similarities can you point out between a chain of newspapers and a network of radio stations?

14. Do you feel that the people in Pittsburgh, Pennsylvania, gain or lose as a result of having three daily newspapers all chain owned?

ADDITIONAL REFERENCES

Barrett, James W., *The* World, *the, Flesh, and Messrs. Pulitzer,* Vanguard Press, 1931.

Bent, Silas, "Adding One Newspaper to Another," *Century,* Vol. 115, November 1927, p. 73.

Bigman, Stanley K., "Rivals in Conformity: A Study of Two Competing Dailies," *Journalism Quarterly,* Vol. 25, June 1948, pp. 127–131.

Bleyer, Willard G., *Main Currents in the History of American Journalism,* Houghton Mifflin, 1927.

Brisbane, Arthur, "William Randolph Hearst," *The North American Review,* Vol. 183, September 21, 1906, pp. 519–525.

Britt, George, *Forty Years—Forty Millions,* Farrar & Rinehart, 1935.

Brooks, Ned, *Chain Newspapers,* Ohio State University Press, 1923.

Casey, Ralph D., "Scripps Howard Newspapers in 1928 Presidential Campaign," *Journalism Quarterly,* Vol. 7, September 1930, pp. 209–231.

Chafee, Zechariah, Jr., *Government and Mass Communications,* University of Chicago Press, 1947, Vol. II, pp. 537–677.

Cochran, Negley D., *E. W. Scripps,* Harcourt, Brace, 1933.

Colleagues and Associates, *The Lee Papers: A Saga of Midwestern Journalism* Star-Courier Press, Kewanee, Illinois, 1946.

Davis, Forrest, "Mr. Hearst Steps Down," *The Saturday Evening Post,* Vol. 211, August 27, 1938, p. 5.

Doan, Edward N., "Chain Newspapers in the United States," *Journalism Quarterly,* Vol. 9, December 1932, pp. 329–338.

Ernst, Morris L., *The First Freedom,* Macmillan, 1946.

Federal Trade Commission, *Newsprint Paper Industry,* July 8, 1930.

Gardner, Gilson, *Lusty Scripps,* Vanguard Press, 1932.

Howard, Roy W., "Newspaper Mass Production," *The North American Review,* Vol. 225, April 1928, pp. 420–424.

King, Marion Reynolds, "A Link in the First Newspaper Chain," *Journalism Quarterly,* Vol. 9, September 1932, pp. 257–268.

Lee, Alfred M., *The Daily Newspaper in America,* Macmillan, 1937, pp. 208–257.

Lippmann, Walter, "Two Revolutions in American Journalism, *Yale Review,* Vol. 20, March 1931, pp. 433–441.

Lundberg, Ferdinand, *Imperial Hearst,* Equinox Cooperative Press, 1937.

McRae, Milton A., *Forty Years in Newspaperdom,* Coward-McCann, 1924.

Millis, Walter, "Hearst," *The Atlantic Monthly,* Vol. 148, December 1931, p. 707.

Mott, Frank L., *American Journalism,* Macmillan, 1950.

Neurath, Paul, "One-Publisher Communities: Factors Influencing Trend," *Journalism Quarterly,* Vol. 21, September 1944, pp. 230–242.

Nixon, Raymond B., "Implications of the Decreasing Number of Competitive Newspapers," in *Communications in Modern Society,* Wilbur Schramm (editor), University of Illinois Press, 1948, pp. 43–57.

Rosewater, Victor, *History of Cooperative News Gathering in the U.S.,* Appleton-Century, 1930.

Schramm, Wilbur (editor), *Mass Communications,* University of Illinois Press, 1949.

Spargo, George H., "Newspaper Paralysis," *The North American Review,* Vol. 226, August 1928, pp. 189–194.

Tebbel, John, *An American Dynasty* (The Medill-McCormick-Patterson family), Doubleday, 1947.

———, *The Marshall Fields,* E. P. Dutton, 1947.

Villard, Oswald G., *Some Newspapers and Newspapermen,* Alfred A. Knopf, 1923.

Weinfeld, William, "The Growth of Daily Newspaper Chains in the United States: 1923, 1926–1935," *Journalism Quarterly,* Vol. 13, December 1936, pp. 368–375.

Williamson, Samuel T., *Frank Gannett,* Duell, Sloan and Pearce, 1940.

Winkler, J. K., *W. R. Hearst,* Simon & Schuster, 1928.

21. GOVERNMENTAL PUBLICITY IN THE NEWS STREAM

INTRODUCTION

Modern American government, a gigantic and intricate public business, occupies a paradoxical position in connection with the process of distributing information about itself. In spite of the fact that one of the basic ideas of the democratic state is constant scrutiny by the citizens of the actions of their representatives, government operates under many restrictions in attempting to tell its story to the public.

These restrictions are applied both internally and externally. The members of Congress have frequently opposed the issuance of publicity by the administrative agencies and this, in turn, forces many agency heads to act with conservatism and caution in informing the public of orders and policies.

On the outside stand the representatives of the media who insist that news about government must be processed by them if the citizens are to be assured a truthful picture. A strong feeling exists among newsmen that government cannot report its own affairs without glossing over errors and emphasizing accomplishments, the end result being propaganda. They argue that they must accept the primary responsibility for scrutinizing the public housekeeping on all levels of government. When the "Voice of America" program was introduced by the State Department after World War II, both the Associated Press and United Press interpreted this doctrine to be worldwide in effect and refused to provide their news reports for dissemination by the government.

Restrictions to the contrary notwithstanding, government officials find themselves forced to issue a great amount of information that affects the news picture. During the last hundred years, government has been transformed from a police to a service instrumentality, possessed of wide discretionary power to cope with an increasingly complex set of problems. The services are provided by agencies established by the legislative arm and no matter how insignificant an office may be, a publicity program is an inevitable part of its functions.

The primary publicity procedure involves a satisfactory working arrangement with the representatives of the media. Major news is disseminated through either press conferences or specially prepared releases. Routine news, on the other hand, quite often is of such a nature as to force the agency to send it directly to the public involved. The same holds true of many announcements concerning new legislation, changes in policy, and requests for co-operation. Journalists' lack of interest in "dull news" is what forces the agency to develop a direct publicity approach.

There are serious problems in the issuance of information by government. The strong and weak points in the conduct of public affairs should be clearly seen by the public. But there is no assurance that any given government official will prove willing to let the publicity chips fall where they may. In fact, there is a strong possibility that he will indulge in self-defense and self-praise in presenting his story to the people. Likewise, there is very little urgent public need for much of the government publicity that is issued. There is an element in bureaucracy that encourages administrative officials to seek to bolster their hold on office through reliance on publicity that goes far beyond their actual needs. The sheer amount of governmental publicity creates another issue. All Washington correspondents agree that it is impossible to keep abreast of the continuous flow of mimeographed releases. The situation makes it easy to write off routine publicity programs as "government by propaganda."

The influence of government publicity on the press and the mass audiences is tremendous. The White House press conference is possibly the most significant news source in the world. It gives a President an opportunity to shape public thinking to a remarkable degree. Stories based on interviews with members of the cabinet and top administrative officials are highly evaluated by the media. Even much of the so-called routine news finds its way into the communications channels. Washington correspondents admit that it would be impossible to "cover" the national capital without mimeographed news releases.

This basic problem remains: can the government effectively tell its story to the public through existing arrangements?

The media answer the question with an emphatic "yes." They insist that they have the resources to report all the news about government worth disseminating.

Voices may be heard, however, on the other side. Why, they ask, should it be wrong to spend the taxpayer's money to give him a direct and official picture of the "biggest business" in the world?

Future years undoubtedly will see an increase rather than a decrease in government publicity. And the media will probably continue to be the primary agency for its distribution. It is the responsibility of all concerned to see that news of the government is a true and fair report.

GOVERNMENT INFORMATION—PRO AND CON

—Zechariah Chafee, Jr., *Government and Mass Communications,* University of Chicago Press, 1947, Vol. II, pp. 752–756, 768–769, 773–776. Mr. Chafee, a professor of law at Harvard University, served as vice chairman of the Commission on Freedom of the Press.

The People Must Be Informed

"Democratic government may indeed be defined as the government which accepts in the fullest sense the responsibility to explain itself."

Justice Frankfurter probably did not have our precise problem in mind when he spoke this sentence at the fiftieth anniversary of the American branch of the Oxford University Press, but its pertinence is plain. He elaborated the idea as follows:[1]

> In the years between the wars few things were more disturbing than the number of citizens who gave up the effort to understand our problems. . . . Education means the power to reduce the number of citizens who give up the effort of disinterested and responsible understanding. . . . For where the effort is made, there citizens are found; and where citizens are found, responsibility is squarely forced upon a statesman to explain, if need be to justify, the policy he proposes. . . . It can operate successfully only when statesmen know not merely that they will be held to account for what they do, but that those who hold them to account can weigh facts and reflect upon their meaning.[2]

Many purposes come to mind which can be promoted through governmental information. The broadest of all, perhaps, is to provide models of discussion that win respect for "talk" as an efficient, or-

[1] The "precise problem" discussed by Professor Chafee in the chapter from which this extract is taken was how the government might better talk to the people.—The Editors.

[2] Felix Frankfurter, "There Is No Middle Way," *The Saturday Review of Literature,* Vol. 30, October 26, 1946, p. 21.

derly means of clarifying goals, trends, and the alternatives among which a choice is to be made. Free government depends in part on maintaining confidence in "talk." Many forms of existing public discussion undermine respect for it. Often the proceedings follow no clear line and seem to provide no more than entertainment or the chance to "sound off" in undisciplined fashion.

Unfortunately, outstanding examples of this very thing are found in many of the deliberations of the Senate and the House, as printed in the *Congressional Record.* If the debates were broadcast, as is occasionally proposed, the frequency of irrelevant interruptions and digressions would have a devastating effect on the public's opinion about Congress. Even if our national legislature does not wish to keep its debates to the point under consideration, as the Speaker of the House of Commons is empowered to do, Congress might do well to present to the people from time to time lucid summaries of what it has been doing. A carefully prepared radio address or printed article might summarize some important bill, describe its aims and the objections raised by its opponents, narrate the stages through which the bill had passed, indicate what proposed amendments were driving at, and in short give citizens an intelligible account of the process of lawmaking.

Instead of rebelling quite so much as it does against the spread of information by administrative officials, Congress would do well to institute an information service of its own. The attempt to give a coherent picture of its proceedings might help to make the proceedings themselves more coherent and better adapted to the task which nobody except Congress can perform. . . .

Possessing as we do the largest electorate in the world, it is very desirable that our citizens should be given an enlightened understanding of what the active participants in governing us are trying to accomplish for our benefit.

Second, many statutes and regulations need to be explained in ordinary English to the honest persons whose lives will be affected thereby. Why not write the laws themselves in plain English in the first place? Because the business to be controlled is complex; because many precise words must be used to reach those who would deliberately evade brief general provisions; because many qualifications have to be inserted to prevent injustice in special situations. Reasons of this sort made it impossible, for example to frame the regulations of the Office of Price Administration in simple terms. Therefore, the authoritative text necessarily baffled millions unlearned in the law who sincerely wanted to know what they should or should not do. The OPA did its best to meet their needs by means of its information service, which periodically translated the legal terminology into common speech. Thus you might say that the government put out the law in two forms—a technical form for bad citizens and a popular form for good citizens.

Third, a good information service may sometimes render it unnecessary to pass any law at all. Suppose conditions create a serious public danger—of inflation, let us say, or hoarding. If the government makes the danger plain to the people, they may be able to ward it off by private action—by restraining their own selfishness and persuading their neighbors to co-operate.

Such situations and many more afford the government the opportunity to make itself a real part of the lives of citizens. In an enormous country like ours with a large and diverse population, the law-makers and officeholders in Washington are likely to be viewed as something distinct, huge, menacing. "Consequently," as T. North Whitehead observes, "activities of the Federal Government are apt to be contrasted in the minds of the people with actions performed by themselves."[3]

A gulf grows up between We and They. An intelligent information service can bridge this gulf. It can bring the daily work of officials before our eyes and ears so that we realize it is an essential part of our own work. It can bring their thoughts and aims into our thinking and emotions. . . .

Objections Raised by the Press

From the newspapers comes a . . . set of objections to efficient government information service, especially a centralized OWI in peace.[4] In so far as the material is distributed to citizens through the press, the fear is that skillful publicity agents will revise releases and prearrange press conferences so as to make it much harder for re-

[3] *Leadership in a Free Society* (1936), p. 256.

[4] Other objections noted by Professor Chafee: (1) "information can easily become propaganda for a cause," (2) "the desire of those in power to stay in power," and (3) the tendency of administrative agencies to by-pass Congress.—The Editors.

porters, correspondents, and editors to break through the reluctance of officials to have the people know about their shortcomings. Among the Nieman Fellows this was a prevalent attitude: "These press agents are paid to present the most attractive sides of their agencies for press consumption, often given to attempting suppression of unsavory sides. Our government must not get to the point where it feels it shall have the right to deal out to the reporters what little amounts it wants them to know. We need full and open records, with open doors to all governmental operations. This extends to diplomatic affairs as well as to domestic issues." And an older newspaperman remarked to us during hostilities: "Byron Price has stated that censorship will stop with the shooting; this should happen to the OWI too. American publicity abroad will continue, of course, but it is to be hoped that domestic handouts will cease. There is no objection to government releases by the various agencies themselves (for instance, the Department of Agriculture), but only to their unification through OWI. Bureau handouts are not objectionable, and there may be consolidation up to the Cabinet level."

A still greater anxiety is expressed in the communications industries that the government may ignore them altogether and go directly to the public in a big way. They do not worry about such accustomed matters as departmental bulletins or even an occasional documentary film, but they are fearful lest emphasis on information services may lead to a national newspaper and a national motion picture board with the vast resources of the Treasury at their disposal, competing with the metropolitan press and Hollywood, much as the Tennessee Valley Authority competes with the private generation of electric power. . . .

The fact that active governmental participation in mass communications is sometimes advocated as a cure for the diseases of the commercial press naturally increases the resentment of newspapermen. This is not the only reason for an information service, of course. Even if there were perfect private media, a government official still has to make his thoughts clear to the people. But the following position taken by a few rebellious Nieman Fellows, though presumably not typical of newspapermen, especially those toward the top, is shared by many outside critics of the press.

"I am less concerned by possible governmental restrictions than by the failure of the press to restrict itself. Press freedom is in danger because the press does not behave responsibly. Responsibility should go with power. Instead, a kind of Gresham's Law operates in the field of journalism. Just as bad money tends to drive out good, so newspapers with poor ethics tend to drive out papers with better standards. The government should act vigorously to make the newspaper press responsible. The existing libel laws fall short of the need. The best way to offset the misrepresentations of the mass-circulation media is to establish *one* government newspaper, *one* government radio station, and *one* government movie producer. This will enable the government to present its point of view to the public."

These advocates of a government-owned press and the newspaper leaders who are so terrified of its coming both seem to me completely off the road, although in different ditches. As to the first group, government ownership is not a satisfactory remedy for the present shortcomings of the communications industries. As already pointed out, the evils of bigness will persist in a big government newspaper, unless indeed it is so unenterprising and dull as to be unread. And, on the other hand, the newspaper leaders who fight all efficient public information because it will give us something like *Pravda* and the British Broadcasting Corporation are either insincere or "fraidy-cats." Given the hostility of Congress toward mild experiments in the information field, the enormous funds required for a national newspaper will not be appropriated in any foreseeable future. It would be more sensible to expect the Federal Theater project of WPA to produce a replica of the Paris Opera House in Washington equipped with teachers of coloratura singing and ballet. The nearest we ever came to a national domestic channel of mass communications was when President Roosevelt was offered a chance to buy the Blue Network and declined. Something can be said for a municipal radio station like WNYC or for broadcasting at a state university; but, so long as high federal officers find nation-wide hookups on all the networks available, any proposal for sending out much more than time signals and weather reports at the expense of the taxpayers is likely to fall on deaf ears in the Capitol. The notion that OWI would develop into a peacetime octopus seems to me ridiculous. If its Domestic Branch was open to blame, this was not because it was continually seeking new worlds to conquer but on the ground of undue caution for fear of what Congress might do. Its denunciators in high press circles have got so excited that they have mistaken Caspar Milquetoast for Boris Karloff.

There is much more basis for the fear that the government will work through the private press with propaganda and careful concealment of official weakness, although the demand for plate-glass objectivity comes with rather a bad grace from some newspapermen who are past masters at shaping facts to suit their own policies. An improvement in the accuracy and fairness of the regular press is likely to be paralleled in the performance of government publicity experts, who have often got their preliminary experience in work for newspapers, broadcasters, etc. As I said about the defects of the communications industries, it is mainly a question of raising professional standards. Not that we want to encourage devious practices in government just because the private media indulge in them, but the fact that some persons do wrong is not a conclusive reason for denying other persons the opportunity to do right in ways which the country badly needs. If Congress were more sympathetic to information services, as I have suggested, the past or potential publicity programs of specific agencies could be examined in relation to their honesty and abstention from objectionable propaganda. Bad actors could be denied funds and public-spirited performers encouraged. This is not a problem to be solved by sweeping formulas.

A final objection to further publicity is that it will add to what is now enormous in bulk. For example, the New York *Times* now gets twenty-one pounds of government handouts every day in Washington and ten pounds more at its home office. One is appalled by the prospect of more tonnage per annum—"Of making many books there is no end; and much study is a weariness of the flesh." Certainly greater quantity can be justified only by distinctly higher quality.

THE NEED FOR EXPLANATION IN GOVERNMENT NEWS

—James B. Reston, "Reporting on Foreign Affairs," *Nieman Reports,* Vol. 3, July 1949, p. 3.

It is remarkable how much progress the United States has made since 1945 in the realm of foreign policy. If that is to be maintained the institutions to interpret foreign policy to the people must keep pace. These are chiefly the press, the President's press conference and the State Department's public relations. But these have not kept pace.

No official in the world has better reason than the State Department official for knowing that a foreign policy is no better than the public understanding and support behind it. Yet the State Department is still trying to implement a modern foreign policy without an adequate system for explaining it to the people.

It is true that the jobs of responsible officials at the State Department and responsible reporters there are in direct conflict, maybe ten percent of the time. Our job is to report, to explain, and to disclose. Their job, part of the time, is precisely the opposite: in the general interest, they cannot always disclose or explain. But 90 percent of the time, the job of the responsible foreign policy official and the job of the responsible foreign policy reporter are complementary, not antithetical.

Most of the time we are the means to the public understanding and support on which their policy in the last analysis rests. Perhaps 90 percent of the time, therefore, the reporter is an opportunity for the State Department, not a problem, though the tendency is to treat the reporter as a problem most of the time.

It is a fact of some importance, I think, that a reporter for a responsible newspaper like the New York *Times* gets more reliable factual guidance on international issues from the representatives of every other major Western country than his own.

There cannot be an adequate system of explaining foreign policy if there is a lack of confidence between officials and reporters at the Department of State, and this confidence does not exist. The negotiations which led to the ending of the Berlin blockade came directly as a result of the enterprise of a reporter's questions to Premier Stalin. Yet when that reporter (Kingsbury Smith of the INS) sent his questions to the Kremlin, the reaction at the State Department was that his questions were an annoyance, an invasion of the province of diplomacy, and an instrument of Soviet propaganda. In the long run, Smith's questions led to the Jessup-Malik conversations, and when reporters sought to check reports that these conversations were proceeding, they were not only evaded (which was all right in the circumstances), but they were misled by a series of half-truths and worse.

Let me emphasize a point here: Reporters have a tendency to wail about the barriers placed before them by officials. Our job is to get all the facts the people need to reach correct judgments and we would be deceiving ourselves if we thought that anybody cares very much about the problems of newspapermen except other newspapermen.

The question of whether these major questions of foreign policy are fairly and adequately explained to the American people, however, goes far beyond the problems of reporters. It is a question which affects the understanding and support of American policy, and I take it this is a fairly wide and important subject.

The problem at the State Department is not that there is a conscious conspiracy to conceal or mislead, though that happens more often than is necessary. There is, however, nobody working directly and intimately with the Secretary of State who knows the needs of newspapers, the strengths and weaknesses of newspapers, or what to expect from newspapers when information is concealed or disclosed. There is nobody in that position who can look over the vast flow of information coming into the Department and define accurately and fairly what part of the information properly falls within the ten percent that has to be concealed and the 90 percent that can be disclosed, to the benefit of the Department and the public.

On routine questions of getting out texts of speeches and communiques, the system at State works all right. The difficulty is that the system of explanation—which is what we are talking about—always breaks down at the most critical time. When things are going along in a routine way, which isn't often these days, officials who know what is happening are available to reporters. But when the big story breaks, the officials you want are almost always tied up on policy matters and very properly cannot take time out in the crisis to explain sensitive questions to reporters. This does not solve the problem, however, for at such times the officials who are available to the reporters do not know what's going on, and those who do know what's going on are not available. Therefore, for lack of a well-informed officer dealing with reporters at such times, the reporters either write inadequate or misleading stories, or if they are wise, get their information from reliable officials of other governments.

The State Department has spent a great deal of time studying the technical problems involved in transmitting information abroad. This is important but it is secondary. The primary problem is not how to transmit information abroad, but what information you transmit at home and abroad. It is the old question of form and substance. The substance is the important thing, for unless you get the substance right, a good transmission system will probably do the nation more harm than a bad transmission system. After all the Voice of America is the President of the United States and all the myriad voices beneath him; it is not merely a radio station.

THE WHITE HOUSE AS A NEWS SOURCE

—A. Merriman Smith, *Thank You, Mr. President,* Harper & Brothers, 1946, pp. 1–3, 8–9, 15–18, 29. Mr. Smith for many years was the chief White House correspondent of United Press.

THE MOST DIRECT channel of communication, the most frequently used line between the President of the United States and the public is the White House correspondent.

Our Chief Executives do not always like the idea, but the American citizen has a direct property right in the Presidency. And it is the reporter assigned to the White House who keeps the people up to date on what and how their property is doing. . . .

There are two varieties of White House reporters. The group I am writing about is small—no more than a dozen. They are assigned to the White House as a day-long, full-time job. They spend eight to ten hours a day in their own White House quarters and are classed practically as members of the White House family, although they are employed and paid by their individual news organizations.

The other group consists of the remaining bulk of the Washington news corps—the men and women who come to the White House usually on Presidential press conference days only, or when there is news breaking at 1600 Pennsylvania Avenue of world-shaking importance.

One never knows in this business, but at this writing I am the White House correspondent for the United Press, one of the three major press associations.

The United Press, the Associated Press and International News Service keep men at the White House each moment the President is working. Between these three organizations they serve directly or indirectly every daily newspaper and radio station on earth. . . .

The White House reporters have an inner clique described as "the regulars." These are the men whose full-time job is reporting the activities of the President and they are on the job in close proximity to the Chief Executive regardless of whether he is in the White House or in Honolulu. The travel with him and serve as the eyes of the world staring coldly at everything he does and telling all about it a few minutes later. . . .

On an average day, the White House closes shop by 6 P.M. or a little after. Negro messengers pass the word from office to office, "He's gone over." Which means the President has left his office and gone to his residential quarters in the White House proper. This word is the signal for most everybody to start for home. The final word to the reporters comes when a press attaché advises "the lid is on."

There is, however, nothing tight about the "lid" at the White House. It can pop off at the most inopportune moments. At two or three in the morning. Or fifteen minutes after you have assured your office that everything is locked up, so it is quite safe for you to go to a cocktail party. When there is hot news, the White House usually puts it out right away. That is, within fifteen or twenty minutes after the news agency and other major radio and newspaper offices have been advised that something big is on its way.

Being a White House correspondent for a wire service is rather like being a doctor when it comes to telephone calls in the middle of the night or hurried trips to town.

Newspaper editors the world over seemingly cherish the idea that when information is unavailable on any given subject at any other source, that puts it up to the White House. These inquiries teletyped from various parts of the nation into our Washington office are telephoned to me and I'm supposed to do something about it.

I only wish some night telegraph editor in Metropolis, U.S.A., who suddenly wonders whether his town is going to get a new sewage disposal plant, could suffer the pleasure of rousing a White House press secretary out of bed at two in the morning with such an inquiry. . . .

One of the most singularly American events at the White House each week is the President's press conference. These meetings between reporters and the Chief Executive have all the qualities of a high school track meet, bear baiting and the third degree administered by heavy-handed plain-clothes men. . . .

The conferences are held in the President's circular office, the reporters standing and filling the room wall to wall. There are no holds barred as far as questions are concerned. The President's answers may not be quoted directly without specific permission from the President. And this permission is given only infrequently for part of a sentence, or just a few words.

When the President speaks for "background only," what he says may be printed or broadcast, but not attributed to him. This is a troublesome classification and few ever understand it clearly. Consequently, it is rarely employed.

"Off the record" means that the President is speaking confidentially and his words must not be publicized in any way. For the most part, what the President says off-record isn't very important. Usually he is explaining why he can't answer a certain question or he is telling about advance plans which for some reason he wants withheld from publication for the present.

Reporters gather in the White House lobby fifteen to thirty minutes before the conference to discuss the news probabilities of the day. At the appointed time, they file into the President's office, showing their passes to watchful Secret Service men and White House police as they enter.

The front row along the President's desk usually is occupied by the working regulars—the men who will do most of the questioning—and most of the writing. They represent the wire services, metropolitan newspapers and the radio networks. There are no assigned places, but rather an understanding by the correspondents that the men who will have to do most of the work should have the best working space.

The conference begins when either Harold Beckley of the Senate press gallery, or Bill Donaldson of the House gallery, shouts "all in" from the rear of the room.

The President makes what formal announcements he has prepared, then says, "That's about all I have today." Then comes the most heard-about part of the conference—the questioning.

Some Presidents in the past, notably Hoover, required written questions to be submitted in advance. There was no questioning from the floor. And in this manner, if a President wished to dodge an embarrassing question, he just ignored it.

But such was not the case with Mr. Roosevelt who really built the press conference into the popular government instrument that it is today. Nor is it the case with Mr. Truman who'll field any ball thrown at him, curve or otherwise.

The reporters can question the President as long as they please. It is their decision when the conference shall end. The questioning actually closes and the meeting is over when the senior wire service man on the White House assignment decides that the reporters have exhausted the news possibilities for that day and says, "Thank you, Mr. President."

The wire service men and some of the radio representatives then break into a mad, scrambling dash to get out of the President's office, through the office of his appointment secretary, then the big lobby and into the press room where wait the hungry telephones.

Newcomers find this reckless race hard to justify. New men assigned to the White House invariably say, "Why can't we take just a little more time to look over our notes and get our facts straight?"

Truth of the matter is that a reporter who has to handle a Presidential news conference on a spot, immediate basis has to keep his notes straight in his mind and get his facts straight in the twenty or thirty seconds he spends getting to his telephone.

When there is a red-hot story in the conference, the wire service men usually are dictating to their offices well within thirty seconds after the "thank you." . . .

The next President—the Republicans and Democrats have different ideas about who he will be or when he will come along—will find it extremely difficult to discard the press conference system. There's no parliament in this country, and the Congress never has an opportunity to question the head of state publicly.

Thus the job is left up to a lot of reporters who take their job seriously—much too seriously on occasion.

Mr. Roosevelt really made the Presidential press conference what it is today—a third degree in white-hot light.

(Uniformly, the White House reporters exercise good taste. They have innumerable chances to trap a President in the political morass of incongruity. But they never do it to his face.)

Mr. Truman wisely elected to go along with the Roosevelt plan. The reading public, the editors and the reporters like the idea.

But should there come some day to the White House a President who thinks he can drop press conferences—well, he's President and he can do pretty much what he wants. But what a skull beating he's in for! His honeymoon will last exactly up to the time he says "No press conference," or "Please submit written questions."

THE DEPARTMENT OF AGRICULTURE

—T. Swann Harding, "Informational Techniques of the Department of Agriculture," *The Public Opinion Quarterly,* School of Public and International Affairs, Princeton University, Vol. 1, January 1937, pp. 84–86, 88–89. Mr. Harding is a veteran government public relations official.

THE ANNUAL REPORT of the Director of Information of the Department of Agriculture, dated September 19, 1936, begins with the following words:

> Information work in the department reflects all its activities, both in research and service, and in the application of old and new principles and policies to farm and other national problems. It is efficient in proportion to the effectiveness which it carries to the farmers, and to other interested groups, a correctly balanced, readily comprehensible, and adequate body of usable knowledge. Needless to say, this ideal of balance, quantity, and utility can only be approximated. New problems sometimes get more than their due share of attention. Sometimes the available facilities do not suffice to carry and properly distribute all the information that agriculture and industry require. Sometimes the complexity of the subject matter baffles the skill of the interpreter and the facts therefore fail to reach their goal in the public consciousness. It may fairly be claimed, however, that the department's informational work meets these complex requirements more adequately today than ever before, and provides means for putting agricultural science into practice along an ever-widening front.

This paragraph is pregnant with meaning, especially for those who may regard the information work of a Federal government department as necessarily publicity or propaganda, using the words in their more invidious connotations, that is, as practically synonymous with ballyhoo. The organic act founding the Department of Agriculture bade it not only discover and collate agricultural knowledge, in the broadest possible sense, but also disseminate that information. . . .

First, foremost, and all the time the information given out by the Department must be authoritative. Both the Department and the Office of Information, of course, have a frame of reference provided by an imperfect political government and a very fallible economic system. For that reason alone, their work will be imperfect, at times even illogical. It would take the broadest kind of planning on an entirely new basis to make a thoroughly logical and scientifically planned informational program operate at 100 percent efficiency, and then, queer beings that we are, we should probably be dissatisfied with it.

But somewhere there must be a final authority on scientific questions in the field of agriculture; somewhere the stream of basic knowledge must be kept pure and undefiled; somewhere there must be plant pathologists, animal specialists, agronomists, and horticulturists who know what they are talking about when they make public statements. The Department must, in its information service, be exact, objective, critical, and detached, even if this seems to make it slow and ponderous as well. It must not make too much haste. It cannot afford to be in error. Its reputation for authority entails heavy responsibility.

Next in importance after accuracy is the necessity for putting facts in the most comprehensible and usable form, and for placing those facts in the hands of those who can make use of them. Every mechanical agency must be called upon to accomplish this—the press, the mimeograph and multigraph machines, the motion picture, the radio. The information must not be emitted in isolated, uncorrelated stabs of fact. It should be related to a general subject. The present trend is to organize the information on a commodity basis.

A commercial publicity agency has a very different duty to perform. A private advertising or propaganda campaign may spend a great deal merely in attracting attention, bringing specific needs to the minds of the public, or even in inventing needs and then offering to fill them. It is not at all unusual for a private concern to spend a million dollars annually in radio advertising for a single product. But the entire informational work of the Department of Agriculture must be financed at about the same cost. Again, though publicity costs in industrial production are usually rated at 5 per cent of the budget, the entire cost of printing all forms, all publications, bulletins, and mimeographs, of buying all machines needed, of distributing this material, and of paying the salaries of editors, writers, and others amounts to less than 1 per cent of the annual budget of the Department of Agriculture.

It is true that in such work as forest-fire prevention the Department has to adopt the attention-attracting technique; the same is true in preventing soil-erosion. But in general the Department is engaged merely in the conveyance of facts to an already interested public. That this public is already interested is indicated by the fact that Department publications are today distributed on a request basis to the extent of 95 per cent. The annual report of the Director of Information for 1929 says:

> But the Office of Information is in no wise a publicity agency in the usual sense of that term. Its purpose is not to acquire prestige for itself or for the Department as a whole, not to "sell" the Department to the public or to advertise the achievements of Department workers, but to make public the results of the Department's manifold activities.

Naturally there is always present the human tendency to break over into an effort to attract attention, but the counter tendency to curb this is also present. These two forces are in chronic conflict, their balance depending on economic and other conditions. But when so great a program must be financed on so little, constant care must be exercised to make the money go far. This is a tremendous job. The Department is required to do more than issue bald announcements of the results of its research in press releases; it must interpret these new developments in their natural scientific context and show their practical utility. . . .

The report for 1935 announced the following activities of the Division of Publications: 220,113 photographic jobs completed wtih drafting work on 2,506; 3,876 printing requisitions drawn for various types of printing for the Department proper, and 2,171 for the Agricultural Adjustment Administration; $2,726.10 received in 17,654 letters requesting publications; 6,522 visitors given 35,315 copies of publications; 510,950 letters handled in the Distribution Section alone; 197,-383 copies of publications sent abroad; 111,167,608 pages of duplicating work done. Approximately 2,450 press releases were sent out this same year. The National Farm and Home Hour was being broadcast by fifty-six stations, and the Western Farm and Home Hour went out over ten stations.

The report for 1936 records that 22,375,132 copies of publications were distributed during the fiscal year covered; 1,466 manuscripts of a scientific, technical, and popular nature were submitted for publication; the output of photographic items numbered 243,976; 79,719,532 pages of mimeographed, 26,642,450 of multigraphed, and 19,054,896 of multilithed material were issued. The output of mimeographed press releases for this year, the last for which records exist to date, was 1,316, not including 716 items distributed for the Agricultural Adjustment Administration, and 30 special statements not mimeographed. The Weekly Clip Sheet was coming into wider usage and increasing editorial recognition was accorded it. . . .

Adverse critics are prone to overlook the fact that this service is given in response to a demand. Very often 3,000 requests for data reach the Office of Information in a single day, and this does not include the hundreds of letters sent directly to the bureaus of the department and handled by their own information sections. The annual report of the Office of Information for 1932 carried a section under the subhead "Millions Request Facts from the Department" and it stated nothing less than the truth.

The availability of free publications is no longer mentioned by the department either in radio or press releases. Yet a million requests for publications come in per month. The report for 1935 noted a further increase in subject-matter requests requiring special replies. Agricultural changes were taking place rapidly, and thousands of families wanted comprehensive, detailed, and perhaps unavailable information. Letters began to come requesting special compilations of statistics, explanations of the economic bases of programs undertaken; advice about locating a particular type of farm in a particular locality, or regarding procedure in obtaining loans, producing poultry or vegetable crops, or supplementing cash income by home production of fruits and vegetables. Such letters merit careful replies and are, of course, far more expensive per unit than bulletins.

"SELLING" GOVERNMENT SERVICES TO THE PUBLIC

—Stanley High, "You Can't Beat the Government," *The Saturday Evening Post,* Vol. 210, November 20, 1937, p. 34. Mr. High has written and lectured extensively on international, national, and religious affairs.

In 1935 . . . Congress passed the Social Security Act, and John G. Winant, former Republican governor of New Hampshire, was made chairman of the board. Governor Winant, so inarticulate himself that his press conferences were complete failures and had to be abandoned, recognized that the first task of his board was in the field of salesmanship. The Social Security Act was and would continue to be so much paper until some way was found to persuade the 26,000,000 people who were eligible for its benefits to register voluntarily. Tipped off by Harry Hopkins, Winant went to New York, called on

Louis Resnick, who was director of publicity and education for the Welfare Council of New York City, and put the job up to him. Resnick, a young man, trained in the newspaper business, but with a remarkable flair for organization, took a $2,000 cut in salary and came to Washington. That was the first of January 1936. While the members of the board twirled their thumbs or sought to ward off the attacks of their critics, Resnick got together a Washington staff of thirty-three, set up twelve regional offices and launched a drive to get the necessary data from 26,000,000 people who knew little about the act, and that little generally unfavorable. By the first of the following January, the last card of the 26,000,000 was in and the board began to function.

Resnick employed all the methods known to the science of persuasion and cajolery. For the weeks prior to and during the big push in November and December of last year [1936] some 1,200 newspapers carried a daily question-and-answer column on the Social Security Act. A series of special articles and a routine daily news release supplemented this service. The aid of the WPA was enlisted. WPA artists were assigned to the job and a succession of social-security posters were painted. Three million, three hundred thousand of these posters were distributed. Three three-minute social security newsreels were made. The three of them were shown in 12,000 moving-picture theaters to an estimated audience of 50,000,000 for each picture. From July 1936 through June 1937 programs for and proponents of the Social Security Act were on the air 3,952 times. Some 400 individual radio stations were and are still being furnished with the 225 electrical transcriptions produced to date by Resnick's organization.

Four long articles on old-age benefits were written for 1,000 foreign-language newspapers and translated, not by the papers but by the government, into twenty different languages, from Yiddish to Chinese.

By this amazing campaign Resnick got his 26,000,000 people on the dotted line. But, as he will readily admit, he did much more than that. He sold the Social Security Act, and, inevitably, the Roosevelt administration, which sponsored it. His newspaper columns were not explanations of, they were arguments for, the Social Security Act. His motion pictures and radio recordings not only told the public what to do, but made it plain what benefits would flow from doing it. His posters, with the United States Capitol in the background and a government check in the foreground, announce: A Monthly Check to You for the Rest of Your Life; or Three Steps to Security in Your Old Age; or Join the March to Old Age Security. That, obviously, is not merely the phraseology of explanation. It is the phraseology of salesmanship.

It is small wonder, in the face of such a drive, that John D. M. Hamilton's last-minute pay-envelope campaign against Mr. Roosevelt was a dud.[1] John Hamilton, whatever the merits of his case, was no match for Louis Resnick plus the government of the United States. . . .

It is possible that the politicians likewise look with relish upon the work of the public relations division of the Federal Housing Administration. The FHA has no such mass mobilization to its credit as the Social Security Board, although its assistance to 1,500,000 home owners in the repair and modernization of their homes is not to be passed over lightly. . . .

The public relations division of the FHA is concerned almost exclusively with the stimulation of more and better home building. Until recently, it had some thirty writers on its staff. At present, in the Washington office, there are probably not more than a dozen. But that modest staff is no measure of its activities.

For one thing, it serves the real estate editors of the country's newspapers. Nearly 2,000 daily papers, 4,900 weeklies and 682 foreign-language publications get its weekly clip sheet. It is sent, however, only on request and every six months a poll is taken as to its usefulness. Papers which do not reply are cut off the list.

The clip sheet is filled with almost everything that might be usable in the real-estate section of a newspaper, from plans for low-priced houses to suggestions for the proper ventilation of attics. Stimulated by this service, some 2,434 publications—most of them newspapers—have run real-estate editions, which are calculated to have produced, to date, some $8,000,000 in advertising revenue. The division also conducts a service for advertising managers designed to aid them in increasing their building and real-estate accounts, and turns out frequent special technical bulletins, some of which have an enormous circulation.

[1] Mr. High refers to one of the activities carried out by Mr. Hamilton, who was chairman of the Republican National Committee, in supporting the candidacy of Mr. Alfred M. Landon in the 1936 national election.—The Editors.

But there is more to the FHA selling program than its printed documents and newspaper releases. Like the Social Security Board, it has gone in, even more extensively, for movies and the radio. More than 500 of the nation's 700 radio stations are using, each week, its recorded programs. It has produced Better Housing News Flashes, a series of ten six-minute motion pictures. These pictures have had a combined total of 361,000 showings in commercial theaters to an estimated audience of 97,000,000 people. The recorded radio programs have cost the housing authority $7,000; the moving pictures, $40,000. For both recordings and movies, the demand exceeds the supply.

And the FHA, like all the other New Deal agencies, has gone on what is probably the wholly accurate assumption that its success depends not only upon the extent to which its program is understood but upon the degree to which it is popularly supported. It, too, has done a work of conversion as well as of explanation. . . .

REVIEW QUESTIONS AND ASSIGNMENTS

1. If you were a member of the House of Representatives what position would you take on publicity issued by administrative departments?

2. What connection do you see between the newer functions of government and the increase in government publicity?

3. Do you believe that the newspaper reader would resent it if his newspaper made frank use of stories issued by the various departments of the Federal and state governments?

4. Clip out all of the stories in one issue of your newspaper that you believe originated from the press services of federal and state departments, and comment on the connection between their subject matter and the general welfare.

5. What distinctions do you see between news stories issued by the Department of Agriculture and news stories issued by the Pennsylvania Railroad?

6. Would you be willing to support a proposal to set up a central agency at Washington that would funnel all administrative news releases to capital correspondents?

7. Consult the annual reports of four or five government departments and chart the publicity activities.

8. What lessons about government publicity, if any, did we learn from our experiences in World War II?

9. What is your attitude toward the "Voice of America" program of the U.S. Department of State?

10. Do you approve or disapprove of the efforts of some state editorial associations to set up rigid bans on all publicity releases, including those of the government?

11. The editor of your local newspaper can supply you with an armful of government publicity releases if you call him and ask him to save them. A survey of such stories should prove profitable.

12. Would you favor or disfavor the use by government agencies of paid advertising to defend policies, rulings, and orders?

13. Discuss the proposal that the government should issue a weekly magazine that would outline its current activities in popular fashion.

14. What conflicts do you see between the traditional methods of news presentation and government issuing of information? Can you suggest any solutions?

ADDITIONAL REFERENCES

Baker, Gladys, *The County Agent,* University of Chicago Press, 1939.

Bendiner, Robert, *The Riddle of the State Department,* Farrar & Rinehart, 1942.

Bent, Silas, *Ballyhoo: The Voice of the Press,* Liveright, 1927.

Catton, Bruce, *War Lords of Washington,* Harcourt, Brace, 1948.

Childs, H. L. (editor), *Propaganda and Dictatorship,* Princeton University Press, 1936.

Corbin, C. R., *Why News Is News,* Ronald Press, 1938.

Crawford, N. A., *The Ethics of Journalism,* Alfred A. Knopf, 1934.

Creel, George, *How We Advertised America,* Harper & Brothers, 1920.

Dewey, John, *The Public and Its Problems,* Henry Holt, 1927.

Essary, J. Frederick, *Covering Washington,* Houghton Mifflin, 1927.

Flint, L. N., *The Conscience of the Newspaper,* Appleton-Century, 1925.

Hulen, Bertram D., *Inside the Department of State,* McGraw-Hill, 1939.

Hyman, Herbert, and Paul Sheatsley, "Some Reasons Why Information Campaigns Fail," *Public Opinion Quarterly,* Vol. 11, 1947, pp. 412–423.

Kent, Frank R., *The Great Game of Politics,* Doubleday, Doran, 1923.

Kiplinger, W. M., *Washington Is Like That,* Harper & Brothers, 1942.

Larson, Cedric, "How Much Federal Publicity Is There?" *Public Opinion Quarterly,* Vol. 2, October 1938, pp. 636–644.

Lasswell, H. D., *Propaganda Technique in the World War,* Alfred A. Knopf, 1927.

Lippmann, Walter, *Public Opinion,* Macmillan, 1922.

Loftus, Joseph, "The Reporter and the 'Information Man,'" *Nieman Reports,* Vol. 2, January 1948, pp. 7–8.

Lowell, A. T., *Public Opinion and Popular Government,* Longmans, Green, 1902.

Lumley, F. E., *The Propaganda Menace*, Appleton-Century, 1930.

McCamy, James L., *Government Publicity*, University of Chicago Press, 1939.

———, "Variety in the Growth of Federal Publicity," *Public Opinion Quarterly*, Vol. 3, April 1939, pp. 285–292.

McMillan, George E., "Government Publicity and the Impact of War," *Public Opinion Quarterly*, Vol. 3, April 1939, pp. 285–292.

Mercey, Arch A., "Modernizing Federal Publicity," *Public Opinion Quarterly*, Vol. 1, July 1937, pp. 87–94.

Merritt, Leroy C., *The United States Government as Publisher*, University of Chicago Press, 1943.

Michael, George, *Handout*, G. P. Putnam's Sons, 1935.

Odegard, Peter, *The American Public Mind*, Columbia University Press, 1930.

Pollard, James E., *The Presidents and the Press*, Macmillan, 1947.

Rogers, Lindsay, "President Roosevelt's Press Conferences," *Political Quarterly*, Vol. 9, July 1938, pp. 360–372.

Smith, A. Merriman, *A President Is Many Men*, Harper & Brothers, 1948.

Stoke, Harold W., "Executive Leadership and the Growth of Propaganda," *American Political Science Review*, Vol. 35, June 1941, pp. 490–500.

22. LOCAL INFLUENCES AFFECTING THE PRESS

INTRODUCTION

That a newspaper is not edited and published in a social vacuum is obvious enough, and that it is molded by the environment in which it is printed is also clear. But just how and to what extent the editors of country weeklies and small-city and metropolitan dailies are affected by local influences in their decision to print or not to print is a matter that is not easy to set forth in general terms. The influence of advertisers and pressure groups has been much discussed, but influences other than these are constantly at work, and they affect the choice of material for news and editorial columns.

Editors vary greatly in their sense of responsibility to society, and in other ethical concepts to which they hold. With the best of conscience editors may take opposite views on the advisability of printing a particular piece of news. For instance, one editor may feel in conscience bound to print the name and actions of a juvenile delinquent, while another editor would feel that he was best serving the interests of the community by printing the facts but withholding the name. In a small town many an editor would withhold both name and facts. There are no clearcut rules by which the editor and reporter may proceed and no units of measurement at hand by which he may gauge the possible effect of a piece of news upon his public. It is true that any well-trained editorial worker can recognize news when he meets it, but it is not true that he can as readily decide whether that bit of news should be printed or withheld. In the end the best-intentioned editor must use his own intuitive judgment upon the matter, and the results often will live to shame him.

Greatest among the local factors influencing choice of news, and one often overlooked by press critics, is the reader for whom the news is edited. The reader is moved by prejudices, antagonisms, and hatreds. He desires to hear his friends, his party, and his own principles praised, and he dislikes to have them attacked. In fact, he is inclined to distrust the paper that doesn't think as he thinks, and he is very likely to refuse to subscribe to it if he can get another. Every newspaperman knows this fact, and trims his stories accordingly. One newspaper is sensational because it tries to appeal to those who like sensational news, and another in the same city is conservative because it attempts to reach those readers whose principles are conservative. The Republican newspaper often caters to Republican ideals, the Democratic paper to the Democratic ideals. The student of the press can see the same catering of newspapers to their readers in greater or lesser degree in countless instances at other times and places.

Most of the selections in this chapter deal with the influence of the reader upon his own newspaper. Pressure groups, which often are local, are discussed elsewhere. The influence of advertisers, likewise, has been cited earlier. In one of the first efforts to measure the relative amounts of control exercised by various groups over local news Swanson has obtained opinions from a city newspaper staff. This citation presents only the opinions of the staff, and inferences should not be made beyond the limited data. Nevertheless these opinions are significant, and they point the way to further similar studies.

Allen enumerates some typical examples of direct pressure groups upon editors, though no indication of the relative weight of such pressure is made. In a judicious analysis Bailey suggests some other aspects of reader influence—how the staffs attempt to guess what readers would like to read in order to supply that desire. How the editor may buck the reader's interest in a limited number of fields concurrently, is explained by Hocking. Too much conflict with the reader's interests leads to rejection by the reader, according to this writer.

Ernst implies that the limited finances of the weekly editor leave him open to the pressure to use free publicity from various concerns. This has been a favorite theme for press critics for many years. The interested student should check other printed sources to see how important this influence is today. In the final citation Johnson states what every editor knows—that the reader is the final censor of what goes into the paper he reads.

CONTROL OF LOCAL NEWS

—Charles E. Swanson, "Midcity Daily: The News Staff and Its Relation to Control," *Journalism Quarterly*, Vol. 26, March 1949, pp. 20, 23–24.

Most American cities have one or more daily newspapers owned by one owner or owning group and edited by the owner and his employees. This pattern has raised a cry of "press monopoly" with its connotation that the power of the owner results in absolute control over the decisions to print or not to print the news.

At least, social conflict over "press monopoly" emphasizes that control of mass media has become "one of the principal sources of political, economic, and social power" in a democratic society.[1] To treat this issue as a problem, control analysis—a branch of the science of communications—requires field studies and data on one-newspaper cities. Thus, the scientist may observe the relative power of owner, employee, and community group in the control of such newspapers and analyze the relations of control to content and effects of these media.

To investigate this general problem of control of a newspaper and its effects in a one-newspaper city, the operations of a daily newspaper were observed from October 1946 to May 1948. This article will describe the social characteristics of the editing-writing group, its values and appraisal of the newspaper, and its relative control, if any, over the power to print.

Twenty-five members of the group (of sub-editors and reporters) completed an anonymous questionnaire with 125 items. This comprised quantitative data on their appraisal of the newspaper and their opinions on its control.

Those individuals and groups in Midcity "whose interests are most important" in deciding "what local news goes in and what stays out of the paper" were ranked in 1-2-3 order. The rankings were weighted in inverse order; a rating of 1 was weighted 10 and so on. Results are shown in Table I.

TABLE I

THOSE WITH MOST POWER OVER LOCAL NEWS

Position	*Weighted Score*	*Individual or Group*
1.	149	Managing editor
2.	97	City editor
3.	73	Editor
4.	70	Residents of city
5.	68	Publisher
6.	55	Advertisers
7.	44	Your personal views
8.	38	Business manager

[1] Louis Wirth, "Concensus and Mass Communication," *American Sociological Review*, Vol. 13, 1948, pp. 1–15.

TABLE 1 (*Continued*)

Position	*Weighted Score*	*Individual or Group*
9.	27	Chamber of Commerce
10.	23	Local businessmen
11.	10	Churches
12.	10	"Business office"
13.	10	"Space" (available in newspaper)
14.	7	Labor unions

These rankings showed the group's opinion that it held most of the control over what local news to print or not to print. It shared this power with the city's residents, the publisher, and the business group. It rated the business group (businessmen, Chamber of Commerce, and advertisers) as the only group of significance outside the newspaper in degree of power over what the *Daily* printed.

However, the staff agreed unanimously that directions never had been given to "slant news without regard for the facts and according to this newspaper's policy."

Eight staff members gave instances where the *Daily* had opposed interests of a "pressure group"—the American Legion, bankers, Republican politicians, state officials, and "big taxpayers." However, one said the newspaper had opposed the "public interest" in its stand on housing.

PRESSURE FROM SUBSCRIBERS

—Eric W. Allen, "The Newspaper and Community Leadership," *The Press in the Contemporary Scene, The Annals of the American Academy of Political and Social Science,* Vol. 219, January 1942, pp. 25–26.

AS THE editor-publisher sits at his desk, hoping to find time to do a little writing, he is interrupted. His anteroom is filling; persons and delegations are waiting. Everybody wants something. Nobody is quite satisfied with the world as it is. All have ideas as to what tomorrow's paper, next week's papers, should do about it, and are hoping to get the editor to fall in line. They are not thirsting to satisfy literary tastes; they are democratic statesmen at the grass roots; they think in terms of action; they want the public mind conditioned so that actual results will follow. The editor's bulky mail is largely in the same spirit.

This visitor wants Monroe Street extended to the waterfront; that one wishes to attack a building ordinance that forbids what seems to him a reasonable structure; another is scandalized by something radical said by a teacher at the Irving School; here is a delegation of farmers inconvenienced by a soil-conservation project; next is a banker and advertiser, a good friend but angry, decrying yesterday's editorial on the branch-banking bill; now a soil-conservation expert from Washington to explain how rapidly the county's soil is seeping away and how urgently something needs to be done; then a pair of labor leaders pointing out a small inaccuracy in yesterday's report of the Iron Works strike, maintaining that it was intentional and important, and demanding a lengthy correction.

This is but the beginning of the day's callers. One by one they come, hour after hour, day after day. Fathers of drafted boys, clergymen, generals in the army, utopian uplifters, sordid self-seekers, politicians, dreamers, certified public accountants, aesthetes, careerists, agitators, Townsend Planners, educational reformers, tax spenders, tax resisters, tax evaders,—these and many others all feel that what is printed will help or hurt a favorite cause, and all bring to bear on the newspaper varying amounts of suggestions and advice, influence or dangerous pressure.

Obviously, tact, experience, and courage are required to reply with a modified "no" to most of the proposals made, and to end the day with the paper, a little more strongly independent, a little better entrenched in public respect—that is, a little more influential—than it was in the morning. This portrait of the editor-publisher is plainly not that of a knight errant hunting for more combats to enter.

Editors, like other people, vary. Here and there is one who has no desire whatever for "social control," who would be happy if he could stay out of all controversies—sit on the side lines, completely uninvolved, and merely describe the battles, the angers, the victories, and the defeats of others so interestingly, so accurately, so fairly, that all concerned would exclaim "How true!" Others respond strongly when they see Good engaged in a precarious struggle with (what seems to them to be) Evil, and they delight to seize a weapon and lend a helping hand.

These two attitudes exemplify two divergent, more or less irreconcilable, ideals of journalism; the hard part of editing is to succeed in both without doing harm to either. The more thoughtful and conscientious editors have been seeking the answer to this problem for generations. Notable progress has been made, but the end is not yet. Perhaps there is no complete answer. Few students of the newspaper would wish either of the two conflicting ideals of journalism to be completely abandoned.

READERS TO BLAME FOR NEWSPAPER FAULTS

—Thomas A. Bailey, *The Man in the Street,* pp. 316–317. Copyright 1948 by Mr. Bailey. Used with the permission of The Macmillan Company. Mr. Bailey, a voluminous writer, is professor of history at Stanford University.

IF A PEOPLE get no better government than they deserve, it is no less true that the subscribers get no better newspapers than they deserve. As Oscar Wilde put it: "Modern journalism justifies its own existence by the great Darwinian principle of the survival of the vulgarest." If the masses did not want vulgar newspapers, the alert publisher, ever keen for profits, would provide something better.

In this so-called freest of free countries, we have a crippling self-imposed censorship of the press. The newspaper does not have space to publish more than a small part of the mountain of material that comes in over the teletypes, and the tendency is to eliminate all except what the Almighty Reader wants, or what the editor thinks he wants. Broadly speaking, the subscriber does not want the truth, but a concoction liberally seasoned with his own bias. The radical wants radical material; the liberal, liberal; the conservative, conservative. "Your favorite newspaper," as Bruce Bliven has said, "is your favorite quite as much because of the things it leaves out as those it prints."

The mass of semiliterates, upon which the Hearst journals and the Patterson-McCormick "newspaper axis" feed, is the greatest barrier to a good press, as it is to good government and a sound foreign policy. Newspaper editors have learned to their cost that nothing is gained by getting out too far in advance of herd thinking; they merely antagonize or bore readers and lose revenue. They have learned, as the *Reader's Digest* has learned, that the people do not want problems over which to puzzle their tired heads; they demand interesting and bizarre facts, but nothing that involves a prolonged consideration of causal relationships.

One unhappy by-product of popular education has been the overthrow, with a few notable exceptions, of the sober newspaper aimed at the upper or middle classes. This has been true in England as well as in America, and one can regret that the press escaped the domination of government in the seventeenth and eighteenth centuries only to fall under the domination of the masses in the nineteenth and twentieth. What good does it do to teach the people to read if they demand only comics, murders, sex scandals, and sports, with a consequent debasement of sound journalism? To argue that the subscribers are seduced into reading sound information by these allurements is to argue that vice is the way to virtue.

Newspaper publishing is a business, but the publisher who sells newspapers clearly has a higher social responsibility than the grocer who sells potatoes. The editor won freedom of the press so that he might champion the rights of the people, and if he abuses his dearly-won privileges, the people may impose trammels upon him. With newspapers becoming fewer and bigger, the press is partaking more and more of the nature of a monopoly, and hence a public utility. Those who do not operate quasi-public utilities in the public interest merely speed the day of regulation.

Yet, in the last analysis, the defects of the newspaper are in large measure attributable to the reader, for the editors, like other businessmen, aim to please the customer. The alleged faults of the press are not so much the faults of the press as of democracy itself. As we raise the educational and critical level of the people, we may confidently expect journalistic standards to rise correspondingly. But this is a slow and painful process. An ignorant and indifferent citizenry is not the stuff out of which to make good journalism, a workable democracy, or a far-visioned foreign policy.

THE PUBLIC AFFECTS EDITOR'S CAMPAIGNS

—William Ernest Hocking, *Freedom of the Press,* University of Chicago Press, 1947, pp. 140–141. Mr. Hocking is professor of philosophy, emeritus, of Harvard University, and was a member of the Commission on Freedom of the Press.

SINCE THE SUBSCRIBERS must be free not to subscribe, and supporters not to support, certain financial pressures upon unwelcome opinions are a normal part of the operation of social judgment. There can be no social presumption that morally courageous newssheets must survive, even if they are also mentally competent. Public irritability, stupidity, and intolerance have cost society many an important idea and will continue to do so until the social principle "no irrelevant penalties" has become a habit. The survival of an independent press in a highly opinionated and impatient society follows no law different from that of any individual commentator: if his judgment commends itself to the public in three points, he may buck the current in the fourth without being rejected; but the public will not allow him to oppose it on all points at once, nor yet to confine himself to a single point, however valuable, on which he exclusively harps. If he disobeys these precepts of pedagogy, the public will slay him, no matter what his merits; both will be the losers, and there is no actionable offense on either side. It is only when financial pressure has the deliberate aim of compelling a speaker or editor to conform in his views *while continuing to speak* that crime occurs. When speaker or editor yields to that pressure, there is a double crime which journalism should join with law and the moral sense of the public to make disreputable.

ECONOMIC CONTROL OF THE WEEKLY

—Morris L. Ernst, *The First Freedom,* pp. 105–107. Copyright 1946 by Mr. Ernst. Used with the permission of The Macmillan Company.

THE ECONOMIC PROBLEM of weekly publishers is generally the problem of small business enterprise. About half the total number of weeklies are run by single families, with perhaps one extra employee. Usually a paper of this type has one linotype machine and a second-hand press. The main source of revenue is a job-printing business—in fact, many weekly newspapers were started as sideliners by job printers who had set up their own printshops. These papers are not expected to be distinguished by their high standards and often reveal their more or less casual production. But they are the product of the people of the community. At the very least they are the training schools and educators of many of our best newsmen.

The better type of weekly is run very much like a small daily, in respect to organization, personnel and equipment. This kind of paper has little or no job-printing, and employs from five to eight persons. From three to five men make up the mechanical staff. The editor, with two or three others, handles the editorial and business offices. Generally the paper circulates to the same public as the small daily and runs the same type of advertising. Some such weeklies operate with annual expenses of $5,000 or less, while the expense of a daily in the same circulation group runs to at least $40,000. With an average per capita income of about $1,000 in the United States, the country editor with an income of $2,500 is often an opulent member of his community.

Advertising is an important economic factor in weekly publishing. Only about 17 per cent of the advertising in weekly papers is national. This fact is consistently deplored by weekly publishers, because national advertising brings in the money, and they have had an uphill fight to secure these campaigns. *American Press* says the average national advertising rate in weekly papers increased by about 6 per cent in 1944. They benefited only slightly from the current wave of institutional advertising. The publishers' representatives who try to secure this advertising for country papers point out that readership is unusually high in this medium, and that it covers many persons who otherwise would not respond to advertising appeals. The heads of advertising agencies live too close to Broadway, Manhattan.

The disadvantages of weekly papers as an advertising medium, from the point of view of the advertiser, are inferior typography and layout, the difficulty of measuring results and the scattered quality of the country press which makes it hard to place ads save through representatives. Moreover, until very recent years publishers would often quote different rates whenever it seemed expedient and those on the economic fringe would run free publicity in the hope of getting ads —which made advertising unnecessary. But these conditions have changed. Advertising agencies have fought against varying rates for years. Now most papers have standard rate cards. Publishers are learning to resist the use of free publicity material, and are learning not to editorialize about products they hope to advertise. Also, many weekly papers now have their circulations audited, which makes them a more computable and dependable advertising medium.

Because the precarious budgets of many weeklies are well known, there has arisen an unfortunate practice of having publicity, and even editorial material, prepared in clip sheets and mat services to be sent to weekly editors. This material, if used, provides the publisher with material at practically no cost or labor. Such services are regularly maintained by such organizations as the National Association of Manufacturers with its *Industrial Press Service*—which the N.A.M. says is used by 5,000 weeklies—the CIO, and the AFL, an organization fighting grade labeling, and many others. Some editors receive as many as ten such mat services weekly and, of course, a flood of publicity releases as well.

THE READER AS THE FINAL CENSOR OF THE PRESS

—Gerald W. Johnson, "Freedom of the Newspaper Press," *The Annals of the American Academy of Political and Social Sciences,* Vol. 200, November 1938, p. 70.

THE REALLY ACTIVE, powerful, and relentless censor of the press is not the politician, not the judge, not the advertiser, but the reader. As Lippmann pointed out fifteen years ago, a newspaper can assail almost any other power and survive, "but if it alienates the buying public, it loses the one indispensable asset of its existence."[1] This is due to the fact that news is paid for indirectly. The cent or two you hand the newsboy does not pay for your paper. That part of the sum which reaches the publisher—much less than two cents, since out of it must come the dealer's profit and the cost of distribution—represents hardly more than the profit; one authority has asserted that the net proceeds of circulation ought to represent the profit; the cost of production is concealed in the price of every advertised article you buy, which is to say in practically everything on the market. It is their ability to reach the buying public that the newspapers sell to advertisers to pay their costs of production. If they have no such ability, they have virtually nothing to sell, for the proceeds from sale of their own products are relatively trifling. As a condition precedent to existence, therefore, the newspaper must obtain and retain the patronage of readers, and this necessity circumscribes its freedom more definitely than any other force.

REVIEW QUESTIONS AND ASSIGNMENTS

1. Consider your own interests. What is it that makes you read the newspaper you now read? Is the paper edited for people with tastes similar to your own?

2. What guides has an editor to the types of news stories and features desired by the reader?

3. What factors contribute to a reader's interest in a particular news item?

4. What evidence is there that advertisers select a newspaper according to the type of reader to which it caters?

5. What types of news should be suppressed on behalf of public interest?

6. Are there any types of news that should be suppressed because of

[1] Walter Lippmann, *Public Opinion,* Macmillan, 1927, p. 324.

the welfare of a single individual or of a single individual and his circle of friends and relatives?

7. Should women and children be given special consideration by the press in its exposition of their shortcomings?

8. What restrictions does the public lay upon the press in its printing of the news?

9. What subjects, if any, should not be discussed in the press? Is it the subject matter or the way in which it is handled that produces trouble?

10. What changes in public taste that have been reflected in the press can you cite? What were the factors in bringing about the change in public taste? To what extent was the press an influence?

11. Is it true that the press must "put on a good show" for the public?

12. To what extent does the public read the newspaper for entertainment rather than for information?

13. Can you cite any cases in which the public has grown weary of a news story? In what way did it show its boredom?

14. Do you know of any news stories that dropped from the press because the public had lost interest?

15. Would you want the press to eliminate all sensational matter? Do you prefer a sensational newspaper or a conservative newspaper?

16. Should the newspaper suppress all news items that promote the financial interests of an individual or corporation? Justify your answer.

17. What examples of newspaper subservience to local pressure do you know? Is your information hearsay, or can you prove it? Do you know that the editor was acting in bad conscience?

18. How much of the news that is suppressed is withheld because of ethical or social conditions?

19. Everyone knows that much news is suppressed, and should be. How much is suppressed that should have been and could have been printed?

ADDITIONAL REFERENCES

Allen, Charles L., "The Press and Advertising," *The Annals of the American Academy of Political and Social Science,* Vol. 219, January 1942, pp. 90–91.

Anonymous, "Daily Newspaper Reading Habits," *Newsweek,* Vol. 11, February 7, 1938, p. 27.

———, "Every Reader a Censor," *Rotarian,* Vol. 53, December 1938, p. 34.

———, "Give Them What They Want," *American Mercury,* Vol. 45, December 1938, pp. 458–463.

———, "Press and Its Readers," *Christian Century,* Vol. 51, December 19, 1934, pp. 1616–1617.

———, "Press vs. the Public; Difference Between Attitude of the Papers and that of Their Readers," *The New Republic*, Vol. 103, September 23, 1940, p. 405.

Calkins, E. E., "Gnats and Camels, the Newspaper's Dilemma," *The Atlantic Monthly*, Vol. 139, January 1927, pp. 1–14.

Casey, Ralph D., "How to Read Domestic News," *Seventh Yearbook of the National Council for the Social Studies*, 1937, pp. 27–32.

Flynn, John T., "News by Courtesy," *Forum*, Vol. 83, March 1930, pp. 139–143.

Johnson, Gerald W., *What Is News?*, F. S. Crofts, 1926.

Kent, Frank R., *The Great Game of Politics*, Doubleday, Doran, 1923.

Lippmann, Walter, *Public Opinion*, Macmillan, 1922, pp. 323–324, 338–357.

Merz, Charles, "What Makes a First-Page Story?" *The New Republic*, Vol. 45, December 30, 1925, pp. 156–158.

Miller, William J., "What's Wrong With the Newspaper Reader?" *Nieman Reports*, Vol. 1, February 1947, pp. 1–2.

Nevins, Allan, *American Press Opinion*, D. C. Heath, 1928.

Poynter, Nelson P., "Economic Problems of the Press," *The Annals of the American Academy of Political and Social Science*, Vol. 219, January 1942, pp. 82–85.

Radder, N. J., *Newspapers in Community Service*, McGraw-Hill, 1926, pp. 152–175.

Ross, C. L., "Interest of Adults and High School Pupils in Newspaper Reading," *School and Society*, Vol. 27, February 18, 1929, pp. 212–214.

Salmon, Lucy M., *The Newspaper and the Historian*, Oxford University Press, 1923, p. 431.

Seldes, George, "News Is Suppressed," *The New Republic*, Vol. 99, August 2, 1939, pp. 351–354.

White, William Allen, in *The Editor and His People*, Helen O. Mahin (editor), Macmillan, 1924.

Yost, Casper S., *The Principles of Journalism*, Appleton-Century, 1924, pp. 31–35.

23. PRESSURE GROUPS AND THE PRESS

INTRODUCTION

ALTHOUGH the characteristic group called a "pressure group" is not a phenomenon of the last two decades, an aroused public interest in the activities of such groups is. It is only recently that their techniques and back-stage manipulations have been thoroughly aired. The work and character of the publicity agent are much better known. Mention of the publicity agent brings to mind the itinerant representative of the circuses, the press agent of Broadway shows, and the ghost writers of Hollywood, while such names as Ivy Lee, Edward L. Bernays, and William B. Shearer are widely known for their individual efforts on behalf of various "interests." Although the pressure groups work through such men, press agent efforts by no means represent the total attempt of pressure groups to influence the newspaper. Quite as often the publicity agent is the representative not of a pressure group but of a single businessman or some other individual in public life. For this reason the work of the press agent will be presented in the next chapter, and that of the pressure group below.

The pressure group works through suppression as well as through propaganda. The latter is commonly understood to imply little more than persuasion, while pressure usually involves considerably more.[1] Most propaganda reaches the newspapers as free "handouts" to be taken or left by the press as it chooses, and much of this publicity immediately goes into the wastebaskets. But pressure group tactics also include promises, and often threats.

An indication of the breadth and extent of pressure group activity is made by Bailey. Among the hundreds of such organizations Bailey singles out a number and tells what their interests are. Smith explains how some pressure groups work. Though these methods were worked out years ago, they have changed little in recent times.

Casey turns the spotlight on a number of pressure groups to illuminate some of their partisan activities. A more detailed glimpse is

[1] R. M. MacIver, "Social Pressures," *Encyclopedia of the Social Sciences*, p. 347.

given by Dakin in his explanation of the working of the Christian Science Committee on Publication. While the Dakin item deals with a selected religious group, one should bear in mind that any church (or comparable institution) can, when it feels the need, exert a strong degree of influence on the content of the media.

The Commission on Freedom of the Press cites an example of one editor who testified that pressure group activities cost his paper 50,000 subscribers. The Commission holds that all boycotts by the public are potentially dangerous. Usually they are organized by pressure groups that have come under the criticism of the press. A corollary idea is presented by Hocking who holds that press columns ought to be open for the expression of all ideas worth expressing, though he is not clear how the selection is to be made.

In the final citation MacNeil explains how the lobbyists of Washington win favors from the capital correspondents. That similar activities also occur in state capitals and elsewhere can hardly be doubted. In the local scene editors are frequently the invited guests of those who would like to influence them.

PRESSURE GROUPS ARE NUMEROUS

—Thomas A. Bailey, *The Man in the Street,* pp. 292–295. Copyright 1948 by Mr. Bailey. Used with the permission of The Macmillan Company.

It is probably fair to say that most Americans belong to some kind of pressure group, whether as farmers, laborers, veterans, manufacturers, or other special interests. A vast number belong to several such groupings. In a broad sense, the American people are a gigantic pressure group, the most powerful in the world. A partial listing of some of the better known organizations will give some idea of the magnitude of the problem.

The hyphenated Americans, through such organizations as the National Jewish Welfare Board and the Ancient Order of Hibernians in America, are better organized to promote the interests of a foreign element than the average American is to promote American interests.

The church groups have formed the Federal Council of Churches of Christ in America, the National Catholic Welfare Conference, and other organizations of huge numbers and impressive power. . . .

The farmers, speaking through the National Grange, the Farmer's Union, and the American Farm Bureau Federation have made their voices heard in regard to tariffs and other matters of primary concern to them. The National Grange, with a membership of some 800,000, threw its weight behind the drive to secure the Kellogg-Briand peace pact.

Commercial and manufacturing interests exert tremendous pressure through the National Association of Manufacturers, the National Foreign Trade Council, and the Chamber of Commerce of the United States. They have not distinguished themselves for a liberal and far-sighted approach to the tariff, and some of them, in their desire for cheap sweat, have pursued selfish aims with regard to immigration.

The manual laborer, working through the American Federation of Labor and other groups, has been keenly alive to the fate of his highly perishable product. The only major affiliate of the League of Nations that we ever joined was the International Labor Office in 1934, partly no doubt out of respect for the labor vote. One should also note that labor organizations have consistently opposed unrestricted immigration, particularly that from the Orient. In 1900 the humor magazine *Puck* had a missionary explain to a puzzled Chinese that the latter could go to the white man's heaven but not to his country because there was no labor vote in heaven. At various times labor organizations have favored the World Court; the withdrawal of marines from the Caribbean; the independence of the Philippines with their competing Filipino labor; noninterference by Washington with labor-sympathizing Mexican regimes; the boycotting of Japanese goods (after the attack on China in 1937); and the opposition through boycotts to Communism or Fascism in any form. Labor unions have not fared too well under the Communists and Fascists.

Veterans' organizations, like the Veterans of Foreign Wars of the United States and the American Legion, have been militantly active. They have generally favored narrow nationalism, patriotic textbooks, suspicion of foreigners (especially Communists), nonrecognition of Russia, the exclusion of aliens; a strong foreign policy, isolation ("Keep Out, Keep Ready" was an American Legion slogan in 1939–1940), a "navy second to none," and a formidable military establishment. The veterans who in their earlier days were thrust into front lines without proper training or equipment do not have to be converted to the idea of preparedness.

The women, represented by the National League of Women Voters and the American Association of University Women, have also been vocal. Taking seriously their duties as citizens and mothers, they have generally sponsored a liberal foreign policy and have campaigned for such objectives as the World Court and international cooperation. Not wanting their sons to die on foreign fields, they have been unusually ardent advocates of peace.[1]

Anglo-American groups, pooling their strength in such organizations as the English-Speaking Union, have labored for better relations between the Mother Country and the Daughter Country, and in pursuance of their program have published hands-across-the-seas literature.

Preparedness promoters, like the members of the Navy League, have long agitated for bigger and better armed forces. Herbert Hoover, who was both peace-minded and economy-minded, ran afoul of the Navy League, which allegedly contributed money to defeat him in 1932 and elect Roosevelt, who was regarded as more "ship-minded."

The pacifists have also been energetic in time of peace, although forced to soft-pedal their zeal in time of war. The best known of these groups is the Carnegie Endowment for International Peace, generously provided with the gold that Andrew Carnegie made from steel. Much of its activity, especially in published form, may be better classified as educational rather than propagandist. Dr. Charles A. Beard has rather angrily charged that the various foundations, through fellowships and other subsidies, have induced academicians to scramble onto the peace bandwagon.

The professional patrioteers, such as the Daughters of the American Revolution and the Sons of the American Revolution, have wielded a powerful tomahawk. They have made their pressure felt for big armies and navies, and against the pollution of the Plymouth Rock stock by foreign immigrants, especially those with dangerous ideologies.

The influence of the super patriots has perhaps been most keenly felt in the writing and adoption of textbooks of history, and to some extent of geography. These groups have been especially vigilant in demanding that our forefathers be generously gilded, and that our ancient enemies be liberally blackened. Boards of education and other adopters of textbooks can avoid much tribulation if they favor eulogistic treatment, and particularly if they see to it that foreign ideologies like Communism are mentioned only to be condemned.

[1] In 1947 several hundred members of the Congress of American Women paraded in Washington against President Truman's proposal for strengthening Greece and Turkey against Russia. Banners proclaimed: "Mothers and Wives Reject Proposals That Lead to New World Conflict."

All countries do the same thing. The chief difference between censorship by dictators and censorship by pressure groups is that the former is more ironclad. In 1927, when naval disarmament was much in the public eye, the Detroit *News* observed: "Disarmament is a help, but what the world needs is a history schoolbook that reads the same in all countries." Another journal remarked: "Beating swords into plowshares won't help if they keep on beating twisted versions of history into the heads of children."

As the American nation has become more sophisticated and less on the defensive, we have permitted our textbooks to become more critical, although there remains room for improvement. In 1945, when the country was still under the spell of wartime cooperationist sentiment, a public opinion poll discovered that nearly nine out of ten adults would like to see an international agency set up to examine our textbooks. More than seven out of ten were willing to change the texts, even as regards Germany, if the accounts were demonstrably unfair.

Certain other nonpatriotic groups are so definitely nonpartisan that they cannot be fairly classified under the heading of pressure or propaganda. Among organizations of this type may be found the Foreign Policy Association, and the Council on Foreign Relations.

Pressure groups, especially those of a hyphenate or ultraliberal complexion, have often hamstrung the work of our diplomats abroad by emitting loud outcries at most inopportune times. In 1945 the State Department, seeking to forestall subsequent criticism, took the unusual step of inviting forty-two of the most important service, educational, and other organizations to send consultants to the San Francisco Conference. The strategy of inviting potential opponents into one's camp undoubtedly contributed to the snowballing of public opinion behind the United Nations Charter.

VARIATIONS IN PRESSURE GROUP METHODS

—Charles W. Smith, Jr., *Public Opinion in a Democracy,* Prentice-Hall, Inc., 1939, pp. 248–250, 252–253, 261–262. The author was an assistant professor of political science at the University of Alabama when he wrote this volume.

THE METHODS used by pressure groups to attain their ends vary from time to time and under different circumstances. The lower the standards of morality, the coarser have been the methods used by those seeking favorable legislation. In Andrew Jackson's day the Bank of the United States loaned money to needy congressmen. Daniel Webster, one of its staunchest champions in the United States Senate, was on its payroll as an attorney. In the 1860's and 1870's, lobbyists not infrequently bought the votes of legislators by the direct use of money, railroad passes, and "other things of value." Since that time the technique has been refined and methods diversified. Outright bribery is no longer common, but money is still effective in influencing the actions of government officials.

Some lobbyists represent pressure groups with large memberships. Others work for interests with large financial resources but small membership. The methods used to influence the government differ decidedly according to the size of the membership of the pressure group. Where the membership is large, the group's leaders and its lobbyists may powerfully influence legislation by working almost wholly with their own group. In elections, they may notify their members that a candidate is favorable or unfavorable, and, if they hold the balance of power, bring about his election or his defeat. When Congress or the state legislature convenes, the mere threat of an organization with a large membership has a strong influence on legislators. If they need to be reminded of the membership's existence and its wishes, the lobbyist can bring down upon them a barrage of letters and telegrams. To legislative ears, the voice of the organized seems much louder than the voice of the unorganized. Such organizations may rely wholly upon the political strength of their own membership and make no great effort to win the support of the general public for the measures they favor.

An organization or a group without a large membership must rely upon money and publicity to give it power. Sometimes it can get what it wants by securing the support of political bosses who control the legislators. This is particularly true in state politics. Contributions to campaign funds may also be made as an investment, and usually the investor is not disappointed. If necessary, a great campaign of propaganda may be launched to win public opinion to the side of the pressure group. Where a genuine public sympathy cannot be created, money and business pressure may win the support of newspapers and bring about the sending of enough letters and telegrams to give the appearance of a public opinion. . . .

More recently, pressure groups have come to place increased reliance upon propaganda designed to influence public opinion. In fact, most of the propaganda that floods the country, aside from commercial advertising, has for its purpose influencing the actions of the government. Whether or not such propaganda actually creates public opinion, it may certainly, as one lobbyist said, "accelerate" it. Large sums of money are spent on the acceleration, or creation, of opinion, because lobbyists assume now that public opinion is supreme in the United States, and the best way to control the government is to control public opinion. They seek to mold the opinions of the electorate, in order that favorable legislators will be elected and the opinion of their constituents will keep them going in the right direction after they are elected. . . .

Newspapers and magazines are sometimes made to fight the battles of special interests, because the press exercises considerable influence and it is still popularly regarded as showing some indication on the trend of public opinion. . . .

Patent-medicine interests have made ingenious use of the newspapers. The maker of a widely advertised catarrh "cure" once disclosed to a meeting of patent medicine makers that his company had discovered an effective way to prevent hostile legislation. The plan was to shift responsibility to the newspapers by inserting in all advertising contracts a clause providing that the contract would be voided if any law was passed in that state prohibiting the manufacture or sale of patent medicines. Then, whenever a threatening bill was considered by the legislature, the company would wire the newspapers urging them to oppose the bill and suggesting that its passage might make necessary the discontinuance of advertising in that state. Another manufacturing company had a clause in its contracts stating that the enactment of state or national legislation adverse to the manufacture or sale of patent medicine would void the contract. Such clauses in a number of cases resulted in powerful newspaper opposition to patent medicine legislation.[1]

DEALING WITH MILITANT PRESSURE GROUPS

—Ralph D. Casey, "The Press, Propaganda, and Pressure Groups," *The Press in the Contemporary Scene, The Annals of the American Academy of Political and Social Science,* Vol. 219, January 1942, pp. 67, 72–73. Mr. Casey is director of the School of Journalism, University of Minnesota.

Criticism that the press carries propaganda will no doubt continue as long as readers have differing views and beliefs. What one group

[1] Edward B. Logan, "Lobbying," Supplement to *The Annals,* Vol. CXLIV, 6, 7.

of intelligent citizens may believe is propaganda will be described by another as news. We are not concerned here over honest differences of opinion. We express, rather, some anxiety over the lack of information possessed by the public in the techniques used by newspapers in subjecting information to scrutiny and analysis before it appears in print, and the failure to discriminate between disinterested news reporting by trained journalists, on the one hand, and propaganda on the other. While the feverish interest in propaganda may have run its course, at least for the present, scars remain. Unjustified distrust of all information service remains in the minds of many lay persons. . . .

The problem of dealing with the ordinary news bureau is never so vexing and difficult . . . as that of coping with militant pressure groups. These groups are usually engaged in a controversy or have a single-minded devotion to a program or doctrine which may not be socially acceptable generally. Each of these groups first creates an active central organization with a body of zealous followers, and next organizes its inevitable press committee. The instability or insecurity of various social classes in our present changing social order produces various ideologies to which groups of persons cling with religious-like devotion. They seek by every method of agitation and propaganda to accomplish their ends. They establish their own propaganda journals, both for their own membership and for such sections of the public as they are able to reach. One experienced editor of my acquaintance has described the tactics and strategy of these pressure-group organizations:

> The propaganda papers of these pressure groups are not sparing in their criticism of the newspapers. They tell their followers how to bring pressure to bear on the press and at the same time inform them that any lack of newspaper support is due to unworthy motives.
>
> It is not hard to understand these tactics. The pressure group is organized on the basis of a common grievance, real or fancied, but in any event the technique is to keep the grievance alive and active. The basic grievance must have the agitating support of minor grievances, and the newspaper is valuable to the agitator, either as an agency of propaganda, if possible, or failing in this, it can be effectively utilized as an object of grievance to increase the sense of injustice on which their groups live.
>
> I am convinced that the multiplication of pressure groups demanding support is in part responsible for the present unthinking criticism of the press. The existence of these pressure groups and the existence of this antagonism toward the press may be coincidental in time and without any causative relation to each other, but I suspect there is a relationship.[1]

[1] Thomas J. Dillon, editor of the Minneapolis *Morning Tribune* since 1920.

The war in Spain, prior to the final Franco victory, was productive of much group pressure, and the press was bombarded with appeals and complaints from American sympathizers on both sides. For a time, the Townsendites and the Coughlinites were a thorn in editorial flesh. The boycott against Japan brought its coterie of zealous persons to editorial sanctums. Mild but insistent pressure comes when groups put on drives for money and support, and it is obviously impossible to fill news columns with publicity material from all headquarters of these minorities. Yet the press is faced as never before by the insistent demands of minority groups for space in the newspapers and also for editorial support. It is a rare body of pressure-group leaders that is content to let the editor judge news values and determine what it is in the public interest to publish.

The nature of the press places upon it the responsibility of presenting both sides of a controversy. Sections of the public, however, will resent equal-handed writing and display of the news, and the publishing of the propaganda of one action group in a controversial situation will, of course, anger and outrage the antagonist. . . .

CHURCH CONCERN FOR PRESS CONTENT

–Edwin Franden Dakin, *Mrs. Eddy: The Biography of a Virginal Mind*, Scribner's, 1929, pp. 392–395. Mr. Dakin was a public relations counsellor in New York City when he wrote this study.

IT WAS REALLY Mrs. Eddy, and not the modern leaders of American "big business," who invented corporation publicity and devised the methods to make it work. The idea of assisting newspaper editors and readers to formulate their opinions through correctly prepared publicity material came to her as she pondered the attacks upon herself and her announced discovery.

When she reorganized her church she devised two important departments to deal with public opinion. One was the Board of Lectureship, whose members were "to include in each lecture a true and just reply to public topics condemning Christian Science, and to bear testimony to the facts pertaining to the life of the Pastor Emeritus."[1] Even more important than this Board was another department, called the "Committee on Publication." This committee consisted only of one man, technically responsible to the Board of Directors of The Mother Church, but, through the Board, to Mrs. Eddy personally. In-

[1] *Manual of The Mother Church,* Massachusetts, 1892, XXXI, p. 2.

deed, Mrs. Eddy specifically reserved the right to appoint this "committee" if she so desired. In addition, she stipulated that a similar "committee" should be maintained by the branch churches in each state of the union and in each county of Great Britain and Ireland. The three largest branch churches in each state or county should unite to select their "committee" and to pay his salary. . . .

Under this remarkable provision Mrs. Eddy had some fifty functioning publicity men scattered through the United States, all employed for the sole purpose of disseminating good news concerning herself and her doctrine. No matter how small a news item in any newspaper in any city or town might be, it invariably came to the attention of the various Eddy "committees." If it met with their disapproval, a statement in correction of the offending item was immediately despatched to the editor. If he failed to publish such a correction, subsequent results were unpleasant. For Mrs. Eddy was entirely prepared against such a contingency. Under the duties of her Boston "committee" she had prescribed the following routine:

> This Committee on Publication shall be responsible for correcting or having corrected a false newspaper article which has not been replied to by other Scientists, or which has been forwarded to this Committee for the purpose of having them reply to it. If the correction by the Committee on Publication is not promptly published by the periodical in which it is desirable that this correction shall appear, *this Committee shall immediately apply for aid to the Committee on Business.*[2]

The italics are the biographer's. Mrs. Eddy, through her own publishing experience, had happened on an important and useful fact. Newspapers are not published merely because their editors and owners like to see their views in print. They are published to earn revenue. Mrs. Eddy's own publications were earning approximately $400,000 a year, including advertising receipts, before she died. It thus became wholly obvious to her that a very short and quick route to an editor's heart would be through his pocketbook. And she was right.

If any city-editor ever dared ignore a communication sent out by the Committee on Publication, the managing editor would shortly receive a telephone call. He would not find the "committee" talking on the other end of the wire. Rather it would be one of his most valued advertisers. The advertiser would be extremely sorry to have learned

[2] *Ibid.*, XXXIII, 2.

that the Unionville *Beagle* was so extremely prejudiced in its news columns. If the managing editor was incredulous, it would be explained that his paper seemed to have a desire to persecute and vilify the religious beliefs of the gentleman who now was speaking. If incredulity was still expressed, the managing editor would be told that he should look at the bottom of column six, on page seven, of his issue last Monday week; that he would find there a news item which was wholly erroneous, unjustified, and an insult to the advertiser who was now expressing complaint. The managing editor would look; would find a stick of type referring to Christian Science as a faith cure; would return to the wire; would try to learn what was the matter. Almost inevitably, before he had hung up he had promised to print anything the gentleman at the other end wished to have published in correction.

The result was that the press was strewn with denials that Christian Science was in any way related to common faith cures; denials that Mrs. Eddy was aught but a luminous and vibrant and godly personality; assertions that her discovery was nothing else than a perfectly divine boon to man. So industrious were these various "publication committees" that editors very quickly came to avoid anything but the most reverent and studied approach to Christian Science, for they learned through bitter experience that the least slip would cause their telephones to begin a steady ringing that would not cease until they either had expressed public regret or had lost an advertiser.

The whole secret of this influence with the press lay not in numbers, but in organization. Mrs. Eddy's "committees" were picked for shrewdness and sagacity; in most instances they combined business acumen with religious zealotry; and they never rested until they cornered the offending editor with the most influential Eddy disciple in the community. They could pick with unerring accuracy exactly the right individual to assist the editor to revise his expressions of opinion.

It was natural that an editor, finding anything which he published on Christian Science subject to the most careful scrutiny, should reach the conclusion that the Scientists must be a remarkably numerous and influential sect; and Mrs. Eddy's "publication committee" encouraged this idea whenever possible. Mrs. Eddy's own hints concerning the millions who responded to her will combined with an editor's actual contacts with her disciples, left no doubt in thousands of editorial minds that the lady had untold legions of adherents. Probably few people would have believed, in 1906, that there were not many more than 60,000 Christian Scientists scattered all over the country.

PRESSURE GROUPS AND BOYCOTTS

—Commission on Freedom of the Press, *A Free and Responsible Press,* University of Chicago Press, 1947, pp. 57–59, 96–97.

PEOPLE seldom want to read or hear what does not please them; they seldom want others to read or hear what disagrees with their convictions or what presents an unfavorable picture of groups they belong to. When such groups are organized, they let the press know their objections to remarks concerning them. The press is therefore caught between its desire to please and extend its audience and its desire to give a picture of events and people as they really are. . . .

Every branch of the communications industry is subject to the same sort of pressure. Publishers who stick to their guns have suffered for it. The managing editor of one of the principal papers of the country testified before the Commission that in his opinion his publication took a drop of more than 50,000 in circulation because of a policy displeasing to a well-organized pressure group.

It would be a mistake to assume that pressure is always bad just because it is pressure. Testimony before the Commission reveals that pressure groups often correct unconscious bias or mistakes and bring into view neglected areas of discussion. But the power of these groups and the importance of the mass media raise a serious question, to which we shall later return: How can a medium of communication which almost by definition must strive to please everybody perform the function which it should perform today? . . .

The people of this country are the purchasers of the products of the press. The effectiveness of buyers' boycotts, even of very little ones, has been amply demonstrated. Many of these boycotts are the wrong kind for the wrong purposes; they are the work of pressure groups seeking to protect themselves from justifiable criticism or to gain some special advantage. The success of their efforts indicates what a revolt of the American people against the service given them by the press might accomplish.

We are not in favor of a revolt and hope that less drastic means of improving the press may be employed. We cannot tell what direction a revolt might take; it might lead to government control or to the emasculation of the First Amendment. We want the press to be free, and a revolt against the press conducted for the purpose of giving the country a truly free press might end in less freedom than we have today.

What is needed, first of all, is recognition by the American people of the vital importance of the press in the present world crisis. We have the impression that the American people do not realize what has happened to them. They are not aware that the communications revolution has occurred. They do not appreciate the tremendous power which the new instruments and the new organization of the press place in the hands of a few men. They have not yet understood how far the performance of the press falls short of the requirements of a free society in the world today.

FREEDOM FOR PRESSURE GROUPS

—William Ernest Hocking, *Freedom of the Press,* University of Chicago Press, 1947, pp. 195–196.

AN IDEALLY free press is free *from* compulsions from whatever source, governmental or social, external or internal: from compulsions—not, of course, from pressures, since no press can be free from pressures except in a moribund society empty of contending forces and beliefs. An ideally free press is free *for* the achievement of those goals of press service which its own instinct of workmanship and the requirements of the community combine to establish; and for these ends it must have command of all available technical resources, financial strength, reasonable access to sources of information at home and abroad, and the necessary staff and facilities for bringing its information and its judgments to the national market. An ideally free press would be free *to* all who have something worth saying to the public; and the selection of the voices thus deserving to be heard must be a free selection, arising from the preparatory processes of free speech, not from the desk of owner or editor alone.

To state these requirements of an ideal freedom is to indicate at once a pulling in opposite directions, from which some of the problems of the contemporary press arise. In fact, these several factors of an ideal press freedom are to some extent incompatible with one another. This will appear more explicitly if we bring together here some of the demands in behalf of freedom we have already made.

Full equipment always makes against free motion, like Saul's armor on David. A press which has grown to the measure of the national market and to the full use of technical resources can hardly be free from internal compulsions. The major part of the nation's press is large-scale enterprise, closely interlocked with the system of finance and industry; it will not without effort escape the natural bias of what it is. Yet this bias must be known and measurably overcome or counterbalanced if freedom is to remain secure

The ideal of the nation-wide press in a growing nation is increasingly difficult—through no one's fault—to combine with the ideal that every voice shall have the hearing it deserves. The extension of the major press toward national scope through consolidation or otherwise automatically renders less operative on a comparable scale the claims of potential issuers who have no press. For this clash there is no perfect remedy. There is relief through the multiplication of new instruments of manifolding and mass expression, and also through the effort of the wider press, somewhat as a common carrier, to assume responsibility for representing variant facets of opinion. But to represent all or any large number of such facets would only multiply confusion. No listening devices of the human mind have yet secured us from a certain wastage of human genius, as the scale of a nation's thinking enlarges. And the contemporary arts of what is called publicity—whose existence itself advertises the wide-felt need of special effort to secure recognition—cannot be acquitted, even at their best, of aiming rather at further lens distortion than at a just and proportionate publication of worth.

PRESSURE CONTACTS IN WASHINGTON

—From *Without Fear or Favor,* copyright, 1940, by Neil MacNeil. Reprinted by permission of Harcourt, Brace and Company, Inc. Mr. MacNeil was an assistant managing editor of the New York *Times* when he wrote this work.

More insidious and more difficult to deal with is the propaganda of the lobbyist and the pressure groups. There is scarcely an industry, a pressure group, selfish or otherwise, or an organization that has dealings with the government that has not its lobbyist or its bureau in the national capital. These work on both the press and the legislators, and their approach to each is much the same. They pass out their handouts and other literature, colored to suit their purposes. They bring pressure of all sorts on members of the Congress, and these in turn may make speeches or statements that cannot be ignored by the press; when Congress acts the press reports it. They attempt to ingratiate themselves with individual correspondents. Sometimes these lobbyists are former newspapermen or former members of the Congress with many personal friends in the press corps.

Many lobbyists maintain homes or offices equipped for elaborate entertainment and have ample expense accounts for this purpose. Some keep open house, and their food and their liquors are of the best. Here the correspondent will meet members of the Congress, high officials, important visitors to Washington, and fellow-workers. There is an atmosphere of good-fellowship and conviviality. There is no mention of the lobbyist's special interest; but some time later the lobbyist may call the correspondent's attenion to an "important" bill among the hundreds before the Congress, and his handouts will inevitably get just a little more attention.

Then the new or inexperienced correspondent in the capital may have a wife with social aspirations or marriageable daughters. Washington without an invitation is a cold city. Just about the time the correspondent's womenfolk are beginning to regret their transfer to Washington, a very charming lady calls, or telephones, to suggest that the wife might enjoy an invitation that would enable her to meet many Washington matrons or the daughters to meet the younger set. She is the lobbyist's wife. The ladies are introduced into Washington society, perhaps only the outer fringe, but the correspondent's ladies are eternally grateful. Life takes on a new interest for them, and the lobbyist's cause has another press friend.

Washington takes its society seriously. With its bounteous crop of diplomats, politicians, military and naval figures, and visiting statesmen, it is probably the most colorful and interesting society in America. There is still much leaving of cards, bowing from the hips, and kissing of hands. There is a constant round of cocktail parties, receptions, dinners, and balls. There is an equally constant flow of gossip, and all of it is about official life, turning on the figures who make events and the policies of the government. The active correspondent must wear his dress suit often, and with ease and grace. He must have his line of small talk for the ladies, for a chivalrous compliment may bring a page-one story.

REVIEW QUESTIONS AND ASSIGNMENTS

1. What evidence can be found that local business interests have attempted to bring pressure upon the newspapers to alter what they print?

2. Look into the articles by Mussey in *The Nation* and set forth the chief weapons used by the Christian Science Church in bringing pressure upon the newspapers. (See bibliography below.)

3. Make a study of the newspapers to see what recent news of interest groups has been published, and then find out under what circumstances it was printed.

4. To what extent do you find the Women's Christian Temperance Union functioning as a pressure group today?

5. To what extent is the honor and integrity of the press involved when an editor accepts the chairmanship of a brewer's publicity committee?

6. How should an editor who believed in abolishing all sales of liquor govern his choice of news and advertisements?

7. What principles should govern the news columns of an editor who is opposed to publicly owned utilities?

8. Does the increased publicity for private ownership of utilities necessarily represent a trend unfavorable to a free public opinion? Justify your answer.

9. Discuss the merits of a federal law that would require the printing of the source of every publicity article used by the press.

10. Is it true that a newspaper always reflects a particular point of view in its columns? Is a truly objective newspaper possible?

11. Discuss the statement that the political parties are pressure groups.

12. To what extent is any administration, as separate from the political party it represents, a pressure group?

13. How great a menace to the press is the total influence of the pressure groups?

ADDITIONAL REFERENCES

Boardman, F., "Helping the Press: Catholic Publicity," *The Commonweal,* Vol. 23, March 13, 1936, pp. 543–544.

Crawford, Kenneth C., *The Pressure Boys,* Julian Messner, 1939, pp. 32–35.

Doob, Leonard W., *Public Opinion and Propaganda,* Henry Holt, 1948, pp. 429–440.

Frank, Glenn, "Pressure Groups and the American Future," *Vital Speeches Magazine,* Vol. 3, March 15, 1937, pp. 331–334.

Hocking, William Ernest, *Freedom of the Press,* University of Chicago Press, 1947, pp. 135–141.

Irwin, Inez Heynes, *The Story of the Woman's Party,* Harcourt, Brace, 1921.

Lowry, E. G., "Special Interests," *The Saturday Evening Post,* Vol. 192, January 31, 1920, p. 5.

Morgan, J. E., "Propaganda: Its Relation to the Child Labor Issue," *Education,* Vol. 46, September 1925, pp. 51–54.

Mussey, H. R., "The Christian Science Censor," *The Nation,* Vol. 130, February 5-12-26, 1930, March 12, 1930, pp. 147–149, 175–178, 241–243, 291–293.

Nevins, Allan, *American Press Opinion,* D. C. Heath, 1928.

Odegard, Peter H., *Pressure Politics: The Story of the Anti-Saloon League,* Columbia University Press, 1928, pp. 231–232, 250–252, 262–264.

Riegel, O. W., "Propaganda and the Press," *The Annals of the American Academy of Political and Social Science,* Vol. 179, May 1935, pp. 209–210.

Smith, B. L., H. D. Lasswell, and R. D. Casey, *Propaganda, Communication and Public Opinion,* Princeton University Press, 1946, pp. 1–117.

Van Name, W. G., "Anti-Conservation Propaganda," *Science,* Vol. 61, April 17, 1925, pp. 415–416.

Wisehart, M. K., "The Pittsburgh Newspapers and the Steel Strike," Section II, *Public Opinion and the Steel Strike,* Interchurch World Movement, Harcourt, Brace, 1921, p. 147.

Zeller, Belle, *Pressure Politics in New York,* Prentice-Hall, 1937.

———, "Lobbies and Pressure Groups," *The Annals of the American Academy of Political and Social Science,* Vol. 195, January 1938, pp. 79–87.

24. PRESS AGENTS AND PUBLICITY

INTRODUCTION

PRESS AGENTS, publicity directors, public relations counsels—whatever the current title—uniformly believe that their occupation has entered into a new type of relationship with respect to their employers on the one hand and employes and the press on the other. They speak now of communication channels, and sometimes go for weeks without writing a publicity release or staging a news-worthy event. In fact, a whole new line of effort is opening up for them—the matter of advising business and professional men how to conduct their affairs so that their actions will be more in accord with what employes or the public will approve. One may well believe that in this effort most of those presently employed may be getting over their depth. However, the history and development of these workers is of considerable interest to the student of the press. The citations that follow sample the various aspects of this field.

The rise of the press agent probably was inevitable. When American civilization achieved its present plane of complex "bigness," the stage was set for him. Each development in the economic, political, and social life of the nation called for a change in the system of record. When corporations, institutions, groups, and individuals discovered that the system of record tended to be static and that they had advanced far beyond the ability of the press to report and the public to comprehend, they called upon the publicity man to fill the gap. To him was assigned the task of giving certain events shape through the utilization of communication channels.

Today, the press agent finds himself part of the news machine. He has discharged his task of serving as the middleman between the interests he represents and the press, as well as other communication media, so efficiently that he apparently has become a fixture. His type ranges all the way from a vice-president in charge of public relations for a major corporation to a shabby paragraph-seeker for a cheap carnival. He assumes various names—public relations counsel, publicity adviser, information man—and, if he is successful at his calling, he usually makes little effort to hide his conviction that he is well paid for selecting and dramatizing news his employer wishes the public to see.

That the rise of the press agent would pose a problem for the press was obvious. The theory of news gathering precludes the possibility of anyone outside the newspaper office gathering and selecting material for publication. For a time in the early history of journalism in America this system did prevail. Once the transformation that marked America's "coming of age" occurred, however, the newspaper faced a choice between accepting the releases of press agents or failing to report many facts needed for the record. Censorship, distortion, and the inaccessibility of much news combined to strengthen the press agent's position and his acceptance by the press was an inevitable albeit discouraging conclusion.

The influence of the press agent on the press has been far-reaching. Biographies, investigations, and research studies all attest to his success. From his personal standpoint, the press agent has performed a vital function. He has helped to make clear many events that might otherwise have gone unnoticed, and he has proved an invaluable aid in cutting away the barriers that so often separate the reporter from the hidden facts. From the point of view of the newspaper, the publicity man is far from being an unmixed blessing. Most editors concede that his assistance is perhaps necessary in making the record complete, but, at the same time, they realize that he will never do more than present the picture which he, or his employer, wishes the public to see. Thus editors see that they have replaced negative censorship with positive censorship while saddling themselves with a propaganda burden that brings anguished cries of protest at all meetings of newspaper organizations.

PUBLICITY AND PROPAGANDA

—Herbert Brucker, *Freedom of Information,* pp. 133–135. Copyright 1949 by Mr. Brucker. Used with the permission of The Macmillan Company.

FORTUNATELY the United States has never yet had a Minister of Propaganda and Popular Enlightenment after the manner of Nazi Germany's Dr. Goebbels. Of course, George Creel of the Committee on Public Information in World War I and Elmer Davis of the Office of War Information in World War II were called Administration propagandists by politicians, editors, and businessmen whose spleens were more active than their brains. But despite the totalitarian pressures of war, and the present universal trend toward centralized government, we have not yet remotely approached official management of the news that makes the world as we see it in our heads.

The shoe is, indeed, on the other foot. Not only is there that preponderant identification of our press, radio, and other media of information with the political and economic old guard . . . but such rigging of the news as we have comes more from business interests and pressure groups than from government; for the United States is the world's most fertile breeding ground of press agents, publicity men, vice presidents in charge of information, and counselors on public relations, who have no other purpose than to alter our mental worlds in the interests of their clients. These unofficial ministers of popular enlightenment have so prospered, multiplied, and become a part of the scheme of things that if you want to start an organization to manufacture widgets, sell peanuts, abolish labor unions, wipe out capitalism, or merely to band together a loyal lodge of undertakers, the first thing is to get yourself a publicity man. No publicity, no organization; for, in a world of mass populations dependent on mass communications, any enterprise whose influence goes beyond walking distance of the home office is lost unless it becomes known, understood, and to some extent approved by its public.

Government, of course, has long since joined the procession, and employs publicity men by the thousand. Their output may be sampled from a table in Washington's National Press Club, where mimeographed releases from government agencies and bureaus arrive fresh every day if not every hour, to provide a governmental publicity smörgasbord. The White House itself has not escaped the habit. The Red Cross, the National Tuberculosis Association, the American Society for the Control of Cancer, and innumerable other causes, all go in for publicity—that is to say, for propaganda on behalf of themselves and their objectives. Even the American Library Association makes awards for "distinguished publicity" to libraries. So unbelievably huge is the resulting barrage of releases that newspaper editors on the receiving end have been frenetic on the subject for a generation. This blast from Edward W. Sowers, co-publisher and editor of the Excelsior Springs *Daily Standard* in Missouri, is typical:

> If all the editors of all the newspapers and periodicals in the United States would do what I am doing . . . we would in twelve months eliminate the . . . paper shortage, lift the post office department out

of the red, save $13,688,340.64 in wasted postage, save an additional $27,376,681.28 in paper and labor gone-for-naught.

Mr. Sowers' remedy was simple: to put all publicity material into the wastebasket instead of into the paper.

Perhaps, however, it is not so simple as that. Publicity and propaganda differ only in degree, and not in kind; and for all the waste involved, propaganda is to a greater or lesser extent effective. The waste of paper in publicity is merely the by-product of the amazing potency of propaganda in favorable circumstances. Samuel Adams, Thomas Paine, and a handful of others committed an undecided majority of the American colonists—almost in spite of themselves—to independence. Again, it was not alone the corruption and confusion of Czarism and war that turned Russia Bolshevist; it was the propagandists Lenin and Trotsky. In the same way the German people did not become Nazis all by themselves; a frustrated nobody with a devilish vision and fanatic purpose led them to it. Or, to descend to a less majestic scale, it was the publicity genius William H. Anderson of the Anti-Saloon League, who, within a few months after his arrival in New York in 1914, changed the entire political line-up of the state. In sum, propaganda and its little brother publicity, alike in that they can channel the wavering minds of men into a predetermined course, have been an exceedingly powerful force throughout modern times.

WHY THE PRESS AGENT EXISTS

—From Walter Lippmann, *Public Opinion.* Used by permission of The Macmillan Company, publishers, 1922, pp. 343–346.

IT WILL BE FOUND, I think, that there is a very direct relation between the certainty of news and the system of record. If you call to mind the topics which form the principal indictment by reformers against the press, you find they are subjects in which the newspaper occupies the position of the umpire in the unscored baseball game. All news about states of mind is of this character: so are all descriptions of personalities, of sincerity, aspiration, motive, intention, of mass feeling, of national feeling, of public opinion, the policies of foreign governments. So is much news about what is going to happen. So are questions turning on private profit, private income, wages, working conditions, the efficiency of labor, educational opportunity, unemployment, monopoly, health, discrimination, unfairness, restraint of trade, waste, "backward peoples," conservatism, imperialism, radicalism, liberty, honor, righteousness. All involve data that are at best spasmodically recorded. The data may be hidden because of a censorship or a tradition of privacy, they may not exist because nobody thinks records important, because he thinks it red tape, or because nobody has yet invented an objective system of measurement. Then the news on these subjects is bound to be debatable, when it is not wholly neglected. The events which are not scored are reported either as personal and conventional opinions, or they are not news. They do not take shape until somebody protests, or somebody investigates, or somebody publicly, in the etymological meaning of the word makes an *issue* of them.

This is the underlying reason for the existence of the press agent. The enormous discretion as to what facts and what impressions shall be reported is steadily convincing every organized group of people that whether it wishes to secure publicity or to avoid it, the exercise of discretion cannot be left to the reporter. It is safer to hire a press agent who stands between the group and the newspapers. Having hired him, the temptation to exploit his strategic position is very great. "Shortly before the war," says Mr. Frank Cobb, "the newspapers of New York took a census of the press agents who were regularly employed and regularly accredited and found that there were about twelve hundred of them. How many there are now (1919) I do not pretend to know, but what I do know is that many of the direct channels to news have been closed and the information for the public is first filtered through publicity agents. The great corporations have them, the banks have them, the railroads have them, all the organizations of business and of social and political activity have them, and they are the media through which news comes. Even statesmen have them."

Were reporting simply the recovery of obvious facts, the press agent would be little more than a clerk. But since, in respect to most of the big topics of news, the facts are not simple, and not at all obvious, but subject to choice and opinion, it is natural that everyone should wish to make his own choice of facts for the newspapers to print. The publicity man does that. And in doing it, he certainly saves the reporter much trouble, by presenting him a clear picture of a situation out of which he might otherwise make neither head nor tail. But it follows that the picture which the publicity man makes for the reporter is the one he wishes the public to see. He is censor and propagandist, responsible only to his employers, and to the whole truth responsible only as it accords with the employer's conception of his own interests.

The development of the publicity man is a clear sign that the facts of modern life do not spontaneously take a shape in which they can be known. They must be given a shape by somebody, and since in the daily routine reporters cannot give a shape to facts, and since there is little disinterested organization of intelligence, the need for some formulation is being met by the interested parties.

The good press agent understands that the virtues of his cause are not news, unless they are such strange virtues that they jut right out of the routine of life. This is not because the newspapers do not like virtue, but because it is not worth while to say that nothing has happened when nobody expected anything to happen. So if the publicity man wishes free publicity he has, speaking quite accurately, to start something. He arranges a stunt: obstructs the traffic, teases the police, somehow manages to entangle his client or cause with an event that is already news.

EDWARD L. BERNAYS

—John T. Flynn, "Edward L. Bernays, the Science of Ballyhoo," *The Atlantic Monthly,* Vol. 149, May 1932, pp. 563–565, 569–570. Mr. Flynn is the author of several books on public affairs and is a frequent contributor to the periodical press.

BY NO SYSTEM of honest elimination can Edward L. Bernays be excluded from a list of representative men in America. He has made an extraordinary success. He has been something of a pioneer. He was conditioning the Mass Mind for Richard Bennett long before Ivy Lee took over the job of merchandising John D. Rockefeller to the American people. He numbers among his clients powerful millionaires, great corporations, even royal personages and governments. He has made a great deal of money—a mark of importance that no American will deny—and, what is more, he has done it in the field of intellectual activity.

For, after all, Bernays is a philosopher, not a mere business man. He is a nephew of that other great philosopher, Dr. Sigmund Freud. Unlike his distinguished uncle, he is not known as a practising psychoanalyst, but he is a psychoanalyst just the same, for he deals with the science of unconscious mental processes. His business is to treat unconscious mental acts by conscious ones. The great Viennese doctor is interested in releasing the pent-up libido of the individual; his American nephew is engaged in releasing (and directing) the suppressed desires of the crowd. He is a social psychologist engaged in carrying out in actual practice and according to newer theories that branch of psychology which Auguste Comte and later Herbert Spencer recognized as having a definite relation to sociology.

He is none the less a philosopher because he does not wear side whiskers and drone in solemn and abstruse dullness, or because he has devised a way of running his philosophy through a meter and sending bills for the service. As a matter of fact, Bernays has both a clear and a very shrewd understanding of his profession. As a Public Relations Counsel he is a liaison officer between Big Business and the Monster. In odd moments he has been a professor in very truth, for until recently he lectured on his system in New York University.

The reader is perhaps aware of the difference between the public relations counsel and the publicity man. The publicity man merely makes a noise in the neighborhood of his client or product to attract attention to it. He beats the drum outside his show. He angles for space in the newspapers. He seldom rises to a higher level of performance than that which Bernays calls "continuous interpretation" or "dramatic high-spotting." If he has bacon to sell, he just keeps repeating, "Eat more bacon; eat *our* bacon."

The public relations counsel manages it differently. He makes use of what the psychologist calls the conditioned reflex. He does not mention bacon at all. He does not mention anything, because he knows no one is interested in what he mentions. He gets a number of physicians to say that people should eat heartier breakfasts. He manages a kind of vogue for heartier breakfasts on grounds of dietetic necessity. That is all. He knows that if people will eat heartier breakfasts they will think of bacon. As for "dramatic high-spotting"—well, when the President of the United States telephones to the President of Peru, and all the newspapers report the event and the conversation, you may be sure that the new long distance service between New York and Lima has been opened, and that the publicity man of the telephone company has been doing the job he is paid for.

Even a public relations counsel may do a lot of this sort of thing. Oddly enough, Bernays himself is perhaps best known for two examples of dramatic high-spotting which were really no more than grandiose, glorified publicity stunts. One of these was Light's Golden Jubilee. Surely you will not have to be reminded of that amazing jamboree which took place when the story of Edison's invention of the incandescent lamp was reenacted in Dearborn, with Edison himself, Henry Ford, and the President of the United States playing the leading roles, while droves of great industrialists and financiers played the parts of villagers and supers in the cast, and radios and newspapers fought for the privilege of broadcasting it. Henry Ford was supposed to be the manager of the show, but the man who set the stage and pulled the strings attached to all the dignified marionettes was Edward L. Bernays. He worked not for Edison or for Henry Ford, but for very important organized commercial interests which saw in this historic anniversary an opportunity to exploit and publicize the uses of electric light. His other outstanding performance was when he spent nearly $70,000 for a single hour's show on the radio to introduce a new Dodge car to the market.

All this was publicity. The Standard Oil Company, which is supposed to have been introduced to the subject by Ivy Lee, was in reality making use of publicity away back in 1888; long before that Jay Cooke manipulated it to sell lots in the West, and earlier still the United States Bank employed it to render the public mind benevolent to its schemes. This sort of thing is probably as old as the human race, but public relations work is new—at least it is new as a conscious and understood science.

And Bernays himself is quite the newest type of public relations specialist, so intelligent and so free from the conventional inhibitions that he assumes almost the character of a phenomenon. He does not ask newspapers to print things. He has not been in a newspaper office in ten years. He creates "events and circumstances" which newspapers are compelled to notice as news. But, more important than this, his chief role is the examination of the relations between his clients and the public. . . .

The phenomenon of shirt-stuffing is now almost a force in our national life independent of any individual designs. Our agencies of communication are all geared as parts of a vast selling instrument.

We have endowed them with so much energy that we have but to feed a name or a thing into them properly to have it taken up and pushed with furious and ceaseless vigor.

Mr. Bernays understands this very well. He has actually analyzed it. He has given the process a name. I had, in my unlettered way, called it the principle of labels; Bernays talks of clichés. Whatever it is called, the meaning of it is simple enough. We have but to put a label on a thing and see that it is set loose in the proper place, and our great, interesting, and interested country will do the rest.

The process is seen best in our daily journals. The daily paper is only incidentally a newspaper. It is primarily a form of entertainment. It is a show, and the men who run it are showmen first and last. It presents to us each day, not so much a play composed of many scenes, but rather a single act in a continuous, serialized drama that has neither beginning nor end. Being a show, it must, of course, have its cast of characters—its villians, its heroes, its funny men, its ingenues, its kind old fathers, its lovers. If these gentlemen do not exist in life and in the news, the paper will invent them. All characters are drawn with heavy, bold, broad strokes—caricatures, in fact—so that a deft sweep of the pen is all that is needed to depict any character in any way.

Now let a man or woman of importance stray into the news, no matter how: the copy desk will pounce upon him and put a label on him suggested by the introductory incident. Once this is done, the label will stand for good. These public performers have a way, too, of accepting their labels and making up for the parts, then playing up to them forever thereafter. Nothing this side of heaven can rescue the victim from that label. Let a more or less talkative old Vermonter wander into the news columns with his lips closed tight and a limited dialogue for the day: the desk promptly labels him "the silent man." He becomes quickly "the strong, silent man." With that label on him he will run through ten thousand editions and a whole career, garrulous, erupting words at every opportunity, but he will always be "the strong, silent man."

As I have already said, Edward L. Bernays understands this well enough. As a masterly practitioner of the New Science of Ballyhoo he knows how to put labels on men, on merchandise, on ideas, on events, and march them properly in front of the reporters and in view of the copy desk. He knows that the desk can be depended upon to act up to form.

GETTING HIS IDEAS BEFORE THE PUBLIC

—Institute for Propaganda Analysis, "The Public Relations Counsel and Propaganda," *Propaganda Analysis,* Vol. 1, August 1938, pp. 62–64.

Now the question arises: How does the public relations counsel get his ideas before the public? Naturally, he does not want to use advertising: The advertisement is obvious special pleading, and obvious special pleading, as has already been noted, is relatively ineffectual. Consequently, the public relations counsel attempts to slip his propaganda into the press as news, features, or editorials; into the newsreels under the same guise; into the magazines as unbiased articles, written by disinterested authorities; into the ether as sustaining radio programs; and into the movies.

His simplest, though not in any sense his most potent, technique is merely to print brochures and pamphlets and to distribute them, under the name of his institute, among the nation's "leaders of public opinion." These are the public officials in every community, the leading business men, bankers, educators, civic leaders, and newspaper editors, who have the respect of their fellow citizens, and whose opinions carry weight. No doubt you have received many of these publications. They come from the American Iron and Steel Institute, the Edison Electric Institute, the National Association of Manufacturers, and hundreds of similar organizations. Not long ago the Sutton News Service was sending them out for the Japanese Chamber of Commerce to combat the boycott of Japanese goods. . . .

The most common technique is the newspaper release (newspapermen call them "handouts," but the counsel on public relations abhors that word). These are mimeographed articles, written in newspaper style, which, the public relations counsel is convinced, have news value. Sometimes they have. They may, for example, describe an important and news-worthy contribution to science and industry that has recently been made by the press agent's client. Or again, the client's employes may have gone on strike; their union naturally has made demands and charges; the newspaper release will outline the company's defense.

On the whole, however, these newspaper releases are simply advertisements written as news. They are printed either because the newspaper does not hire enough reporters and is, therefore, short of copy, or else because the publisher thinks he will be able to get advertising from the company if his paper runs its propaganda.

Occasionally, when his client has done nothing of news-interest and he wants to get more space in the papers than he can with releases that are blatant advertising, the public relations counsel will make news. He may stage luncheons, dinners, or conferences, at which prominent men will speak. (The speakers, it goes without saying, will always express the very ideas that he wants to pound into the public's mind.) He may hold contests, like the soap-sculpture contest of the Cleanliness Institute; he may arrange for the award of scholarships to worthy high school graduates; he may arrange such events as the "Golden Jubilee of Light," at which Thomas Edison re-enacted the invention of the incandescent lamp.

New refinements in the press agent's technique are the "news bureaus." These masquerade, though not always with success, as regular news agencies like the Associated Press, the United Press, and the International News Service. They distribute news, pictures, features, and editorials without charge to any paper that would rather save on its editorial budget than print legitimate news. One such organization is Six Star Service, maintained by the National Association of Manufacturers. Among its products is the feature "Uncle Abner Says." Another is the Health News Service, which supplies news of developments in the field of public health—in order to boost the consumption of milk. Still another is the Fashion Worth News, which supplies news of fashions—in order to boost the sale of Cluett Peabody Co. shirts. The Foremost Feature Service sends eleven or twelve news pictures each week to any paper that wants them, but three or four of the pictures are really disguised propaganda.

And do you read the "Letters to the Editor" column in your paper? Surely there can't be propaganda there: just letters from readers with an idea. Yet, according to Walter Winchell, an investigation by New York City editors recently showed that half of the letters they received had originated in one publicity office. And the American Newspaper Publishers Association has frequently pointed out to its members the amazing similarity between letters that supposedly have been written by several different people.

Pick up your newspaper again. Scattered through it are pictures of pretty girls with slender ankles, shapely legs. Most of them are skimpily dressed—in bathing suits, perhaps—and they are swimming, playing tennis, surfboard riding, dancing at (the captions are careful to mention) Spring Lake, N.J.; Sun Valley, Idaho; Old Point Comfort, Va.; Miami and Miami Beach, Fla. Most of those girls are professional actresses. Many of them were posed for the photographs by Carl Byoir, Steve Hanagan, or Hamilton Wright. . . .

This article is not intended to indict the business of public relations. Our society is run by public opinion; daily, institutions clash with institutions, and ideas with ideas, for public favor. In this war of propagandas, as the Institute has pointed out in previous letters, we all participate. What other people do poorly, the public relations counsel does well. If his methods seem rather shoddy, at times—and they do—the fault lies not so much with him as with the conditions that make those methods efficacious: the willingness of the press and radio to coöperate with the public relations counsel, the readiness of the average man or woman to get on the band wagon, the fact that we often let our biases and prejudices, rather than our minds, think for us.

PRESS AGENTS IN ACTION

—Federal Trade Commission, *Utility Corporations:* Summary Report, Resolution No. 83, 70th Congress, 1st Session: *Efforts by Associations and Agencies of Electric and Gas Utilities to Influence Public Opinion,* U. S. Government Printing Office, 1934, pp. 92–97.

THE ORGANIZATION of E. Hofer & Sons of Portland, Oreg. (the San Francisco office and the Salem [Oreg.] office were closed and combined with the office at Portland) is briefly explained in a letter from E. Hofer & Sons, to Mr. A. R. Gwinn, Central Illinois Public Service Co., May 26, 1925, in which it was stated:

> The service of the Manufacturer and Industrial News Bureau is an outgrowth of work started in Oregon, largely in the interest of public utilities, 13 years ago, when, as a matter of self-preservation, utility and other industrial companies found it necessary to get facts before the public in order to counteract the destroying influence of proposed destructive legislation.

About 1924, a conference in Mr. C. A. Coffin's apartment in New York attended by R. M. Hofer and representatives of the utilities including E. A. Coffin, retired chairman of the board of directors of the General Electric Co., Randall Morgan of the United Gas Improvement Co., C. E. Groesbeck, S. Z. Mitchell, W. E. Breed, and E. K. Hall of the Electric Bond & Share Co. group resulted in expanding the Hofer service to the entire country, reaching 14,500 to 15,000 newspapers, particularly country papers, whereas it had formerly reached newspapers in only 15 states in the West.

The annual book gotten out by E. Hofer & Sons for the year 1925 stated:

> The work started by the Manufacturer and Industrial News Bureau in Oregon in 1912 has gradually grown until today, instead of reaching some 200 papers in 1 state with an editorial discussion of the subjects as outlined, we are reaching some 14,000 papers in the 48 states.

Before the New York conference referred to above, so close was the relation between the N.E.L.A. (National Electric Light Association) and this service that in at least one instance a geographic division of the N.E.L.A. collected the Hofer subscriptions from its members and paid them over to the Hofer people. Following this conference, the utilities supported the service to the extent of $84,820.80 a year, to have the Hofer aims, shown below, disseminated through the press of America:

> To help counteract conditions that interfere with the lawful development of business and industries.
>
> To help minimize regulation of industry that is unnecessary or hurtful.
>
> To discourage radicalism in all its forms.
>
> To fight for reasonable taxation by city, county, state, and federal governments.
>
> Straight-from-the-shoulder arguments against socialistic propaganda of whatever nature, because socialism does not square with our American industrial system and is contrary to the very foundation principle of our constitutional form of government.

Although the Hofer service was also supported by contributions from other industries in an amount about equal to that of the utility companies, a letter from E. Hofer & Sons, on May 26, 1925, to A. R. Gwinn, manager, industrial department, Central Illinois Public Service Co., stated:

> . . . the leading utilities of the country have made it possible for us to conduct this work.

On May 16, 1927, R. M. Hofer wrote P. S. Young, vice-president of the Public Service Co., Newark, N.J.:

> It is necessary to depend on those interested in this undertaking to continue subscriptions and to help us get an additional one as opportunity offers. The original subscribers who sponsored this work 4 years ago are still its strongest supporters and have continued subscriptions as in the past, with some substantial increase where new companies have been acquired. . . .

Robert M. Hofer testified that the policy pursued by the Hofer service was persistently to oppose municipal operation of utility plants and government participation in business.

Referring to the value of this service in this respect Mr. Coffin's views were:

> The Hofer service has been of especial value to public utilities. Hofer has pointed out in the clearest way and over again the dangers of municipal ownership, and the value of customer ownership; he has fought to a finish the Bone bill in the State of Washington and largely contributed to the defeat of the California power bill. He effectively shows the unwisdom of tax-exempt bonds. The telephone company at first brought this to my attention, with the statement that Hofer had done great service in changing the attitude of the legislatures in the Northwest and North Pacific counties toward the telephone company.

One of the most outstanding articles of this nature appearing in the *Manufacturer*, the monthly publication, included a map issued by N.E.L.A. showing comparative percentages by states of the generating capacity and population served, between privately owned electric light and power systems and municipally operated electric plants. This map showed that 90 per cent of the population was served by private companies which represented 94.5 per cent of the total generating capacity of the 48 states. Six hundred newspapers reproduced this story from the *Manufacturer*.

The *Manufacturer* from September 1926 to May 1928 contained articles similar to those in the weekly news sheet, relating to socialism, customer ownership, disparagement of the Ontario hydroelectric situation, government ownership, the Swing-Johnson bill, sale of municipal plants, Muscle Shoals, views of Martin J. Insull on holding companies, views of Samuel Insull on private initiative, and articles in disparagement of municipally owned street railways.

The following captions are illustrative of hundreds of a similar character of material contained in the weekly bulletin:

Why Special Legislation.

A Practical Answer (relating to Muscle Shoals).

Note Taxes Paid.

Records Speak for Themselves.

Utilities Fight for Private Rights (statement by George B. Cortelyou, chairman of joint committee).

Municipal Ownership Limits Service.

Purchased Power Cheapest.

Taxpayer Pays for Experiments (statement of Alexander Dow, president of Detroit Edison Co.); relating to municipal ownership.

The Socialistic Drive in California (*re* California Water and Power Act).

Would Destroy Industrial Opportunity (relating to socialism).

Customer Ownership Increasing.

Utility Securities Inspire Confidence (relating to customer ownership).

The Public Utilities (comments of President Sloan of Brooklyn Edison Co., *re* putting Federal government into the electric power business).

Too Many Umpires (statement of Representative Charles A. Eaton, of New Jersey, *re* political bureaucracy and government interference).

New Profession Develops in Generation (address of P. H. Gadsden, vice-president United Gas Improvement Co., concerning customer ownership constituting a strong protection against radical and ill-considered changes in policy).

105 Municipal Plants Sold During Year (quotations from N.E.L.A. report showing 1,234 municipal plants sold or abandoned).

A large part of the weekly service sent out is editorial in form and has been reproduced as editorials in great numbers of papers throughout the country, without indicating the Hofer source. The following quotation shows Mr. Hofer's claim relative to this editorial achievement:

> Reproduction of our articles appear almost invariably as original editorials, as we ask no credit.

A letter from G. W. Curren, secretary United Gas Improvement Co., to H. S. Whipple, vice-president Rockford Gas Light & Coke Co., June 10, 1927, also makes the claim that

> The articles are reproduced extensively as original editorial and news.

What their character was and what their appeal was that lured

$84,000 per annum from the private utility groups and companies are thus stated:

> We show the blighting effect government or public ownership has on private initiative and enterprise. We show that drastic and radical rate regulation which kills utility development hurts the community worse than the company; we show that exorbitant taxation of business is simply indirect taxation of the consuming public.

In addition to the service, Mr. Hofer also carried on correspondence with editors giving at some length arguments against municipal ownership of utility plants.

E. Hofer & Sons furnished three different services or publications. The newspapers receiving these Hofer services did not pay for them, nor was it disclosed to them that the service was paid for by the persons who contributed $170,000 yearly. They published a monthly industrial trade journal magazine known as the *Manufacturer,* also a weekly mimeographed *Industrial News Bureau Bulletin,* which consisted of from 2 to 4 sheets of editorial matter discussing problems affecting basic conditions in the country and in each state. The third was a weekly state industrial review, which was sent to the papers of each state, and which accompanied the *Industrial News Bureau Bulletin,* and which amounted to 2,496 original reviews per annum.

In the rural press the reproductions of articles appeared almost invariably as original editorials, and constituted

> a vigorous and continuous drive in favor of business and industrial stability, and counteracted radicalism in all its forms.

Notwithstanding its 50 per cent support by utilities, the Hofer service represented itself to be

> an independent publication dissociated from direct connection with any industry,

and

> doing a highly intensive and scientific line of publicity work which is reaching more people continuously with the industrial idea through the country daily and weekly newspapers of this nation than are being reached by any other single agency.

The place for any results from such an alleged "independent" service was expressed in a letter written on September 27, 1926, by R. M. Hofer to J. D. Pettegrew, Nebraska Power Co., Omaha:

> The Nebraska Utilities Information Committee and the information bureau of the N.E.L.A. can give authentic information on statistics, management, operation, etc., of electric light and power companies. These organizations represent the industry and speak with authority on matters of fact. After such information has been issued it is then a question of getting it commented on editorially and thoroughly understood by the general public.
>
> At this point our organization begins to function. As an independent publication not directly and primarily affiliated with electric-light companies, but discussing various industrial problems, we can take up many legislative, political, taxation, and government ownership questions and discuss them as they affect public utilities. In other words, a third-party opinion is often accepted with less bias in an editorial discussion than a statement from parties directly interested.

The utility source of some of this "independent" matter appears in a letter of March 5, 1925, which A. W. Flor, publicity man for the Electric Bond & Share Co., wrote C. E. Groesbeck, vice-president of the same company and also a member of the 1924 conference in New York, which arranged for expanding the service to cover the entire country. In this letter Mr. Flor stated that he had gotten in touch with Mr. Hofer when he was in town and spent an afternoon with him preparing a story for use in his service which was sent to 14,000 papers. This story was published in the weekly bulletin and bore the caption "Inevitable Rate Raise Occurs in Cleveland," referring to Cleveland's municipal electric plant.

On March 7, 1928, P. H. Gadsden, vice-president of the United Gas Co., wrote to P. S. Young, vice-president of the Public Service Corporation, Newark, N. J., expressing satisfaction with the results attained, as follows:

> I have kept in close touch with the Hofer service and have become very much impressed with the value of the publicity work which is being done. We have on several occasions asked Mr. Hofer to send us clippings for various states in which we were interested and I have been astonished at the volume of it.
>
> Recently I spent an hour with Mr. Hofer going over his work, and I am more than ever satisfied that he is performing a very valuable service not only to the public utilities of the country but to business interests generally.

N.E.L.A. also approved this work. The association clipped editorial articles, written by the Hofer service, from local papers and credited the local editor. Concerning the effect of this, Mr. Hofer said:

Such recognition of a local editor, by an organization as well known as the N.E.L.A., encourages newspaper editors to advocate sound and constructive ideas.

Favorable indirect as well as direct results were apparent soon after the 1924 meeting in New York of Mr. Hofer and utility executives, for the 1925 edition of the annual book published by E. Hofer & Sons contained the following statement:

> There is one effect of our service the importance of which cannot be estimated, namely, its influence in causing editors who read it but never use our articles to consider questions from a more conservative viewpoint and refrain from running much radical material which would otherwise appear in their papers. It has had that effect in many instances which have come to our observation.

In correspondence at various times, Mr. Hofer stated the quantity of material reproduced in the rural press from 1924 to 1927, and showed that for 17 months ending October 1924, reproduction in all states was estimated to be 27,000,000 lines or about 25,000 pages; for 1926, the amount of publicity obtained was estimated to be 2,318,964 inches, or about 19,325 solid pages, and for 1927, the total estimated inches were 3,111,420.

Inasmuch as Mr. Hofer testified that the policy of the service was persistently to oppose municipal operation of utility plants and government operation in business, it is safe to assume that a major portion of the reproduced articles carried this viewpoint, and related particularly to the utilities.

SOME FAULTS OF THE PRESS AGENT

—Lee Trenholm, "Press Agents Irritate the Press," *The Public Opinion Quarterly,* School of Public and International Affairs, Princeton University, Vol. 2, October 1938, pp. 671–677. Mr. Trenholm is a public relations counsellor.

WHAT NEWSPAPERMEN invariably call press-agentry but what we publicity people insist is public relations has come a long way since Tody Hamilton's day, but evolution of its technique has barely begun. This becomes apparent upon inquiry into today's tactics of many of the publicity fraternity.

Seek as we may to dignify our status and our methods; conscientiously strive as many of us do for a forthright bearing and reputation; regret as we must the undeniable obloquy into which numbers of our colleagues have fallen—twenty years' observation as both newspaper and publicity man, coupled with a current consensus of typical editors, convinces me that the craft's conduct by and large hardly becomes a group aspiring to professional or semi-professional recognition.

As William H. Vanderbilt's petulant execration of the public was thought to represent the typical capitalistic outlook, so it may be paraphrased into "the press be damned" to summarize the astounding attitude most public relations practitioners appear to share. Arising primarily out of selfishness, indifference, or ignorance, it is nonetheless as inexpedient as if it partook of the active hostility it usually excites in the Fourth Estate.

Most public relations people will deny that such an attitude exists. What we choose to believe, however, matters little beside the unflattering view actually held by countless key executives of newspapers, press associations, magazines, newspicture services, feature syndicates, newsreels, the radio, and the other portals to public opinion through which we must everlastingly tread.

When newspapers, if they refer at all, speak depreciatingly of the press agent, one cannot wonder that a more and more publicity-wise public has come to entertain the same uncomplimentary notions. If the press, which knows us best, thinks ill of us, how can the public be expected to regard us otherwise? It is strange, perhaps significant, that as a whole we have done for ourselves, our principles, and our functions one of the poorest public relations jobs. There is probably good and sufficient reason for our shunning the very light we seek for others. Our professional self-effacement stands well advised beside what unsought and usually unwelcome inquiry into our methods customarily reveals.

The two most sincere attempts of public relations men to organize have been successfully frustrated by public relations men themselves. Nor is it reassuring that a present move in the same direction, fostered by professional trade-association promoters, is already involved in an unduly prolonged and potentially fatal effort to formulate a code of ethics. This may appear less puzzling when it is remembered that one of this embryonic organization's directors was openly accused by the Publishers Association of New York City of handling a client's fund of $12,000 for distribution among "deserving" editorial workers.

One occupying an executive chair in any press organization knows the motley procession in public relations masquerade that troops endlessly before him. With the majority's tricks, their evasiveness, and their incompetence he is painfully familiar. Separating the sheep from the goats is a process so complex and precarious that it is not worth while. As a result, all are suspect *per se.*

Newspapers are still the basic avenue to public opinion. Our activities accordingly impinge upon theirs more often than upon any other publicity medium. So it behooves us to keep constantly fresh our understanding of their separate and collective requirements, their problems, and their attitude toward us personally and toward the public relations school in general.

On the one hand we find the inflexible view of the American Newspaper Publishers Association. As an organization, itself admittedly pleading a special cause and with the advertising department obviously uppermost in mind, it considers us utterly indefensible. Regardless of merit as judged by the strictest editorial standards, whatever we offer must be advertising simply because it comes unsolicited, the Association contends, and as such has no place in the editorial columns.

The A.N.P.A.'s thirty years' strumming of this melody has struck responsive chords in many an editorial breast, as is notably manifest in the cooperative embargoes on publicity agreed upon by the newspapers of Atlanta, Los Angeles, Nashville, Binghamton, and other cities. Its hostility achieved emotional heights in the Virginia Press Association's recent symbolic bonfire of publicity releases on the beach at Old Point Comfort.

"Pufflicity" is a pet item in the Association's lexicon of damnation. Repeated with emphasis on every page of the anti-publicity tracts with which its membership is circularized at least once each week are shibboleths such as "They won't pay for it if you give it away!" and "The press agent is an unfair competitor." Many an unsuspecting public relations counsellor would blush with surprise and chagrin at the incisive aspersions cast upon him individually and by name in these well-informed leaflets—or to see how utterly silly one of his handouts looks when set verbatim as a display advertisement!

It would be salutary for us to reflect occasionally upon this proposition that the press agent is commercially a competitor rather than professionally a collaborator of the press and to gauge our press relations accordingly. Almost any publicity prospectus or report confirms this theory by pretensions to deliver or to have achieved fabulous values in advertising for fees representing a small percentage of what the same space would cost the client at the usual rates. Funds so diverted to press-agent pockets, in the Association's inveterate argument, are substantial losses to advertising revenue. We would not gainsay it if we could!

Few editors rigidly practice what the A.N.P.A. so eloquently and tenaciously preaches. For the most part they subscribe to the late Adolph S. Ochs's truism that source of origin in no way affects true news values. To publicity people about whose dependability they have satisfied themselves, countless editors look for welcome tips, acceptable copy, printable pictures.

But editors one and all, apparently without exception, concur in the Association's cardinal accusation—that publicity people employ tactics uniformly indirect, frequently disingenuous, often downright furtive. "Nom-de-press-agent" is another A.N.P.A. turn of phrase to stigmatize the guise publicity too often endeavors to assume to mask its true sponsorship and goal.

That is a charge we find hard to refute. Yet there seems little justification, even if there be explanation, for it. Why must we interminably "put one over" on the press? Isn't it enough that through it we merely attain our ends? Frankness and directness, rather than deception and obliquity, should prove the more effective permanent policy; certainly it would be the simpler. Surely the events of Inner-Sole Week suffer no diminution of news value, if any, because they are openly sponsored by the Inner-Sole Manufacturers Association rather than by a so-called Inner-Sole Institute.

Success of the first 10,000 such devices in offsetting a deficiency of that essential newsworthiness no doubt explains their immortality in a thousand forms. They are as varied and as crafty, it is said, as the schemes of tax-dodgers. Their very antiquity, however, and the increasing irritation and resistance they meet from the press would seem to better the chances of other, fresher recourses.

Distinctiveness of approach to press and public is easy to achieve against so trite and inept a background. To an editor up to his ears in manifold publicity pressure in behalf of overlapping Grandpa Day, Nutcracker Week, Pogo-Stick Month, the open-faced proffer of an honest-to-goodness news story from Pussywillows, Inc., comes as an appreciated breath of candor in a miasma of dissimulation.

A great many publicity workers obviously mistake indirection for cleverness. The more involved the fruition of their ideas, the more effort is entailed and the greater the display of industry to keep the client impressed. Intrigue seems to be an ingrained habit of the publicity mind which colors all thought and endeavor. It is no doubt needed in many cases to hide the dubious hue of the client or his purposes. Public relations counsellors, like counsellors at law, are known largely by the clients they keep and our reputation would be a lot prouder, it would appear, if we avoided those requiring an underhand or mendacious approach to press consideration and public favor.

Gross ignorance of editorial requirements appears next among the main complaints of editors against publicity practitioners, even those of unchallengeable integrity. Copy and suggestions ideal for feature use are offered as straight news to the city desk; potentially usable items of strictly news nature are submitted to Sunday magazine editors, and otherwise acceptable departmentalized material finds its way into the wastebasket as much for submission to the wrong desk as for inherent unavailability. Deceased and transferred editors preponderate on most publicity distribution lists, judging by the amount of material bearing their names. It is an unwritten rule in many editorial offices that obsolete addressing of that kind is *prima facie* proof of uselessness.

One out of ten press agents, some editors estimate, fully understands the importance of the time element.

Publicity copy generally is regarded as too discursive. Little of it is as factually rich as newspapers and magazines demand.

Especially is this so when it comes to client mention. Names are dragged in by the heels apropos of nothing, and great indignation is expressed if they are deleted or if a definite commitment is not forthcoming that they will be used as is. An appropriate and not constrained reference or two to the client is not a source of objection from most editors in truly worthy copy or suggested stories. But just how far some of us would have them go is illustrated by a recent masterful release announcing a new cosmetic in which the product was mentioned by trade-name eight times and its manufacturer five times in a single page!

Inaccuracy, bugaboo of all who go to the public in print, is of course another source of editorial grievance. Editors worn with vigilance against their own errors find inaccuracies in publicity material particularly irritating—and it requires no hawk-eyed copyreader to discover an abundance of them among a specimen assortment of releases received any day by any newspaper. Many errors arise from overstatement.

Misinformation seems to creep as much into abbreviated copy accompanying photographic material as into larger textual matter. Perhaps because they must be brief, captions seem to convey a higher percentage of erroneous impressions. That pictures usually represent a much greater investment of effort and money than other forms of publicity suggests that time is wisely spent in the careful composition and thorough verification of the explanatory text which supplements them.

In the photographs themselves, picture editors see room for immeasurable improvement. Good picture subjects are often as not photographically massacred; excellent treatment is wasted on impossible topics; highly acceptable prints reach picture desks 50 per cent of the time so late that their value is largely dissipated, and they even come uncaptioned.

Such is the cream of complaints about our operational shortcomings which newspaper, magazine, press association, and picture service editors voice and which feature syndicate, newsreel, radio, and other desks in one form or another echo. Lesser irritants are legion: absence from releases of unequivocal identification of their source; attempts to apply pressure through the business office or editorial superiors; an overreadiness to dispute the definition of indefinable "news"; bothersome requests for "tear sheets" and for the return of unusable material; unwarranted personal appeals for "cooperation," and copy frequently so illegible that one Puckish Midwestern daily reports that government handouts from Washington "are so neatly printed that their backs can be used for copy paper while most private press material is so badly offset that it has to go directly into the wastebasket."

Imagine the maladroit short-sightedness of the publicity organization promoting foreign travel which requested papers and magazines finding its offerings unsuitable to so advise it so that their names might be removed from the mailing list! To one editor who affirmatively complied, this appreciation was dispatched:

> We are pleased to inform you that we shall be delighted to take your name from our list. We have the most serious doubts whether your

publicity would be of any value to us, regardless of whether the publicity or advertising you carried were free or paid.

Organized public relations may some day evolve a code of ethics for its collective guidance. It will be a revelation many of us await with as much misgiving as interest. Unless the concepts and conduct of most of us undergo decided prior change it will probably prove a meaningless summarization of high-sounding theories calculated to throw the cloak of idealism about practices still unidealistic.

Meanwhile, a few will have foresight enough, and in the eyes of their cleverer confreres will be naïve enough, to hold and act upon the conviction that their standing with the various publicity media shapes and limits accomplishment for their clients. Consciously or otherwise they will adjust their press attitudes and actions to policies approximating these:

> They will serve no cause requiring misrepresentation; they will speak for no one except with candor and frankness; they will guard their press reputation more jealously than their most valued clients; they will inform themselves in detail of the editorial standards, policies, and requirements of at least the major publicity outlets with which they deal; they will spare no effort to make accurate and to verify every detail of statement and fact offered in their clients' behalf; they will conduct their press dealings with all the art of human relations at their command.

When all or a majority of us are fundamentally guided by similar considerations, press and public alike will view us with less disrespect. Greater sympathy and cooperation will be extended, and our individual and aggregate lot should be happier, healthier, and more prosperous.

CASE EXAMPLE OF PUBLICITY

—Ralph D. Casey, "The Press, Propaganda, and Pressure Groups," *The Press in the Contemporary Scene, The Annals of the American Academy of Political and Social Science,* Vol. 219, January 1942, pp. 69–70.

THE PROBLEM every newspaper faces in separating news from propaganda is trying and difficult. Nowadays almost every organized group has some knowledge of publicity techniques, and the issues these groups seek to promote gain for their cause an advantage usually involving much greater matters than the trivial events reported by the press agents of an older generation.

Perhaps the problem can best be illustrated by describing a minor event in which an effort was made to manipulate the news. The reader will perceive at once that questions of greater importance for an editor arise when major events are stage managed by propagandists, especially when the latter are highly placed in government or industry.

Last October a chap named Hopkins, hitherto an obscure parachute jumper, dropped from a plane to the top of Devil's Tower, Wyoming, bailing out above the monolith and spilling his 'chute as required until he reached the top of his lofty goal. The jump was clearly a promotional stunt. The resulting mild controversy between a Rapid City, South Dakota, managing editor and a Fairmont, Minnesota, editorial writer as to whether a photograph of the leap should have been sent to the press by a news association picture service, illustrates the dilemma faced by newspapers even in such an inconsequential item as this.

The Fairmont editor referred to the affair as "the cheapest kind of a purposeless publicity stunt, something quite different from a legitimate news happening." And he inquired, "If this conclusion isn't correct, how come the news writers and picture takers happened to be there just at the right moment?" To which the Rapid City *Journal* replied a few days later:

> There was no deception involved in the Devil's Tower affair. Hopkins did go aloft in a plane, did bail out, and did land on Devil's Tower. That was newsworthy and, of course, local newspapermen and photographers were on hand to record the event, just as the Fairmont *Sentinel* staff would have been on hand had Hopkins undertaken a similar stunt in that city.
>
> Had everything gone according to schedule, Hopkins' leap would have been a story of local and minor interest, soon forgotten. But the unexpected happened. He couldn't get down. That was news . . . and as such it was given wide play in newspapers throughout the country.

Every editor has to determine whether an event is sufficiently interesting to warrant publication. This is the real test. The Fairmont *Sentinel* probably had no compunctions in publishing the exciting adventure of Leonard Coatsworth in escaping from the toppling Narrows bridge near Tacoma a year or two ago, an episode not inspired by a publicity man; yet Hopkins' rescue was no less interesting than Coatsworth's mad scramble to safety. The benefit an individual or group receives as a result of publicity cannot, moreover, serve as a final test of its legitimacy. To reject all propaganda-inspired material at the threshold of the news room is hardly a satisfactory solution of the problem. The fact that a news story benefits someone, whether written by a reporter or a publicity man, is hardly a test, since much of the news is likely to have values for some persons or groups.

Furtive sponging on the press is easy to circumvent, but newspapers cannot disregard interesting and important events simply because the master hand of a propagandist is behind the scenes pulling strings. Neither can they post a warning sign over what appears to be propaganda, since sometimes the journalist would run grave risks in judgment. . . .

REVIEW QUESTIONS AND ASSIGNMENTS

1. What signs are there that press agentry has entered a new era?

2. In attempting to explain the rise of the press agent, prepare a list of types of news that regular reporters might have difficulty in obtaining. Explain why the difficulties would exist.

3. Show the relationship between the rise of "big business" and the appearance of the press agent. Why did business need a voice? Why couldn't the regular press serve as a voice?

4. Discuss this statement: "If the publicity man wishes free publicity, he has, speaking quite accurately, to start something." Can you cite examples?

5. Interview a publicity man in your city and try to find out his theories on dealing with the press, news values, relations with clients, and his position in the community.

6. Do you see any distinction between the work of a government press agent and a public relations counsel for the Pennsylvania Railroad?

7. Select any major event recently sponsored by some group in your community and prepare an account of the way in which its publicity was written and distributed.

8. How would you state the case for and against the press agent from the standpoint of a newspaper editor?

9. Do you see any way in which the newspapers might effectively eliminate the press agent?

10. Study your local paper for one week and then prepare an estimate of how much and what kind of news the paper printed from what you consider to be press agent sources.

11. If you were the editor of a daily in a city of 100,000, what position would you take toward the press agent? What distinction would you make between the press agent for the ministerial association and the press agent for the theater managers?

ADDITIONAL REFERENCES

Bailey, Thomas A., *The Man in the Street,* Macmillan, 1948, pp. 291–303.

Batchelor, Bronson, *Profitable Public Relations,* Harper & Brothers, 1938.

Bent, Silas, *Ballyhoo: The Voice of the Press,* Liveright, 1927.

Bernays, Edward L., *Crystallizing Public Opinion,* Liveright, 1923.

———, "Engineering of Consent," *The Annals of the American Academy of Political and Social Science,* Vol. 250, March 1947, p. 113.

———, *Propaganda,* Liveright, 1928.

———, "Speak Up for Democracy," *Current History,* Vol. 52, October 1940, p. 21.

Broughton, Averell, *The New Profession,* E. P. Dutton, 1943.

Casey, Ralph D., and Glenn C. Quiett, *Principles of Publicity,* Appleton-Century, 1934.

Cerf, Bennett, "Sweet Are the Uses of Publicity," *American Mercury,* Vol. 59, October 1944, p. 436.

Doob, Leonard W., *Public Opinion and Propaganda,* Henry Holt, 1948, pp. 269–270, 323–325, 367–370, 429–440, 552.

Fine, Benjamin, *College Publicity in the United States,* Bureau of Publications, Teachers College, Columbia University, 1941.

Fiske, Frances, *So You're Publicity Chairman,* Whittlesey House, 1940.

Fitzgerald, Stephen E., "Public Relations: A Profession in Search of Professionals," *Public Opinion Quarterly,* Vol. 10, Summer 1946, p. 191.

Goldman, Eric F., *Two-Way Street,* Bellman, 1948.

Griswold, Glenn, and Denny Griswold, *Your Public Relations,* Funk & Wagnalls, 1948.

Hocking, William Ernest, *Freedom of the Press,* University of Chicago Press, 1947, pp. 130–131.

Irwin, Will, *Propaganda and the News,* McGraw-Hill, 1936.

Johnston, Alva, "Hundred-Tongue Charley, the Great Silent Orator," *The Saturday Evening Post,* Vol. 208, May 30, 1936.

Kienle, Edward C., "Press Relations and a Wedding," *Public Opinion Quarterly,* Vol. 1, October 1937, p. 136.

Lee, Ivy L., *Publicity,* Industries Publishing, 1925.

Lockwood, Arthur, "Press Agent Tells All," *American Mercury,* Vol. 49, February 1940, p. 173.

MacNeil, Neil, *Without Fear or Favor,* Harcourt, Brace, 1940, pp. 300–317.

Merton, Robert K., *Mass Persuasion,* Harper & Brothers, 1946.

Miller, John C., *Sam Adams, Pioneer in Propaganda,* Little, Brown, 1936.

Overstreet, H. S., *Influencing Human Behavior,* W. W. Norton, 1925.

Plackard, D. H., and Clifton Blackman, *Blueprint for Public Relations,* McGraw-Hill, 1947, pp. 7–30.

Regier, C. C., *The Era of the Muckrakers,* University of North Carolina Press, 1932.

Riegel, O. W., "Propaganda and the Press," *The Annals of the American Academy of Political and Social Science,* Vol. 179, May 1935, pp. 203–204.

Riis, R. W., and C. W. Bonner, Jr., *Publicity, a Study of the Development of Industrial News,* Dodd, Mead, 1926.

Sills, Theodore, and Lesly, Philip, *Public Relations,* Richard D. Irwin, 1945, p. 255.

Sorrells, John H., *The Working Press,* Ronald Press, 1930.

Walker, Stanley, *City Editor,* Frederick A. Stokes, 1934.

Wright, J. Handly, and Byron H. Christian, *Public Relations in Management,* McGraw-Hill, 1949.

25. RADIO AS A NEWS MEDIUM

INTRODUCTION

THE LINES of struggle between press and radio grow clearer with each passing year. At first the press fought with every ounce of its strength to keep radio from becoming a newscaster. It failed. Later it tried to prevent its new rival from becoming a news gatherer. Here, too, it failed. But the evidence appears to prove that this fear of radio as a news disseminator was in large part groundless, for radio listening seems to increase newspaper reading, rather than decrease it. However, what the press would never have believed could come about has happened—a large part of the citizenry is quicker to believe the radio than the press on numerous points. Other surprising trends are also noted in the citations in this chapter.

The early history of the conflict between press and radio is traced by Carskadon. In a fast-changing industry this struggle is almost ancient history, but it is nevertheless important. Schramm and Huffer in a pioneering press-radio study reveal how some segments of the population now depend entirely upon the radio for certain types of information. They also reveal the extent to which various groups believe the information received from press and radio.

In one of the interesting events of recent days, radio has developed a program in which certain metropolitan newspapers are put on the spot for their errors of omission and commission. A discussion of this program is presented by Don Hollenbeck of CBS. One of the first efforts to compare press and radio treatment of an outstanding news story has been done by Lillian Gottlieb in her article on the Heirens murder case. Although but one radio station and five daily newspapers were studied, the analysis is worth scrutiny because it also is a pioneering effort at coming to a better understanding of the relative merits of press and radio.

Many people are concerned by the centralization of radio ownership and by the ownership of broadcasting facilities by the press. This is particularly true where the single local daily also may own the sole local radio station. This problem is discussed by Brucker. Some of the effects of the competitive struggle, particularly for advertising revenues, are set forth by Kinter. White analyzes another problem in the same area—the extent to which press and radio are free from dominance by advertisers. In the case of the radio, advertisers control both advertising copy and programs, according to White. The reader of this chapter should keep in mind that disinterested research in the area of press-radio struggle is just getting underway.

RADIO STRUGGLE FOR A FOOTHOLD

—T. R. Carskadon, "The Press-Radio War," *The New Republic,* Vol. 86, March 11, 1936, pp. 132–135. The author is a member of the executive staff of The Twentieth Century Fund and is in charge of the Fund's educational program.

THE BATTLE between newspapers and the radio goes on. It has elements of high comedy, utmost seriousness, and coarse vulgarity, but the fact remains that every bit of news you receive from whatever source today is increasingly colored and conditioned by radio. For years newspaper publishers have fought the bad fight, using boycotts, reprisals, intimidation, ridicule, and injunctions in a relentless effort to make radio shut its many-tubed mouth, but the end is failure. Today the major press services are selling direct to radio stations; the largest newspaper chains, Hearst and Scripps-Howard, are busily lining up radio chains, and there are now more news broadcasts on the air than at any time since De Forest and other workers with the vacuum tube made broadcasting possible and mediocrity audible.

Things were not always thus. When radio emerged in the early nineteen-twenties newspapers received it with thoughtless enthusiasm. Here was a brand-new industry mushrooming into being, advertisements for receiving sets were coming in, and it was just as well to help the thing along by printing daily program schedules and stray bits of gossip about radio activities. As commercial broadcasting developed, it was thought that listing sponsored programs was a pleasant way of complimenting prospective advertisers. This beneficent attitude endured throughout the golden era of Calvin the Silent and Andrew the Tax-Returner until the arrival, seriatim, of Herbert Hoover, 1929, and the crash.

Came the depression, and came trouble for the newspapers. Radio by that time had produced some remarkable selling programs, such as Amos 'n' Andy's campaign for Pepsodent, and radio was new, gadgety, and (comparatively) cheap. Harassed advertising managers, confronted with drastically shrunken budgets, were of a mind to try radio and get theoretically equivalent coverage for only the fraction of the cost of printed media. The result was that in 1930 and even more in 1931, while newspapers were showing vicious and in some cases disastrous drops in advertising revenue, the big radio chains marched on to ever greater profits.

The resulting howls from newspapers was no less gentle for being human and understandable. Their revenues were dropping, radio's were mounting—*ergo:* radio must be stealing the business from the newspapers. To make matters worse, a new type of program was coming to great popularity. This was the news broadcaster or commentator, led by the trigger-tongued Floyd Gibbons, the Chicago *Tribune's* gift to journalistic exhibitionism. Contemporary with him were such figures as William Hard, David Lawrence, H. V. Kaltenborn, and others who fed the public's growing appetite for news and comment over the air. Radio was not only hamstringing advertising receipts, but it was dishing out free what newspapers had to sell.

After a futile attempt to maintain the too-proud-to-fight, or thou-worm attitude, the newspapers finally lashed out and belted radio on the nose. Early in 1931 the papers said, in effect, that they would be good and damned if they were going to give free advertising to commercial concerns who deserted them for radio, and henceforth all commercial names were to be omitted from program listings. Thus the Atwater Kent program became "concert hour" and the Clicquot Club Eskimos became "Eskimos orchestra" and radio news items and supplementary publicity were practically abolished.

Things rode along until the spring of 1932, when a crisis was precipitated by the kidnapping of the Lindbergh baby. That whole episode was and continues to be a ghastly affair, but it was unquestionably the biggest news story since the World War. The big networks were on the air practically twenty-four hours a day. Radio regularly ran ahead of the fastest newspaper distribution by minutes, hours, and even days. Here, beyond any question, was the news-disseminating agency of the future.

Newspapers, however, represent vast and powerful vested interests. Radio stations, allowed to exist solely by reason of ninety-day renewable licenses issued by the federal government, were by no means eager for a trial of strength with the newspapers. Far from following up its advantage, radio did everything possible to recede from newscasting and tried to placate the press. History worked against the attempt. The two national conventions, the bonus marchers, the political campaign, kept radio on the air with more and more news—delivered with eyewitness immediacy and color.

The newspapers were beside themselves with rage. Not only was radio wildly and flagrantly invading the field, but here in mid-1932, in the very valley and bottom of the greatest depression the world had ever known, when any legitimate business should be honestly and decently losing its shirt, the big radio networks kept marching right straight ahead to still greater receipts and still greater profits. The newspapers now came up with blood in their eyes. Following the annual meeting of the national association of newspaper publishers in the spring of 1933, the papers asserted their property rights in the news and flatly decreed that no news should be broadcast unless it was directly gathered by the networks or individual stations themselves.

This precipitated chaos. In the good old days, news commentators got their material largely by buying late editions of the afternoon papers, jotting down a few notes and marching up to the microphone. This process was given some refinements as the news broadcasts grew enormously in popularity and such present-day favorites as Lowell Thomas, and Boake Carter, and Edwin C. Hill began to appear, but even so, the simple act of "lifting" news from late papers remained a prime factor in radio procedure. With this source closed, the big networks faced the necessity of gathering their own news or taking their very popular and lucrative newscasters off the air.

The networks decided to fight. By collecting hand-outs and by the judicious use of telephone calls to governors, mayors, chiefs of police, and others, radio achieved an astonishingly complete news coverage.

The Columbia Broadcasting System, always fast on its feet, saw an opportunity and made the most of it. Under the leadership of Paul White, veteran of the United Press, Columbia set up its own news service, with correspondents in American and foreign cities, an able editorial staff, leased wires, and a fast, terse coverage of world news. They got under way late in the summer of 1933, and within a month it was obvious that they were going places. As a matter of fact, in the fall of 1933 radio had the newspapers licked. The broadcasters were operating independently of the established news services, and they were daily getting on the air with spot news before the newspapers could get copies on the street.

In the midst of victory came the call to retreat. There were three main reasons for this. First was the old and never dying fear of newspaper agitation against monopoly. (The federal government in allotting to a radio station one of the very limited number of available wave lengths does, in fact, without charge confer a monopoly privilege which is thereafter exploited for private profit.) The second reason was that whereas Columbia had a complete news service, its older and larger rival, the National Broadcasting Company, had none, and was thus more disposed to negotiate. The third reason was that in 1933 the depression finally caught up with the big networks. For the first time since they were founded, their receipts and profits showed a drop—it was both slight and temporary, but a drop, none the less—and this made them less arrogant.

There ensued the famous "Biltmore Conference" of December 1933. In smoke and hate-filled rooms in the Hotel Biltmore in New York City, radio and the newspapers came to terms. But alas, what was hailed officially as radio's Locarno turned out to be radio's Versailles. The two big networks must withdraw completely from gathering their own news, they must restrict their newscasters to "interpretation" and "comment," and the actual broadcasting of news must be confined to two five-minute periods daily, one in the morning and one at night. This news would be supplied free by the major wire services to the Press-Radio Bureau ("For further details read your daily newspaper"), and the broadcasters would bear the administrative and transmission costs of the Bureau. News announcements must not be sold commercially, must be limited to thirty words per item, and special bulletins were to be issued only on news of "transcendental" importance.

Such savage restrictions were an open invitation to revolt. It came. The two big networks dutifully signed the agreement and it was arranged that the Press-Radio Bureau would start operations on March 1, 1934, but the independent stations were howling bloody murder. It must be remembered that out of a total of approximately 600 radio stations in America, fewer than 200 are affiliated with the big networks and only a small percentage of these are wholly owned and wholly controlled by the networks. Disgruntled affiliates, independent stations, regional groupings such as the Yankee Network and a Northwestern group centering around Seattle, all set out to gather their own news.

By far the most potent entry in this field was Trans-Radio Press Service. This was headed by Herbert L. Moore, a dynamic young Southerner who had worked with Paul White in building up the Columbia News Service and who refused to let a good idea go to waste. Starting with the proverbial shoestring and aided by some Columbia veterans, he was ready to offer a rival service when the Press-Radio Bureau began operations on March 1, 1934. By the end of the year, Trans-Radio was clearly leading the independent field, and the Press-Radio Bureau, under pressure of actual broadcasting experience, had removed such silly restrictions as the thirty-words-per-item rule, had allowed more convenient time schedules and was giving very liberal interpretation of the word "transcendental" in determining the importance of items to be released as bulletins for immediate broadcast. Along came the Hauptmann trial early in 1935. Radio, by the simple elimination of paper, type, and presses, was ever and always first with the actual flash news, and the newspapers began to see the inevitable coming.

It was simply impossible to keep news from the radio stations, and the established wire services might just as well sell it to them and thus prevent further radio encroachments in the field of actual newsgathering. This was the most momentous decision in the long history of the press-radio wars, and it was announced following the annual meeting of the American Newspaper Publishers Association last year. On April 29, 1935, Mr. Hearst's two organizations, International News Service and Universal Service, and the Scripps-Howard child, United Press, offered to sell their services to all radio comers. The Associated Press, a cooperative non-profit organization, was by its charter prevented from selling news, but by paying a certain premium percentage of their annual assessment, member newspapers that own radio stations may use Associated Press for their own broadcasts.

Many newspaper publishers hoped that the entry of the old-line wire services into the field would crush Trans-Radio, but Trans-Radio is now serving some 250 stations, or practically as many as those served by all the old-line agencies put together. Trans-Radio has its own correspondents and staff in principal American cities and European capitals; makes free use of the technique of direct telephone to the scene of news; maintains the only twenty-four hour open-wire service in the world; and above all keeps its channels always open for flash headline news, without clogging the system with the endless columns of background, supplementary, feature, and "dope" material that so impede the flow of the old-line wire services. Trans-Radio has scored some notable "beats," such as the Dillinger escape, the correct Hauptmann verdict, and the Italian invasion of Ethiopia, and its fast, skeletonized service points to the way of news coverage of the future —by radio.

After years of bitter opposition, newspapers are beginning to see the light and there is now a formidable movement toward ownership or alliance with radio stations. Hearst Radio now controls six stations outright, Scripps-Howard owns a station in Cincinnati, and both the Hearst and the Scripps-Howard chains are embarked on active campaigns to build up radio alliances. All told, out of 632 radio stations in the United States, there are now 143 that are owned or controlled by newspapers.

Radio networks heatedly deny any censorship of news, other than on the grounds of good taste, meaning the elimination of gory, sordid, or nauseous details in stories that are going to families that contain small children, families that are seated at dinner. While there is no overt censorship as such, it is fair to say that radio as a whole parallels the large newspapers as a whole in the—often unconscious—class bias in favor of big ownership.

Thus, radio and the newspapers are facing the future in a state that might be called armed good will. Science will be the deciding factor. Already the laboratories have developed facsimile transmission to the point where it is now possible to send through the air and print in an attachment to the receiving set in your own home a daily newspaper. It may be some time before any such device comes into general use, but ultimately the newspapers are tied to the horse and buggy. It is radio that has the automobile end of this particular argument.

RELATIVE RELIANCE ON PRESS AND RADIO

—Wilbur Schramm and Ray Huffer, "What Radio News Means to Middleville," *Journalism Quarterly*, Vol. 23, June 1946, pp. 179–181. Mr. Huffer is a radio news writer for the Associated Press. Mr. Schramm is now dean of the Division of Communications at the University of Illinois.

THE WEEKLY NEWSPAPER in Middleville was recently suspended because of the publisher's health. That circumstance gave an opportunity to find out what happens to a community's listening and reading habits when it loses its newspaper. Only a few of those facts are pertinent to this report. In brief, the story seems to be that the county seat daily has come in with Middleville correspondents and filled most of the hole left by the suspended weekly. Almost 100 per cent of Middeville say that they now turn to the daily for local news. Twenty-five per cent say that they spend more time listening to radio news, now that the weekly is gone, and 33 per cent say that radio is doing some of the job the weekly used to do. Farmers, however, turn almost entirely (88 per cent) to radio for crop and price reports, and farmers and other residents (87 per cent of them) depend on the radio for weather news. If the radio were to satisfy some of Middleville's often expressed desire for more local news, the dailies might have still more competition.

The people of Middleville read 1.65 daily newspapers a person, one person out of ten reads a newsmagazine, and three persons out of ten read weekly newspapers. Asked whether they would be more likely to believe radio or newspaper, if the two sources did not jibe, they reported as follows:

	Believe Radio	*News-paper*	*Un-certain*
Housewives	55%	17%	28%
Working women	62	19	19
Town working men	28	39	33
Farmers	38	31	31
Male students	75	22	3
Female students	72	25	3

The breakdown of these answers by ages is interesting. Of the persons who were young enough (30 or under) to grow up with radio, 70 per cent said they would believe radio, 26 per cent newspaper, with only 4 per cent uncertain. The older persons who had grown up before radio gave radio 40 per cent and newspaper 25 per cent, with 35 per cent uncertain.

When the people of Middleville were asked, "If you had to give up either radio news or newspaper, which one could you get along without more easily?" 64 per cent of them said they could get along better without newspaper.

"After you have heard a radio newscast, for what kind of news do you turn to the newspaper?" they were asked. These were the commonest answers in relative order of frequency (the first item being arbitrarily set at 100):

General news	100
Local news	82
More details	60
Comics	56
Sports	43

Among the concrete suggestions as to how the newspaper might make itself more useful, now that so much radio news is available, the following were most often heard:

What to write: more documentation, more news in summary form, more feature and human interest material, concentrate more on local news.

Pictorial features: more pictures, more maps, more graphs.

News handling: quit writing the inverted pyramid story, "boil 'em down," don't skip stories from the first page to an inside page.

If there was any thought that Middleville listeners might divide their news intake between radio and newspaper on the basis of categories of news, this study blasted that. Middleville gets all kinds of news from radio and all kinds of news from newspapers. It gets far more local news from newspapers, but radio stations carry little local news for Middleville, and Middleville wants them to carry more. The difference is rather when they get the news (usually first from radio) and how much they get (more details from newspapers). This was checked not only by categorical questions, but also by finding out where people got their information on several important stories of the time. In most cases, the headline news had come from radio, the pictorial treatment and more details from the newspaper, and sometimes at the end of the cycle an editorial opinion from a radio commentator.

Three conclusions were uppermost in the minds of the persons who made the survey and those who analyzed the reports.

In the first place, the importance of radio news to the village of Middleville (which, it may be well to repeat, is not its real name) was impressively demonstrated. The fact that 88 per cent of the homes and 43 per cent of the business places have radios, that every radio in the town is used for newscasts, that the average person in Middleville who listens at all hears between two and three newscasts a day and spends within ten minutes as much time on radio news as on newspapers, that the majority of people are more inclined to believe radio than newspaper news, and that almost all people depend on radio for weather forecasts and almost all farmers depend on it for market reports—these facts do not mean that radio is replacing the newspapers, but certainly that, in the informational pattern of a village like Middleville, radio news has assumed an importance akin to that of the newspaper.

In the second place, Middleville's strong interest in local news by radio is something that should be taken into account by radio news editors, and by station managers who are contemplating FM installations.

In the third place, there are signs that a generation with a somewhat different attitude toward radio may be growing up. Persons 30 or under have been exposed to radio for most of their educational life. When some of the statistics from Middleville are broken down in terms of people under 30 and people over 30, the results are extremely interesting. For example, persons under 30 are significantly less opposed to crime stories on the air, less disturbed by gruesome details on the air. Does this indicate that material of this kind is developing scar tissue in its hearers, and that a different kind of listener is beginning to appear? Furthermore, there is a significant difference in the attitude of Middleville people under 30 toward the newspaper. Seventy per cent of those persons under 30 say that, in the case of conflicting news, they would be inclined rather to believe radio than newspaper; only 40 per cent of persons over 30 felt that way. Sixty-nine per cent of persons under 30 indicated that they could more easily give up newspaper than radio news; only 56 per cent of persons over 30. There is no attempt in this report to equate Middleville to the entire United States, and the persons who made the survey were well aware that a prestige factor might be operating in favor of radio. But even with those allowances, the suggestions of a new radio-mindedness developing in the younger generation have implications far beyond Middleville.

RADIO DIAGNOSES THE PRESS

—**Don Hollenbeck, "CBS Views the Press,"** ***The Atlantic Monthly.*** Vol. 182, September 1948, pp. 49–51. Mr. Hollenbeck, who has worked on newspapers in Omaha and San Francisco, is a news commentator for CBS.

"CBS Views the Press," a weekly fifteen-minute broadcast over the Columbia Broadcasting System's key station WCBS in New York, has been on the air for more than a year. During that year, in its discussion of how the New York newspapers handle stories ranging from an international crisis to a tie-up in the subway, the program has aroused the sympathetic interest of the public and has won five major radio awards. But what did the press think of this innovation?

"Man-bites-dog act slays N.Y. press; dailies' reaction big $64 question," said *Variety*. "The worm turns," said the headline over an editorial in *Editor & Publisher*. The Jamaica (N.Y.) *Leader-Observer's* editorial said, "Thou hypocrite, cast out first the bean (*sic*) out of thine own eyes." Not all of the printed reactions to the premier performance of "CBS Views the Press" had the charm of a typographical error in a misquotation from the sixth chapter of St. Luke, but most of them had that burden.

What man bit what dog? "CBS Views the Press" is a cooperative venture, the result of a study by a number of men and women. Three men are assigned to the job almost full time—Joe Wershba, Edmund Scott, and I—but the entire CBS news staff contributes ideas, opinions, and research. There are nine New York daily newspapers to be read; there are in addition the news magazines and other publications when their contents have to do with news. Sometimes the topic for the week dictates itself: the coverage of the national conventions, for instance, or the Hearst newspapers' crusade for General MacArthur for President. Often a story will be in the process of development for several weeks before we feel that enough material is in hand to prepare a satisfactory broadcast.

CBS correspondents overseas are called upon when the story involves foreign reporting, as in the case of Maxwell Anderson's visit to Greece. The playwright made a quick trip to that country, talked to a number of persons, and subsequently prepared for the New York *Herald Tribune* a series of articles on the Greek problem. As Mr. Anderson saw it, and as he wrote for the *Herald Tribune*, the problem was all Red. The late George Polk, CBS's Middle East correspondent, was requested to put Mr. Anderson's article into a truer perspective.

The raw material for a broadcast of "CBS Views the Press" is made the subject of an editorial conference, the direction is set, and a 2500-word broadcast is written, carefully checked as to accuracy, and put on the air. Accuracy is the program's bogeyman; the beam in one's own eye sometimes looms large. In one case, the wrong first name of a New York *Sun* reporter survived all checking of the manuscript, and the reporter's pained but restrained letter of protest brought an apology the next time we were on the air. In larger matters, the program has maintained a consistent reputation for accuracy.

There is often heated argument as to what the attitude of "CBS Views the Press" should be in a debatable matter. One of the warmest discussions arose over a political story. When Senator Robert A. Taft was launching his candidacy for the Republican Presidential nomination, he made a cross-country trip to see important people and to get the wheels turning. About the time the Senator's trip was being arranged, a national food-saving plan had been announced, and the Senator himself had commented that we should eat less meat and eat less extravagantly. Political enemies of Senator Taft made the most of that one. The New York *Post* listed for seven days the complete menus of the hearty meals eaten by Senator Taft, with price tags attached where possible. Most of them had been served him as a guest at clubs and hotels by Republican groups interested in Mr. Taft's candidacy, but some of them were dining-car meals. The story was intended to show that Senator Taft's advice was hypocritical, and that behind his talk of saving food he was gorging himself.

The question was, was this a fair political attack? After much wrangling, it was concluded by the majority of the CBS staff that it was not: that Senator Taft had been on a political tour, that entertainment and meals for him had been planned in advance by his hosts, that it was not for him to dictate what should or should not be set before him, and that it would have been boorish in the extreme—besides being politically unwise—to have made an issue of it among the people whose votes he was interested in.

Out of such general discussions and arguments come the weekly "CBS Views the Press" programs designed to help readers of newspapers get their own perspective on what they see in print.

Radio has done other adult jobs while growing up, and for several years the type of program known as the documentary has been acknowledged to be one of the finest forms of comment on current problems. Radio news presentation, radio drama, have been received approvingly, and without wonder. Criticism of the radio was instrumental in improving radio's performance. But when radio presumed to criticize the sacrosanct press, that was too much.

"How long do you think you'll get away with it?" is the tenor of many letters. "They'll get you, they'll fix your wagon." This skeptical attitude is depressing because it indicates the low esteem in which radio has been held for a quarter of a century when a program such as "CBS Views the Press" is greeted with such skepticism.

The reaction of working newspaper men and women to "CBS Views the Press" was somewhat different: hopeful welcome tinged with cynicism. This sort of program simply could not exist. Now they help enthusiastically when their assistance is enlisted in getting a particular story together for the program, but at first they helped with an air of looking carefully over their shoulders to be sure that they were not being followed.

The Columbia Broadcasting System gave air time to a spokesman for the New York *Sun* when that paper considered it had a grievance over our discussion of its handling of the supposed theft of atomic energy secrets from Oak Ridge. John T. McManus asked in *PM*, "Is surrender ahead for 'CBS Views the Press?' " The editor of a Newspaper Guild publication called to get some facts for the obituary he was writing for the program.

The broadcast of an article prepared on the efforts of the management of Time, Inc., to censor the outside writing of its employees was delayed for a couple of weeks while we debated the question of whether differences between management and personnel of a publication came within the scope of our program. We concluded that since these differences might have an important effect on the publication, or on books and articles by the writers involved, such differences were well within our sphere, and the story was broadcast. But during the delay, word got around the publishing business that CBS was due for a fall this time. You just couldn't go on the air with anything critical of Time, Inc., and get away with it. The obituary writers got busy again.

This apprehensive attitude is depressing for a second reason. It reflects an almost unconscious view that one might as well abandon the search for truth; that to discuss with honesty an institution so venerable and so powerful as the press is suicidal. Too many people seem too ready to give up without a struggle their right to free speech and open discussion. They are glad when a program such as "CBS Views the Press" fights to keep that right alive, but they are glad with a wry smile, as if to say, "There goes Don Quixote at the windmills again."

Last fall, the program dealt with the New York newspapers' treatment of the trial at Nuremberg of twenty-three top officials of the I. G. Farbenindustrie. The names of some extremely big American firms were linked with Farben in the testimony, and in many of the newspapers those names were not even mentioned. That fact was so stated on "CBS Views the Press," and the following week the mail increased greatly. The keynote was surprise and praise for our "audacity," and there was the old postscript: "Better look out, you're monkeying with hot stuff, and they'll be getting you." The following week's broadcast dealt with a really monumental fumble by the press in reporting a Federal court opinion on a Standard Oil patents case in which the name of Farben also figured. At that, the amazement of some of our listeners knew no bounds: two in a row, think of it!

Now there really seemed to be little audacity involved in what was a straight reporting job on how the New York newspapers treated two particular stories, and yet the nature of the stories was such that to many people the mere mention of them seemed to constitute bravery and audacity.

What is happening? Are the American people willing to see free speech and honest discussion vanish? Are they to salute with despair any attempt to keep alive that free speech and honest discussion, and are they ready to write off such attempts as forlorn hopes and windmill-tilting? Maybe they are, because so far as we know, the only radio station of any size or influence in the country which broadcasts a program critical of the press is WCBS in New York.

Radio stations all around the country regularly get copies of the scripts; they hear transcriptions of the programs; they see the venture discussed in their trade publications; they are keenly aware of the great public interest in it, and, wise in promotion, they are professionally aware of the critical recognition given it. They read in *Variety* that other stations may soon be putting on similar programs in their communities, and yet those programs don't come off, or they haven't at this writing. Why not?

One general conclusion emerges—that the local presentation of such a program would be much more effective than any network presentation, and for obvious reasons. The listener in any community must with ease relate such a broadcast to what he sees in his own newspapers. Listener and broadcaster must establish a rapport, each must know what is being talked about.

There have been many thoughtful and provocative critical studies of the press as a whole: the Hutchins committee's findings on the freedom and responsibility of the press; the Nieman Fellows' conclusions as to what an ideal newspaper should be like; Morris Ernst's excellent book, *The First Freedom;* A. J. Liebling's *New Yorker* articles collected under the title of *The Wayward Pressman*—all offer much valuable discussion and information as to the current state of the American press. But they do not and cannot do what a local critique of the press can do: they cannot establish that rapport which is so necessary for the communication and reception of useful criticism. Their contributions must of necessity be in general terms, and although Mr. Liebling's discussions come the closest to being specific, they have an inevitable tendency to fade and, to readers outside New York, not to mean much.

It is the constant treatment of the local performance which begins to make the listener think a little more about the newspaper he reads. And about those he doesn't read, too, but which he sees on the newsstands every day or clutched in his fellow commuters' hands. "I've read one paper for years," a correspondent wrote in. "It never occurred to me that news could be presented in so many different ways, or simply not presented at all. I never heard of the Dorothy Lawlor story, because the paper I read never printed a line of it." Our correspondent was referring to the case of the young woman on Long Island who early this summer got a lot of newspaper space around the country by going through the motions of advertising in a New York newspaper for a husband with ten thousand dollars cash. The advertisement was turned down by the business office, but ethics were thrown right out the window by the editorial department. It faked an advertisement, reproduced it in its news columns, and the resulting publicity was something to shudder at.

"CBS Views the Press" discussed some of the journalistic antics, and our correspondent pointed out that since he read the New York *Herald Tribune* in the morning and got his news from a very conservative radio analyst in the evening, he had never heard of the thing. Not that he wanted to, he hastened to add; he'd keep right on reading the *Herald Tribune*. But it made him think about how newspapers do or don't report news, and he wondered if there were other things of more importance going on of which he was unaware.

We reminded him of the now celebrated case of the Mississippi Bureau of Investigation: a secret police force was last year empowered to make arrests without warrants in crimes of violence, under legislation which made the possession of explosives by persons who do not use them in normal business prima-facie evidence of possession for purposes of crime; and for the bombing of transportation facilities, the death penalty was provided, whether or not anyone was killed. Enactment of the legislation had followed some strike violence in Mississippi.

A secret police force of this character and power in any one of the forty-eight states should be of interest and concern to all Americans, no matter how far from Mississippi thcy live. And yet until A. J. Liebling found out by reading the New Orleans *Times-Picayune* what was going on and wrote an article about it for the *New Yorker*, and "CBS Views the Press" took it up where he left off, the story had had no circulation at all; the press associations sent out squibs which gave one no idea of the real story and its importance, and as a consequence, editors didn't bother to print them. This was a case of a regional blockade. Press association editors reason that news originating in the South is of interest only to Southerners, and the same theory applies in other regions.

It is the job of the critic of the press to ferret out these cases, and to report them on the basis of how the local newspapers did or did not treat them. Discussion of the Associated Press means little to the readers of the Emporia *Gazette* or the Philadelphia *Inquirer;* it is what those newspapers did with the Associated Press copy they got that can be made of interest to them. That's why criticism of the press is best done locally; it means more personally to those who hear or read it.

The suggestion has often been made that "CBS Views the Press" should be a daily broadcast, done, perhaps, in the cool of the evening, with all the day's newspapers close at hand, and a little time for sober assessment of the news after the strain and confusion of going to press are over. From the critic's point of view it is a horrible thought—enough care is involved in getting out a weekly product; and yet from the interested listener's standpoint, it must be admitted that here would be almost the ideal criticism of the press. The ideal would be the same criticism by the press itself.

RADIO-PRESS NEWS TREATMENT COMPARED

—Lillian Gottlieb, "Radio and Newspaper Reports of the Heirens Murder Case," *Journalism Quarterly*, Vol. 24, June 1947, pp. 98–99, 106–108. Miss Gottlieb was a member of the staff of the Columbia University Bureau of Applied Social Research when she wrote this article.

THIS SPECIFIC STUDY compared the newspaper and radio treatment in Chicago of the apprehension, investigation, and eventual conviction of William Heirens in the Suzanne Degnan and other murders.

Employing the technique of content analysis, comparisons were made between newspaper and radio treatment of the story in two different ways:

1. The comparative prominence given the story by the two media;
2. The objectivity with which the developments of the case were presented.

A thorough survey was first made of all of the events involved in the case from the time that William Heirens was apprehended to the time that he was convicted. The five major developments in the case during this period were then chosen for analysis. These developments and the days on which they were reported over the air and in the local press were:

1. Apprehension of Heirens on a burglary charge and the subsequent matching of his fingerprints with those found on the Degnan ransom note. (June 29 through July 2, 1946.)
2. The uncovering of evidence possibly connecting Heirens with other murders—Francis Brown and Josephine Ross—and several assaults. (July 13 through July 17, 1946.)
3. The indictment of Heirens for murder and his unofficial confession. (July 25 through July 28, 1946.)
4. Heirens' official confession. (August 6 and 7, 1946.)
5. The trial and sentence. (September 4 through 6, 1946.)

The treatment of these developments in the columns of the five Chicago daily newspapers—the *Tribune, Sun, Herald-American, Times,* and *Daily News*—and on the news broadcasts of radio station WBBM, the CBS outlet in Chicago was then analyzed.

One edition of each newspaper was analyzed for each of the days chosen, except for the *Daily News* which does not publish on Sundays.

Only the scripts of news broadcasts originating locally were analyzed. The scripts used included the fifteen-minute newscasts at 9 a.m. and at 12 noon or 1:45 p.m., and the five-minute news summaries at 11 p.m. It was not always possible to obtain for each day the scripts of the three news broadcasts. However, we had at least one script for each day, and an average of two scripts for each day was available.[1]

The scripts of news commentators were not analyzed because, by inspection, it was observed that none of them was concerned with the Heirens case. Of the thirty-nine scripts used in the analysis, the thirteen morning broadcasts were sustaining; the remaining twenty-six sponsored.

This gave a total of eighty-five newspaper issues and thirty-nine radio scripts. All written material dealing with the case which appeared in these newspapers and radio scripts was included in our analysis. . . .

Although one way of testing the objectivity of a news report is to determine to what extent each side of an issue is aired, it is also important to study to what extent the stories contain items which although not necessarily prejudicial in themselves, are couched in such terms by the staff reporter as to slant or "color" the news.

In making the analysis, therefore, the investigators first classified all statements as to whether they were neutrally stated (*i.e.*, matter-of-factly) or slanted, and then went on to classify all slanted statements as having a positive implication (in favor of Heirens) or a negative implication (against Heirens).[2]

Such items as the following were coded as having a negative implication, *i.e.*, colored, or slanted in a way unfavorable to Heirens:

> Heirens . . . regarded the judge with the unblinking eyes of a cat. —*Sun*, 7/17

[1] The files of radio news scripts kept by station WBBM were incomplete, and although they sent all they had for the days specified, fifteen of the desired fifty-four scripts were lacking. Five of the morning scripts, three early afternoon newscasts, and seven evening scripts were not available. However, there is no reason to believe that the results of the analysis would have been different had all the desired scripts been available.

[2] It is important to note here that what was taken into consideration was the handling of the news items by the newspaper or radio staff. Thus, if a policeman was quoted as saying "Heirens is guilty," this was not classified as having a negative implication. The subject categories (*e.g.* guilt, innocence, etc.) are wholly independent of the "slant" classification.

> William Heirens signed the name "Wilhelm Heirens von Lincolnwald" in his school textbooks and had a copy of Friedrich Nietzsche's *The Superman,* sometimes called the "Bible" of Nazi Germany, in his bookcase.—*Times,* 7/2

> Whether William Heirens, 17, despite his youth, is one of the most ruthless criminals of modern times, or whether he is a victim of abnormal mentality caught in a web of circumstances which he is powerless to resist, authorities last night said that it is doubtful whether the state is in a position to charge him with the Degnan kidnapping and demand the death penalty.—*Tribune,* 7/13

> William Heirens, 17-year old crime riddle . . . —*Herald-American,* 7/13

Much rarer were statements with a positive implication, *i.e.,* slanted in favor of Heirens.

> In (Heirens) bedroom, the youth's trophies adorned the walls—several rifles, sports pictures, and other things that decorate countless boys' rooms like it all over town.—*Times,* 6/29

A comparison of the relative frequencies of neutral, negative, and positive statements for WBBM and the newspapers is shown in Table VIII.

TABLE VIII

Per Cent of Statements which Were:	*WBBM*	*Sun*	*Tribune*	*Times*	*News*	*Herald-American*
Neutral	97	93	88	89	84	87
Negative	3	6	12	10	16	13
Positive	—	1	—*	1	—*	—*
Total	100%	100%	100%	100%	100%	100%
	(136)	(1102)	(1213)	(1015)	(726)	(1384)

* Less than one-half of one per cent.

In this respect WBBM did a more objective job in reporting the Heirens story than any of the newspapers; the only newspaper which was almost as unbiased was the *Sun.*[3]

In order to determine which subjects were most frequently given a negative implication by the press or radio, the investigators measured the percentage of each subject-category which was slanted negatively toward Heirens. There was a significant proportion of

[3] If feature stories are excluded from this table and only regular newspaper stories considered, the results are not consistent for all the newspapers. The *Sun* has a lower percentage of negative statements in its regular stories; the *Tribune, News, Herald-American* a higher proportion; and the *Times* the same proportion of negative statements in both types of news stories.

negatively colored statements only among those items dealing with facts about the Degnan, Ross, and Brown murders, Heirens' crime record and pathology, and Heirens' guilt in the Degnan, Ross, and Brown murders.

Quite a few of the statements giving facts about the murders were colored by the *Sun, News,* and *Herald-American.* A sizeable proportion of statements dealing with Heirens' crime record and pathological background were slanted against Heirens by all, but especially by the *News.* As for statements maintaining that Heirens was guilty of any of the three murders, only WBBM and the *Herald-American* did not slant any of them negatively.

A similar analysis was done to see whether there was any tendency to slant statements emanating from some sources more than others. The statements from each source were measured to see what percentage of each was colored against Heirens.

All the newspapers except the *Sun* slanted the majority of those statements whose source was not ascertainable against Heirens, and a significant proportion of those originating from their own staffs as well. Statements coming from Heirens were also colored to an appreciable degree by the *Tribune.* In this respect, WBBM did a far more objective treatment than any of the newspapers.

In summary, then, the findings indicate that although both media treated most of the statements about the Heirens case neutrally, the newspapers exhibited a greater propensity toward slanting or coloring the news against Heirens than did WBBM.

The results having been presented in detail, one final question should be raised in relation to the degree of "sensationalism" exhibited by the station and the papers. "Sensationalism" was measured in terms of two indices: "over-emphasis" and "lack of objectivity."

It might well be asked why mass media should be objective toward someone who is suspected, on the basis of good evidence, of having committed a series of vicious murders, and who eventually confesses that he has indeed committed these extremely inhuman crimes. The best answer is that it is a basic tenet of civil liberty that everyone is presumed to be innocent until a court has found him guilty. It is necessary to act in accordance with this principle in every case, lest the public and mass media do not respect it in regard to political, social, and religious issues, where its abnegation is of more extensive import.

The radio station differs from the newspapers in different directions as regards "prominence" and as regards "objectivity." The station did not play up the murder case, that is, it gave it less prominence, but when the station did deal with murder it was less objective toward the suspect by one index, than were the newspapers. This may be due to a stronger moralistic tradition in the philosophy of the radio industry, or to a general characteristic of all restraints: that they become weakened at those points where their applicability is not so obvious.

The total result of this case study, however, favors the radio station. Compared to the average newspaper in the same city, the radio is shown to have exercised restraint in handling a murder case. The radio did not subordinate important news stories to the Heirens case to the degree that the newspapers did, and the radio did not willfully slant its news against the suspect.

EFFECTS OF PRESS-RADIO JOINT OWNERSHIP

—Herbert Brucker, *Freedom of Information,* pp. 83–87. Copyright 1949 by Mr. Brucker. Used with the permission of The Macmillan Company.

THERE ARE, naturally enough, two opposing views of joint control of newspapers and radio. Those who fear the march toward monopoly accept the premise that if a relatively small group holds in its hands a substantial share of the instruments through which the public gets its news, then it will color that news in its own interest. Like medieval robber barons perched in strongholds on the hilltops, the barons of publishing and radio dominate the news traffic that passes by. Therefore—according to this view—they will inevitably make us all their mental slaves by giving us only the picture of the world they want us to have.

The opposing point of view is that the experience and discipline inherited from three centuries of journalism, that is, the Fourth Estate's fumbling but fundamentally valiant battle in search of the truth, plus its established position and economic stability, combine to make newspapers peculiarly fitted to operate the sister service of radio. After all, this argument runs, journalism is journalism. What difference does it make whether its agent happens to be a rotary press or a broadcasting transmitter?

By nature the New Deal accepted the first of these opposing

views. But since newspapers were protected by the First Amendment from government molestation, it could not get at them. Radio was different. Because room on the air is limited, radio cannot be open to all, even in theory. Hence radio had to be made subject to government regulation, and exists today under the administrative supervision of the Federal Communications Commission. And since in prewar days the Commission had a five-to-two New Deal majority, it made a handy tool not only to get at the suspicious liaison between newspapers and radio, but in so doing also to peep into the forbidden preserves of the newspapers themselves. And while FCC acted with an outwardly punctilious respect for its nonpartisan obligations, many newspaper and radio people convinced themselves that the Commission, and notably James Lawrence Fly, its chairman at that time, were essentially hatchet men sent out by the New Deal to get them. The line-up was, in short, much like that in the contemporary battle between the Department of Justice and the Associated Press.

The question of joint newspaper-radio affiliation had long been agitated, but Chairman Fly took as the immediate occasion for his inquiry the fact that by June 30, 1941, forty-three or nearly half, of ninety-nine applications for FM radio licenses before the Commission came from newspaper interests. "These newspaper applications," he said, "raise the common question of the extent to which and the circumstances in which grants to newspapers will serve the public interest." So it was that on March 20, 1941, the FCC directed itself, through its Order No. 79, to look into the matter. Before long there began a series of hearings that stretched from July, 1941, to February, 1942. Some 3,500 typed pages of testimony were put into record by both sides.

The burden of the testimony offered by witnesses called by the FCC make it clear that the Commission was conducting not so much an investigation as a prosecution. It sought to get into the record reasons that might justify rulings that would divorce newspapers from radio. But the FCC's case rested not on evidence that joint ownership did in fact result in twisted news, but on showing the extent of affiliation between newspapers and radio, and in then arguing on the assumed premise that such overlapping was *ipso facto* evil. Typical of the host of Commission witnesses was Morris L. Ernst, New York lawyer and associate counsel for the Civil Liberties Union, who began his argument by expounding what was essentially the theory of a free press. . . . As he put it, "We are gambling in this country and our society on the thought that if there is a market place in thought, truth will win out." But, he said, newspaper-radio affiliation automatically cut down the number of items offered in the market place of thought:

> I don't think you can maintain our philosophy of the market place of thought, that the truth will win out there, unless you have as decent and as complete a market place as society permits; and the best way to prove it is that nobody would favor having all of the radio stations owned by the newspapers . . . So the only dispute is at what point should we be frightened, at what point should we stop—300 out of 800, or should we wait until 700, 600? There can be honest differences of opinion as to just where is the frightening point. I am telling you my prejudices. I am frightened when I see one. I am frightened if I think of the motion picture companies owning television. I am frightened as to any interlocking of the controls because I want the greatest possible variety of prejudices in that market place, whether I agree with them or not, and then they are going to correctly criticize each other.

Ernst described the newspapers, radio, and other means of communication as pipe lines to human minds. We could not maintain the Bill of Rights, he contended, if the number of persons who controlled those pipe lines got to be fewer and fewer.

Another of the many witnesses who expressed preference for separate ownership, though he declined to take sides on the question of a flat rule forbidding newspaper ownership of radio stations, was Professor Zechariah Chafee, Jr., of Harvard. A Commission witness, Professor Chafee nevertheless made an observation that must be scored on the newspapers' side. The FCC, he said, was not in charge of the national welfare as a whole, but in charge of radio only. Not only that, but the Commission was fighting its battle on the border line between two industries, one of which—the newspaper industry—was outside its field. "The use of a political power established for one purpose in order to produce a result of a different sort," said Professor Chafee, "is always risky."

When the time came for witnesses on the publishers' side to speak, they made more of this point. In particular, Arthur Garfield Hays, national director of the Civil Liberties Union, forcefully expressed this thesis, thus opposing his fellow apostle of civil liberties, Morris Ernst. It surprised many to find a veteran battler for the underdog, like Hays, turning up on the side of the Bourbons of the press; but he did so because of his convictions on the fundamental political issue involved. His argument makes required reading for anyone who wonders how the historic principles of democracy apply to the society of today. For example:

> What I am afraid of is an extension by law, or by any Commission, which would lead to a violation of rights, because of a desire to bring about more equal opportunities. I feel that, under a democratic system . . . so long as we have equal rights under the law, most of us can take care of ourselves . . .
>
> If everybody is given equal rights, it is up to those who want radio stations to run them properly and convince the Commission that they are the people who are best qualified to have them.
>
> Just as soon as you favor one group over the other, under the law, whether it is to protect somebody or help somebody, it seems to me you are denying the underlying principles of democracy.
>
> Of course, everybody who starts out with the idea of denying these principles, does it with good motives. The purpose, unquestionably, is to bring about a desired end. But the theory of democracy is that, if you let people alone, they will get farther by their own efforts, so long as you treat them alike, and that no government can safely lay down methods that will bring about as beneficial results as giving people equal rights under the law.[1]

[1] *Freedom of the Press,* a selection of testimony from witnesses before the FCC Newspaper–Radio hearings (New York: Newspaper–Radio Committee, American Newspaper Publishers Association, 1942), p. 66.

So the arguments went. Innumerable facts, statistical and otherwise, subtle theories as to the functions of administrative agencies as distinct from legislative bodies, journalistic history, radio history, all were put into the record. Many distinguished persons testified. At length, on February 6, 1942, Chairman Fly recessed the hearing *sine die.*

The fundamental fact that emerged from the hearing was that there was no concrete evidence of bias stemming from newspaper control of radio. FCC investigators had been sent out on a nationwide hunt to get the goods on newspaper-owned radio. They searched the stations of the country through and through with fervor and diligence, but still they could find no example of monopoly-colored news caused by joint newspaper-radio control. They did bring into the hearings, to be sure, a suspicious situation in Charleston, South Carolina. Here radio station WCSC had complained about its local competitor, WTMA, which was owned by the two newspapers in town. And the newspapers had, for a time, published the program listings of their own station but not those of the rival—an old habit of the years when the press fought radio that still persists in some areas, hardly reinforcing the newspapers' protestations of purity and objectivity. Even so, the most strenuous efforts of the FCC produced nothing in the way of evidence of bias in the general dissemination of news and opinion. One witness for the complaining station (State Senator Cotesworth P. Means) probably put his finger on the truth of the whole matter when under cross-examination he said that the monopoly dangers complained of were feared for the future rather than evident in what had happened to date.

A comparison of what actually goes out over the air from newspaper as against non-newspaper stations can be found in a study made by the Office of Radio Research, affiliated with Columbia University, at the request of the publishers' Newspaper-Radio Committee. This study compares news and educational programs as broadcast by newspaper and non-newspaper stations, and also the political allegiance of newspapers with radio affiliations and without any. It is based on the output of fifty newspaper-owned stations, fifty non-newspaper stations, and fifty newspapers without radio connection, all matched as closely as possible. The assumption was that any differences that appeared might be due to the newspaper-radio connection or lack of it.

This study revealed that in towns with only one paper and only one station, where each was independent of the other, the papers tended to discriminate against the stations by not printing a log of all their programs—the vicious and shortsighted policy on the part of publishers noted in Charleston. But so far as the quality and quantity of news and social service programs was concerned, and also the time of day at which they were broadcast, there were only negligible differences. All in all, this study, one of the tiny bits of factual light on this much agitated question, proved little. It did hint, however, at what anyone familiar with journalism and radio would suspect in the first place: that individual newspapers and individual radio stations are pretty much what circumstances and their owners make them, and that affiliation between the two makes little difference one way or another.

COMPETITION AMONG COMMUNICATION MEDIA

—Charles V. Kinter, "Economic Problems in Private Ownership of Communications," *Communications in Modern Society,* Wilbur Schramm (editor), University of Illinois Press, 1948, pp. 29–34. Mr. Kinter, a former financial writer, is now lecturer in the School of Commerce at Northwestern University and an economist for Shaw, Isham and Company.

THOSE WHO lament the decline of competition in the communications field on an over-all basis often are not referring to competition in an economic sense at all. Competition for the advertiser's dollar probably never was keener than in 1948 despite the decline in the number of newspapers in the last few decades and the concentration of control of the type described by Mr. Ernst and the Commission on Freedom of the Press. Keenness of competition in recent years is indicated by the fact that the newspaper, which had $964 million in advertising revenue in 1946, compared with $760 million in 1928, actually received only about 31% of the advertising dollar in 1946, compared with 68% in 1938. On the other hand, the share of the advertising dollar received by radio has climbed from around 2% in 1928 to more than 15% in 1946.

Competition for an audience also has intensified. The rise of the news magazine, the radio, and the picture magazine has meant an invasion of the realm of the newspaper as purveyor of news, comment, and interpretation. Competition for attention apparently has just started. Television and facsimile apparently will cut into the audience of the newspaper, radio, and moving pictures. As one writer described it the new inventions in the radio field, such as FM, facsimile, and television, should "herald an increasingly vital democracy in which each man, in his own parlor, will occupy a ringside seat at national affairs."

In some phases of communications, the competition has indeed become a battle between titans, but it would appear that the intelligent individual has ample sources of information and expression. Too much stress, perhaps, has been placed upon the decline in the number of newspapers. Any gap left by the contraction of the newspaper field appears to have been filled by the rise of new media.

Let us look briefly at the competitive situation within several of the communications industries. The number of daily newspapers has, except for a few years, been in a decline since 1909 when a peak of

2,600 was reached. However, newspaper circulation has been in a steady rise. Dr. Nixon discusses this situation at some detail in this volume. It is interesting to note that the large majority of daily newspapers which passed out of existence between 1929 and 1946 either did not have enough circulation to weather the economic storms of the 1930's or were published in cities no longer able to support a daily newspaper due to a change in fundamental economic factors.

The experience in Chicago provides another example. According to a study by George C. Blohm, there have been 63 Chicago newspapers which have been consolidated with other papers or have failed since 1833, until now only six remain. Thirty-one of the 69 were absorbed into the entities of the six papers which now serve Chicago.

The decline in the number of newspapers has been regarded as all the more serious because of the number of towns left without newspaper competition. Roughly only one in twelve towns has competing daily newspapers. The weekly field also has been hard hit by mortality with the number declining from around 16,000 in 1910 to roughly 10,000 now.

In his column, *The Editor's Notebook*, John S. Knight, editor and publisher of the Chicago *Daily News* and publisher of several other newspapers, aired some of the economic problems of newspaper and periodical businesses and the obstacles to free competition in these fields. Among the problems mentioned by Mr. Knight were the following:

1. Ever increasing demands for higher wage rates have been made by the printing trades and the American Newspaper Guild while at the same time production has steadily declined. "If we could really get what we pay for, the wage rate would not be so important," he said.

2. The newsprint situation has been critical for many newspapers. This situation is closely related to the shrinkage of the newsprint market, as already mentioned, in the face of heavy foreign and domestic demand.

Despite the problems faced by publishers, Mr. Knight ended an open letter in his column to Senator James E. Murray on this cheerful note: "Frankly, Senator, to use the words of my small-town newspaper friends, there is nothing wrong with the newspaper business that better production and an adequate supply of newsprint won't cure."

Now let us turn to the radio industry where we shall see that competition is becoming much more intense. Far from decrying the encroachment of government on the rights of the press, some radio operators have criticized the Federal Communications Commission for being so liberal in granting licenses to newcomers in the industry.

In our discussion of competition in the radio field, we cannot turn entirely away from the economic problems of other communications media. As we have noted, the percentage of all advertising going to radio has been rising while the share of newspapers has fallen except for what may have been a very recent and possibly temporary upturn in newspaper volume. The loss of advertising volume to radio has been chiefly in the national advertising field. However, radio is beginning an all-out invasion of the local advertising field. Due to the restricted territories of FM stations and small AM stations, we can expect this competition for local advertising to intensify.

Although there are but four major networks in the United States, competition nevertheless is keen in radio broadcasting. In its recent "Economic Study of Standard Broadcasting," the FCC emphasized this expanding competition. The report envisioned 2,000 standard (AM) broadcasting stations on the air by the end of 1948, or roughly 200 more stations than there are English language daily newspapers. The FCC pointed out that it has encouraged competition within the industry by its licensing policy, which follows the principle of free competition laid down by the Communications Act. Despite the financial pain such a policy will cause some stations, the Commission believed the good results will outweigh the bad.

This brings us to an impending battle for advertising revenue. Considering licenses granted and those still pending, the FCC anticipated that there might eventually be 1,350 postwar standard radio stations, in addition to the 909 authorized in 566 communities as of October 8, 1945. It was expected that the 1,350 postwar stations would require $131,000,000 annual revenue, or slightly less than $100,000 a station. A large portion of this revenue was seen as coming from local advertising, a field, as we have seen, long dominated by newspapers. Increased competition for revenue within the industry, as well as with other media, was regarded as inevitable.

While newspaper advertising volume made gains over radio when newsprint became in better supply after World War II, the FCC pointed out that the decline in the number of small city newspapers has helped radio in the competition for local advertising. One factor intensifying competition between the radio and the newspaper is that a large portion of postwar stations are being located in small communities previously lacking stations. This is so in regard to AM stations and will be important as more and more AM stations are established.

But all of the radio story has not been told. The rise of the Frequency Modulation (FM) broadcasting industry illustrates also the growing competition within the communications field. Late in 1947, an official of the FM Association estimated that there were 306 FM stations in operation, compared with 66 a year earlier. In addition, 622 FM stations had been authorized and 100 applications were pending. Dr. W. R. G. Baker, a vice-president of General Electric, has estimated that there is room in the United States for between 3,000 and 5,000 stations. . . .

The private owners of radio stations have been running head on into the cost problem despite their advantage due to the relatively smaller investment in a radio station compared with a newspaper plant. During the immediate postwar period, the rise in talent costs and other expenses convinced station operators that higher rates were necessary. Complaints from advertisers were loud and instances were recorded of smaller allocations of advertising dollars to radio. Competition of magazines and newspapers also was being felt as paper became available.

It should be mentioned that the growing television industry, while still in its infancy, appears certain to be a major factor in the communications field. At the end of 1947, there were about 20 television stations in operation, against 11 at the end of June, and 9 in 1945. In addition, 80 license and construction permits for additional stations in 36 cities had been issued.

RELATIVE FREEDOM FROM ADVERTISERS

–Llewellyn White, *The American Radio*, University of Chicago Press, 1947, pp. 224–227.

THE AUTHOR has indicated that he does not believe that the broadcasters could make much progress along the lines of program improvement which he has suggested unless and until they first radically changed their relationship with the advertising men. It is possible that they would also have to change their relationships toward one another, toward the government, toward the other media of mass communication, and toward the public. This, in turn, suggests improved relationships toward the broadcasters on the part of the government, of the other media, and of the public. Finally, it suggests a clarification of the proper functions of the various interested agencies of government in their relations with the broadcasters, with the public, and with one another.

1. *The broadcasters need to achieve, immediately, that degree of arm's-length relationship with the advertisers which fairly characterizes all but a submarginal handful of newspapers and magazines.*

The author has set forth to the best of his ability the reasons why he believes this step is of the first order of priority for the broadcasters. The broadcasters have given him a dozen reasons why they profess to believe that such a step should not or could not be taken. Let us examine some of them.

It has been said that advertisers dictate policy in the print media, also. The studies of the Commission on Freedom of the Press indicate that the Commission does not believe this to be the fact in the vast majority of instances. Certain facts, however, seem too obvious to permit of debate. One is that the advertisers do not actually prepare the reading matter in the print media or weave their sales messages into the reading matter. Another is that the bulk of newspaper and magazine publishers do not regard the sale of goods and services as their only or even their primary reason for being.

It has been said that it makes no difference whether A, who writes radio shows, B, who produces them, C, who directs them, and D, E, and F, who act them, are on the pay roll of a broadcasting station or on the pay roll of an advertising agency. They would be the same people, the broadcasters say, and so they would be bound to write, produce, direct, and act in precisely the same way. To say this is, it seems to the author, to miss completely the point made above.

It is hard to rationalize the statement. One invariably asks himself: Are they ignorant of the basic human desire to please whatever bosses man has, or is this a tacit admission that the broadcasters' goals are, in fact, the same as the advertisers': to sell goods and services? It is like saying that Frederick Lewis Allen, Ben Hibbs, and Virginius Dabney would be just as satisfactory editors for *Harper's*, the *Saturday Evening Post*, and the Richmond (Virginia) *Times-Dispatch*, respectively, if they were employed by a national advertising agency. It discounts, perhaps through ignorance, the classic "war" between editorial people and the "front office." Indeed, it skims over the constant struggle between the creative people in radio, both those who work for the broadcasters and those who work for the advertisers, payroll-wise, and their masters—the advertiser and the advertiser-cowed broadcaster.

The truth is, as hundreds who have done it can testify, that a newspaperman *does* express himself differently when he becomes an advertising man. He even thinks differently. Or perhaps it would be more correct to say that, if he finds he cannot think differently, he goes back to newspaper work, breathing imprecations and maledictions against the whole advertising fraternity.

To change from one to the other is rather like changing goals in a football game. It does not involve the question of whether the men in the blue jerseys are any better than the men in crimson. The fact is that the two teams are facing in opposite directions, aiming for goalposts separated by the length of the playing field, each determined to reach one set and frustrate every attempt of its rival to reach the other. A man who ran first this way and then that or who hesitated uncertainly in midfield would not be regarded as a very useful football player. For precisely the same reasons an advertising man who subordinated the selling of goods and services to other interests would not be a very effective advertising man, from his employer's standpoint. And a broadcaster who subordinated other interests (presumably, in his case, informing and entertaining the public) to the selling of goods and services would not be a very good broadcaster, from the public's standpoint. In the circumstances, therefore, it might be useful to number the players and give them different-colored jerseys.

It has been said that if any attempt were made to exclude advertising men from the preparation of radio's "reading matter," the advertising men (including the sponsors) would simply abandon radio to economic starvation. Here we are asked to believe either that radio is not really so effective as an advertising medium as the broadcasters have been telling us and that the sponsors who have been using it were prompted solely by charitable motives; or that their advertising messages could not stand on their own merits, as they are obliged to do in the other media, but must be slipped over on a public which otherwise would reject them; or that people do not listen to the commercials at the beginning and end of programs but only to middle commercials.

It is difficult for the author to reconcile these things with the broadcasters' repeated claims that radio is far and away the most effective medium for the advertisement of certain types of goods and services, that listeners actually "like" the commercials, and that the majority of them do not turn their sets off or down during the commercials between programs, even when these commercials are what are known as "local station-break spots" and are therefore wholly unrelated to the programs preceding or following them.

REVIEW QUESTIONS AND ASSIGNMENTS

1. Did the radio threat to the press arise because of inadequate news coverage by the press or because radio offered a quicker method of reaching the public?

2. How many newspapers now operate radio broadcasting stations?

3. Who finances radio stations, and how are they affecting newspaper revenue?

4. Did the radio handling of the Heirens murder case prove the seriousness of rivalry by the radio?

5. What is the policy of the FCC on newspaper ownership of broadcasting facilities?

6. Which has the greater freedom from advertising pressure, press or radio?

7. Has the newspaper "extra" been eliminated by the radio? If not, under what circumstances are "extras" now printed?

8. If the newspaper cannot compete with the radio in speed, what, if any, is its special province?

9. What results are to be expected from programs such as "CBS Views the Press"?

10. What advantages do radio news broadcasts enjoy over the newspaper other than speed?

11. Has the newspaper more to fear from the facsimile newspaper than from radio?

12. What signs are there that the press is trying to avoid the mistakes in dealing with facsimile reproduction that it made in battling the radio?

13. What effect does replacement of the press by the radio have upon the reading and thinking habits of the public?

14. Is the nation more or less open to propaganda if it depends on the radio rather than on the press?

15. What will the wide adoption of television do to the press as it is known now? To the listening public?

ADDITIONAL REFERENCES

Anonymous, "A.P. and Radio," *Newsweek,* Vol. 11, May 9, 1938, p. 28.

———, "Broadcasters and Newspaper Make Peace," *Newsweek,* Vol. 2, December 23, 1933, p. 18.

———, "Compact Between Broadcasters and the Daily Press," *The New Republic,* Vol. 77, January 3, 1934, p. 209.

———, "Newspapers Versus News Broadcasts," *Fortune Magazine,* Vol. 17, April 1938, pp. 104–109.

———, "Radio Stations Under Newspaper Control," *Christian Century,* Vol. 54, February 24, 1937, p. 237.

Barnett, Stanley, "The Press and the Radio: Past and Future," *Journalism Quarterly,* Vol. 20, December 1943, pp. 326–330.

Bent, Silas, "Radio Takes Over the News," *American Mercury,* Vol. 35, October 1935, pp. 228–230.

Bickel, Karl A., *New Empires: The Newspaper and Radio,* J. B. Lippincott, 1930.

Bickford, Leland, *News While It Is News,* Manthorne & Burack, 1935.

Churchill, Winston, "You Get It in Black and White," *Collier's,* Vol. 96, December 29, 1935, p. 32.

Coase, R. H., *British Broadcasting—A Study in Monopoly,* Harvard University Press, 1950.

Commission on Freedom of the Press, *A Free and Responsible Press,* University of Chicago Press, 1947, pp. 40–41.

Davis, Jerome, *Capitalism and Its Culture,* Farrar & Rinehart, 1935, Chapter 17, "A Radio Monopoly."

Desmond, Robert W., *The Press and World Affairs,* Appleton-Century, 1937, (Index).

Doob, Leonard W., *Public Opinion and Propaganda,* Henry Holt, 1948, pp. 462–497.

Ernst, Morris, *The First Freedom,* Macmillan, 1946, pp. 125–180.

Gorham, Maurice, *Television—Medium of the Future,* Macmillan, 1949.

Hammargren, R. J., "The Origins of Press-Radio Conflict," *Journalism Quarterly,* Vol. 13, March 1936, pp. 91–93.

Kaltenborn, H. V., *Fifty Fabulous Years,* G. P. Putnam's Sons, 1950.

Kinter, Charles V., "How Much Income Is Available to Support Communications?", *Journalism Quarterly,* Vol. 25, March 1948, pp. 38–42.

Lazarsfeld, Paul F., *Radio and the Printed Page,* Duell, Sloan and Pierce, 1940, p. 276.

Michael, Rudolph D., "History and Criticism of Press-Radio Relationship," *Journalism Quarterly*, Vol. 15, June 1938, pp. 178–184.

Munro, W. O., "Newspaper by Radio," *Current History*, Vol. 47, December 1937, pp. 40–45.

Potter, R. D., "Newspapers by Radio," *Science News Letter*, Vol. 34, September 3, 1938, pp. 154–155; Vol. 87, Supplement 11, February 18, 1938.

Seldes, Gilbert, *The Great Audience*, Viking Press, 1950.

Siepmann, Charles A., *Radio, Television and Society*, Oxford University Press, 1950.

Whiteside, Thomas, "Reading and Writing Arithmetic," *Harper's Magazine*, Vol. 193, July 1946, p. 48.

Whittcmorc, C. W., "Radio's Fight for News," *The New Republic*, Vol. 81, February 6, 1935, pp. 354–355.

26. THE NEWSPAPER GUILD AS AN INFLUENCE

INTRODUCTION

ORGANIZATIONS of employees of communications media have appeared in one form or another in this country ever since the close of the Civil War. During the last half of the nineteenth century, before the press became a complex business undertaking, organizations usually known as "press clubs" flourished in many cities. From time to time newspaper editorial workers attempted to organize unions patterned after the International Typographical Union, a potent force in the mechanical department ever since it succeeded the National Typographical Society in importance. Most of these "labor units" proved failures, and it was not until 1933 that a professional organization of editorial workers gained sufficient strength and permanency to make itself an influence in the conduct of newspaper establishments.

Late in 1933 a small group of editorial workers organized the American Newspaper Guild with the expressed purpose of giving newspaper workers the benefit of certain of the social legislation enacted by the Congress in the early years of President Roosevelt's first New Deal administration.

The late Heywood Broun, recognized as one of the "founding fathers" of the Guild, wrote a column for the Scripps-Howard New York *World-Telegram* on August 7, 1933, which stands as a landmark in the formation of an organization of editorial workers. In answering "Reporter Unemployed" (undoubtedly Mr. Broun), who asked why "editorial department boys will continue to work 48 hours a week because they love to hear themselves referred to as 'professionals' and because they consider unionizing as lowering their dignity," Mr. Broun wrote:

"But the fact that newspaper editors and owners are genial folk should hardly stand in the way of organization of a newspaper writers' union. There should be one. Beginning at nine o'clock on the morning of October 1, (1933) I am going to do the best I can in helping get one up. I think I could die happy on the opening day of the general strike if I have the privilege of watching Walter Lippmann heave a brick through a *Tribune* window at a non-union operative who had been called in to write the current 'Today and Tomorrow' column on the gold standard."[1]

The first leaders of the Guild, most of whom were on the staffs of metropolitan newspapers, took advantage of several developments in the post-depression years in putting the Guild on a firm footing. They were undoubtedly helped by the dismissals and wage reductions effected by many newspapers in the economic upheaval which followed the 1929 Wall Street crash. The passage of the National Industrial Recovery Act in the spring of 1933 with its famous Section 7-A on labor bargaining provided a strong impetus. The enactment in 1936 of the National Labor Relations Act proved even more stimulating. The legislation and the spirit of the times played directly into the hands of editorial workers who long had resented salary scales and working conditions not on a par with fellow workers in the composing room and in other fields.

The trend of the Guild, following a preliminary period devoted largely to discussion of improved professional standards, has been toward labor unionizing. The early years, with their emphasis on purely local and autonomous bargaining negotiations, produced few results and at the June 1936 national convention the Guild voted affiliation with the American Federation of Labor and thereby placed itself squarely in the ranks of organized labor. One year later, the Guild dropped out of the A.F. of L. and joined the Congress of Industrial Organizations. At the same convention, the Guild voted to include all newspaper workers except those already enrolled in other unions as eligible members.

The influence of the Guild on the press has been widely felt. Its leaders have concentrated on bargaining at the expense of other aims and have succeeded in obtaining numerous contracts guaranteeing higher wage scales, severance notices and pay, improved working conditions, and more stable tenure. These accomplishments have aided the drive for new units and more members. The Guild has not hesitated to use the strike as a weapon. In several cases, it has forced the temporary suspension of papers; in 1947 J. David Stern, one of the earliest publishers willing to recognize the Guild, blamed the sale of the Philadelphia (Pa.) *Record* and Camden (N.J.) *Courier* and *Post* on a stalemated Guild strike.

[1] Reprinted in *The Guild Reporter*, Vol. 16, December 9, 1949, p. 5.

There are two aspects of Guild influence that have received attention ever since the organization was founded. One concerns the desire of the Guild to obtain as many "Guild" or "closed" shops as possible in contracts it signs with publishers. Publishers have vigorously resisted on the ground that the arrangement would nullify to some extent at least the meaning of freedom of the press. Another factor concerns the fear on the part of some members of the press that Guild membership tends to destroy a reporter's objectivity in those cases where he is assigned to cover a story dealing with organized labor. Some editors have said that they would not assign a Guild member to report a C.I.O. strike. The Guild's answer has been that the charge doesn't mean anything unless concrete evidence of coloration or bias can be proved against a Guild member covering a strike.

The Guild is not without competitors in its effort to defend the interests of "front office" employees. The American Press Society, organized in 1936, seeks to pursue a set of professional objectives without any emphasis on a labor union program. The American Editorial Association, formed in 1940 under the auspices of the American Federation of Labor, is more directly competitive. Neither organization, however, has been able to dim the lustre of the Guild.

WHY THE GUILD ATTRACTS MEMBERS

—Henning Heldt, "The End of a Legend." Reprinted by permission of the publishers from *Nieman Essays, 1941–1942, Newsmen's Holiday.* Cambridge, Mass.: Harvard University Press, 1942. Mr. Heldt wrote this article while a Nieman Fellow at Harvard and while on leave as a reporter for the Jacksonville (Florida) *Journal.*

IT TOOK the Great Depression of the early 1930's to wake the average newspaperman out of the fond dream that he was different from "Labor"—to destroy his willingness to accept "the pat on the back and the by-line" in lieu of dollars and cents for the privilege of participating in the high and honorable profession of journalism. The starvation wages and layoffs of those depression years soon convinced many a reporter and desk-man, however, that the time had come to discard his long-nourished aloofness and individualism, that each must join in union with his fellows or starve, that only organized effort could guarantee decent pay checks.

The tradition of "individualism" dies hard. Even today many a newspaperman prefers to hold himself apart from the collective efforts of his fellow workers to better their lot through union organization. Too often these "individualists" are but the selfish and ambitious confident of their own ability to get ahead, whether it be through personal ability or talent as an apple polisher. There is still plenty of "I'll get mine, to Hell with the other fellow" philosophy in the ranks.

The first great surge away from the anti-joining complex of the average newspaperman took place more than eight years ago, following formation of the American Newspaper Guild. Organized in December, 1933, as an organ through which working newspapermen might seek more favorable provisions in an NRA code for the newspaper industry than those proposed by the American Newspaper Publishers Association, the Guild soon found its ranks swelled by thousands of editorial workers. A few years later the union opened its membership to all newspaper workers not under jurisdiction of the mechanical printing trades—but the membership still continues predominantly editorial.

Concern over the size of his weekly pay check, his working hours, and his lack of job security powerfully motivated the average newspaper worker who joined the Guild. Most of the growth of this union took place during the stern years in which this country climbed painfully up from the 1932–33 nadir of the Great Depression. Editorial workers who had experienced drastic salary cuts, longer working hours without extra pay, and frequent staff reductions had finally begun to realize that lack of organization placed them at terrific disadvantage to unionized workers in the printing departments when newspaper owners began looking around for departments in which they could cut expenses.

Then, too, editorial department employees were becoming more and more aware of the discrepancy between the professional skill required by their work and the wages paid. Many a college-educated reporter with years of experience found himself working for less than a linotype operator. The lesson was clear. If unionism had brought the linotype operator relatively high wages and kept them high right through the depression, it would do the same for the editorial worker. The rush to join the Guild began.

There was a motive beyond the economic which brought newspapermen by the thousands into the Guild. Close to the hearts of many new members lay the conviction that this new organization should strive to raise the standards of American journalism. This group hoped to make it an agency to combat the distortion of news, the opening of news columns to publicity and free advertising, and the suppression of stories in which large advertisers and friends of newspaper owners figured in a bad light.

A large proportion of editorial workers felt that their profession had fallen to a disgracefully low level and wanted to do something about it. Keenly aware that the average publisher of today is a businessman and/or politician, news writers realized that this development often adversely affected the honest practice of their profession. Publishers kowtowed increasingly to the dictates of their advertisers. They often suppressed stories. They killed news involving their friends and business associates in scandal. Stories of industrial strife usually gave one side of the trouble—and it wasn't labor's. Publishers and editors often put pressure on reporters to use their influence with public officials to gain special favors for friends.

These abuses naturally did not exist on every paper. But they were widespread. There was little the individual news writer could do to combat them. Often he was the unwilling tool of an unscrupulous executive. To refuse to be a party to such abuses might mean the loss of his job. To refuse was not so hard when jobs were plentiful. But in bad times, with the prospect of having to join the hundreds of newspapermen already roaming the streets in search of jobs, it was a more difficult matter to say no.

The establishment of the American Newspaper Guild offered hope to many a newspaperman not yet prey to the cynicism which had become almost an occupational disease. In such an organization he saw the possibility of an effective weapon to combat the abuses which sapped his integrity as a journalist. The desire to dedicate the Guild to such an end, in addition to its use to improve the economic status of the newspaper worker, is shown in a resolution adopted at the Guild's second annual convention, held at St. Paul, Minnesota, in 1934:

"Resolved that the American Newspaper Guild strive tirelessly for integrity of news columns and the opportunity for its members to discharge their social responsibility; not stopping until the men and women who write, graphically portray or edit news have achieved freedom of conscience to report faithfully, when they occur—and refuse by distortion and suppression to create—political, economic, industrial and military wars." . . .

The struggle for recognition and bargaining rights, the efforts to raise contract standards and their members' wages to levels more nearly in line with the degree of intelligence and technical skill required, the necessity of waging several long and costly strikes—all these factors have diverted the American Newspaper Guild from its second objective, the raising of professional standards. Little has yet been done in this field. It seems unlikely that much will be done until the Guild has achieved far greater national strength and a greater degree of economic well-being and security for the average newspaperman than he yet enjoys.

Guildsmen accept the primacy of the economic objective. First things must come first. But many look forward to the day when their union will be able to turn to the much-needed job of raising professional standards. Here and there some work has been done by individual Guild units. In Youngstown, Ohio, for instance, the local unit has twice organized and conducted a school in practical journalism in line with the national objective of raising newspaper working standards. The national organization itself has established an annual award, dedicated to the memory of Heywood Broun, for the best piece of writing by a Guild member.

But it cannot be denied that the Guild has neglected the subject of professional standards. The subject gets little space in the semimonthly *Guild Reporter*; it has seldom come up for discussion at Guild conventions after those of 1933 and 1934, and only once in awhile does it creep into Guild contracts. Occasionally a phase of it is represented in a contract clause providing that news writers in articles appearing under their by-lines need not conform to the editorial policy of their papers, should that policy be contrary to their own beliefs.

COLLECTIVE BARGAINING AS SEEN BY THE GUILD

—Eva Jollos, "Guild Setting Pace for Industry with Gains in Contracts," *The Guild Reporter,* Vol. 16, December 9, 1949, pp. 5, 8. The author is a member of the American Newspaper Guild Contracts Committee.

"THE fundamental purpose of the Guild is to bargain collectively with publishers, to preserve the vocational interests of its members, and to improve the conditions under which they work and live."

Thus the ANG's first constitutional convention in St. Paul in 1934 spelled out the Guild's aims. But it was to take three years before the Guild started to hit its stride in collective bargaining and signed contracts became the accepted rule rather than the rare exception. . . .

Nationally, the Guild at first took a hands-off attitude on collective bargaining. The first constitution, adopted at the founding convention in Washington in December 1933, contained an outright prohibition against national interference in local negotiations.

By the time of the St. Paul convention the following June, complete local autonomy had proved impractical, and the national Guild was given authority to intervene in any negotiations carried on in violation of the constitution. . . .

On the wage front, in order to get data on editorial earnings, the Guild launched a national survey on wages and hours in co-operation with NRA economists. Previously some locals had made their own studies.

The combined results, published in October 1934, gave a devastating answer to the contention of many publishers that editorial employes were specialized professionals who could not be "regimented" by codes setting up minimum employment standards.

In many cities the average pay for veteran newsmen was revealed to be just slightly above that for garbage collectors. The figures also provide an interesting comparison with conditions today.

The median weekly wage for reporters revealed by the study was $30.70. (Median wage represents the mid-point in the scale, above which and below which an equal number are paid.)

While the published results did not include actual average weekly salaries for the various editorial classifications, they did give a breakdown of average hourly rates which showed that reporters earned an average of 71 cents and worked an average of 41.6-hour week for an average weekly salary of $29.47.

Moreover, 53 percent of the reporters were found to earn below $32 per week. Only six of the 1,042 reporters covered by the study (0.57 percent) earned $100 or more per week. Twenty percent of the reporters earned under $20 per week, and 84.2 percent under $50.

While no accurate comparison can be made on a salary basis, present minimums alone point up how far the Guild has come in improving wages in its organized jurisdiction.

Editorial departments currently are covered by contract on 170 papers.

On 38 of these the reporter minimum is $100 or better, and while this represents only a relatively small portion of the papers covered, they represent about 55 percent of the Guild's entire organized jurisdiction.

On 90 papers the minimum is $85 or more, and there are only 25 papers (total coverage about 500 employes) on which the minimum is under $75. . . .

Three contracts were signed during 1934. The first, signed April 7, was with the Philadelphia *Record,* followed by a contract covering the *Capital Times* and *Wisconsin State Journal* in Madison on Sept. 14, and the Cleveland *News* on Dec. 20.

Madison three years later became the first local to sign a contract covering commercial departments, after the Guild had voted to join the CIO and extend its jurisdiction.

The agreement, signed Aug. 14, 1937, covered the *Capital Times* commercial employes. Today the Madison contract covers *Capital Times* editorial employes only, the *Wisconsin State Journal* employes having set up a company union two years ago, and commercial coverage was lost this fall in an election in the merged commercial departments of both papers.

The first Madison contract provided for a $35 top minimum after two years for all editorial employes; a maximum of one month "dismissal notice" after one year; a closed shop and a 48-hour week.

The latter provision came in for considerable criticism nationally, but for the employes involved it meant reductions from an average 55 to 45-hour week. The contract was silent on vacations and sick leave, provided overtime pay at the rate of 75 cents an hour or equal time off computed on a monthly basis, and provided that work on non-publishing holidays was to be treated as overtime.

(The latest contract provides a $80 top minimum after four years and the starting rate now is $5 higher than the top minimum in the first contract. Employes now get three-week vacations after 10 years, a maximum of 25 weeks severance pay, sick leave with full pay for the duration of any illness, and double-time pay for Sunday and holiday work. The 40-hour week was established in 1937, and the closed shop converted to a Guild shop in 1938.)

The first Cleveland *News* contract established a $40 top minimum after four years for the main editorial classifications. It provided the 5-day 40-hour week and an 8-hour day including an hour for lunch; a maximum of 12 weeks severance pay after nine years; equal time off for overtime, settled every six months, with the publisher having the option of paying for 25 percent of the accumulated time at straight-time rates; a clause giving the publisher absolute right to discharge any employe at any time, except for Guild activity, and a clause permitting the publisher considerable latitude in making pay cuts above the minimums. There were no provisions for vacations, holidays, or sick leave.

(The latest contract, which expired Nov. 1, has a top minimum of $97.50 for key editorial classifications, with $40 to start; 30 weeks severance pay; three-week vacations after five years, and standard holiday sick leave and overtime provisions.)

Elsewhere that year pressure by local Guilds led to posting of conditions of employment by managements and a number of verbal commitments which established the 40-hour week and restored paycuts in some instances.

Severance pay (then called "dismissal bonus") was born early in 1934 when the Newark Guild vigorously protested repeated firings on the *Star-Eagle,* won one reinstatement and a verbal commitment from Publisher Paul Block to pay severance thereafter on a graduated schedule running to six months pay after 10 years service.

The principle caught on quickly, and locals throughout the country soon made it part of their own demands.

Nationally, the Guild did not adopt a collective bargaining program until 1937. The 1934 convention, which went on record that "it is better to have no contract than a bad one," provided locals with an outline of demands, but it was purely an advisory move.

Negotiations continued on a purely local basis in many cities during 1935 and 1936. A few more contracts were signed, more bulletin board statements made their appearance, but each local continued pretty much on its own. The lack of co-ordination was so complete that the 1936 convention complained that it could not make a complete report on all agreements in existence because ANG had no records, and ordered the national executive secretary henceforth to keep track of contracts and report on them every six months.

A year later, with 30 contracts and 33 bulletin board agreements on the books, locals had found out that the autonomous approach was becoming harmful, with publishers quick to utilize substandard agreements elsewhere in their own negotiations.

The 1937 convention, "for the protection of the majority," therefore rewrote the constitution to require submission to ANG of all contract proposals and final drafts, and national supervision of collective bargaining. These constitutional provisions have remained virtually unchanged since that time.

Sparked by the extension of Guild jurisdiction to the commercial departments, 1937 saw the greatest increase in contracts of any year before or since.

Thirty of the agreements signed that year are still in effect. Of the contracts signed in 1935 and 1936, only those with the Boston *Herald* and *Traveler,* Cleveland *Press,* New York *News* and New York *Post* still survive.

While a national collective bargaining program, spelling out uniform conditions and requiring locals to propose them was adopted in 1937, it was not until 1945 that wages were tackled on a national basis.

The Guild's first national wage program called for a uniform $65 top minimum for reporters and key classifications in the other departments. At that time the highest reporter minimum in the country was $64.75, and many locals (along with the publishers) threw up their hands in horror, terming it fine for the metropolitan papers but "impossible to achieve on the smaller ones."

Eighteen months later the minimum goal had been established or bettered on some 60 papers, and the Scranton convention adopted the second wage program for a $100 minimum and a basic floor of $50 for any experienced adult worker.

THE GUILD'S CODE OF ETHICS

—George A. Brandenburg, "Newspaper Guild Adopts Ethics Code," *Editor & Publisher,* Vol. 67, June 16, 1934, pp. 7, 41. Mr. Brandenburg is a staff writer for *Editor & Publisher,* with headquarters in Chicago.

THE COMMITTEE ON ETHICS, headed by Paul Comley French, Philadelphia, brought in the following report (at the St. Paul national convention of the American Newspaper Guild in June, 1934), which was adopted as a basic policy of the Guild:

1. That the newspaperman's first duty is to give the public accurate and unbiased news reports, and that he be guided in his contacts with the public by a decent respect for the rights of individuals and groups.

2. That the equality of all men before the law should be observed by the men of the press; that they should not be swayed in news reporting by political, economic, social, racial, or religious prejudices, but should be guided only by fact and fairness.

3. That newspapermen should presume persons accused of crime of being innocent until they are convicted, as is the case under the law, and that news accounts dealing with accused persons should be in such form as not to mislead or prejudice the reading public.

4. That the Guild should work through efforts of its members or by agreement with editors and publishers to curb the suppression of legitimate news concerning "privileged" persons or groups, including advertisers, commercial powers, and friends of newspapermen.

5. That newspapermen shall refuse to reveal confidences or disclose sources of confidential information in court or before other judicial or investigating bodies, and that the newspaperman's duty to keep confidences shall include those he shared with one employer even after he has changed his employment.

6. That the news shall be edited exclusively in the editorial rooms instead of in the business office of the daily newspaper.

7. That newspapermen shall behave in a manner indicating independence and decent self-respect in the city room as well as outside, and shall avoid any demeanor that might be interpreted as a desire to curry favor with any persons.

Your committee also urges the condemnation of the following practices as being harmful to the public interest, the newspapers and newspapermen:

1. The carrying of publicity in the news columns in the guise of news matter.

2. The current practice of requiring the procuring or writing of stories which newspapermen know are false or misleading, and which work oppression or wrong to persons and to groups.

3. The acceptance of money by newspapermen for publicity which may be prejudicial to their work as fair reporters of news. Your committee urges the particular condemnation of the practice of writing paid publicity by staff political writers, and the acceptance by sports editors and writers of money from promoters of alleged sporting events.

4. The practice of some newspaper executives in requesting newspapermen to use influence with officials in matters other than the gathering of news.

THE PUBLISHERS' OPPOSITION TO A GUILD SHOP

—Arthur Robb, "Firm Stand Against Guild Closed Shop Voted by Eleven Newspaper Groups," *Editor & Publisher*, Vol. 70, July 3, 1937, pp. 3–4.

UNALTERABLE OPPOSITION to the closed shop, in news and editorial departments of newspapers, not as an economic issue, but because it deprives the responsible newspaper operator of the right to select his staff, was expressed in a formal resolution by representatives of 11 publishers' and editorial associations meeting here today [Chicago, June 29, 1937]. . . .

The resolution, as passed, follows:

The newspaper editors and publishers from all sections of the United States individually and through their cooperative associations listed below are gathered here to take action upon the American Newspaper Guild's recent declaration for the closed shop in editorial and news departments. We recognize the fact that when a problem of major importance is presented to us, the public is entitled to a statement.

This meeting is by no means one of opposition to collective bargaining, better hours, pay, or working conditions for newspapermen and women.

We are here to discuss the closed shop as a matter of journalistic and public principle, not as an economic issue.

Established for the benefit of all the people are four fundamental rights in the Constitution, freedom of religion, freedom of speech, freedom of press, and freedom of assembly. Experience has proved and even now is demonstrating in Russia, Italy, and Germany that the interference with one of these fundamental rights means the curtailing of others—the collapse of liberty itself.

Freedom of the press is not an exemption accorded by the Constitution for the benefit of publishers; it is but one of these four guarantees. It is a publisher's responsibility, a citizen's right—one which entitles him to an accurate statement of what is taking place in order that he may have the facts wherewith to judge matters of public policy and take whatever action may be necessary to protect himself and that which he holds dear.

There has never been a time in our history when uncolored presentation of news was as vitally important as today.

The extension of the great press associations serving news to newspapers of varying social, economic, political, and religious beliefs has emphasized this development of impartial news treatment. Thousands of men and women are devoting their lives to the gathering and presentation of the news without bias.

Only on such a foundation of factual reporting can sound public opinion and wise public policies be based.

This vital service of the press to the public can be performed properly only when those who are responsible for the publication are free to choose the persons whom they deem best qualified to report and edit the news.

This responsibility cannot be discharged if some outside authority, beyond their control, determines whom they shall or shall not employ. That is precisely what the American Newspaper Guild seeks by its demand. And that demand is the more serious because the Guild is now committed to a number of definite political objectives.

The recent American Newspaper Guild convention in St. Louis by resolution took positions on such debatable subjects as the war in Spain, the Court bill, and the support of a particular political party. In the same convention the Guild as an organization enlisted as a partisan in the tremendous public dispute now involving the entire labor movement in this country.

Following the expression on public policies enumerated, the Guild laid down mandatory rules calling for a closed or Guild shop. The closed shop is present in mechanical departments of many newspapers, absent in some.

We unite now, however, in unswerving objection to the closed shop for news and editorial department workers, not because we regard it as a labor issue involving questions of wages, hours, and working conditions, but because we are unwilling to turn over the news columns to any group already committed as an organization on highly controversial public questions.

We make no charge that bias is found *per se* in the work of a Guild member. To do so would imply bias *per se* in a non-Guild worker. Neither is true. Bias arises, however, among any group respecting any policy common to the group. No newspaper can command confidence in the fairness of its news presentation if it selects all its employees from only one political party, one religious denomination, or any one group devoted to a single cause.

We do not deny that causes require champions, and that progress springs from the genius of its advocates. Equally important to society, however, are those who report the controversial scene. It is the newspaper man's job to do that, not as a partisan but as an objective observer.

Therefore, be it resolved, that as editors and publishers here assembled from all parts of the United States we declare our unalterable opposition to the closed Guild shop or any other form of closed shop for those who prepare and edit news copy and pictures for newspapers, and we hereby express our determination not to enter into any agreement upon such basis.

American Society of Newspaper Editors; Pacific Northwest Publishers Association; New England Daily Newspaper Association; New York State Publishers Association; Inland Daily Press Association; California Newspaper Publishers Association; Pennsylvania Newspaper Publishers Association; Texas Newspaper Publishers Association; Ohio Newspaper Association; Southern Newspaper Publishers Association; and the American Newspaper Publishers Association.

WHY ONE EDITOR OPPOSED THE GUILD

—Malcolm W. Bingay, "An Editor's Case Against the Guild," *Editor & Publisher,* Vol. 70, June 26, 1937, p. 12. Mr. Bingay is a well-known editor on the staff of the Detroit (Michigan) *Free Press.*

I HAVE ALWAYS believed in good wages and working conditions for newspapermen because I realize that brains, energy, and ambition on the part of a staff are what make a paper a success and lead to the establishment of journalism not as a "game" but as a profession.

Higher wage levels and better working conditions will keep such men in the editorial departments and bring about the things for which I have always fought—to have journalism take its rightful place in professional standing along with law, medicine and engineering.

A newspaper guild built on such basic principles is one thing, however, and a union labor organization is strictly another. In fact, the plan of a labor union defeats the very purposes of a professional guild. It is a step down and not up. It destroys the spiritual essence of our work, lowers the levels of personal achievement, and makes the day's job a thing of factory routine.

In the long run it will reduce the standards of journalism and will not raise the average salaries. The least competent will be benefited and the more capable will be paralyzed. Individual effort will go for naught because in any regimentation of workers the good men must carry along the hewers of wood, the carriers of water, and the drones.

This is not true of mechanical departments or in any other factory work where production can be determined without question. There the work can be thoroughly standardized.

In an editorial department, however, it is not a case of mere typing. If it were, any stenographer could do the job. In editorial work the intangible values of brains, judgment, imagination, character, personality, are so completely interwoven that no man's work can be judged by a day's output.

I know of no way by which brains can be measured by a yardstick. Nor can loyalty, imagination, enthusiasm. One idea for a story may be equal to a whole week's work in the estimation of an understanding city editor. The human equation enters into every phase of editorial activity so completely that to regiment brains brings the whole business down to a subsistence level, with the lowest common denominator determining the character of the group.

In a composing room a loafer can be spotted in a few hours and will be as promptly repudiated by his foreman. Incompetence can be as readily proved. But not so readily in an editorial department. We all know how reporters can agree to "syndicate" and loaf on a beat. We all know that a man can write a routine story about which the city editor cannot complain; or, he can put a sparkle into it that will make the whole office hum with appreciation. A newspaper reporter who does not want to work and has no ambition can get by for a long time without having his derelictions detected by even the best of city editors.

The human equation makes completely different the work of the editorial man and that of the union labor man. There is no analogy.

THE GUILD AND FREEDOM OF THE PRESS

—United States Supreme Court, *Associated Press v. Labor Board,* 301 U. S. 103.

(EDITORS' NOTE: *On April 12, 1937, the United States Supreme Court, by 5–4 decision, upheld the constitutionality of the Wagner Labor Relations Act as applied to the Associated Press. The opinion was deliv-*

ered by Justice Owen D. Roberts. The case originated in 1935, *when the Associated Press discharged one Morris Watson, an employee in the New York headquarters. The American Newspaper Guild filed a charge with the National Labor Relations Board alleging that Watson's discharge was in violation of Section* 7 *of the National Labor Relations Act, which confers on employees the right to organize, to form, join, or assist organizations, and to bargain collectively through representatives of their own choosing. The Labor Board, after hearings, ordered the Associated Press to cease and desist from discouraging membership in the Guild and to reinstate Watson with back pay. The Associated Press refused, and the case went to the Court of Appeals on the Labor Board's petition for enforcement. The court upheld the board, and the case went to the Supreme Court. The material here is from Justice Stone's discussion of the relationship of the Wagner Act's bargaining provisions to freedom of the press.)*

. . . IT IS insisted that the Associated Press is in substance the press itself, that the membership consists solely of persons who own and operate newpapers, that the news is gathered solely for publication in the newspapers of members.

Stress is laid upon the fact that this membership consists of persons of every conceivable political, economic, and religious view; that the one thing upon which the members are united is that the Associated Press shall be wholly free from partisan activity or the expression of opinions, that it shall limit its function to reporting events without bias in order that the citizens of our country, if given the facts, may be able to form their own opinions respecting them.

The conclusion which the petitioner draws is that whatever may be the case with respect to employes in its mechanical departments it must have absolute and unrestricted freedom to employ and to discharge those who, like Watson, edit the news; that there must not be the slightest opportunity for any bias or prejudice personally entertained by an editorial employe to color or to distort what he writes, and that the Associated Press cannot be free to furnish unbiased and impartial news reports unless it is equally free to determine for itself the partiality or bias of editorial employes.

So it is said that any regulation protective of union activities, or the right collectively to bargain on the part of such employes, is necessarily an invalid invasion of the freedom of the press.

We think the contention not only has no relevance to the circumstances of the instant case but is an unsound generalization. The ostensible reason for Watson's discharge, as embodied in the records of the petitioner, is "solely on the grounds of his work not being on a basis for which he has shown capability." The petitioner did not assert and does not now claim that he had shown bias in the past. It does not claim that by reason of his connection with the union he will be likely, as the petitioner honestly believes, to show bias in the future. The actual reason for his discharge, as shown by the unattacked finding of the board, was his guild activity and his agitation for collective bargaining.

The statute does not preclude a discharge on the ostensible grounds for the petitioner's action; it forbids discharge for what has been found to be the real motive of the petitioner. These considerations answer the suggestion that if the petitioner believed its policy of impartiality was likely to be subverted by Watson's continued service, Congress was without power to interdict his discharge. No such question is here for decision.

Neither before the board, nor in the court below, nor here has the petitioner professed such belief. It seeks to bar all regulation by contending that regulation in a situation not presented would be invalid. Courts deal with cases upon the basis of the facts disclosed, never with non-existent and assumed circumstances.

The act does not compel the petitioner to employ any one; it does not require that the petitioner retain in its employ an incompetent editor or one who fails faithfully to edit the news to reflect the facts without bias or prejudice. The act permits a discharge for any reason other than union activity or agitation for collective bargaining with employes.

The restoration of Watson to his former position in no sense guarantees his continuance in petitioner's employ. The petitioner is at liberty, whenever occasion may arise, to exercise its undoubted right to sever his relationship for any cause that seems to it proper save only as a punishment for, or discouragement of, such activities as the act declares permissible.

The business of the Associated Press is not immune from regulation because it is an agency of the press. The publisher of a newspaper has no special immunity from the application of general laws. He has no special privilege to invade the rights and liberties of others. He must answer for libel. He may be punished for contempt of court.

He is subject to the anti-trust laws. Like others he must pay equitable and nondiscriminatory taxes on his business.

The regulation here in question has no relation whatever to the impartial distribution of news. The order of the board in no wise circumscribes the full freedom and liberty of the petitioner to publish the news as it desires it published or to enforce policies of its own choosing with respect to the editing and rewriting of news for publication, and the petitioner is free at any time to discharge Watson or any editorial employe who fails to comply with the policies it may adopt.

PROGRAM OF THE AMERICAN PRESS SOCIETY

—Foreword to booklet on the Constitution of the American Press Society, published by the Society.

Organization of a professional association of American and Canadian journalists, now functioning internationally as the American Press Society, grew out of a conversation in August 1936 among five members of the staff of the New York *Times.*

The conversation had become a discussion of the disturbing fact that throughout the world, even in the United States, ambitious men, backed by unscrupulous cliques, all greedy for power, were seeking by deceptive means to gain domination over their fellow men. Collective action, made compulsory by law and necessary by circumstances, was being seized upon by them and used as an instrument to further their selfish ends.

The newspaper men discussing this grave situation agreed, with unanimity of expression, that they individually and collectively were being attacked, their rights and liberties threatened, and that there existed a compelling need for an effective organization to protect their independence as journalists and to keep the channels of public information clear.

The group found, on careful inquiry among other members of their own and other editorial staffs of New York newspapers, that they were not alone in their anxiety. Determination was expressed everywhere that the high-handed tactics of demagogic racketeers should not be allowed to force the profession into the industrial war, then at its height.

Thirty-eight of those in first contact with the group contributed one dollar each toward the formation of an organization that would be not industrial, but professional. This money was to be used to test sentiment throughout the nation. Notices that a movement was under way to organize on a strictly professional and ethical basis were sent to 400 newspapers, the notices to be posted on bulletin boards.

The response was immediate and enthusiastic. Reporters copyreaders, editors, cartoonists wrote us that if a satisfactory constitution and program could be evolved, they would join us.

An open meeting was called for Oct. 7 at the Hotel Astor, New York. Eighty-five persons were invited to attend—sixty-six were present, a proportion so high as to be noteworthy. Five or six were openly inimical, but despite their efforts to hamper proceedings, the meeting went on record that such an organization was timely and needed. Oliver Holden, of the New York *Times*, was designated organization chairman and O. D. (Don) Donaldson, also of the *Times*, provisional treasurer. A committee to propose an economic policy was named.

Discussion at the meeting had shown a firm belief that, once organized as are the medical, legal, and engineering professions, newspaper workers not only improve their status economically, but also take a higher place in the social structure of the nation. There was precedent for this conviction: Professor Harold F. Clarke of Columbia University found that lifetime earnings in various groups averaged as follows: medicine, $108,000; law, $105,000; dentistry, $95,-400; engineering, $95,300; architecture, $82,500; journalism, $41,500; ministry, $41,000; skilled trades, $28,600; unskilled labor, $15,200.

Point may be added to these figures by recalling the evolution of the barber-surgeon. The craft split, the barbers eventually becoming trade unionists and the surgeons organizing on a professional basis, placing ethics, research, skill, prestige, accomplishment, and dignity above other considerations. The eventual reward for improving the quality of their product—their services—is demonstrated by Professor Clarke's figure.

Dentistry, engineering, and architecture, although younger as professions than medicine or the law, show twice the income of such unorganized professions as journalism and the ministry. Even these, however, show nearly 50 per cent more income than the skilled trades, which have been organized for years on a trade union basis, and nearly three times as much as that of unskilled labor, which in organizing makes no allowance for skill. Moreover, in all organizations which put money first, it is found that a standard wage eventually results, and recruits of ability seek some other occupation rather than be limited to the standard.

Bearing in mind, then, that improving the quality of the product—skill and character—would enable news workers to obtain for their services higher rewards, the economic committee met on Oct. 23 and drafted recommendations for subordinating any economic program to the ethical side of the Society's task.

A close study was made of the charters or constitutions of such organizations as the American Medical Association, American Bar Association, the American Society of Civil Engineers, the British Institute of Journalists, the National Press Club of Washington, and Sigma Delta Chi Journalistic fraternity.

In addition, analyses were made of some thirty or forty previous attempts, local and national, to organize newspaper men and women, nearly all of which had run into trouble. These studies took in the New York Newspaper Club, the Boston Newspaper Union, and others.

It was found that the apparent causes of failure were many, but that one factor was present in every instance of failure—the reluctance of the working newspaperman to devote any considerable part of his spare time to the burdens and routine of maintaining his organization and its integrity. Instead of actively helping, newspaper men permitted individuals willing to attend conventions and otherwise carry out the work of the organization to act for them; most of these "willing workers" went into action because they had an axe to grind, either a commercial cause, or some quixotic, crusading cause which had little or nothing to do with journalistic standards, ethics, or welfare. As a result, the organizations fell into disrepute and ultimately ceased to exist.

The drafters of the American Press Society's constitution endeavored to meet this situation by eliminating conventions and by setting up administrative machinery to assure constant control by the members, acting through a Board of Governors, whose actions the voting membership can check at any time by the simple processes written into the constitution.

Some of the organizers advocated a minimum of ten years' experience for membership. Others thought one year sufficient. A compromise on four years was reached, with provision for a non-voting junior membership and for recognition of distinguished journalistic work by an honorary rank, that of Fellow. Protection of any material interests acquired by members was assured by creating a non-voting Associate Membership for those who leave the news-room temporarily or permanently. Also Honorary Membership for distinguished public service having no direct relation to journalism was provided with a limitation of five new honorary members in any one year and a requirement of unanimous approval of the Board.

After the constitution was drafted the task of placing the Society and its objectives before the newspaper men and women of the United States and Canada was begun. This necessarily has been slow, as the Society was determined not to place itself under obligation to anyone but its own members and therefore was unwilling to ask help which might have strings tied to it. Money with which to do this work was lacking at the start and has been limited throughout. Nevertheless applications for membership, accompanied by dues payments, trickled in week by week, until by the middle of July 1937 the Society had a nation-wide and well-established membership. And on every staff where the Society gained substantial membership, friction subsided and confidence and serenity were restored.

On July 15, 1937, a provisional Board of Governors was designated and on October 1, 1937, the first national officers and permanent board were elected. In November, the first concrete service to members was established in the form of a placement bureau. In December the Society voted to establish a legislative committee in Washington to press for inquiry into and exposure of propaganda activities in the United States and Canada and to urge legal protection of the professional status of newspaper workers. . . .

The first autonomous affiliate of the Society was organized by members in Pittsburgh, Pa., on May 5, 1938. This was followed shortly thereafter by a New York section.

Although the Society is improving its finances steadily and therefore its ability to serve its members and establish its reputation, it is not expected that the growth will ever be speedy or sensational. The Society does not coerce or even urge any one to join.

With a selective membership, the organizers and officers feel that the Society is destined to become a powerful instrument for preserving and fostering integrity in journalism, and therefore for serving well both the public and its members.

THE AMERICAN EDITORIAL ASSOCIATION

—Anonymous, "National Newswriters' Union Formed by AFL," *Editor & Publisher*, Vol. 73, October 26, 1940, p. 46.

(EDITORS' NOTE: *Representatives of federal local unions, affiliated with the American Federation of Labor, established a national organization of newspaper men and women under the name of the American Editorial Association at a meeting in Chicago on October 23, 1940. The delegates represented 15 locals, with a membership of 1,500.*)

THE AEA council adopted the following declaration of principles:

The American Editorial Association dedicates itself to the advancement of the economic and social welfare of all editorial workers on newspapers of general circulation and on accredited news services in the United States and Canada.

Convinced that certain subversive forces are working to destroy our democratic American form of government, the Association declares itself unalterably opposed to Communism, Nazism, Fascism, and all other alien isms. It declares as a matter of fundamental policy that no person espousing the doctrines of any of these alien isms shall be admitted to membership in the Association.

The Association holds that freedom of the press, freedom of speech, of assembly, and of religion are vital to the preservation of democracy and democratic institutions, and pledges itself to fight unceasingly to preserve, protect, and maintain them. It proclaims the right and duty of newspaper editorial employees to present the news without bias, fear, or favor, free from any political, economic, or social domination.

Recognizing that editorial workers have a highly specialized ability and a distinct community of interest, the Association holds that they can best be served through unions of members of their own occupation, and we invite the editorial workers of America to join with us in the formation of such unions.

The Association further pledges itself to raise the standards of the editorial workers' calling in every way; and particularly by giving encouragement, guidance, and assistance to the younger newspaper editorial employees.

REVIEW QUESTIONS AND ASSIGNMENTS

1. What factors would you cite to explain adequately the rise and growth of the American Newspaper Guild?

2. Do you believe that the Guild erred when it affiliated with the Congress of Industrial Organizations, the C.I.O.?

3. Make a study of the present executive personnel of the Guild and then discuss the often repeated charge that the leadership of the organization is "leftist."

4. Trace the developments in three outstanding strikes involving the Guild and publishers and then state your conclusions about the issues involved.

5. Examine three recent Guild-publisher contracts and state your conclusions concerning the provisions.

6. Do you feel that the Guild can deal in a satisfactory fashion with the so-called professional aspect in communications activity?

7. If you were an editorial worker on a newspaper that had been successfully organized by the Guild but that had not signed a contract, would you join the Guild? Defend whichever point of view you take in answering this question.

8. Discuss realistically the Guild "closed-shop" issue. Work out a comparison of the positions taken by the publishers and the Guild before attempting to reach conclusions.

9. What are your conclusions regarding the Associate Guild program which the A.N.G. has tried to organize among journalism students?

10. Do you feel that the Guild and other organizations of press workers represent threats to freedom of the press?

11. What position do you think the schools and departments of journalism should take toward organizations like the Guild and the American Press Society?

12. What do you think of the charge that a reporter who is a member of the Guild is likely to inject a pro-labor bias into stories he writes about strikes involving C.I.O. unions?

13. Prepare an outline of the labor affiliation picture in radio.

14. Write a brief paper on the contributions made by the late Heywood Broun in the founding and development of the Guild.

ADDITIONAL REFERENCES

Annual Reports, National Labor Relations Board.

Bliven, Bruce, "Union Card Journalist," *The New Republic,* Vol. 88, September 9, 1936, pp. 125–126.

Broun, Heywood, "An Army with Banners," *The Nation,* Vol. 140, February 13, 1935, p. 154.

Chafee, Zechariah Jr., *Government and Mass Communications,* University of Chicago Press, 1947, Vol. 2, pp. 517–536.

Collective Bargaining in the Newspaper Industry, National Labor Relations Board Bulletin No. 3, October 1938.

Guild Reporter, published semi-monthly by the American Newspaper Guild.

Howard, Nathaniel R., "The Guild and the Labor Situation," in *Problems of Journalism,* American Society of Newspaper Editors, 1944, pp. 28–35.

Keating, Isabelle, "Reporters Become of Age," *Harper's Magazine,* Vol. 170, April 1935, p. 601.

Kramer, Dale, *Heywood Broun,* A. A. Wyn, 1949.

Labor Research Association, *Labor Fact Book,* International Publishers, 1939.

Lee, Alfred M., *The Daily Newspaper in America,* Macmillan, 1937, pp. 666–699.

Levinson, Edward, *Labor on the March,* Harper & Brothers, 1938.

Luxon, Norval Neil, "The Guild and Education," *Nieman Reports,* Vol. 3, October 1949, pp. 9–11.

Lyons, Louis M., "The Character of the Newspaper Job," *Nieman Reports,* Vol. 3, October 1949, pp. 18–21.

Minton, Bruce, and John Stuart, *Men Who Lead Labor,* Modern Age, 1937. (Contains chapter on Heywood Broun.)

Mott, Frank L., *American Journalism,* Macmillan, 1950.

Nicolet, C. C., "The Newspaper Guild," *American Mercury,* Vol. 39, October 1936, p. 186.

Pringle, Henry F., "The Newspaper Guild," *Scribner's,* Vol. 105, January 1939, p. 21.

Seldes, George, *Lords of the Press,* Julian Messner, 1938.

The Philadelphia Record *Case,* Hearings Before the Committee on Education and Labor, House of Representatives, 80th Congress, First Session, Vol. 1, U.S. Government Printing Office, 1947.

Werne, Benjamin, *The Law of Labor Relations,* Macmillan, 1949.

Woytinsky, W. S., *Labor in the United States,* Social Science Research Council, 1938.

27. PRESS TRENDS AND POSSIBILITIES

INTRODUCTION

IN BRINGING together the materials for a critical appraisal of the American press, it has been necessary to cite certain early writings, upon which the passing years have thrown a peculiar light. Alarmists have been proved to be unduly alarmed, and prophets have been shown not to be true prophets. These early citations are vitally important in showing what the press was at various periods in the past, as well as what the hopes and fears of critics were at those times. With their aid a valuable perspective is established that shows a distinct evolution in the press, in which notable improvements in accuracy, independence, and service to the reader have been made. Further, the weaknesses that once appeared to some critics to endanger the newspapers have proved to be the source of their strength —for example, their dependence upon advertisers for financial support. Current writings of exacting journalists suggest that readers have every reason to hope for continued improvement.

Before leaving the study of the press, it is good to look ahead and see what changes are indicated by forces now active, insofar as that can be done in a world that finds itself in unusual turmoil. The first citation, the work of Nixon, presents the best analysis to date of the effects of the decreasing number of dailies in the United States, and of the trend toward concentration of ownership. A different interpretation has been made by Ernst in his *The First Freedom*, and the student should read the citation referred to in the bibliography. Lack of space prevented the editors from doing justice in this chapter to Mr. Ernst's point of view.

Whether or not new daily newspapers can be founded to fill the needs perceived by some critics of the American press is a question that has been discussed with increasing social references for at least fifty years. Two of the most recent are presented here. Liebling, the tongue-in-cheek critic, and Wolseley, student of the religious press, present some of the possibilities and improbabilities inherent in such ventures.

What will radio, FM, television, facsimile, and ultrafax do to the press? These are questions that have concerned publishers as each device has appeared to threaten newspaper circulation. Because radio has had a nationwide acceptance for more than two decades, Lazarsfeld is able to give an interesting revelation on the effect of radio. Beville, who speaks with intimate knowledge of the other electronic wonders, suggests some of the possibilities in FM, television, facsimile, and ultrafax.

In an able discussion of objective reporting, Brucker explains how this concept has been a cultural invention of the American press. Slowly growing, it has gradually enveloped greater and greater areas of the printed news. Although he indicates a need for considerable improvement, Brucker says that there is reason for satisfaction with the trend of the years. The desirability of instituting channels of self-criticism is set forth by Hocking in his study for the Commission on Freedom of the Press. Fortunately, at this date the press is the subject of more first-rate criticism than at any other time in its history. In the last citation the editors of this book refer to some of the more outstanding sources of such analyses.

Finally, the student of the press should not lose sight of the fact that the American press as it is now constituted and with whatever shortcomings it is endowed is possible only under the present form of government. The editors have made some observations on this point in the last article.

IMPLICATIONS OF DECREASING DAILIES

–Raymond B. Nixon, "Implications of the Decreasing Numbers of Competitive Newspapers," *Communications in Modern Society,* Wilbur Schramm (editor), University of Illinois Press, 1948, pp. 50–53. See also Mr. Nixon's press ownership study in the *Journalism Quarterly,* June 1945, Vol. 22, p. 97.

WHAT, THEN, are the implications that reasonably may be drawn today from the decreasing numbers of competitive newspapers?

1. *The number of competitive daily newspapers will continue to decline.* Even though the total number of dailies may increase, through the establishment of new papers in the faster-growing small cities, the percentage of communities having more than one general-circulation paper or one publisher will not increase at any time in the near future. Spiralling costs, which affect the advertiser, and the

reader as well as the publisher, will discourage the establishment of new publishing ventures in the larger cities. A severe depression would have a similar effect, as it did in the thirties.

2. *The one-publisher town is not an evil in itself—it all depends on the publisher.* To quote Mr. Lindley again, "a community is no worse served by one poor newspaper than by several poor papers," but "certainly it is better served by one good newspaper than by two or three poor ones." We cannot improve the situation merely by multiplying mediocrity. But a responsible "monopoly" publisher, as I observed in my 1945 article, can dedicate his paper to the principles of intelligent and objective reporting, giving all groups a fair hearing. Extensive research is needed on this point. A preliminary report of an investigation at Columbia (published in the June 1948, *Journalism Quarterly*) indicates that except in the very large cities competing papers tend to be merely "rivals in conformity."

3. *The "monopoly" omnibus daily is here to stay.* The new methods of "cold-type printing," which do away with expensive linotyping and stereotyping, will make it easier for many smaller communities to support local newspapers. Moreover, these cheaper processes will enable private groups in the larger cities to operate their own special-interest papers as outlets for minority views. It is doubtful, however, whether either such publications or facsimile papers will offer any serious competition to the established general-circulation dailies that do a good job of supplying the wide variety of expensive news, opinion, features, and advertising that readers have come to demand. "A young man could start a daily newspaper in New York City today along the line of the *Sun* of 1883, a four-page one-cent sheet, and he could do this on small capital," writes Dr. Alfred M. Lee. "But . . . the whole job would attract few purchasers even at one cent in competition with today's *Daily News* (or) . . . *Times*. . . . Part of the press's institutionalism, a very powerful part, is in the minds of subscribers."[1]

4. *Competition from the new electronic media will increase.* The growing number of both AM and FM stations together with the advent of television and facsimile newspapers is filling the gap left by the "disappearing dailies." This new competition for the advertiser's dollar will tend to hold newspaper advertising rates at a reasonable level and thereby stave off any demand for regulation solely because

[1] A. M. Lee, "The Basic Newspaper Pattern," in *The Annals of the American Academy of Political Science,* Vol. 219, January 1942, p. 52.

of economic practices. Even "monopoly" publishers are having their troubles today in keeping revenue ahead of expenses and readers and advertisers know it.

5. *This new competition does not necessarily promise any improvement in quality.* On the contrary, as the struggle for survival becomes more intense, the temptation may increase for the weaker units to accept border-line advertising and to attract readers or listeners through sensationalism and "sure-fire" features at the expense of good reporting and diversified opinion. Excesses of this kind might lead to a far more widespread demand for regulation than we have had up to now.

We are faced, then, by a curious paradox. Although we seem to be on the verge of getting the increased competition on which Mr. Ernst has pinned his faith, it actually may lead to more of the evils and dangers he deplores.[2] We are back to the premise on which most teachers of journalism started long ago: namely, that if we wish to improve newspapers, regardless of their number, we must raise the social responsibility and professional competence of the men who run them. At the same time we must educate a more enlightened generation of newspaper readers, who will demand, and in turn receive, a better product.

Mr. Ernst will insist, of course, that what he wants is a competition of ideas, not merely a competition for revenue. I agree with him that diversity is desirable. I believe we shall have more and more of it without any of the additional laws he advocates. That is, provided we can avoid a war or a severe economic depression that would bring a curtailment of all our democratic liberties. But where he makes his mistake is in taking his stand that "the important issue is solely the need of competition." Economic diversity alone can never "make available to the peoples of the world the kind of communications content that will enable them to maintain a peaceful and productive society." What is needed, above all, is a higher *quality* of content coupled with a journalistic *effectiveness* that will assure this content of being read and understood. The greatest enemy of a free press and of a democracy is not "monopoly," but too much "threadbare traditionalism" in determining both *what* to print and *how* to print it.

Even the Commission on Freedom of the Press ignored the second half of this basic problem. At least the Commission's formal report

[2] Morris L. Ernst, *The First Freedom,* pp. 57–124.

reveals an almost complete unawareness of the need for effective communication. One large Southern newspaper that printed the report almost in its entirety did not receive a single letter of comment from its readers. Obviously not many of those readers read or understood the report, or were affected by it.

The history of American journalism may be divided into four major periods. The first was the period of the fight for freedom, during which both newspapers and readers were fighting for that freedom from governmental restrictions which was essential before the press could fill its role in a democracy. The second was the period of political party domination during which party leaders, rather than the editors themselves, usually dictated the policies of the papers. The third was the period of personal editorial leadership, in which editors like Horace Greeley became independent moulders of opinion. The fourth was the period of business office emphasis, in which the growth of the modern daily into a complex economic enterprise made the publisher, rather than the editor, the dominant figure in journalism. In each of these periods the press has responded to changes in its economic, social, and political environment.

I firmly believe we are now entering a fifth major period: a period in which the emphasis will be increasingly upon *scientific direction.* The mere fact that so many papers are "monopoly" papers trying to satisfy all kinds of readers under conditions that hourly grow more complex, would tend to make us depend more and more on scientific direction, even if common sense did not tell us it is imperative. Public opinion polls, readership and readability studies, experiments with new processes of printing, the scramble for television and facsimile licenses, the Nieman fellowships and the American Press Institute, the accrediting program for schools of journalism—all these are unmistakable signs of the new trend.

POSSIBILITIES FOR NEW DAILIES

—A. J. Liebling, *The Wayward Pressman,* Doubleday & Company, Inc., 1947, pp. 271–274. Mr. Liebling conducts the "Wayward Press" column for *The New Yorker.*

I BELIEVE that labor unions, citizens' organizations, and possibly political parties yet unborn are going to back daily papers. These will represent definite, undisguised points of view, and will serve as controls on the large profit-making papers expressing definite, ill-disguised points of view. The Labor Party's *Daily Herald*, in England, has been of inestimable value in checking the blather of the Beaverbrook-Kemsley-Rothermere newspapers of huge circulation. When one cannot get the truth from any one paper (and I do not say that it is an easy thing, even with the best will in the world, for any one paper to tell all the truth), it is valuable to read two with opposite policies to get an idea of what is really happening. I cannot believe that labor leaders are so stupid they will let the other side monopolize the press indefinitely.

I also hope that we will live to see the endowed newspaper, devoted to the pursuit of daily truth as Dartmouth is to that of knowledge. I do not suppose that any reader of the *Magazine* believes that the test of a college is the ability to earn a profit on operations (with the corollary that making the profit would soon become the chief preoccupation of its officers). I think that a good newspaper is as truly an educational institution as a college, so I don't see why it should have to stake its survival on attracting advertisers of ball-point pens and tickets to Hollywood peep shows. And I think that private endowment would offer greater possibilities for a free press than state ownership (this is based on the chauvinistic idea that a place like Dartmouth can do a better job than a state university under the thumb of a Huey Long or Gene Talmadge). The hardest trick, of course, would be getting the chief donor of the endowment (perhaps a repentant tabloid publisher) to (a) croak, or (b) sign a legally binding agreement never to stick his face in the editorial rooms. The best kind of an endowment for a newspaper would be one made up of several large and many small or medium-sized gifts (the Dartmouth pattern again). Personally, I would rather leave my money for a newspaper than for a cathedral, a gymnasium, or even a home for streetwalkers with fallen arches, but I have seldom been able to assemble more than $4.17 at one time.

A provision of the Taft-Hartley Act (Section 304), aimed primarily at labor-union newspapers, prohibits any non-profit publication from publishing political news or opinion. This would, of course, also stop any endowed newspaper.

It will also, I believe, outlaw or severely limit the *Christian Science Monitor*, published by the Church of Christ, Scientist, and several hundred church and diocesan publications, a circumstance which Mr. Taft will surely regret before he is much older.

Non-profit publications supported by corporate funds will also be barred from writing about politics, according to the senatorial author of the Act in a debate on June 6, but newspapers, although corporations, will be allowed to continue as usual because: "They get their money from advertising." This is a curious qualification of freedom of the press; only mediums of ballyhoo will be allowed to express an opinion. Senator Taft has not yet explained whether a newspaper will be stopped from discussing politics until its advertising begins to support it—in some cases a period of several years. Mr. Howard's *Telegram,* for example, would not have been allowed to peep about politics from the time he bought it, in 1927, until 1932, when, by virtue of an assist from the Pulitzer brothers, it began to pay. Even at that, the disastrous Ohio statesman has not explained whether such a newspaper will be considered profitable until it has paid off all of its debts. He has not said, either, whether old-established papers will be enjoined from writing about politics if they start to lose money and have to draw on corporate funds to keep going. How much grace will they receive before being ruled "non-profit" publications: five minutes? five months? five years?

This provision, from a long-range view perhaps the most important in the bill, received virtually no publicity in the regular daily press, which may have seen in it an aid to its own continued monopoly. I never read anything about it myself until President Truman mentioned it in his veto message. It was the old story of the correspondents at London asking an outside power to crack down on their competitors. The foremost enemies of freedom of the press are its chief beneficiaries. The newspaper publishers, those avowed great enemies of government regulation of the press, have now tacitly supported government regulation of an important part of it. They favored the Taft-Hartley Bill almost unanimously. I am against government-owned newspapers and government interference with privately owned ones. But monopoly invites regulation, and when a large city has only one newspaper, the paper becomes as much a public utility as the gas company. The publishers' hope for continued independence lies in keeping the way open for the rise of new newspapers. By sealing off the potential sources of new papers, the Taft-Hartley Act would insure the eventual regulation of those that remain.

POSSIBILITIES FOR RELIGIOUS DAILIES

—Roland E. Wolseley, "A National Religious Daily." Reprinted by permission of *The Christian Century* from the issue of December 29, 1948, pp. 1426–1428. Mr. Wolseley is professor of journalism at Syracuse University.

FROM TIME TO TIME church bodies urge the establishment of a daily religious newspaper. Now and then a layman will propose the launching of a great Protestant or Catholic daily. Generally the people who put forward this idea hope to supply a corrective for the sins of the regular press. They believe that the kind of paper they visualize would demonstrate to the journalistic profession that acres of comic strips, charm columns and crime stories are not essential to the success of a 20th century newspaper.

This idea, for example, was advanced in 1940 by Theodore F. MacManus, who proposed to the convention of the Catholic Press Association that all the diocesan publications be merged into one big national Sunday paper. The merged publication was to have foreign correspondents, the reports of the major wire services, and room for the right kind of comics and for society, sports and other types of general news. MacManus conceived it as "a national newspaper edited as Catholic newspapers ought to be edited." Nothing came of the proposal.

In the same year Bishop G. Bromley Oxnam told the Methodists that "for the present a national newspaper appears to be a colossal and unwise undertaking." Writing in the *Christian Advocate* of February 1, 1940, he asked for a group of six papers, one for each of his church's jurisdictions. However, he reported that "there is a demand for a national Methodist paper." Neither the national paper nor the jurisdictional papers materialized.

The most famous experiment in the way of a great religious paper is, of course, the *Christian Science Monitor*. This daily, however, is presented not as a religious publication or denominational journal, but as a superior secular paper sponsored by a religious body. A memorable incident in this phase of journalism is Charles M. Sheldon's week of editorship of the Topeka (Kan.) *Daily Capital*. He edited the paper as he thought Jesus would have done it had he been bodily on the scene in March 1900. During that week, the Topeka paper reported at the time of Dr. Sheldon's death three years ago, "the circulation of the *Capital* soared to astronomical heights," and to this day "people write from everywhere on the globe asking for copies."

Church people who occasionally examine their regular papers to see how well they stand the test of religious sincerity seem to be searching for a paper that measures up to the ideal advanced by Mr. MacManus, Bishop Oxnam, and Dr. Sheldon. Thus a churchwoman, Dorothy Rickard, took a look at a small daily in Pennsylvania and concluded that it proves that "Methodism is workable seven days a week in business."

Miss Rickard, writing in a recent issue of the *Christian Advocate,* did not say that the Philipsburg (Pa.) *Daily Journal* is edited exactly as Jesus might edit it. But she did make quite clear that Methodism involves high ideals and that this paper lives up to them. The *Daily Journal* may indeed be a remarkable paper. However, we must judge it by the picture drawn by its biographer. What are its characteristics, as pointed out by Miss Rickard?

It refuses to print crime news. It allots "at least 10 per cent of the news matter printed each week" to church news. It does not use advertisements, pictures and reading matter "that might be harmful to our young readers." (This means that "no beer or liquor advertisements have ever appeared . . . nor have advertisements of Sunday sports or other forms of Sunday entertainment ever been allowed." Pictures of celebrities shown drinking are not published. And "the sports editor has strict orders not to write up any Sunday baseball or football games for the Monday columns.") It reports few court cases. ("About once every five years a case comes up . . . of such intense local interest it cannot be ignored.")

Are these the principal policies to which other editors must adhere if their newspapers are to be as good as the Philipsburg daily? Evidently so, since no other positions or viewpoints are mentioned. Are these standards a religious test of good journalism? Might the *Daily Journal* be a model for a "great Protestant daily" or a "national religious newspaper?"

The Philipsburg formula outlines a relatively easy means of journalistic grace. Most of the 11,000 daily and weekly newspapers of the United States could follow it without much trouble. Some, of course, if deprived of certain types of advertising, might collapse quickly. But virtually all could prove in a short time that religion, Methodist or any other type, is workable seven days a week in business and make themselves model newspapers if all they need do is to imitate the Pennsylvania paper's policies. The fact is, however, that these policies are practically no test at all and certainly offer no pattern for a church-sponsored national newspaper.

What standards might more nearly determine the religious earnestness of American editors and publishers? The answer can best be arrived at by asking certain questions.

Does the paper, through its editorials, fight the forces of evil in the local community? Does it expose political chicanery, police dishonesty and inefficiency, and other forms of community mismanagement if they exist in its territory? Or does it wink at violations of the law committed by the "best" people? Is it silent about all but the most trivial issues?

Does the paper print not only news about the town's or city's churches but also fair-minded news about the local cooperative, Socialist or other minority party meetings, labor rallies and other neglected or unpopular activities? Does it go out of its way to see that minority groups are given the chance to reply to editorial charges, so that readers will know that there are dissatisfied or rebellious people in the community and the reasons for their rebelliousness?

Does it print enough crime news and court reports to serve as a thorough record of community criminal action, so that possible victims are warned and criminals are put under the spotlight of publicity?

Does it seek to apply Christian principles by attacking and exposing racial discrimination, misrepresentation of individuals by name-callers and gossips, vigilante groups that take the law into their own hands, and religious bigots?

Naturally there are other tests, but these are a sample of what Miss Rickard seems to have overlooked, if it is granted that such standards have anything to do with religion. That the tenets of any church demand more than refusing to print crime news, allowing generous space for church news, ignoring Sunday sports, and turning down liquor and certain other kinds of advertising is clear from an examination of basic church laws and the actions of church governing bodies. In the case of the Methodists, the *Discipline* and the work of the 1948 General Conference in Boston show that Philipsburg is hardly doing enough. Miss Rickard either did not use a broad definition of the tenets of her church or her article was cut. The tests listed above, it would seem, are far more penetrating and important than strict orders to the sports editor "not to write up any Sunday baseball or football games."

Of course it may be that the Philipsburg daily stands up very well under our tests. If so, it is indeed a superior newspaper, and more nearly a product of religious idealism than any other now being published. There is no American newspaper, church-sponsored or otherwise, so full of virtue as to meet the tests set forth here. There may never be. But there certainly could be a greater approximation to the perfect than now exists.

Journalists or teachers of journalism frequently are asked to name the five or ten "best" newspapers in the country. There is no such thing, of course, as a "best" newspaper any more than there is a "best" church or a "best" book or a "best" university. Best for what? Scrimmage University may be best for football teams and Notabene University best for its journalism department. But Reredos University may have a very fine theological school while the dental school at Molar College may be tops. Thus with newspapers. Most tabulations of the "ten best" include the New York *Times*, the New York *Herald Tribune,* the St. Louis *Post-Dispatch,* the Louisville *Courier-Journal,* the *Christian Science Monitor*. If George Seldes compiles the list he omits all these, and if Roy Roberts compiles it he includes all these. Seldes believes that the entire press is corrupt and says so in his books, whereas Roberts, head of the Kansas City *Star* and a champion of the newspapers, sees the press as a great and noble institution.

But perhaps neither is right. The *Monitor* does little with local news whereas the *Post-Dispatch* is known for its exposés of local corruption. The *Times'* foreign service is magnificent and far to be preferred to the overseas coverage of the *Courier-Journal,* but the Louisville paper's editorials stir the brain with their vigor instead of dulling it with wordiness.

None of these prominent papers, excellent as they are in many ways, could qualify as evidence that religious principles in general are workable journalistically, and none could prove that it adheres closely to the tenets of any church. If any denomination owned any one of them it would not be advancing the cause of religion much more than the Philipsburg *Daily Journal* is doing. None of them is a truly religious paper. In short, a "truly religious paper" is a myth.

To be sure, the *Christian Science Monitor* is sponsored by a church.

But outstanding as that publication has become throughout the world, it falls short not only of Methodist but also of Christian Scientist tenets. Not so far short as the average paper—say a Pulcipher (Neb.) *News Gazette* or a Middleage (Ohio) *Journal-Union*—but still short. The *Monitor* has numerous blind spots, such as its refusal to print most disaster news and its attitude on narcotics and even on psychology. Presumably the *Monitor's* editors are, theoretically at least, as zealous for fairness in the treatment of human beings as is demanded by the tenets of the church that owns the paper. Yet the *Monitor* is hardly known as a crusading daily, as a paper in which the unwashed, the underprivileged, the unpopular and the other standard minorities can find a generous and encouraging outlet for their political and economic views. It is a decent and clean paper, but it also is a smug and contented paper.

The reason why the religious principles of Methodism, Roman Catholicism, Christian Science or any other church body will never be proved workable through a newspaper can be understood from the *Monitor's* experience. That paper must either please enough readers to remain solvent or make do with the funds that the Mother Church, as its underwriter, is willing to furnish. Americans and Britons, who are the principal readers of the *Monitor,* never have responded to the relatively high quality of its content in sufficient numbers to prove that a "good" newspaper is a paying proposition. And there is some reasonable doubt that the *Monitor* is the ideal "good" newspaper.

Most newspaper readers will want lots of comics, crime and charm. Not only must the human beings who run newspapers observe closely the interests of the human beings who do the buying and thereby support the press; they also inevitably suffer from their own tendencies as human beings. Newspapers are the work of people, not entirely of machines. A newspaper is not produced as unchangeably as chewing gum, with the same size and stretchability day after day. Two issues, even two editions, are never quite the same. A newspaper is very much the product of human judgment, subject to the pull of human prejudice. Men decide what shall go into its columns. Men decide what news shall be emphasized. Men decide what point of view the editorials shall take. And men are men.

When human behavior has become ideal and human thought transcendent, newspapers may serve as examples of workable religion.

Until then they can only approximate the ultimate. And since the ideal society is free of war, prejudice, unemployment and faulty educational methods, no Christian or any other citizen can be satisfied by a newspaper of today. No Christian should go out of his way to compliment a paper whose claim to perfection, even in the limited form of "workable Methodism," is based on little more than that it refuses certain kinds of advertising and plays down crime news.

When the day arrives that the public will support a "great Protestant daily" such a daily will not be needed. Until it can be assured of support, launching such a paper will be merely another adventure in subsidized journalism, like that of the Christian Scientists with their general paper and the average church with its denominational weeklies. To succeed in our economy a "great Protestant daily" would have to imitate and excel the standard papers. Otherwise it would be as superficial religiously as Miss Rickard's Pennsylvania daily evidently is, or as ineffectual as the bulk of the denominational press. By and large, church people are bored with their papers and the unchurched are not reached by them.

INFLUENCE OF RADIO ON THE PRESS

—Paul F. Lazarsfeld, "Some Notes on the Relationship Between Radio and the Press," *Journalism Quarterly*, Vol. 18, March 1941, pp. 10–13.

THE GREATEST single change which radio has helped to bring about is the greatly increased interest in news all over the country. Of course it is not possible entirely to disentangle the role which European events have played from the fact of easier access to news due to radio. But it is safe to say that without radio the steadily increasing participation in current events would not have come about so quickly and so thoroughly.

Thanks to this interest in news, it is not likely that the reading of newspapers has decreased as a result of radio's coming onto the scene. In addition, there is fairly positive evidence that people who used to read newspapers are not reading less because they can now listen to the radio. The old newspaper reader uses radio as a supplement to his reading. As time goes on, it is even likely that new newspaper readers are recruited through radio. For a number of psychological reasons, persons who *hear* a news item are often inclined to want to *read* it just because radio has brought it to their attention. This relationship, however, is probably a different one in different situations. In a crisis situation, follow-up reading is much more frequent than in times of a news lull, when radio news seems to indicate that not much can be expected from reading the newspaper. (In general it has been found that the same people listen to and read about conventions, public discussions, and so on.)

Whereas thus far the radio has been not detrimental but probably even beneficial to newspaper reading, it has cut very heavily into the advertising budgets of newspapers. Between 1928 and 1939 expenditures for advertising in newspapers decreased from 760 million dollars to 525 million; expenditures for radio advertising increased from 20 million dollars to 170 million in the same period. These financial changes are really the ones which might bring about major effects in the structure of the newspaper trade. The actual measures which those who want to defend newspaper interests will have to take will be contingent on a careful estimate of a number of psychological and sociological factors.

One of these factors is a change of function which the radio is likely to bring about. The newspaper cannot compete with the radio in speed; the "scoop" aspect of news will more and more be monopolized by radio. The newspaper will probably have to stress the "intelligence" aspect of news. As in earlier times, people will turn to the paper for details on and interpretation of news—news they will already have heard by radio. A similar distribution of function might come about in the advertising field. There is no reason why the radio should not announce the existence of a product and then refer, "for further details," to current advertisements in newspapers and magazines. Such a development would find strong popular backing from the side of the average radio listener who is annoyed by "too much advertising" on the air.

Furthermore, it is likely that the most efficient use of an advertising budget does not lie in putting all available money into radio, but in creating a "clinching effect" by using radio and print-media so that the consumer can find confirmed in one medium what he has been made aware of in the other. An advertising message in two media probably attains much more than a double effect from this mutual backing. Unfortunately there are no studies yet available on this point, but general knowledge of the psychology of attention and memory would make such studies advisable.

Until recently printed media have had a monopoly of communications, and therefore have not done much research work to back their claims. Radio, an upstart, has used research much more skillfully, and to its own advantage. It is research into the yet unexploited potentialities of print rather than into political activities of pressure groups that will help to keep a healthy balance among the different media. One suggested avenue of investigation which seems most hopeful arises from the fact that reading has certain advantages over listening which will make it always desirable for the person who has acquired enough reading skill to read without difficulty. We can read at a time we choose, at a speed appropriate to the topic; we can skip one page in reading and dwell upon another. These are advantages which the less flexible radio program does not have. The future development of competition between radio and print will therefore depend partly upon the progress in the general reading skill level of the population. If the great extension of formal schooling which has come about during the last decades continues, it will help the newspapers to point to an ever-increasing market for their output. On the other hand, newspaper associations would do well, in their institutional promotion, to link the press with educational movements and organizations of all kinds.

In efforts to tie the newspapers in with the general social and cultural trends of our times, both media—radio and print—have much left to do. Contrary to early expectation, radio has not become a channel of general information for the masses. People on lower educational levels (and 50 per cent of the American population has not gone beyond grade school) who do not read because they have not acquired the necessary skill, do not listen to serious broadcasts. They obviously lack the conceptional skill to make use of serious information in whatever form it appears. Here radio has not seen its task clearly and has not achieved as much as in the commercial field. A prevalent misconception was that informative programs on the air would be picked up by the masses of radio listeners. This has proved not to be the case. The printed media still have the chance of extending their cultural services and putting in a claim for public support, which they would not and should not get merely by deploring the technological progress which shifts employment and income from one group of the community to another.

News interests which radio arouses are somewhat different from corresponding interests in the pre-radio area. The new type of news consumer who cares for current events as the result of his exposure to radio news seems to know less, to have a more episodic and a less deep-rooted concern with current events than the person who was brought up on a newspaper diet. A similar phenomenon can be found in the field of music. There is no doubt that radio has greatly increased the number of those who listen to and care for serious music. But their attitude toward serious music is rather different from what we were accustomed to find in middle-class homes where traditional musical education prevailed. Whether one wants to call the radio-created music lover less expert and less systematic, or whether one wants to see in him a modern American type as good, in his way, as the older type who mainly took over the European musical tradition, is a matter of general philosophy. In the news field it is of significance to be aware that radio has greatly increased the number of people who view public affairs somewhat as a spectator watches sports, and who might exhibit some of his characteristics in a crisis situation.

The newspaper trade cuts itself off from one very important source of information by not handling its own circulation figures in an adequate way. Elaborate efforts have shown that the vast area of circulation figures available at this moment is not used and is hardly usable for studying the effect of radio. It would be advisable, and easy, to keep circulation records in a form in which they can be matched with the shifting scene of broadcasting. Newspaper circulation in times of crisis should be compared with circulation in times of relative quiet on the news front; comparisons between urban and rural circulation, between morning and afternoon papers, between areas covered by radio networks as compared with areas of local broadcasting, and many another analysis of this kind would help greatly to furnish a glimpse into the future.

A final group of questions likely to become of prominence centers around the problem of joint ownership of stations and newspapers. At this moment about a third of American stations are professedly owned by newspaper interests. What is the advertising policy resulting from joint ownership? How is news of social importance, such as that of labor disputes and racial problems, handled under varying ownership structures of newspapers and radio stations?

The student of radio expects another problem to grow large in the not too distant future, although it is scarcely discussed at present.

Due to its fleeting nature, radio needs an outlet through which its services can be announced in advance so that audiences can do more planning for their listening. As the novelty of radio wears off, and as it extends its function more and more from mere entertainment to general informational services, it will become more and more evident that people need to know in advance what to expect on the air. Improved schedule information and discussion of past and future programs will become as important as they now are in the motion picture field, for example.

If the unsettled relationships between radio and the press persist much longer, then radio will be forced to look for its own outlets in print, and the question of newspaper-owned stations will turn into the question of station-owned newspapers. It would not be surprising if the situation which developed between the song publishers and the radio industry were to repeat itself in the relationship between radio and the printed page.

INFLUENCE OF TELEVISION, FM, AND FACSIMILE

—Hugh M. Beville, Jr., "The Challenge of the New Media: Television, FM, and Facsimile," *Journalism Quarterly,* Vol. 25, March 1948, pp. 3 ff. Mr. Beville is director of research for NBC.

America is now entering a new era of electronic mass communication. These new vehicles of electronic communications will have a tremendous impact on all existing means of mass communication—not only on radio broadcasting—but on the printed media and the motion picture.

The new media are television, frequency modulation broadcasting, and facsimile broadcasting. Television and FM are daily enlarging their influence in the field of mass communications. Facsimile stands at the threshold of commercial field development. Truly we can say that the field of mass communications faces a period of evolution—if not revolution—which will be comparable to the combined effect of introducing the rotary press and the motion picture camera to the world simultaneously. . . .

Since any communication medium depends for its true value upon what service the public receives, a brief summary of television programming and its future potentialities would seem to be in order.

It is often said that by adding sight to sound, television has done the same thing for radio that the addition of sound accomplished for the silent motion picture. This is a highly inadequate analogy. Actually, the addition of living pictures to sound has produced in television a new and unique medium of mass communication. It delivers something far beyond an addition of sight to existing radio broadcasting or the possibility of seeing present-day movies in the home. Television has often been characterized as "bringing the world into your home." More truly, television takes the viewer from his home to the very scene of the telecast. The viewer gets a feeling of "being there," of immediacy which gives to telecasts authority and significance possessed by no other medium of mass communication. No one who saw the telecast of President Truman's short message to Congress on the Greek-Turkish aid program, and who viewed the grim countenances of Mr. Truman, the Cabinet, and Congressional leaders, could have escaped the fact that this was indeed a dramatic event which marked a radical change in the whole course, not only of American foreign policy, but of history itself.

As a means of educating and informing the American public on important international, national and local issues, television is in a field by itself. The availability of television networks was the paramount factor in the determination of the Democratic and Republican National Committees to select Philadelphia for their 1948 conventions.

Television has already demonstrated its ability as a teaching aid. Successful demonstrations have been made whereby surgical operations performed in a hospital have been telecast and transmitted to televison screens viewed by groups of surgeons and students at a remote point. The New York City Board of Education has definite plans to include television in all future school buildings. Such plans call for large screens in auditoriums and for viewing rooms where visual demonstrations can be seen. . . .

The greatest significance of FM to those interested in the field of mass communications lies in the fact that it permits many more broadcasting stations to be operated than has been possible with the AM system of broadcasting. This is going to introduce greater competition in broadcasting than the newspaper field has ever known; it is going to make local radio stations services available to many hundreds of communities which heretofore had to depend on distant stations for service; and it is bringing into broadcasting many new interests as stations operators. Among the new licenses of FM stations are to be found educational institutions, local public school systems, trade unions, and publications of various sorts. Once a substantial number of FM receivers are in the hands of the public, these new independent FM operators will have an opportunity to demonstrate what they can do in the way of building audiences by creating new types of programming, and by developing fresh talent at the local community level. . . .

There is little question in the minds of most students of radio that FM will be the standard sound broadcasting system of the future. Its technical superiority seems to insure this. (The only exception is to be found in remote rural areas which cannot be reached by FM stations due to the technical limitations on the service range of FM transmitters.) Despite the bright future for FM as a sound broadcasting system, it would be folly to believe that FM will revolutionize broadcasting. The American public possesses today more than 65,000,000 receivers which will receive only AM stations and such receivers are currently being bought by the public at the rate of a million per month. It will surely be 10 years or more before FM can hope to reverse the picture which we have today and establish itself as the primary system of sound broadcasting.

The bright promise of a newspaper printed in your home has occupied a firm place in the bag of tricks with which prophets of the electronic future have delighted their audiences for many years. This service is to be made possible by facsimile broadcasting—the transmission of reproductions of printed matter and pictures by radio into the home.

In contrast to TV and FM, facsimile is still considered by the FCC to be in the experimental phase of development. Although facsimile has undergone a number of years of laboratory development, thorough testing under field operating conditions is just beginning. . . . The introduction of frequency modulation has greatly stimulated improvement in facsimile because FM's wider broadcasting bands permit greater printing speeds for facsimile.

An important step which must be taken before we can expect facsimile to grow greatly is the establishment of standards by the FCC. The setting of standards will assure the public that all facsimile broadcasting stations will use uniform transmission systems. Prior to taking the step, the FCC has requested that further experimental operation and demonstration be conducted to determine public preference relative to certain features of the proposed system. . . .

At the present time the cost of facsimile receivers, which are made on a special order basis, is something more than $600 per set. The cost of a 400-foot roll of chemically treated paper which is used in the Hogan recorder is now $3.85, or approximately one cent per foot. This roll of paper is good for 24 hours of reception, which means that the paper for a four-page edition costs approximately four cents. Hogan anticipates that recorders may ultimately be turned out on a mass production basis for $100 to $200, while the paper supply may be obtained at a cost of one cent per four-page edition.

A study of the above figures will indicate that the newspaper in the home may still be a long way off. Facsimile offers a timely newspaper service, but whether it can successfully compete with sound broadcasting for speedy news bulletins and with the more complete coverage of a newspaper which can be picked up at the front door for a nickel a day or less, is still a challenging question.

Because it offers newspapers extensive promotional opportunities, facsimile development in the next year or two will more than likely follow the pattern established by the Philadelphia *Inquirer* and the Miami *Herald,* with installations of recorders in public places where the volume of traffic and the number of viewers may make it economical as a newspaper adjunct. Its developers, however, are looking ahead to the days when facsimile will enter the home and thus truly become a new mass media. They see in it the possibility to render not only bulletins of important news items, but also specialized newspapers for the minority interests which get limited attention in today's dailies. In this category we may include the housewife, the school child and the farmer. Therefore, instead of the present-day single newspaper with many departments, these departments would become special editions, broadcast at times to suit the reading convenience of audience—early morning for the man of the family, mid-morning for housewives with shopping news and women's features, noon time for the farmer with market and weather reports, and mid-afternoon for school children with comics.

In addition to permitting speedier facsimile printing, the advent of FM has benefited facsimile in another important respect. FM has brought into existence a thousand stations, *all of which* are potential facsimile broadcasters.

These stations can become facsimile broadcasters in one of two ways:

1. By broadcasting facsimile at various times when they are not broadcasting sound—early morning or late at night. It is not inconceivable that these stations might periodically interrupt sound broadcasting to put out facsimile transmissions for 15 minutes.

2. By simultaneously broadcasting sound and facsimile—a technical accomplishment known as "multiplexing." Multiplexing can now be done only at the expense of degrading the sound service. Nevertheless, further engineering developments may reduce the effect of multiplexing on the quality of sound to a point where the FCC would approve such simultaneous operation, at least during periods of talk programs which are least affected by multiplexing.

The fact that FM stations will be located in many smaller cities now served by only one or by no local daily newspaper may encourage them to develop facsimile services. At least we can look forward to experiments in this direction, as certain FM stations find that competition in sound broadcasting is so keen as to jeopardize their economic future. Of course, all of this is predicated upon the development of inexpensive home receivers and expanded cheap paper supply. The accelerated momentum of television today will surely postpone the arrival of facsimile as a mass medium of communication.

Before leaving the subject of facsimile, I cannot refrain from a brief mention of a new and even more revolutionary advance in communications developed by the RCA Laboratories. I refer to ultrafax, a combination of television, radio relay and high-speed photography. Ultrafax can handle the transmission of documents, messages and printed pages at the rate of a million words a minute. Photographs, maps and other illustrations can be flashed through the air at a speed of 30 pages a second. Electronic communications are thus prepared to serve society in an age of ever greater potentials—of supersonic speed of travel and of atomic sources of energy. . . .

The fourth challenge of the new media is their potential impact on all existing media of communications—newspapers, magazines, radio, and motion pictures. Just as in the early days of radio's growth there were many dire predictions as to what news by radio would do to newspapers and what music by radio would do to the phonograph record business, there are today forecasts that these new means of communications will disastrously affect existing media. Major motion picture producers fear the growth of television. We hear the question asked, "Who will continue to listen to sound broadcasting when the public can get sight plus sound via television?" Even some of the magazines are giving serious thought to the new competition in the home for the eyes of their readers which will come from the video receiver.

The answers to the questions regarding radio's effect upon other media of communications are available for all to study as pertinent evidence on these questions. In 1930, the total weekly amount of time given to news on New York's four major stations was one hour and twenty minutes. Last week these same four stations broadcast seventy-one hours and forty-five minutes of news programs. Nevertheless, during this period there has been a steady increase in newspaper circulation in New York. Outside of helping to kill the "EXTRA" edition, which was probably never a profitable operation for publishers, radio's principal effect on the newspaper has been to increase people's interest in news and thus aid in the building of newspaper circulation. Although the phonograph record business was seriously affected during the depression years, probably by economic factors rather than by radio, this industry has in each of the past two years sold more than twice the number of records turned out in 1921, the previous year of peak sales. Certainly the magazines and motion pictures have hit new highs in circulation and audiences in recent years.

This suggests that all of these new media may ultimately find a place for themselves in the communications structure without seriously disrupting any existing media. There are many social factors which account for this phenomenon. Among these are our constantly increasing population; the steady improvement in educational levels; higher average family income and living standards; the greatly increased amount of leisure time; and the interest which one media stimulates in another.

To those who question whether we need these new media in mass communications, I would like to say that I am among those who believe that an increased knowledge and a truer understanding of social, political, and economic problems on the part of the American public is vital to our future democracy. When we find, as George Gallup did last November, that 60 per cent of the American public had no real knowledge of the Marshall Plan, and that 39 per cent had not even heard of the Taft-Hartley Law, we must recognize that here is a real challenge to all of us. The new media present us with unrivalled opportunities to overcome public ignorance and apathy concerning crucial issues of our times.

TREND TO OBJECTIVE REPORTING

—Herbert Brucker, *Freedom of Information,* pp. 267–270, 275. Copyright 1949 by Mr. Brucker. Used with the permission of The Macmillan Company.

CURIOUSLY, the critics of our press, as one man, overlook the significance, promise, and even the very existence of the tradition of objective reporting. One reason is, no doubt, the spate of frankly opinionated columns, features, and editorials that exists side by side with it in our papers. Another is the fact that the good of unbiased reporting is partly obscured by the surviving vulgarity, sensationalism, and headline thinking that still characterize the news pages of our papers. I hope I have made it clear in the brief historical sketch above that the vulgarity, growing out of an interest in the news as news, as something interesting to the mass of men, contributed notably to the rise of objective reporting. But we still cannot see the forest of objectivity for the trees of journalistic superficiality. Perhaps, if we cannot see it on today's front pages, we can appreciate it by looking back with the advantage of hindsight. To us Joseph Pulitzer, for example, is far enough in the past to be seen for what he was, both a panderer to the vulgar and a pioneer in changing the press from its nineteenth to its twentieth century form. Yet a contemporary, even in Pulitzer's later days when he was already abandoning yellow journalism to conduct one of the outstanding American liberal newspapers, could see only the bad in him. Thus, in 1903, C. C. Buel, assistant editor of the *Century Magazine,* protested earnestly to Columbia University at its soiling its hands by accepting Pulitzer money to found a school of journalism that might help raise the standards of the profession. When Pulitzer acquired the *World* in 1883, Buel declared, Bennett's *Herald*—another pioneer on the way to objective reporting—had been for many years "an easy-going prostitute in the journalistic field, with few or no imitators." But then came Pulitzer:

> At first all reputable journalists were shocked, and many of them stood out against the new practices, but little by little, the tone of nearly

the whole press began to change, for the *World* steadily grew in wealth and influence, and as each year new men from the colleges poured into newspaper square, journalism that could produce wealth became more and more the beacon-light of success . . .

Pulitzer has made yellow journalism a necessity of human life, because human nature is too weak in the mass to resist the enjoyment of the sins and follies of its fellows.

Buel added that Pulitzer had brought him to believe "that the fast rotary press is the greatest curse that ever fell on civilization." Perhaps that reveals the extent of his understanding of democracy.

In Europe too, even today, it is the fashion to look down upon the American press as vulgar. General assignment reporters on the American model are unknown on the Continent. Fires, police news, the courts, and all the trivia of the American press, from Hollywood scandals to kittens rescued from trees, are beneath the dignity of the Continental editor. The result is, to be sure, that Europe's newspapers are less cluttered than ours with the tinsel and baubles of the passing show. But it is equally true, and far more significant, that twentieth century Continental journalism bears a remarkable likeness in the political partisanship of its news to the American party press of the dark age in the first third of the nineteenth century. A European looks to his paper not for an unbiased report, but for a window on the world that is heavily stained with his own prejudices.

Even the relatively new Soviet press, which takes a severely holier-than-thou attitude toward our press, simply does not understand the obligation to be impartial in reporting news. For example, Tass, the Soviet news agency, in reporting the discussion during the long sessions of the Paris Peace Conference of 1946 over whether Albania should be invited to attend, told Russian readers that Anglo-Saxon speeches against the invitation "provoked *quite reasonable* objections from Vishinsky. . . . Immediately after this the Greek Prime Minister Tsaldaris made a speech in which he put forward *rude and unjust accusations* against Albania."

No American reporter could have written the words I have italicized. Trained in the American tradition, he would automatically have been content simply to record what Mr. Vishinsky's objections were, letting the reader judge for himself whether they were "quite reasonable" or wholly unreasonable. In the same way he would not have made the distinctly editorial comment that Mr. Tsaldaris was "rude and unjust," but would merely have reproduced the accurate substance, if not indeed the essential words themselves, of the Greek minister's remarks.

This point is so important to a determination of what to do about the future of the American press, and is so consistently overlooked by the critics of our press, that it is well to make the contrast clearer with an American example. Two quotations do not make a case; but no one familiar with European journalism and American journalism can doubt that Tass' editorializing of the news and the following sample of American news writing are wholly representative of these two utterly different journalistic traditions. The example I choose is from my own paper, the Hartford *Courant,* although almost any spot-news story on a reasonably controversial subject from any other American paper would do as well. The item concerns a local strike, in which the two opposing sides inevitably had different opinions and different emotions as to the rights of the matter. Under the headline "Royal Union Makes Issue of Security," the story began:

> Maintenance of "union security" and the method and extent of future arbitration are the two key issues in the Royal Typewriter Company contract dispute negotiations, Union President Joseph Chesery revealed Saturday when details of the dispute were aired publicly for the first time by both sides.
>
> According to the union, negotiations have ended, and about 3500 Royal employees will vote whether or not to strike for their demands at 10 a.m. Monday in the State Theater.
>
> After each of the six issues that follow, the management's viewpoint as stated by Charles B. Cook, company vice-president and factory manager, is found in the first paragraph; the union stand, given by Mr. Chesery, is in the second.

The story went on to give the details in exactly this fashion, without any hint as to whether the reporter, or his superiors, held the management's or the union's cause to be the more just. I repeat that this is nothing unusual. It merely typifies what is done every day, in the vast majority of news stories, as a matter of course.

Prewar France made a distinction between the *journal d'information* and the *journal d'opinion*; the first was supposedly devoted to news more or less on the American pattern, while the second was frankly in the tradition of the European, and the dark-age American method of reporting the world according to a preconceived point of view. It is true that the *journaux d'information,* like the prewar

Matin, did publish more general news in the American pattern than other French papers. Yet the worst of today's American transgressors against objective reporting are pure by comparison. And it is precisely this that the critics of American newspapers, foreign and native alike, refuse to credit.

Instead, the critics concentrate on two things: the surviving violations of the American tradition by American newspapers, and the many editorials, columns, features, and other matter in our papers that are openly devoted to opinion. There can be little doubt that most American newspapers slant these deliberate expressions of opinion in a conservative direction. That is, as we have long since noted, what is wrong with the twentieth century press. But I submit that we cannot find ways and means of righting this balance without starting from the surprising fact that our editors and publishers go as far as they do in keeping their prejudices out of their news columns. Rather than criticize them for their remaining offenses against objectivity, we must recognize that their achievements in this direction are, when measured against the journalism of our own past and against that of most of the rest of the world even today, nothing short of extraordinary. . . .

Rather than complain about the remaining imperfections of our press, then, we ought to marvel that it is as objective as it is; and, having looked back upon more than a century's steady progress toward honest journalism, we must remind ourselves that the journey is not yet ended. The journalism of today is not America's final, best product. We are simply midway, perhaps much farther than midway, along the road. Right now our papers are still marching along that road by making still firmer the obligation to be impartial in news reports and by carrying that obligation into fresh areas hitherto reserved to opinion. They will go farther in that direction, no matter how impatiently critics who are ignorant of journalistic history damn them for their unquestioned faults, no matter how the Chicago *Tribunes* and *PMs* alike cling to the journalistic vices of the past. And our newspapers and their critics alike will find that no doctrine imported from abroad, no inspiration dreamed up in Washington, no theory invented in an academic ivory tower, points the way ahead. That way lies in following to the end the same natural, spontaneous course into the future that we have followed in the past.

SELF-CRITICISM AND IMPROVEMENT

—William Ernest Hocking, *Freedom of the Press,* University of Chicago Press, 1947, pp. 206–207.

THE PRESS is capable of a more adequate self-regulation than it has hitherto exercised. It alone can hold itself to the positive standards of performance; it needs perhaps chiefly to have pointed out to it how fundamental its work is. Its major defects are within reach of a measure of prompt correction. Incompetent reporting and comment on grave public issues cannot be wholly avoided, since reporters cannot be omniscient, and they must preserve, as Arthur Brisbane advised, their "superficiality"—their attachment to the current and visible phase of things. But they can be encouraged to use conscience, and they can achieve the grace of modesty and warn their readers that their version of truth is tentative. The photographers' outrageous violations of public meetings and personal privacy can be curbed without damage to their inestimable gift of the graphic record. A maturer responsibility can be taken for the educational possibilities of the qualitative aspects of the press, especially those that have to do with the stabilities of social faith and the level of art and entertainment within the press including the cartoon. A readiness of the press to co-operate with private agencies and of private agencies to assume a greater measure of initiative in advising on press standards contain large promise of advance.

But within the community at large, also, there must be a profounder sense of responsibility for one's own thinking and for the level of emotional life, in recreation and the use of leisure. The agencies of amusement and art touch the most potent springs of that emotional unity in which alone, through the meeting of minds, public discussion can be fruitful. This is why degradation of the arts through commercialized vulgarity, claiming the cover of freedom, stands out as so vital a blow to freedom. What men decide to enjoy is not purely a private concern. A vulgarized art elicits disintegrating rather than uniting emotions; and emotion is the energy of the will. If the agencies of amusement and art could recover a sense of dignity of their social function, that of restoring vagrant feeling to a free acceptance of the good, the instinct of regulation—like an awkward gesture for recovering a lost balance—would be put to rest.

Unless in such ways as these the lifting element within our culture, which is by necessity spiritual and free, can find a route to its indispensable work, there is no certitude that a free press can or should remain wholly free.

We know now because of events and trends abroad that a free press can exist only in a free land, that the only free peoples are democratic peoples. We know that the truth can be told only among free, democratic peoples. In all other lands the people are lied to, tricked, and deceived, as a matter of conscious national policy. In all these lands the press has gone off the honor basis. In these lands the greatest lie has become the greatest national service. The more the press deceives its readers, the more it profits the state. Yet not only the nationals suffer; their neighbors suffer as well.

Present authoritarian states do not and cannot allow the press to be free. The more authoritarian the country, the less the freedom of its press. Further, whenever a non-authoritarian state moves toward absolutism, its press at once is shackled in a like degree. It is a danger to be watched in every democratic country, for either step is a measure of the movement along the other line.

This country will find that the more it perfects itself in democracy, the more perfect will become the press; and the farther away it moves from democratic ideals, the more the stature of the press will shrink, and integrity and honor will be sacrificed to whatever national aims exist at the moment. Present imperfections of the press are a reflection of an imperfect society and an imperfect democracy. But they are the flaws of society that consciously seeks to improve itself, to administer greater freedom, justice, security, and well-being for all. It is the only type of human society of which that can be said.

DEMOCRACY AND PRESS TRENDS

—A conclusion by the editors.

The years since the end of World War II and the advent of the Atomic Age have seen a number of heartening developments in the realm of the mass communications media in this country.

Whatever the trends are on other continents and among other peoples, in the United States a greater effort is being made to understand and evaluate the functions of the media and their influence upon the mass audience than in any other period in history. This statement would imply little, indeed, if volume of attention were the only index. More significant by far is the fact that efforts to appraise—in order to improve and perfect rather than to use—the press are of a much higher quality than ever before, and also of wider scope. Few, if any, aspects of the media have escaped the searching questions of the research workers.

It is important in a world that has become so unsatisfactory to so many to know that there is encouraging growth at some points. This is particularly true when applied to the press, the greatest single safeguard of American freedom and security.

In 1936, Dean Carl Ackerman of Columbia told the A.N.P.A. that "we need a journalism foundation in the United States dedicated to the study of the daily newspaper and government. We need scientific studies of the press, by the press, and for the press, which will contribute to the progress of journalism as the great educational foundations have advanced medicine." In recent years, the requirements he stated have increasingly been met.

Scholarly, scientific studies of the press, by the press, and for the press, are coming from the schools and departments of journalism, and from the progenitors of the foundation that Dean Ackerman anticipated in his address. Outstanding among the latter is the University of Illinois Institute of Communications Research. Under the direction of Wilbur Schramm, it has initiated a program of research that has begun to produce results. The group of papers published in 1948 under the title of *Communications in Modern Society* indicates the promise of this institute. Already highly productive is the Columbia University Bureau of Applied Social Research, of which Paul Lazarsfeld is director. Concerned somewhat more at this time with the radio than with the newspaper, this group of research workers is uncovering data of great significance to the newspaper. Nor should the seminars held at Columbia University by the American Press Institute be overlooked. This movement, financed by the newspapers and the University, for several years has brought together leading newspaper executives for the purpose of analyzing the operation, influence, and cultural setting of the newspaper for the purpose of self-improvement.

Other productive studies have developed from the Nieman Foundation of Harvard University. Its quarterly publication prints some of the most thoughtful essays on journalism. Among other publications, *The Annals of the American Academy of Political and Social Science,* in such issues as the one devoted to 'The Press in the Contemporary Scene," Vol. 219, January 1942, has printed and continues to publish helpful essays on the press. Pre-eminent in the field is the *Journalism Quarterly*, which under able editorship is regularly publishing the most penetrating studies of the press and society.

Wherever students of the press turn, they find an expanded and lusty growth of research in journalism. Better texts, concerned with influence and significance as much as with techniques, are being made available by teachers of journalism. The schools and departments are enriching and extending their curricula with the social sciences. Also, some of them have already set up or have started to set up special research efforts in the broad field of communications; Minnesota and Illinois have been pioneers in this field.

To our mind the most important and concerted effort to understand, evaluate, and make recommendations for improvement of the press is the work of the Commission on Freedom of the Press under Robert M. Hutchins. The work of this commission has resulted in the publication of *Freedom of the Press,* by William Ernest Hocking, *Government and Mass Communication,* by Zechariah Chafee, Jr., *Freedom of the Movies,* by Ruth A. Inglis, *Peoples Speaking to Peoples,* by Llewellyn White and Robert D. Leigh, *The American Radio,* by Llewellyn White and the summary report, *A Free and Responsible Press.* In spite of the affronted reception of some of these reports by certain newspaper people, the work of the commission deserves to be compared with that of the Wickersham Commission on Law Observance and Enforcement and with that of the Hoover Commission exposing inefficiency in the American Federal government. It will be recalled that the recommendations of none of the three were universally accepted. A detailed criticism of the findings in the joint report of the Hutchins Commission may be studied in *Prejudice and the Press,* written by Frank Hughes, a member of the staff of the Chicago *Tribune,* and published in 1950.

The editors contend that the outlook for the American press is generally encouraging—economically, politically, and socially. The current introspection of the press augurs well. Further, the press has never been so free in America as now. The results of the anti-trust action in the case of *United States v. Associated Press* extend rather than restrict the growth of the press, while freedom from contempt proceedings has broadened in recent years. Though the rights of the press may be said to be always in flux, because of restrictions that legislatures or courts may seek to put into effect, actually the general area of press freedom in America has been extended. There seems to be no reason to believe that the present status will be changed for the worse in the near future, barring the advent of a war or minor setbacks in localized actions. In the latter kind of restriction the press is able to protect itself through the processes of appeal.

REVIEW QUESTIONS AND ASSIGNMENTS

1. Are there any signs that concentration of newspaper ownership is now breaking up?

2. Has the development of automatic composition lived up to its early promise?

3. To what extent are newspapers printed in the home?

4. What are the natural limitations against which "radio newspapers," or home-printed newspapers, must battle?

5. Do you see any influence from *Time* or *The New Yorker* in your local newspaper?

6. Is there any noticeable change in the style of news writing in the past ten years? Do you predict any? If so, what?

7. Explain the growth of the columnists. How far do you think this trend is likely to go?

8. What is the effect of the influence of columnists upon the old influence of the editorial page?

9. Do you find an increasing use of pages of interpretation and summary?

10. Cite any demands from readers that are not met by the newspapers. Why are they not met?

11. To what extent has the radio injured the newspaper? Give proof.

12. What do you predict will be the influence of the radio upon the press in the next few years? Of television? Of facsimile?

13. In how many countries is the press now free to print uncensored news?

14. Do you believe an uncensored press can exist in any type of country other than a democracy? Justify your answer.

15. What is the justification for censorship in time of war?

16. Which type of censorship is preferable if one must be imposed, government-directed or self-imposed?

17. Discuss the statement that the defects of the press are but reflections of an imperfect society.

18. Would you say that the press was more or less completely "civilized" than other institutions of society?

ADDITIONAL REFERENCES

Anonymous, "Can a Daily Be Lithographed?" *Business Week,* December 2, 1938, pp. 24–26.

———, "Chain of Facsimile Newspapers," *Business Week,* March 11, 1939, p. 28.

———, "New Kinds of News," *Business Week,* July 27, 1940, p. 32.

———, "Newspaper Readers Get the Whole Story on Page One," *Newsweek,* Vol. 7, February 29, 1936, p. 20.

———, "Press Has a Future," *The Saturday Evening Post,* Vol. 210, November 27, 1937, p. 22.

Barnhart, Thomas F., *Weekly Newspaper Makeup and Typography,* University of Minnesota Press, 1949, pp. 246–263.

Beazell, William P., "Tomorrow's Newspaper," *The Atlantic Monthly,* Vol. 146, July 1930, p. 30.

Bliven, Bruce (editor), *20th Century Unlimited,* J. B. Lippincott, 1950.

Brucker, Herbert, *The Changing American Newspaper,* Columbia University Press, 1937, pp. 6–7.

———, *Freedom of Information,* Macmillan, 1949, Chapter 17.

Davis, Donald W., "The Newspaper of Tomorrow–A Summary of Probabilities," *Journalism Quarterly,* Vol. 22, June 1945, pp. 144–150.

Davis, W., "Next Step in Newspaper Work: Microfilming," *Vital Speeches Magazine,* Vol. 3, September 1, 1937, pp. 695–697.

Dewey, E. A., "Twilight of the Press," *The Commonweal,* Vol. 28, August 5, 1938, pp. 380–381.

Ernst, Morris L., *The First Freedom,* Macmillan, 1946, pp. 62–124, 245–271.

Garnett, Burrett P., "Changes in the Basic Newspaper Pattern," *The Annals of the American Academy of Political and Social Science,* Vol. 219, January 1942, pp. 53–59.

Gorman, A., "Era of Big City Dailies," *Scholastic,* Vol. 32, March 25, 1938, pp. 4–6.

Haskell, W. E., "Everchanging Newspaper World," *Vital Speeches Magazine,* Vol. 3, August 15, 1937, pp. 665–667.

Hodgins, Eric, "A Definition of News for the World of Tomorrow," *Journalism Quarterly,* Vol. 20, December 1943, pp. 273–279.

Hotaling, Burton L., "Facsimile Broadcasting: Problems and Possibilities," *Journalism Quarterly,* Vol. 25, June 1948, pp. 139–144.

McCambridge, W. J., "Technical Developments and the Future of the Press," *Journalism Quarterly,* Vol. 20, December 1943, pp. 331–333.

MacNeil, Neil, *Without Fear or Favor,* Harcourt, Brace, 1940, pp. 396–408.

Merz, Charles, "The Editorial Page," *The Annals of the American Academy of Political and Social Science*, Vol. 219, January 1942, pp. 139–144.

Pratt, F., "Propaganda Captures the Newspapers," *American Mercury*, Vol. 44, August 1938, pp. 450–458.

Riegel, O. W., "Propaganda and the Press," *The Annals of the American Academy of Political and Social Science*, Vol. 179, May 1935, pp. 201–210.

Robb, Arthur, "The Ideal Newspaper of the Future," *The Annals of the American Academy of Political and Social Science*, Vol. 219, January 1942, pp. 169–175.

Svirsky, Leon (editor), *Your Newspaper: Blueprint for a Better Press*, Macmillan, 1947, pp. 161–194.

Walker, Stanley, *City Editor*, Frederick A. Stokes, 1934, pp. 33–34.

INDEX

B

C

D

F

G

O

P

R

S